Families as Partners in Education

Tenth Edition

Families as Partners in Education

Families and Schools Working Together

Mari Riojas-Cortez
Professor, The University of Texas at San Antonio

Eugenia Hepworth Berger
Professor Emerita, Metropolitan State College of Denver

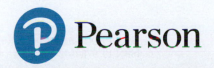

Director and Publisher: Kevin Davis
Executive Portfolio Manager: Aileen Pogran
Portfolio Assistant: Maria Feliberty
Executive Field Marketing Manager: Krista Clark
Executive Product Marketing Manager: Christopher Barry
Content Producer: Megan Moffo
Development Editor: Krista McMurray
Operations Specialist: Deidra Headlee
Cover Design: Pearson, CSC

Cover Art: Valarti/Fotolia
Media Producer: Autumn Benson
Editorial Production and Composition Services: Pearson, CSC
Editorial Project Manager: Mirasol Dante, Pearson CSC
Full-Service Project Manager: Prince John William Carey, Pearson CSC
Printer/Binder: LSC Communications, Inc./Willard
Cover Printer: Phoenix Color/Hagerstown
Text Font: Palatino LT Pro

Acknowledgments of third party content appear on appropriate pages within text.

Photo Credits: Mari Cortez-Riojas, p. 3; Chris Robbins/Photodisc/Getty Images, p. 3; VOISIN/PHANIE/Alamy stock photo, p. 3; Kian Khoon Tan/Alamy Stock Photo, p. 3; Carla Mestas. Pearson Education, Inc., p. 4; Photodisc/Getty Images, p. 5; Chubykin Arkady/Shutterstock, p. 8; Mari Riojas-Cortez, p. 12; Fuse/Corbis/Getty Images, p. 13; logoboom/Shutterstock, p. 18; Armando Cortez, p. 18; Guy Cali/Corbis/Getty Images, p. 22; ZouZou/Shutterstock, p. 25; Noam Armonn/Shutterstock, p. 29; Szefei/Shutterstock, p. 29; Jupiterimages/Stockbyte/Getty Images, p. 41; Mari Riojas Cortez, p. 43; Thinkstock/Stockbyte/Getty Images, p. 43; PacoRomero/E+/Getty Images, p. 51; Comstock Images/Stockbyte/Getty Images, p. 59; Rawpixel.com/Shutterstock, p. 61; Lloyd Smith/Shutterstock, p. 69; Eugenia Berger, p. 71; Eugenia Berger, p. 72; Istomina Olena/Shutterstock, p. 72; Bettmann/Getty Images, p. 75; Dean Mitchell/Getty Images, p. 79; David Kostelnik/Pearson Education, Inc., p. 90; Armando Cortez, p. 92; Judy Bellah/Alamy Stock Photo, p. 98; Pearson Education, p. 101; Exactostock-1557/Superstock, p. 109; Merrill Education, p. 111; Mari Riojas-Cortez, p. 128; Studio 8/Pearson Education Ltd, p. 131; matka_Wariatka/Shutterstock, p. 134; Steve Debenport/E+/Getty Images, p. 137; Shorrocks/Getty Images, p. 149; Kali Nine LLC/Getty Images, p. 150; Ariel Skelley/Blend Images/Alamy, p. 162; Jim West / Alamy Stock Photo, p. 164; Merrill Education, p. 174; Mark Bowden/Getty Images, p. 181; Rawpixel.com/Shutterstock, p. 190; Studio 8/Pearson Education Ltd, p. 190; Merrill Education, p. 195; Gideon Mendel/Corbis/Getty Images, p. 198; David Mager/Pearson Education, p. 201; Oleg Kozlov/shutterstock, p. 202; Stockbyte/Getty Images, p. 219; Jupiterimages/Stockbyte/Getty Images, p. 227; Chad Baker/Jason Reed/Ryan McVay/getty Image, p. 239; Diyana Dimitrova/Shutterstock, p. 240; Robin Sachs/Photo Edit, p. 241; George Dodson/Pearson Education, p. 245; Denis Kuvaev/Shutterstock, p. 254; Mari Riojas-Cortez, p. 256; Monkey Business Images/Shutterstock, p. 261; Suzanne Clouzeau/Pearson Education, Inc, p. 265; Denis Kuvaev/Shutterstock, p. 278; Armando Cortez, p. 291; Jules Selmes/Pearson Education Ltd, p. 292; Scott Camazine/Alamy Stock Photo, p. 299; Mediscan/Alamy Stock Photo, p. 304; Karen Grigoryan/Shutterstock, p. 304; st-fotograf/Shutterstock, p. 304; Stephanie Rausser/The Image Bank/getty Image, p. 305; SPL/Science Source, p. 305; GIRAND/BSIP SA/Alamy Stock Photo, p. 305; Geo Martinez/Shutterstock, p. 325; Monkey Business Images/Shutterstock, p. 329; Creativa Images/Shutterstock, p. 332; Wavebreakmedia/Shutterstock, p. 332

Library of Congress Cataloging in Publication Control Number: 2018052082

1 18

ISBN 10: 0-13-519672-8
ISBN 13: 978-0-13-519672-4

Dedicated with cariño (affection) to all families who are separated by different circumstances. May kindness and humanness be granted.

—Mari Riojas-Cortez

About the Authors

MARI RIOJAS-CORTEZ became interested in family engagement when she was a bilingual teacher working with young children in San Antonio, Texas. She learned early in her career that families play a very important role in children's development, and she developed strong relationships by welcoming families to her classroom and inviting them to participate in different aspects of their children's education. Mari understood the challenges that many Latino families faced because her own parents faced the same cultural and linguistic barriers when they arrived in the United States from Mexico. After completing a master's degree in educational leadership, Mari's interests in early childhood education and bilingual education led her to The University of Texas at Austin, where she received a doctorate in curriculum and instruction with a concentration in early childhood education and bilingual education in 1998. Currently, she is Professor of Early Childhood Education at The University of Texas at San Antonio (UTSA), where she continues to collaborate with local school districts and early childhood agencies in various capacities. Additionally, Mari's work has been published in a variety of journals including *Journal of Early Childhood Research, International Journal of Early Childhood Education, Young Children, Early Child Development and Care, Journal of Early Childhood Teacher Education, Language Arts,* and the *Bilingual Research Journal*, among others. Mari Riojas-Cortez also serves as Editor for *Dimensions of Early Childhood* (a journal published by the Southern Early Childhood Association).

EUGENIA HEPWORTH BERGER became interested in parent involvement when she and her husband, Glen, became the parents of three children who attended public schools. A professional in early childhood education, sociology, family life education, and parent education for more than 35 years, she has two master's degrees and a Ph.D. in sociological foundations of education. Eugenia has been active in many professional organizations, including the Association for Childhood Education International, the National Association for the Education of Young Children (life member), and the National Council for the Social Studies. She served on the board for the National Association of Early Childhood Teacher Educators, the Colorado Association for Childhood Education, the Colorado Association for the Education of Young Children, and was president of the Rocky Mountain Council on Family Relations. After finishing her doctorate at the University of Denver, she became a faculty member at Metropolitan State College. She retired in December 1997 and is now professor emerita of education.

Preface

This edition of *Families as Partners in Education: Families and Schools Working Together* highlights the changes in U.S. society and effective ways for teachers and other professionals to understand and work with families. For the last 30 years, we have seen major changes in families. In particular, we have seen an increase in the number of diverse families. The beauty of this change reminds us of the diversity of our nation. Learning to work with diverse families, including those with diverse family structures, requires an understanding of who we are as individuals and educators, and that we acknowledge the values and beliefs that our own families have taught us.

Among other themes, this edition still emphasizes the importance of *funds of knowledge* (Moll et al., 1992) for children's development and for effective partnerships with families. We have also acknowledged the concept of "funds of identity" as a catalyst for educators to understand their own identity which will in turn help understand and work with others. It is not only important for educators to understand and know child development theories, but also how children develop within the context of their families.

Creating strong partnerships involves the understanding and willingness to work with all families, including families that are different than our own. Once educators understand the value of families for healthy development, they can begin to create strong partnerships to assist children in successful educational experiences. This edition continues to highlight important parent involvement programs and that such programs are often successful because of an asset-based view of families, particularly of those that are diverse, as well as those with children with special abilities.

New to this Edition

This edition includes updated material and additional coverage of many subjects. Of particular interest are

- Updated measurable learning outcomes (every chapter) on which to focus.
- Updated tables and figures.
- Real voices of families.

- Description of family theories (Chapter 1).
- Expanded explanation regarding diversity of families (Chapter 3).
- Inclusive historical overview of families (Chapter 4).
- Expanded section on school climate in order to create positive partnerships with families (Chapter 5).
- Focus on leadership for teachers working with families (Chapter 7).
- Updated information regarding school- and home-based family engagement programs (Chapter 8).
- Updated information regarding child abuse and domestic violence (Chapter 11), as well as newer photos.
- Revised chapter on advocacy based on the concept of social justice (Chapter 12).

Guidelines and Strategies for Working with Families

The tried-and-true how-to ideas and means to help parents and educators join together include:

- Communication, an essential element in providing an environment where learning and caring coexist.
- An understanding of diversity in different contexts.
- Ideas to help build a partnership of home, teacher, and school.
- Ways to set up an environment that is respectful to cultural, linguistic, and ability diversity where learning can take place.
- Historical development of views on children and how those views affect family life.
- Activities and programs to enrich parent–school collaboration.
- Awareness of the needs of special abilities or special needs for families.
- Methods needed to welcome families in the schools.
- Practices to develop working relationships with diverse families.

Orientation to the Text

Interdisciplinary Approach. The text studies family engagement from an interdisciplinary approach and looks at home–school partnerships from educational, anthropological, sociological, and psychological perspectives. In this edition, there is a strong effort to view families from a diverse perspective.

Theory and Research. Theory and research underpin each chapter of the text. New research emphasizes the need for home–school partnerships, particularly as they relate to culturally and linguistically diverse families.

Practical Application. A parent, student, teacher, or administrator can pick up this book and find suggestions and descriptions of specific programs that will enable collaboration between families and schools.

Readability. Reviewers and students have commented on the readability of the text in its comprehensive coverage. An easy-to-read style makes it convenient to share ideas from the book directly with parents who are not professional educators.

Figures and Tables. Numerous helpful figures and tables are included in the text to help illustrate content.

Photos. Many new photographs that depict culturally and linguistically diverse children, families, and teachers, as well as families with children with special needs, enrich the content of the book.

Special Features

Situational Vignettes. Vignettes bring alive situations that typically occur in parent–school relationships. Co-author Mari Riojas-Cortez has woven some personal vignettes throughout the book based on her experience from her professional work with children and families as well as her personal experience. Other examples are also highlighted to demonstrate inclusion and diversity.

Diverse Families. Suggestions and activities about how to work with diverse families, including a special focus on families affected by autism, are given.

Immigrant Families. Descriptions and explanations of situations that affect immigrant families are provided, including suggestions on how best to develop partnerships.

Advocacy. Preparation and suggestions on advocating for children give families and educators the knowledge they need to encourage them to be actively involved in advocacy issues.

Historical Outline. A historical outline highlights education and parent education milestones, and succinctly illustrates family engagement throughout different eras in the U.S.

Instructor's Resources

The following ancillaries are available for download to adopting professors via www.pearson-highered.com from the Educators screen. Contact your Pearson sales representative for additional information.

Instructor's Resource Manual. This manual contains activity ideas to enhance chapter concepts.

Test Bank. The test bank includes a variety of test items, arranged by chapter.

PowerPoint Slides. PowerPoint slides highlight key concepts and strategies in each chapter and enhance lectures and discussions.

A Note About Census Data

Although every effort was made to include up-to-date information in this 10th edition, we strongly suggest that readers check the American Fact Finder on the U.S. Census website for the latest data.

Acknowledgments

Eugenia Hepworth Berger had a vision when she developed *Families as Partners in Education: Families and Schools Working Together*. Her vision carried this book through seven editions—30 years of sharing ideas with educators and administrators on how to enhance parental involvement to strengthen home–school partnerships. I hope to expand her vision in this tenth edition where we further our understanding of collaborating with diverse families, and I offer my sincere gratitude for her trusting me again with her book.

I want to thank all of the previous contributors to the book as well as my university students who provide me with opportunities to stay informed regarding the realities of many families.

I want to thank the staff of Pearson for their guidance, patience, and support, and in particular: Aileen Pogran, Executive Portfolio Manager, for her trust, patience, guidance, and encouragement although we just met for this edition; Krista McMurray for providing guidance and feedback on chapter content although she was herself starting a family, and congratulations on her baby; and Mirasol Dante, project manager at SPi Global, Inc., as well as the amazing copyeditors for the production services.

I also want to thank all the reviewers who took the time to read and provide feedback for this edition. Their diverse insights and expertise have strengthened it: Gwen Walter, Forsyth Technical Community College, Retired; Robin Fox, University of Wisconsin, Whitewater; and Tisha Rivera, California State University, Fullerton.

Finally, I want to acknowledge my husband, Armando Cortez, and our three extraordinary children Marisol, Rodrigo, and Miguel for their love, patience, and understanding while this project was completed, they are my inspiration.

—*Mari Riojas-Cortez*

Brief Contents

Contents

Chapter 1

Family—Essential for a Child's Development

The family is the entity that assists children in their development. Families bond as they guide children in their development using their funds of knowledge.

Mari Riojas-Cortez

Learning Outcomes

This chapter stresses the importance of the family as the main influence in children's development. Respecting and valuing families acknowledges their importance for children's healthy development. After completing the chapter, you should be able to do the following:

1.1 Identify the influence of families on children's development.

1.2 Discuss and examine the concept of funds of knowledge as it relates to children's development and families.

1.3 Identify and describe different attachment theories in relation to child development and families as systems of support.

1.4 Analyze the role of the family in a child's brain development.

The Influence of Families on Children's Development

Families play a major role in their children's development. They provide food, shelter, care, love, opportunities for play, education, and much else. Families that provide these necessities are strong families. Strong families are essential because they help create a nurturing society, transforming the society by actively participating in systems that in turn help them, the family members, have a healthy, successful life. Regardless of how nurturing the society, sometimes even strong families face difficulties that test their well-being, such as parents working multiple jobs to meet the basic needs of their children, or facing the challenges of divorce. Although family stressors such as these are difficult for children, families that are strong are often resilient and learn to work out problems because they care for each other, particularly their children. This strength allows families to help children in their development.

Defining the Term *Parent*

Throughout this book, the term **parent** includes those who act in a primary caregiver or parent role, whether they are the biological parent, a relative, adoptive parent, foster parent, or nonrelated caregiver. In fact, parents can be one person or a group of individuals, such as those that form part of support systems, who help meet the cognitive, linguistic, physical, socioemotional, and cultural needs of children.

1

The Role of the Extended Family

The role of the extended family has evolved over time. The extended family often focuses on gathering on major occasions such as *quinceañeras*[1], weddings, bar mitzvah celebrations, or religious holidays. Today many families "gather" on social media and send congratulatory messages, and some even communicate through Instagram or Facebook. How often have you encountered *Abuelita*[2] or Grandma give advice to new parents? How often does an auntie provide care for her sister's children while her sister works? Because families are so important, resources must be provided to support their needs, specifically their children's needs. Extended family members like grandparents, who often have the responsibility of taking care of the children, are an important support for families. However, their role is also to provide guidance and *consejos*[3] or advice to ensure children are cared for appropriately, largely based on their own cultural practices. The support that the extended family provides helps create a caring environment for children.

The definition of the extended family depends on the cultural background of the family. For example, many countries in Africa and Asia consider what we know in the U.S. as extended family to be their nuclear family. In the following example, Ndimande describes the concept of Family of the Zulu people of South Africa (where he is from):

> *Zulu people do not use the Western notion of traditional family, although now things are gradually changing. But when I was growing up, for example, my uncle, antie, especially grandparents would live with us. They were not regarded as "extended" family. They were family, period. So, the notion of nucleus family was fluid, it was not defined by biological parents. But also we did not have old age homes as we are now beginning to have. This is the reason I like that your Mama lives with you and Armando. So, for Zulu people, she is family, not necessarily extended. The same goes to the children of your brothers, sisters (if they live with you, they are your children). You did not need an authorization from the government or anything. The good thing about this type of extended family, individuals retained their original last names, irrespective of who they live with. And it makes the family stronger.*

It is clear from this example that what is considered the extended family in the U.S. is not considered seen the same way in some cultures in Africa. A strong family seems to be one that takes care of each other regardless of biological ties.

In some societies, such as in some Asian Indian cultures, the success of individuals comes from having strong ties to the family as explained by Kalpana, a mother of two teenagers and who is from India but has lived in the U.S. for many years:

> *Asian Indian people, along with their immediate family (i.e. parents, siblings, and grandparents) attribute their success and achievements to extended family members. Indians live in a system called joint family (which is the opposite of the western nuclear family system), where there is space/scope for lateral relationship building for psychological well being of the young adults. Indian culture is complex and intricate with influences from outside of the family that they refer to as extended family support.*

For Kalpana, family has also a different definition and the family functions as a system that is complex. In the Indian culture there appears to be a cohesive system where many members have the responsibility to support young children.

Latinos in the United States regard the extended family as being just as close as the nuclear family; the members have strong bonds and attachments with each other. When I was growing up in Mexico, my *madrina*, or godmother, came to our house every day. My mother and she would spend hours talking. In fact, my *madrina* was an influential person for my sisters and I to attend kindergarten, or *jardín de niños*, because as my mother put it, "*era muy importante el jardín de niños para que pudieran aprender más*" [kindergarten was very important so that you all could learn more].

The extended family influence extends from intangible things such as values, traditions, concepts, and principles but also to tangible things such as housing and adult- and childcare. For example, household composition varies not only depending on the cultural background but also on the resources that are available within a household. The extended family often assists when other resources are not available (LaFave & Thomas, 2014) this is particularly true for low-income families, immigrant families (with and without documents), and those who have children with special needs.

---

[1]Celebration of a girl's 15th birthday throughout Latin America and Latinos in the U.S.
[2]Abuelita is a Spanish term for Grandmother.
[3]Consejos is a Spanish term for advice.

Funds of Knowledge

Caretaking and teaching other people's children are tremendous tasks. Teachers must have the desire to teach children who come from a variety of cultural and linguistic backgrounds as well as children who are not developing typically. Often teachers are told that they need to be aware of the differences in language and culture of the children they teach, but merely being aware of cultural and linguistic differences is not sufficient to work effectively with families. Awareness implies knowledge but not action. When working with culturally and linguistically diverse children, teachers must know about the children's families, including but not limited to their cultural practices, childrearing practices, traditions, and each individual family's **funds of knowledge**.

A family is a child's first teacher, passing on their concepts, or funds of knowledge, to help them grow and thrive (Moll et al., 1992). These concepts can be passed along from generation to generation, and new ones can be developed as new families are formed.

For early childhood educators, the importance of understanding the concept of funds of knowledge is crucial, because they must understand why families do the things they do. Often educators criticize parents if their ways of raising their children are different from theirs, and this creates a dissonance that prevents teachers from truly collaborating with parents. We must remember that children learn from their parents first, and the learning and teaching that occur in the home are great assets for children in school—particularly when teachers value the children's funds of knowledge. When teachers value parents' funds of knowledge they encourage parent engagement (Gregg, Rugg, & Stoneman, 2012) because parents feel valued and respected.

Mari Cortez-Riojas

Chris Robbins/Photodisc/Getty Images

VOISIN/PHANIE/Alamy stock photo

Kian Khoon Tan/Alamy Stock Photo

Strong families influence, nurture, socialize, and educate and teach their children through funds of knowledge.

Examples of Funds of Knowledge

I have seen funds of knowledge "in action" in different settings. For example, while eating at a local restaurant, a father was observing his son, who had Down syndrome, figure out the amount of tip to leave for the server. This exercise taught the young man an important social skill while fostering his independence. When I was a teacher, many parents would send their preschool children to school dressed in their Sunday best. Girls would wear black patent shoes and ruffled dresses, while the boys would wear dressy pants and a nice shirt. After my initial meeting with them before school started, I knew they valued education, and by sending their children to school looking their best, they were asserting this value. This truly was "funds of knowledge" in action. By understanding a family's funds of knowledge, teachers are also engaging in social justice because they want to create opportunities for those children and families who are often underrepresented and marginalized.

Part of my funds of knowledge include my father's teaching regarding the value of social justice while growing up in Mexico. He taught me the value of being fair and equitable, particularly with those who work with and for you. My father, who was actively involved in the *sindicato obrero*, or the "blue collar" union, fought for workers' rights. My sisters and I were used to listening to my father talk about how to make sure the workers would get treated fairly,

Funds of knowledge can be passed along from generation to generation, and new ones can be developed as new families are formed.

which is something that has become part of my philosophy of teaching—providing fair opportunities so all children can learn.

Another example of funds of knowledge is derived from an interview with an African American family. The interview showed that the family wanted to teach their children about "Black pride"—they wanted their children to know their history so they would continue to advocate for each other. They taught their children about different African American historical figures, but they also talked about their own family and how they make a difference in their community. The funds of knowledge learned by the children in this family included the need to participate in advocacy for their community.

Families who immigrate to the United States often use their funds of knowledge to learn to live in a new culture, but oftentimes, the child takes the role of the teacher and the parent the learner. When visiting a school on the east side of Austin, Texas, I recall listening to a mother having a conversation with her young daughter, who was probably about 10 years old, regarding the papers needed to register her, the child, in school. The child spoke English and had to translate the process to register for school for the mother. Another time, I witnessed a family at an auto parts store, and the young son was translating for his father what the salesperson was telling him in English. The father was a mechanic. In both instances, the children had knowledge of the vocabulary used in their native language (in both cases it was Spanish).

Examples of funds of knowledge vary between cultures, as well as between individual families. Funds of knowledge can be observed in different situations. In schools or childcare centers, examples can be found in children's play that include language, values and beliefs, ways of discipline, household care, and the value of education (Riojas-Cortez, 2001). Teachers can observe children during play, particularly sociodramatic play, to recognize cultural traits and identify funds of knowledge. For instance, a teacher who arranges the dramatic play area to reflect the children's experiences, such as setting up the area to resemble a neighborhood restaurant, creates an opportunity to observe a family's funds of knowledge. Children's family backgrounds are indeed the basis for their development.

Attachment Theories in Relation to Child Development and Families as Systems of Support

It is important to understand how children develop in order to work better with families. However, it is also important to understand family theories as they help us understand families' ways of being. Child development theories often help us understand the basis for educational and childrearing practices (Charlesworth, 2014) while family theories help with the understanding that families are dynamic groups that change for a variety of reasons.

Rosalind Charlesworth, Professor Emerita of Child and Family Studies, explains that in recent years, the cultural relevance of child development theories has been criticized. The way to interpret the theory is to look at its premise and then adapt it to the child's situation in the United States. The adaptation of the theory is crucial so that the child is not assessed from a deficit perspective. The theories described in this chapter focus on the role the family has in child development. In particular, the emphasis is on attachment theories and child development.

Attachment Theory

Ecological systems should be nurturing environments where children have opportunities to develop socially and emotionally. A nurturing environment allows children to create bonds and attachments. The development of positive parent–child relationships is based on the quality of attachments the child has developed. **Attachment** is defined as a form of behavior that has its "own internal motivation distinct from feeding and sex, and of no less importance for survival" (Bowlby, 1988, p. 27).

Since the 1930s, there has been increasing research on bonding and attachment. Experts recognize attachment as an essential ingredient for a healthy personality. Attachment behavior is the behavior a person exhibits to obtain and maintain proximity to the attachment figure, generally the mother, but also the father—and in the absence of either parent, someone the child knows;

in many culturally and linguistically diverse families, the grandparents may take that role. This attachment is strongest when the child is sick, tired, or frightened, but is crucial throughout the life cycle.

Psychoanalysts Skeels, Spitz, and Bowlby recognized the importance of the first few years in the development of attachment, as evidenced through studies of children who did not thrive. These psychoanalysts did not conduct controlled studies that gave some children love and withheld it from others, but instead they looked at what had happened to children who had failed to thrive. Why had this happened? What did these children lack that the other children had?

Skeels

During the 1930s, questions about the importance of human attachment in young children were raised. Harold Skeels, a member of the Iowa Group of child researchers, studied the effect of environment on the

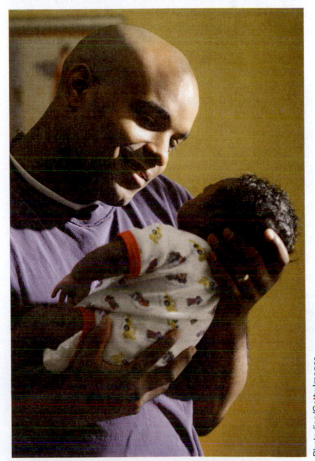

Eye contact between father and child fosters human attachment, a necessary component for healthy development.

development of children during a period when most researchers (e.g., Gesell and Watson) were studying maturation or behaviorism. One study, a natural history investigation, had startling findings (Skeels, 1966). Skeels placed 13 infants and toddlers from a children's home in a mental health facility. The 13 children— 10 girls and 3 boys—ranged from 7.1 to 35.9 months and had IQs from 36 to 89, with a mean IQ score of 64.3. Children in the control group of 12—also chosen from children in the children's home, between 12 and 22 months old—had IQs of 50 to 103, with a mean IQ of 86.7 points. The children placed in the mental health facility were showered with attention by the attendants and supervisors. They were cared for, played with, loved, and allowed to go along on excursions. Almost every child developed an attachment to one person who was particularly interested in the child and his or her achievements. The control group of children in the children's home, however, received traditional care with no special treatment. When retested, after varying periods from 6 to 52 months, the children in the mental health facility had gained 27.5 IQ points, but those left in the orphanage had lost an average of 26.2 IQ points.

Although the research could be criticized because variables were not controlled—there were more girls than boys placed in the homes—and changes in IQ can be partially explained by statistical regression, the results were so dramatic and unexpected that the effect of early environment had to be considered. Skeels (1966) followed up on the subjects of this research almost 20 years later and found evidence to reinforce his initial findings. Of the 13 children in the experimental group who had been transferred to the mental health facility, 11 had been adopted and reared as typically-developing children. Twelve of the 13 had become self-supporting adults, achieving a median education level of 12 years of schooling. Of the control group of children who had been left in the orphanage, four were still in institutions, one was a gardener's assistant, three were employed as dishwashers, one was a floater (performed different types of jobs as needed), one was a part-time worker in a cafeteria, and one had died. Only one individual had achieved an educational level similar to that of the experimental group—a man who as a child had received different treatment from the others. He had been transferred from the children's home to a school for the deaf, where he received special attention from his teacher.

The children who had been placed in an institution and later adopted received love and developed human attachments. They had achieved a lifestyle more typical of children outside the orphanage, whereas those left in the orphanage had only a marginal existence. Evidence strongly supports the importance of a nurturing early environment and also indicates that a poor initial environment can be reversed by enriched personal interaction (Skeels, 1966). Interestingly, these findings also indirectly support the importance of funds of knowledge, which are gained through nurturing interactions between the child and immediate and/or extended family in a caring environment, regardless of income level and cognitive ability.

Spitz

In *The First Year of Life* (1965), René Spitz describes his research into and observations of the psychology of infants. He studied babies in different situations: private families, foster homes, an obstetrics ward, a well-baby clinic, a nursery, and a foundling home.

Both the nursery and foundling home were long-term institutions that guaranteed constancy of environment and dramatically illustrated the necessity of human attachment and interaction. Both institutions provided similar physical care of children, but they differed in their nurturing and interpersonal relationships. Both provided hygienic conditions, well-prepared food, and medical care. The foundling home had daily visits by a medical staff, whereas the nursery called a doctor only when needed. The nursery was connected to a penal institution where what they called "delinquent girls," pregnant on admission, were sent to serve their sentences. Babies born to them were cared for in the nursery until the end of their first year. The mothers were primarily socially challenged minors. In contrast, some of the children in the foundling home had well-adjusted mothers who were unable to support their children. Others were children of single mothers who were asked to come to the home and nurse their own and one other child during the first 3 months.

Spitz (1965) filmed a representative group of the children he studied in both institutions. He studied 203 children in the nursery and 91 in the foundling home. The major difference in the care of the two sets of children was the amount of nurturing and social interaction. The nursery, which housed 40 to 60 children at a time, allowed the mothers or mother-substitutes to feed, nurse, and care for their babies. The infants had at least one toy, and they were able to see outside their cribs and to watch the activities of other children and the caregiving mothers. These babies thrived. In the foundling home, however, the babies were screened from outside activity by blankets hung over the sides and ends of their cribs, isolating them from any visual stimulation. They had no toys to play with, and the caretakers were busy tending to other duties rather than mothering the children. During the first 3 months, while they were breast-fed, the babies appeared to be developing typically. Soon after separation, however, they progressively deteriorated. Of the 91 foundling home children, 34 died by the end of the second year.

Spitz (1965) continued to follow up on 21 children who remained in the foundling home until they were 4 years old. He found that 20 could not dress themselves, 6 were not toilet trained, 6 could not talk, 5 had a vocabulary of two words, 8 had vocabularies of three to five words, and only 1 was able to speak in sentences. Spitz attributed the deterioration of the infants to lack of mothering. Although the children in the nursery had mothering, those in the foundling home did not, thus finding themselves in an emotional starvation stage (Spitz).

Bowlby

In 1951, John Bowlby reviewed studies of deprivation and its effects on personality development. In a systematic review for the World Health Organization, he described those works that supported theories on the negative aspects of maternal deprivation. In a monograph, Bowlby (1966) stated: "It is submitted that the evidence is now such that it leaves no room for doubt regarding the general proposition that the prolonged deprivation of the young child of maternal care may have grave and far-reaching effects on his character and so the whole of his future life" (p. 46).

DEVELOPMENT OF ATTACHMENT. Bowlby (1982) described attachment in a family setting. Most babies about 3 months old show more attention and are more responsive to their primary caregiver than to others by smiling at, vocalizing to, and visually following their parent or other primary caregiver. At about 6 to 8 months of age, infants develop stranger anxiety. They become concerned about being near their caregiver and fearful of those they do not know. This attachment to primary caregivers continues and strengthens in intensity from 6 to 9 months, although when the child is ill, fatigued, hungry, or alarmed, the intensity increases. During the same period, the infant demonstrates attachment to others as well, primarily the father, siblings, and caregivers. Attachment to others does not reduce the attachment to the mother or primary caregiver. At 9 months, most children try to follow primary caregivers when they leave the room, greet them on return, and crawl to be near them. This behavior continues throughout the second year of a child's life and into the third. When children reach about 2 years 9 months to 3 years of age, they are better able to accept a parent's temporary absence.

Bowlby (1966) emphasized that the greatest effect on personality development is during the child's early years. The earliest critical period was believed to be during the first 5 or 6 months, while the mother figure and infant are forming an attachment. The second vital phase was seen as lasting until near the child's third birthday, during which time the mother figure needs to be virtually an ever-present companion. During the third phase, the child is able to maintain the attachment even though the nurturing parent is absent. During the fourth to fifth year, this tolerable absence might extend from a few days to a few weeks; during the seventh to eighth year, the separation could be lengthened to a year or more. Deprivation in the third phase does not have the same destructive effect on the child as it does in the period from infancy through the third year.

Maternal or Human Attachment?

Prominent child psychiatrists Rutter (1981) and Bower (1982) questioned whether the term *maternal deprivation* was too restrictive to cover a wide range of abuses and variables. They suggested that maternal deprivation was too limited a concept—that human attachment and multiple attachments should be considered and that warmth as well as love be regarded as vital elements in relationships. Rutter argued that the bond with the mother was not different in quality or kind from other bonds. In addition, individual differences among children resulted in some children being more vulnerable to mother deprivation.

Tizard and Hodges

Questions regarding the irreversibility of deprivation were raised. Would sound childrearing reverse early deprivation? It appeared that good childrearing practices and a good environment would be of some help to the child, but early deprivation continued to be a problem, and deprived infants often remained detached. Tizard and Hodges (1978) studied children raised in an institution to see if the lack of personal attachment had lasting effects. Children who were adopted did form bonds as late as 4 or 6 years of age, but they exhibited the same attention and social problems in school as those who remained in the institution: "Being one in a class of many other children may for the child have repeated some of the elements of the nursery 'family group,' leading to a similar pattern of competitive attempts to gain the attention of the teacher and poor relationships with other children" (Hodges, 1996, p. 71).

Ainsworth

Mary Ainsworth's (1973) seminal work regarding classifications of attachment provides a deeper understanding of Bowlby's critical period of attachment. Ainsworth identified three classifications of attachment—avoidant/insecure, ambivalent/insecure, and securely attached—during a controlled experimental procedure known as the Strange Situation procedure (Shore, 1997).

Brazelton and Yogman

In their extensive studies of infants, Brazelton and Yogman (1986) analyzed the process of early attachment and wrote specifically about the interaction between infant and parent, covering even the effects of experiences in utero. The child appears to be born with predictable responses, including the ability to develop a reciprocal relationship with the caregiver.

Brazelton and Yogman (1986) described four stages vital to the parent–infant attachment process, which lasts from birth to 4 or 5 months. In the first stage, the infant achieves homeostatic control and is able to control stimuli by shutting out or reaching for stimuli. During the second stage, the infant is able to use and

The brain is affected by nourishment, care, and stimulation. Early attachment and nurturing are essential for a child's development.

attend to social cues. In the third stage, usually at 3 to 4 months, the reciprocal process between parent and child shows the infant's ability to take in and respond to the information as well as to withdraw. During the fourth stage, the infant develops a sense of autonomy and initiates and responds to cues. If the parent recognizes and encourages the infant's desire to have control over the environment, the infant develops a sense that leads to a feeling of competence. This model is based on feedback and reciprocal interaction and allows for individual differences (Brazelton & Yogman, 1986).

The Brazelton Institute

The Newborn Behavioral Observation (NBO) is a family-centered observation set that is designed to be used by clinicians at the Brazelton Institute as they focus on individual infants and observe their individuality and competencies, because early months of infancy, from birth until the third month, are important periods in the infant's adaptation to his or her environment. In addition to strengthening the relationships between infant and parent as well as parent and clinician, the NBO provides information to the parents that helps them be better caregivers. The parents learn to read their baby's communication cues, understand their baby better, and are able to respond with appropriate care (Brazelton Institute, 2005).

Challenges

Although most families successfully develop attachments with their children, a few find different

Classifications of Attachment

Attachment Classification	Description	Example
Avoidant/insecure	Child shows no reaction when separated from the mother.	Child is dropped off at daycare and shows no reaction to mother leaving.
Ambivalent/insecure	Child shows high levels of distress when separated from the mother.	Child cries himself to sleep when mother drops him off at daycare.
Secure	Child shows signs of distress.	Child is comforted by caregiver.

challenges for a variety of reasons. Five groups of parents may typically face challenges when developing parent–child attachments. The first group are parents who have never had models of good parenting or have been reared in abusive homes. They need help in learning how to nurture and care for children as well as eliminate violence from their lives. Organizations such as the National Coalition Against Domestic Violence provide useful resources for families. The second group contains parents who tend to be isolated and insecure and do not have a support system. These groups could be helped by home-based programs such as Parents as Teachers, HIPPY, and Project CARE. The third group includes parents who are busy and away from home for extended periods and must find trusting caregivers for their children. The fourth group consists of parents who are raising a child with a special need and need financial and emotional assistance. Such parents may be able to get help from organizations such as Easter Seals (children's services) or Through the Looking Glass Project (see Colmer, Rutherford, & Murphy, 2011). The fifth group contains adolescent (teen parents) parents. The majority, if not all, of the parents in this group need guidance in prenatal care and early maternal-infant attachment (Feldman, 2012).

The importance of early bonding and attachment development is so critical that parents must be aware of the consequences of not devoting time to their young children. Children who lack attachment from infancy on may have enormous difficulty with social interaction. This can result in them having difficulties making and keeping relationships, not only between a parent and a child with insecure attachments, but also with peers. These children are often aggressive in their relationships with other children in a school setting. The attachment process and the early life of a child are the first steps in the child's total growth. They provide the necessary emotional trust that allows the child to continue to develop relationships. Providing parents with helpful tools to enhance their understanding of how to interact with and relate to their child is important. Researchers Zeanah, Berlin, and Boris (2011) provide a list of different types of attachment interventions that may help families, including Child–Parent Psychotherapy (CPP), Video-based Intervention to Promote Positive Parenting (VIPP), The Circle of Security (COS), and Attachment and Biobehavioral Catch-up (ABC).

Culture and Attachment

The research regarding attachment across cultures is still scarce according to Mesman et al. (2016). Because attachment theory developed in the Western world, it is important that other studies are conducted with families in non-western cultures. Interestingly the Mesman et al. study focused on 26 cultural groups from 16 countries. The researchers found (not surprisingly) that cultural group membership remains a significant predictor of variations in maternal sensitivity (p. 385). Socioeconomic background and demographic factors also contributed to the variation. Of importance are the findings regarding cultural specific aspects. Although at times we may not understand different cultural aspects, we as educators must find ways to learn about them to better understand children and families.

Family Theories

Family theorizing involves discussing different perspectives regarding family behavior or ways of being. Families are dynamic systems that change and evolve over time. Knowing different theories allows teachers to better understand families and such understanding helps creates stronger partnerships between home and school. Each theory has its own focus so it is difficult to prescribe to one but it is important to be aware what each one theorizes. Table 1.1 provides a brief overview of some family theories.

Family Ecological Systems Theory

One of the family theories that educators often refer to is the Family Ecological Systems Theory. This theory will be discussed in the context of this book. It is well known that both children and parents are affected by the family system in which they participate. Family systems are guided and influenced by their cultural and historical backgrounds. When a family undergoes a transitional event such as the birth of a child, a move to a new location, or an illness of a family member, the system will need to adapt to accommodate the change. Change occurs in a variety of ways. It may be sudden or gradual, positive or negative. The change may be minimal or shattering. Divorce is one common change that causes children to lose the family system as they knew it and adapt to an entirely new one. Changes may also occur at the local, state, or federal government level.

Table 1.1 Family Theories

Theory	Concepts	Examples
Social Exchange Framework	Focus is on individuals making selections for the ultimate rewards. Thibaut & Kelley, 1959	Families sending children to school for an education in order to get a better job and contribute to the family income.
Symbolic Interaction	Focus is on a person's consistent interaction, with significant others in particular (Potts, 2015).	Husband-wife conversation during family dinnertime.
Life Course Development	Focus is on the life trajectories and changes that occur but influenced by social and cultural constraints (Elder, 1998).	Oldest son graduating from high school and first in family attending college.
Critical Theory	Focus is on how to overcome the oppression and marginalization of people (Horkheimer, 1972).	Advocating for DACA or Deferred Action for Childhood Arrivals program to keep families together.
Ecological Framework	Focus is on adapting to changes but support is given or provided by systems (Bronfenbrenner, 1979).	Grandparents taking care of children while parents work.

Teachers need to know not only what is happening in a student's family but also how changes in policies may affect children and families, so they can respond in an appropriate manner and be helpful to the child.

LEVELS OF ECOLOGICAL SYSTEMS. A child's development is related to experiences in the entire environment. Bronfenbrenner (1979, 1986) recognized five levels, as shown in Figure 1.1.

1. The microsystem includes face-to-face relations with family and peers, with parents as the major influence on a child's interactive ecological system (O'Callaghan, 1993). Examples include interactions with parents, peers, or teachers.

2. The mesosystem involves face-to-face relationships with more formal organizations. Examples include school, family, peers, health-care services, religious institutions, and the playground.

3. The exosystem, although further removed from personal interaction, still influences children through their parents. Examples include the parents' employment and government actions.

4. The macrosystem includes the attitudes and ideologies of the culture. Examples include environmental events and cultural traditions, laws, and customs.

5. The chronosystem includes the element of time as it relates to changes in a child's environment. Examples of the chronosystem include the child getting older and the aging or death of a parent or family member.

The parents' role in their children's early years is significant in many ways, but it requires the support of different systems as stated by Bronfenbrenner. The support systems have a tremendous responsibility to meet the needs not only of the child but the family as well. For example, the needs of families who are living with high levels of stress due to violence, homelessness, and chemical dependence (Swick & Williams, 2006) are different from those of families that also have high stress due to different circumstances—such as a child with a special need, a parent who works two jobs, parents that have demanding jobs, families who are not authorized to live in the U.S., and families whose first language is not English.

For children from culturally and linguistically diverse families, some of the systems may not work so successfully (Riojas-Cortez, 2017). A criticism of this theory is that for culturally and linguistically diverse children, the mesosystem and the exosystem often do not value their culture, and their funds of knowledge are considered deficits. For example, a study found that resiliency in nine Native American teenagers was influenced by individual and environmental factors related to the family and extended family support (Feinstein, Driving-Hawk, & Baartman, 2009) or microsystem, but there was no mention of how the mesosystem and exosystem have helped Native American children. In another study, Chen and Abenyega (2012) found that conflicts between entities in the mesosystem prevented parents of kindergarten students in China from truly becoming involved in their children's education.

As indicated in the previous paragraphs, it is important to acknowledge how family theories help us understand the different behaviors that occur within the family. As educators we must develop this understanding in order to be better prepared to develop partnerships with families, allowing the entities within the microsystem to better work for children.

Figure 1.1 Bronfenbrenner's Ecological Theory

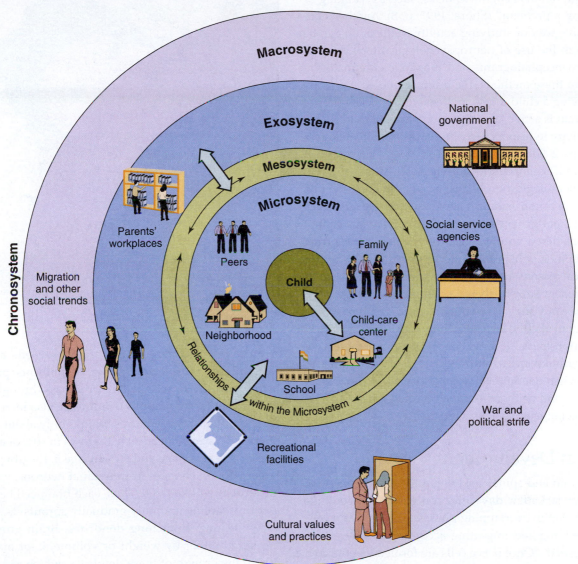

Source: Based on *Making Human Beings Human: Bioecological Perspectives on Human Development*, U. Bronfenbrenner, 2005, Thousand Oaks, CA: SAGE.

Families Influencing Brain Development

Families indeed play a significant role in the development of children and their behavior and the dynamics need to be strong for children to have healthy development. Children's lifelong learning depends on how well their brain has developed. Genes play an important part in brain development as well as the environment and early experiences. Children's early learning experiences provide the foundations of learning (Petersen, 2012).

Research on brain development emphasizes the importance of the first years of life and the role that families play when interacting with their children (Bernier, Calkins, & Bell, 2016). Stressful conditions such as poverty affect brain development (Dike, 2017). Brain research uses different technologies such as ultrasound to study fetal brain development and neural functioning and scanning techniques such as magnetic resonance imaging (MRI) and positron emission tomography (PET) to learn how the brain works after the child is born. "Functional MRI provides information about changes in the volume, flow, or oxygenation of blood that occur as a person undertakes various tasks, including motor activities, such as squeezing a hand, but also cognitive tasks, such as speaking or solving a problem" (Shore, 1997, p. 8). Another non-invasive way of studying activity in the brain can be through the use of neuropsychological tools such as electroencephalograms and magnetic encephalography. In these methods, the brain is studied indirectly by giving a child a task and examining which part of the brain is active, and also observing the child's level of activity in response to different stimuli (Shonkoff & Phillips, 2000).

A PET scan, employed when a child is thought to have neurological problems, requires an injection of a tracer chemical, making it an invasive procedure, which researchers generally avoid. Since PET scans cannot be considered noninvasive, the research comes from situations in which the child has needed the scan for medical reasons. By analyzing the results of PET scans, researchers have furthered scientific knowledge: "Scientists can visualize not only the fine structures of the brain, but also the level of activity that is taking place in its various parts" (Shore, 1997, p. 9). Prior to these technological advances, brain research was accomplished only when operations were performed or people had strokes, and neither situation revealed what was happening in the brain at specific times.

Brain Development

The brain and spinal cord begin their developmental journey just a few days after conception and continue to develop in overlapping phases, with the brain cells multiplying and migrating according to where they are needed: "Once nerve cells are formed and finished migrating they rapidly extend axons and dendrites and begin to form connections with each other, called synapses" (Shonkoff & Phillips, 2000, p. 186). The nerve cells are able to communicate with one another. The synapses are refined through maturation and pruning followed by myelination, the formation of a protective and supportive tissue surrounding the cells.

The brain does not develop one area and then the next in a straight, linear pattern. It develops in an integrated and overlapping fashion. Structures that control cognition (thinking), perception (sensing), and action (moving) develop at the same time but not in lockstep fashion. They are linked by a network of interconnections, separate but functioning parallel to one another (Goldman-Rakic, 1996).

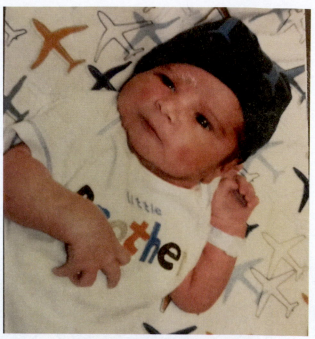

Mari Riojas-Cortez

The brain of an infant develops at an exhilarating rate.

The development of the brain proceeds at an exhilarating rate. The number of neurons peaks before birth (new neurons are produced throughout life, though far less rapidly). Brain size also increases more gradually. A newborn's brain is only about one-quarter the size of an adult's. It grows to 80% of adult size by 3 years of age and 90% by age 5. Its growth is largely due to changes in individual neurons, which are structured like trees. Thus, each brain cell begins as a tiny sapling and only gradually sprouts its hundreds of long, branching dendrites. Brain growth, measured either by weight or volume, is primarily due to the growth of these dendrites, which serve as the receiving point of synaptic input from other neurons. Another way of measuring brain growth is speed processing. Newborns are considerably slower than adults—16 times less efficient—and the brain does not reach maximum size until about 15 years of age (Zero to Three, 2001).

GENES AND THE ENVIRONMENT. The environment and the genes play a very important role in brain development. Interactions between the genes and the environment are crucial for brain development and they play different roles. Genes form all cells and make general connections for the brain regions and they help children adapt to their environment (Zero to Three, 2001, p. 1). According to Diamond (2009), it is experience that helps to wake up the dormant genes; therefore "the environment participates in sculpting expression of the genome" (p. 1).

EARLY INTERACTIONS AND BRAIN DEVELOPMENT.   Engaging children from infancy is extremely important, as it is estimated that the number of synapses reaches adult level by age 2, and by age 3, a child's brain is two and one half times more active than the brain of an adult. It is estimated that by age 3, the child's brain has a quadrillion synapses. The number holds steady for the first decade. After the child reaches 19, the synapses decline in density, and by late adolescence, half of the synapses have been discarded and 500 trillion remain (Shore, 1997). Elimination varies according to the area of the brain. Huttenlocher (1979, as cited in Shonkoff & Phillips, 2000) researched the production of synapses and the pruning that reduces the amount of synapses to adult level. He estimated that various areas of the brain have different patterns of synapse development and pruning. The visual cortex production occurs about midway through the first year, followed by a gradual reduction by the middle of the preschool period. The part of the brain responsible for language and hearing is similar but somewhat later. In the prefrontal area, which contains higher-level cognition, the proliferation of synapses begins around the first year, but adult level is not reached until middle to late adolescence.

As infants continue to develop, their need for exploration increases. Soska, Adolph, and Johnson (2010) indicate that the infant's motor and perceptual abilities help with exploration. The more opportunities for exploration and movement the infant is given, the greater the chances for acquisition of new skills. Therefore, the early

For children to achieve their potential, it is essential for families and educators to show support and caring.

experiences that parents provide for their children are crucial for their development, though individual experiences for children will vary depending on their families.

The Wiring of the Brain

Experience is critical in the "wiring" of a child's brain. When a stimulus activates a neural path, the synapses receive and store a chemical signal. If synapses are used repeatedly, they are strengthened, reach a threshold level, and become permanent. If not used repeatedly, they are pruned and eliminated (Shore, 1997).

The Importance of Family Interactions for Brain Development

Parenting experiences for young children help shape children's brain development (Morgan, Shaw, & Forbes, 2014). Children learn and develop on their own timetable, but they need interaction with their caregivers, mothers, fathers, and others to help in that development. When one realizes how rapidly the newborn infant's brain develops, a question emerges: How should the mother, father, and caregivers respond to best aid the child's development?

LANGUAGE INTERACTIONS WITH PARENTS OR CAREGIVERS.   Providing a safe environment helps infants and young children as well as families feel valued and respected. It is also important to develop a secure and positive relationship with the infant by holding him or her in a loving and comforting manner. Babies need cradling, gentle touching, and eye contact. They also need to hear a voice, whether singing or talking to them, while they are being dressed or fed. Be sure to respond to the baby's sounds; they too will try to imitate the sound they hear. This will help them develop a sense of language.

It is also important for families to continue to share their cultural values with their children, because these values are assets to their children's development. For example, parents can play culturally relevant music for their children. Interestingly, Soley and Hannon (2010) found that infants appear to prefer music that has culture-specific meaning—music from their native culture. Nursery rhymes in the child's heritage language assist young children in learning the sounds of that language. For example, many families in the U.S. recite Mother

Goose rhymes which help increase language awareness and are fun to repeat! Young children also enjoy looking at colorful picture books and reading books with their caregivers, particularly when they can relate to the book themselves. A great example is Sandra Cisneros's book *Hairs/Pelitos*, in which the main character talks about the different types of hair of family members.

Providing a safe environment is important so that infants and young children, as well as families, feel valued and respected. It is also important for families to continue to share their funds of knowledge with their children because these are assets to their children's development.

EMOTIONAL AND COGNITIVE INTERACTIONS WITH PARENTS AND CAREGIVERS.   According to Dowling (2010), there is a link between feelings and brain development that is crucial in the early years. Children who have healthy emotional development have supportive families that guide them through different emotions in order to develop strong cognitive skills such as problem solving, perception, and reasoning.

Six levels of developing emotional and intellectual health in children are described by Greenspan (2002). At the first level, when a familiar caregiver touches and talks with the infant, the child responds with interest and pleasure. This helps the child develop a feeling of security and also helps the child organize his or her senses and motor responses. When children do not receive interaction from their caregiver, they withdraw and become apathetic and despondent.

The second level of development occurs by 4 months, when infants begin to respond to a parent's smile. Emotional responses precede the child's motor ability. These emotional responses can be observed by watching a 4- or 5-month-old baby smile in response to another's smile. By 9 months, there are early forms of communication and thinking. Two-way communication, with the mother talking and the baby responding, occurs.

The emotional abilities developed earlier become the building blocks in the third level at 12 to 18 months. The child has a greater ability to problem solve. The fourth level focuses on the toddler who increasingly needs to develop the use of emotional cueing, more often referred to as affect cueing.

The fifth level includes symbols that have purpose and meaning, as seen in make-believe play. The sixth level finds the child able to use cause-and-effect thinking, recognizing others' ideas with his or her own intentions and feelings. This level allows impulse control, judgment, and reality testing (Greenspan, 2002).

Positive Environment, Healthy Families, and Children

As already discussed, a child's brain is not fixed at birth but rather is affected by the nourishment, care, and stimulation it receives. The interactions that children have with their families and other support systems are crucial for a healthy development.

Because the environment has an impact on the brain even before birth, trauma and abuse can harm it and interfere with its development. For example, exposure to nicotine, alcohol, or other drugs affects the child before and after birth. It influences not only the child's general development but also the wiring of the brain. For educators, it is important to understand that early experiences such as interactions help stimulate brain activity. Nourishing young children means that adults actively engage with them. With new technologies, caution should be taken since early exposure to screen media may have negative effects for young infants (Napier, 2014). All this shows the importance of promoting nourishing, caring, responsive environments for healthy brain development.

Early Experiences

Children are primed for learning during the early years. Their experiences in the first three years affect their growth and abilities for the rest of their childhood and as adults. According to Newman (1996), "Early stimulation is essential to normal development" (p. 15)—both normal brain development as well as emotional development. This is because when the environment is nurturing and stimulating, it results in both neurological brain development and human attachment (Brazelton & Greenspan, 2000). Parents must be able to read their babies' cues and respond to infants' feelings, knowing when they need stimulation, when they need to be left alone, and when they need comforting.

Summary

Strong families have strong parents who know how to meet the needs of their children regardless of the stressors they face. Families need to know that what they offer their children—their funds of knowledge—are valued by the school and other extended systems. In order to identify funds of knowledge, teachers must know the family's cultural and social background. When working with diverse families in an early childhood program, it is very important to keep in mind ethnicity and national origin, language, religion or spiritual practice, special needs, socioeconomic status, and sexual orientation, as these characteristics of families help in the creation of funds of knowledge. It is important to keep in mind too the different family theories in order to understand the situations that vary related to the circumstances in the family.

Parents are their child's first educators and are responsible for providing an environment that facilitates attachment and brain development in their child, but parents often rely on the entire family to assist with the development.

Child attachment theories help teachers and parents identify appropriate and quality interactions for children. Theories of attachment help parents understand that when they provide children with strong attachments from birth, children will develop a healthy understanding of friendships and relationships that may last a lifetime. The Ecological Systems Theory provides parents and educators with a blueprint regarding how the community, the school, the teacher, and the family work together to promote children's overall development.

Suggested Class Activities and Discussions

1. Make a list of the funds of knowledge that have been given to you by your family. Interview two families different than your own. Make a list of their funds of knowledge. Find similarities and differences between families. Share with the class.

2. Using the book *Cuadros de Familia* (or *Family Pictures*) by Carmen Lomas Garza, make your own book with your family pictures. You can draw the pictures or use real photographs. Write in the text that describes your family's traditions, beliefs, and cultural practices. Develop an attachment statement that shows how your family creates attachments. Share with the class.

3. Using Family Ecological Systems Theory concentric circles, look for resources in your community that collaborate with families. Make a list including addresses, phone numbers, and websites to begin creating a Support Systems Resource Guide. Add information as needed.

4. Take the quiz regarding brain development on the Zero to Three website to test your knowledge of brain development.

Useful Websites

National Center for Families Learning
Zero to Three

National Association for the Education of Young Children

Glossary Terms

Attachment: Bond created between mother/father with baby.
Funds of knowledge: Those skills that families pass to their children to help them survive and thrive.

Parent: Someone who takes care and provides for a child, can be biological or adoptive.

Chapter 2
The Diversity of Families

Understanding, valuing, and respecting diversity of families helps teachers create a nurturing and inclusive environment for children and promotes family engagement.

Mari Riojas-Cortez

Learning Outcomes

In this chapter on the diversity of families, you will find information that will help you examine the strengths and challenges of diverse families. After completing the chapter, you should be able to do the following:

2.1 Define the term *family*.

2.2 Examine the diversity of families.

2.3 Identify current trends within the diversity of families.

2.4 Describe the functions of families.

2.5 List and describe the five stages of parenthood.

Families

The U.S. Census Bureau (2010) defines a **family** as "a group of two or more people who reside together and who are related by birth, marriage, or adoption," while a **household** is defined as "all people who occupy a housing unit as their usual place of residence" (see Figure 2.1 for different types of households from 1970 to 2012). The percentage of married households has declined in the U.S. since the 1940s and nonfamily households have seen a steady increase (see Figure 2.2). Families live within households and vary significantly. Since the family is a socially constructed concept (Weigel, 2008), the variations are endless and depend on variables such as nationality, culture, traditions, and socioeconomic status, among others. As such, these families are diverse and dynamic. This definition of *family* fits many families today, and includes those that are culturally and linguistically diverse, come from diverse backgrounds, and those who are raising children with special needs.

The importance of the family unit in the socialization of children cannot be overstated. It is essential that children have a supportive, interactive environment that provides loving, caring relationships so that children develop emotionally, intellectually, and physically. Although families in the United States and around the world must live with change, the essence of the family remains stable. Family members need a permanent relationship on which they can count for consistency, understanding, and support. Qiu, Schvaneveldt, and Sahin (2013) found in a cross-cultural study that children believed that the function of a family was to provide "affection, nurturance, interaction, and support" (p. 10). If the family provides for the basic needs of its members and its members are connected, reducing isolation and alienation, then the family will flourish. Nothing is more important than the family as the provider for and socializing agent of children. Regardless of the structure, the family is a viable, working system that gives the nurture and support needed by its members. The school needs to respect families in this role.

Figure 2.1 Different Types of Households from 1970 to 2012

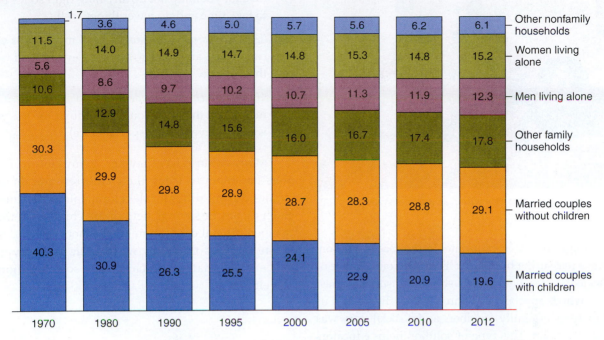

Source: U.S. Census Bureau, Current Population Survey, Annual Social and Economic Supplement, selected years, 1970 to 2012.

Families across cultures have different ways of displaying affection, but children cannot thrive physically or emotionally without the nurturance of those who love and care for them. This is particularly true of children with special needs. For example, my son, who has autism, does extremely well when people who work with him praise him and respond to his hugs. This is important to note, because in our family we like to give hugs and praise one another as part of our funds of knowledge. Depending on the age of the child, though,

Figure 2.2 Percentage of Married Households Since 1940s

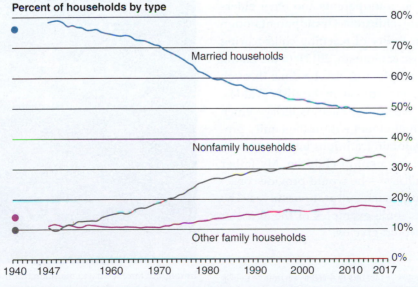

Source: U.S. Census Bureau, Decennial Census, 1940, and Current Population Survey, Annual Social and Economic Supplements, 1968 to 2017.

logoboom/Shutterstock

Unity helps families operate within a variety of systems.

hugs might not be appropriate. In the case of my son, when a reassuring hug might have been out of place or unwelcome, teachers would show him social stories[1] about who is appropriate to hug. His teachers asked us for pictures of family members and a social story was created for him. This type of solution helps educators increase their cultural understanding of a family's socialization practices in order to collaborate with them and thus provide safe and healthy experiences to assist in the child's development (Casper, Cooper, & Finn, 2003; Nelson, Leerkes, Perry, O'Brien, Calkins, & Marcovitch, 2013). Understanding a family's socialization practices will help create stronger bonds between families and educators.

Just like educators and parents, extended family members such as grandparents and other elders provide support for children. Grandparents often take on the responsibility of teaching child-rearing practices (Backhouse & Graham, 2012). In the Latino community, for example, this can be done through *consejos* which means advise in English (Valdés, 1996), or cultural narratives such as *dichos* which means "sayings", that elders within the family provide not only to maintain traditions but also to help in the healthy development of children. My father used to "speak in *dichos*"—he would provide consejos or advice through such cultural narratives. The following includes some examples of the *dichos or sayings* my father would give us.

---

[1]Social stories include photos or pictures that create a narrative to help children on the autism spectrum with different social situations.

1. "*El que mucho abarca poco aprieta*" means that if you do a lot you may not do anything right so it's best to take time and do fewer things well.

2. "*A la fuerza ni los zapatos entran*" means that you can't force anything to happen; events will take their course.

3. "*El que mucho se despide pocas ganas tiene de irse*" means that the more you say goodbye, the less you want to leave (from a special place).

Many cultures have sayings. In my culture, families use them to teach their children morals and values during different developmental milestones. Such dichos or sayings help guide children in their socioemotional development. Teachers can find out if the families that they work with have sayings or consejos that guide children's socioemotional development.

Armando Cortez

Immigrant families try to maintain traditions for the socioemotional well-being of their children.

The Diversity of Families

The structure, stage of family development, religion or faith, family size, socioeconomic background, language, culture, ages, and gender of children contribute to the makeup of each unique family. According to Knopf and Swick (2007), families in today's society are very different from those of previous generations. With the increase of diversity in families, it is imperative not only to increase awareness but also engagement as this will help to create stronger partnerships.

The families presented in the following vignettes represent a few examples of the diversity—especially the diversity of structure—encountered in many families. Think about your own family and the families you work with and see if any are similar to the ones presented in these examples.

The Single-Parent Family

Tina is a young divorced mother with one son, Tommy, age 3. They live with Tina's parents. In addition to working part-time at a department store, Tina takes 6 hours of classes at a community college. Each morning she prepares breakfast for Tommy and herself, bundles him into his coat during cold weather, hopes that her aging automobile will start, and heads into her long day. First, she drops Tommy off with her sister, Georgia, who runs a family childcare facility in her home. She feels fortunate to have a relative who enjoys children to care for Tommy, who has been anxious ever since his father left. The security of spending his days at Aunt Georgia's helps compensate for his loss.

Tina's ex-husband, Ted, does not send support money consistently, and Tina knows her parents' resources are limited. As she works as a clerk in the department store, she dreams of the time when she will earn enough money to give Tommy the home and opportunities he needs. Tina figures that with family help and her part-time job, she will be able to graduate in a little more than two years, just about the time Tommy will start school.

The School-Age Mother

As Sherrill thinks back, she can't remember when she didn't want a baby. "When I have a baby," she thought, "I'll be treated like an adult by my mother, and I'll also have a baby all my own who will love me." At

3 months, though, Gerald has already become more than she can handle.

Sherrill turned 15 yesterday, and instead of being able to hang out with her friends, she had to take care of Gerald. "If only my mother hadn't had to work," Sherrill complained, "I would have had a couple of hours between feedings just to get out. I never dreamed a baby would be so demanding. What makes him cry so much?"

The school down the street offers a program for teen mothers and their infants. Sherrill is on the waiting list and plans to enroll at the end of summer. "I never thought I'd want to go back to school," she says, "but they help out by caring for my baby while I'm in class and my mother says that I need to be able to make a living for Gerald. Temporary Assistance to Needy Families will help me for only 24 months. I really don't like school, but I guess I'd better go. If only Gerald would start being more fun."

The Two-Parent Family Experiencing Homelessness

When Barbara married Jed, the future looked good. Young, handsome, and hardworking, Jed thought his job at the plant would last forever. Who would have expected the layoffs? Jed's father worked at the plant for 25 years before he retired. Now Jed and Barbara, along with Jessie, age 2, and Bob, age 6, are moving west in hopes of finding work.

It's hard to live out of a car. Barbara worries about Bob because he is missing first grade. She and Jed put him in school whenever they are in a city for any length of time, but schools want his permanent address. It embarrasses Barbara to say their family is homeless, so she finds out the name of a street near the school and pretends they live there. Bob doesn't like school anyway. He says the children make fun of him and the teacher gives him seatwork that he doesn't understand.

Jed feels as if he has failed as a father and provider for his family. If he could just find a good job, his family would not be homeless. Minimum wage doesn't give him enough to pay for rent, let alone buy clothing and food. Last month they spent time at a church-run mission for the homeless. Jed was glad they were in a town far from home so that none of his old school friends would recognize him and Barbara. Jed hopes that maybe a good factory job will turn up, but the fact that he does not have technology skills or a high school diploma presents a challenge.

The Two-Income Family

"Joe, the alarm. It's your turn to get up and start breakfast," Maria says as she turns over to get 10 more minutes of sleep before the drive to school. Each day, Maria teaches 28 second-graders in the adjoining school district. Joe teaches mathematics at the local middle school. Their children, Karen and Jaime, stay with a neighbor until it is time for them to walk to school. Joe and Maria take turns dashing home early enough in the afternoon to supervise the children after school.

At times, the stress of work and the demanding days get to Joe and Maria. Some days their schedules do not blend and they scurry to find someone to care for the children after school. Karen and Jaime occasionally have been latchkey children, providing for themselves with no adult supervision in the afternoon. Neither Joe nor Maria want the children to be left on their own. They see too many children in their classrooms in similar situations who feel as if no one cares. Joe tries to be a nurturing father who helps with the home, but he relies on Maria to clean, shop, and cook.

Summers are the best time for the family. Joe works for a summer camp and Maria is able to spend more time at home, enjoying the children and organizing for the coming year. Periodically, she thinks about how much easier it would be for her to quit teaching, but then reality sets in. They could not make the house payments if they were not a two-income family.

The Immigrant Family

The Gonzalez family moved to the United States from San Luis Potosí, México, ten years ago when their two older children were very young. After Juan and Leticia married, they decided to move to the United States to provide a better life for their children. Although lacking proper documents, the newlywed couple decided to venture to a new country where life is very different from their life in rural Mexico. Juan found work in construction, while Leticia worked as a babysitter for children from an affluent neighborhood. Because Leticia and Juan work long hours, they have not been able to attend English as a Second Language, or ESL, classes at their local church, although they have tried. Their two oldest children have to translate for them when they receive notes from school or go to the doctor. Juan and Leticia have thought about going back to their home country, but they know life would be harder. Here, they live in a community close to their own family, and

Leticia's aunt takes care of their youngest two children. The Gonzalez family is saving money in order to hire an immigration attorney to help them get the necessary papers to obtain permanent residency but with the current immigration policy and the reversal of the DACA or Deferred Action for Childhood Arrivals, they are living in fear of being deported.

The Grandparents Family

Wolf is a sixth-grader who is being raised by both maternal grandparents. Wolf's parents divorced when she was very young and her grandparents were given custody of her and her two siblings. She also has stepsiblings who live with other family members. Wolf's mother became involved with drugs when she married her husband, and was arrested and sent to prison. Unable to take care of the children, she gave up her parental rights to her parents. Although Wolf's grandparents are actively engaged in her education, Wolf often shows negative behaviors that get her in trouble with her teachers. She also appears to have difficulty interacting with other children. The grandparents are worried and have been talking with the school counselor and social worker to get her the help she needs, to try to prevent these behaviors from becoming more difficult as she gets older.

The LGBTQ Family

Rosie and Linda met in college but married other people. After they had children and their marriages ended, they moved in together and decided to raise the children from their previous marriages as a family. Although neither family was supportive of Rosie and Linda's lifestyle at first, their respective families eventually understood that they needed to be a part of the children's lives. Often Rosie and Linda find themselves in difficult situations particularly at school because some teachers and other parents do not agree with their lifestyle. Sometimes their children do not understand why others do not invite them for play dates and birthday parties.

The Family with a Child of Special Abilities

Alan and Miranda were very excited to have a boy as they already had a daughter, and Johnny was the perfect baby boy when he was born. Both parents worked, so Miranda's parents took care of Johnny. Nothing seemed to be out of the ordinary until Johnny was around 10 months. His family noticed he wouldn't point or babble or turn when they called him like other children his age. Johnny's parents communicated this to his pediatrician, who referred them to one of the local organizations for screening. In the meantime, the doctor asked them to go to the Autism Speaks website to learn the signs of autism and take the M-CHAT-R, the Modified Checklist for Autism in Toddlers (Revised) available on that site. Alan and Miranda have to take turns taking Johnny to different specialists, causing them to ask for time off from work.

The Family of Muslim Faith

Fatima and her husband Ahamed are Muslim. They have two children: a daughter Noor who is 5 years old, and a son Hassan who is 8. Both children love attending school but are often bullied because of their faith. The children laugh at Noor when they see her wearing a hijab. Fatima's daughter is now asking not to wear the hijab to school because she doesn't want others to laugh at her. For Fatima and Ahamed, faith is very important and they are considering switching their children to another school, even a private one.

The Co-Parent Family

Susan and Kevin were inseparable. People often used to refer to them as the perfect couple. After three children, completion of graduate school, the death of a parent, and financial stress, things began to change. The arguments in the household increased. Both Susan and Kevin felt that it was better to divorce, particularly for their children, than to live in constant stress. After a very difficult divorce Susan and Kevin began the process of co-parenting. For about two years, they had to learn to live with each other but separately and with respect. Family dinners were still a ritual on Sunday evenings but their children spent their time split between Kevin's apartment and Susan's house. The children had to learn to live in two homes but have accepted the situation and are happy that they get to see both parents every day.

KNOWING DIVERSE FAMILIES.   The preceding examples show some of the variety in family structure. The vignettes are based on real-life family situations. Regardless of the structure, most families have support groups such as extended family to provide love and care when parents are not present. Even when families deal with difficult situations, strong families learn to cope with difficulties because they want to see their children succeed in school. Unfortunately, not all families have

support systems to help them in difficult situations. It is imperative that the schools find ways to support families for the healthy development of children.

It is important for educators to understand how each of these structures, and others not discussed, affects families. All families need guidance but in different ways, depending on their needs and family structure. For instance, families not familiar with the school system, such as immigrant families, will need more guidance to understand the school's expectations. Teachers should ensure that information is relevant for all families, regardless of their structure. Teachers can make things easier for parents by making school routines and procedures parent-friendly. It is never a good idea to scold parents who do not follow procedures, because this only creates barriers between the home and the school.

Current Trends in the Diversity of Families

The next section provides more information regarding current issues of the diversity of families. At this point, it is important to remember that diversity goes beyond culture and language, although both are of critical importance. Diverse families face similar situations and challenges. However, diversity of families is a broad spectrum of situations. The real-life vignettes provide an opportunity for teachers to reflect on their perceptions of diverse structures within families. Our perceptions as educators build a positive or negative foundation for the development of family partnerships.

Fatherhood

The National Center for Fathering (2018) lists the following situations for many fathers in the United States today: adoptive dad, at-home dad, divorced dad, noncustodial dad, single dad, stepdad, traveling dad, special needs–kids dad, and urban dad. Also very important is the married dad. Regardless of their specific circumstance, fathers play an important role in a child's development. From before Puritan times until well after industrialization, a "good" father was the breadwinner and provider of moral guidance. Fathers have long held these two roles, but in the 20th century, the importance of fathers' roles in their children's development underwent change based on social conditions and beliefs as well as research in child development. In

All children need a nurturing relationship with their fathers.

the 21st century, fathers exhibit a willingness to expand their role, becoming companions, caregivers, standard setters, guidance counselors, play partners, teachers, providers, and role models.

The Children's Bureau, established in 1912, provides information to families about caring for their infants in their publication *Infant Care*. Historically, although fathers were mentioned in the publication, the advice was directed to mothers. Fathers were not considered as important to the child's development until the 1940s. Awareness of the father as a gender role model came about toward the end of World War II, but it was not until the 1970s that the role of nurturant father was emphasized (Lamb, 1997). In the last two decades, the number of intervention and support programs for fathers has increased (Bronte-Tinkew, Burkhauser, & Metz, 2012).

Some advocates for fathers argue that in the 20th century fathers were viewed as superfluous: "The retreat from fatherhood began in the 1960s, gained momentum in the 1970s, and hit full stride in the 1980s" (Horn, 1997, p. 24). In the 1990s, however, organizations that focused on fathers emerged, including the National Institute for Responsible Fatherhood and Family Development, Promise Keepers, National Center for Fathering, and the National Fatherhood Initiative. These groups responded to data about the negative aspects of being raised without a father, including that children are "three times more likely to fail at school, two to three times more likely to experience emotional or behavioral problems requiring psychiatric treatment . . . three times more likely to commit suicide as adolescents . . . five times more likely to be poor" (p. 27). Even when the families came from the same socioeconomic background, children without a father present had more challenges than those who had both parents (Horn, 1997). In two-parent families, it is important that family members are supportive of one another and that conflict and abuse be absent. For children growing up without a father, having a male as a father figure, such as an uncle or grandfather, has a positive effect on their lives.

In today's society, many fathers are looking for ways to get involved (Goldberg, Tan, Davis, & Easterbrooks, 2013) as research shows, father involvement has positive outcomes such as higher IQs, advanced language and cognitive skills (Ancell, Bruns, & Chitiyo, 2018). The number of children living only with fathers in 2017 increased (see Figure 2.3). Indeed, the presence of the father is significant in children's lives.

Figure 2.3 Children Under 18 Living with One Parent

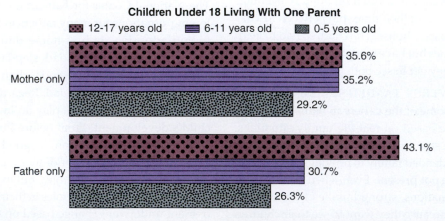

Source: 2017 Current Population Survey Annual Social and Economic Supplement www.census.gov/topics/families.html.

Current studies suggest that fathers' involvement can help offset negative effects on child development when mothers are not as supportive (Martin, Ryan, & Brooks-Gunn, 2010). Even when mothers are supportive, research shows that fathers' more physical style of interacting with their children supports and adds to the nurturing and verbal style of the mother (Horn, 1997; Lamb, 1997). As a father's parental role grows beyond just that of a breadwinner, so do the father's attitudes toward parenting. In a national survey conducted by Zero to Three (2010), it was found that fathers today are not satisfied with their work/family balance, find challenges in a variety of parenting situations, and need more information regarding social development. Modern day fathers show increased engagement and affection, which help children with their socioemotional development (American Psychological Association, 2018).

High levels of father involvement indicate positive outcomes in cognitive and socioemotional development (Halme, Astedt-Kurk, & Tarkka, 2009). The Fathering Indicator Framework (Gadsden, Fagan, Ray, & Davis, 2001) provides six positive fathering indicator categories: 1) father presence, 2) caregiving, 3) children's social competence, 4) cooperative parenting, 5) father's healthy living, and 6) material and financial contribution. Operational categories accompany the fathering indicator categories. These are used by programs to guide research regarding the importance of a father in a child's life, as well as how a father's participation creates a change of behavior in the child and family, and how these effects are threaded together to help men become more positively involved in their children's lives (National Center on Fathers and Families, 2011).

Heightened interest in fatherhood goes hand in hand with the increasing number of women who work outside the home. Many young fathers see the expression of love toward their children as a way toward fulfillment in their own lives through meaningful relationships. Some fathers are full-time homemakers and care for the children while their wives work outside the home.

Although fathers and mothers are similar in their connection with their children, fathers tend to be more physically stimulating through unpredictable play, whereas mothers tend toward containment and soft, repetitive verbal expression. Although this will vary depending on the individual. A father's physical play largely benefits the child's socioemotional development (Fletcher, St. George, & Freeman, 2013). Furthermore, fathers of children with special needs have a tremendous responsibility in making sure they bond with the child and yet maintain a strong bond with their other children (Huhtanen & Huhtanen, 2008). Figure 2.4 from the U.S. Census provides a snapshot of today's dads.

In the National Association for the Education of Young Children (NAEYC) accredited childcare programs, fathers preferred involvement in (a) family activities, (b) Daddy and Me programs, (c) activities for both parents to learn about their child's future, (d) activities for both parents to learn about child development, and (e) sporting events (Turbiville, Umbarger, & Guthrie, 2000). Parker and Livingston from the Pew Research Center (2017) list six important findings regarding fathers: 1) Parenting is central to identity; 2) There has been an increased involvement in childcare; 3) It is now less common to be the breadwinner; 4) Work-family balance is a challenge; 5) Public perceptions of the father's role as opposed to mother's can be challenging; 6) Most adults believe it is important for the father to bond with baby. More than half of the fathers surveyed by the Pew Center indicated that they find parenting essential for their identity, very rewarding, and enjoyable all of the time.

SUGGESTIONS FOR EDUCATORS TO SHARE WITH FATHERS

1. *Be there.* Engage in activities with your child, from the early caregiving bathing and bedroom routines to the later reading, storytelling, and playing together activities.

Figure 2.4 Fatherly Figures

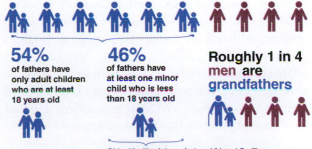

Roughly 6 in 10 men are fathers

Of the 121 million men age 15 and over in the United States, about 75 million are fathers to biological, step, or adopted children.

54%
of fathers have only adult children who are at least 18 years old

46%
of fathers have at least one minor child who is less than 18 years old

Roughly 1 in 4 men are grandfathers

Of the 35 million fathers of minor children, 1.7 million (roughly 2 percent) are "single" fathers who are living with at least one child under 18 with no spouse or partner present.

Source: Fatherly Figures: A Snapshot of Dads Today. U.S. Census Bureau. Retrieved on July 22, 2018 from https://www.census.gov/library/visualizations/2018/comm/fathers-day.html

2. *Accept your child.* Accept your child for who she or he is. Each child has an individual personality. Trying to change a quiet child into a boisterous one or an uncoordinated child into an outstanding athlete makes the child feel unaccepted.

3. *Use positive parenting.* Praise is better than punishment in guiding children. Help the child express anger constructively.

4. *Share parenting.* Work as a team with your spouse or with the mother of your children.

5. *See fathering as worthwhile and satisfying.* Fatherhood can be a prideful role. Think about how you can influence the future by working positively with your child.

6. *Be there for your children.* Be involved in your children's education from early childhood on. Listen to the needs and interests of your children and show interest in what they like. The PTA (Parent Teacher Association) is a good way to connect to your child's education.

The first step in getting fathers, brothers, uncles, and other male role models involved is to keep in mind that the term *father* extends to all father figures. Because many children do not have a father in the home, the inclusion of father figures is extremely important. Encourage family friends, uncles, grandfathers, stepfathers, and interested others to become support systems for children.

Many schools and centers have developed ways to involve fathers and other male role models. Fourteen of these programs are described in *Getting Men Involved* (Levine et al., 1993), but there are more current examples. For example, there is the National Fathering Network, which has affiliates in 35 states and provides different opportunities for involvement. Another example is the Kindering Center in Bellevue, Washington, a support group for fathers raising children with special needs. The Parents as Teachers program in Ferguson-Florissant, Missouri, has established programs for teenage parents and parents-to-be. The FRED (Fathers Reading Every Day) program focuses on reading. AVANCE also offers a father involvement program that focuses on increasing father interactions with children and decreasing violence in the home (AVANCE, 2018). Another current program is the Fatherhood Project sponsored by the Department of Psychiatry at Massachusetts General Hospital (MGH).

The mission of this project is to "improve the health and well-being of children by empowering fathers to be active, informed and emotionally engaged with their children and families" (The Fatherhood Project, 2018). This project provides different opportunities for community organizations to engage parents, workshops, research, and other resources.

Divorce

The divorce rate in the United States has fluctuated between 2000 and 2011, with the highest rates in 2000 and 2002 (see Figure 2.5). The economic status of parents who divorce changes drastically—about one quarter, or 24.6%, of all custodial parents and their children had incomes below the poverty level in 2007. Issues such as health care and child support that custodial and non-custodial parents face affect their and their children's economic well-being (Grall, 2009).

Divorce involves change for both parents and children but can be particularly difficult for children. Children are usually ashamed of the divorce and feel rejected because of a parent's departure, but the effects of divorce on children are related more to the previous situation and the subsequent events that affect the child than to the divorce itself. Despite most children's negative feelings about their parents' separation, divorce can improve the situation for a child when a successfully reestablished single-parent family or a remarriage provides the child with a good quality of life. Oftentimes, too, children's initial adverse feelings reduce over time; their risk at school is much lower even just a year after the divorce than immediately following it. Parents must continue to do positive parenting, limit conflicts, and increase the quality of parent—child interactions to make separation or divorce less difficult on children (Clark, 2013).

Children of all ages respond to the divorce of their parents; some children are more resilient than others. When I was a teacher, one of the most challenging times I had with a child was when her parents were going through a divorce. The father had decided to go back to his home country so the mother had to go back to work, thus spending less time with her daughter. As a teacher, I had to learn how to adjust my classroom environment to ensure the child felt safe and nurtured by engaging with in her favorite centers which ere the dramatic and art center.

Another part of helping children adjust to divorce is to reassure them they are not the cause of it. They also

Figure 2.5 Provisional Rate of Divorces and Annulments: United States, 2000–2016

Year	Divorces and annulments	Population	Rate per 1,000 total population	Year	Divorces and annulments	Population	Rate per 1,000 total population
2016[1]	827,261	257,904,548	3.2	2007[3]	856,000	238,352,850	3.6
2015[2]	800,909	258,518,265	3.1	2006[3]	872,000	236,094,277	3.7
2014[2]	813,862	256,483,624	3.2	2005[3]	847,000	233,495,163	3.6
2013[2]	832,157	254,408,815	3.3	2004[4]	879,000	236,402,656	3.7
2012[3]	851,000	248,041,986	3.4	2003[5]	927,000	243,902,090	3.8
2011[3]	877,000	246,273,366	3.6	2002[6]	955,000	243,108,303	3.9
2010[3]	872,000	244,122,529	3.6	2001[7]	940,000	236,416,762	4.0
2009[3]	840,000	242,610,561	3.5	2000[7]	944,000	233,550,143	4.0
2008[3]	844,000	240,545,163	3.5				

[1]Excludes data for California, Georgia, Hawaii, Indiana, Minnesota, and New Mexico. [2]Excludes data for California, Georgia, Hawaii, Indiana, and Minnesota. [3]Excludes data for California, Georgia, Hawaii, Indiana, Louisiana, and Minnesota. [4]Excludes data for California, Georgia, Hawaii, Indiana, and Louisiana. [5]Excludes data for California, Hawaii, Indiana, and Oklahoma. [6]Excludes data for California, Indiana, New York City, and Oklahoma. [7]Excludes data for California, Indiana, Louisiana, and Oklahoma.

Note: Populations are consistent with the 2000 census.

Note: The term "provisional" in this context indicates that the statistics are constantly changing.

Source: National Center for Health Statistics, CDC. www.cdc.gov/nchs/nvss/marriage_divorce_tables.htm

need to know by the parents' actions and words that they will continue to have their parents' love. Adapt your caring for children to their level of development—their understanding and response are related to their age and maturity (Leon & Cole, 2004).

Teachers and administrators must recognize that during the period of divorce, the family may be in turmoil. Children will bring their distress with them to the classroom. The school can offer the child a stable and sensitive environment—one the child can count on. The school can also provide support and

understanding by trying to meet the family's needs. Talk with both parents to help the child feel safe, secure, and accepted. Keep positive expectations for the children. Be kind, but encourage them to keep up with their classwork. Find ways that the child can contribute to the class. Use special projects or activities that may interest the child. Provide a "Talk About Feelings" learning center where children can talk to you about their feelings, or write or draw what they are feeling. The center should also include books about feelings or developmentally appropriate videos to help the children reflect on their feelings. Opportunities to learn about and express their feelings provide children with tools to handle their emotions.

Single-Parent Families

Single-parent families are not a new phenomenon. From the 1860s until the mid-1960s, there was no increase in the proportion of single parents because the growing divorce rate was offset by the declining death rate. Young children in the last half of the 1800s and first half of the 1900s were raised in single-parent families, most often because the mother was widowed; 25% had lost a parent to death (Amato, 1994). According to the U.S. Census, in 2011 there were 32 million one-person households in the U.S. (you can also refer

ZouZou/Shutterstock

This single parent supports her child's education by coloring with him.

back to Figure 2.3). Grall (2009) indicates that 27% of custodial single mothers and their children live in poverty, whereas 12.9% of custodial single fathers and their children live in poverty. In 2012, 24% of children in the U.S. lived with only their mother, while 4% lived only with their father (Federal Interagency Forum on Child and Family Statistics, 2013).

Gender differences exist for mothers and fathers. For example, during the period that a mother is raising her children alone, she has a much higher risk of poverty. Twelve percent of single parents who work full time find themselves in poverty; 49% of those who work part time are also poor. Almost 74% of single parents who do not work are in poverty, and 79% of single parents are in the labor force (Litcher & Crowley, 2002). Most divorced parents remarry, however, making it possible for 80% of children to live in two-parent homes with a reduced risk of poverty. Figure 2.6 shows living arrangements for children under 18 years old (U.S. Census Bureau, 2018). Interestingly, the number of children in 2017 who lived with just their father increased to 16.1%.

Teachers need to show empathy for families who are going through life-changing events such as divorce, as this will increase the opportunity for collaboration. In addition, parents' marital status is not for teachers to judge; instead, they must learn how to best work with each parent or important caregiver in a child's life. This empathy is particularly significant in the lives of young children as they are developing attachments with adults.

Parents and teachers need to communicate throughout a child's education, but it is essential during periods of change to know what is happening both at home and at school, and to help children overcome the isolation and distress they might feel. Although approximately only one in every five children will be from a one-parent family at any given time, half of all children will spend part of their childhood in a one-parent family. Thus, it is important for teachers to offer convenient times for parent–teacher conferences, so ask the parents for their best times for availability. It is important to learn parents' names by checking records because the names of the children and the parents might not be the same. Calling the parents by their correct names is a simple gesture of courtesy. Find ways that single parents can be involved without putting great stress on the family. Parents who work outside the home might be able to attend early morning breakfasts, especially if childcare is provided and the children get breakfast, too. Keep the number of parents at each breakfast small so you can talk with each parent individually. Find out how

---

Figure 2.6 Living Arrangements for Children Under 18 Years Old

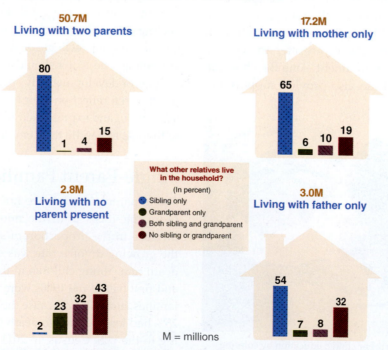

M = millions

Source: U.S Census Bureau. (2018) 2016 Current population survey annual social and economic supplement. Retrieved on November 9, 2018 from https://www.census.gov/library/visualizations/2016/comm/cb16-192_living_arrangements.html

they would like to be involved, what their needs are, and if they have any ideas for their partnership with the school. Acknowledge their suggestions for improved home–school collaboration.

Acknowledge and communicate with noncustodial parents. If noncustodial parents receive report cards and other information, they likely will be more interested in the child's work and can be better involved with the child. Most noncustodial parents are men, and the percentage of men who pay child support is low. Schools can help sustain or even increase the father's interest by keeping him informed, if such communication is specified in the custody papers.

Use care in communication. In all partnerships with parents, one of the most important elements of cooperation and understanding is the ability to communicate. The first objective is to have effective communication. The second objective is to prepare written materials that project positive and knowledgeable feelings toward the parent. Take care when preparing invitations to programs. Perhaps you may wish to encourage the participation of one particular group, but make sure the child and parent know they do not need to have a father, mother, or grandparent to attend. For example, saying, "Bring your grandparent or a grand-friend to class next week" implies that the visitors, not their titles, are important. At the program, make sure you have some get-acquainted activities so no one feels left out or alone. Activities also encourage networking among parents, and might be the best opportunity for new single parents in the neighborhood to become acquainted with others.

Be aware that if the parent remarries, the child is affected again, and concerns can arise regarding the loss of the parent as the sole caregiver, and a change in the strong relationship that may have developed between parent and child. There could also be issues with relationships between the stepparent and the children.

Blended Families

There is a complex social organization in blended families. In remarried families, some children might be the offspring of the mother, some of the father, and the remaining might be born to the remarried couple. A child could be living in a home with a brother or sister, a stepbrother or stepsister whose biological parent is the mother or father in the home, and a half-sister or half-brother who is the child of the remarried couple. In addition, they may have a similar situation with their other biological parent and have another set of siblings, stepsiblings, and half-siblings when they are living or visiting there. It is estimated that one in six children lives in a blended family (Parenting in America, 2015). In fact, families could have as many as 30 configurations (Manning & Wootten, 1987). In addition, there is an increase in families that have blended cultures.

When two people marry and one or both have children from a previous relationship, the road to a secure, happy family becomes more challenging. The members of the new family come with different backgrounds, have no family history together, and have no established way of doing things. Building a strong new family can be accomplished, but the initial excitement of the children and acceptance of the new arrangement by ex-spouses are complicated by the realities of the situation. A typical complication occurs because both parent and child have come from single-parent family status (even if the single-parent stage is short-lived). During the single-parent stage, parent and child tend to become extremely close. The parent may have turned to the children for emotional support and decision-making help in the absence of the former spouse. Children of the newly married couple often see the remarriage as a double loss: First they lost a parent through divorce, and now they are losing their special relationship with the other parent by having to share their custodial parent with a new stepparent.

Papernow (1993, 1998) breaks down the development of the blended family into three stages: fantasy, which includes fantasy, immersion, and awareness; restructuring; and solidifying. In the first two stages, the family is generally divided according to biological lines, but by the third, the family has created a new bond. During the fantasy phase of the first stage, parents visualize that the new marriage will provide a supportive, loving family; however, the children often want their biological parents back together. Papernow (1993) explains that "because the adults in the new family adore each other, [they assume] stepparents and stepchildren will also" (p. 13). In the second phase of the first stage, immersion, the nonbiological parent becomes the outsider parent, not able to relate in the same way a biological parent does to the biological children. Because of this and other tricky situations in the immersion phase, the parents may be concerned about the family's unity because of the emergence of negative feelings. During the last phase of the first stage, awareness, parents become more able to understand the dynamics of the new relationship. Once the outsider parent acknowledges the bond between biological parent and child, they are ready to go to the next stage. If parents can recognize the areas of concern in each of the three phases and deal with them successfully, the family will probably thrive, but if they get stuck in any of these first three phases, the family will probably dissolve.

The middle, or restructuring stage, includes mobilization—during which the airing of differences occurs—and action, during which power struggles are resolved and new agreements are made, with resulting changes in family structure and new boundaries. In this stage, "Every family activity is no longer a potential power struggle between insiders and outsiders" (Papernow, 1993, p. 16).

The final stage, solidifying, includes contact, during which intimacy and authenticity in real relationships are forged: "The marital relationship becomes more of a sanctuary and source of nourishment and support, even on step issues" (Papernow, 1993, p. 16). Finally, resolution occurs. Although issues can recur and the family may re-experience the stepparenting cycle, the family is able to go forward. Differences no longer threaten the family.

Though by the final stage the family unit is set, the entire blended-family cycle affects the children. They may go through stages of grief similar to those experienced after divorce, death, or moving away from loved ones. During the first stage, while the children are still feeling a loss, their participation in school often suffers. Children may act out in class, they may be despondent, and they may have no interest in schoolwork. For school-age children, the school is a stable environment and can be a support for them. Staying in the same school with their friends can ease the transition.

The stages of the blended-family cycle affect the adults as well. During the early stage, stepparents become aware that they are not able to nurture children in the same way biological parents do, because biological parents already have a strong bond with their children. Parents develop an awareness of these family pressures. Both partners recognize what they can handle and which attitudes need to be changed. In some cases, the family is never able to restructure their lives, and many of these marriages do not succeed.

The restructuring period of stepfamily development allows for more openness in discussion of change.

Parents and children continue to have strong biological ties, but the differences lead to action. In this action phase, family boundaries are clarified and the couple attempts to work together to find solutions.

Keep in mind that blended-family stages cannot be rushed, and that "learning how to work as a team is crucial to stepfamily integration, and usually essential for a close couple relationship to develop and grow" (Visher, 2001, p. 4). The biological parent can help the stepparent become part of the family by showing understanding of the stepparent's position: "Requiring civility within the household allows relationships to have the opportunity to develop, and demonstrating love and caring for both his or her children and new partner is an important element in the success of the family" (p. 3). Be patient with this process—Papernow (1993) found that 4 to 7 years were needed to complete the entire cycle; without patience, some families may never be able to develop their blended family into a strong family. This patience will pay off, because when issues are resolved and the blended family develops into a strong family, children will rebound and will resume normal behavior, including being more engaged in school. For teachers it is important that they are aware of these stages as they will see children experiencing varied behaviors.

Families Headed by Grandparents

Grandparent caregivers may also be an integral part of a family. In 2000, this role was acknowledged by the U.S. Census, which, for the first time ever, included questions regarding the grandparents' part in childrearing. Results of this census showed that the number of grandparents maintaining families doubled from 2.2 million in 1970 to 4.5 million in 2000, and care for grandchildren was maintained by 2.4 million grandparent caregivers. This equates to 3.9% of all households in 2000. Of these families, 19% had incomes below the poverty level. These are families in which parents may live with the family, but where the grandparents provide the financial support, which is different from families who have a grandparent move in with them (Simmons & Dye, 2003). These statistics mean that schools will have some families in which the children's grandparents are the primary caregivers, oftentimes for extended periods of time. Only 12% had their grandchildren less than 6 months; 11% cared for their grandchildren for 6 to 11 months; 23% for 1 to 2 years; 15% for 3 to 4 years; and the most, 39%, for 5 or more

When grandparents drop off or pick up their grandchild or grandchildren at school, be available to talk with them, just as you would with other key figures in the child's life. Make telephone calls or send a text to share something the grandchild has done that was a positive contribution. This could include such accomplishments as a painting, drawing, story, or just an interest in a subject. If there is a grandparent support group, encourage the grandparents with children in your class or school to attend. If there isn't a support group in your school, start one or find one nearby. Invite them to visit the class and help out! The experience of grandparents can be used as a great resource for projects.

Today, one child in 10 lives with a grandparent; about 41% of those are primarily raised by a grandparent (Livingston & Parker, 2010). By 2009, 2% of White and Hispanic children lived with grandparents (and no parents) and 5% of African American children lived with their grandparents (Kreider & Ellis, 2011). Byers (2010) indicates that Native American grandmothers have the highest percentage of rearing grandchildren than any other ethnic group. The U.S. Census estimates that 51.1% of American Indian and Alaskan Native grandparents are responsible for their grandchildren (U.S. Census Bureau, 2018).

The research indicates that the majority of grandparent-maintained families differ from households maintained by parents. These differences include the educational level of the grandparent, who may not have graduated from high school, and the grandparent's profession, which may not be high income. Even when grandparents work and have health insurance, the insurance programs often do not cover grandchildren living with them. In 2010, President Barack Obama

Funds of knowledge are also transmitted by grandparents, who often take care of children.

years (Simmons & Dye, 2003). In 2009, the U.S. Census reported that the majority of the children who live with only their grandparents live in poverty (Kreider & Ellis, 2011 [U.S. Census report]). It is important to provide resources for grandparents as they become responsible for raising their grandchildren so they can provide a stable, healthy, and nurturing environment for them while confronting interpersonal and environmental challenges (Doggett, Marken, & Caldwell, 2014). In 2018, nearly 1.5 million grandparents must work to support grandchildren as Figure 2.7 shows.

Grandparents need help in obtaining accurate information about, and assistance with, support services for themselves and their grandchildren. These services may include counseling, mentoring, and tutoring for the children. The grandparents might need counseling also, as well as information on legal and financial matters. Information given should be easy to understand. The information needs to be presented so all grandparents, regardless of their ethnic, cultural, or educational backgrounds, can understand and use.

Grandparents play a significant role in raising children in different cultures.

Figure 2.7 Grandparents in the Labor Force

Grandparents must work to support grandchildren.

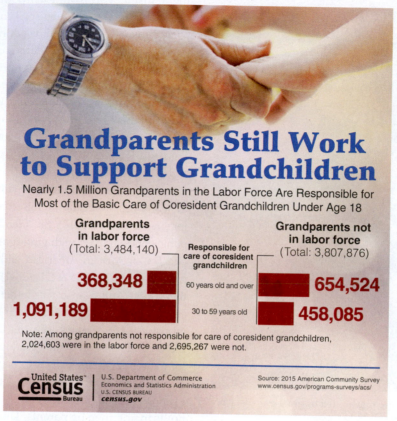

Source: United States Census. (2018). Grandparents still work to support grandchildren. Retrieved on November 9, 2018 from https://www.census.gov/content/dam/Census/library/visualizations/2017/comm/grandparents-day.pdf

signed into law the Patient Protection and Affordable Care Act. This law became highly controversial, but it sought to provide health care insurance for families who otherwise would not be able to obtain coverage.

Poverty and Families

Poverty is defined in the United States according to the income of the person or family. Poverty implies that people lack resources for what they need (Cancian & Reed, 2009). In Figure 2.8, we can see how poverty (number of people and rate) has fluctuated in the United States from 1959 to 2016. The number of children living in poverty increased between 2008 and 2009, from 19% to 20.7% (DeNavas-Walt, Proctor, & Smith, 2010). According to the National Center for Children in Poverty (2018), 21% of all children live in families with incomes below the federal poverty level. Many families live in poverty due to unemployment or loss of employment, a change in family structure, lack

of education, addictions, or health problems, among other reasons.

The economic downturn in 2007 increased the poverty rate due to the loss of employment and earnings (Cancian & Danziger, 2009). According to Cancian and Reed (2009), researchers associated with the Institute for Research on Poverty, changes in family structure and single-parent homes also increased the likelihood of poverty. In fact, the researchers state that single-mother families are five times as likely to be poor as married families. Most single mothers qualify for government assistance programs, including income support programs such as cash welfare and food stamps. Furthermore, the high rate of divorce and the fact that more people are opting not to marry increase the chances that a family will live in poverty (Cancian & Reed, 2009). Policies that specifically help such families increase their economic well-being open the doors for young children to participate in experiences that will help them grow and develop by obtaining assistance

Figure 2.8 Number in Poverty and Poverty Rate 1959–2016

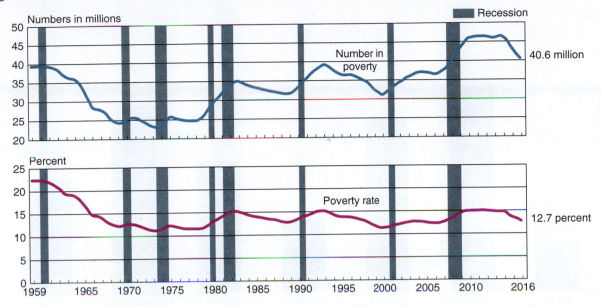

Source: U.S. Census Bureau, current Population Survey, 1960 to 2017 Annual Social and Economic Supplements.

through different programs and agencies as their parents struggle to find a better life. Following are a few of the nonprofit organizations that help people live in poverty. An online search will easily locate their websites.

YMCA

Catholic Charities

Salvation Army

American Red Cross

United Jewish Communities

Goodwill Industries International

Boys and Girls Clubs of America

Feed the Children

Habitat for Humanity International

Shriners Hospitals for Children

Food for the Poor

Throughout history, discrimination has had a negative effect on the social and economic well-being of culturally and linguistically diverse families such as African Americans, Latinos, and Native Americans. According to Cancian and Danziger (2009), half of the nation's poor are African American or Latino. From 2008 to 2009, the poverty rate increased for all groups except for the Asian population, as shown on Figure 2.9 (DeNavas-Walt, Proctor, & Smith, 2010).

According to Ratcliffe and Kalish (2017), poverty is persistent across generations of Black families as compared to white.

Currently, there are about 15 million children living in poverty in the U.S., creating a major health problem (Hanson, Hair, Shen, Shi, Gilmore, Wolfe, & Pollak, 2013). To exist in the culture of poverty often means to feel depressed, powerless to effect change, and unable to control one's destiny. Alienation, anomie, isolation, and depression are common partners of poverty, as well as information processing in infants (Hanson et al.). Although poverty has a look of despair, many families work together to provide the best for their children. Education and training appear to be the keys in helping families in poverty. Many face issues such as lack of insurance and lack of medical care, live in neighborhoods where crime is prevalent, and have negative school experiences due to their socioeconomic status. Many government agencies, such as the Administration for Children and Families, under the U.S. Department of Health and Human Services, provide programs such as Head Start and Temporary Assistance for Needy Families (TANF) to help families survive and hopefully break the cycle of poverty.

Families who have always been self-sufficient and suddenly find themselves without employment face

Figure 2.9 Percentage of Children Under Age 18 Living in Poverty, by Race/Ethnicity: 2012

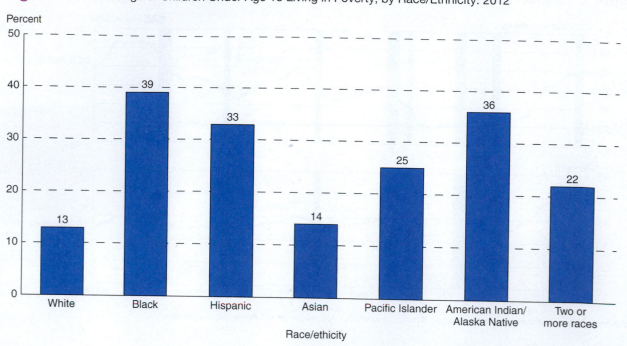

Note: The measure of child poverty includes families in which all children are related to the householder by birth, marriage, or adoption. Race categories exclude persons of Hispanic ethnicity.

Source: U.S. Department of Commerce, Census Bureau, American Community Survey (ACS), 2012. *See Digest of Education Statistics 2013*, table 102.60.

tremendous psychological adjustments, as well as difficulty in providing shelter and food. Have a resource guide posted on the school's website or on a bulletin board so parents can obtain numbers without feeling embarrassed or ashamed for doing so.

For some families, using social welfare is an acknowledgment of defeat and they would rather do without some necessities than accept such help. If they are open to suggestions, help by providing information on social services. The school can also provide exchange options where outgrown clothes can be substituted for ones that fit.

Recommend community agencies for parents who need additional help. If your school has a parent liaison, put him or her in contact with parents needing help. Children in poverty are likely to have poor health and inadequate care.

WAYS TO COUNTERACT POVERTY.   Poverty is multifaceted and it is often difficult to end its cycle, which is commonly known as chronic poverty. Stereotypes of families in poverty in the media portray these families as having numerous children, chronic unemployment,

and associations with drugs and violence (National Center for Children in Poverty, 2018)

To counteract the stress of poverty on families, parents and children need at least the following:

- A decent standard of living (jobs that pay enough to adequately rear children)

Families need healthy salaries to provide the basic necessities for their children. For the 21st century, the basic necessities include food, clothing, and shelter, as well as access to running water, electricity, phone, and technology. The median family income varies between states. Figure 2.10 shows the disparities between the states. For example, the median household income in 2016 for Virginia and Maryland was more than $60,000, in contrast with Arkansas and Mississippi, where the average income was less than $45,000. Examine Figure 2.10 and compare the states that have the highest poverty rates with the states that have large number of minority populations, Latino and African American in particular.

- Flexible working conditions so children can be cared for, and flexible childcare hours

Figure 2.10 Median Household Income in the Past 12 Months for the U.S. and Puerto Rico: 2016

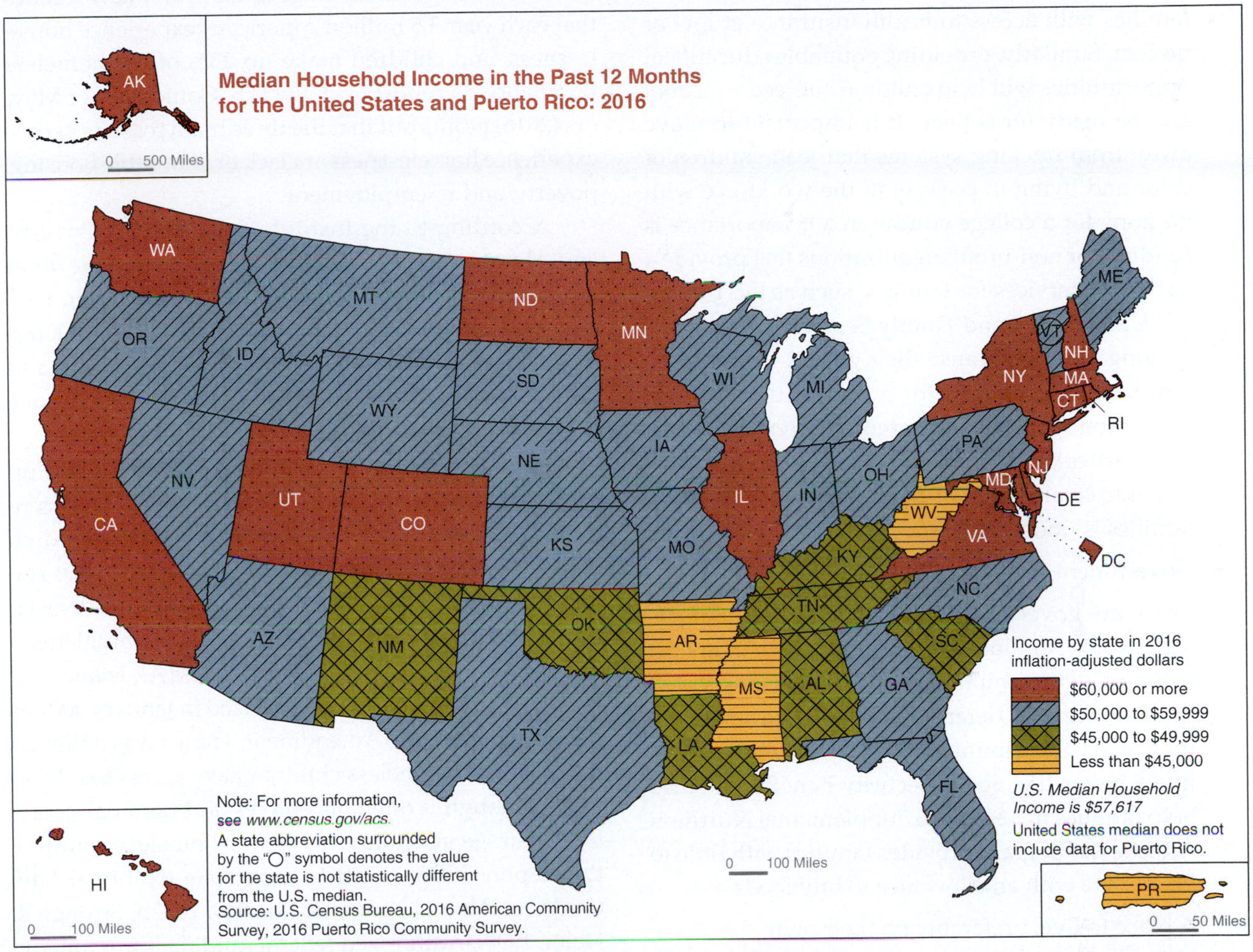

Median Household Income in the Past 12 Months for the United States and Puerto Rico: 2016

Income by state in 2016 inflation-adjusted dollars

- $60,000 or more
- $50,000 to $59,999
- $45,000 to $49,999
- Less than $45,000

U.S. Median Household Income is $57,617

United States median does not include data for Puerto Rico.

Note: For more information, see *www.census.gov/acs.* A state abbreviation surrounded by the "O" symbol denotes the value for the state is not statistically different from the U.S. median. Source: U.S. Census Bureau, 2016 American Community Survey, 2016 Puerto Rico Community Survey.

Source: Guzman, G. G. (2017). Household income: 2016 American Community Survey Briefs. Retrieved from U.S. Census Bureau, on November 20, 2018 from https://www.census.gov/content/dam/Census/library/publications/2017/acs/acsbr16-02.pdf.

It has been said that providing good employment opportunities for women helps children. Flexible working conditions for families—in particular for those that have women as head of the household—are crucial for a family's financial health. I know women who work 2 p.m. to 10 p.m. so that they can be available for their children's school activities. Women working these hours must have systems that help with the children after school, such as after-school programs that help children with their homework, and provide dinner and extracurricular activities. In addition, these women must have a system of support that can pick up their children from the after school program and get them home safely. Families of infants and toddlers also need flexible schedules so that they can maximize the time they can spend with their children. That means that childcare centers must have different schedules to meet the needs of the parents. Large cities often have childcare providers who have flexible schedules as well. When flexible working and childcare hours are not available, at least one parent has to care for the children, and this can lower the family's income.

- An integrated network of family services

Urie Bronfenbrenner believed in the importance of systems to help children (Bronfenbrenner, 1979). An integrated framework of services that can assist with children's needs includes systems such as the family, the school, the community, businesses, and the government. Each system needs to provide opportunities particularly for families in poverty so that they can stop the cycle. Children and families must be healthy in order to attend school and work. Health programs such as Medicare, Medicaid, CHIP, and the Affordable Care Act provide families with access to health insurance at low or no cost. Similarly, providing equitable educational opportunities will help children succeed in school and be ready for college. It is important to move away from tracking systems that lead children of color and living in poverty to the workforce with no hope for a college education. Of importance is funding for non-profit organizations that provide a variety of services for families, such as the YMCA, the United Way, and Family Services Association (among others) because their goal is to empower families and children for a better future. Legal protection for undocumented children and families, particularly those who have DACA status, is imperative although at this time the fate of such families is undetermined.

- Government policies to help families in poverty

There are government policies that help counteract poverty. Minimum wage laws help workers get better pay from employers because the lowest permissible wage is determined by the government. Increasing the minimum wage can help families live a better life. Social Security benefits can also help families in need. The Supplemental Nutrition Assistance Program provides families with little to no income with an allowance to buy foods.

- A place to live, preferably on their own

Affordable housing is a right and not a privilege. However, many families cannot afford a place to live. In addition, families who are poor are often placed in subsidized housing in neighborhoods that are high in crime. Families should be able to live in peaceful neighborhoods where children are safe from violence. Good planning by local governments can provide families with such opportunities. It is important for city officials to create neighborhoods where children who live in poverty have access to clean and environmentally friendly parks so that they can play and stay physically healthy.

Homelessness and Families

What are your perceptions of people who are homeless? It is important to understand that often people's circumstances can render them incapable of affording shelter, through no fault of their own. The National Law Center on Homelessness and Poverty (2018) states that each year 3.5 million Americans experience homelessness, and children make up 23% of the homeless population. A report from the U.S. Conference of Mayors (2016) points out that the three main reasons people experience homelessness are lack of affordable housing, poverty, and unemployment.

According to the Institute for Children, Poverty, and Homelessness (2018), currently there are over 1.35 million children who are homeless. Children who are homeless have acute and chronic health problems, experience emotional and behavioral problems, and have issues with school performance (Interagency Council on Homelessness, 2010).

Estimates say that families with children make up 40% of those who are homeless. Schools are directly concerned with single- or two-parent families with children who should be in school, as well as children who run away and have dropped out of school. Federal legislation has been passed to help mediate these problems.

The Stewart B. McKinney Homeless Assistance Act of 1987 (P.L. 100-77) was reauthorized in January 2002 as the McKinney-Vento Amendment. The act was designed to ensure that homeless children have access to education. Although it offers incentives and nominal grants to encourage states to provide for homeless children, the responsibility is left to each state (National Law Center on Homelessness & Poverty, 2002b; Stronge & Helm, 1990). Authorized federal funding is $70 million. The minimum amount of funding any state receives is $150,000 (National Law Center on Homelessness & Poverty, 2002b).

The National Law Center for Homelessness & Poverty recognizes some issues that need to be addressed to help people who are homeless. Less than 30% of the people eligible for low-income housing receive low-income housing. Only 11% of the 40% eligible for disability benefits receive such benefits. Only 37% of homeless people have food stamps, even though most are eligible for them. Similarly, most are eligible for welfare benefits, but only 52% receive them (National Law Center for Homelessness & Poverty, 2002a, pp. 1–2).

Children and youth who are considered homeless include those who are living with someone who cannot afford a home or who has lost his or her home, whether that person is a friend, relative, or someone else. It also includes those staying in a motel, hotel, or emergency shelter because they do not have adequate accommodations (National Law Center on Homelessness & Poverty, 2002b).

The McKinney-Vento Act states that children without homes must have the same educational services provided to other students. These include Head Start availability, Individuals with Disabilities Education and Child Find for early identification of needs, Title I for those at risk of failing in school, and free and reduced-price meals. Students in homeless situations also have specific protection for school selection (National Law Center on Homelessness & Poverty, 2002b, pp. 1–6). Regrettably, in spite of the law, 12% of homeless children are still denied their education (National Law Center for Homelessness & Poverty, 2002a, pp. 1–2).

When families are dislocated because of losing their home, they might move to various locations, such as shelters or relatives' homes, which may be in other school districts. Not only do the children lack the security of living in a stable environment, but if the school will not accept them because of residency requirements, they also lack the stability provided by attending the same school.

Children who are without homes also have a higher risk of nutritional deficiency and other health problems, including delayed immunization, poor iron levels, and developmental difficulties. In a study of children without homes compared with low-income children who had homes, it was found that the children without homes were delayed in their growth (Fierman et al., 1991). It may be a combination of factors—malnourishment, diarrhea, asthma, elevated lead levels, or social factors including family violence, drug exposure, alcohol abuse, mental disorders, and child abuse and neglect—that affect the child's growth (Bassuk, 1991; Fierman et al., 1991).

Administrators and teachers should be particularly aware of this and other special concerns of homeless children, including the opportunity for education, acceptance by staff and peers, and referrals as needed for special services. They should also be aware that homeless children may suffer from learning difficulties, speech delays, behavioral problems, depression and anxiety, short attention spans, aggression, and withdrawal (Bassuk & Rubin, 1987; Klein, Bittel, & Molnar, 1993; McCormick & Holden, 1992). Children experiencing homelessness who come to school are usually ashamed of living out of a car, tent, or shelter and of not having a home instead. They need support, not blame; they need acceptance, not rejection; and

they need a curriculum that allows them to succeed. They may need special tutoring and a buddy assigned to help them learn the routine. If they are continuing in the same school that they attended before becoming homeless, they need to be assured that they are still valued. Administrators and teachers should keep in mind that because the family and children are under a lot of stress, it is better to let them offer information than to inquire into personal concerns.

In a research survey (McCormick & Holden, 1992), parents without homes indicated they would like assistance with transportation, developmentally appropriate childcare, opportunities to share with others, flexible opportunities to be involved, respite opportunities, mental health self-esteem groups, information on services, an easy intake process for preschool participation, and classes.

The McKinney-Vento Act (Sec. 722[g][4]) offers the following standards for parents:

Standard 4. Parents or persons acting as parents of homeless children and youth will participate meaningfully in their children's education.

4.1. Parents or persons acting as parents will have a face-to-face conference with the teacher, guidance counselor, or social worker within 30 days of enrollment.

4.2. Parents or persons acting as parents will be provided with individual student reports informing them of their child's specific academic needs and achievement on academic assessments aligned with state academic achievement standards.

4.3. Parents or persons acting as parents will report monitoring or facilitating homework assignments.

4.4. Parents or persons acting as parents will share reading time with their children (i.e., parent reads to child or listens to child read).

4.5. Parents who would like parent skills training will attend available programs.

4.6. Parents or guardians will demonstrate awareness of McKinney-Vento rights.

4.7. Unaccompanied youth will demonstrate awareness of McKinney-Vento rights.

Homes for the Homeless (2011) developed the American Family Inns, where parents and children can live for a year, establishing stability in the family and allowing the parents to become self-sufficient. The American Family Inns program meets the educational needs of each parent; children have supplemental help to compensate for skills they need to develop; and infants and preschoolers go to child development centers, giving the children a jumpstart. Recreation and cultural programs are also provided. Similar programs have been established across the country. These programs give single mothers and two-parent families the time to develop skills and establish stable lifestyles.

The extra effort works. After a family moves from an American Family Inn to their own permanent housing, they are provided with aftercare services for an additional year. Studies show that approximately 94% of those who lived in an American Family Inn were still self-sufficient and living independently 2 years later (Nuñez, 1996, p. 76). The continuing concerns for families and their children affected by homelessness require giving top priority to schools and programs that help these families survive and flourish. The United States has more of a challenge compared to many other nations: Although the U.S. provides many successful and effective programs to help the poor, more improvement is needed because the United States ranks 21st among industrialized countries for low birth weight rates, 28th in infant mortality rates, and last in relative child poverty (Children's Defense Fund, 2011).

All of these suggestions can help the family, but families need time to develop skills and stability. Due to the way homeless shelters are usually set up, the family can stay only a limited time. Some programs have begun to recognize that this does not provide homeless families enough time to gain skills for employment or enough stability to provide for the family.

Teachers should create an environment where children have empathy for all, but particularly for those who need it the most. Establishing a buddy system in the classroom can help promote empathy and collaboration. Providing a place where children can keep their school materials and a supervised area where homework or enrichment activities can be completed at school will help children who are homeless have a place of their own. Encourage parents to become involved. Let the parents of homeless children participate in the classroom. As with all parents, they will need to know how you want them to participate. Plan a workshop for parents, or mentor them individually. Their involvement will not only provide extra help in the classroom, but it can also become an educational program for parents. They may learn more about how they can help their children.

The Functions of Families

Families have different functions in the development of children. The way that these functions occur is as diverse as the families themselves. Swick (1986) described these roles as "(1) nurturing, (2) guiding, (3) problem solving, and (4) modeling" (p. 72). Cataldo (1987) described similar roles: providing "care, nurturance, and protection"; socialization; "monitoring the child's development as a learner"; and supporting "each youngster's growth into a well-rounded, emotionally healthy person" (p. 28).

The family functions occur at different times and no one function is better than the others. However, it is true that families need first and foremost to provide nurturing by supplying the basic needs of nutrition, protection, and shelter, as well as the emotional needs of interaction, love, and support. The family has a responsibility to see that the child receives adequate care but also a right to rear the child as it sees fit; this is part of guiding children. This is important to remember because families in the United States are becoming more diverse as more families come from different countries and as American families (with children and parents born and raised in the United States) develop new childrearing practices and beliefs, including how to engage in problem solving. For instance, Latino immigrant families living in a bicultural context adapt to a different socialization process where flexibility is key (Aldoney & Cabrera, 2016). African American families focus on racial socialization as parents teach their children positive self-concept even when faced with racism and hostility (Thomas & Blackmon, 2015). Most have to show their children how to find solutions to such issues. Educators need to understand the differences and challenges faced by families. When differences are understood—particularly cultural differences—educators open the door to create partnerships with families to aid in the healthy development of children. It is important for parents to model for their children how to get along and relate well with others.

Part of understanding cultural differences is having knowledge of how parents socialize their children according to their native culture's norms. Socialization varies, depending on the culture. For example, respect for elders is a norm in most cultures, but in others, such as Latino and Asian cultures, it is especially important in the socialization process. Another example is the role the extended family plays in the raising of children—for some cultures, the role is very integral, whereas in others, extended families may be more distant. There are also variations within cultures that result from how the parents were raised. For instance, in some African American families, speaking Ebonics (some refer to as Black English" or "African American Vernacular English") is very important (Boutte & Strickland, 2008). Whatever the rearing process, most children learn and internalize their parents' value system.

The Stages of Parenthood

The stages of parenthood, developed by Galinsky (1987), divide parenthood into six levels of development, much like the child's stages of development. Although this is a good model that may be applied to many families in Western society, it is important to contextualize the six stages within the child's cultural and socioeconomic background.

The first stage, **image making**, takes place before the birth of a child. Images are formed and preparation is made for the birth. This is where parents may get the nursery ready and buy clothes for the infant. Family members and other systems can help those parents who might not be able to provide for the infant. The second stage, **nurturing**, is when attachment develops during infancy. Parents and infants begin to develop their relationship through different types of interactions such as breast-feeding, playing, reading, singing, and just holding the baby. In the third stage, **authority**, families teach children rules and consequences. Parents discover the type of authority they want to use with their children. Parents learn that setting limits and enforcing the rules become important for positive guidance. During the **interpretive** stage, which is the fourth stage, parents and children learn to interpret their social reality. Children throughout elementary and middle school practice social skills that will help them at home and school. As children get closer to the teen years, they tend to question rules and consequences. The **interdependent** years make up the fifth stage of family development. This stage occurs during high school or the teen years. Parents during this stage learn to reinforce authority in order to help children grow emotionally but responsibly. For example, during the high school years, children develop a different type of independence that allows them to go out in the world to practice what they learned throughout their childhood. When the children are ready to go out into the world for themselves, the parents enter the last stage: **departure**. During each of these stages, parents self-evaluate their parenting skills. This is when others reassure parents that if they trust in the values instilled in their children, the children will follow them. Once the children leave home, parents evaluate their children's experiences by measuring them against what they taught them. Depending on the family's culture, children physically leave home or stay to help their parents and contribute to the household.

Parenting Styles

Parents play a key role in ensuring that their family creates a strong bond regardless of the family structure. The roles that a parent plays are largely based on his/her parenting style, which is also culturally based. Parents display an array of behaviors and interactions with their children, which can be described as their parenting style (Laukkanen, Ojansuu, Tolvanen, Alatupa, & Aunola, 2013). Parenting styles (some of which are more effective than others) are often identified as *authoritative, authoritarian*, or *laissez-faire* (see Table 2.1).

Each of these types has different ways of handling issues and concerns within the family. In addition, depending on the circumstance, responses even in families with the same parenting style may vary. The style

Table 2.1 Parenting Styles

The manner in which families socialize their children varies. Three major styles—**authoritative**, **authoritarian**, and **laissez-faire**.

Family Type	Characteristics
Authoritative	Democratic decision making Guidelines and parameters Effective communication Problem solving Self-discipline and responsibility
Authoritarian (might be overprotective)	Demanding parent Absolute rules Restrictive environment Punitive control Strong guidelines
Laissez-faire (might be very indulgent)	Anything goes Neglectful parent No one cares Withdrawal from parental responsibilities
Dysfunctional (includes authoritative, authoritarian, and laissez-faire families)	Alcohol or drug-addicted Neurotic or mentally ill abusive

recommended by parent educators is the authoritative, democratic style because it is thought that children raised under that style will achieve, be dependable and responsible, and feel good about themselves. A child's temperament also influences parenting styles.

Children raised with authoritative parents will be allowed to analyze and recognize the issues confronting them. Guidance will be available but will not be dictated. Children will learn to make decisions. Through working and talking together, they will be able to learn why angry, quick decisions are not effective.

Children with authoritarian parents are expected to mind their parents without any question about what precipitated any given issue. The children do not get an opportunity to resolve a conflict or learn from actions, except to learn that punishment will follow no matter what the situation. They receive little training in decision making. Under this parenting style, children may learn to mind, but they also learn to avoid being caught, and perhaps to lie when they get caught.

Children of laissez-faire rearing often think that their parents are not interested in them. The children may be depressed, act out, or take risks because they do not feel their parents care. In addition, they get little to no guidance to help them make decisions. While children may think they enjoy the freedom of a laissez-faire parenting style, too much freedom makes it possible for children to think that they do not matter.

There are also two subtypes that do not fit into the three major types. One is the overprotective parent, who can often become authoritarian. The other is the indulgent parent, who may not guide the child. Dysfunctional families—including those that are abusive, have parents who are addicted to drugs or alcohol, or where the parents are mentally unstable. These families might fluctuate between authoritarian (to the point of abuse) and laissez-faire, with abdication of parental roles. One of the most difficult issues children in dysfunctional families face is the inconsistency. Dependable families in which children understand the guidelines and can communicate with and rely on their parents are extremely important to children's mental health.

If the types of families are multiplied by the number of configurations of families (single-, two-parent, and blended) and the individual personality differences of each child and parent, it becomes clear that to work effectively with parents, teachers and child-care workers must individualize their suggestions and responses. Ashiono and Mwoma's study (2015) seems to agree with this statement, as they found no significant relationship between parents' marital status and parenting styles (p. 69). Teachers awareness of parenting styles would help him/her work more effectively with parents.

Summary

The population of the United States has increased dramatically in the last 50 years. Along with growth in numbers, several trends are evident, such as the diversity within families that form part of the U.S. society. Diverse families include traditional two-parent, single-parent, divorced, blended, homeless, and immigrant families, as well as families living in poverty, among others. All families have the responsibility to provide for their children, so each family has functions it must exercise in order to ensure that children's needs are met. Parents also have different parenting styles that affect children's development. Grandparents play an important part in raising children in today's society, because not only do families depend on them for taking care of the grandchildren, but also many parents need the grandparents to take custody of their children. Fathers need to have a strong presence in their children's lives in order for children to have healthy relationships. Homelessness and poverty affect many diverse families, but there are laws that protect such families so their quality of life can improve.

Suggested Class Activities and Discussions

1. Survey your class and find out the different types of family structures represented.

2. Interview different types of families. Ask them questions, including what kinds of things help them be a family, some of their favorite things to do, the challenges they face on a daily basis, and what keeps them together.

3. Who are the immigrant families in your city? Do a search for your city and discover where families live and the conditions in which they live. Compare your answers with another classmate and see what he or she found.

4. List ways that fathers can become involved in a school or childcare center.

5. Examine the Personal Responsibility and Work Opportunity Reconciliation Act (PRWORA). Is it working? Is it causing hardship for children? What are the changes to the PRWORA?

6. Count the number of residential moves the members of your class have made. Why have they moved? Where have they moved? How many times have they moved?

7. Research the effect of Temporary Assistance for Needy Families (TANF) on childcare and families. What services does it provide? Has it been helpful? Are there any concerns? Learn where the TANF office is located in your community.

Useful Websites

Institute for Research on Poverty (IRP)
Interagency Council on Homelessness (ICH)

National Fatherhood Initiative

Glossary Terms

Family: A group of people living together and supporting each other.
Household: The place where a family gathers.

Poverty: Scarcity, lacking materials or money.

Chapter 3
Learning About Culturally and Linguistically Diverse Children and Families

It's not about accepting those who are different than us; it is about valuing fellow human beings.

Mari Riojas-Cortez

 Learning Outcomes

In this chapter, you will find information and strategies that will assist you in understanding and working with culturally and linguistically diverse children and their families. After completing the chapter, you should be able to do the following:

3.1 Explain the terms *culture* and *diversity*.

3.2 Explain why examining one's own identity (including one's own ancestry, culture, and values) is important before beginning work with culturally and linguistically diverse families and children.

3.3 Discuss immigrant families in the United States.

3.4 Identify dual-language learners and programs that support their learning.

3.5 Discuss culturally responsive pedagogy in the context of families.

As I was waiting to visit one of my students at a local elementary school that offers a dual-language program, I found myself listening to a very upset parent. The parent asked questions and his tone reflected irritability and frustration. His concern was that a note sent home in English and Spanish—normally a good thing—had grammatical mistakes in Spanish, and he felt someone should have caught the mistakes. The parent stated that a note with grammatical mistakes in English would never have been sent home. He argued that his home and native language was very important to both him and his family because it formed a large part of their identity. The administrative assistant assured the parent that all notes were checked for errors but sometimes people who spoke fluent Spanish were not available. Interestingly, there were teachers who were fluent Spanish speakers and who were present during this event, but they stayed quiet, not knowing how to best respond.

How would you have responded to this parent? Why is it important to address his concerns? As educators, we need to acknowledge what we missed and find solutions that enhance our partnerships with parents. The example is not only about learning how to work with parents but also about taking an in-depth look at how much value we place on identity issues of culturally and linguistically diverse families. Throughout this chapter, you will see how teachers' understanding of culture, diversity, and identity is critical to offer quality experiences to all children and their families in the schools, particularly those who have often been marginalized because of their cultural and linguistic background. Knowing the family's identity will help teachers determine how to best integrate culturally responsive pedagogy for children of color and dual-language learners. While reading this chapter, it is important to keep in mind the previous discussion on funds of knowledge.

Culture and Diversity

Our nation is very diverse. This diversity is due to family configurations, ethnic groups, socioeconomic backgrounds, religion, sexual orientation, and urban and rural settings. Very often, the term **culture** gets confused with the term **diversity**.

Diversity—differences in characteristics, qualities, traits, values, beliefs, and mannerisms in self and others based on predetermined factors (e.g., gender and race) and changeable features (e.g., language and citizenship). (Hernández-Sheets, 2005)

Culture—the learned and shared values of a society; a system of beliefs, attitudes, and control mechanisms that shape behavior (Geertz, 1973, as cited in Hernández-Sheets, 2005, p. 15).

Knowing the difference between the two terms can help teachers better understand the diversity of the students they teach and their families (Nieto, 2008). One misconception some teachers have is to say something like, "I don't see color, all children are the same." I hear this statement in classrooms, conferences, and workshops, and it makes me wonder if these teachers understand they need to see the color of children, because color is one way to understand the experiences and funds of knowledge of children and families.

The term **culture** is most easily understood when viewed as a way of life. Other descriptions are "blueprints for living" and "guidelines for life." It is the knowing, perceiving, understanding, and learning one brings to a situation (Nieto, 2008). Although culture refers to the way life is lived—including housing and clothing—it is much more than that. Culture is a way of life that is learned and that is shared through values (Boyer, 2013). It is a process that is multilayered, connecting language, values, beliefs, and behaviors (Ovando, Combs, & Collier, 2006).

The term diversity is often only equated with race or ethnicity when it entails much more. Diversity is largely the different identities of a population including color, ethnicity, national origin, gender, beliefs, sexuality, abilities, socioeconomic background, age, family structure, and many more. For those who have a narrow lens on diversity, they can't see how in fact they are diverse as well. A friend from Mexico who immigrated to the U.S. once made a comment that he was not diverse because he was Mexican. The fact that he was an immigrant made him diverse.

It is important for us as teachers of young children to understand the concepts of culture and diversity because we are not only helping children develop physically, socially, linguistically, and cognitively, but we are also helping them develop culturally (Ovando, Combs, & Collier, 2006) through organization of their learning (Boyer, 2013) but we also help them to understand their differences. We, as educators, must lead by example. How do we assist culturally and linguistically diverse children in our effort to make school relevant for them? Fisher (2006) suggests that "the challenge of cultural analysis is to develop translation and mediation tools for helping make visible the differences of interests, access, power, needs, desires, and philosophical perspective" (p. 363). Furthermore, there are certain norms of behavior that teachers expect of all children regardless of their background. This is problematic because

Jupiterimages/Stockbyte/Getty Images

Culturally and linguistically diverse families adopt the traditions and values of the new culture.

of the cultural dissonance that occurs between schools and homes of diverse children, particularly with families of lower socioeconomic backgrounds (Smith, 2012). As educators we must understand that culture is the way in which life is perceived, and because of this, it can be stereotyped. A too-common example of cultural relevancy is foods that families eat and how children eat them. I have often heard teachers reprimand children because they use their fingers to eat. It is important to find out cultural practices from the home in a subtle way so as not to offend parents. One way is to talk about the expectations of the school at the beginning of the school year and provide examples of those expectations. If you know that the home practices differ from those of the school, try to work with the parent to make sure they feel valued so that they feel safe enough to share their practices and traditions.

A reflective approach to diversity issues will enhance the quality of experiences for children. Reflect on the following questions:

1. Who am I? What is your identity? Do you know your culture, values, and beliefs? Do you have biases toward others? As a teacher, you must examine your own beliefs before you can reflect on others' differences and learn to value them.

2. Who are my students? How do I make an effort to know them? Is my classroom an environment of acceptance, encouragement, and inquiry? Does my classroom reflect the diversity of my students?

3. Do I know the term funds of knowledge? How do I find out the funds of knowledge of my students? How do I collaborate with parents? Do I have a "tourist approach" to knowing a culture? A tourist approach is one that only focuses on the traditional tangible items of a culture, such as Chinese lanterns or Mexican *sarapes*. In this approach the items would only be for display purposes. A non-tourist approach incorporates the children's funds of knowledge such as in the dramatic play center where culturally relevant items may be placed and children use those items to role-play scenarios from their culture.

Identity

"I really don't have a culture. I'm just a simple American. I was born here and my parents are from here. I heard my grandmother's parents came from France but I never really thought about it. My last name is Morales, but I am not Hispanic. I was born in Louisiana. I don't speak Spanish."

This quote represents a preservice teacher's understanding of her identity. Note that the preservice teacher is not prejudiced toward "Hispanics"[1] or people who speak Spanish—in fact, in the same conversation, the student talked about how she wished she spoke Spanish. Yet her understanding of the Hispanic culture and her own was limited. Interestingly, she stated that she was from Louisiana and therefore couldn't be Hispanic. I asked her if she knew the history of Louisiana, which includes Spanish and French influence. The student said that she had never thought about it—she always thought that Hispanic people just came from Mexico. I eventually asked her to visit the oldest cemetery in New Orleans to observe the last names represented. This conversation prompted her to begin looking for her own ancestry and thus her own identity. If you can't see your own identity, can you see and understand others?

Identity is defined as knowing who we are and to what groups we belong (Hernández-Sheets, 2005; Dutro, Kazemi, Balf, & Lin, 2008; Sollberger, 2013). Knowing who we are very often helps us understand who others are. This is particularly important for teachers who work with diverse learners (Clark & Flores, 2001). However, since the majority of teachers in the schools are White (Ford & Sassi, 2014), it may be challenging for them to see and understand "other people's children" (Delpit, 1996). One way around this is by examining our own ancestry, which allows us to begin to understand and explore the differences between diverse groups (Bekerman, 2009).

Taking a look at your own family history, you can begin to understand values, social practices, and traditions that your family has passed down through generations. What internalized values really came from childhood and the manner in which you were socialized? How much do you model after your parents, other relatives, or friends? Do you know your funds of knowledge? Examine the lives of those who have been significant to you—family, teachers, friends, or maybe even someone famous. What was their cultural background? What did they believe? What values did they live by? Have they influenced you? Ask yourself challenging questions to uncover prejudicial

---

[1]*Hispanic* is a term used by the U.S. Census, but a more appropriate term is *Latino*.

Mari Riojas Cortez

Latino families value all levels of education.

feelings. If you do, you may be able to examine them, recognize that they are not based on fact, and eliminate them so you can be more understanding of your students and their families. For teachers, it is imperative that they look into the psychosocial factors that influence their own perception and thinking such as ethnic identity, beliefs, acculturation, efficacy, and motivation (Flores, Clark, Guerra, Casebeer, Sanchez, & Mayall, 2010).This should remind us of the concept of funds of knowledge discussed earlier in this text.

Practice Discovering Your Identity

Following the concept of funds of knowledge, Guitart and Moll (2014) developed the concept of **funds of identity**, which is used to refer to the accumulated cultural and social resources that contribute to a person's self-expression, self-understanding, and self-definition. All of these are needed to discover and develop our own personal identity. Subero, Vujasinovic, and Guitart (2017) discuss how to mobilize funds of identity in and out of school. The authors stress the importance of recognizing that "any inclusive pedagogy has to positively affirm the pupils' identities and their sociocultural legacies" (p. 15).

The challenge, as the authors point out, is to bridge experiences and funds of knowledge in and out of school.

In many early childhood classrooms, the topic of self is an important one to cover. Teachers often use circle time to have children talk about themselves. When I was a teacher, I used a mirror and a tape recorder and encouraged children to describe themselves by talking into the tape recorder. Amazingly, many of my preschoolers would not only describe their hair and eye color but they would describe the color of their skin. Since I taught in a bilingual class with Latino children, the children would say, "*Mi piel es blanca*" (my skin is white) or "*Yo soy moreno*" (I am dark).

One activity that may help you on your journey to understanding yourself is to answer the question, "Who am I?" Draw a picture of yourself and on the back of the paper, make a list of who you are. List the main points of how you see yourself, writing whatever comes to mind first. Do not dwell on what the answers mean. List five to ten items on your list. Now, look at the list and see what you placed first. When you think of yourself, what roles are paramount? Was it teacher, mother, father, husband, or wife? Your view of who you are may change, depending on what stage of life you are in. You may not even agree with the list you just made. Are there other roles more important to you? What is important in this exercise is that you review the roles and think about what they mean to you. This is also an activity you can do with your students, particularly those who are very young and who are learning about themselves. Parents might also enjoy this activity and would probably appreciate the chance to participate.

Another activity both you and your students can work on is making a family tree. There are many websites

Thinkstock/Stockbyte/Getty Images

In many immigrant families, elders help children create strong bonds and attachments.

that provide free templates to create one. In order to include children who are adopted or in foster care, have them make a tree with the people who are important in their life. After making the family tree, students may choose to make a family history album. Talk with relatives and people of importance to the child and find out what you can about the family. Record the stories they share. Children who are adopted or are from a foster family can write about their adopted, extended, or foster family.

Invite family members to your classroom and share stories and pictures of their families. This activity will highlight the diversity within families by including extended families.

You can provide children with the opportunity to create their own personalized books by using a variety of software if you have access to a digital tablet such as an iPad. You can download any of several apps for free (such as StoryKit) that children can use to create their own books. Diversity in your classroom will be valued when a collection of digital stories are on display. You may also want to tell your own story.

If you have a computer and Internet access, an activity you can do using this book as a basis is to use a family history website to research your family. You can even suggest this activity in a parent newsletter! Using this information, you can write a narrative about your family. Use a scanner to scan old photos of your relatives. You will learn a lot about your family and yourself. The parents that you work with can also do this activity to discover their ancestry.

Teachers can also encourage children to create their own community books by taking photos of the community and creating stories around those photos. Children can act as illustrators by creating their own books.

In order to know more about the community where they teach, teachers can obtain information from the U.S. Census and see the different languages, ethnic, socioeconomic, and family backgrounds represented and then find appropriate resources. This information is important so that the existing curriculum can be developed to reflect culturally and developmentally appropriate practices.

The use of children's literature is another strategy to use when addressing identity issues (Kelly, 2012). Very often, teachers like to teach concepts of identity through the use of books and stories. Using children's literature to teach these concepts is an effective strategy to use because children can read the book for themselves after it is presented and continue thinking about the concepts. For example, the children's book, *The Color of Us* (1999) by Karen Katz is a book that can help children think about different shades of skin. Another children's book that can be used is *My People: My People with Photographs* (2009) by Langston Hughes. Langston Hughes wrote the classic poem, *My People*, which was used to create this book, in the late 1920s, a time when Blacks were not accepted by society, as a way to celebrate the pride he felt about his people as a Black man.

The classic children's book *Family Familia*, by children's author Diane Gonzales Bertrand (1999), is a good example of a book to read to children about family history because it touches on the topic through a family that is attending its family reunion. Although the book reflects the experience of a Mexican American family, it can be used for all children to discuss what their family is like.

Similarly, *Aunt Flossie's Hats (and Crab Cakes Later)*, by Elizabeth Fitzgerald Howard (1991), describes two African American sisters who visit their great-great-aunt Flossie to try on her hats, hear her stories, and eat crabs.

Remember other aspects of diversity such as religion. *Golden Domes and Silver Lanterns: A Muslim Book of Colors* by Hena Khan (2012) is a children's book that highlights Muslim traditions, including important artifacts. An example of a children's book for diversity in family structure includes Justin Richardson's and Peter Parnell's *And Tango Makes Three* (2005). Riojas-Cortez and Cataldo (2016) discuss the benefit of using children's literature to teach and talk about family values, traditions, and beliefs.

Using culturally relevant children's books helps [children] make connections between their experience and the experience of the characters in the books. This in turn validates the children's experiences, particularly those children who are culturally and linguistically diverse.

Immigrant Families in the United States

We all have heard the poem that is inscribed at the Statue of Liberty in New York. The poem was written by Emma Lazarus in 1883 and it is titled "The New Colossus." The most famous lines of this poem include:

"Give me your tired, your poor, Your huddled masses yearning to breathe free, The wretched refuse of your teeming shore. Send these, the homeless, tempest-tost to me, I lift my lamp beside the golden door!"

Figure 3.1 Foreign-Born Population by Region of Birth: 1960 to 2010 (Numbers in millions)

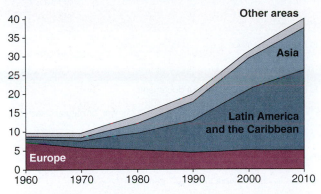

U.S. Census Bureau, Census of Population, 1996 to 2000 and the American Community Survey, 2010

According to an article by Walt Hunter published in *The Atlantic* (2018), the poem has become a symbol for many different interpretations, including the welcoming of immigrants to the U.S. Starting from its inception the U.S. has been as a nation of immigrants, from the Spanish, Dutch, and English to later groups such as the Italian, Irish, and Asian immigrants of the nineteenth and twentieth centuries, and continuing today with people from all over the world, including Southeast Asia, India and Pakistan, the Middle East, and Latin America. López and Radford from the Pew Center (2017) report that there are approximately 43.2 million immigrants living in the U.S. as of 2015. Figure 3.1 shows the foreign-born population by region

of birth from 1960 to 2010, and Figure 3.2 shows foreign-born population by country of birth. These figures show how the U.S. has become even more diverse with time. Many people dream about immigrating for reasons such as looking for a higher standard of life and education, wanting to be with family, or escaping violence and war in their country of origin.

There are different terms that we need to be familiar with as we work with diverse immigrant families. Table 3.1 shows these terms and their definitions. Becoming familiar with the terms allows teachers and administrators to better understand a family's immigration status. Regardless of our political stance, as educators we should have the disposition to get to know the issues that immigrant families face, regardless of their legal status in the U.S. These efforts will only strengthen partnerships, which in turn will enhance children's success in school. Immigrant families form part of the diverse population in the U.S. Therefore, teachers' dispositions regarding immigrant families will help families meet the challenges faced by the children and increase parental engagement (Pedro, Miller, & Bray, 2012).

In my own experience, I remember when my family and I immigrated to the United States in 1978. We originally lived in a metropolitan city in Mexico called Monterrey, which is approximately 300 miles from San Antonio, Texas. I remember very clearly the day that we went to the bus station with the only belongings we were able to take on the bus. Our friends from church went to the bus station to say goodbye. For a

Figure 3.2 Foreign-Born Population by Country of Birth: 2010

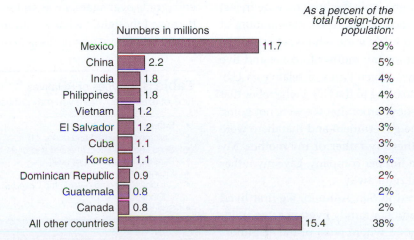

U.S. Census Bureau, American Community Survey, 2010

Table 3.1 Terms and Definitions

Common immigration terms and definitions within the context of the U.S.

Term	Definition
Immigrant	A person who goes to another country to live permanently.
Permanent Resident Alien	An immigrant who has documents such as a green card.
Undocumented immigrant	A person who goes to another country to live permanently but without documents.
Refugee	Someone who has been forced to leave his/her country of origin because of violence, war, or natural disaster.
Migrant	A person who moves from place to place for seasonal work.
Unaccompanied minor	Children under 18 who arrive at a country without an adult.
Green Card	Permanent resident card that allows individuals to live and work in the U.S. permanently.
Passport	A travel document that allows individuals to travel to other countries.
Visa	Permission from a country given to foreigners in order to travel into that country.

12-year-old girl the experience was traumatic. I had just finished one year of middle school. I had my own set of friends and so did my two sisters, who also had boyfriends at the time. I remember traveling with my mother to the states of Tamaulipas and Coahuila to get original birth certificates. I also remember going to the U.S. consulate to get physicals showing that we were healthy. Once we got all of the paperwork in order, we sold all of our belongings, gave some of our things away, and embarked on an unknown journey. After six months of preparation that included getting all of the documents necessary on May 22, 1978 we left Mexico for the U.S.

When we crossed the border at Laredo, Texas, we were taken to a room where my parents showed agents all of the documents. After that, our photos were taken for our Resident Alien Cards, or what are more commonly known as Green Cards (because they are in fact green). The process took an unprecedented amount of time, about six months. My aunt, who was born in the U.S., filed a petition for my mother to come and live there. Table 3.2 shows which types of relatives a U.S. citizen can petition to bring to the U.S. I remember that my parents had to show proof that we were not going to be a burden to the government and that there were jobs waiting for either my father or my mother. My uncle, who owned a lumber company, gave my father a job so we qualified right away.

When we arrived in San Antonio, we first lived with my aunt. She and her family lived in a very middle-class neighborhood where most of the neighbors did not speak Spanish. The houses were very big as were their yards, and we never saw anyone outside. This was something that we were not used to, as we lived in a working class neighborhood in Monterrey and we knew everyone in our neighborhood. We cried every night because we wanted to go back to Monterrey. We missed our life there because the food, values, and ways of life were so different.

When it was time to start school, we were surprised at the size of the middle and high schools. When my mother took me to Longfellow Middle School to register me, I had completed seventh grade in Monterrey, with very good grades. Because my aunt spoke English, she came with us to the school and translated for my mother. Interestingly, she served as my advocate when my mother was told that they were going to put me two years behind because I didn't speak English. In the end, the administrators only made me do seventh grade over again. I was still so mad and frustrated because I thought, "what would my friends in Mexico think?" But there was nothing I could do.

Table 3.2 Types of Relatives

Type of relative for whom you may petition to bring to the U.S.

- Spouse
- Children (unmarried and under 21)
- Sons and daughters (married and/or 21 or over)
- Parents, if you are 21 or over
- Siblings, if you are 21 or over
- A fiancé(e) residing outside the United States and children of fiancé(e) under 21
- Spouse
- Children of spouse (unmarried and under 21)

Office of Homeland Security. (2018). Family of U.S. citizens. U.S. Citizenship and Immigration Services. https://www.uscis.gov/family/family-us-citizens.

The experience was awful. I had to be pulled out from several classes so a paraprofessional could translate work for me. At that time, speaking Spanish was not cool and many Latino students shied away from it. Surprisingly, I got excellent grades in math because numbers is a language of its own (except when it came to word problems). I had three teachers who were Latinos that had different levels of Spanish, but all were willing to help, and each would translate some content for me.

The kids were another story. It was very difficult to make friends, not only because of the language barrier, but because my parents were very strict and wouldn't let us go out with anyone for fear that something would happen to us. Throughout my years in middle school I was laughed at, called "wetback," and ridiculed. High school was a bit better but it was still very difficult to fit in. What I wanted the most was to finish high school and start college because I thought college would set me free. As I learned to navigate the world of high school, I quickly became aware that I didn't know what to do in order to go to college as no one would talk to me about it. In fact, in my senior year I approached two administrators, the principal and the counselor, and asked them to sign a form for me—something dealing with college—and they both laughed, saying, "You want to go to college?" They signed and then dismissed me. Years later, I recall seeing that counselor in some administrative offices when I had to attend a meeting after I joined the faculty at my current university. It brought back many bad memories. Although I had some wonderful teachers and a few good friends, I know that there were many things that I missed because of the language and cultural barriers.

My family story as immigrants is no different from others. Many of us struggle with language and cultural barriers. Many struggle because they are not so fortunate to have papers that will allow them to provide for their children the basics: food, clothing, shelter, and an education. The Pew Research Center indicates that as of 2018, there were approximately 34 million immigrants with documents in the U.S. According to Child Trends (2014), the population of first- and second-generation immigrant children grew by 51% between 1995 and 2014. Children who are Hispanic or Latino comprise about 55% of all immigrant children (Child Trends, 2014; see Figure 3.3).

When I was a bilingual prekindergarten teacher at a school district in San Antonio, the majority of my students were children of immigrant parents. My relationship with the parents was always very positive because we spoke the same language and we had similar experiences growing up in Mexico. This supports Adair's (2016) study of immigrant teachers who displayed their

Figure 3.3 Percent of Immigrant* and Non-immigrant Children Under Age 18 by Race/Hispanic Origin, 2014

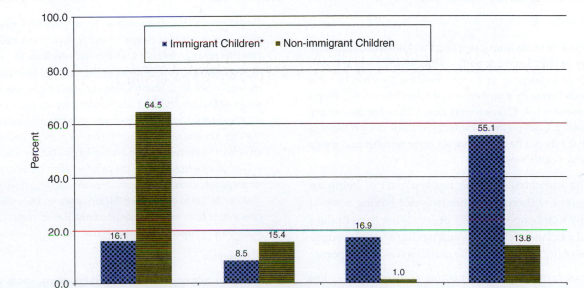

*Child Trends' original analyses of data from the current population survey, March Supplement.

strongest affection for immigrant families and communities. In other words, immigrant teachers empathize with immigrant families because they share similar experiences.

For many undocumented families, living in the shadows is part of their daily reality. Regardless of your personal views on immigration, as teachers we must empathize with families because our commitment as educators is to collaborate with families in order to enhance children's educational experience.

Have you ever spoken with someone who is undocumented? Would you know if someone is undocumented? Do you think a parent's legal status affects children? I want to introduce you to Teresita. She lives "somewhere in the United States" with her four daughters. Because of her legal status I am using a pseudonym and I am not revealing where she lives. Teresita is from a small rural town in Puebla, Mexico. She indicated that she didn't know how to read or write. In fact, she mentioned that her first language was not Spanish but Nahuatl, a pre-Columbian language from her region of Mexico. I asked Teresita what it meant to be an immigrant in the U.S., and this was her response:

> *Bueno ser inmigrante para mi pues he tenido dificultad más que nada número uno es en el trabajo pues casi ahorita para ir a trabajar en una compañía una tienda pues nos están pidiendo un número de seguro bueno y si no pues no so puede trabajar y he encontrado trabajos creo que por mi capacidad si puedo trabajar yo he ido a entrevistas pero mi problema es que no tengo un seguro bueno entonces pues no, no he podido pues trabajar bien.*

Translation

[Well, to be an immigrant, for me, I have had difficulty more than anything with finding work because I can't go to a company or a store, because they ask us for a social security number, and if I don't have one, then I cannot work. I have found jobs, I think because of my ability. I have gone to interviews but my problem is that I do not have a social security number and that's why I can't work well.]

Teresita indicated that the hardest part of being an immigrant without documents is not having a social security number because this prevents her from finding a good job. I also asked how not having a social security number affects her family life and this was her response:

> *Pues la verdad es que es un gran cómo le explico es una gran batalla pues que uno no se puede expresar como uno*

quisiera pero no se puede. Porque también tengo una niña de 16 años me la traje entonces ella tampoco trae documentos y con ella pues es un poquito más difícil como ahorita ella ya está para ir ella tiene que ir a la universidad y allí o sea ella no puede hacer muchas cosas por lo mismo que no tiene seguro social. Pero ahorita tampoco es imposible hay mucha ayuda en este país si es una gran diferencia entre una persona que tiene documentos bien y otra que no tiene. Tiene más oportunidad la que tiene que la que no tiene.

Translation

[Well, the truth is, how can I explain, it is a great battle because you cannot express yourself as one would like, you cannot. Because I also have a 16-year-old girl I brought her with me. She also does not bring documents with her and it is a little harder now that she is getting ready to go to college. She has to go to the University and there she cannot do many things for the same reason, that she does not have a social security number. But right now it is not impossible either, there is a lot of help in this country. But there is a great difference between a person who has good documents and another who does not have them. You have more opportunities if you have documents than when you do not.]

Teresita knew about the difficulties of not having documents, particularly for her daughter, who is close to going to college. The realities of not having documents make all things more difficult for families.

I asked Teresita about the most important thing she learned from being in the U.S. as an immigrant and her response was:

> *Bueno pues en mi experiencia yo llegue pues hace muchos años pues la realidad es que no puedo decir nada malo de este país porque gracias a Dios he salido adelante yo vengo de una familia muy humilde no tuve estudio ni nada así que no sabia nada. Pero he aprendido que aquí en este país pues me ha dado la oportunidad de aprender pues ir a una escuela un poco lo poco que he ido pues he aprendido muchas cosas trabajar sin que yo tuviera una carrera pues he trabajado en diferentes partes eso es lo que me ha ayudado mucho este país si yo estuviera en México yo no pudiera trabajar pues no tengo una carrera y pues allí te piden comprobantes para trabajar lo único que hice en México pues yo trabajaba en casa y aquí pues he trabajado en compañías en restaurants en diferentes cosas donde yo he podido hacer.*

Translation

[Well, in my experience, I arrived many years ago and the reality is that I cannot say anything bad about this country because thanks to God I have come out ahead. I come from a very humble family. I did not study or anything so I did not know anything. But this country has given me the opportunity to learn because I have gone to a school—well, a little bit, because I have learned a lot of things, like to work without having a career, because I have worked in different places. This country has helped me a lot. If I was in Mexico I could not work because I do not have a career and they ask you for proof to work. The only thing I did in Mexico, I worked cleaning homes and here I worked in companies at different restaurants doing things that I could do.]

Teresita was thankful for the opportunities she found in the U.S., although it has been a difficult journey. She indicated that in Mexico she would not have had the same opportunities she had in the U.S. because of her lack of education. This is something with which I can empathize as the same thing happened to my father in Mexico, and the main reason for our move to the U.S. was economic. Still, she lives in fear of being deported and is unsure of her future and her daughters' future, particularly her oldest, Jacqueline, who considers herself a "DREAMER." Jacqueline told me that she is a junior in high school, and she is part of a program that helps high school students to pursue their dream of attending college. This program is called Educators for Fair Consideration (E4FC) and its mission is to empower undocumented youth to achieve educational and career goals. Jacqueline considers herself a dreamer because *"muchos tenemos el sueño de hacer algo por nuestra vida por la educación . . . "* [many of us have dreams about doing something in our life for our education . . .]

Policies for immigrants vary but particularly affect those who are undocumented. In 2001 and 2002 the DREAM Act (Development, Relief and Education for Alien Minors Act) was introduced in the House of Representatives and the Senate but it was never enacted. This act proposed to give provisions for citizenship for undocumented youth. Different versions of the act were proposed between 2003 and 2008, according to Venegas et al. from the Pullias Center for Higher Education (2017). In 2010 this act passed the House of Representatives but not the Senate. Venegas et al. indicates that in 2012, former President Barak Obama gave an executive order allowing some undocumented individuals to defer action from deportation. This executive order is known as DACA, or Deferred Action for Childhood Arrivals. The individuals that fall within this order are known also as DREAMERS because of the DREAM Act. See Figure 3.4 for DACA timeline.

The status of many immigrant families is diverse. Some, like my family, have documents; others do not. In some immigrant families, the entire family (mother, father, and children) may not have documents. In others, the mother may have documents but the father may not, while the children are American citizens. This is the case for Mr. Gutierrez, who makes cedar furniture for a living "somewhere in the U.S." and his family. His wife was born and raised "somewhere in the U.S." and they had four children. Other cases are more complicated; for instance, both parents and one child are undocumented but the rest are U.S. citizens. Many families do not seek the help that they need because of fear of deportation (Landale, Thomas, & Van Hook, 2011). The cases become more complex and immigration laws and policies must work for immigrant families in order to achieve well-being.

Do you think that there are differences in working with immigrant parents? If you do, you are correct. Two of the major differences when working with immigrant parents are cultural and linguistic. Many immigrant parents, regardless of their legal status, have not been part of the U.S. education system and may not know the appropriate procedures or protocols. The following list provides ideas and suggestions for teachers and schools when working with immigrant families.

1. Always be empathetic and do not judge. Think about the definition of a family and the diversity within each. Having an open mind and being willing can help the child, the family, and the school.

2. Reflect the ethical behavior of a professional and act accordingly. The National Association for the Education of Young Children (NAEYC) (2011), ethical core values remind us that as early childhood educators we must "Respect the dignity, worth, and uniqueness of each individual (child, family member, and colleague)" (p. 1).

3. Provide a translator and liaison. Often other parents who have gone through similar situations are willing to help others.

4. All materials sent home should be in the language that the parent understands. Look at universities and colleges for available translators; often students have to do service learning projects and translating simple documents can be done to meet that requirement.

Figure 3.4 DACA Timeline

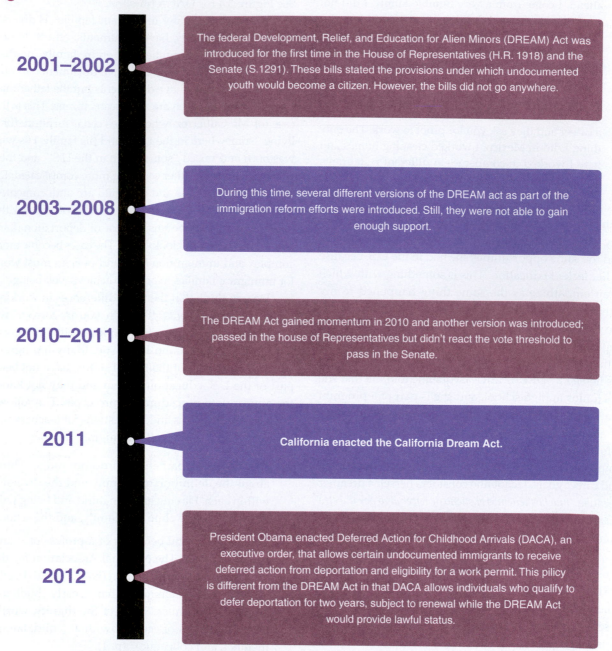

2001–2002 The federal Development, Relief, and Education for Alien Minors (DREAM) Act was introduced for the first time in the House of Representatives (H.R. 1918) and the Senate (S.1291). These bills stated the provisions under which undocumented youth would become a citizen. However, the bills did not go anywhere.

2003–2008 During this time, several different versions of the DREAM act as part of the immigration reform efforts were introduced. Still, they were not able to gain enough support.

2010–2011 The DREAM Act gained momentum in 2010 and another version was introduced; passed in the house of Representatives but didn't react the vote threshold to pass in the Senate.

2011 California enacted the California Dream Act.

2012 President Obama enacted Deferred Action for Childhood Arrivals (DACA), an executive order, that allows certain undocumented immigrants to receive deferred action from deportation and eligibility for a work permit. This pilicy is different from the DREAM Act in that DACA allows individuals who qualify to defer deportation for two years, subject to renewal while the DREAM Act would provide lawful status.

Source: Pullias Center for Higher Education. (2017). *Understanding DACA and the implications for higher education*. University of Southern California. Adapted from Pullias Center for Higher Education. (2017). Understanding DACA and the implications for higher education. University of Southern California

5. Learn about the country and culture of the family, and find out its values and traditions. Parents are always willing to share something from their home culture.

6. Avoid stereotypes. Usually stereotypes lead to making fun of someone for being different.

7. Find out the funds of knowledge of the family, as this will help in teaching their child in school.

Dual-Language Learners and Bilingual Programs

Many children in the United States are considered culturally and linguistically diverse. We have children who are biracial, bicultural, and bilingual, meaning they are growing up in two worlds (Pérez, 2004). Many

Table 3.3 Population Estimates
Population estimates by race and hispanic origin.

Race and Hispanic Origin	
White alone, percent, July 1, 2016	76.9%
Black or African American alone, percent, July 1, 2016	13.3%
American Indian and Alaska Native alone, percent, July 1, 2016	1.3%
Asian alone, percent, July 1, 2016	5.7%
Native Hawaiian and Other Pacific Islander alone, percent, July 1, 2016	0.2%
Two or More Races, percent, July 1, 2016	2.6%
Hispanic or Latino, percent, July 1, 2016	17.8%
White alone, not Hispanic or Latino, percent, July 1, 2016	61.3%

Source: U.S. Census Bureau. (2018). Quick Facts United States. Population Estimates. Retrieved on March 18, 2018 from https://www.census.gov/quickfacts/fact/table/US/PST045217#viewtop.

Immigrants come to the U.S. because it is a "land of opportunity."

PacoRomero/E+/Getty Images

of these children are minorities or are from traditionally underrepresented groups, such as Latinos and African Americans. There are also those who are multicultural because their families are so varied in their ancestry. Also represented in the United States are children who are monolingual speakers of other languages, or what we know as **English language learners (ELLs)**, and more recently as **dual-language learners (DLLs)**. In fact, the children of immigrants are the fastest growing population in U.S. schools (Calderón, Slavin, & Sanchez, 2011).

The U.S. Census estimates that by the year 2043 the U.S. will be a more diverse nation where no majority group will prevail. The U.S. Census predicts that the Hispanic population will double, while the African American population will increase slightly. The Asian population is expected to more than double by the year 2060. Table 3.3 shows numbers that indicate the diversity of our nation. With diversity comes diversity of language with individuals being labeled second language learners.

Who Are English Language Learners?

English language learners come from different backgrounds. If you examine Table 3.3, you can see the different races and Hispanic origins. Within that population we can find families that speak another language

besides English or in addition to English, as shown in Figure 3.5. The majority of the children who are ELLs are of Latino descent or are immigrants. The second-largest group of children who are ELLs are of Asian descent. It is also important to remember that Americans of different cultural and language descents, who have been in the U.S. for generations, may also speak two languages at home. Although most of the U.S. population is English proficient, the U.S. Census shows that Spanish and Chinese are the two most popular non-English languages spoken in U.S. homes. See Figure 3.6 for non-English-language households.

Table 3.4 shows the number of dual-language learners by state. The State of California has the largest number of ELLs, followed by Texas. Other states have also seen a growth in the number of ELLs enrolled in their schools. Since the number of ELLs continues to increase, some school districts are realizing that effective programs and strategies need to be implemented in order to meet the needs of these students. When school districts do not comply with meeting the needs of English language learners, then the Office of Civil Rights gets involved in order to provide basic rights to language-minority students (Ovando, Combs, & Collier, 2006).

Learning a Second Language

Understanding how a second language is learned becomes important not only for teachers but for parents as well, who very often want their children to quickly learn English at the expense of their native language (Wong-Fillmore, 1991). It is not that the parents want their children to lose their language—it is that they want their children to have better opportunities, and

Figure 3.5 Household Language[1] of Children Ages Birth to Age 17: 2004–2013

	2004	2005	2006	2007	2008	2009	2010	2011	2012	2013
Number of Children (millions)										
English Only	52.6	51.8	51.8	51.7	51.5	51.3	50.6	50.2	49.7	49.9
All Languages other than English[2]	20.3	21.4	21.8	21.9	22.2	22.9	23.3	23.4	23.7	23.4
Spanish	13.5	14.3	14.7	14.8	14.9	15.5	15.6	15.7	15.8	15.7
Other Indo-European	3.5	3.5	3.5	3.5	3.6	3.6	3.7	3.7	3.7	3.6
Asian and Pacific Island	2.4	2.5	2.5	2.6	2.5	2.8	2.8	2.8	2.9	2.9
Other	0.9	1.0	1.1	1.1	1.1	1.1	1.2	1.2	1.3	1.3
Percent of Children										
English Only	72.2	70.8	70.4	70.3	69.9	69.1	68.5	68.2	67.7	68.0
All Languages other than English[2]	27.8	29.2	29.6	29.7	30.1	30.9	31.5	31.8	32.3	32.0
Spanish	18.5	19.6	20.0	20.1	20.3	20.9	21.1	21.3	21.6	21.4
Other Indo-European	4.8	4.8	4.8	4.7	4.9	4.8	5.0	5.0	5.1	4.9
Asian and Pacific Island	3.3	3.4	3.4	3.5	3.4	3.7	3.8	3.9	4.0	3.9
Other	1.2	1.4	1.4	1.4	1.5	1.5	1.6	1.7	1.7	1.7

[1]Children in non-English households live with at least one person (relative or non-relative) who speaks a language other than English; such children may speak English only.

[2]Languages in the "Other Indo-European" category include most European languages (such as German and Russian), as well as languages from India, such as Hindi. Persian and Urdu are also included in this category. Languages in the "Asian and Pacific Island" category include the languages of East Asia (such as Chinese and Korean), as well as Pacific Island languages such as Tagalog and Hawaiian. Turkish is also included in this category. Other languages include American Indian and African languages, Hungarian, Arabic, Hebrew, and Finnish.

Source: Child Trends original analysis of the 1-year American Community Survey Public Microdata Sample (ACS PUMS)

Adapted from Child Trends' original analyses of the 1-year American Community Survey Public Microdata Sample (ACS PUMS).

Figure 3.6 Of All U.S. Children (ages birth to 17), Percentage Living in a Non-English-Language Household*: 2004–2013

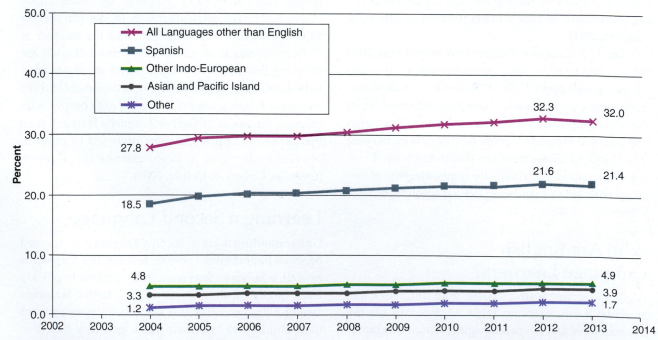

*Adapted from Child Trends analysis of the American Community Survey.

Table 3.4 Number and Percentage of Public School Students Participating in English Language Learner (ELL) Programs, by State: Selected Years, Fall 2004 Through Fall 2014

State	Number of public school students participating in programs for English language learners							Percent of students participating in programs for English language learners						
	2004	2009	2010	2011	2012	2013	2014	2004	2009	2010	2011	2012	2013	2014
1	2	3	4	5	6	7	8	9	10	11	12	13	14	15
United States	43,41,435[1]	43,64,510[1]	43,70,004[1]	43,89,325	43,97,318[1]	44,60,956[1]	45,59,323[1]	9.1[1]	9.1[1]	9.1[1]	9.1	9.2[1]	9.3[1]	9.4[1]
Alabama	14,801	19,497	17,559	17,895	17,837[2]	17,457	17,863	2.0	2.6	2.4	2.4	2.4[2]	2.3	2.4
Alaska	21,533	14,581	14,894	14,538	14,824	14,923	15,078	16.2	11.1	11.3	11.1	11.3	11.4	11.5
Arizona	1,85,050	78,793	70,716	70,527	58,512	63,242	60,171	20.2	8.2	7.5	7.5	6.2	6.7	6.4
Arkansas	18,642	29,735	31,457	32,671	33,745	35,814	37,587	4.0	6.3	6.6	6.9	7.1	7.5	7.8
California	15,74,397	14,68,815[3]	14,45,496[2]	14,15,623	13,91,913	13,92,871	13,90,316	25.2	24.1[3]	23.6[2]	23.2	22.8	22.7	22.4
Colorado	90,364	94,391	98,809	1,01,262	1,01,913	1,05,856	1,02,359	11.8	11.4	11.8	12.0	12.0	12.2	11.7
Connecticut	26,865	29,266	29,671	29,318	30,077	30,261	33,525	4.9	5.4	5.6	5.6	5.8	5.9	6.6
Delaware	4,846	7,615	6,766	6,972	7,280	7,927	8,092	4.3	6.5	5.6	5.9	6.1	6.6	6.6
District of Columbia	4,771	4,203	3,741	3,745	4,530	4,716	4,882	7.7	9.6	8.4	8.4	10.3	10.5	10.6
Florida	2,14,450	2,30,440	2,29,659	2,34,347	2,42,133	2,50,296	2,52,172	8.1	8.8	8.7	8.8	9.0	9.2	9.2
Georgia	60,334	86,668	80,965	83,400	87,104	90,481	97,670	3.9	5.2	4.9	5.0	5.2	5.3	5.7
Hawaii	17,017	18,097	19,092	24,750	16,474	15,949	14,425	9.3	10.0	10.6	13.5	8.9	8.5	7.9
Idaho	20,986	15,931	15,361	15,143	16,615	13,147	12,657	8.3	6.0	5.8	5.7	6.1	4.7	4.6
Illinois	1,70,941[2]	1,79,850	1,74,335	1,70,626	1,91,738	1,91,057	2,09,959	8.2[2]	8.6	8.4	8.2	9.4	9.3	10.3
Indiana	50,843	48,364	48,574	50,082	50,750	54,364	56,097	5.0	4.7	4.7	5.0	5.0	5.4	5.6

(continued)

Table 3.4 Number and Percentage of Public School Students Participating in English Language Learner (ELL) Programs, by State: Selected Years, Fall 2004 Through Fall 2014 (*continued*)

State	Number of public school students participating in programs for English language learners							Percent of students participating in programs for English language learners						
	2004	2009	2010	2011	2012	2013	2014	2004	2009	2010	2011	2012	2013	2014
1	2	3	4	5	6	7	8	9	10	11	12	13	14	15
United States	43,41,435[1]	43,64,510[1]	43,70,004[1]	43,89,325	43,97,318[1]	44,60,956[1]	45,59,323[1]	9.1[1]	9.1[1]	9.1[1]	9.1	9.2[1]	9.3[1]	9.4[1]
Iowa	14,606	20,867	21,733	22,503	21,839	23,137	25,875	3.1	4.2	4.4	4.5	4.4	4.6	5.1
Kansas	26,041	38,011	39,323	41,052	42,590	45,530	47,209	5.6	8.0	8.1	8.5	8.7	9.4	9.5
Kentucky	10,471	14,244	16,351	16,878	18,761	19,594	20,708	1.6	2.1	2.4	2.5	2.7	2.9	3.0
Louisiana	12,916	12,499	11,617	12,348	13,105	14,438	17,473	1.8	1.9	1.7	1.9	2.0	2.2	2.6
Maine	2,814	4,467	4,792	5,104	4,980	5,194	5,174	1.4	2.4	2.5	2.7	2.7	2.8	2.9
Maryland	21,706	43,179	45,500	51,574	55,343	56,047	60,705	2.5	5.1	5.3	6.0	6.4	6.5	6.9
Massachusetts	48,098	49,612	52,610	62,354	63,917	66,640	70,212	5.9	6.3	6.7	7.9	8.1	8.5	9.0
Michigan	57,820	53,565	50,773	52,811	56,865	63,322	70,231	3.5	3.5	3.5	3.7	4.1	4.6	5.2
Minnesota	54,013	54,349	40,778	54,034	50,837	55,875	57,980	6.7	6.8	5.1	6.8	6.3	6.9	7.2
Mississippi	3,365	6,061	5,617	6,175	8,485	6,574	7,773	0.7	1.2	1.1	1.3	1.7	1.3	1.6
Missouri	18,745	19,393	20,411	23,169	24,455	25,149	26,731	2.0	2.2	2.3	2.6	2.7	2.8	3.0
Montana	6,716	3,806	3,299	3,318	3,750	3,311	3,299	4.6	2.7	2.3	2.3	2.6	2.3	2.3
Nebraska	16,124	19,323	20,062	17,532	16,895	15,416	17,494	5.7	6.6	6.7	5.8	5.6	5.0	5.6
Nevada	71,557	67,868	83,351	84,125	67,970	67,640	74,521	17.9	16.0	19.4	19.6	15.7	15.5	17.0
New Hampshire	2,569	3,821	3,965	3,892	3,709	3,506	3,592	1.2	1.9	2.0	2.0	2.0	1.9	2.0

Table 3.4 Number and Percentage of Public School Students Participating in English Language Learner (ELL) Programs, by State: Selected Years, Fall 2004 Through Fall 2014 (*continued*)

State	Number of public school students participating in programs for English language learners							Percent of students participating in programs for English language learners						
	2004	2009	2010	2011	2012	2013	2014	2004	2009	2010	2011	2012	2013	2014
1	2	3	4	5	6	7	8	9	10	11	12	13	14	15
United States	43,41,435[1]	43,64,510[1]	43,70,004[1]	43,89,325	43,97,318[1]	44,60,956[1]	45,59,323[1]	9.1[1]	9.1[1]	9.1[1]	9.1	9.2[1]	9.3[1]	9.4[1]
New Jersey	53,300	55,450	52,580	53,543	57,838	60,655	65,997	3.9	4.1	3.8	4.0	4.3	4.5	4.8
New Mexico	62,386	51,257	52,029	53,071	51,554	49,917	47,626	19.1	15.5	15.7	16.1	15.8	15.3	14.6
New York	1,88,682[2]	2,00,433	2,07,708	2,04,898	1,97,594	1,84,562[4]	1,86,694	6.7	7.4	7.8	7.8	7.5	7.0[4]	7.1
North Carolina	68,063	1,05,651	1,02,397	98,264	97,338	93,726	92,589	5.0	7.3	7.1	6.7	6.6	6.5	6.3
North Dakota	2,033	3,031	2,788	2,589	2,667	2,749	3,111	2.0	3.3	3.0	2.7	2.7	2.7	3.0
Ohio	27,176	36,527	35,170	35,729	37,207	40,195	42,016	1.5	2.2	2.1	2.2	2.3	2.5	2.6
Oklahoma	44,433	39,259	41,431	44,593	46,155	46,736	47,605	7.1	6.0	6.3	6.7	6.9	7.0	7.1
Oregon	64,603	61,625	58,662	63,790	50,181	49,543	49,311	11.7	11.0	10.5	11.3	8.9	8.8	8.7
Pennsylvania	36,663[2]	44,359	44,729	44,242	44,017	44,777	47,443	2.1[2]	2.6	2.7	2.7	2.7	2.8	3.0
Rhode Island	8,508	6,340	7,161	7,724	7,856	8,562	9,180	6.0	4.9	5.5	6.1	6.2	6.8	7.3
South Carolina	12,523	34,661	36,360	38,986	40,876	40,087	42,133	1.8	4.8	5.1	5.4	5.7	5.5	5.7
South Dakota	4,179	4,005	4,383	4,736	4,999	4,251	4,676	3.3	3.2	3.5	3.7	3.8	3.3	3.5
Tennessee	27,875[2]	27,550	29,680	30,996	32,331	34,397	36,398	3.0[2]	2.8	3.0	3.1	3.3	3.5	3.7
Texas	6,76,857	7,08,615	7,18,350	7,22,043	7,39,639	7,65,952	7,72,843	15.6	15.0	15.0	14.9	15.1	15.5	15.4
Utah	44,981	46,591	41,805	32,423	31,810	32,775	36,175	9.2	8.5	7.7	5.9	5.7	5.7	6.3

(*continued*)

55

Table 3.4 Number and Percentage of Public School Students Participating in English Language Learner (ELL) Programs, by State: Selected Years, Fall 2004 Through Fall 2014 (*continued*)

State	Number of public school students participating in programs for English language learners							Percent of students participating in programs for English language learners						
	2004	2009	2010	2011	2012	2013	2014	2004	2009	2010	2011	2012	2013	2014
1	2	3	4	5	6	7	8	9	10	11	12	13 14	14	15
United States	43,41,435[1]	43,64,510[1]	43,70,004[1]	43,89,325	43,97,318[1]	44,60,956[1]	45,59,323[1]	9.1[1]	9.1[1]	9.1[1]	9.1	9.2[1]	9.3[1]	9.4[1]
Vermont	1,989	1,525	1,510	1,447	1,427	1,348[5]	1,442[5]	2.1	1.7	1.6	1.6	1.6	1.5[5]	1.7[5]
Virginia	66,748	86,475	87,752	91,431	92,937	93,995	97,397	5.6	7.0	7.1	7.4	7.4	7.5	7.7
Washington	75,103	65,101	90,282	82,070	93,940	99,650	1,07,197	7.4	6.3	8.7	7.9	8.9	9.4	10.0
West Virginia	1,774	1,605	1,786	1,914	2,084	1,878	2,704	0.6	0.6	0.6	0.7	0.7	0.7	1.0
Wisconsin	26,616	45,041	43,562	44,362	43,189	42,711	42,259	3.1	5.2	5.0	5.1	5.0	4.9	4.9
Wyoming	3,543	2,098	2,602	2,706	2,733	2,756	2,697	4.2	2.4	2.9	3.0	3.0	3.0	2.9

[1]U.S. total includes imputation for nonreporting states.

[2]Imputation for survey nonresponse. State-level imputations were based on the percentages reported by the state for other years applied to the enrollment for the given year.

[3]Based on data reported by the California Education Agency (http://www.cde.ca.gov/ds/sd/cb/cefelfacts.asp).

[4]For 2013, New York data on participation in programs for English language learners are from U.S. Department of Education, National Center for Education Statistics, EDFacts file 046, Data Group 123, extracted December 2, 2015, from the EDFacts Data Warehouse (internal U.S. Department of Education source).

[5]Includes students enrolled in all types of school districts.

NOTE: Includes students served in regular school districts, excluding regional education service agencies and supervisory union administrative centers, state-operated agencies, federally operated agencies, and other types of local education agencies, such as independent charter schools.

Source: U.S. Department of Education, National Center for Education Statistics, Common Core of Data (CCD), "Local Education Agency Universe Survey," 2004–05 through 2014–15.

speaking English opens the door to many opportunities, such as education and employment.

Unfortunately, what happens to many children is that in an effort to learn English, their native language is lost. Language loss increases family challenges since parents (and other family members such as grandparents) can no longer communicate with their children, which creates issues of separation (Wong-Fillmore, 2000). Often, in the case of many Mexican-American families who have been in the U.S. for generations, Spanish has been lost and the fluency varies depending on how often the language is spoken to children by adults. I have often heard many Mexican-American friends say, "I don't speak the correct Spanish, it's Tex-Mex," because the Spanish they heard at home was different than those who came from Spanish-speaking countries.

There are many theories of how children develop language, including behaviorist, nativist, cognitivist, social interactionist, and information processing (Hulit, Howard, & Fahey, 2011). Similarly, there are second-language acquisition theories, including environmentalist theories, Schumann's Acculturation Model, nativist theories, and Krashen's Monitor Model (Freeman & Freeman, 2001). Krashen's Classic Monitor Model of Second Language Acquisition focuses on the importance of the learner to have low anxiety as he or she learns a second language. Krashen (1981) discusses five hypotheses regarding second-language acquisition that have helped educators understand the process: (1) acquisition/learning distinction, (2) the natural order hypothesis, (3) the monitor hypothesis, (4) the input hypothesis, and (5) the affective-filter hypothesis. This theory emphasizes the natural order of language acquisition and the importance of giving the learner time and support.

A seminal theory, proposed by Cummins (1979), indicates there are two time periods that a child usually goes through when learning a second language: Basic Interpersonal Communication Skills (BICS) and Cognitive Academic Language Proficiency (CALP). In the BICS stage, children use language for social functions, to give information, to project situations or to guess future situations, to control themselves and others, and to direct attention and memory. In the CALP stage, children are listening, speaking, reading, and writing within a content area (Gonzalez, Yawkey, & Minaya-Rowe, 2006). These skills are usually practiced within a classroom setting and take 5 to 7 years to master (Gonzalez et al.).

These two skill stages have become guidelines for teachers to understand the process of second-language acquisition and the importance of teaching children in their native language in order for them to continue learning academic concepts. It is important also for teachers to explain to parents that their children will learn to speak English, but they need academic instruction in their native language as they learn English.

Communicating with Parents Regarding Second-Language Learning

We encourage teachers to provide language support for dual-language learners and their families. Understanding the benefits of bilingualism, teachers can be advocates for children and families to ensure that children maintain their home language while learning English in a developmentally appropriate manner (Magruder, Hayslip, Espinosa, & Matera, 2013). Teachers can give parents the following tips to explain how to support young children's language development:

- Talk to your child in your home language.
- Sing to your child in your home language.
- Tell your child traditional stories from your culture in your home language.
- Read culturally relevant books to your child in your home language.
- Play traditional children's games from your culture.
- Have your child send letters, e-mails, or texts in their home language to family members, such as grandparents.
- Use your native language in social media.
- Encourage grandparents to speak to your child in their native language.

Programs for English Language Learners

The type of programs that research has shown helps ELLs not only learn English but learn academic content are bilingual programs with an English as a Second Language, or ESL, component. Bilingual programs are usually offered in school districts that have a large number of students with the same language background. Table 3.5 provides a list of Bilingual Education Program Models.

Table 3.5 Bilingual Education Program Models

Program	Description
Transitional Bilingual Education	This program focuses on transitioning children quickly from their native language to English. The home language is used from prekindergarten until third or fourth grade. It is usually accompanied by English as a Second Language instruction.
Maintenance or Late Exit	There are few programs that focus on maintaining the home language through early childhood and elementary schools. Schools that have maintenance or late exit use the home language for instruction until fifth or sixth grade.
Dual-Language and Two-Way Immersion	Different models are used in these types of programs. Usually, emphasis is placed on the home language in the early grades with some instruction in English. The most popular model is the 50/50 in which half of the instruction is in English and half in Spanish, but not simultaneously. Some subjects are taught in the native language and others in English.

Source: Herrera, S. G. & Murry, K. G. (2011). *Mastering ESL and Bilingual Methods: Differentiated Instruction for Culturally and Linguistically Diverse (CLD) Students*, 2/E. Upper Saddle River, NJ: Pearson.

TWO-WAY IMMERSION OR DUAL-LANGUAGE PROGRAMS. Two-way immersion, or dual-language programs seem to be getting more popular because of the inclusion of home-language speakers as well as English speakers. Teachers play a key role in that they learn how to negotiate between languages for academic and social purposes (Gort & Pontier, 2013).

Two-way immersion programs are beneficial for children. The children who are English speakers learn about their identity because they learn about the identity of others. Noteworthy is the fact that many children and families have lost their native language because, historically, language minority groups, such as Chicanos, were prohibited from speaking their language and were harshly punished (Valencia, 2002). Dual-language or two-way immersion programs assist children in developing both languages and help in maintaining attachment to their families, particularly those who do not speak English (Block, 2012). The Center for Applied Linguistics provides additional information on the principles of two-way immersion programs.

Children in two-way immersion programs also score higher in reading and math achievement tests compared to those children in transitional programs (Marian, Shook, & Schroeder, 2013).

ENGLISH AS A SECOND LANGUAGE. Schools that do not offer bilingual programs often offer some type of English as a Second Language program, such as an ESL class, ESL pull-out, sheltered instruction, or structured immersion (Calderón, Slavin, & Sanchez, 2011). It is important for teachers to understand the difference between bilingual programs and ESL programs because one is asset-based, meaning that the native language of the child is valued for academic learning,

while the other one focuses on rushing children to learn English quickly. The parents are the ones who decide if they want their children in a bilingual or ESL program. Therefore, it is imperative that the teachers assist parents in making an informed decision.

Additionally, programs should value and build a cultural and linguistic capital of English language learners. This means that the children's native language, as well as their culture, need to be respected in order to let parents know how they and their children are valued (Brooks & Karathanos, 2009).

Bilingual Education Outlook

According to Kelly (2018), the U.S. does not have a "policy for language education" (p. 6). Under the Lau v. Nichols (1974) law, school districts across our country have the right to select the language of instruction. Although California and Arizona had adopted an "English-only" emphasis in the 1990's, there are some proposed bills in each state to expand dual language education (Kelly, 2018). These bills bring back the importance stance of bilingual education. Bilingual education promotes excellence and equity, allowing children to use their native language to learn academic concepts while at the same time learning English (which is one of the goals of bilingual education), thus becoming biliterate—a goal in itself that is a fundamental advantage (Goldenberg, 2014).

For very young children, bilingual education programs are crucial for their healthy development. When early childhood programs describe themselves as "developmentally appropriate," they need to take into consideration the child's primary language. For example, in 2009, a Head Start program in Washington

State decided to make changes in its curriculum to create a strong foundation in the children's primary language in order to help children succeed. Previously, they had used English immersion, but the teachers and administrators realized that English immersion was not helping children be successful in school (Youngquist & Martínez-Griego, 2009). The children's language production increased as a result of allowing them to use their native language. This important finding supports previous research regarding the need for children to be allowed to interact in their home language in early childhood.

Interestingly, there seems to be a movement across the U.S. where private preschool programs are opening their doors to families who wish their children to grow up bilingually. In southern Texas, the number of Spanish-immersion private preschool programs has increased in the last five years and so has the need for early childhood educators to know more about culturally responsive pedagogy in order to meet the needs of young children from all backgrounds.

Advocacy for appropriate programs that promote the child's native language for instruction is very important. Just as important is for the bilingual programs to provide literacy experiences for children that will allow them to become biliterate. What does it mean to be biliterate? Someone who is biliterate can read and write in two languages. For children who are growing up in the U.S., becoming biliterate is a must for family as well as economic reasons. Many immigrant children and children of immigrant parents have a first language which in most cases is not English. As immigrant families strive to become part of the U.S., they also learn the importance of speaking the language. Teresita, in the example in the previous section, was very proud to say that she knew enough English that she could get by. However, just as important is for Teresita to become biliterate so that her opportunities can broaden. Although many schools promote bilingualism, many are promoting biliteracy, such as those that have dual language programs. These programs expect children to be bilingual and biliterate so that they can reap the benefits of being fully literate in two languages. The field of biliteracy is starting to grow with many researchers (e.g., Perez, Escamilla, Lindholm-Leary, Soto Huerta, among others) seeking to see how well children develop biliteracy skills, particularly those in dual language programs. There are family biliteracy programs that focus on the whole family's biliteracy skills, such

as the Migrant Education Family Biliteracy Program. Based in California, this program promotes the "academic, language, social, and cross-cultural challenges of school that prepare migrant children for kindergarten (California Department of Education, 2018). The program focuses on migrant families who may be or not documented.

Culturally Responsive Pedagogy

Culturally responsive pedagogy has truly changed the way teachers work with students. It is defined as a "theoretical model that not only addresses student achievement but also helps students accept and affirm their cultural identity while developing critical perspectives that challenge inequities that schools (and other institutions) perpetuate" (Ladson-Billings, 1995, p. 469). Often teachers misinterpret culturally responsive pedagogy as a cultural celebration (often the tourist approach), something that creates a dissonance in students' learning (Sleeter, 2012).

Culturally responsive pedagogy, or CRP, is important for all culturally and linguistically diverse children. CRP provides opportunities to enhance learning, particularly for minority groups, such as African Americans and Latinos, who have been marginalized from the school system for many years, causing them to be less successful than White students (Howard, 2003).

Culturally responsive pedagogy allows teachers to reflect on their practices and provide a curriculum that is relevant to all children in order to increase learning opportunities (Milner, 2013). A curriculum that is

Children's culture is an asset for school learning.

Comstock Images/Stockbyte/Getty Images

culturally responsive means it reflects the children's experiences, identity, culture, and abilities in the lessons (Rychly & Graves, 2012). Such a curriculum also includes parents and sees families from an asset perspective. For example, while doing a project or unit on transportation, a preschool teacher can find out how many different types of transportation children use when they go visit their families during the summer or school holidays. Teachers must understand the cultural and socioeconomic background of the children. Having discussion regarding the children's daily lives is a good way to get to know them. For instance, teachers can ask the children how they get to school, who lives with them, or daily routines that may be part of their traditions.

Culturally Relevant Curriculum: Antibias

Antibias education focuses on the notion of "practice of freedom," which is how cultural consciousness has the power to transform reality (Lin, Lake, & Rice, 2008). An antibias classroom respects, values, and takes pride in the children and their families (Derman-Sparks & Olsen Edwards, 2012). One book written for preschool teachers and their students that can be useful in learning about and implementing antibias education is *Anti-Bias Education for Young Children and Ourselves* by Derman-Sparks and Olsen Edwards (2010). This book, now in its second edition, has made an impact on issues of equity by providing ideas, questions, and strategies to use in the classroom. It encompasses what developmentally and culturally appropriate practices are all about: taking into consideration culture, language, religion, country of origin, and gender.

The foundation of antibias education is understanding how "young children construct their personal and social identities, [and] how they think about differences and absorb messages about prejudice and social advantage or disadvantage" (Derman-Sparks & Olsen Edwards, 2012, p. 11). The four goals of antibias education guide educators to develop an understanding of discriminatory actions by actively promoting principles of social justice in a language that young children understand.

The antibias curriculum seeks to avoid the trap of the "tourist" examination of cultures, in which holidays and customs are the only ventures into cultural identity. An antibias curriculum also uses the children's funds

of knowledge as a resource for learning. A preschool that follows antibias goals includes a curriculum that:

1. Uses children's books that reflect differences in gender, race, disabilities, geographic location, and socioeconomic class.
2. Offers opportunities for dramatic play with different peers.
3. Plays different genres of music that represent different groups in the U.S., such as rap, hip hop, jazz, *conjunto*, and country, among others. It is also a good idea to play traditional music from countries around the world.
4. Displays a variety of art that represents different artists from the United States and around the world, allowing children to explore their own creativity.
5. Engages children in different types of traditional children's games from the United States and around the world.
6. Invites parents and/or other family members to join in the children's learning, not only at home but at school as well.

In order for children to experience healthy development, social inequities and biases must be eradicated, and early on. Derman-Sparks and Olsen Edwards (2010) point out that children notice gender and racial differences as early as the second year of life, and by age 3 may already have been exposed to biases that the authors call "preprejudice." For children to have an equitable education, it is important for educators and administrators to create antibias classrooms that focus on the reality of children's lives, taking into consideration the many cultural aspects of all of the children in the class. Building and maintaining strong relationships between teachers and families will help ensure the effectiveness of this antibias classroom.

Culturally and Linguistically Diverse Parents, Children, and the Community

The first and most important thing to remember when working with culturally diverse groups is to avoid stereotyping. Very often, information about different ethnic groups is learned from the media, which may portray groups from just one perspective (Gay, 2010).

Many culturally and linguistically diverse families are second, third, and fourth generation Americans that have acculturated to a variety of traditions.

Unfortunately, this perspective leads to stereotypes that prevent teachers from communicating effectively with parents.

Culturally responsive teaching promotes active communication with parents by following the protocols of communication associated with the family's culture (Gay, 2010). One way to get to know the families in the community, in addition to inviting them to the school, is to go out into their community. School personnel should get acquainted with the school neighborhood before school starts. Taking "block walks" or attending special events in the community can give teachers an idea of what the community is like. In order to get to know the community deeper, teachers can conduct a community study. A community study motivates teachers to look into different aspects of the community, such as the type of businesses, churches, schools, and other resources that are present. It also helps teachers understand other people's way of life (Ek, Machado-Casas, Sánchez, & Smith, 2011), including beliefs about how children develop and how they learn to assimilate and acculturate in a different world (Riojas-Cortez, 2008). When I was a teacher, I remember visiting my students' homes and that allowed me to become familiar with the community. I developed a different perspective regarding children's lives. I saw some very shocking things such as children eating from the floor as the crumbs of food fell, but most importantly, I learned how much

parents valued their children regardless of their income. That gave me a more humane perspective for parents and helped me work more closely with them without judging or stereotyping.

While some schools promote Parent Teacher Association (PTA) meetings, others, like a school in South Central Texas, decided that PTA night did not work. So they decided to create parent/teacher workshops for one hour after school or at a time that was most convenient for parents in each classroom. Some schools have tried "Family Nights" for ESL families but often with little to no success (Guo, 2009). To make sure such events are a success, teachers need to use principles of culturally relevant pedagogy to make families feel welcome and safe at school. Other schools have events such as open houses on the weekends, because they have found that more parents visit when the parents do not feel pressed for time. Teachers and administrators must know their families in order to know what works for them.

When learning about the community, it is imperative that teachers keep an open mind and begin by looking at positive aspects of the community and by avoiding stereotypes. For example, not all Latinos are immigrants from Mexico and other Latin American countries. Many Latinos have been in the United States for generations. The same is true for people of Asian descent.

By getting to know the community, teachers can use Bronfenbrenner's Ecological Systems Theory to understand how children are seen in the community and how each system supports their development. Rather than just giving information, teachers can truly collaborate with culturally and linguistically diverse families by understanding the important role that parents have in their children's lives and how they truly want to participate in their children's education (Valdés, 1996). The following list gives best practices regarding how to effectively communicate with culturally and linguistically diverse families (Araujo, 2009):

- *Incorporate funds of knowledge.* Connect the children's world with the school by using the knowledge they gain at home within the curriculum.

- *Practice culturally responsive teaching.* Use parents' knowledge to provide relevant lessons. Use native language for instruction.

- *Foster effective communication.* Send newsletters in the student's native language, make phone calls to give positive feedback (use a translator if necessary), make home visits, talk to parents about how you need their help reinforcing rules and policies, and ask parents to visit the classroom just to see how the school and the classroom operate.

- *Extend and accept assistance.* Provide information regarding community resources, create parent liaisons within the school to assist parents who may not be familiar with the school system, and have a pool of translators who can readily communicate with parents.

Summary

Understanding the differences between terms such as culture and diversity will help teachers understand how to incorporate culturally relevant teaching in their classroom. Exploring one's own culture, ancestry, and values helps create empathy for others. Teachers and administrators identify the needs of culturally and linguistically diverse children by providing programs that promote the use of their native language for instruction. When that is not possible, they provide programs that will help children achieve not only English proficiency but also academic proficiency. Culturally relevant pedagogy lets teachers use the children's funds of knowledge in their lessons, thus providing the opportunity for children not only to learn content but also to learn it in a way that they can internalize it more effectively. The antibias curriculum shows teachers and administrators the importance of knowing how to effectively use developmentally and culturally appropriate practices with children and their families. Knowing how to work with culturally and linguistically diverse families will help teachers enhance children's learning by using them as a resource for teaching.

Suggested Class Activities and Discussions

1. List the values and strengths you look for in a family. Why did you choose them?

2. Discover your heritage by researching your family's past. If you were adopted and your heritage was not revealed to you use your adoptive family heritage..

3. Invite parents of different cultures to share family traditions with the class.

4. Visit various places of worship. Invite ministers, priests, rabbis, or other clerics to share beliefs and ideas with the class.

5. Have a class discussion about family traditions and beliefs.

6. Visit museums in the area. What is revealed about beliefs or cultures of different time periods?

7. Investigate methods and curricula that schools are using to include culturally relevant pedagogy.

8. Complete the *Play Memories* handout on page 63 to understand differences and similarities in children's traditions.

Play Memories

Directions: Please complete the following form regarding how you and your family play(ed) together.

Who am I?

When I was young, I liked to play with

When I was young, my favorite games were

Today I like to play

My parents' favorite games were

When my parents were young, they used to play

Today they play

When my grandparents were young, they used to play

Today they play

©1999 by Mari Riojas-Cortez

Useful Websites

Center for Applied Linguistics (CAL)
National Association for Bilingual Education (NABE)
Migration Policy Institute

Child Trends Hispanic Institute
Pew Research Center

Glossary Terms

Antibias: Approach in early childhood education that discusses the importance of embracing diversity and differences in a fair and equitable manner.

Culture: The learned and shared values of a society; a system of beliefs, attitudes, and control mechanisms that shape behavior.

Culturally responsive pedagogy: Pedagogy that recognizes the importance of incorporating culture in students' learning.

Diversity: Differences in characteristics, qualities, traits, values, beliefs, and mannerisms in self and others based on predetermined factors (e.g., gender and race) and changeable features (e.g., language and citizenship).

Dual-language learners: Children acquiring two languages simultaneously.

English language learners (ELLs): Students who are learning English usually in U.S. schools.

Funds of identity: Resources we use to describe ourselves.

Identity: Defined as knowing who we are and to what groups we belong.

Immigrant: A person who goes to another country to live permanently.

Chapter 4
Family Engagement: History and Social Influences

Learning about the past gives us an opportunity to understand our future.

Mari Riojas-Cortez

Learning Outcomes

In this chapter, you will learn how family involvement in children's lives has evolved over time. After completing the chapter, you should be able to do the following:

4.1 Define family engagement from a historical context.

4.2 Reflect on the views of children throughout history.

4.3 Explain the influence of social thinkers regarding views of children throughout history.

4.4 Identify social changes that influence family engagement.

4.5 Examine the influence of digital technology in family engagement.

4.6 Describe the focus on healthy living for families.

Family Engagement: Historical Overview

Parents have always been an important influence in children's lives. Their role as active agents has evolved over time. In the last 20 years, educators wanted parents to become "involved" with their children; today educators call for parents to be "engaged." **Engagement**, according to Ferlazzo (2011), means a commitment, while involvement indicates taking part in something. Engagement has an emotional undertone, while involvement is detached.

Parents become actively engaged with their children from a very young age and attachment helps nurture this engagement. Being actively engaged with children means giving them the unconditional attention they need in order to have a healthy development. Parents engage with their children emotionally as they meet their children's immediate needs, such as providing food and shelter.

In order to understand the history of **family engagement** we must understand and accept the differences between families in our nation and throughout the world. It would be a mistake on our part to view the history of parent engagement only through a Western lens. We must also understand parent engagement from a variety of cultural groups and from families' funds of knowledge.

Throughout history, we can see how parents engaged with their children. The engagement varied depending on the period of time and the influences that families endured during that period. For instance, agrarian families needed children to help with the daily chores of the farm, while families that worked in factories needed children to help with the daily chores of the home. Older children often took care of the younger ones while the father worked outside the home and the mother took care of the household, sometimes in addition to a factory job, farm chores, or other work. Interestingly, parents had to learn to accept the importance of school for children. For many other families, however, school was a way out of poverty, a way to improve their standard of living. As school attendance became mandatory, parents had to find other monetary support because they wanted their children to have more opportunities than they did. For minorities and children of poverty, school attendance is still a struggle, particularly for older children who have to take on adult responsibilities, making school attendance for them logistically difficult.

Today, family engagement happens every day across the United States and the world. In the United States, we see most families getting their children to school each day regardless of the challenges they face. Some families particularly those of low-income background struggle with odd work schedules that create obstacles for active engagement with their children, including nonstandard sleeping schedules leading to tardiness, difficulty staying awake and on task, strong reliance on fast food for nutrition, and absenteeism from school. Clearly, families in the U.S. and across the globe face many challenges and somehow they still function together, involving each other in different aspects of their lives. Situations such as hunger, war, immigration, discrimination, poverty, violence, abuse, disease, and unemployment often bring families together, but other times can take them apart.

Families across cultures have different views of children, and this often dictates the amount of engagement families have with their children. These views are often based on historical perceptions that are passed down through the generations and have acculturated within societies. Teachers must explore historical events to have a clear understanding of how such events affect parental engagement.

Views of Children and Family Engagement Throughout History

History shows that perspectives regarding children vary depending on the era. For example, in primitive times, children were valued for their contribution to survival and for their implied continuance of society. Greeks viewed children as a link to the future, the conveyors of culture and civilization, as well as valued members of the family. Artwork depicts Egyptians as holding their children in high esteem. In some societies, adults showed affection for their children by holding them on their laps and embracing them. Children were also portrayed in art as carefree—running; playing with balls, dolls, and board games; and playing leapfrog and hopscotch (Bell & Harper, 1980; Osborn, 1991).

The perspective of children mentioned in the previous paragraph influenced education. Formal systems of education existed in ancient India, China, and Persia, as well as in the pre-Columbian Americas, especially in the cultures of the Mayas, Aztecs, and Incas. The Aztecs regarded their children highly, but as the youths got older, parents were strict with their punishments. While the Mayans believed that children had a duty to help out their families, particularly their elders, punishment was not harsh for their children unless their actions presented danger. During the Middle Ages in Europe, from about the year 400 to 1400, children ranked very low among society's priorities; therefore, there was no system of education and very little family life.

During medieval Europe (around the 15th century), living conditions did not provide poor people with an opportunity for privacy or time with their families. European societies in the 16th century, emerging from a time of suffering and hardship and influenced by the Protestant Reformation and the Catholic Counter-Reformation, viewed the child as one in whom evil must be suppressed and the soul nourished (Bell & Harper, 1980). The modern parent educator did not begin to emerge until the 17th and 18th centuries, and the general population was not affected until the 19th century (Bell & Harper, 1980).

The Influence of Social Thinkers on Views of Children and Family Engagement Throughout History

Social thinkers such as Comenius, Locke, Rousseau, Pestalozzi, and Froebel developed new ideas about education and the importance of the home in the education of children. Their theories help us understand why some views of children have evolved and why some remain the same. It is important for teachers and other educators to understand these philosophical views because this knowledge helps teachers become aware of how parents perceive their children and thus engage in their development.

John Amos Comenius (1592–1670).   Born in Moravia in 1592, Comenius was a member and bishop of the Moravian Brethren, who believed in the basic goodness of each child. This belief is reflected in his writing about education methodology. In *Didactica Magna*, a large treatise on education, he discusses the importance of the infant's education: "It is the nature of everything that comes into being, that while tender it is easily bent and formed, but that, when it has grown hard, it is not easy to alter. Wax, when soft, can be easily fashioned and shaped; when hard it cracks readily" (Comenius, 1967, p. 58). In *School of Infancy*, written in 1628, he emphasized that education begins at home and described in detail the manner in which young children should be educated. Comenius also wrote textbooks for children. *Orbis Pictus (The World in Pictures)* is considered the first picture book for children (Woo, 2016). Although a prolific writer, Comenius was unable to change the direction of education during his lifetime.

However, Comenius's ideas as they relate to parental involvement are now extremely important. First, believing that children are inherently good helps families work with their children in harmony. It helps families understand that children go through phases and their behavior will change but that they can help mold that behavior through guidance and discipline (not necessarily spanking). In contrast to this, if families believe that children are born bad, then the undesired behavior becomes their focus, rather than teaching for teaching's sake. Such families often spend a great deal of time disciplining rather than teaching their children. Often, children who are playful, loud, or mischievous are categorized as "bad." An adult student in one of my classes once told me that he believed that children were "bad." He told me that he spanked his 2-year-old because she had disobeyed him and had run away at the grocery store. He believed that his daughter disobeyed him on purpose, not realizing that such behavior is typical of toddlers.

Comenius also believed in the importance of infant education—perhaps not education in the formal sense of the word, but in the sense that parents teach children

many things that we now define as funds of knowledge. This was a revolutionary premise because infants during Comenius's time were not believed to be able to learn anything. Today we see parents praising their infants when they reach a milestone, and many look for different toys, books, and activities to help their children grow and develop, thus teaching their children from an early age. We also see families struggling to find quality childcare because of the great emphasis that has been placed on early childhood development in the last decade.

John Locke (1632–1704).   Locke, an Englishman, had far-reaching and innovative ideas concerning government and education. He probably is best known for the concept that the newborn's mind is a *tabula rasa*, or blank slate, at birth. All ideas develop from experience; none are innate. Therefore, it is up to the family and teacher to provide valuable experiences and the optimum environment for the child's mind to thrive.

Some parents hold belief that they have to "fill" their child's mind with information, and thus some parents work with their infants steadily to get them to reach milestones sooner, while others send their infants to schools that emphasize academic development at an early age. I have often heard parents indicate that their child is like a "sponge," absorbing everything they see and hear. This idea shows their belief that infants need to be filled with ideas in order to understand and interact. In contrast to this concept is that children learn by doing and imitating because they have the cognitive skills to understand such concepts. For example, when my son Miguel was an infant, he would like to give *besitos*, or kisses, to pictures of family members. We never taught him to give kisses to the pictures, but we had taught him to love his family and to kiss to show affection. Miguel was imitating his family's behavior and at the same time he was able to cognitively process the social interaction by showing his understanding of this cultural practice. Recently, while waiting to catch a flight, I saw three different families with young children teaching them different things as they tried to keep the children entertained while waiting to board the plane. One mother would cheer when her baby clapped her hands; the more the parent cheered, the more the baby clapped. When parents teach, they are more than involved—they are engaged.

Locke, who lived during the period when "hardening" the child was in vogue, was a staunch supporter of this concept. If children were exposed to cold baths and other methods of hardening, according to the belief, they would become more resistant to diseases and ailments. In essence, this view tells parents that the more the child suffers, the better he or she is going to be equipped for life. We still see this idea when parents allow children to get hurt (but not badly), such as letting them touch things that are hot so they can learn not to do it again. I remember my father telling my sisters and me when we were growing up in Mexico that we needed to "suffer" to understand the value of things (i.e., studying and working), and if we didn't suffer to get something, we would not appreciate its value. The belief of the "hardening" of the child is one that helps children become "strong," and parents very often want their children to be strong. This thinking can lead parents to be engaged in a different way, more as "watchdogs" over their children than people who believe and trust in what they do.

Although parents who value instilling this type of strength in their children ultimately have the children's best interest in mind, they should bear in mind that children should never be allowed to be in danger in order to learn something. It is our duty as parents and teachers to guide children to become strong and productive individuals who care for others, but it is also our duty to prevent harm and danger in their lives.

Jean Jacques Rousseau (1712–1778).   Rousseau, a Frenchman, was another giant in the development of European social thought. As thoughts of greater freedom for human beings evolved, stirrings of freedom for children also emerged. As a political analyst, Rousseau wrote *Social Contract* in 1762, in which he described government through consent and contract with its subjects. This desire for freedom extended into his writings concerning children. In *Emile*, also written in 1762, he urged mothers to "cultivate, water the young plant before it dies. Its fruits will one day be your delights . . . Plants are shaped by cultivation and men by education" (Rousseau, 1979, p. 38).

Rousseau's ideas began to show the importance of the mother teaching her children. There are many early childhood programs that work with mothers (and recently have extended to fathers) to show them how to educate their children. For example, the organization Zero to Three provides brochures and other resources for parents to work with their infants and toddlers (these materials are offered in English and Spanish). For parents who do not have access to the Internet, teachers and other caregivers can make copies or share the information during workshops.

Johann Heinrich Pestalozzi (1747–1827).   Pestalozzi believed in the natural goodness of children, and struggled for many years to teach and care for poor children in his home in Switzerland. Pestalozzi based his teaching on the use of concrete objects, group instruction, cooperation among students, and self-activity of the child. To teach mathematics, he used beans and pebbles as counters and divided cakes and apples to demonstrate fractions. The child's day also included recreation, games, and nutritious snacks and meals (Gutek, 1968).

There are many examples of how parents today use "manipulatives" to teach children, such as when they go to the grocery store to buy fruits and vegetables. They might teach older children measurement by using an infant's bottle to measure the milk. Parents, even those who have no formal education, use different methods. I recall a father who participated in one of my research projects teaching his child about weight using the tools from his mechanic shop.

Though his method of teaching through tangible objects is still prevalent, Pestalozzi is most remembered for his writings. In his first successful book, *How Gertrude Teaches Her Children*, he emphasized the importance of the mother and included teaching methods for parents. It was the first comprehensive education book for parents—Pestalozzi truly can be hailed as the father of parent education.

Friedrich Wilhelm Froebel (1782–1852).   Froebel, known as the father of kindergarten, was born in Germany in 1782, 35 years after Pestalozzi. Froebel is most noted for his development of a curriculum for the kindergarten, but he also recognized the importance of the mother in the development of the child. He saw the mother as the first educator of the child and wrote a book for mothers to use with their children at home. Froebel's book *Mother Play and Nursery Songs with Finger Plays* included verses, pictures, songs, and finger plays still used today, such as "pat-a-cake." Froebel's plan for education was developed around a concept of unity. He organized his curriculum to follow the natural unfolding of the child, with the mother assisting in the development. *Mother Play and Nursery Songs with Finger Plays* was translated into English, giving a large number of parents an opportunity to use Froebelian activities in their homes. In 1870, there were only four books on

Parent involvement in the 1800s focused on families working together for survival.

kindergarten, but by the end of the decade, five more had been translated into English; four more had been written; many articles had been printed and distributed; and two journals, *The Kindergarten Messenger* and *The New Education*, were flourishing (Vandewalker, 1971).

Froebel's development of the kindergarten curriculum has had a significant effect on the current philosophy of education. Instead of a prescribed curriculum designed by the adult to teach the child to read, write, and be moral, the curriculum was developed from the needs of the child. The concepts of child development and teaching to the individual levels of each child were a radical departure from lockstep education.

Identifying the needs of their children is what many parents do today. When they become aware of their children's needs, parents can engage in their children's development by meeting those needs in different ways. Communication and awareness are two crucial skills to teach children social and emotional skills. For example, reading, singing, and even just conversing with their children are important activities for parents to do and oftentimes come naturally, perhaps because their parents taught them such skills (funds of knowledge). My mother, who only had a sixth-grade education and attended beauty school, taught us that talking and singing to infants were crucial for their language development. I still sing to my children the same lullaby that my mother sang to my sisters and me and to all of her grandchildren. I also often listened to my daughter sing the lullaby in Spanish to her dolls when she was young.

Sociohistorical Influences on Family Engagement: Decades of Change for Families

The emphasis on childrearing and education helped to develop a climate in which the learning interactions between child, parent, and family became important for children's development. For instance, the Child Study Association of America (CSAA) was formed in 1888 by a group of New York City mothers; the American Association of University Women (AAUW) was founded in 1882 by college graduates; the National Congress of Mothers, later changed to the National Congress of Parents and Teachers (the PTA), was organized by women who gathered from across the nation at a meeting in 1897; and the National Association of Colored Women was established in 1897.

The associations founded in the 1880s and 1890s had a lasting effect on parent education in the United States. Throughout its history, the CSAA has emphasized child study and parent education. It was the oldest and largest organization solely committed to the study of children. Its earliest programs were studies by authorities of the time: Spencer, Rousseau, Froebel, and Montessori (Brim, 1965). The organization engaged in a variety of activities and services—all related to children and parents (Brim, 1965; Fisher, 1933; National Society for the Study of Education, 1929; Schlossman, 1976). The AAUW implemented a diverse educational program, including the study of children and parent education. The PTA has been concerned with parent–school relationships since its inception. The National Association of Colored Women has focused on civic service, social service, and education with committees on home and the child, mothers, and legislation. Another group, the General Federation of Women's Clubs, formed in 1889, ushered in an even greater interest in women's roles as leaders. These organizations, with the exception of the CSAA, are still actively involved in the field of education and provide resources for many parents.

The Early 20th Century and Childrearing

The early part of the 20th century centered on the family, with well-defined roles for the father and mother (in middle class families). The father's duty was to financially support the family while the mother's duty was to focus on the home. Mothers were idolized as the epitome of purity and goodness, and children were taught to model the mother in their character development. It was important then that the mother be the right kind of person. For this reason, women's clubs flourished. Well-to-do mothers were able to join the many clubs available to them, and those who were on a lower socioeconomic level were served by settlement houses and the Free Kindergarten Association.

Poverty-stricken children in the United States were often forced to work under horrendous conditions at a very young age. These children, who were undernourished, neglected, or abused, prompted a rising social concern. As a result, the first White House Conference on Care of Dependent Children was called in 1909. The Children's Bureau was created in 1912 as a consequence of the conference, a first step in government concern for children.

Soon after the 1909 White House conference, the government began disseminating information on childcare. The first book, *Infant Care*, which would become a popular parent education book on childcare for infants, was published in 1914 by the federal agency that is now the U.S. Department of Health and Human Services.

Interestingly, although the population of the United States was diverse, the study of childrearing focused mostly on Americans of European descent. Minorities' childrearing experiences were not taken into consideration until the Civil Rights Movement raised awareness of issues such as African American slavery, reservations and boarding houses for Native American children, punishment for Mexican American children for speaking Spanish, and similar examples.

Establishing High-Quality Childcare

Twelve faculty wives at the University of Chicago—with guidance from the university—established the first parent cooperative in the United States in 1916. The women wanted high-quality childcare for their children, parent education, and time to work for the Red Cross during the war (Taylor, 1981). This cooperative, the only one established in that decade, followed the tradition of English nursery schools established in 1911 by Margaret McMillan.

McMillan originally designed an open-air school for the poor in England. She emphasized health, education, play, and parent education, rather than mere child watching. The concept of the nursery school was welcomed by middle-class American families, as illustrated by the cooperative in Chicago. Thus, parent cooperatives and the growth of nursery schools in the United States strengthened and promoted parent education with an emphasis on social development.

Changes in Social Skills

While the period of 1890 to 1910 stressed love and freedom, the period of 1910 to 1930 emphasized strict scheduling and discipline. Changes in the philosophical view of children had prompted school authorities to suggest that in order to ensure character development, discipline through punishment was necessary. The increased attention to strict childrearing was illustrated by the first issue of *Infant Care*, issued by the Children's Bureau. Mothers were told to expect obedience, ignore temper tantrums, and restrict physical handling of their children. The recommended changes started early, as seen in the shift in attitude toward breast-feeding. Although breast-feeding was still highly recommended, a supplemental bottle could be given at 5 months, and the child was supposed to be completely weaned by the end of the first year (Wolfenstein, 1953). These severe attitudes continued into the 1920s, when all magazine articles on the topic recommended strict scheduling of infants rather than responding to the infants' needs (Stendler, 1950).

The 1920s Through the 1950s

During the 1920s, many teenagers and young adults were viewed as reckless, overindulged, and spoiled (Schlossman, 1976). To reverse this scandalous situation, children were to be trained early to be responsible, well-behaved individuals. Watsonian behaviorism, the belief that humans can modify behavior through environmental conditioning, was beginning to be felt (Trawick-Smith, 2010). This childrearing theory was mixed in the 1920s with the learning-by-doing theories of Dewey, a small portion of Freudian psychology, and Gesell's belief in natural maturation and growth. Although each theorist had a different approach, all recognized the importance of early experiences and the influence of the environment on the child's development.

The 1923 edition of *Infant Care* admonished parents that "toilet training can begin as early as the end of the first month . . . The first essential in bowel training is absolute regularity" (Vincent, 1951, p. 205). Although breast-feeding was recommended for 6 to 9 months, once weaning was commenced it was to be accomplished in 2 weeks. If the parents insisted on substitution to "artificial food . . . the child will finally yield" (Wolfenstein, 1953, p. 125).

An explosion of parent programs accompanied the prosperity of the 1920s. The era reflected a swing from parent education offered by settlement houses for immigrants and free kindergartens for the underprivileged to the involvement of many middle-class parents in study groups for their own enlightenment and enjoyment.

Parent Cooperatives

The parent cooperative movement, which developed rapidly in California but grew more slowly elsewhere until after World War II, was a way for parents to obtain high-quality education for their children (Osborn, 1991). Parent cooperatives emerged in five locations in the 1920s: Cambridge, Massachusetts; the University of California at Los Angeles; Schenectady, New York; Smith College in Northampton, Massachusetts; and the American Association of University Women in Berkeley, California. To participate, parents had to share

Rural families, such as the one pictured here, were the norm in the United States. Many immigrants also settled in the cities.

Eugenia Berger

responsibilities, which not only helped the cooperatives function, but was an excellent example of parent involvement.

Parent Education

Organizational membership growth also illustrated increased interest in parent education. PTA membership expansion depicted, in terms of sheer numbers, the growth in interest in parent programs. The organization grew from 60,000 in 1915 to 190,000 in 1920, to 875,000 in 1925, to nearly 1.5 million in 1930 (Schlossman, 1976). AAUW membership rose to 35,000 in the 1920s, and each issue of its journal contained a column on parent education. Concurrently, the Child Study Association of America, recognized as the educational leader in parent education during the 1920s, grew from 56 parent groups in 1926 to 135 in 1927 (National Society for the Study of Education, 1929).

The Child Study Manual

Across the country, many school systems implemented parent education and preschool programs. The Emily Griffith Opportunity School (part of the Denver public school system) initially funded a parent education and preschool program in 1926. Its early emphasis on health education for families expanded to childrearing theories and other parenting skills as interests and needs changed. Also in the 1920s, Benjamin Gruenberg published *Outlines of Child Study: A Manual for Parents and Teachers*, a text on childrearing that many parent groups used as a study guide. Succinct discussions on issues of child development were included in each chapter (Gruenberg, 1927).

The Coming of the Depression

As the 1920s drew to a close, middle-class parents were active in parent groups; optimistic about the future; and concerned about health, nutrition, and shaping their children's actions. That all changed with the financial crash of 1929, which forced a tremendous shift in the lifestyle of many families and set the stage for the Great Depression of the 1930s. Poverty made it very difficult for families to provide for their children during these years, and there was a need to support families by offering information on budget, clothing, health, physical care, and diet. The decade began with the White House Conference on Child Health and Protection

in November 1930. Results included rehabilitation projects, such as the Works Progress Administration (WPA), which offered a forum for mothers who were not active in women's clubs or Parent–Teacher Associations to learn about home management practices. Established in October 1933, the Federal Emergency Relief Administration (FERA) authorized work-relief wages for unemployed teachers and others to organize and direct nursery schools; about 75,000 children were enrolled during 1934 and 1935 (Goodykoontz, Davis, & Gabbard, 1947).

This time of change also reflected varying viewpoints on childrearing, ranging from strict scheduling to self-regulation. *Character formation* began to take on broader meanings. Whereas it had meant moral development earlier in the 1900s, articles in magazines now included personality development (Stendler, 1950).

This mother reading to her children illustrates the emphasis on parent education, which expanded in the 1920s and continued into the 1930s.

Families struggled to survive in the 1930s.

Regardless of their viewpoints, many parents maintained involvement with parent education, with numbers continuing at a high level during the first half of the decade. During this time, parents in the United States were receiving information through the mass media, including radio series, lectures, magazines, and the distribution of more than 8 million copies of *Infant Care*. The Pennsylvania Department of Public Instruction's (1935) Bulletin 86, *Parent Education*, reported that parents were also being reached through study groups, with more than 700,000 parents involved in group participation.

Bulletin 86 stressed the importance of parent education, noting that:

> The job of the school is only half done when it has educated the children of the nation. Since it has been demonstrated beyond doubt that the home environment and the role played by understanding parents are paramount in the determination of what the child is to become, it follows that helping the parent to feel more adequate for his task is fully as important from the point of view of public education and the welfare of society as is the education of the children themselves. Moreover, an educated parenthood facilitates the task of the schools and insures the success of its educational program with the child. (p. 12)

Discrimination and Segregation

During the 1930s, people of color suffered tremendously. Not only were they not allowed in public places as whites were, but organizations such as the Ku Klux Klan (KKK) tormented and terrorized families of color (Pegram, 2011). Many families from diverse backgrounds lived with bullying and harassment. Many were killed, while others were burned out of their homes. The Klan harassed individuals who in their eyes were inferior and "sinful," including people of color, Jews, immigrants, and Catholics, among others. This creates a very interesting scenario, because not only were diverse families affected, but the families and children of the men that belonged to this group were certainly affected as well.

Division and segregation prevailed during the 1920s and 1930s, particularly in regard to education for people of color, usually African Americans, Native Americans, and Latinos. Organizations such as the League of United Latin American Citizens (LULAC) were created in 1929 to help promote education among Latinos and end segregation. It was not until 1954 that the U.S. Supreme Court declared the practice of segregation a violation of the Constitution. Latino children, mostly Mexican Americans, also suffered from prejudice, with many not being allowed to speak in their family's native language. In some schools, teachers even punished children who spoke their native language by hitting them. For Native American children, the negative view of their cultures continued to exist, although there were some movements to assist tribes to improve quality of life. Such movements still could not undo what had been done to many families for over 100 years (Carlisle, 2011). In general, the view of children of color was not positive during the 1920s and 1930s.

Changing Views on Children

The tendency of parents in the 1920s and early 1930s to follow the specific rules of behaviorists changed in the 1940s when parents began to recognize that no one answer could work for all situations (Brim, 1965): "The swing from the 'be-tough-with-them, feed-on-schedule, let them cry-it-out' doctrines of the twenties and thirties was almost complete" (Brim, 1965, pp. 130–131). The emotionally healthy child was the goal for professionals and parents, with a new emphasis being placed on self-regulation, which allowed the development of trust and autonomy in the young child.

Vincent (1951) suggested that the decade between 1935 and 1945 could be called the "baby's decade," with the mother "secondary to the infant care 'experts' and the baby's demands" (p. 205). By the early 1940s, mothers were told that children should be fed when hungry, and bowel and bladder training should not begin too early. Babies were to be trained in a gentle manner after they developed physical control. The latest version of *Infant Care* depicted children as interested in the world around them and viewed exploring as natural.

Mead and Wolfenstein later described the change in attitude toward the basic nature of human beings:

> One of the most striking changes in American thinking about children from the nineteenth and early twentieth centuries to the more recent past and the present is the radical change in the conception of the child's nature. From the 19th-century belief in "infant depravity" and the early 20th-century fear of the baby's "fierce" impulses, which, if not vigilantly curbed, could easily grow beyond control and lead to ruin, we have come to consider the child's nature as totally harmless and beneficent. (Mead & Wolfenstein, 1963, p. 146)

Spock

Shifts in beliefs about children were reflected in the childrearing practices of the period. In 1946, Benjamin Spock, a best-selling author and parent educator, published *The Common Sense Book of Baby and Child Care*. He believed the rules and regulations imposed on parents during the 1920s and 1930s caused undue pressure, and he advised parents to enjoy their children and the role of parent.

Spock's book answered questions on feeding, sleeping, clothing, toilet training, management, and illnesses. He had answers for almost all the questions a new parent might have. His writings continued to have great influence on childrearing through the 1950s and beyond as children raised by Spock's methods became parents.

Parent Groups

Both the Great Depression and World War II brought federal support for children's services at younger ages. FERA regulated the childcare funds originally, followed by WPA, and, during World War II, the Federal Works Agency (Goodykoontz et al., 1947). The need to provide childcare for families during the Depression emanated from the necessity for parents to work to get back on their feet and support their families. During World War II, women needed childcare services so they could join the war effort.

The 1940s, although consumed by the U.S. involvement in World War II, saw no reduction in offerings in parent education, though research and training in child development did decline (Brim, 1965). Parent groups continued in public schools, county extension programs prospered, and parent education found added direction in the 1940s through the mental health movement. In 1946, the National Mental Health Act authorized states to establish mental health programs and related parent education (Goodykoontz et al., 1947). The need to understand oneself and one's children was recognized as necessary for healthy parent–child interaction.

Many young adults had postponed marriage and family during the war, but the 1950s were years of relative calm, allowing for an emphasis on children and family life. This is when the "baby boom" began gathering more steam. Schools were feeling the increase in numbers of children and were rapidly expanding to meet their needs. The PTA had more than 9 million members and thousands of study groups among its 30,000 local chapters. Parents were involved with the schools as "room parents" and fundraisers for special projects. The view "Send your child to school—we will do the teaching; your responsibility as a parent is to be supportive of the teachers and schools" prevailed as the basic philosophy between school and parents.

The Emphasis on Family Life

Parent education and preschool programs, part of adult education in many school districts, continued as a vital source of childrearing information. In fact, a survey by the National Education Association revealed that family life was the topic of 32% of adult education classes (Brim, 1965). Pamphlets from the Child Study Association, the Public Affairs Committee, Science Research Associates, and the Parent Education Project of Chicago, plus books by authorities such as Arnold Gesell, Erik Erikson, B. F. Skinner, Benjamin Spock, Lawrence Frank, and Sidonie Gruenberg, were used as curriculum guides.

This trend continued through the 1950s. During this time, James L. Hymes wrote his first book on home–school relations. James L. Hymes author of the book Teaching the Child Under Six and other titles was a child and parent development specialist and advocate. His work focused on how to raise and teach young children. Caring for children became a very important focus. The fifth White House Conference on Children in 1950 focused on developing mental, emotional, and spiritual characteristics to be happy and healthy (Children's Bureau, 2018).

Orville Brim, sponsored by the Russell Sage Foundation and the Child Study Association, examined the issues involved in parent education in *Education for Child Rearing* (1965). His analysis of the effects of parent education continues to be relevant to the study of parent education today.

Erikson

Erikson (1986) popularized the eight stages of personality development in *Childhood and Society*, first published in 1950. His neo-Freudian theories emphasized social and emotional development based on interdisciplinary theories from biology, psychology, and sociology. His theory outlines eight stages of growth, from infancy to adults over 60. The stages begin with the development of trust versus mistrust for infants, autonomy versus shame and doubt for toddlers, initiative versus guilt for preschoolers, and industry versus inferiority for school-age children. The later stages involve adolescents forming identity versus identity diffusion; for young adults, intimacy versus isolation; for adults, generativity versus self-absorption; and for mature adults, integrity versus despair. Erikson's developmental stages and the childrearing practices of the 1950s reflected the belief that social and emotional health were of utmost importance to the child.

Analysis of Parent–Child Relations

The decades between the 1920s and 1950s provided different ideas regarding child development and parental involvement based on the new ideas and beliefs shown by child psychologists and educational philosophers. In a content analysis of *Ladies' Home Journal*, *Good Housekeeping*, and *Redbook* from 1950 to 1970, Bigner (1985) found articles primarily concerned with parent–child relations, socialization, and developmental stages. Spanking was condoned by some in the early 1950s, but by the end of the decade it was consistently discouraged and described as an inefficient and barbaric method that does no more than show the youngster that parents can hit. Most articles encouraged self-regulation by the child. Parents were told it was important that children feel loved and wanted and were advised to hold, love, and enjoy their children and to rely on their own good judgment in making childrearing decisions. Parents were also encouraged to provide a home life that was supportive of individual differences and allowed each child to grow into a well-adjusted adult. Development was a natural process, and maturation could not be pushed. Gesell's work on development in psychomotor and physical areas supported the theory that children proceed through innate developmental stages. As a consequence, parents were encouraged to provide a well-balanced, nutritional diet and an environment that allowed children to grow and learn at their own rate.

The 1960s: Civil Rights and the Family

Great changes in the American family took place between 1890 and 1960 as the country changed from a basically rural nation to an urban one. The majority of families had been self-sufficient rural families with authoritarian parents in the earlier part of the century, and children were economic assets who helped their parents with the family farm or business. As the century progressed, children became financial liabilities, costing $20,000 to raise from infancy to 18 years of age (Hill, 1960). It was not just the children's role but also the roles of the parents that shifted during this time, including increased numbers of women entering the labor force to supplement their husband's income or increase their own economic freedom. For many women who were single parents or were a supporting member of a two-parent family, working was an economic necessity. Because of the social climate during this time, it was common for all institutions—family, education, religion, economics, and government—to be questioned and to undergo change.

However, human rights became the focus of the 1960s.

Father Involvement

During the 1960s, the importance of the father's relationship with his children was also stressed, and although his expected obligations to his children were not the same as the mother's, early interaction with his newborn baby was recognized as very beneficial.

Information for Parents

Parents of the 1960s had many childcare books and booklets from which to choose. Publications from the Child Study Association, Science Research Associates, and public affairs pamphlets covered many of the problems parents faced. Benjamin Spock continued to publish books on childcare, and in them he advised firm, consistent guidance of the child. Spock's efforts were aided by psychologist Haim Ginott (1965), who

The Civil Rights Movement brought about changes in families.

Bettmann/Getty Images

offered parents a method for talking about feelings and guiding the child in a manner that avoided placing guilt, and which helped the child understand the parents' feelings, thus disciplining the child in a positive manner.

The War on Poverty

Although prosperity was within reach for most U.S. citizens and the standard of living had steadily improved to the highest in the world, minorities, people with disabilities, and other groups were still underemployed, often poverty stricken, and largely ignored. The government had high hopes for the Great Society envisioned by President Johnson in eliminating poverty for all citizens. The War on Poverty was legislation introduced by President Johnson to support his belief in increasing social welfare programs, including education and health care. In the War on Poverty programs, children of the poor—who were undernourished, in ill health, did not have proper housing, and lacked educational opportunities—as well as minority children in need, were chosen as a major target to realize hope for the future.

Works of behavioral scientists and educators presenting overpowering evidence that early environment has a profound effect on a child's development, coupled with the national mood of equality and opportunity in the 1960s, propelled the country to respond to the needs of the poor (Bloom, 1964; Hunt, 1961; Skeels, 1966; Spitz, 1965; see Chapter 1). One of the most effective responses was to provide educational intervention for the children of the poor. If children could be given equal environmental opportunities, the cycle of poverty could be broken. The stage was set for the birth of Head Start.

Head Start

In 1965, the Office of Economic Opportunity began an 8-week summer program for preschool children from low-income families. The proposed project had a two-pronged approach: The child would benefit from an enriched early education program, and the parents would be an integral part of the program as aides, advisory council members, or paraprofessional members of the team. As a result of these beliefs, the first Head Start centers were opened in the summer of 1965 as part of the War on Poverty. Head Start was a comprehensive program of health, nutrition, and education, as well as a career ladder for economically disadvantaged families. Migrant Head Start, a program for children of migrant workers, had the first center-based infant–toddler program.

The Elementary and Secondary Education Act

Shortly after the formation of Head Start, the Office of Education and the Department of Health, Education, and Welfare undertook direction from the Elementary and Secondary Education Act (ESEA) of 1965. Two of the title projects under ESEA were:

1. Title I, which assisted school districts in improving the education of educationally deprived children. From its inception, parents were involved in the program.

2. Title IV-C (formerly Title III), which promoted the innovative programs that enrich educational opportunities. Many of these projects included home visitation programs for preschool children, the identification of children with developmental delays before school entry, and working with parents for the benefit of their children.

Concern about continuity of educational success after Head Start resulted in the implementation of the Follow Through program as part of the 1967 Economic Opportunity Act. Designed to carry the benefits of Head Start and similar preschool programs into the public school system, parent participation was a major component of the program, and, as with the Head Start program, parent advisory councils were mandated.

Developmental Continuity

Concern about the link between Head Start and the public school resulted in funding for developmental continuity. Two program designs were investigated. One was based on a cooperative model with both Head Start and the schools working out a continuous educational program for the child. The other design caused change within the existing school system and included programs for children ages 3 years and up as part of the school system, as well as a curriculum structured for preschool through age 8. Both programs involved parents throughout the children's preschool and school years.

The Civil Rights Act of 1965

Although not directly connected with parent education, the Civil Rights Act of 1965 had a great influence on the role of minorities and women during subsequent decades, and through this, it affected the family. Affirmative action, requiring minorities and women to be treated equally in housing, education, and employment, resulted in psychological as well as empirical, observable changes in conditions for these populations.

The 1970s: Advocacy and Action

The decade of the 1970s could be described as the era of advocacy. Groups were no longer willing to sit and wait. They had learned in the 1960s that the way to help is through self-advocacy and intensive activism. Parents of children with disabilities—individually and through organizations such as the Association for Retarded[1] Children, the Council for Exceptional Children, and the Association for Children with Learning Disabilities—advocated equal rights for the special child and won. Advocate groups for children sprang up across the land with training sessions on political power and the means to implement change and protection for children.

The public schools were not immune. Parents began to question programs and their participation with schools and teachers. Forced integration and required busing were issues confronting schools and parents.

Research

Studies conducted in the 1970s consistently demonstrated the importance of an enriched early home environment to the child's school success (Hanson, 1975; Shipman, Boroson, Bidgeman, Gart, & Mikovsky, 1976; White, Kaban, Attanucci, & Shapiro, 1973). Shipman et al. (1976) studied African American children of low socioeconomic status and found that the mother's educational aspirations and expectations were higher for children who scored high in reading than for those who scored low in reading. A higher level of parental education was also associated with children's overall academic success.

In 1975, the Consortium for Longitudinal Studies (1983) set out to determine the effect of the experimental early intervention programs of the 1960s on children. The consortium selected 11 research groups for analysis. Although the programs differed, they were all well designed and well monitored.

The consortium's findings emphasized the importance of early intervention (Consortium for Longitudinal Studies, 1983; Gray, Ramsey, & Klaus, 1982; Lazar et al., 1982; Levenstein, 1988; Spodek, 1982). In a summary of the findings, Lazar et al. (1982) discussed two important points. A good preschool program pays off in two ways: first, benefits for children's development and financial savings as a result of less special-education placement; and second, "closer contact between home and school and greater involvement of parents in the education of their children are probably more important" than generally realized by administrators (p. 464).

A follow-up study of Weikart's Perry Preschool Program vividly illustrated the effect that early educational intervention can have on children's lives (Berrueta-Clement, Schweinhart, Barnett, Epstein, & Weikart, 1984). The Perry Preschool Program followed children to age 19, four years beyond the report published by the Consortium. Berrueta-Clement et al. compared children who had attended the Perry Preschool with children who had not. The researchers found that former Perry Preschool students grew up with more school success, placed a higher value on school, had higher aspirations for college, had fewer absences, and spent fewer of their school years in special education than children in a control group.

With the results of the research came increased programs. In 1972, 16 Home Start programs serving 1,200 families were launched, and 11 Child and Family Resource programs serving 900 families were started in July 1973. These programs promoted "continuity of service by including all children in the participating family from prenatal stage through age 8, and broaden[ed] the program focus from the age-eligible child, to the entire family" (U.S. Department of Health, Education, and Welfare, 1974, p. iii).

Over the years, parent involvement in school decision making diminished, but when formal education joined with informal education, parents still had decision-making rights in regard to their child's schooling. The decade closed with school, government, social agencies, and families concerned with educational programs and support systems for children and parents.

---

[1]The term "retarded" was commonly used during this decade it is no longer acceptable as it is derogatory.

The 1980s: Focus on the Family

The 1980s commenced with the White House Conference on Families, which took place in July 1980 at three locations: Baltimore, Minneapolis, and Los Angeles. Interest was high. Families were important to the citizens, but divisive interests complicated the work. Despite this, the conference approved 20 recommendations to support families, including flexible work schedules, leave policies, job sharing, more part-time jobs, and more childcare services. However, it did not have a great impact on reducing divorce or improving marital harmony.

Family Concerns

Families in this decade were under stress caused by financial pressure, the lack of available time, high mobility, the lack of an extended family in proximity, drugs, abuse, violence on the streets and on television, health concerns, inadequate nutrition, and difficulty in obtaining or providing adequate childcare. On the positive side, inflation steadied in the 1980s. Those who did not have housing, however, were caught in a crunch. Home buyers were faced with high down payments or extremely high monthly payments. Many could not afford any housing, and the number of homeless increased to become a national crisis.

Poverty existed in all parts of the United States—32.5 million people were poor, 12.5 million of whom were children. One child out of five lived in poverty. The ratios were even higher for two minority groups: Nearly one in two African American children and one in three Latino children lived in poverty (Children's Defense Fund, 1989). Poverty was most evident in the inner cities. Relief came in the form of shelters and churches offering warmth to the homeless on cold nights and food lines set up by many private and church groups. In rural areas where poverty was not so evident, little hope was available. Many children attended school without their basic nutritional needs being met. Having access to school lunches was a means of survival for them.

Dealing drugs became more prevalent during this time. Children and families living in inner cities with high crime rates and widespread drug abuse needed comprehensive support to enable them to realize a more promising future (Schorr & Schorr, 1988). The "Just Say No" campaign was implemented to deter children from doing drugs, but it is uncertain the impact this campaign had on children and adolescents. Another important event that focused on children and youth keeping a healthy drug-free life, and which originated in the 1980s, is Red Ribbon week. During this week, students in schools across the U.S. pledge to stay free from drugs.

Along with drugs, there were other major problems that put children at high risk. One was the increased numbers of teenage pregnancies. Very young mothers were not prepared physically, educationally, or mentally to rear children, yet one in five infants was born to a teenager (Hymes, 1987). A second problem was the increased numbers of single mothers due to divorce, death of the spouse, or by preference (did not want to marry or have a partner) also heightened the risk of poverty. Still another problem was that acquired immunodeficiency syndrome (AIDS), first recognized in the early 1980s, frightened the entire society.

In sharp contrast, the 1980s were also characterized by great affluence. High salaries were available for those in business, technology, and communication. In more than half of two-parent families in the United States, both parents worked outside the home (O'Connell & Bloom, 1987). This gave families a higher financial standard of living. However, time became a precious commodity, and some families found it difficult to save time for themselves and their children. Articles on handling stress and programs for stress reduction continued to grow in popularity. Parent education programs such as STEP, PET, and Active Parenting were offered by schools, hospitals, and social agencies.

Parent Education

The country was divided throughout the 1980s, just as it had been during the White House Conference on Families: The far right decried public interference in the rearing of children, but polls showed that most people favored family-life education.

The decade ended with little movement toward achievement of these recommendations. Few companies offered flexible work schedules and job sharing, and Congress defeated the Family and Parental Leave Act in 1988 (this later was approved and became the Family and Medical Leave Act of 1993).

1990s: Emphasis on Family Involvement

From focusing on mothers in the 1950s and both the father and mother in the 1960s and 1970s, a shift occurred toward viewing the entire family environment as the most important factor in a child's education. The Department of Education emphasized the strengthening of families and issued a paper, *Strong Families, Strong Schools: Building Community Partnerships for Learning* (1994). Family partnerships with schools were encouraged, and in 1990, the Center on Children, Schools, Families, and Children's Learning was established.

Federal influence on schools continued with federal programs such as Title I, Even Start, and the Elementary and Secondary School Act. The introduction of *Goals 2000: Educate America* and the development of national standards were criticized by some as taking away the constitutional rights of states to control education, but, at the same time, parents were given more power to influence the education of their children. Many schools began restructuring and turned to site-based management, an educational design in which parents worked with school personnel to establish goals and direction. There was also a movement for choice in school selection. Charter schools became available in many states starting in 1996 and 1997. Parents could elect their own board and choose their own curriculum for their charter schools, funded by the school district in which they were located. The field of early childhood education had great interest in constructivism and Reggio Emilio philosophy, which emphasized the importance of children learning by doing.

Family Resource Centers

During the 1990s, the creation and funding of family resource centers helped strengthen and empower families. The centers designed their programs according to the needs of their populations with offerings that might include parent education, programs for children, and literacy programs. Family literacy programs were established to help those who could not read, including immigrants who did not speak or read English or those who had not learned to read in school. Family literacy programs recognized that parents could help their children more if the parents themselves were able to read.

Homeschooling

Homeschooling became more popular during the 1990s, and support groups helped parents who wanted to teach their children at home. States enacted certain requirements for parents to continue homeschooling. For example, children must take tests every three years and place no lower than the 19th percentile. It was recommended that schools work with homeschooling parents so that children could participate in activities that the home is unable to offer, such as band, chorus, and athletics.

The Family and Medical Leave Act

Congress finally passed the Family and Medical Leave Act in early 1993, providing 12 weeks of unpaid leave for employees with such family concerns as childbirth, adoption, or the serious illness of a child, spouse, or parent. The bill required all companies with 50 or more employees to guarantee jobs and provide health benefits to workers when they returned after the leave.

Temporary Assistance for Needy Families

Welfare was revamped in 1996 with the Personal Responsibility and Work Opportunity Reconciliation Act. AFDC (Aid to Families with Dependent Children) had provided assistance for poor, single-parent families since 1935. It was replaced with Temporary Assistance for Needy Families (TANF), which provides block grants to states who run their own programs within federal guidelines. The law requires mothers to join the workforce if they have received assistance for more than two years. It placed a 5-year lifetime limit on eligibility for assistance. Some concerns have emerged as the law was carried out, including lack of childcare, insufficient health care, the poor job skills of some former AFDC recipients, and childcare workers who earn low wages.

Dean Mitchell/Getty Images

Families that interact in different ways teach their children many skills and concepts.

The 21st Century: Children's Readiness and Family Involvement

The 21st century opened with a continued emphasis on education. Programs that had originated in the 1960s from the War on Poverty, such as the Elementary and Secondary Education Act and Head Start, continued into the new century. The importance of families in the education of children was emphasized, and programs for the very young child were increased. A new law, the No Child Left Behind Act of 2001, was signed into law on January 8, 2002. The new law was "considered to be the most sweeping reform of the Elementary and Secondary Education Act since it was enacted in 1965" (U.S. Department of Education, 2002). President Obama's Health Care Act became a very important (and controversial) act to provide insurance at an affordable cost for all qualified Americans, including families and children.

Partnerships for Family Involvement in Education

The U.S. Department of Education offered information and support through the establishment of Partnerships for Family Involvement in Education. In addition, the Center on Families, Communities, Schools, and Children's Learning, which was established at Johns Hopkins University, continued to provide research, policy, and the National Network of Partnerships. A number of promising practices policies put out during this time resulted in various improvements in the schools, including goals built around school readiness and parental involvement.

The Family and Medical Leave Act Revised

The Family and Medical Leave Act, which offers 12 weeks of unpaid leave from work, was favored by most citizens when it was passed in 1993. It was found, however, that 78% of those who needed leave were unable to take it because one salary was not enough to support their families. Some states looked at options that would supplement the one salary, which allowed the parent staying home with the infant to take out unemployment benefits or temporary disability insurance. In 2000, the U.S. Department of Labor adopted regulations encouraging states to provide unemployment benefits to working parents who take leave to care for newborns or newly adopted children (Asher & Lenhoff, 2001). This act was also amended in 2008 and again in 2010 to include military personnel. The final amendment to this act changed it to cover military families for special leave and also includes a special provision for air flight crew employees (United States Department of Labor, 2013).

Living in a Digital World

We are living in a digital world. Households not only have computers but all kinds of digital devices that open up the world to children and youth. The number of computers in the schools increased from 250,000 in 1983 to 8.6 million in 1997. In 2008, 100% of all U.S. public schools had computers with Internet access (National Center for Education Statistics, 2010). According to the 2010 U.S. Census, 68.7% of U.S. households owned a computer with Internet access in 2009, while in 2011 75.6% of households reported having a computer at home (File, 2013). Today, it is not only important to have a computer at home, but families must also have Internet access. Figure 4.1 shows the increase in number of computers and Internet access in the U.S. from 1984 to 2011.

Access to technology in this digital age is important for academic achievement (see, for example, Shapley, Sheehan, Maloney, & Caranikas-Walker, 2011; Bester & Brand, 2013; Bursal, 2013; Eyyam & Yaratan, 2014). Low-income minority children do not have access to the same types of technologies that middle class children have. Some figures show that the disparities might be changing somewhat, but the gap remains prevalent. African American and Latino households still have less access to computers and the Internet compared to White and Asian households (see Figure 4.2). In addition, the use of smartphones and other digital devices like tablets has increased the amount of information that children are exposed to at an early age. Families have access to such devices because the prices are more affordable. Many families have different views regarding the use of technology, but the fact is that all children need to be exposed in order to conquer the digital divide. The National Association for the Education of Young Children (NAEYC)

Figure 4.1 Household Computer and Internet Use: 1984–2011 (In percent)

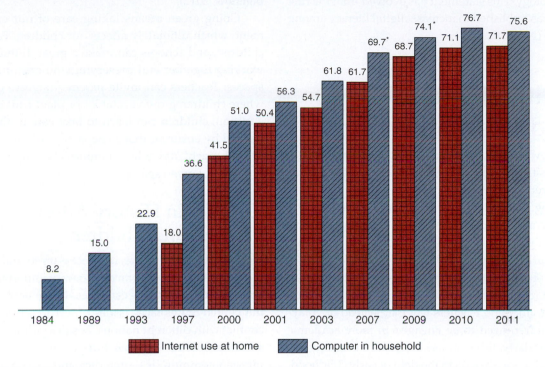

Note: In 2007 and 2009 the Census Bureau did not ask about computer ownership. The estimates presented here for 2007 and 2009 reflect estimates made based on the ratio of computer ownership to Internet use in 2003 and 2010, respectively.

Source: U.S. Census Bureau, Current Population Survey, selected years.

Figure 4.2 Household Internet Use by Race and Ethnicity: 2000–2011 (In percent)

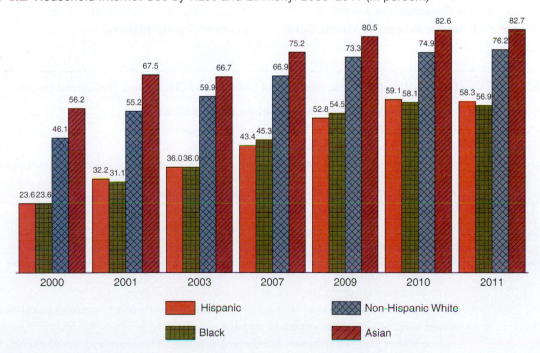

Source: U.S. Census Bureau, Current Population Survey, selected years.

has issued a statement focusing on the appropriate use of technology. This statement has evolved from the first time it was published to increase digital literacy among children (NAEYC, 2014).

Healthy Living, Get Outdoors, and Go Green

In this new century, the threat of diabetes, heart disease, and obesity are very real, and there has been increasing awareness of the importance of healthy living and exercising. It is not unusual to see families out in parks, bicycling and walking. However, not all families and children live in areas where this is possible. In addition, food security and choices also exacerbate health issues such as obesity. Furthermore, recess or outdoor play has been removed from many school schedules. Often, administrators and teachers feel that instead of "playing," children need to be engaged in more academic work. Similarly, teachers use recess as a consequence for misbehavior. Experts in the field of early childhood, such as David Elkind, warn about taking physical play out of a child's life and the negative consequences this may bring to a child's development (Elkind, 2007). Other researchers in the fields of health and medicine also agree that limiting children's outdoor physical play will have serious consequences overall to children's development (Ergler, Kearns, & Witten, 2013;

Söderstörm, Boldemann, Sahiln, Martensson, Raustorp & Blennow, 2012).

Going green means taking care of our environment, which ultimately affects our children. Families, children, and schools can make a great difference by working together and preserving and creating green spaces. Teachers can invite parents to create gardens where children grow vegetables or plant fruit trees. In addition, children can learn to take care of the playground by ensuring that there is no trash and having a "bash trash" day where families clean up the playground and green spaces.

Changes in History Affect Families and Children

To understand the future, it is necessary to understand the past. Table 4.1 offers an overview of important ideas about children over the centuries. In the new century, the United States faces issues of terrorist threats and conflict with different nations. Besides political unrest, social problems such as hunger, genocide, drug-infested communities, prejudice and racism, and the lack of health care and educational opportunities prevail around the world, affecting families abroad and in our own backyard. Many families live in dire conditions that need to be eliminated. As challenges abound, it is important for us all to consider how we, as well as our nation and the world, will respond to create better experiences for all children.

Table 4.1 Events and People Who Influenced Ideas About Children and Childrearing Throughout History

6000–5000 B.C.	Primitive cultures developed. Parents modeled behavior for children to learn.
5510–3787 B.C.	Egyptian children were educated in their homes in the Old Kingdom of Egypt.
3787–1580 B.C.	Schools outside the home developed in Egypt.
427–347 B.C.	Life of Plato, who questioned theories of childrearing, suggesting that a controlled environment would promote good habits. Infanticide was practiced by Greeks, Romans, and others.
384–323 B.C.	Life of Aristotle, father of the scientific method, who promoted childrearing and education by the state.
204–122 B.C.	Life of Polybius, who noted the importance of the family in developing good Roman citizens.
106–43 B.C.	Life of Cicero, who emphasized the family's role in the development of the Roman citizen.
A.D. 318	Emperor Constantine declared infanticide a crime.
A.D. 400–1400	The Roman Empire declined and the feudal system emerged. Wealthy children were apprenticed to nobles; commoners were apprenticed to tradesmen. Peasants worked in the fields.
A.D. 1450	The printing press was invented, but books were available only to the wealthy.
1483–1546	Life of Martin Luther, who introduced the Ninety-Five Theses and began the drive for all to learn to read the Bible.
1500–1671	Etiquette books began to include etiquette for children.
1592–1670	Life of John Amos Comenius, a Moravian educator, who wrote books on progressive educational theories.

1632–1704	Life of John Locke, who believed the newborn's mind was like a blank slate—everything is learned.
1697	Mother Goose tales were published.
17th and 18th centuries	Wealthy European children were cared for by wet nurses. Colonial American children were taught to follow Puritanical religious beliefs and were trained to be obedient and faithful.
1703–1791	Life of John Wesley, founder of Methodism, who was raised by his mother, and who believed in breaking the will.
1712–1778	Life of Jean Jacques Rousseau, author of *Emile*, who wrote that children should grow up untainted by society.
1747–1827	Life of Johann Heinrich Pestalozzi, father of parent education, who developed a curriculum based on concrete objects and group instruction, cooperation among students, and self-activity.
1782–1852	Life of Friedrich Froebel, who developed a curriculum for the young child based on the concept of unity. He is regarded as the father of kindergarten.
19th century	American parents began to rely on American publications in addition to European ideas and the tenets of the church.
1815	Parent group meetings were held in Portland, Maine.
1854	Henry Barnard, U.S. Commissioner of Education, supported Froebelian concepts.
1856	A German-speaking kindergarten was established in Wisconsin by Margaretha Shurz.
1860	Elizabeth Peabody established the first English-speaking kindergarten in the United States.
1861-1865	During the Civil War, women were encouraged to replace men as teachers.
1870	The National Education Association was founded.
1870–1880	A great extension of the kindergarten movement and parent education occurred.
1871	The first public kindergarten in North America was established in Ontario, Canada.
1873	Susan Blow directed the first public kindergarten in the United States, opened by Dr. William Harris in St. Louis.
1882	The American Association of University Women was established.
1884	The Department of Kindergarten Instruction of the National Education Association was formed (later the Department of Elementary-Kindergarten-Nursery Education; dissolved in the mid-1970s).
1888	The Child Study Association of America was founded.
1889	The General Federation of Women's Clubs was founded. G. Stanley Hall began the first child study center.
1890–1900	Settlement houses were established to aid the poor and new immigrants.
1892	The International Kindergarten Union (now the Association for Childhood Education International) was established.
1895	Patty Smith Hill and Anna Bryan studied with G. Stanley Hall.
1896	The Laboratory School at the University of Chicago was started by John Dewey. The National Association of Colored Women was established.
1897	The Parent Teachers Association (PTA) was founded.
1898	*Kindergarten Magazine* was first published.
1905	Maria Montessori established Casa dei Bambini in Rome. Sigmund Freud wrote *Three Essays of the Theory of Sexuality*.
1909	The First White House Conference on Care of Dependent Children was held.
1911	Margaret McMillan designed an open-air nursery for children of the poor in England. Arnold Gesell started the Child Development Clinic at Yale University.
1912	The Children's Bureau was established. It published the first edition of *Infant Care* in 1914.
1916	The first parent cooperative was established in Chicago.
1917	The Smith–Hughes Act was passed. The Iowa Child Welfare Research Station was established.
1920s	Twenty-six parent education programs were established.
1920	The Child Welfare League of America was founded. Watson, a behaviorist, believed that children should be strictly scheduled and not be coddled.
1922	A nursery school was established in Boston by Abigail Elliot. Benjamin Gruenberg wrote the *Child Study Manual*.
1925	The National Council of Parent Education was established. Patty Smith Hill began the National Committee on Nursery Schools (now the National Association for the Education of Young Children).
1927	The first Black nursery school in the United States was founded by Dorothy Howard in Washington, D.C.
1928	The nursery school movement expanded from 3 schools in 1920 to 89 in 1928.
1930	The White House Conference on Child Health and Protection recommended parent education as part of the public school system.
1932	Parent education courses were offered in 25 states.

(continued)

Table 4.1 Events and People Who Influenced Ideas About Children and Childrearing Throughout History (*continued*)

1933	The Federal Emergency Relief Administration authorized work-relief wages for nursery school teachers.
1934–1938	*Parent Education*, the journal of the National Council of Parent Education, was published.
1940s	A new emphasis on mental health for children emerged.
1940	The Lanham Act provided money for childcare so mothers could join the war effort.
1946	Benjamin Spock published *The Common Sense Book of Baby and Child Care*.
1949	*Your Children from 6 to 12* was published by the Children's Bureau.
1950	Erik Erikson wrote *Childhood and Society*, which included the eight stages of personality growth. James Hymes wrote *Effective Home–School Relations*.
1952	Jean Piaget's work *The Origins of Intelligence in Children* was translated into English.
1957	After the launching of *Sputnik*, new emphasis was placed on children's intellectual development. *Parenthood in a Free Nation* was published by the Parent Education Project of the University of Chicago.
1960	The Golden Anniversary White House Conference on Children and Youth was held. The Parent Cooperative Preschools International was founded.
1960	The Day Care and Child Development Council of America was founded.
1962	J. McVicker Hunt wrote *Intelligence and Experience*, which questioned the concept of fixed IQ.
1963	The White House Conference on Mental Retardation was held.
1964	The Economic Opportunity Act of 1964 began the War on Poverty.
1965	The Civil Rights Act was passed. Head Start was established. The Elementary and Secondary School Act was passed; Title I provided money for educationally deprived children.
1967	The Follow Through program was begun to provide continuity for former Head Start students.
1970	The White House Conference on Children and Youth was held.
1972	The National Home Start program, which involved parents in teaching, was initiated.
1975	The Education for All Handicapped Children Act, P.L. 94-192, was passed.
1980	The White House Conference on Families was held.
1987	P.L. 99-457, designed to serve handicapped children with disabilities up to age 2, was passed.
1990	National Education Goals 2000 was established.
1993	The Family and Medical Leave Act of 1993 was passed.
1996	Temporary Assistance for Needy Families (TANF) replaced Aid to Families with Dependent Children (AFDC).
1997	The White House Summit on Early Childhood.
1997	The Individuals with Disabilities Education Act of 1997 was reauthorized.
2001	The No Child Left Behind Act of 2001 was passed.
2010	The Affordable Care Act provided families with affordable insurance coverage.
2011	Natural disasters such as tornadoes and tsunamis affected families in the U.S. and around the world, creating public awareness of the plight of children impacted by such tragedies.
2012	Penn State former coach was indicted in multiple cases of child abuse, raising awareness of such crimes and their cover-ups, and moving an enraged public to insist action be taken.
2012–2014	The number of Americans without health insurance dropped as a result of the Affordable Care Act.

Summary

Historically, the family provided the first informal education for the child through modeling, teaching, and praising or disciplining. From the times of early Egyptian, Sumerian, Hebrew, Greek, and Roman days, parents were actively involved in the selection of teachers and the education of their children.

Family life in the United States was able to flourish from the early days. Childrearing practices varied according to the country of origin, but they were basically tied to the religious background of the family. The parent education groups in the early 1800s were based on the need to rear children according to these religious principles.

The 1920s were the most productive in terms of the establishment of parent education programs. Change had also come in terms of childrearing practices. Although authorities in the 1890s and early 1900s emphasized love and affection in the formation of character, the 1920s focused on strict scheduling and discipline. During the 1940s, parent education programs continued, bolstered by childcare money for mothers working in the war effort. The 1950s showed more concern for the mental health of the child.

In the 1960s and 1970s, Americans were confronted with great social change. The 1980s began with the first White House Conference on Families, attended by men and women representing diverse philosophical beliefs about families. Parent involvement was recognized as an important element in a child's success at school. Monetary support for family support programs, however, decreased in the 1980s. Societal problems included increased drug and alcohol abuse by school-age children and poverty for one in five children.

The 1990s saw the Family Medical Leave Act pass in 1993. Family resource centers, family literacy, and Even Start supported parents in their search for literacy and family strengths. In 1996, welfare was revamped as Temporary Assistance for Needy Families (TANF), which replaced Aid to Families with Dependent Children (AFDC). The 21st century arrived with many challenges.

Suggested Class Activities and Discussions

1. Ask a librarian to help you find books from art museums throughout the world. Examine these for trends in childrearing practices and beliefs.

2. Find a library that has federal publications. Look through books published by the Children's Bureau. Examine the changes in beliefs about child development.

3. Get a copy of the *Twenty-Eighth Year Book, Parts I and II, Preschool and Parent Education* by the National Society for the Study of Education. Compare the programs on parent education in the 1920s with today's programs in 2010.

4. Concern about the poor was strongest during the 1890s, the early 20th century, the 1930s, and the 1960s. What were the differing causes of poverty? Why did the concern seem to lessen in intervening decades?

5. Identify some of the Native Americans' nations. How has their way of life changed over the past 150 years?

6. Examine your community. How many types of programs for children have begun since Head Start was initiated in 1965?

7. Describe immigration. How have various immigrant groups differed in their treatment after arriving in the United States?

Useful Websites

Smithsonian National Museum of American

Smithsonian Kids

Glossary Terms

Engagement: Commitment to do something.

Family Engagement: Commitment of families to do something with their children.

Chapter 5
Creating Effective Partnerships: Families, Schools, and Community

That responsibility begins not in our classrooms, but in our homes and communities. It's family that first instills the love of learning in a child.

President Barack Obama
(*Winning the Future, State of the Union, 2011*)

Learning Outcomes

In this chapter, you will learn how to create positive relationships between the home and school, to enhance the education of young children.

5.1 Define the meaning of school climate and school culture.

5.2 Identify how to create family–school collaborations and the roles of the different stakeholders.

5.3 Describe school activities and resources that help in building collaboration with families in the community.

5.4 Explain how to create pathways for family engagement that build family strengths.

5.5 Discuss ways that families can become volunteers in schools and centers.

A Positive School Climate and Culture for Effective Family–School Collaboration

When you walk into a school, preschool, or childcare center, are you able to sense its spirit? Does it seem to invite you in? Or does it make you feel unwelcome? Can you pinpoint the reasons for your feelings? Each school differs in its character (usually set by the administrators) and reflects the morale and attitudes of the personnel. Some say, "Come—enjoy this exciting business of education with us!" Others say, "You are infringing on my territory. Send us your children. We will return them to you each evening, but in the meantime, let's each keep to our own responsibilities." In the first instance, there is joy in the educational spirit. In the second, fear and avoidance are dominant. Within the context of different social issues, it is the role of teachers and administrators to make every effort to keep a positive school climate that empowers families. We know that in the wake of school violence schools have to increase their security and at times this may be perceived as negative. However, the creation of a positive school climate involves the safety of students and others.

School climate has a positive effect on children's learning (McCoy, Roy, & Sirkman, 2013); therefore, the majority of schools look for ways to promote it. When children first attend school, they may feel apprehension and fear. Administrators and teachers must take those feelings into account and create an environment where safety and trust are the norm. Rather than mocking young children for crying or admonishing older children for taking their time going to class, teachers and administrators must show an attitude of respect and guide children to feel safe and secure in a new environment. For older children, such as those in middle school, climate relates to the way teachers teach the curriculum (hands-on and dynamic), the type of extracurricular activities offered, and the student–teacher relationships (students value teachers who respect them) (Conderman, Walker, Neto, & Kackar-Cam, 2013). It is important for administrators and teachers to understand how children perceive school in order to create a positive school climate that will yield higher academic results because children value school as a place where they belong.

Similarly, when teachers feel valued and respected by administrators, they feel motivated and excited about teaching. I have often heard teachers express disappointment in the way administrators lead the school because they use a top down approach or speak to teachers as if they were inferior. A principal once told me that it's the small things that help her build a positive school climate with her teachers, such as relaxing the dress code and allowing teachers to wear the city's professional basketball team's t-shirt on special occasions, for instance, if the team goes to the finals. This principal felt that she wanted her teachers to know that she was listening to them and thus helped with job satisfaction. A teacher named Miriam also shared this principal's opinion, although they are at different schools:

> School climate is important because you want to feel welcomed. You don't want to go to a school where teachers and staff are frowning/scowling. The principal I had before was always present, rarely in his office. He was at breakfast, lunch, hallways, and dismissal. Parents and students loved him because he knew most by name. We would have meetings and discuss all students, not just the ones that needed help. He would visit classrooms a lot too.

Miriam's opinion regarding school climate begins with the principal. A positive tone from a leader helps others to follow in making sure everyone feels welcome, thus developing positive relations with faculty and staff and in turn helping to increase collaboration with families.

Collie, Shapka, and Perry (2012) found that stress level, job satisfaction, and teaching efficacy have been shown to affect school climate. Therefore, it is important that administrators find ways to support teachers through the creation of a positive school climate to promote academic achievement.

Another important term to remember within school climate is school culture. Although some educators seem to use the terms *climate* and *culture* synonymously, according to author Anthony Muhammad (2017) they are different. Culture deals with behavior within the context of a school, the way things are done. In contrast, the climate of the school is how people feel. Using Miriam as an example, the culture of her school is the presence of the principal in the daily routine of the school and his close interactions with teachers, students, and parents. She believes that the resulting positive school climate makes people feel "welcomed" so that means it makes them feel "good."

A school culture can be positive or toxic. A positive school culture is one where all stakeholders, teachers, students, parents, and staff feel responsibility for what happens in their school. They strive to work collaboratively by being empathetic and respectful. Diversity and culture are valued and included. In a school with positive culture, immigrant families will feel safe and valued. Military families will be provided the support that they need when their loved ones are deployed. LGBTQ families will know that they will not be judged for their lifestyle. In positive culture schools, stakeholders engage in deep reflective thinking to help them keep a positive view (Muhammad, 2017). Unfortunately, there are schools where the culture is toxic. In these schools, gossip and negative behaviors are dominant. Administrators and teachers argue and talk about one another. Principals are hardly seen in the classrooms and are never available for parents. Teachers complain to parents about the negative culture of the school and this infiltrates their teaching, affecting children. Principals shy away from the challenge of restructuring a toxic school culture as they feel this is something that is difficult to accomplish (Gruenert & Whitaker, 2017). According to Gruenert and Whitaker,

"Culture is much bigger than climate. Culture is the personality of the building. It is the professional religion of the group" (p. 4). As culture influences climate, they are connected. None of the activities that are considered part of the climate of the school can be successful when the culture of a school is toxic.

Last year I was able to attend a meeting where positive school culture was evident. The parent meeting was at one of our local elementary schools. Parents had been invited to attend the meeting to learn about possible new changes. School administrators scheduled two meetings and both were very well attended. Each meeting had a brief introduction by the vice principal and then the parents were asked to form 10 focus groups and to join based on the number given at the beginning of the meeting focus groups. Parents in my group mentioned they had attended the meeting because they were worried that the values of the school were going to change (school culture) and they did not want that. Interestingly, the reason the meetings were organized was to hear the parents' voices about how the programs that the school offered could be enhanced. Some parents were worried because they misunderstood the purpose of the meetings. Transparency is part of having a positive school culture. The principal was very transparent at the meeting and this transparency helped ease the parents' feelings and emotions. Some parents mentioned that they really appreciated the meeting and were looking forward to hearing the results from all of the focus groups. The school began implementing some changes that the parents wanted to see to improve the school. This is an example of how school culture and school climate connected with one another.

Family Attitudes Contribute to the School Climate

Other stakeholders that must be considered are the parents or the family in general. School administrators and teachers build a climate where parents feel safe and valued. Parents' perceptions of school climate affect how children view school and will affect their engagement in school (Schueler, Capotosto, Bahena, McIntyre, & Gehlba, 2014). Parents bring different attitudes into the home–school relationship. One parent may feel excitement and anticipation about a forthcoming visit to the school or center, whereas another may be struck with dread over a required conference. If past school experiences were pleasant and successful, parents are likely to enjoy visiting schools again. If the experiences were filled with failures and disappointments, the thought of school is depressing; if they do approach the school, it is with trepidation. To help make the idea of visiting the school exciting for parents, teachers should strive to recognize, understand, and respect parents' cultural and social backgrounds. This will make educators more likely to succeed at bringing those parents into a partnership with the school (Riojas-Cortez & Flores, 2009a).

Coupled with the parents' past experiences are current social pressures. In some districts, the burden of poverty will consume the parents. Parents concerned with mere subsistence may have little energy left for self-fulfillment or for meeting their children's emotional and educational needs; however, in my experience as a public school teacher, the parents who had fewer resources were the most eager to help in any way they could because their children's education was very important to them. Consequently, parents contending with unemployment, limited income, and social change will need special understanding. In particular, immigrant parents face many challenges, and the schools need to provide an environment that respects, values, and welcomes them and their community (Suárez-Orozco, Gaytán, Bang, Pakes, O'Connor, & Rhodes, 2010). Teachers and administrators can change the climate as it relates to immigrant students by creating an environment that integrates children and parents regardless of their social status (Crawford & Witherspoon, 2017).

All parents have had different experiences with schools—some positive, some negative. Figure 5.1 shows how parents may respond to involvement in the schools based on their past experiences and current situations.

The importance of parents' engagement in their children's growth and education has been recognized for many years and is imperative for academic achievement and positive school climate. In a classic reading, Hymes (1974) eloquently described the parent–child–teacher relationship in the following quote:

> Show your interest in a child and parents are on your side. Be casual, be off-handed, be cold toward the child and parents can never work closely with you . . . . To touch the child is to touch the parent. To praise the child is to praise the parent. To criticize the child is to hit at the parent. The two are two, but the two are one. (pp. 8–9)

Figure 5.1 Parent Attitudes

Parents respond to schools based on their past experiences and their current situations.

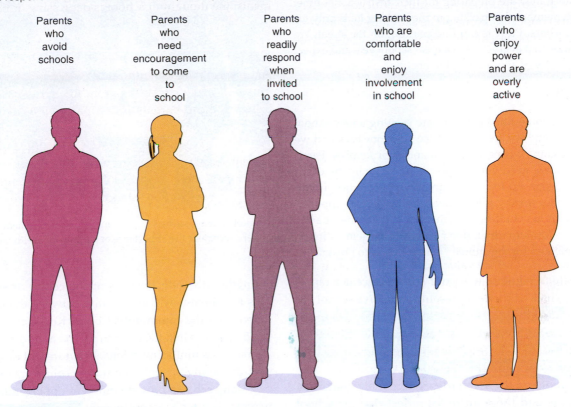

| Parents who avoid schools | Parents who need encouragement to come to school | Parents who readily respond when invited to school | Parents who are comfortable and enjoy involvement in school | Parents who enjoy power and are overly active |

It is important to note that, in a few instances, parents may appear to want to have control over every single aspect of the school or center, but the principal or director can guide that quest for power into more productive causes, such as giving the parents a special project in which they take the lead. It is good to remember that although parents may be eager to help, they need to do so in the context of the needs of the school, since disagreements between administration and parents may create a negative school climate. On the other hand, parents who tend to stay away will need time to overcome negative experiences and learn to appreciate that the school or center will welcome them and their efforts. If the school has an inviting and responsive climate, the three groups of parents in the middle of the figure will feel welcome. These groups, which encompass the largest portion of parents, will soon begin contributing to the school's activities. They can also form a supportive advocacy for school plans.

Offering a variety of tasks and different degrees of involvement assures parents that they may contribute according to their talents and availability and allows all of them to be comfortable about coming to school and enjoying involvement in the educational process. It is up to the teachers and administrators to develop a school or center that welcomes parents by creating a positive school climate. They must be aware of their own feelings and ability to work with and support parents as they develop their plans.

Family–School Collaboration and the Roles of Different Stakeholders

Consider the following letter to parents:

"Welcome to a new school year. We are excited that your child will be coming to our school. We warmly ask you to drop her/him off and quietly leave the building. Teachers do not have time to speak with you since they are preparing for their instructional time. Remember that parking in the parking lot is only for teachers. Parents can find parking on the street. We hope that everyone has a great school year and expect to see you at our first PTA meeting."

OR

"Welcome Mustangs! We are starting a new school year and we are happy to see everyone back and we welcome our new children and their families. Families, we need your help—please come by the office and sign up for our volunteer opportunities. If you cannot stop by, please check our website for opportunities to volunteer and other news. If you are a parent of a kindergartner, don't leave. Please join us in the cafeteria for the annual "Parent Boo-Hoo Breakfast."

Which vignette will your school or center represent? Which vignette represents a positive school climate? The attitude of the personnel is reflected in the way parents are met in the principal's or director's office, the friendly or unfriendly greetings in the hall, and the offerings in the school. If visitors walk into the school and the secretaries ignore them, that body language and those attitudes reflect that the school would prefer that they not visit. If schools want to collaborate with parents, they must make sure the office is staffed by people who support a positive school climate and can make parents feel welcome. This, along with positive school policies and services, indicates whether the school recognizes families as important and will help build collaborations between school and families.

Family–school collaboration brings the strengths of the home and the expertise of the center or school into a working partnership. As we have stated before in the book, a family's funds of knowledge help children perform in life and in school. It is crucial for teachers and administrators to respect and value a child's culture and background because children bring the ideas, feelings, strengths, and weaknesses of the home into their life at school and will help to promote a positive school climate. Because of this, every school issue, concern, and educational goal should involve the child's family. Knowing the life and the family culture also involves knowing their community. If homes and centers are connected through the children, this partnership will

Support systems, such as schools and child development centers, recognize the importance of partnerships with families.

strengthen the effectiveness of the center or school. This is a three-way collaboration between the family, school, and the community. Collier, Keefe, and Hirrel (2015) mention that the teacher, parent, and community interaction is multidimensional in nature and this helps with the family–school–community collaboration.

Many schools provide different opportunities for parents to attend school events. It is important for schools to remember to meet the parents' needs and offer programs that are convenient and easy to participate in. If the school offers a variety of activities, then parents will be able to select what best fits their situation. Parent–school partnerships are highly necessary from birth through high school (Epstein, 1996, 2001, 2005; Epstein & Sheldon, 2002; Loucks, 1992; Meyerhoff & White, 1986; Moles, 1987, 1996a, 1996b; National Association of State Boards of Education, 1988, 1991; Warner, 1991; Wherry, 2009). Truly, home–school partnerships are essential to moving education forward, particularly for minority children (Gillanders, McKinney, & Ritchie, 2012) and children with special needs.

The Leader's Role in Family Engagement

The leader's role in family engagement is crucial as they need the support from district leaders and community organizations to ensure this is a success. Organizations such as the National PTA and the National Network of Schools in Partnership are two organizations that provide needed support. The National Parent Teacher Association (National PTA) recognizes the important role of leaders to create positive partnership and engagement opportunities, and has recently created the Center for Family Engagement. The mission of this center is to use transformative family engagement practices that take into consideration the changing needs of families (National PTA, 2018). This center will provide ideas that educational leaders may want to adopt for their schools. The National Network of Schools in Partnership works with public, private, charter schools through implementation support, leadership, and advocacy (2018). Both organizations work closely with leaders to improve their family–school–community partnerships.

The administrator as a leader needs support in order to create a positive school climate. School climate or ecology—the atmosphere in the school or center—reflects the principal's or director's leadership style. The administrator and leader of a school must take five different roles that will assist with the development of effective school–family interaction and involvement.

1. The spirit of the school or center and the enthusiasm of its staff reflect the administrator's role as *morale builder*. Supportive guidance, with freedom to develop plans based on individual school or center needs, allows the principal or director to function with productive autonomy. The principal or director builds staff morale by enabling staff members to feel positive, enthusiastic, and secure in their work with children and parents. Authoritative leaders seem to be best suited to nurture relationships with teachers and parents (Marsh, Waniganayake, & De Nobile, 2014).

2. As a program designer, the principal or director needs to recognize the importance of family–school–community relationships in the success of the educational program and strive toward implementation of such a working relationship. If the principal or director allows teachers the autonomy to work with parents, using them as volunteers and aides in the development of individualized curricula, the school is on its way to an effective program of parent engagement.

3. The development of an effective principal–parent relationship or director–parent relationship is crucial for positive climate. The principal or director determines whether the school ecology makes parents feel welcome. Besides influencing the general spirit and morale of the school, the principal or director is responsible for maintaining an open-door policy, scheduling open houses, providing and equipping resource areas for parents, arranging parent education meetings, developing parent workshops and in-service meetings, and supporting the PTA, PTO, or family organization (Riojas-Cortez, Flores, & Clark, 2003).

4. The principal serves as a program coordinator. Individual teachers may develop unique programs using the talents of parents, but the achievement of continuity requires the principal's or director's knowledge and coordination of parent-engagement programs.

5. The principal or director has a leadership role in developing site-based management and directing advisory councils and decision-making committees. This new role needs strong leadership ability to encourage and enable teachers, staff, and parents to work together and develop an educational program specific to their community's needs. Childcare center directors can develop a site-based management program that fits the center's individual needs.

An administrator or principal needs to be transformative. She has to acknowledge the type of school climate in her school, as a principal it is critical for effecting change for school reform (Sanders, 2014). An administrator uses collaborative or shared decision making with other members of the staff and with the community, including parents, in order to reach and support important decisions that will ultimately benefit children. Principals become proactive participants in the development of strong school–family partnerships (Flynn & Nolan, 2008) by taking on different roles that will assist them in becoming more effective leaders.

The Teacher's Role in Family Engagement

In order for teachers to engage parents in the education process, they must not only develop sociocultural

Armando Cortez

Knowing children's favorite family activities will help educators strengthen family relations.

consciousness but also empathy and understanding. In other words, they need to understand the inequities in society (Villegas & Lucas, 2007) as well as the hardships associated with other family issues. Teachers need to develop this understanding because they need to learn how to reach parents and how to get rid of negative stereotypes. Before teachers develop this type of understanding, they must know their own identity and biases; then they can understand and even appreciate the children they teach and their families. Family knowledge may include students' family structure, favorite activities, challenges, traditions, strengths, family history, and of course the family's *funds of knowledge*.

Families that have children with academic and behavior issues may have difficulties in engaging with teachers in the schools. As such, teachers must be prepared to work with these families. Unfortunately, many of these children are in classrooms where the teacher needs help changing his perception to engage families more (Herman & Reinke, 2017). Often these teachers need the help of a strong leader who can guide them in providing resources and support. The leaders may be other teachers who act as role models in working with families. Additionally, other families can also be of help

for teachers because they can reach out to the parents to become engaged in different ways.

Teachers have different roles in the lives of children and their families. These roles can include facilitator, counselor, communicator, program director, interpreter, resource developer, and friend, in addition to teacher. Because they touch the children's lives in so many capacities, being conscious of the background of children and their families becomes crucial in order to assist them to have a successful school experience.

Teacher Attitudes and Feelings

The school needs personnel who accept parents and families, but sometimes teachers and administrators are unaware of how they feel toward parents and families. It is known that teachers' attitudes towards a student (and thus his family) are based on the characteristics of the children they teach and the neighborhood where the children live (Miller, Kuykendall, & Thomas, 2013). In a study of Black families who lived in a predominantly White suburban neighborhood, it was found that these families faced microaggressions from school officials and community members (Posey, 2017). These Black families encountered class, gender, and racist microaggressions despite their positive engagement with their children. Many minority families experience these types of microaggressions that may be intentional or unintentional. Very often teachers (and other individuals) are not aware they are being aggressive, but the minority individual, in this case the parent, recognizes those behaviors. It is imperative that others speak up and let teachers and school officials know when they are using microaggressions so that they can learn and change their attitude and provide respect for families and children.

The questions in Figure 5.2 were developed to help teachers assess their attitudes toward parents. As an educator, try to answer these questions truthfully to see if you may have a bias towards parents using "As a teacher I . . ." first and then "As a teacher I should . . ." This will provide the teachers with a way to compare their current practices with what they should be doing. It is also helpful for teachers to discuss their work with another person. I once heard a teacher say, "I can't wait till I retire. I have only two more years and I'm out. I'm tired of parents thinking they are entitled!" I could hear the teacher's frustration, but this attitude could be prevented if principals or directors provide transformative systems to provide assistance for teachers regarding their attitudes and feelings. For instance, teachers can talk to a close colleague about what they value in their work with students and parents. They can then reflect on how their own ideal values compare to the values that they act on in their daily work. They could ask a close colleague to evaluate apparent values and compare their real with their ideal values. This will help teachers focus on their attitudes about working with parents. There are no right or wrong answers; the purpose is to recognize attitudes and perhaps anxiety about engaging with parents or even having parents in the classroom. If a teacher feels anxious about having parents in the classroom, he can organize or structure volunteer activities where the tasks

are clearly delineated. For example, he can provide a list of different tasks for parent volunteers. This will assist him in maintaining predictability and the anxiety factor will decrease. Some of the roles that parents can take include homeroom parent, storyteller, field trip sponsor, learning center volunteer, and outdoor play partner, among others.

The Roles of Parents

Within each school, parents may assume a variety of roles (see Figure 5.3). Most commonly, parents observe what the school does with their children in the educational process. In many schools, you see some parents

---

Figure 5.2 Teacher Self Assessment
Teachers can assess how they feel about collaboration with parents by answering these questions.

As a Teacher I . . .	How You See Yourself		How You Wish You Were	
	Yes	No	Yes	No
1. Feel that parents are more work than help.	❑	❑	❑	❑
2. Feel tense when parents enter my room.	❑	❑	❑	❑
3. Prefer to work alone.	❑	❑	❑	❑
4. Compare brothers and sisters from the same family.	❑	❑	❑	❑
5. Feel threatened by parents.	❑	❑	❑	❑
6. View parents as a great resource.	❑	❑	❑	❑
7. Believe that low-income children have parents who do not care.	❑	❑	❑	❑
8. Enjoy working with several outside persons in the classroom.	❑	❑	❑	❑
9. Have prejudiced feelings about certain groups.	❑	❑	❑	❑
10. Feel that parents let children watch too much television.	❑	❑	❑	❑
11. Feel that parents are not interested in their children.	❑	❑	❑	❑
12. Work better with social distance between the parent and myself.	❑	❑	❑	❑
13. Believe parents who let their children come to school in inappropriate clothing are irresponsible.	❑	❑	❑	❑
14. Feel that a close working relationship with parents is necessary for optimal student growth.	❑	❑	❑	❑
15. Am pleased when all the parents are gone.	❑	❑	❑	❑
16. Anticipate parent conferences with pleasure.	❑	❑	❑	❑
17. Feel that parents have abdicated the parental role.	❑	❑	❑	❑
18. Enjoy working with parents.	❑	❑	❑	❑
19. Value my students' funds of knowledge.	❑	❑	❑	❑
20. Work with parents of inclusion children.	❑	❑	❑	❑

(continued)

Figure 5.2 Teacher Self Assessment (*continued*)

	As a Teacher I . . .			As a Teacher I Believe That I Should . . .	
	Always	Sometimes	Never	Essential	Not Important
1. Listen to what parents are saying.	❏	❏	❏	❏	❏
2. Encourage parents to drop in.	❏	❏	❏	❏	❏
3. Give parents an opportunity to contribute to my class.	❏	❏	❏	❏	❏
4. Have written handouts that enable parents to participate in the classroom.	❏	❏	❏	❏	❏
5. Send newsletters home to parents.	❏	❏	❏	❏	❏
6. Contact parents before school begins in the fall.	❏	❏	❏	❏	❏
7. Listen to parents 50 percent of the time during conferences.	❏	❏	❏	❏	❏
8. Contact parents when a child does well.	❏	❏	❏	❏	❏
9. Allow for differences among parents.	❏	❏	❏	❏	❏
10. Learn what objectives parents have for their children.	❏	❏	❏	❏	❏
11. Learn about interests and special abilities of students.	❏	❏	❏	❏	❏
12. Visit students in their home.	❏	❏	❏	❏	❏
13. Show parents examples of the student's work.	❏	❏	❏	❏	❏
14. Enlist parent volunteers for my classroom.	❏	❏	❏	❏	❏
15. Ensure a caring environment.	❏	❏	❏	❏	❏
16. Encourage both mother and father to attend conferences.	❏	❏	❏	❏	❏
17. Make parents feel comfortable coming to school.	❏	❏	❏	❏	❏
18. Include parents in educational plans for their children.	❏	❏	❏	❏	❏
19. Try to be open and honest with parents.	❏	❏	❏	❏	❏
20. Send notes home with children.	❏	❏	❏	❏	❏
21. Include students along with parents during conferences.	❏	❏	❏	❏	❏
22. Let parents sit at their child's desk during back-to-school night.	❏	❏	❏	❏	❏
23. Keep both parents informed if parents are separated.	❏	❏	❏	❏	❏
24. Consider parents as partners in the educational process.	❏	❏	❏	❏	❏
25. Encourage English language learners to use their first language.	❏	❏	❏	❏	❏

Figure 5.3 Possible Roles for Parents in Schools

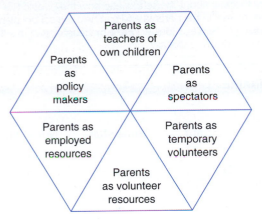

Note: These roles for parents in schools are typical of those that emerge in the interaction of parents and schools. It is important to have parents involved as more than just spectators.

involved in the PTA, while others go to the classroom on a daily basis, attend field trips, help with fundraising, and more. However, it is important to note that the role of parents is to be parents first and foremost. As educators, we must be willing to accept new and transformative engagement of families. When I was a teacher I had parents who were willing to help in different ways. One year, back in the 1980s, I had a parent who worked for Sony and would bring us cases of computer paper for us to use for drawing. Another parent was a baker and would bring us eggshells to paint to use for *cascarones* (confetti eggs) during *FIESTA*[1] time in San Antonio, Texas. I was very fortunate to have families throughout my years of teaching that were engaged with their children, and were very aware of their role as a parent. They met their children's physical needs as well as their emotional needs. The majority of the parents were low-income and many were immigrants (some with documents and others without), and they faced many struggles but their children were always their priority.

It is the teacher's responsibility to provide engagement opportunities. The room parent, for example, may be the parent who organizes parties or field trips, brings snacks, and helps the teacher create decorations for the classroom. Volunteers can provide needed services, but their involvement is geared only to a specific time and task. The parent questionnaire in Figure 5.4 asks the parents what they want to know about the school or center, as well as how they would like to be involved. Each classroom can develop an appropriate

questionnaire that would be based on the plans in the classroom and the opportunities available for parents as they volunteer in the school.

Increasingly, parents are serving as more regularly scheduled resources to the schools. Some parents spend a morning or a full day each week working in the resource center, developing materials, and sharing with other parents. You may find others making books with children's stories or listening to children read and discussing ideas with them. Still others work as unpaid aides in the classroom. Because many employed parents use a childcare center, their contributions will need to be geared to their availability. Some centers have an occasional activity on Saturday with those parents in mind.

Parents may also help make policies. For example, school boards have been composed of community leaders charged with making educational policy for many years. Early control of schools was accomplished by community leaders who were generally the elite of the area. At least 50% of the Parent Advisory Councils in Head Start must be composed of parents served by the program (U.S. Department of Health and Human Services, 2010). Parent engagement, including input into the program, is recommended. With this representative membership, policy control has reached down to the grassroots of the constituency being served, with the decisions of policy-making parents directly affecting the schools their own children attend.

Collaborative decision making brings parents of children in the schools into the decision-making process. Clearly, parents are teachers of their own children. Through funds of knowledge, parents teach children a variety of skills including language, problem solving, socioemotional, and physical skills. For example, setting the table and putting away the dishes involves the classification of objects. Teaching children a traditional song from their culture helps children develop not only language awareness but also cultural pride and awareness. Very often, parents are aware of their role in teaching their children, but they may not be aware of the connection between home and academic learning; therefore, teachers must show parents how the two are connected (Riojas-Cortez & Flores, 2009a). It is important that the teachers practice what is known as cultural humility so that they can learn more about the children's family background (Veseley, Levine Brown, & Mehta, 2017) and that the partnership that develops is strong, based on mutual respect and understanding.

[1]FIESTA is an annual festival in San Antonio that takes place in April.

Figure 5.4 Parent Questionnaire

This questionnaire is a simplified needs assessment of what parents want to know about the school and how they would like to be involved. Asking these questions at the beginning of the year shows interest in the parents and can help the school plan meetings and activities. The questionnaire can also be done using apps such as Survey Monkey where the teacher can use the questions from the parent questionnaire but parents would have a chance to complete digitally.

PARENT QUESTIONNAIRE

1. What I want to know about the school:

	Very important	Somewhat	Not at all
1. What curriculum will my child have?	❑	❑	❑
2. How is the school organized?	❑	❑	❑
3. What is the procedure for seeing school personnel?	❑	❑	❑
4. If I have a problem with the school, not the class, whom do I see?	❑	❑	❑
5. How is reading taught?	❑	❑	❑
6. What books are used in the school?	❑	❑	❑
7. What books should I use with my child?	❑	❑	❑
8. How are subjects taught?	❑	❑	❑
9. How should I help my child with different subjects?	❑	❑	❑
10. Other	❑	❑	❑

2. How I would like to be involved with the school:

	Very interested	Somewhat	Not at all
1. Be a classroom volunteer	❑	❑	❑
2. Serve on policy committees	❑	❑	❑
3. Make games for the classroom	❑	❑	❑
4. Help with money-raising events	❑	❑	❑
5. Collect resources for the classroom	❑	❑	❑
6. Be a room parent	❑	❑	❑
7. Organize a volunteer program	❑	❑	❑
8. Share expertise or experiences	❑	❑	❑
9. Work in family resource room	❑	❑	❑
10. Other	❑	❑	❑

Comments: _____

Ways to Enhance Center–School–Home Relationships

Why does one school or center have superb relationships with parents and a community, whereas one nearby does not? Most often, the leadership of the administration and individual teachers from such schools have made the school responsive to the parents and families, and therefore the parents supportive of the school. The relationship with the community plays a very important role in the development of positive relations with parents.

Schools or centers usually do not change overnight, but gradually the school, home, and community can become united in a joint effort. Many of the techniques geared to improve center–school–home relationships are already in place. Increasing collaboration within schools must focus on five areas: (a) the center–school atmosphere and involvement of parents, (b) activities and resources for parents, (c) contact early in the school year, (d) meeting the needs of the school or center area, and (e) volunteers.

Multiple methods of communications can increase contact between family, center, and school. Communication can range from a simple note sent home to communication through websites, blogs, forums, and workshops (Williamson & Blackburn, 2010). Nowadays most schools use Facebook, Twitter, texting, different apps such as Class Dojo, and other mass social media to communicate with parents, who seem to appreciate readily available information. Some schools have YouTube channels where teachers communicate with parents about updates in their classrooms, and some even do lessons. The use of the strategies mentioned in this chapter along with effective communication can help increase the quality of partnerships with families.

Welcoming is only one aspect of restructuring needs. Elimination of discrimination and inclusion of culturally and linguistically diverse groups, immigrants (documented or undocumented), and other marginalized groups set the stage for all to participate meaningfully in a democratic society. Supporting and recognizing all families and children will be necessary before schools or centers can meet their challenge.

An Open-Door Policy

An open-door welcoming policy is more an attitude of the school than a series of activities, although periodic open houses, forums, coffee hours, and interactive seminars can add to the receptive climate of the school. Parents are welcome at any time in schools with an open-door policy. Schools that have a closed-door policy and are unpleasant or that require appointments to visit the principal, teachers, or classrooms are saying, "Come only by request or when you want to discuss a problem." Schools and parents need to avoid the problem-conference syndrome. Dialogue between parents and schools should occur before a problem develops. This can be done through coffee klatches and seminars. Parents can give suggestions and get answers; school personnel can ask questions and clarify school procedures and curricula long before an issue develops into a problem. By establishing an open-door policy early, the climate is set for parents and schools to work together

on behalf of, rather than to suffer a confrontation over, a child.

Parent Advisory Councils and Site-Based Management

Title I of the Elementary and Secondary Education Act was developed to improve the academic achievement of children of underrepresented groups and to "ensure that all children have a fair, equal, and significant opportunity to achieve a high quality education and reach, at a minimum, proficiency on challenging State academic achievement standards and State academic assessments" (U.S. Department of Education, 2002, p. 1). All schools can establish parent advisory councils. Title I components establish two parent advisory councils: a districtwide council and a local council for each involved school. The councils give input on the planning, implementation, and evaluation of the Title I program. Head Start and Home Start have had participatory advisory councils since the 1960s, but public schools were not required to have such parent participation until 1974. Fifty percent of council members should be selected from among parents of students receiving Title I services (U.S. Department of Education, 2002).

The success of parent advisory councils in Head Start, Home Start, and Title I programs has demonstrated that parents can be involved in policy and decision making in a meaningful and constructive way. Although schools can implement a parent advisory council related to their own situation, they can also learn from the Title I experience, in which schools actively solicit parents' participation and give them the information and training needed to become effective policy and decision makers. Working together with schools and centers through site-based management increases home–school–community relations.

Site-based management has been established in schools across the nation. The site-based management theory lies in the belief that those closest to an issue are the ones who can make decisions and find the most appropriate answer. For instance, teachers must be given the opportunities to emerge as leaders who can affect school policy (Mayer, Donaldson, LeChasseur, Welton, & Cobb, 2013). Site-based management, also known as school-based councils, seems to work best when the principal actively facilitates parental involvement (Shatkin & Gershber, 2007) and provides the opportunity for parents to participate in important school decisions.

Strategies for Supporting and Involving Culturally and Linguistically Diverse Families

A strong home–school connection is crucial for student success. For culturally and linguistically diverse families, "collaborative efforts" as described by Ishimaru (2014) send a strong signal that parents and families are needed to support and improve student learning (p. 1). Nelson and Guerra (2010) developed a plan for three of the most common types of home–school connections including involvement, engagement, and empowerment. Each of these connections varies depending on the backgrounds of the children and their family, but will help teachers and principals or center directors develop cultural awareness in their school or center:

Involvement—Actions at home provide support for children's education.

> *Example:* Encourage parents to use their funds of knowledge to teach children skills (i.e., singing, dancing, gardening, cooking, playing an instrument, or fixing things).

Engagement—Teachers and parents work collaboratively to meet a school's broad goals.

> *Example:* Meet regularly with parents to discuss the children's progress and how they can help their children at home. Use native language for effective communication.

Empowerment—Parents, teachers, and school administrators participate in all aspects of decision making, working as partners.

> *Example:* All parents, particularly of those underrepresented groups, participate in giving input and taking action to create more educational opportunities for children in all aspects of learning. Parents work with one another, empowering themselves. One person should be working with the parents to ensure that the empowerment occurs.

Home–School Continuity

Continuity between home and school is a necessary and important support system for families today. President Obama eloquently explained the importance of continuity in his State of the Union 2011 address: "Our schools share this responsibility. When a child walks into a classroom, it should be a place of high expectations and high performance." Families cannot afford to be caught in an adversarial position with the school. They need cooperation, support, and facilities that make it possible to supply their children with a stable environment. If you do not know their needs, you will not be able to respond to them. For instance, the number of immigrant families has increased dramatically, and in order to better provide continuity for their children, it is important to understand their backgrounds, including traditions, beliefs, and funds of knowledge.

A good way to improve relationships between school and home is to do a needs assessment or survey to determine what the families in the school area desire. The questionnaire shown earlier in Figure 5.4 is just an example. If you know several of the parents or have access to the parents' addresses, asking them what topics they want or need included on the questionnaire would make the assessment more meaningful.

Community outreach that continues to help families even when school is not in session is a positive step toward achieving continuity. Continuity needs to be a cooperative effort. Groups such as recreation program leaders, library services personnel, special after-school teachers, and artists-in-residence should be enlisted to help extend the school day to accommodate parents' schedules. Parents who are not employed outside the home could volunteer or be paid to help with before-and after-school programs. The coordination of school programs with social agencies, recreation departments, and other community resources will greatly enhance the chance of successful continuity.

Home–school activities should be culturally relevant.

Judy Bellah/Alamy Stock Photo

Family Rooms

Families need a place within the school where they can meet, share information, work, and relax. Ideally, families will have a room similar to that traditional haven, the teachers' lounge, as well as a space within each classroom. The family room can be equipped and stocked by the families. Typical items include a sofa, comfortable chairs, table, coffeepot, microwave, computer or digital tablet, bulletin board, storage area, supplies, and reading materials. If a room is not available, a small area shared in a workroom or an area in an unused hall, would give at least minimal space. In each, both storage space and a bulletin board for notices should be available.

Teachers can help families develop a base in each classroom. An extra desk, corner, or bulletin board lets families claim a spot within their child's classroom. If the area contains information on current assignments, new curriculum ideas, activities to be used at home, taped messages from the teacher, or a display of children's work, parents will make a point to stop by. Families of preschool, kindergarten, and elementary children can use the corner to find activities, to talk or work with individual children or small groups, or to find ways to continue the educational experience in the home. Teachers can use the corner for short conferences with families. The *families' room* implies that parents are not only welcome but are part of the school—there is a place for them to stop and a base from which they can reach out in their involvement. Providing a special place for parents and families allows for a positive school climate because it values the presence of families in the school.

School Activities and Resources

Family engagement fosters interest and support of children's education. We encourage teachers and administrators to select those activities that will meet the parents' needs. Very often, schools continue to offer activities that are not of interest to parents or activities that parents cannot attend. Remember the teacher at the beginning of the chapter, Miriam? She shared the following activities regarding how her school tries to keep parents engaged,

"We have many, many school activities after school and in the evening, flight club (airplanes), coding club, Project Acorn (outdoors), robotics, choir, solar cars. We just had a Math Madness night that was very successful and we got lots of positive feedback. This year, teachers have a Twitter account to let parents and community know what is happening at our school and classrooms. We're trying to reach [families] using different platforms since flyers get lost sometimes. We are a Title I school, lots of young parents. We try to communicate through newsletters, flyers, robo calls, etc."

Miriam's school is a good example of a school trying to provide parents different activities that are often considered involvement, and as families and schools increase their trust, collaboration and partnerships evolve and hopefully this would turn into engagement. These activities are important as they tend to improve school climate.

Parents as Resources

Parents should be asked early in the year about their talents or experiences, and which ones they would like to share with classes. Parents might share information about their careers, or they might have a hobby that would spark student interest or supplement learning programs. Storytelling is an art that is often overlooked. Invite some senior citizens to tell about their childhoods. The resources in the community are unlimited.

Back-to-School Nights

A time-tested school event, the back-to-school night, has proved very successful. This type of evening program has improved home–school relationships from preschool through secondary schools. Parents enjoy sitting in the desk normally occupied by their child, viewing the curriculum materials, observing the displays in the room, and listening to the teacher tell them about school programs. Following a presentation of the course objectives, there is usually a period for questions and answers. Back-to-school night is not a time for talking extensively about individual children, although the teacher should identify which parents belong to which students. It is a good time to set up a special conference if you have concerns about the progress of a student.

A variation on the back-to-school night is the Saturday morning session. Some working parents have difficulty attending evening programs, and offering an alternative time can increase parental participation. The Saturday morning activity can be a workshop with parents participating in their children's normal activities, or it can be a presentation and discussion similar to the evening session. Saturday morning programs work well for childcare centers and preschools, as well as schools. The programs can become a meaningful educational experience for both children and families by involving a series of parent–child programs.

Parent Education Groups

Parent education groups can be conducted in different forms. Meetings can range from a one-day workshop to an organized series of workshops throughout the year. Individual teachers use the parent group meetings for in-service training of volunteers in their rooms, dissemination of information to parents, or presentation of programs that answer parents' needs. Parents become real resources for the school through parent education meetings, which teach them to become effective tutors and school volunteers.

Parent education may be offered whenever the need arises. The school can have a list of workshops available or determine the needs of the community. Many districts do a "massive phone call or text" where the principal calls all of the listed numbers and gives them information about upcoming events. The school website is also a good resource for families to find a variety of information.

Parent education meetings offered by schools are viable for those with children at any age level. The parent of a young child may be interested in child development, enrichment activities, and promotion of creativity. Middle and high schools have very few parent education groups, but the parents of these students are vitally concerned about their children's futures. Parents of children of all ages are concerned about drugs and alcohol. Parent education groups are an essential part of the educational program because they allow parents to meet and discuss common concerns.

Schools need to offer parent education. In doing so, they strengthen parent–school–community relationships. An advocacy group for children and parents also can be formed to outline responsibilities and guidelines for students, as determined by parents and students in a specific community, that can support parents in the rearing of their children.

Parent Networks

Parent networks may form naturally out of parent education groups, but many parents with no interest in parent education might want to join a network group of parents. When I was a teacher, there were many parents who were very interested and had the time to help, so the parents organized themselves to provide assistance to all of the teachers. Parents began to work together on bulletin boards, making games, and even going to the classroom to work with the children. In addition, the parents created a network of friends that provided support for one another and they also learned how to share resources with those who needed them most.

Home-School Activity Packets

Parents appreciate knowing activities and enrichment ideas that support the school curricula. Teachers can make calendars that describe what the child will be learning at school. Sending home packets with activities that support the curriculum enhances parents' involvement in their children's education (Riojas-Cortez, Flores, & Clark, 2003; Tobin, 2017). The activities need to be relevant to the curriculum within each class and each school. These packets may be supported by workshops in which parents learn about the activities, or they may be ongoing informational packets related to what the child is learning at school.

One workshop could be developed in which parents make tote bags their children can use to bring ideas and materials for the activities to be done at home. At this workshop, the ideas behind the take-home activity kits could be explained and discussed. Some families have difficulty completing home–school activities. Communicate with them—develop quick activities for parents who do not have a lot of time, and try to encourage interactions between parent and child that are positive and fun. Some early childhood classrooms send home a stuffed teddy bear, asking the family to include the bear in their weekend activities and then write a story about the bear's adventures. Other schools send home fish, gerbils, or other live animals to be cared for during breaks. These activities are similar to those in school–home activity packets, but the kits usually include many educational activities, with some (but not all) related to the family. For example, children might measure their parents' height, design the week's menu, plan a garden, calculate the number of times each person can jump while playing jump rope, or write a story about their family. Think about the children and families with whom you work. Recognize their interests and their needs, and plan how to organize school–home activities that are culturally appropriate for the children such as the ones included in the following list:

1. School–home activity packets should emphasize developmentally appropriate practices for young children and play.

2. Activities should be interesting and enjoyable for the parent and child. Stress that the activities are to be enjoyed. If they cause stress rather than a positive interaction, do not insist they be completed.

3. Make sure the activity is culturally relevant for families (for examples, see Smith & Riojas-Cortez, 2010).

4. Send home clear instructions included in English and the children's native language. Be available to answer questions by telephone or e-mail.

5. The packets should include any special materials needed to complete the activity.

6. Activities that do not require materials are often more fun than those that do because there is no stress related to finding the materials.

7. Ask parents to complete an evaluation form that is included with the instructions that is easy to follow and complete.

8. If the activity kit has permanent equipment, make sure it is returned in a timely manner, such as a week. Remember this activity packet is for families to interact with the child. Materials are always replaceable. If you feel you cannot part with a specific material, don't include it in the activity pack.

School Programs and Workshops

Parents from the community can plan and implement some of the workshops, and speakers can be obtained from outside sources. Local universities may be good places to ask for resources. Often, professors are ready and willing to work on projects of interest to the families (Riojas-Cortez & Flores, 2009a).

A project in which parents make books of their children's work can be a great success and also create memories to be kept for years. Simple construction-paper books, as well as hardback books, can be developed.

Volunteering at school assists with home–school relationships.

Books containing stories and poems composed by parents or children can be placed in the library and classroom for all students to use. Using culturally appropriate activities during workshops ensures that parents continue to participate and attend (for examples, see Riojas-Cortez, Huerta, Flores, Clark, & Perez, 2007; Khailova, 2012).

Try to arrange alternate times to offer workshops. If you offer meetings during the day, in the evening, and on Saturdays, parents will be able to come to the ones that fit their schedules. In addition, encourage parents to bring young children, allowing them to participate without the hassle of needing to find childcare.

District or School Conferences

Professionals go to conferences to gain information and be stimulated to try something new. Why not have the same kind of conference for parents? Instead of a workshop, plan a half-day or full-day conference where teachers and other professionals hold sessions for parents and community personnel to attend. These sessions could include such subjects as play, social development, literacy, math, music and movement, art, language arts, social studies, science, and computers. Other topics of interest for parents of young children include guidance, brain development, nutrition, and infant and toddler development, among others.

If a conference is planned, get resources from the district and the community to ensure that information from different organizations is given to parents. For example, a mini conference on how children learn

Pearson Education

and develop can involve district curriculum specialists, but also pediatricians or nurses, speech and/or occupational therapists, personnel from education service centers, university professors, and even other parents and grandparents. Often, retired teachers and retired administrators are also willing to share their expertise with parents.

An example of a conference that focuses on family learning is the National Center for Families Learning or NCFL. The NCFL mission is to "envision a world in which all families are provided opportunities to improve their lives and become strong contributors to society" (National Center for Families Learning, 2018). This organization focuses on literacy and education.

School Projects

Enlist parent help if you plan to add to the playground or build a reading loft in your classroom. For example, at my daughter's public school, there was a nonprofit organization (Friends of Bonham) created by a group of parents to support the school's mission to provide a dual-language program, emphasize outdoor science, and support the arts. The organization works with the school administration and teachers to ensure that they provide the needed support to enhance children's learning.[2] Fundraising was very important to obtain items that otherwise the school would not be able to get, such as a new playground. With the help of all parents, this organization was able to replace the school's existing playground and donate it to another school. This is an excellent example of how different systems such as schools, with the help of the community, can develop positive relations that enhance children's overall development and at the same time involve parents.

Most parents enjoy contributing their time for something permanent, and children will be proud that their parents helped build the jungle gym or plant the elm tree in the schoolyard. Working on a project can start a relationship that brings them into a partnership with the school, such as when sessions are offered on different schedules to accommodate parents' busy schedules. Welcoming fathers and not creating gender stereotypes will certainly help with the school climate for all parents and families.

PTO or PTA

The tradition of parent–teacher associations (PTAs) extends back to the 1890s, and their influence on parent–school relationships has been demonstrated over the years (National Parent Teacher Association, 2018b). The PTA publishes material for parents and strives for parent–school cooperation. Many parent–teacher groups, generally called parent–teacher organizations (PTOs), do not join the national PTA, but have similar structures and interactions with the schools. Both PTAs and PTOs can serve as avenues toward greater parent–school interaction. Many school PTAs have their own websites where they provide parents with a variety of information. The National PTA's website offers grants, resources in Spanish, and ideas for fundraising (National Parent Teacher Association, 2018a).

FAIRS, CARNIVALS, AND SUPPERS. Traditionally, the PTO or PTA sponsors spaghetti or enchilada suppers, potluck dinners, dinner theaters, or similar activities that promote a community spirit, give families a night of fun together, and usually increase the treasury. Parents and children flock to school to attend a carnival produced by parents and school staff. Money earned is generally spent on materials or equipment for the school program. Sometimes schools have competitions so that the best-decorated booth gets a special prize such as a pizza or ice cream party. Often teachers recruit parents to engage in this activity.

EXCHANGES. As children grow, new clothes are needed, toys get tiresome, and books are read. Why not have an exchange? A popular exchange in some communities is to have children bring boots, heavy jackets, and raincoats to school to be traded or sold. Boots seldom wear out before they're outgrown, so a boot exchange works very well. Toys can also be exchanged. How often have you seen toys sit for months without being used? Some schools have children bring two toys, one for an exchange and one to give to another child. Children swap the toy they brought for a different one. It is very important to remember, however, that very young children may not be able to let go of their toys; therefore, adults need to be sensitive to their feelings. Children also tire of some books and can exchange their old ones for books they have not read. A parent volunteer checks in the books and issues tickets to be used to "buy" another one. Children look through the books until they find a book they want and then use the tickets to buy it.

---

[2]For more information, go to the Friends of Bonham Facebook page.

Note: Teachers should proceed with this activity with caution, particularly if there are children who are homeless or from very low income families and so may not be able to participate.

BOOK AND TOY DONATIONS. Teaching children the value of sharing can be practiced by asking them to bring the toys and/or books they do not use to donate to a children's shelter or donate to those children who may not have any. This can be done at the beginning of the school year and during the holidays. Parents can get involved by making sure the toys and books donated are in good condition and that the children actually get involved in taking the toys and books to children who need them the most.

CARING-CARDS EXCHANGE. Parents can organize a caring-cards exchange and take the cards to the children who are sick in hospitals. Parents can ask teachers to involve their children in a service learning activity in which they become "pals" with a child in a hospital who is ill. They can exchange cards that they each make, and the parents make sure that the cards get mailed out.

Learning Centers

Parents or volunteers from the community can be put in charge of learning centers. Use the resource room to furnish ideas and supplies for parents, or have a workshop to demonstrate how to plan and prepare a learning center. Learning centers can include the following:

- A place for games
- A dramatic play center
- A reading center
- A center for writing and making books
- A puzzle center
- A center for problem-solving activities
- A science area
- A talk-and-listen center
- A place for music and tapes
- A weaving center
- An art project center

Rules and regulations for using the center should be posted. Parents can help create the poster.

Telephone Tutors

The school can set up a tutor aide program through telephone calls in the evening. Volunteers or teachers can answer the telephone in the afternoon at the school. Later calls can be forwarded to the homes of a volunteer or paid aide working with the children that night. In a well-coordinated program, the volunteer could know what curriculum is being covered in the class. If the entire district uses the telephone tutor, special numbers could be assigned for mathematics and language arts. If students have access to the Internet, the school can set up "chat sessions" where the children with their parents "chat" about their homework needs with a volunteer who may be a parent or someone who has passed a thorough criminal background check.

The Internet

Many families have access to the Internet. E-mails may be sent to each child in each classroom or to all the children in the school if their families are willing to share their e-mail addresses. In addition, the school could have its own web page with descriptions of upcoming school events or information about achievements and activities in the school and individual classrooms. They can also create blogs or chat rooms where they discuss their homework. Creating a LISTSERV helps disseminate information pertinent to different classrooms.

Resource Rooms

When parents see they can contribute to a project that has obvious benefits for their children, some will become more actively involved. A resource room can be beneficial to both school and parents. Resource materials located in an empty room, a storage closet, the corner of a room, or a metal cabinet can be a great help to teachers. Involve parents in developing a resource center by holding a workshop to describe and discuss the idea. Brainstorm with parents and other teachers on ideas that might be significant for your school. Parents can take over after the workshop to design, stock, and run the center. Later, as assistants in the classroom, they will use it. They can help supply the center with articles on teaching, ideas and materials for games, and recycled materials to use in activities.

ARTICLES ON TEACHING. Parents and community volunteers check old magazines related to teaching and classify useful articles according to subject and student age level. These are filed for use by teachers and aides. In searching for and classifying the articles, parents learn a great deal about teaching activities for home and school, so the exercise is beneficial for the parent and the school. Internet access to academic journals and educational magazines gives parents opportunities to learn more about school and children's learning.

GAMES.   Parents check books, magazines, and commercial catalogs for ideas for games and adapt them to the school's needs. Volunteers make universal game boards for reading, spelling, and math from poster board or tagboard. Felt markers are used to make lines and note directions. Games are decorated with artwork, magazine cutouts, or stickers. Game materials should be laminated or covered with clear plastic.

RECYCLED MATERIALS.   Volunteers collect, sort, and store materials for classroom teachers. Items such as egg cartons, wood scraps, wallpaper books, cardboard tubes, felt, fabric remnants, and plastic food holders are used for many activities. Egg cartons, for example, can be used to cover a dragon, make a caterpillar, store buttons for classification activities, and hold tempera paint for dry mixing. Milk cartons are used for making various items, from simple computers to building blocks. Science activities are enriched by a collection of machines—for example, motors, radios, computers, clocks, and typewriters. The articles can be used as they are or taken apart and rebuilt. Recycling is limited only by a person's imagination.

Libraries

A collection of magazines and books can be useful to parents or teachers in the development of teaching aids—such as games and learning activities—or for information on how children learn. From ideas therein, a toy lending library, an activity lending library, a book and magazine library, or a video lending library can be developed. Items can be checked out for a week or two. Checkout and return are supervised by parent volunteers.

TOY LENDING LIBRARY.   The toy lending library was developed with educational toys for young children (Nimnicht & Brown, 1972) or with a collection of toys for older children. The toys for young children can be built and collected by parents. Some parent programs like AVANCE have special toy making classes that guide parents to use their creativity for the benefit of their children. Toys for older children can be collected from discarded toys left over after the toy exchange, or they can be built by parents and children.

ACTIVITY LENDING LIBRARY.   Games and activities developed by parents and children can be checked out for a week or two. A parent volunteer can assist in organizing and maintaining the lending library.

BOOK AND MAGAZINE LIBRARY.   Discarded magazines and books can be collected and used to build a comprehensive lending library. Professional magazines have many articles on child development, education, and learning activities. Booklets distributed by numerous organizations can also be lent. Pamphlets and articles cut from magazines can be stapled to file folders and loaned to parents. To keep track of the publications, glue a library card pocket in each book or on each folder. Make a card that states the author and title of the publication, with lines for borrowers to sign their names. As each is taken, have the borrower sign the card and leave it in the card file. When the publication is returned, the name is crossed out, and the card is returned to the pocket.

APP LISTS.   The school may ask parents to create an app list so the children can use their digital tablets that contain apps that are educational and thus enhance what teachers have taught in the classroom. A list of free apps is usually helpful for parents so that they can readily and freely access appropriate educational activities. Some schools allow parents to checkout digital tablets for their children.

VIDEO LENDING LIBRARY DVDS.   DVDs made by teachers to illustrate their lessons on math, social studies, language arts, art, physical education, music, and other subjects or activities can be very helpful to parents. Homework or "homefun" assignments can be explained on the videos. Teachers can also share creative activities that families would enjoy together. This would be especially beneficial during breaks or weekends.

Actual classes can also be the subject of videos so that parents can see their child at work or play during the school hours. This type of video is often used to accompany parent–teacher conferences but could also be available in the family resource room. Selected videos and videos of student activities would offer a look at students at school; homefun or homework assignments; educational movies; videos on educational programs, such as language, writers' workshops, mathematics, geography, or science; and age-appropriate movies for entertainment. YouTube videos about lessons can be safely uploaded where only the intended participants can watch them.

Other educational DVDs can also be provided for parents to check out. These do not have to be commercial DVDs, but they can have educational value such as documentaries or National Geographic programs.

PUBLIC LIBRARY PROGRAMS.   Public libraries are great resources for families as they are free, except for some fees for a library card. Some libraries have programs that help families get their library cards for free. Libraries provide programs, classes, and technology (mostly computers and electronic tablets). The most common programs found in public libraries are reading programs for children. For example, many local public libraries have toddler or preschool reading time. Others have specific programs such as those that work with Latino children. Such programs are important because often families' cultural traditions and life experiences are not reflected in children's books. The Stories to Our Children program sought to bring parents together to create authentic children's literature that reflected Latino/a cultural groups (Rosado, Amaro-Jiménez, & Kieffer, 2015). The books were developed and published by parents and reflected culturally relevant experiences. The library has the book as part of their collection. Another example of a program is one from Australia that focuses on parents of young babies. This is a family literacy program called Better Beginnings. The program is a partnership between public libraries, health professionals, and local governments (Barratt-Pugh, Anderson, & North, 2013). The librarians transformed their thinking about working with families of young children. They understood the importance of collaborating with other professionals such as nurses. The libraries began to offer open spaces for families. Because of the success of the program, the librarians decided to start focusing on engaging families who traditionally would not visit the library (Barratt-Pugh, Anderson, & North, 2013). These two programs are unique in that the library works together with other stakeholders to ensure collaboration that engages parents.

Summer Vacation Activities

Parents can keep students, particularly elementary-age children, from losing academic gains during the summer. Research shows that the parents who are involved by teachers and childcare leaders become more positive about them and rate them higher in interpersonal skills and teaching ability. Some children have opportunities to attend summer programs, while others do not. Families can still ensure a positive summer experience by engaging children in different activities or chores for the summer. Activities differ depending on the age of the child. For very young children a stroll in the park may be a good way to interact with the environment while for older children taking care of plants and picking up trash from the community park will help children interact with the environment and with their family.

Shared Reading

A practice that has had promising results is inviting parents, community celebrities, and school personnel to share a book they enjoy with the children in the class. The book, of course, needs to be one that fits the developmental level of the children and that is short enough to be read in one session. It is also very important to select a book that reflects the children's culture as well as their native language. Parents and grandparents enjoy the opportunity to visit the class to read a story to the children during sharing time. Principals can use this as an opportunity to get to know children better. Afterward, children will be able to relate to the principal as someone who spent time reading with them and who respects them. Children are excited to meet a "celebrity" who comes to share with them. But most importantly, children's self-esteem will be positively affected if they see their parents or grandparents or any family member reading to them and their friends. Following the visits, letters by the children may be written to thank the contributor.

Book Publishing

One of the most beneficial activities that has developed from the emphasis on reading, writing, and writing workshops is the opportunity for parents to be involved in helping children publish their own books. The activity may be done at home or at school. Some schools have the equipment that allows the parent to volunteer to be a book publisher. The child may develop a story during a writing workshop period, a language arts lesson, or traditional reading and writing sessions. After the story is completed, it can be published with or without editing, although editing helps the child learn conventional spelling and grammar in a positive situation. If parents are available, they can help with the process. The following steps are usually taken:

1. The story is written during a writing workshop or (for the younger child) the story is dictated to the parent.
2. The story is edited by the student, by the student and the parent, or by the parent alone. In some

classes, an editing panel is established and students edit together.

3. The story is typed on a computer by the student or parent. If the story is to be published in handwritten form, this step is eliminated. Copies of the stories may be made on a copy machine.

4. If the book is going to be handled and read by many students, the pages should be laminated. A laminating machine or clear contact paper can help make the book permanent.

5. The book is bound. Many schools have spiral binding equipment available for the parent to use. In other schools, binding may be done by simply stapling the pages together and covering the book with heavy paper. Traditional bookbinding can also be accomplished by parents. A bookbinding workshop would show parents how to sew the pages together and make the outside cover. The outside sheet between the cover and the inside pages is a plain sheet of construction paper. The construction paper is glued to the outside cover. Depending on the material used, the outside cover can also be laminated.

6. The completed works should then be recognized and shared. Some schools have complete libraries of children's books displayed in the front halls or rooms. Others have classes that keep their published books in their own rooms. One school has the books circulate from room to room with an insert that allows children to write that they have read the book and to add a compliment so that the young writer receives recognition for the work.

7. An alternative to creating a paper book can be creating a book with an app such as StoryKits.

Career Day

Plan a day or a series of days when parents and community volunteers come in and explain their careers. Rather than have parents talk to the whole class, let them work at a center. Have them explain their careers, the pros and cons, the necessary skills, and the satisfaction obtained from their work. If feasible, the parents can provide some activities the children could do related to the career. For example, a carpenter could bring in tools, demonstrate their use, and let the children make a small project, supervised by the carpenter and an aide or another parent. Another parent who works in retail may choose to bring some items that are necessary to do their job such as an inventory list.

Talent Sharing

Let parents tell stories, sing folk songs, lead a creative theater project, or share another talent. You might persuade some to perform before the class; some may wish to work with a few children at a time and let the children be involved. Some parents may have a collection or a hobby to share. Quilting is popular and could be followed by a lesson in stitchery. Some parents love to do different types of art such as basket making, growing orchids, stamp collecting—all these provide opportunities for enriching the classroom learning experiences. Cooking or baking can also be part of these sessions. Some parents have organized to offer Zumba classes or some other type of exercise such as bike riding. Others may play an instrument or have a special talent that may often go unrecognized. Ask the parents and bring those educational and fun lessons out to enjoy. These activities may also allow for parents to share their funds of knowledge.

Children Learn at Home

Reading at home throughout the year should be encouraged. Figures 5.5 and 5.6 illustrate a way to get parents involved in a home reading program. First, a letter is sent to parents describing the program (Figure 5.5). An explanation could also be given at back-to-school night or during a workshop. A poster can be created by the teacher and/or children and sent home to put up on their refrigerator to remember to read. Each teacher sends home a list of books that are appropriate for the child to read. Bookmarks with the titles of books related to the age of the child are a good idea. In addition, books from the school library can be checked out and taken home. It is important to note that the books should be culturally and linguistically appropriate for children and their families. A certificate of accomplishment can be distributed each week or month to acknowledge readers. Certificates can be created using simple templates that can be downloaded free from the Internet.

Families need to be encouraged to use their first language when reading stories to children. A library with a variety of culturally and linguistically appropriate children's literature needs to be provided. The Barahona Collection is located in the library of the California State University in San Marcos and it houses thousands of books in Spanish for children and teens. The Cooperative Children's Book Center in the School of Education at the University of Wisconsin-Madison provides

Figure 5.5 Parent Sample Letter
Encouraging parents to be involved in their child's reading is a positive way to accomplish good reading habits and communicate with parents.

[School Letterhead]

Dear Parents:

The more your child reads with you the more s/he is going to develop good reading habits. I want to encourage you to read to your child every day. You can read books, you can choose a website that is appropriate for your child to read with you, you can share the book that you are reading, or your favorite magazine or newspaper. Our school and/or local library are good resources to use. I will also be sending literacy backpacks for you to enjoy with your child. We also have a classroom library where you can check out books and magazines. I'll be Tweeting the titles of different books so that all children can know the title of the books. Don't forget to update your Twitter account and share books that you have enjoyed reading to your child.

Please let me know if I can be of any assistance to you by calling the school (xxx) xxx-xxxx or e-mail to janesmith@school.edu. You can always reach me on my cell phone at (xxx) xxx-xxxx.

Let's read together!

Ms. Jane Smith

Estimados padres de familia:

Cuanto más que su hijo lea con usted más que él/ella va a desarrollar buenos hábitos de lectura. Quiero animar a leer a su hijo todos los días. Usted puede leer libros, se puede elegir un sitio web que sea apropiado para su niño a leer con usted, usted puede compartir el libro que está leyendo, o tu revista favorita o de un periódico. Nuestra escuela y/o en la biblioteca local, son un buen recurso a utilizar. Voy a twittear los títutlos de diferentes libros para que todos los niños puedan saber el títulos de los libros. No olvide actualizar su cuenta de Twitter y compartir libros que le hayan gustado leer a su hijo(a). También voy a estar mandando mochilas de alfabetización para que disfruten con su hijo. Contamos con una biblioteca de aula donde se pueden sacar libros y revistas. ¡También puede leer esta carta a su hijo!

Por favor, díganme si puedo ser de alguna ayuda para usted llamando a la escuela (xxx) xxx-xxxx o por correo electrónico a juanita.garcia@school.edu. Usted siempre puede comunicarse conmigo a mi celular al (xxx) xxx-xxxx.

¡Todos a leer!

Maestra Juanita Garcia

variety of lists of children and adolescent literature. Another resource can be found on line at the library of the University of Kansas. This resource is a collection of children's literature in Spanish, which is offered on line and some of the books may be downloaded in pdf format. In addition, the website offers links to other virtual resources in Spanish. The de Grummond Children's Literature Collection at the University of Southern Mississippi focuses on special collections of American and British children's literature with special collections and highlights of international fairy tales and folktales, an African American collection, and fables.

Figure 5.6 Sample Poster
Attractive posters highlight the importance of reading.

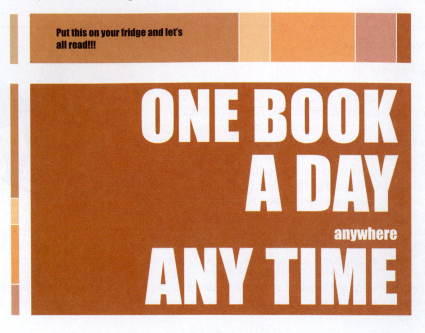

Welcoming Families Before School Starts

Many teachers have found that early communication is well worth the time it takes, even if it is during summer vacation. It is quite common for kindergarten teachers to invite the new kindergarten class and their parents to a spring orientation meeting. Generally, these functions are scheduled in the hope that the strangeness of school will diminish and that, as a result, subsequent entry into kindergarten will be more pleasant. Just as important is the message to the parents that the school cares. This idea can be carried over into other levels of education with results that are just as gratifying.

Letters in August

Some teachers send letters, with pictures of themselves enclosed, to each new student coming to their classes. The student and parents learn the teacher's identity and know that the teacher cares enough to write. A good rapport between teacher and home is established before school begins. E-mails or texts are also beneficial for children and parents to begin to know the teacher and the school.

Neighborhood Visits

Rather than waiting until the regular conference period arrives or a problem arises, teachers should contact each parent early in the year. Visits to the neighborhood are excellent ways to meet parents.

Block Walks

Try a block walk while the weather is warm and sunny. Map the location of all your students' homes (this may be a class project) and divide the area into blocks. Schedule a series of block walks and escort the children living in each block area to their homes on a selected day. Have the students write letters or notes in advance, indicating you will visit a particular block. Choose an alternate day in case of rain. On the appointed day, walk or ride the bus to the chosen block. Meet the parents outside and chat with them about school. You may also accumulate some teaching materials such as leaves, sidewalk rubbings, or bits of neighborhood history to be used later by the children in the classroom. This initial contact with parents will be positive and possibly make a second meeting even more productive. You can reinforce the positive aspect of an early meeting by making an interim telephone call to inform the parents of an activity or an interesting comment made by their child.

Bus Trips

An all-school project, with teachers riding a bus to tour the school's enrollment area, allows parents and teachers to meet before the opening of school. A parent network can be used to approach all parents and create positive connections between them and the school. Parents that know the community are great assets to increase parental involvement.

Picnics

A picnic during the lunch hour or while on a field trip during the early part of the year will afford teachers the opportunity to meet some parents. Plan a field trip to a park or zoo and invite the parents to a bring-your-own-lunch gathering. Have another picnic after school for those who could not come at lunchtime. After the lunch or picnic, call to thank those who came. Because some parents work and will be unable to attend either picnic, you might wish to phone them for a pleasant conversation about their child.

Parent behaviors that support the child's cognitive development include the following:

- Talk with children and listen to their concerns.
- Read to children and listen to them read.
- Establish daily routines that include study time for homework in an area conducive to study (if the child is old enough to have homework).
- Provide opportunities for exploring and play.
- Eat meals together.
- Have appropriate bedtime schedules.
- Guide and monitor out-of-school time.
- Model good values and positive behavior.
- Have high expectations of achievement.
- Gain knowledge of child development and parenting skills.
- Use authoritative rather than authoritarian control.
- Take a strong interest in the schools.
- Communicate with the teacher.
- Children do better in school if their parents help them. The children also behave better and are more diligent than children whose parents do not involve themselves.
- Teachers and principals show greater respect to parents who participate in school activities and

Positive interactions from infancy help build strong relationships.

also have better attitudes toward the children of these parents.

- When teachers involve families, they rate the parents more positively and do not stereotype single parents or those with less education. The teachers recognize that parents are equally willing to help and follow through at home. When they do not work with single parents or parents with less education, they rate these parents as less willing to help and follow through at home.
- Work at home with one subject—for example, reading—result in increased scores in that subject but do not transfer to other subjects—for example, math.
- Parents are able to influence and make a contribution to the education of their children.
- Students, parents, and school personnel all agree that parent involvement is important.
- The way teachers work with parents is more important than the family background, including class, race, marital status, and whether both parents work (Epstein, 1996). Socioeconomic status is not

Exactostock-1557/Superstock

the primary causal factor in school success or lack of success; it is parental interest and support of the child.

Parents can do many things at home to help their children succeed in school. They do this through their daily conversations, household routines, attention to school matters, and affectionate concern for their children's progress. Conversation is important. Children learn to read, reason, and understand things better when their parents use their funds of knowledge as well as:

- Read, talk, and listen to them.
- Tell them stories, play games, and share hobbies.
- Discuss the news, TV programs, and special events.
- Provide books, supplies, and a special place for studying.
- Observe a routine for meals, bedtime, and homework.
- Monitor the amount of time spent watching TV, playing with the computer or digital tablets, and doing after-school jobs.
- Discuss school events.
- Help children meet deadlines.
- Talk with their children about school problems and successes.
- Build positive attachments that create strong relationships.

But above all, children will positively react to love and affection.

Assisting Families with Their Needs

Schools can make a special effort to help families function more effectively. Some parents travel constantly; the stay-at-home partners in those families have many of the same problems that a single parent has. A parent with a disability may need help with transportation or childcare. An early survey of families will disclose what parents need and suggest ways the school can encourage participation.

Worksite Seminars

Meet the needs of parents by offering seminars and parent education at companies and businesses during the lunch hour. Some corporations hire a parent educator to set up a program for their employees. School personnel could coordinate with them and be a resource for the parent educator. Topics for seminars range from school activities and parent–child communication to child development. If the company does not have an employee to set up the program, the school could offer seminars on an ongoing basis.

Telephone Trees, E-mail, Blogs, or Chats

A telephone tree set up by the PTO or PTA can alert parents quickly to needs in the community. One caller begins by calling four or five people, who each call four or five more. Soon the entire community is alerted. Depending on the availability of the Internet, e-mail can be used to send information to parents and children. Chats or blogs can be used to have multiple ways of communicating important information.

Transportation

If a parent group is active, it can offer transportation to those who need help getting to the school or to places like the doctor's office. Those in need might include people with disabilities and families with small children or a child who is ill.

Parent-to-Parent Support

Parents without an extended family living nearby can team up with other parents. The parent organization can set up a file on parents that includes their needs, interests, children's ages, and location, with cross-references for parents to use. Parent education group meetings tend to promote friendships within the group. Isolated parents are often the ones who need the help of another parent the most. One parent may be able to manage the home efficiently, whereas another needs tips and help. Some parents were not exposed to a stable home environment and need a capable parent as a model. Although educators may not want to interfere in the lives of parents, they must remember that they meet and work with all parents and thus have the greatest access to the most parents of any community agency.

Childcare

Childcare can be offered to families with young children during conferences. Older children can participate

Merrill Education

Providing childcare helps families attend school events.

in activities in the gymnasium, while young children can be cared for in a separate room. It is difficult for some parents to arrange for childcare, and a cooperative childcare arrangement with parent volunteers would allow greater participation at conferences. It is particularly important to also offer childcare for parents who have special needs children so that they can feel included in these conferences.

Crisis Nurseries

A worthwhile project for a parent organization is the development of a crisis nursery. Schools would have to meet state regulations for childcare to have a nursery within the school, but it provides a great service and a chance to meet parents and children before school starts. An assessment program, similar to Child Find, might alert parents and schools to developmental problems, such as hearing loss or poor sight and even behavior or emotional concerns.

A neighborhood home can also be used as a crisis base. If a parent with several children must take one child to the doctor, the crisis center can care for the other children during the parent's absence. Abusive parents can use the crisis center as a refuge for their children until they regain control of their emotions.

After-School Activities

Schools can become centers for the community. One step toward greater community involvement is an after-school program. With so many working parents, many children become latchkey kids, going home to an empty house. If schools, perhaps working with other agencies, provide an after-school program for children

of all ages, a great service is accomplished. Teachers should not be expected to be involved in after-school programs. However, recreation workers, trained childcare workers, and volunteers can implement a program that supplements the school program. Children can be taught how to spend leisure time through participation in crafts, sports, and cultural programs.

Although it is generally recognized that young children need supervision, the needs of secondary students are often overlooked. Older students may have three to four unsupervised hours between the time they are out of school and the time their parents arrive home, and that time may be used in ways that will not enrich the child. If you look at community structure, it becomes clear that schools are the major link between the family and the community; therefore, it is important to include all parents, even the ones who may have limited educational experience.

Family Literacy Programs

Families who read with their children instill the love of reading. Once children love to read, then they love to learn. Family literacy programs are needed for all families. It is the school's responsibility to find the best literacy program that fits the needs of the families. For example, family literacy workshops for families who are learning English as a second language provide opportunities for different families to meet one another and learn from each other. It also provides opportunities for families to learn English in order to expand employment opportunities. Different topics for the family literacy workshops include how to select authentic children's literature, how to tell a story, or something as simple as conversing with your child. There are different organizations that have different initiatives and often provide funding opportunities, such as the National Center for Families Learning. Volunteers can help find organizations that would fund the school's family literacy initiative. Solicit volunteers from the community, including retired teachers who might enjoy the challenge.

Skills Training

Offer workshops that provide skills training for the amateur as well as for the person who needs a skill to get a job. Courses in computer training, financial management, organizational skills, and English as a second language would all be appropriate workshops to help the parents in the community. Some underemployed parents may need to develop more skills to become self-sufficient. Offer life-skills training, such as classes on parenting, relationships, anger management, and leadership. Other workshops can include social issues that families from the neighborhood may be experiencing.

Emotional and Educational Support for Families Experiencing Homelessness

Families who experience hardship truly need the support and opportunities that the school provides. Remember that a positive school climate can really help parents learn to be engaged in the school, even those who are experiencing extreme hardship. The following tips provide ideas regarding how to work with families who may be experiencing homelessness.

1. Attitude counts. Be sure the classroom accepts and values all children regardless of living conditions, including homelessness.
2. Make it easy for a family to enroll in the school with friendly, immediate, and trouble-free registration procedures.
3. Provide free or reduced-priced breakfasts, snacks, and lunches.
4. Provide child-development centers for infants and toddlers.
5. Offer early childhood classes for preschoolers.
6. Provide parent education and parent participation programs.
7. Provide English as a Second Language (ESL) courses.
8. Provide family literacy programs in the family's native language.
9. Offer classes or find classes that can help the parent become ready for employment.
10. Provide support meetings that help parents deal with depression and anxiety.

Advocacy

Advocacy is an important aspect of family engagement. Families need to feel they have support from the school for many aspects of their life. The following include tips to advocate effectively for families.

1. Assign a teacher, staff member, or liaison to *help* the child and family during a crisis.

2. Advocate for the family, if necessary, to get needed services.
3. Help with job search and placement.
4. Mentor the family.

The preceding lists were adapted from Eddowes, 1992; Klein et al., 1993; McCormick & Holden, 1992; Nuñez, 1996; Swick et al., 2001; Stronge, 1992.

Building Family Strengths

All families have strengths. These are their funds of knowledge. They are expressed in a variety of ways, but the approach that schools and agencies must take when working with families is to focus on their strengths and, through this focus, eliminate their problems. Research shows that parents respond positively to schools that set out to collaborate with them. During 2001–2008, many families had breadwinners who were out of work or had difficulty finding work that allowed them to provide for their families. Other families have both parents working, so time becomes a scarce commodity. Schools can help make this dual role easier for parents by providing or allowing other agencies to use the school building to provide before- and after-school care.

We tend to look at the half-full glass as half empty. Even if a majority of both parents will be working outside the home, there are still many families who have one parent as caregiver at home with the children. Others can provide the needed security and support their children need to make the school's responsibility of educating easier. Programs such as the Building Family Strengths program, designed at the University of Nebraska, focus on areas that parents need to address to keep their families strong. These include the following:

- *Communication*. Effective communication in strong families involves clear, direct channels between the speaker and listener. Families develop complicated ways of communicating. Strong families have learned to communicate directly and use consistent verbal and nonverbal behaviors.

- *Appreciation*. Appreciation involves being able to recognize the beautiful, positive aspects of others and letting them know you value these qualities. It also means being able to receive compliments yourself.

- *Commitment.* Commitment in strong families means that the family as a whole is committed to seeing that all members reach their potential.

- *Wellness.* Family wellness is the belief in positive human interaction. This belief helps family members trust others and learn to give and receive love. Family wellness is not the absence of problems. Strong families have their share of troubles, but their trust and love enable them to deal with their problems effectively.

- *Time together.* Spending time together as a family can be the most rewarding experience for humans. Two important aspects of time together are quality and quantity. Members of a strong family spend a lot of meaningful time with each other. This gives a family an identity that can be had in no other way.

- *The ability to deal with stress, conflict, and crisis.* All the previous strengths combine to make an inner core of power for families. This core serves as a resource for those times when conflict and crisis come.

Developing these strengths takes time and energy, but realizing their significance can help a family focus on the important interactions within the family. Many families do realize the importance of spending time together, communicating clearly with one another, and showing appreciation. However, these last two strengths take no extra time; they may take practice, but clear communication and showing appreciation can become a natural part of family life.

Families benefit from programs offered at the school or from home visits by school personnel who are able to share ideas about developing family strengths, discipline, school activities, and "homefun."

Parents as Volunteers

Parents want the best for their children. Most will respond to an opportunity to volunteer if the options for working are varied and their contributions are meaningful. When both parents work, short-term commitments geared to their working hours will allow and encourage participation from this group. Although the world is a busy place, time spent at school can bring satisfaction and variety to a parent's life. Volunteerism has been criticized by some as inequitable and an exploitation of "woman power." To avoid such accusations, try to choose volunteers who can afford the time, or allow busy parents to contribute in such a way that they enjoy the time away from their other obligations. If education and training are included in your volunteer program, the participants can gain personally from the experience. For many, volunteering in school may be the first step toward a career.

If you are alert to the needs of parents, using them as volunteers can become a means of helping their families. If you work with them over a period of time, listen and use your knowledge of community resources to support the families in solving their problems. Volunteerism should serve the volunteer as well as contribute to the school.

Who Should Ask for Volunteers?

Volunteer programs vary in their scope and design. Individual teachers may solicit volunteers from parents, individual schools can support a volunteer program, or school districts can implement a volunteer program. A volunteer program can help parents create systems that will support children in families. For example, the school where I taught began developing their parent program because there were parents who would come to the school because they wanted to help but did not know how. It only took the tenacity of one parent to get everyone organized and assist the teachers to create more developmentally appropriate environments for the children.

All teachers can benefit from the services of volunteers, but they should first determine the extent to which they are ready to use the assistance. A teacher who has not used aides, assistants, or volunteers should probably start with help in one area before expanding and recruiting volunteers for each hour in the week. In preschools, the free-choice period is a natural time to have added assistance. In elementary schools, assistance during art projects is often a necessity. Add to this initial use of volunteer help by securing extra tutors for reading class. In secondary schools, recruitment for a special project provides an excellent initial contact.

Easing into use of volunteers may not be necessary in your school. Because most preschools and primary grades have used assistance for many years, their teachers are ready for more continuous support from volunteers. Yet, involving other people in the classroom program is an art, based on good planning and the ability to work with and supervise others. Successful involvement of a few may lay the groundwork for greater involvement of others at a later time.

Recruitment of Volunteers by Individual Teachers

Many teachers have been successful in implementing their own volunteer programs from among the parents of their students. If you have used volunteers previously and parents in the community have heard about your program from other parents, recruitment may be easy. Early in the year, an evening program, during which the curriculum is explained and parents get acquainted, is an effective time to recruit parents into the program. If parents have not been exposed to volunteerism, encourage them to visit the room and give them opportunities to participate in an easy activity, such as reading a story to a child or playing a game with a group. Ask them back for an enjoyable program so they begin to feel comfortable in the room. Sharing their hobbies with the children introduces many parents to the joys of teaching. Gradually, the fear of classroom involvement will disappear, and parents may be willing to spend several hours each week in the classroom.

Invitations that Work

Suppose you write notes or publish an invitation in the newsletter inviting parents to visit the school or childcare center, but nobody comes. If you have had this experience, you need a "parent-getter." Judge your activity and invitation by the following questions:

- Does the event sound enjoyable?
- Is there something in it for the parents?
- Are the parents' children involved in the program?
- Does the program have alternate times for attendance?

The first criterion, making the event sound enjoyable, can be met by the wording of the invitation. The second and third vary in importance; one or the other should be addressed in each bid for parent attendance. Scheduling alternate times depends on your parents' needs.

One teacher complained that the parents at her school were just not interested in helping. Only three had volunteered when they were asked to clean up the playground. When asked if there were any other enticements for the parents to volunteer to help, the teacher said no. "Would you have wanted to spend your Saturday morning cleaning up the playground?" she was asked. The teacher realized she would not have participated either if she had been one of the parents. An excellent means of determining the drawing power of a program or activity is your own reaction to the project. Would you want to come? Had the Saturday cleanup project included the children, furnished refreshments, and allowed time for a get-together after the work was completed, the turnout would have been much better. Make it worth the parents' time to volunteer.

Performances

Many schools have children perform to get parents to turn out. The ploy works—parents attend! Some professionals discourage this method because they believe that children are being exploited to attract parents. However, it is probably the manner in which the production is conceived and readied rather than the child's involvement that is unworthy. What are your memories of your childhood performances? If the experiences were devastating, was it the programs themselves or the way they were handled that led to disappointment? If the performance is a creative, worthwhile experience for the child and does not cause embarrassment, heartache, or a sense of rejection for the child who does not perform well and if all children are included, this method of enticing parents can be valuable for both children and parents. Experience in front of an audience can develop poise and heightened self-concept—and be fun for the child. Parents invited to unpolished programs enjoy the visit just as much as if they had attended refined productions. Small, simple classroom functions, scheduled often enough that every child has a moment in the limelight, are sure to have high parent turnout. The more parents come to school and get involved with the activities, the better chance you have of recruiting assistance.

Field Trips

Use a field trip to talk with parents about volunteering in the classroom. Parents will often volunteer for field trips, during which teacher and parent can find time to chat. See if the parents' interests include hobbies that can be shared with the class. Be receptive to any ideas or needs that parents reveal. The informal atmosphere of a field trip encourages parents to volunteer.

Want Ads to Encourage Sharing Experiences and Expertise

Parents have many experiences and talents that they can share. Who lived on a farm? Who just traveled to Japan? Who knows how to cook spaghetti? Who can knit? Who has a collection of baseball cards? Who can speak a different language? Who has some stories to tell? Who is a geologist? Who is a food server? Ask parents to share their talents, hobbies, and experiences with your class. Send home a want ad to parents (see Figure 5.7) and ask them to return a tear-off portion, or call them and ask them personally to come to the school. Schedule each parent at a time that is convenient for parent and teacher. If possible, a follow-up in class of the ideas presented will make the visit even

Figure 5.7 Volunteer Positions
One way to solicit school volunteers is through a want ad.

Help Wanted
Positions Available

Tutor for Reading
Do you have an interest in children learning to read? Come tutor! We will train you in techniques to use.

Good Listener
Are you willing to listen to children share their experiences and stories? Come to the listening area and let a child share with you.

Costume Designer
There will be a class presentation next month. Is anyone willing to help with simple costumes?

Tour Guide
Do you have memories, slides, or tales about other states or countries? Come share.

Talent Scout
Some talented people never volunteer. We need a talent scout to help us find these people in our community.

Good-will Ambassador
Help us make everyone feel an important part of this school or center. Be in charge of sending get-well cards or congratulatory messages.

Reader of Books
Read to the children. Choose a favorite book or read one chosen by the teacher.

Photographer
Anyone want to help chronicle our year? Photographer needed.

Collector
Do you hate to throw good things away? Help us in our scrounge department. Collect and organize.

Game Player
We need someone who enjoys games tospendseveral hours a week at the game table.

News Editor
Be a news hound. Help us develop and publish a newsletter. The children will help furnish news.

Book Designer
The class needs books written by children for our reading center. Turn children's work into books.

Volunteer Coordinator
The class needs volunteers, but we also need to know who, when, and how. Coordinate the volunteer time sheet.

Construction Worker
Are you good at building and putting things together? Volunteer!

Computer Programmer
Share your expertise with the class.

SIGN UP IN YOUR CHILD'S CLASSROOM OR RETURN THIS FORM WITH YOUR INTERESTS CHECKED.

Tutor_____ Listener_____ Costume Designer_____ Tour Guide_____ Talent Scout_____ Ambassador_____
Reader_____ Photographer_____ Collector_____ Game Player_____ News Editor_____ Book Designer_____
Volunteer Coordinator_____ Construction Worker_____ Computer Programmer_____ Other_____

_____ _____ _____ _____
Name   Address   Telephone   E-mail

more meaningful. After the presentations, write thank-you notes with suggestions that parents might come to class again, providing another means of recruiting potential volunteers.

Invitations to Share

Sending home invitations with the children asking parents if they are interested in volunteering is a direct way to recruit. Each teacher should design the invitation to fit the needs of the class. A letter that accompanies the form should stress to parents how important they are to the program. Let them know the following.

- Teachers and children need their help.
- Each parent is already experienced in working with children.
- Their child will be proud of the parents' involvement and will gain through their contributions.

Friendly requests along with suggestions enable parents to respond easily. Be sure to ask parents for their ideas and contributions. You have no way of knowing what useful treasures you may find! Let parents complete a questionnaire, such as the one in Figure 5.8, to indicate their interests and schedules. Perhaps a parent cannot visit school but is willing to make calls and coordinate the volunteer program. This parent can find substitutes when regular parent volunteers call in to say they must be absent. Others who are homebound can aid the class by sharing childcare, making games and activities at home, designing and making costumes, writing newsletters, and making phone calls.

Parents who are able to work at school can perform both teaching and nonteaching tasks. Relate the task to the parents' interests. Nothing discourages some volunteers as much as being forced to do housekeeping tasks continually, with no opportunity for interaction with the children. The choice of tasks should not be difficult, however, because the opportunities are numerous and diversified, as the following lists indicate.

TEACHING TASKS.

School, Preschool, or Childcare Center
   Supervise learning centers.
   Listen to children.
   Play games with students.
   Tell stories.
   Play instructional games.
   Work with children with learning disabilities.
   Help select library books for children.
   Read to children.
   Take children to the resource center.
   Assist in learning centers.
   Share a hobby.
   Speak on travel and customs around the world.
   Demonstrate sewing or weaving.
   Provide computer training.
   Demonstrate food preparation.
   Show DVDs about subjects of interest.

School
   Help children prepare and practice speeches.
   Supervise the making of books.
   Show children how to use different software.
   Supervise the production of a newsletter or newspaper.

NONTEACHING TASKS.

   Make games.
   Prepare a parent bulletin board.
   Repair equipment.
   Select and reproduce articles for the resource room.
   Record grades.
   Take attendance.
   Collect lunch money.
   Plan a workshop for parents.
   Grade and correct papers or write comments.
   Organize cupboards.
   Help with book publishing.

CONTRIBUTIONS FROM HOME.

   Serve as telephone chairperson.
   Develop a classroom or school website.
   Collect recycling materials.
   Furnish refreshments.
   Furnish dress-up clothes and costumes.
   Wash aprons.
   Make art aprons.
   Design and/or make costumes.
   Repair equipment.

Figure 5.8 Parent Interest Questionnaire
Questionnaires are another way to obtain parents' interests and schedules.

Please Share with the School or Center

Dear Parents:

We need volunteers to help us with our school. You can share your time by helping while you are at home or at school. If you want to share in any way, please let us know.

Are you interested in volunteering this year? _____ Yes _____ No

Check the ways you want to help.
_____ In the classroom
_____ In the resource center
_____ At home

WHAT WOULD YOU LIKE TO DO?

_____ Share your hobby or travel experience	_____ Tell stories
_____ Help children in learning centers	_____ Check papers
_____ Be a room parent	_____ Check spelling
_____ Work in a resource room	_____ Help with math
_____ Supervise a puppet show	_____ Read to children
_____ Go on field trips	_____ Make games
_____ Care for another volunteer's children	_____ Listen to children read
_____ Substitute for others	_____ Play games with children
_____ Develop a learning center	_____ Make books
_____ Tutor reading	_____ Share your recipes

Any other suggestions? _____

_____

Comments _____

When can you come?

Monday	Tuesday	Wednesday	Thursday	Friday
AM | PM	AM | PM	AM | PM	AM | PM	AM | PM

Can you come each week? _____ Other _____

What time can you come? _____

How long can you stay? _____

_____   _____   _____
Name   E-mail   Telephone

Make games.

Care for another volunteer's child.

Write newsletters.

Coordinate volunteers.

Teaching embraces creative ideas and methods. Volunteers, responding to the challenge, can provide a vast reservoir of talent and support. Book publishing is an excellent example of an effective volunteer activity that is both a teaching and a nonteaching role.

Management Techniques

Use management skills in organizing and implementing your volunteer program. A parent coordinator can be very helpful in developing effective communication between teacher and parent. Two types of charts—schedules and volunteer action sheets—can clarify the program and help it run more smoothly.

SCHEDULES. Schedules can be adjusted if weekly charts are posted at school and sent home to parents. When parents can visualize the coverage, the class will not be inundated by help in one session and suffer from lack of help in another.

VOLUNTEER SHEET. Because volunteers are used in many ways, developing an action sheet that describes each person's contribution is helpful. Figure 5.9 illustrates the scope of involvement within one classroom. With this list, the parent coordinator can secure an effective substitute for someone who must be absent. If the teacher needs games constructed, the parent coordinator can call on parents who have volunteered for that activity. Special help in the resource center or with a student project may be found quickly by calling a parent who has already indicated an interest in helping this way. The responsibility for the volunteer program does not need to rest solely on the teacher's shoulders. Parents and teachers become partners in developing a smoothly working system.

Increasing Volunteer Usage

Although permanent volunteers are more effective in establishing continuity in a program than periodic contributions by occasional volunteers, both are needed. As the year progresses, some parents may find they enjoy teaching immensely. These parents may extend their time obligation and, in doing so, bring more continuity to the program. Ideally, an assistant should tutor a reading group or a child for several sessions each week rather than just one. When initiating a program, it is best to start out with easily handled time slots and then expand the responsibilities of parents after they become secure and familiar with the class, the objectives, and the material.

Volunteer Training

Suppose that several parents have indicated interest in being permanent volunteers in your classroom. What is your next step? The time spent explaining your routine, expectations, and preferences for teaching will be well worth the effort in the parents' abilities to coordinate with you in your classroom. Most teachers have specific preferences for teaching that they will want to share with the volunteers helping them. These, in addition to some general guidelines, will help prepare the volunteer. The following humanistic guidelines for working with children are appropriate for all volunteers:

- A healthy, positive self-concept is a prerequisite to learning.
- The act of listening to a child implies that you accept the child as a worthwhile person.
- The child will develop a better sense of self-worth if you praise specific efforts rather than deride failures.
- Provide tasks at which the children can succeed. As they master these, move on to the next level.

Many children who need extra help with their work also need their self-concepts strengthened. Volunteers can provide an extra touch through kindness, interest, and support.

The Teacher's Responsibilities to the Volunteer

As teachers enlist the help of volunteers, certain responsibilities emerge. The teacher's responsibilities are as follows:

- Make volunteers feel welcome. Smile and reassure them.
- Explain class rules and regulations.
- Introduce volunteers to the resources within the school.
- Explain the routine of the class.
- Describe your expectations for their participation.
- Remember that volunteers are contributing and sharing time because of satisfaction they receive and to help their child.
- Give volunteers reinforcement and recognition.
- Meet with volunteers when class is not in session to clarify, answer questions, and, if needed, give instruction and training.
- Appreciate, respect, and encourage volunteers.

Awareness of these points will make the cooperative effort of teacher and volunteer more fulfilling for both.

Figure 5.9 Volunteer Action Sheet

Volunteer action sheets help organize an orderly volunteer program.

Name	Telephone or e-mail	Classroom Regularly	Classroom Substitute	Special Presentation	ChildCare	Make Games at Home	Work in Resource Center: Help Students	Work in Resource Center: Develop Resources: Type	Work in Resource Center: Develop Resources: Make games
Names of volunteers	555-5555								
" "	x							x	
" "		x	x						
" "		x	x						
" "	x		x						
" "		x	x		x				
" "	x				x				
" "				x	x				
" "						x	x		
" "	x								
" "	x								
" "	x		x						
" "						x	x	x	
" "	x								
" "	x		x		x	x			
" "				x					
" "		x							
" "		x							
" "		x			x				
" "		x							
" "		x			x				
" "				x					
" "				x					
" "			x	x					
" "					x				
" "		x				x	x	x	
" "		x							
" "		x		x					
" "			x	x					

The Volunteer's Responsibilities to the Teacher

If parents or others in the community volunteer to help in the school, they accept certain responsibilities, which include the following:

- Be dependable and punctual. If an emergency requires that you miss a session, obtain a substitute or contact the volunteer coordinator.

- Keep privileged information concerning children or events confidential. Do not discuss children.

- Plan responsibilities in the classroom with the teacher.

- Cooperate with the staff. Welcome supervision.

- Be ready to learn and grow in your work.

- Enjoy yourself, but do not let your charges get out of control.

- Be fair, consistent, and organized.

Volunteer aides are not helpful if they continually cancel at the last moment, disrupt the room rather than help it run smoothly, or upset the students. They are immensely helpful if they work with the teacher to strengthen and individualize the school program.

Recruitment by Schools and School Systems

Many schools and school districts assist teachers by recruiting volunteers for their classes. The first step in initiating a volunteer program for a school or school system is the development of a questionnaire to ascertain the teachers' needs. The teachers complete a form based on the curriculum for each age level of students. After the forms are completed, the coordinators can determine the requirements of each room.

After teachers have indicated their needs, the coordinator begins recruitment. Many avenues are open for the recruiter. A flyer geared to the appropriate age or level of children, asking people to share their time with the schools, can bring about the desired results.

Organizations can also be contacted. The PTA or PTO, senior citizen groups, and other clubs have members who may want to get involved as volunteers in the school.

The points discussed earlier for obtaining volunteers for the individual classroom are also appropriate for volunteers who are solicited on a larger scale. The major differences are organizational and include the following:

- Teachers should contact the volunteer coordinator or reply to the coordinator's questionnaire if they want a volunteer.

- Districts usually require volunteers to fill out an application stating their background, giving references, and listing the hours they are available.

- Many school districts have an extensive compilation of resource people who have agreed to volunteer in the schools. An alliance with businesses encourages companies to allow their employees to visit schools and tell students about their careers. These resource people and experts can share their knowledge with classes throughout the school district. Lists of topics with resource people available to share expertise can be distributed throughout the district. Teachers can request the subject and time they want a presentation.

- Outreach, such as a community study hall, can be initiated and staffed by the volunteer program. Volunteers can tutor and work with children after school hours in libraries, schools, or other public facilities (Denver Public Schools, n.d.).

- Certificates or awards distributed by the district offer a way to thank the volunteers for effort and time shared with the schools.

Individual teachers tend to use parents as aides and resource people in the room. The district most often furnishes resource people, drawn from the total population, in schools throughout the district. The school's volunteer coordinator uses both approaches, enlisting volunteers to tutor and aid in the classroom and recruiting resource people from residents of the school's population area to enrich the curriculum.

Summary

Understanding parents' feelings and concerns provides the basis for creating effective home–school relationships. Schools have character—some invite parents to participate while others suggest they stay away and it all depends on the school culture and climate. Parents have feelings about schools that range from a desire to avoid the school to such a high interest that they are overly active. Parents participate in schools as spectators, accessory volunteers, volunteer resources, paid resources, policy makers, and teachers of their children.

Schools can develop attitudes that welcome parents and conduct activities that invite them into the school. Personnel in the school need to understand and examine their own attitudes toward parents. The use of questionnaires helps in the recognition of these attitudes.

An open-door policy with open forums, coffee chats, and seminars invites comments from parents. Initial contact should be made early in the year or even during the summer before the school year begins. Suggestions for early contact include neighborhood visits, telephone calls, texting, school and/or classroom websites, home visits, and breakfasts.

A resource room, established and staffed by parent volunteers, makes parents significant educational resources. The resource room includes articles on teaching, games, recycled materials, and a lending library for toys, books, and games. A family center gives parents a place to stop and a base from which they can reach out to help children.

Parents today are more involved as policy makers than in the past. Parent advisory councils are part of Title I, and parents confer with school administrators on program planning, implementation, and evaluation.

Schools can become community centers and meet the needs of families in the area by organizing parent volunteers for parent-to-parent groups, childcare centers, crisis centers, and after-school programs. If schools focus on family strengths, they will help families develop and keep effective communication, commitment, wellness, time together, and the ability to deal with stress, conflict, and crises. Parents and others from the community can also be included in the schools as volunteers. Teachers need to develop skills to recruit, train, and work with volunteers as part of an educational team.

Suggested Class Activities and Discussions

1. Interview a school principal and ask him or her about ideas regarding school–community relations.

2. Contact the president of the PTA or PTO in a neighborhood school. What are his or her goals for parent involvement in the school? Which programs have been planned for the year? Which direction would he or she like the PTO or PTA to take?

3. Discuss why some parents may feel intimidated by schools and why some teachers may be reluctant to have parents involved. Role-play the teacher and parent roles and share your feelings.

4. Describe an ideal parent–teacher relationship. List five things a teacher can do to encourage such a relationship. List five ways a parent can work with the school.

5. List what makes you feel comfortable or uncomfortable when you visit a center or school.

6. Visit a school and look at bulletin boards, notices, and family centers that might welcome parents. Make a list of things that might invite parents, as well as things that might intimidate parents.

7. Examine the offerings of a school system or an individual school. What programs or activities does the school offer? List and describe the offerings, including programs such as Head Start, family literacy, telephone tutoring, resource rooms, exchanges, prekindergarten programs, and parent advisory council.

8. Do a community study in which you analyze the different families you might find in the school in your neighborhood and in a different neighborhood. What are their living arrangements, their values, their ambitions, their hopes for the future? What businesses are around the school/center that

provide services to families? Are there other community resources that families from the neighborhood use?

9. Design a want ad or letter that invites parents to become volunteers in the classroom.

10. Search the community for resources that can be used in the school. Include specialists, materials, and places to visit.

11. List the strengths that help families. What other strengths might you add? How would you help families build their strengths?

Useful Websites

National School Climate Center
Parents as Teachers National Center (PATNC)

National Center for Families Learning
National Network of Schools in Partnership

Glossary Terms

Family–School Collaboration: the way families and schools work together for a cause.
Parents as Volunteers: parents that agree to participate in different school-related activities.

School Climate: the environment or ecology of a school.
School Culture: within the context of a school, behavior; the way things are done.

Chapter 6
Effective Teacher–Family Communication: Types, Barriers, Conferences, and Programs

Communication allows educators to learn from families in order to offer the best experiences for children.

Mari Riojas-Cortez

Learning Outcomes

In this chapter on communication, you will find methods for effective communication that will enable you to do the following:

6.1 Discuss effective communication.

6.2 Identify one-way and two-way communication strategies.

6.3 Describe roadblocks to communication.

6.4 List and describe parent education programs that use effective communication with families.

6.5 Discuss important communication characteristics of positive family–teacher conferences.

Effective Communication

What do you have in mind when you think of effective communication? Is it the transmission of feelings, information, and signals? Is it the sending and receiving of messages? Is it a verbal exchange between people—for example, parents and teachers? We know that a positive school climate is only positive when there is effective communication between schools and families (Stone Kessler & Snodgrass, 2014). In addition, partnerships can only be created when effective communication occurs between families and schools (Palts & Harro-Loit, 2015). Farrell and Collier (2010) agree that the main purpose of family–school–teacher communication is to promote family engagement.

Examine the following e-mail communication between a parent and a teacher.

Parent: Thank you for your invitation, Mrs. Garza, do you think you can change the time for the celebration after school? Many of us parents work until 5 p.m. and we can't take time off. Not only would I be penalized financially, but I will get "written up" and I could lose my job.

Teacher (Mrs. Garza): No, absolutely not. I cannot change it. An administrator has to be in this event because it's after school and he can't stay very long after school so it has to be 4–5 p.m. I will make sure I videotape your child with all of the other parents and then share it with you. I also have to be at my child's soccer game. Oh, I know! Don't worry, your child takes the bus so we will send all of the goodies with him so he doesn't miss out. Have a great week!

How do you think the parent felt? How do you think the teacher felt? Words can make us or break us. The words that we use as teachers with families give parents the sense of whether they are valued or not. If we use words that make families feel worthless, then we are failing at the most important ingredient to create effective partnerships with families: communication.

Most definitions of **communication** encompass more than mere interchanges of information. Communication entails the active participation of the sender to convey a **message** or thought to the receiver, who in turn may or may not reciprocate the action by acknowledging that information. Communication is achieved when an understanding, but not necessarily an agreement, is reached. Is the message received with the meaning that the sender intended to convey? In working with families, it is essential that messages are sent and received as intended, particularly if we don't speak their language or know their culture.

Messages

Gamble and Gamble, in 1982, formulated the theory that in communication each message has at least three components: (a) the words or verbal stimuli—what a person says; (b) the body language or physical stimuli—how a person gestures; and (c) the vocal characteristics or vocal stimuli—a person's pitch, loudness or softness, and speed. However, now communication occurs most often through digital media where messages can be interpreted differently from what was intended. All individuals vary in the way that they convey their messages but also in how they understand a message; therefore, in the context of family and school relations it is important for teachers to know the families that they work with in order to find ways to send (and receive) messages appropriately to help increase communication for effective partnerships.

Important elements of effective communication include the sender giving a message and the message being received and interpreted by the receiver. If the intent of the message is accurately received, effective communication has occurred. For this to happen, the listener must be an active participant. The listener must be able to hear the message and understand its feeling and meaning. For example, in the preceding scenario, how would you evaluate the different messages sent by

the teacher and the parent? Each player has its own interpretation of the conversation and will express feelings according to that interpretation. How might the message change if this were a face-to-face conversation? Furthermore, in order for effective communication to occur there should be some reflection (positive or negative).

Communication includes speaking, listening, reflection of feelings, and interpretation of the message. It is a complicated process because so many variables are involved. The sender's voice and body language, the message itself, the receiver's reaction to the sender, and the receiver's expectations all affect the message and are all culturally based. To be effective in communication, speakers need to understand their own reactions and the reaction of others to them, and they must listen to the meaning of the message.

Since we live in the digital age, communication also includes texts, e-mails, Facebook, Twitter, blogs, and any other social media (Ozcinar & Ekizoglu, 2013). Feelings and emotions may not be communicated effectively through such media. Messages communicated through social media need to be carefully conveyed, otherwise the consequences can be dire. The receiver must correctly interpret the meaning of the message and the sender's intent. If the message—or the receiver's response—is misinterpreted, miscommunication occurs. This very often happened in parent–teacher conferences and now happens even more through digital messaging.

Miscommunication can be overcome, but the sender or the receiver must understand how to recover from it. The receiver can check his or her understanding by rephrasing and recycling the conversation or by further questioning the sender within the context of the subsequent discussion. As pictured in Figure 6.1, the message (filtered through values and past experiences) goes to the receiver (where it also is filtered through values and past experiences), is decoded, responded to, and sent back to begin the cycle again. Communication is a dynamic, continuous process that changes and evolves. For instance, regarding the earlier example, the parent might feel left out, desperate, anxious, or hurt, while the teacher might feel frustrated and be completely unaware he or she has offended the parent. Researchers such as Thompson, Mazer, and Grady (2015) indicate that in order to better understand communication with parents in the digital age, the use of a framework such as the Media Rich Theory, or MRT, is needed. Originally developed by Daft & Lengel (1986) the MRT provides a framework for clearer communication between sender and receiver. The richness is based

Figure 6.1 Communication Process
Messages are filtered through the receiver's value system and experiences before they are decoded and responded to. Communication is a dynamic, continuous process.

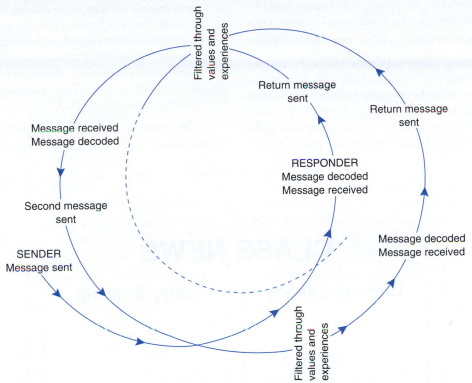

on immediate feedback, cues, variety in language, and the intent of the message towards the receiver.

One-Way and Two-Way Communication Strategies
One-Way Communication

According to *The Oxford Dictionary of Media and Communication* by Daniel Chandler and Rod Munday (2016), **one-way communication** is a message where feedback or interaction is minimal. Typical examples of one-way communication include class lectures, commercials, and YouTube Videos.

One-way communication is very important in the context of teachers and families. It allows the teacher or the parent to convey an easy message. For instance, some early childhood teachers send a note home every week telling parents what their child did. Infants' teachers have to send a note home every day so parents know what happened during the child's day. Examples of one-way communication include notes, phone messages, and newsletters, among others. Many schools call parents

frequently and leave a voice message with important information regarding events or holidays in the form of "robocalls." Robocalls are phone calls that have prerecorded messages, often from the principal, to all parents to inform or remind them of important information. Another example of one-way communication includes text messaging through regular smart phones or through an app such as WhatsApp. Some teachers use apps like Class Dojo, Remind, Bloomz, BuzzMob, The Teacher App & Grade Book, Collaborize Classroom, Remind 101, TeacherKit, or Running Start—and the list of apps to send mass or individual messages or classroom information to parents continues. School districts are also using technology for other purposes such as registration and grades. Recently, one of our local school districts created an online registration website. This allowed parents to register their children from the convenience of their own digital device. After completing the registration form, the parents received a text message (or phone call, depending on the parents' choice) notifying them whether they were successful in registering their children.

These are simple forms of one-way communication. The format varies with the goals and objectives of the school or teachers. For example, newsletters can have different designs ranging from a very simple notice to an elaborate and professional layout. Similarly, before phone, phone messages must be clear and concise and follow a short script where the principal or director reads the announcements that must be made for the parents. Look at the following example of a phone message for families:

"Good evening, Mustang parents! I hope you are having a nice weekend! This is your principal, Mr. Castillo. We want you to be aware of the field day the children will participate on Wednesday, May 23. We need water bottles, juices, and fruit. You may also make a cash donation. Please contact our parent liaison Mrs. Green for more information or just drop off your donation in our office."

"*¡Buenas noches, padres de nuestros Mustangs! Espero que estén pasando un buen fin de semana. Este es su director, el Señor Castillo. Queremos avisarles que los niños van a participar en un día deportivo el Miércoles, 23 de Mayo. Necesitamos botellas de agua, jugos y fruta. Si prefieren pueden también contribuir con donaciones en efectivo. Por favor contacten a la Sra. Green para más información o lo pueden colocar en la oficina.*"

The phone message is above is brief and tells the parents exactly what the school needs. If there are dual

Figure 6.2 Newsletter Template
Newsletters can take many forms, ranging from this informal design to very sophisticated publications.

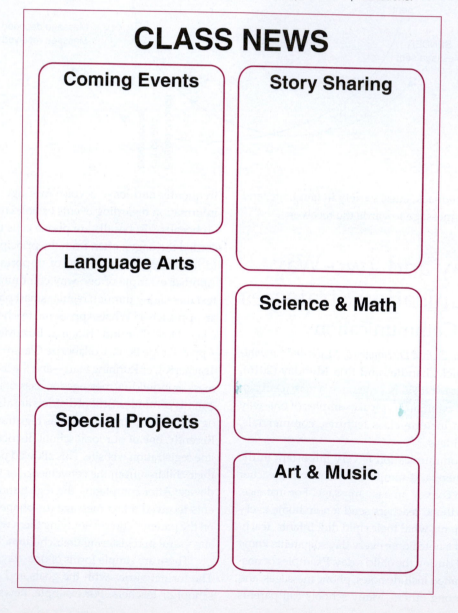

language learners, the message should also be in their first language. In the case of the example above, the message was also supplied in Spanish, as the child's home language should be used if possible. The teachers can follow up with a note that reminds parents about the donations needed. The office staff needs to be notified and, together with the parent liaison, coordinate the best way to communicate with parents. Of great importance is the way that the staff communicates with parents as they bring donations. It is important that the staff and administration know positive communication strategies in order to enhance parent engagement, particularly for an activity such as this one.

SIMPLE NEWSLETTERS. The more newsletters you develop, the easier they become. The design can vary from a simple notice that is hand-printed and photocopied (see Figure 6.2) to a letter created through a desktop publishing program on the school computer (see Figure 6.3) to one that is developed using a free downloadable template. The format is important because it attracts the reader (in this case, the family) to look through the newsletter. The content is

Figure 6.3 Sample Parent Newsletter
If you regularly collect anecdotes and children's work, you will easily have enough material for a four-page newsletter for parents.

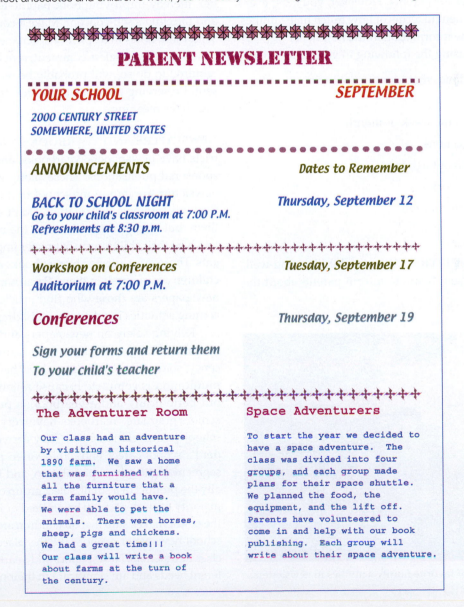

just as important. Articles can feature the children's activities in curriculum areas such as math contracts or contests, reading projects, group presentations in social studies, hands-on work in science, practice in music skills, art experiences, field trips, care of classroom pets, contributions by resource people, creative drama experiences, and accomplishments or remarks by individual children (teachers must ensure that parents give permission to use their children's work in the newsletter). In addition, topics can include information important to parents, such as parent–teacher conferences, back-to-school nights, and parent breakfasts, among others.

If you regularly collect anecdotes and children's work, you will easily have enough material for a four-page newsletter for parents. However, you must exercise your judgment in terms of how much time families have to read the information in the newsletter.

Consider using the following in your newsletter:

- Clear headlines that identify the topic
- Color
- Calendar of the week or month
- Book suggestions
- Recognition of birthdays
- Children's work
- Quotes from children
- Artwork

NOTES AND LETTERS.   When a child is doing well, an "upslip" is sent home to inform parents about the

Mari Riojas-Cortez

Include photos of favorite family activities in newsletters.

child's performance in different aspects of school (see Figure 6.4). It is a good idea to buy small sheets of paper with space enough for a one- or two-line note. If you write too much, you might be forced by time limitations to postpone the incidental note, and thus the positive effect of timeliness is lost.

Letters sent prior to the beginning of school also help establish good communication. They should include reminders, as well as information about significant dates and school events (see Figure 6.5).

Many teachers like to use "good news notes," happy faces, "happy grams," or similar forms periodically to report something positive about each child. The concept behind each of these formats is the same—to communicate with parents in a positive manner, thereby improving both parent–teacher relations and the child's self-concept. Make a concerted effort to send these notes in a spirit of spontaneous sincerity. A contrived, meaningless comment, sent because you are required to do so, will probably be received as it was sent. Preserving good relations requires that the message have meaning.

NEWSPAPERS AND YEARBOOKS.   Most school districts have newspapers, yearbooks, and other school-sponsored publications. These, along with the district newsletter, are important school traditions and effectively disseminate information. Don't stop publishing them, but always remember that the newsletters that touch on their children are of greater importance to parents. Those most affected by yearbooks are those whose children are pictured in them. Parents most affected by newspapers are those who find articles in them concerning activities in which their children are involved.

Relying solely on newspapers and yearbooks for communicating with parents can promote complacency; some administrators and teachers assume communication is complete because a newspaper comes out periodically and a yearbook is published when seniors graduate. Yearbooks have very little effect on school–home relationships. They arrive after the student's school career ends, they often picture a small segment of the school population, and they are generally the product of a small, select group of students. The majority of students may be omitted or ignored, unless the editor makes sure that all children are included. The school newspaper cannot take the place of individual class newsletters. Newspapers and yearbooks meet different needs and are significant in their own way, but to

Figure 6.4 Written Communication Messages

Happy grams, "upslips," and short notes are appreciated by parents and child. Newsletters are a chance to communicate with families; therefore the use of their home language is very important and preferred. Although some languages may not be as familiar as others, teachers still must do everything they can to use the students' native language. Having a bilingual newsletter will help families feel welcomed and valued.

establish a real, working relationship between parents and schools, the school's publication must concern the parents' number one interest—their own children.

MEDIA.   A formal and effective means of reaching parents is through the Internet, e-mail, websites, Facebook, Twitter, text messages, the community newspaper, television, and radio stations. Some schools and teachers also have their own YouTube channel, which is popular with children and families. Use a *who, what, when, where, why,* and *how* information format to send press releases to television and radio stations. Be brief, but include a contact name and phone number. Many districts connect with their families by sending text and e-mail messages. Paper media can still be used for those parents who do not have access to electronic media. Use these opportunities to inform the community about events at school. These can include conferences, sports events, musical performances, debates, theater, school board meetings, community meetings, back-to-school nights, and carnivals. For example, the San Antonio Independent School District provides short video clips to highlight activities throughout the district. The video clips enable parents and the community to learn more about their school district. Remember to assign someone, a teacher or staff, to always keep the information current on social media.

Figure 6.5 Friendly Letter Sample
Friendly letters sent prior to the opening of school can set the stage for a cooperative and pleasant school year.

Dear Families:

All the teachers and staff at Jefferson Elementary are excited about the beginning of school. Now you can follow us on Twitter or like us on Facebook and Instagram. Teachers now have the ability to use WhatsApp to communicate with parents.

Everyone responded so enthusiastically to the new Family Resource Room last year that we have decided to expand it in the coming year. We will have a planning meeting on Thursday, September 24 at 10:00 a.m. Call if you are interested in attending.

Don't forget Back to School Night on Tuesday, September 15. Gather at 7:00 p.m. for refreshments. At 7:45 p.m. parents may go to their children's classrooms to meet with their teachers. We are looking forward to seeing you there.

Summer was a busy time for all the staff. Several teachers worked on special projects and curriculum for their classes. Mr. García was able to get donations for our community garden and a certified master naturalist will be helping us grow our plants. We also need your help on the weekends to keep our gardens healthy. Enjoy the last few days of summer!! We shall start the school year refreshed and ready to go.

Best wishes, Mrs. Zapata, Principal

SUGGESTION BOXES.   A suggestion box placed in the hallway encourages parents to share their concerns and pleasures with the school anonymously. Although this is really a one-way communication system, it effectively tells parents, "We want your suggestions. Let us know what you feel," and encourages them to respond. A way to let parents know that their suggestions were read is to have a "response corner" on a bulletin board close to the suggestion box. That way parents can see how their suggestion has been considered. Remember to place the box where it can be easily seen. There are apps that schools can purchase (some are free) that have different features that allow parents to provide anonymous feedback.

HANDBOOKS.   Handbooks sent home before the child enters school are greatly appreciated by parents. If sent while the child is a preschooler, the school's expectations for the child can be met early. If given to parents at an open house during the spring term, they can reinforce the directions given by the teacher at that time. Handbooks can help parents new to the area by including information on community activities and associations for families. Many school districts and centers are sending the handbooks electronically for parents to download and read. A district handbook designed to introduce parents to the resources in the area—with special pages geared to each level of student—can be developed and used by all teachers in the district. Moles (1996a) suggests the following handbook inclusions:

- Statement of school goals and philosophy
- Discipline policy and code
- Operations and procedures regarding
   a. Grades and pupil progress reports
   b. Absence and tardiness

c. How to inquire about student difficulties

d. Emergency procedures for weather and other events

e. Transportation schedules and provisions for after-school activities

- Special programs at the school, such as after-school enrichment or childcare programs

- Parent involvement policies and practices at the school, with items that describe

  a. "Bill of Rights" for parents

  b. "Code of Responsibilities" for parents

  c. Open house and parent–teacher conferences

  d. Involvement opportunities, such as volunteer programs, advisory councils, and PTAs

- A calendar of major school events throughout the year: holidays, vacations, regular PTA meetings, report card periods, open houses, and other regularly scheduled school–home contacts

- Names and phone numbers of key school contact people

- Names and phone numbers of parent leaders (e.g., members of advisory councils, key people in parent organizations, and room parents)

- A tear-off response form allowing parents to ask questions, voice concerns, and volunteer at the school

In addition, consider the following items when you compile your handbook:

- Procedures for registration
- Invitations to visit the school
- Testing and evaluation programs
- The decision-making process, advisory committees, and site-based management
- Facilities at the school (cafeteria, clinic, library)
- Summer programs
- Recreation programs
- Associations related to families and children
- Community center

SPECIALIZED HANDBOOK. A special handbook related to the child's grade level and academic program can be an effective way to gain parents' cooperation. If it is sent out early in the school term, include the teacher's name and a short autobiography.

Two-way communication improves partnerships.

Studio 8/Pearson Education Ltd

The handbook can include a special section related to the curriculum in the child's grade level and can be developed by classroom teachers at each level and inserted for children assigned to their classes. This is especially important when the school is changing the manner in which the curriculum is taught. For example, for early childhood classrooms, an explanation about the importance of play for children's development can be included to inform parents of the benefits of play. Another section of the handbook can include ideas for activities that parents can do at home with their children that will support the school's curriculum. A list of developmentally and culturally appropriate children's literature complements the specialized handbook.

SUMMER HANDBOOK OR NOTE. If a handbook does not give individualized personal information, a note from the teacher mailed to the home during the summer will be appreciated by the family and will set the tone for a successful home–school relationship.

Families often have different preferences in the way they like to obtain information from the school. In a study conducted by Hoffman, Podikunju-Hussain, and Ridout (2015) English and Spanish speaking families of Head Start and Even Start children preferred hard copies over electronic materials. Regardless of the preference, one-way communication strategies should be used, as these are important resources that help teachers collaborate with parents and eventually partner with parents.

Two Way Communication

Although one-way communication is important, two-way communication is essential because it involves dialogue (Chandler & Monday, 2016). It is possible only when school personnel meet the children and their family. The school principals or center directors set a positive climate that values children and their families. Positive views of children's families will increase the level of family engagement, as families feel welcome and valued.

Increased involvement is necessary for a true partnership. Telephone calls, e-mails, phone apps, home visits, parent visits at the school, parent–teacher conferences, and school activities encourage continued parental involvement. It is also important for teachers to send a brief message to parents privately letting them know how their child is doing and allowing for parents to answer. When they do, this can turn into an electronic dialogue that is very beneficial for both teachers and parents. The more this practice is used, the better the chances of increasing communication.

Visits to the classroom allow parents to become acquainted with their child's educational environment, the other children in the room, and the teacher. Parents need to feel welcome at all times. The teacher can send parents a calendar letting them know of special projects, testing dates, and other important events so they know the best time to visit. If a teacher finds a parent that always wants to be in the classroom, put that parent to work and officially name him or her the "homeroom parent." Ask this parent to assist you in the classroom doing things like working in a learning center, making classroom games, or working on the newsletter—the possibilities are endless. Participation in school activities allows parents to become working members of the education team.

When one stakeholder, parent or teacher, initiates communication and it is reciprocated, then two-way communication has occurred. Usually, the teacher makes that initial communication, which, depending on the quality, may be reciprocated (or not). The benefits of two-way communication include the ability for teachers and families to engage in meaningful dialogue about the child's learning. In addition, two-way communication allows families to discover ways that they can be engaged in that learning, and informs the teacher how families and children engage in learning at home. Many families, particularly those who are of diverse backgrounds, find two-way communication helpful as they can learn more about the school system and programs that are offered by asking questions. In a study conducted by Thomas-Duckwitz, Hess, and Atcherly (2013) it was found that two-way communication allowed Mexican immigrant mothers to better understand their role in their child's education in the United States (which culturally is different than in Mexico). Some two-way communication examples are listed below.

E-MAIL.   Individual messages can be used for specific correspondence between the school and the student or the student's family. Sending e-mails to families whose children have been ill and unable to attend school can help the children keep up with schoolwork. When children are ill, it is often difficult for parents to get to the school to get assignments. E-mail provides a way for families to get the documents that they need.

CHATS.   The school or school district can set up safe chat rooms for children to communicate with one another regarding their homework. The chat rooms should include security devices to make sure children can safely discuss their questions with other friends, teachers, and volunteers. Many libraries, for example, provide help with homework through a live chat online.

YOUTUBE CHANNELS.   Permanent explanations and discussions of academic assignments could be available in a video through YouTube. Teachers can videotape their lectures and assignment instructions. YouTube channels allow students to access the information or lecture they need to complete assignments or homework. YouTube channels can promote interactive communication and discussion once video is watched.

TELEPHONE CALLS.   If it is impossible to visit a parent in person, rely on a telephone call! A telephone call early in the school year produces many benefits from appreciative parents. Be aware, however, that most parents will wonder what is wrong when their child's teacher calls. This is quite an indication of our communication methods; parents are generally contacted only when something is amiss. Change that practice by setting aside a short period each day for making telephone calls to parents. Begin the dialogue on a positive note. Early in the year, calls can include information about who you are, why you are calling, and a short anecdote about the child. If each call takes five minutes and you have 30 children in your class, the calls will consume two and a half hours—a small amount of time for the results you will see. Divide the time into segments of 20 to 30 minutes each evening. Parents also appreciate a note sent home saying you hope to call and asking for a convenient time. A sample letter is shown in Figure 6.6.

Figure 6.6 Sample Parent Note

Asking parents when they are available for telephone calls and letting them know when they can call you encourages communication.

Dear _____:

    During the school year, I will be making periodic telephone calls to parents of my students. I am able to call on Tuesday evening from 7:00 P.M. to 9:30 P.M. or on Wednesday afternoon from 3:30 P.M. to 5:00 P.M. Could you mark the time that would be most convenient for you?

    Should you want to call me, you will find me available on Thursday evenings from 7:00 P.M. to 9:00 P.M. Feel free to call my home at _____ if you have questions or would like to talk. You can also text me or send me an email to sue.green@sisd.net

    I am looking forward to visiting with you this year.

Best wishes,

_____

Telephone call preference

Tuesday: ❑ 7:00 to 8:00 P.M.   Wednesday: ❑ 3:30 to 4:00 P.M.
             ❑ 8:00 to 9:30 P.M.   ❑ 4:00 to 5:00 P.M.

If none of these times are convenient, please let me know.

HOME VISITS. Some teachers make the effort to visit their students' homes early in the school year. This might be the only way to reach parents who have no telephone. It is also a rewarding experience for any teacher who can devote the time required. Not all parents are receptive to home visits, however, and some are afraid that the teacher is judging the home rather than coming as a friendly advocate of their child. Take precautions to avoid making the family feel at ease. Always let the family know you are coming. It is a good idea to write a note in which you request a time to visit or, possibly, give parents the option of meeting at another place. Once home visits become an accepted part of the parent-involvement program, they become less threatening, and both parents and children look forward to them. Some schools require teachers to visit children before they begin school. This allows the teacher and the families to meet each other in a setting that helps the teacher understand the parent. Teachers should never criticize a family's home. Instead, they should be objective and focus on the goals of the home visit.

VISITS TO THE CLASSROOM. The traditional visit with parents invited for a specific event works very well in some school systems. In other schools, special events are complemented by an open invitation to parents to participate in ongoing educational programs.

Outside the classroom or just inside the door, hang a special bulletin board with messages for parents. It might display assignments for the week, plans for a party, good work children have done, requests for everyday items to complete an art project, requests for special volunteer time, or just about anything that promotes the welfare of the room. Parents can plan and develop the bulletin board with the teacher's guidance. Some schools keep up with their website, which can be full of resources for families in all schools, but in particular for those schools where security is tight.

PARTICIPATION VISITS. Directions for classroom participation are necessary if the experience is to be successful. Parents or other visitors feel more comfortable, teachers are more relaxed, and children benefit more if parents or visitors are given pointers for classroom visits. They can be in the form of a handout or a poster displayed prominently in the room, but a brief parent–teacher dialogue will make the welcome more personal and encourage specific participation.

The best welcome encourages the visitor to be active in the room's activities. Select activities that are easily described, require no advance training, and contribute rather than disrupt. You might want to give explicit directions on voice quality and noise control. If you do not want the parent to make any noise, request that a soft tone be used when talking with students in

Visitors can encourage children to work together.

the room. Or you might want to ask the parent to work in a specific area of the room. Most visitors are happiest when they know what you want.

If it bothers you that some parents tend to give answers to students rather than help the students work out their own problems, suggest the method of instruction you prefer. You might give them a tip sheet describing your favorite practices for working with students. Making activities simple for "drop-in" participants will keep problems to a minimum. If some parents prefer to sit and observe, don't force participation. As they become more comfortable in your room, they might try some activities. Selecting and reading a story to a child or group, listening to a child read, supervising the newsletter center, playing a game chosen from the game center with a student, supervising the puzzle table, or talking with students about their work are appropriate activities for new volunteers.

VISITS BY INVITATION.   A special invitation can be sent to parents of a different child each week, asking them to visit as "Parents of the Week" or VIPs—very important parents. A memo from the administration that explains the objective of the visit should accompany the invitation, which is written by the child or teacher. Have the child bring in information about brothers and sisters, favorite activities, and other interesting or important facts about the family. Place a picture of the family on the bulletin board that week. The family could include parents, grandparents, special friends (young or old), and younger siblings. Parents and guests are asked to let the teacher know when they plan to visit.

You could also improve a child's self-concept by making the child "Student of the Week." Not only do the children have a chance to feel good about themselves during their special week, but it also helps children get to know one another better. Feedback from parents after a visit is important. A reaction sheet is given to parents asking them to write their impressions and return it to the school. Comments range from compliments to questions about the school. This process encourages two-way communication.

STUDENT–PARENT EXCHANGE DAY.   An idea similar to the student visiting the parent's place of employment is to have the parent take the place of the student at school. This can be done in several ways. The parent can accompany the student to class and spend the day with the child, or the parent and child can exchange places for the day. Exchanging places for the day works best for an older student who can fulfill some obligation at home or go on a field trip while the parent goes through the student's exact schedule. The parent is responsible for listening to the lecture or participating in the class and doing the homework. The parent learns about the school program, becomes acquainted with the teacher, and is better able to relate to the child's school experience. If the child is young and the school and parent prefer participation without the child, the process is possible if the parent hires a babysitter or if the school provides a field trip for the children in the class.

BREAKFASTS.   Engage the cafeteria staff or volunteers to make a simple breakfast, you can invite parents to an early breakfast. Many parents can stop for breakfast on their way to work. Plan a breakfast meeting early in the fall to meet parents and answer questions. Breakfast meetings tend to be rushed because parents need to get to work, so schedule a series of breakfasts and restrict the number of parents invited to each. In this way, real dialogue can be started. If a group is too large, the personal contact that is the prime requisite of two-way communication between school and home is prevented. Breakfasts also support parent-to-parent communication. It is important that parents get an opportunity to meet the parents of their children's friends. It should be made clear to parents the potential advantage of attending the breakfasts.

Roadblocks to Communication

Examine the following phone conversation scenario:

Parent: *Hello, I would like to make an appointment to see the principal.*

Office Assistant: *Hmmm, what is this about?*

Parent: *I would like to talk to her about the prekinder program. I'm very concerned that my child is not learning.*

Office Assistant: *She won't be available for two weeks, and besides, you have to follow protocol. You have to talk to the assistant principal and if the issue doesn't get resolved, then you can try to make an appointment, but right now she is very busy.*

Parent: *So I can't see her at all?*

Office Assistant: *No, you have to follow protocol. I'm telling you she's not available.*

In the scenario presented above, what are the roadblocks that the parent is encountering? A roadblock impedes progress toward something. In the case of school–family partnerships, roadblocks emerge particularly in communication. Roadblocks in communication with parents might include differences in language, culture, beliefs, and opinions, among others. Some roadblocks are used to protect positions, and others occur because the participants are unable to understand one another's positions. Teachers and administrators play a different role from the parent and as such they need to be willing to listen and work with parents. Alejandra Barreza, a Head Start Director, indicated this very eloquently:

> Some of the roadblocks to communication really have to be placed on the administrator or the teacher. We always have to be willing to understand when a parent is upset. We have to make sure to listen with intention to resolve the concern of the parent. At times, we can get defensive but we have to understand that at the end of the day, a parent only wants the best for their child. Administrators have to be available. The roadblocks that we put is when we make parents wait or have them make appointments or when they call and it takes us more than a day to respond to them. Parents want to be heard.

Both school personnel and parents set up roadblocks but as teachers and administrators we must put the child and the parent first and remove those roadblocks. I remember once, when I was a prekindergarten bilingual teacher, that I forgot to send home a book order form (mistake #1). Since we often received those forms, I didn't think too much about it (mistake #2) until one of the mothers came to my room very upset because the family had been saving money to purchase several books, and due to my mistake, they missed the deadline. When the mother came to ask about it, I just apologized and affirmed that I would send the next form to her (mistake #3). The mother was very upset (rightly so!), so she went to speak with the principal who reassured the mother that it was just a mistake and would not happen again (mistake #4). Unfortunately, all of these "mistakes" created roadblocks to communication with this particular parent. It took a long time for her to learn to trust me or even talk directly to me—for a while she would speak to my assistant regarding any issue dealing with her child. I was so inexperienced in working with parents that I wasn't sure what to do and no one guided me on how to best handle the situation. In retrospect, I could have visited the family's home and talked with the mother to sincerely acknowledge the parents' feelings, offer an apology, and truly listen to her concerns. Home visits, according to research, help increase communication, creating strong partnerships with parents (Risko & Walker-Dalhouse, 2010; Sawchuck, 2011).

Roadblocks to communication occur because, as families and teachers, we have different characteristics that can hinder the process. In the following sections, you are going to read about parents' and schools' characteristics that can hinder communication.

Parent Roadblocks

As you look at this section, it is important to think of these roadblocks not as something negative or a way to criticize parents, but as a way to identify those traits that hinder effective communication.

THE "MY OWN AND MY CHILD'S GUARDIAN" ROLE. Many parents, often subconsciously, view their children as extensions of themselves. "Criticize my child and you criticize me" is their message. They might also think things like "Are you saying that I did not rear my children correctly?" or "Is my child slow in school because I am the parent?" or "Is there something that I should have done differently in my childrearing?" Families of children who have special needs but who have not been formally diagnosed often experience this type of situation.

When a parent puts up a shield against perceived criticism, it becomes very difficult to communicate. When parents are hurt by a child's inability to progress satisfactorily in school, they may withdraw from open, honest communication in an effort to protect their child and their own self-esteem.

A parent's vested interest in the child can be channeled in a positive direction. Effective communication, with positive suggestions for encouraging the child, can help the parent become a partner with the school.

THE "I DON'T BELONG" ROLE.   Many parents do not feel comfortable talking with school personnel. These parents avoid going to civic events—including events that take place at schools—because they do not feel as if they belong. If parents feel inadequate, they avoid coming in contact with the schools. If they do come, they find it difficult to communicate their desires or feelings to the staff. These parents can benefit from encouragement so that they can contribute and be involved. Very often, parents of children who are English-language learners experience this type of role mostly because the school or the teacher has not reached out to them. It is not enough to send out notes in their home language. It is just as important to interact and give families a sense of belonging.

THE AVOIDANCE ROLE.   The avoidance role can include self-assured parents who do not respect the school or the way it treats parents and students. It also includes parents who had a difficult time in school when they were growing up. Perhaps they dropped out of school—the building might bring back bad memories. Schools must reach out to these parents by caring and offering activities and services that the parents need and desire.

THE INDIFFERENT PARENT ROLE.   It seems more difficult today to be a concerned, involved parent because of financial and time pressures. Although most parents want what is best for their children, some are willing to shift their parental responsibilities to others. The institution where children spend most of their parents' working hours is the school. When children are reared by indifferent parents their futures can be devastated. If no one cares, why should the children care? Parents might be facing problems that prevent them

from focusing on the children. Drug and alcohol abuse, divorce, financial troubles, illness or health issues, and criminal behavior can be evidence that parents are facing major problems in their life.

THE "DON'T MAKE WAVES" ROLE.   Many parents are unwilling to be honest in their concerns because they do not want school personnel to take it out on their child. They believe that the teacher or principal might be negative toward their children if they make suggestions or express concerns. This represses communication.

THE "CLUB-WAVING ADVOCATE" ROLE.   Sometimes parents get carried away with their devotion to their children, and they exhibit this through power play. These advocates can become abrasive in their desire to protect their children or change school policy. These parents are the opposite of the "I don't belong" or the "don't make waves" parents. "Club-waving" parents express their concerns through confrontation. Schools must acknowledge these concerns and change the situation when it is sensible to do so. In addition, give the parents opportunities to be leaders in areas where they can contribute.

School Roadblocks

Many times, schools install roadblocks to effective communication without even realizing it. Sometimes they do so intentionally. The stress of educating and working with many children and families, the pressure to accomplish many tasks, and the desire to be seen as efficient all get in the way of unhurried, effective communication. Nevertheless, there is no excuse for creating roadblocks for families. The following roles describe some of the roadblocks that hamper communication between home and school.

THE "AUTHORITY FIGURE" ROLE.   School personnel who act as chief executive officers all too often hinder communication. These teachers and administrators claim to be the authorities, ready to impart information to the parent. They neglect to set the stage for the parent to be a partner in the discussion. If staff members take all the responsibility of running the school without considering the parents' backgrounds and knowledge, there seems to be no reason to communicate. Parents are locked out of the decision-making process. Schools that ignore or criticize parents destroy communication between parents and schools. Such schools tend to have low morale and thus a negative school climate.

THE "SYMPATHIZING COUNSELOR" ROLE.

School personnel who focus on the inadequacy of the child in a vain attempt to console the parent miss a great opportunity for communication. Parents want to solve their concerns through constructive remediation or support. Parents and schools both need to focus on the achievements that can be attained through cooperation and collaboration.

THE "PASS THE BUCK" ROLE.

Communication stops when school personnel refer the concerns of the parent to another department. They might say things like "Sara may need help, but we cannot schedule her for tests for five months" or "It is too bad that Richard had such a bad experience last year. I wish I could help, but he needs special services." Sometimes parents think the school is deliberately stalling while their child falls further and further behind. Lately, some schools wait to test a child until first or second grade, and this is crucial time lost, particularly for children who have developmental disabilities.

THE "PROTECT THE EMPIRE" ROLE.

A united, invincible staff can cause parents to think no one cares about their needs. School personnel need to work together and support one another, but they also need to listen to the parent and should advocate for the parent as they formulate an educational plan for the student.

THE "BUSY TEACHER" ROLE.

Perhaps the greatest roadblock to good communication between parent and teacher is time. If you are harried, you do not have time to communicate with your students or their parents. Both teachers and parents need to reduce stress and set aside time for communication. Reorganize schedules to include on-the-run conferences, telephone calls, and short personal notes to parents and children. Principals and directors could perhaps take over the classroom occasionally so teachers can make telephone calls to parents. The principals and directors would then also get to know the children in the classes and the importance of teacher–parent interaction would be emphasized. Roadblocks can be overcome.

Communicating with Culturally and Linguistically Diverse Families

Because communication is culturally based, teachers and administrators need to learn the culturally appropriate ways to communicate with families who are culturally and linguistically different. When I was a teacher, I learned to ask parents for special things we needed. I taught in a bilingual prekindergarten classroom where the majority of the children were immigrants and unfamiliar with the American education system. As such, it was imperative that I knew how to communicate not only policy and procedures to parents but also about their child's learning. Effective communication is particularly important with culturally and linguistically diverse families and those families who have children with special needs (Francis, Haines, & Nagro, 2017).

Although it is imperative that teachers and administrators find translators who can communicate to families the information that needs to be given, they need to understand the families' cultural practices for effective communication. The idea of funds of knowledge needs to be taken into consideration when communicating with parents. Possible ideas to enhance communication would be to learn about the culture from different organizations—for example, in San Antonio, Texas, we have different cultural arts centers that focus on particular ethnic groups such as the Guadalupe Cultural Arts Center that focuses on the Latino community and the Carver Community Cultural Center that focuses on the African American community. Additionally, recruiting other parents who speak different languages to become translators would be important because not only would they know how to talk with the parents, but they would also encourage these parents to participate and become involved in the school even if they don't speak English. Although some carefully planned events such as Parents' Night might work for a certain group of parents, for other parents whose background is different, these

Teachers need to effectively communicate with culturally and linguistically diverse parents.

Steve Debenport/E+/Getty Images

types of activities might not be effective (Guo, 2009). Therefore, it is imperative that teachers and administrators find ways to increase communication with parents who are of diverse backgrounds but who have been marginalized by society, as well as those parents unfamiliar with the education system.

Effective communication starts with effective leadership. Effective administrators recognize that in order for children's school experiences to be successful, the parents must be informed to be involved. To achieve effective communication, parents and teachers need to recognize roadblocks to their success. At the same time, they can increase their communication skills by practicing positive speaking, rephrasing, and attentive listening. Trust is built from constant communication between parent and teacher.

When teachers talk with parents, they communicate in many ways—through their words, their body actions, and their manner of speaking. Nonverbal communication is important since messages can be conveyed through body actions and gestures.

Effective Communication Skills

Teachers can establish rapport with parents by using effective communication skills. Effective communication is honest and open and takes time. Good communicators listen, rephrase and check out, and avoid criticizing and acting superior.

Teachers are good communicators when they do the following:

1. Show respect for the parents. They recognize that their concerns, opinions, and questions are significant factors in mutual understanding and communication.

2. Give their total attention to the parents. They establish eye contact (if appropriate based on cultural expectations) and clearly demonstrate through body language that their interest is focused on what is being said.

3. Use culturally appropriate communication. Their strategies focus on respecting and accepting the ways families communicate.

4. Listen and restate the parents' concerns. They clarify what has been said and try to discern the speaker's meaning and feeling to be sure they understand it correctly. They avoid closed responses or answering as a critic, judge, or moralist.

5. Recognize the parents' feelings. How much can they discuss with parents? Perhaps they need to establish a better parent–teacher relationship before they can completely share their concerns for the child.

6. Tailor discussions to fit the parents' ability to handle the situation.

7. Do not set off the fuse of a parent who might not be able to handle a child's difficulties. They don't accuse. Instead, they spend more time with the parent via other modes of communication and through conferences.

8. Emphasize that concerns are no one's fault. They understand that teacher and parents have to work on problems together to help the child. They use concerns as forums for understanding one another.

9. Remember that no one ever wins an argument. Calmly, quietly, and enthusiastically they discuss the *good* points of the child before bringing up any concerns.

10. Focus on one issue at a time. They are specific about the child's progress or concerns.

11. Tackle barriers when working with a parent with a disability (Stalker, Brunner, Maguire, & Mitchell, 2011).

12. Become allies with parents. They work in harmony since the goal of the partnership is the child.

Parents become partners in the educational process when they do the following:

1. View the teacher as a source of support for their child and themselves.

2. Listen carefully and give total commitment to the teacher.

3. Show respect for the teacher—recognize that the teacher's concerns, opinions, and culture questions are significant to mutual understanding and communication.

4. Recognize that the teacher has a difficult challenge to meet the needs of all students, and help the teacher succeed.

5. Rephrase and check their understanding of messages given during conversations or conferences.

6. Speak openly and honestly about the child.

7. Use concerns as forums for understanding the school and teacher.

8. Become allies with the teacher.

Positive Speaking

If your message is positive, the parent is more likely to want to listen. The relationship between teacher and parent is enhanced. A positive statement needs to be accompanied by attentive behavior, good body language, and a warm tone of voice. Add clear articulation, and you have the recipe for effective communication between parent and teacher.

Listening

Effective leaders are good listeners (Kayser, 2011) and this helps create a positive school climate. As teachers, we always remind children that, "they need to listen." We even include it as one of our classroom's rules! Interestingly, teachers often do very little listening with families, but **listening is the heart of effective communication**. Listening is more than hearing sounds. It is the active process of interpreting, understanding, and evaluating spoken and nonverbal communication as a meaningful message. Listening, not speaking, is the most-used form of communication. Forty-five percent of verbal communication is spent listening, 30% speaking, 16% reading, and 9% writing.

In education, much attention is given to the ability to write; yet there is very little training for listening. Greater understanding and retention of information would occur if an appropriate amount of time were spent on helping people listen effectively. Smith (1986) recommends these steps to improve listening skills:

1. *Be receptive.* Listeners encourage the speaker by being receptive and providing an environment where the speaker feels free to express ideas and feelings.
2. *Pay attention.* Make an effort to concentrate on what is being said.
3. *Use silence.* Communicate that you are listening through attentive behaviors while remaining silent.
4. *Seek agreement.* Look for the broader meaning of the message rather than focusing on isolated facts.
5. *Avoid ambiguity.* Ask questions to clarify, look for main ideas, and focus on intent as well as content.
6. *Remove distractions.* Eliminate daydreaming, remove physical barriers, and delay other important messages to make the climate clear for listening.
7. *Be patient.* Don't rush the speaker. Allow time for the message to be completed.

Table 6.1 Characteristics of Good Listeners

• Listen carefully to the other person.	Observe the speaker and have a facial expression that shows interest.
• Have good eye contact.	Respond with attentive body language, such as leaning forward or touching.
• Encourage the speaker by using body language and verbal expressions such as "yes."	Rephrase the substance and meaning of the message they receive from the speaker when appropriate.

Teachers and parents communicate when they work together to help the child. Although most effective communication traits are culturally based, the following list provides some examples of what is often valued and practiced in American society. Table 6.1 shows characteristics of good listeners.

Open Responses and Closed Responses

An **open response** encourages communication to continue. Open responses can vary from positive body language (demonstrated by a nod of the head or a smile indicating you wish the speaker to continue) to a verbal response in which you indicate your interest. If a child comes into a home or classroom with a caterpillar in hand, ready to display the treasure to mother or teacher, an open response would be a smile, a nod, or a question such as "Where did you find such a marvelous caterpillar?" A closed response would be a frown or a comment such as "Take that caterpillar away this very minute." What child would dare to explain that the caterpillar was a treasure?

Should a child prove a problem to a teacher, the easy response to a question by the parent would be a **closed response**. For example, a parent asks, "Why does John have trouble with math?" A closed response would be "If you would help him with his homework, he wouldn't have so much trouble." The conversation is finished. No one has sought to communicate and find out the best way to handle the situation and judgment was passed. Whereas an open response might be, "I think I have an idea but I would like to speak with you to see if you are seeing at home what I'm observing here at school. Just let me know what date and time is convenient for you." This response is an effective way to communicate.

Reflective Listening

Reflective listening is the ability to reflect the speaker's feelings. The listener's response identifies the basic feelings being expressed and reflects the essence of those feelings back to the speaker. Reflective or active listening is used in several parent programs, such as the Parent Effectiveness Training (PET) (Gordon, 1975, 2000), Active Parenting (Popkin, 2002), Parent's Handbook, Systematic Teaching of Effective Parenting (STEP) (Dinkmeyer, McKay, & Dinkmeyer, 1997), and Teaching and Leading Children (Dinkmeyer, McKay, Dinkmeyer, & Dinkmeyer, 1992). These programs are described in the next section. The examples illustrate the use of active or reflective listening.

REFLECTIVE LISTENING AND REFLECTIVE RESPONSES. Reflective listening encourages open responses. A reflective response is effective if the listener recognizes the feelings of the speaker and is able to respond accordingly. The parent asks, "Why does John have trouble with math?" A reflective response would be, "You are concerned about John's ability to do his math?" The parent at that point probably would agree.

To practice reflective listening, think of the following three steps:

1. Use attending behavior. Make eye contact. Lean forward and be interested.

2. Listen for the feeling behind the message.

3. Respond with a statement of that feeling.

I–YOU–WE MESSAGES. One useful communication skill relies on *I messages instead of you messages*. A "you" message places the responsibility on the person receiving the message, and it is often a negative message. With a parent, it might be used in the following way: "If you would just help John with his homework, he would be more successful at school." To change that statement to a more positive "I" message, use words like those described in the following three steps:

1. "When [describe the behavior that is bothering you],

2. I feel [state how you feel about the concern]

3. Because [describe what you think might happen]."

For example, you might say, "*When* John does not finish his homework, *I feel* worried *because* I am afraid he will fall behind and not be able to catch up." Gordon (1975, 2000) introduced the "I" message, and Dinkmeyer and McKay (1997) and Popkin (2002) use "I" messages in their parenting programs. There are times when a "we" message is more appropriate than an "I" message: "When Mary does not finish her homework, we have real concerns because she may fall behind her classmates." By using a "we" message, the teacher acknowledges that the parent is also concerned.

REPHRASING. **Rephrasing** is restating the intent of the message in a condensed version. There are three steps in rephrasing. First, the listener must determine the basic message and the intent of the message. Second, the listener restates the intent of the message. Third, the listener confirms the accuracy of the rephrasing.

When listeners seek to confirm or clarify a statement by saying something like "It sounds as if you feel . . ." or "I'm hearing you say . . .," they are rephrasing the statement. With rephrasing, communicators can avoid misunderstanding the message by checking the accuracy. Confusion and ambiguity in communication are avoided. The interest displayed by rephrasing also shows caring and builds trust (Center for Family Strengths, 1986).

REFRAMING. **Reframing** involves taking the sting out of the negative description of a child. When communicating with parents, if your answer reflects your understanding of parents' concerns, the conversation will remain open, but the words you choose can bring either desirable or disastrous results.

A teacher with good intentions and great concern for a child once opened a conference with a parent by referring to the child's "problem" of not staying on task. The antagonized parent struck back: "I think you're obnoxious!" The family was already overwrought by strain and worry over the child. The rest of the conference time had to be devoted to rebuilding a working relationship, allowing no time for productive dialogue about the child and leaving both teacher and parent with emotional scars.

Instead of focusing on the negative aspects of an individual start with positive comments. Then, reframe the child's troublesome quality into an acceptable or even positive trait. Had the teacher started the conference with some friendly remarks and then stated, "I have some concerns about John that we should work on together," the parent might not have responded with such anger.

Table 6.2 shows examples of phrases that reframe a "problem" as a concern about the child.

Table 6.2 Examples of Phrases that Reframe the Problem

Problem	Concern	Examples
loud and boisterous; gives others' answers	very active; can't help sharing	"Linda seems to be very active." "Juan is so excited about participating that sometimes he can't help himself . . ."
steals	takes without asking	"When Britanny plays, she takes toys without asking."
won't follow rules	has own agenda, or is determined	"Tanya is very independent even when she needs to follow my lead."
shy	self-contained	"I noticed that Izumi likes to play by herself."
talks too much	likes to share with others	"Isabella has a lot of information to share."
does not pay attention	is preoccupied	"Amira seems to be preoccupied with other things during circle time."

It is particularly important during parent-teacher conferences to reframe the way negative behavior is framed so that communication can occur more effectively. There might be times, however, when the teacher may need the help of the principal or the family specialist particularly if the child's negative behavior escalates. In such cases, the teacher still needs to be professional and treat the parents with respect. More than likely the parents are also experiencing such behavior at home. Having a list with possible solutions will help the parents know that the teacher and the school are doing everything possible to help the child overcome obstacles and be successful.

Parent Education Programs—PET, STEP, and Active Parenting

Many parent education programs incorporate the child-drearing suggestions in Parent Effectiveness Training (PET), Systematic Training for Effective Parenting (STEP), or Active Parenting. Excerpts from these programs illustrate the materials and communication techniques each uses.

Parent Effectiveness Training: The Proven Program for Raising Responsible Children

In Parent Effectiveness Training (PET), Gordon (1975, 2000) discusses many topics, including active listening, "I messages," changing behavior by changing the environment, parent–child conflicts, parental power,

and "no-lose" methods for resolving conflicts. The following excerpt relates to problem ownership and active listening.

In the parent–child relationship, three situations occur that we will illustrate with brief case histories:

1. The child has a problem because he or she is thwarted in satisfying a need. It is not a problem for the parent because the child's behavior in no tangible way interferes with the parent's satisfying his or her own needs. Therefore, *the child owns the problem.*

2. The child is satisfying his or her own needs (he or she is not thwarted), and his or her behavior is not interfering with the parent's own needs. Therefore, *there is no problem in the relationship.*

3. The child is satisfying his or her own needs (he or she is not thwarted). But his or her behavior is a problem to the parent because it is interfering in some tangible way with the parent's satisfying a need of his or her own. *Now the parent owns the problem.*

It is critical that parents always classify each situation that occurs in a relationship. Which of these three categories does this situation fall into?

When parents accept the fact that problems are owned by the child this in no way means that the parents cannot be concerned, care, or offer help. Professional counselors have real concern for, and genuinely care about, each child they are trying to help. But, unlike most parents, the counselors leave the responsibility for solving the child's problem with the child. They allow the child to own the problem. They accept the child's having the problem. They accept the child as a person separate from herself or himself. And they rely heavily upon and basically trust the child's own inner resources for solving the problem. Only because they let the child own the problem areas, the professional counselors are able to employ active listening.

Active listening is a powerful method for helping another person solve a problem that that person owns, provided the listener can accept the other's ownership and consistently allow the person to find the solutions. Active listening can greatly increase the effectiveness of parents as helping agents for their children, but it is a different kind of help from that which parents usually try to give.

Paradoxically, this method will increase the parent's influence on the child, but it is an influence that differs from the kind most parents try to exert over their children. Most parents are tempted to take ownership of their children's problems rather than allow children to learn to resolve problems. Active listening is a method of influencing children to find their own solutions to their own problems. This will help children develop self-regulation and responsibility for their actions. It is important, however, that parents remind children that they are always there for them but that taking responsibility for their actions will help them become prepared to face different situations.

Systematic Training for Effective Parenting

The Systematic Training for Effective Parenting (STEP) program offers a variety of training programs (STEP, 2018). Offered in several languages including English, Spanish, German, Japanese and French, these programs focus on developing healthy relationships. There are four programs: the original STEP, dealing with issues of children 6 to 12 years old including a choice of STEP Biblically for those who adhere to biblical values; Early Childhood STEP; STEP/Teen; and STEP Spanish. Kits are offered for every program and include a leader's resource guide, DVDs, and parents' handbook. The goal of the program is to help parents learn to understand their child and themselves by engaging in topics that include listening, encouraging, learning to cooperate, and understanding emotions and beliefs.

Active Parenting

The Active Parenting program is similar to both PET and STEP in that it is also based on the theories of Alfred Adler and Rudolf Dreikurs. Goals of misbehavior, logical consequences, active communication, exploring alternatives, and family council meetings are described. The programs are offered in kits and include DVDs, parent and leader manuals, and other resources. The Active Parenting program also provides an online learning center that includes an Active Parenting Online Video Library, Online Leader Training Workshops, and an Active Parenting Online Group (Active Parenting, 2018).

Parent–Teacher Conferences

A parent–teacher conference is a collaborative effort to coordinate the best possible effort for the education of the child in the classroom. It is a time for listening and sharing on the part of the school staff and the parents (Manning, 1985; Moles, 1996a; Elmore, 2008; Hoerr, 2014). To accomplish the greatest cooperation between home and school and provide the greatest benefit for the student, the conference needs to continue the communication between the parent and school, based on agreed-upon goals for the child throughout the year. Teachers and parents need to build a "relationship of respect and cooperation" (Saylor, 2007). "Personalizing" the school can help increase partnerships with parents (Esparza, 2007).

Start the school year with a positive interchange between teacher and parent by reaching out to parents through social media to initiate the parent–school partnership. Stephens (2007) states that it is important to ask parents what they would like to talk about and where they can hold the meetings. Some alternative ideas for parent conferences include meetings online using Facetime, Skype, or Zoom. Some parents still appreciate teachers calling and visiting their homes. When I was a prekindergarten bilingual teacher we would use the first two weeks at the beginning of the school year to make home visits but the initial contact was through a phone call. The first exchange was to introduce myself and the goals of the program. This helped set goals for the children's learning. I asked the parents what they wanted their child to learn, and the majority said they wanted the children to learn to like school. The goals should reflect what parents want and what is best for the child (Akers, 2005). The first conference can be a progress and planning session based on those goals.

Parent–teacher conferences are personal opportunities for two-way communication between parent and teacher or three-way communication among parent, teacher, and student. Parents as well as teachers recognize the conference as an excellent opportunity for clarifying issues, searching for answers, deciding on goals, determining mutual strategies, and forming a team in the education of the student. Most schools schedule conferences two or three times a year for typically-developing children; for children with disabilities, it is important that teachers conference with parents more often (Kroth & Edge, 2007). Parent–teacher conferences are an excellent way to begin engaging parents in conversation that will lead to partnerships. Teacher preparation programs as well as school administrators must provide training for teachers that show effective ways to engage in effective conferences that lead to positive home–school relations and avoid the typical "client orientation" type of conference (Lemmer, 2012).

Collaborative Conversations

Collaborative conversations can help develop cooperation and resolution of issues. Koch and McDonough (1999), using an example of a young child who hit and bit other children, describe five stages to improve parent–teacher conferences through collaboration of all parties as part of the team:

Stage 1. *Development of trust.* It is essential that a trusting relationship be developed. This can be enhanced prior to the conference at back-to-school nights, home visits, and informal interactions at school.

Stage 2. *Invite.* Extend an invitation that promotes cooperation and involvement. For example: "When would be a good time for us to talk together about Mary? Would you prefer to talk at school or at your home? Is there anyone else involved with Mary who could join us? Between now and the time we meet, let's all notice when Mary expresses her feelings safely" (p. 12).

Stage 3. *Set a mutual goal.* Facilitate or have a facilitator establish a cooperative atmosphere. Focus on the positive actions of the child when he or she appropriately handled the situation. Come to an understanding of your goal to enhance the positive.

Stage 4. *Listen to all viewpoints and expand understanding.* Allow all participants to express their feelings and ideas. The discussion moves from "identification of and observations about the effects of the problem to a dialogue about the unique outcomes/exceptions and the significance of these for all persons concerned" (p. 14).

Stage 5. *Restate the goal, measure it, and decide what to do about it.* Collaborative conversations "create an atmosphere filled with possibilities and ideas that enhance the lives of children and the adults that care for them" (p. 14).

Invitations and Schedules

The invitation to attend a conference sets the tone. If it is cordial, shows an awareness of parents' busy lives and obligations, and gives the parents time options for scheduling the conference, the teacher has shown consideration of the parents and a desire to meet with them. Most school systems have worked out procedures for scheduling conference periods. Release time is usually granted for teachers. Originally, most conferences took place in the afternoons. Children attended school in the mornings, and classes were dismissed at noon, with conferences between school personnel and parents—usually mothers only—occurring in the afternoon. With the increase in the number of working parents and single-parent families, and the growing number of fathers becoming more directly involved in their children's education, many schools are scheduling more evening conferences, while retaining some afternoon options.

To prepare the schedule, send notes to parents asking for their time preference. The formal note should be direct and list specific options for the time and place of the conference. A sample note is found in Figure 6.7. After the responses have been returned, staff members, including teachers in special areas of education, meet to schedule back-to-back conferences for parents with more than one child attending the school.

A telephone call from the teacher to each parent adds a personal touch. These calls, made either before or after the invitation has been sent, can clarify questions and let the parents know they are really welcome.

Figure 6.7 Sample Parent-Teacher Conference Schedule Note
Send a note home to schedule a conference.

Dear _____:

    We are looking forward to meeting with you and discussing _____ experiences and progress at school. Will you please let us know when a conference would be most convenient for you? Please check the date and time of day you could come.

Thank you,

_____

Teacher's name

Could you give a first and second choice? Please write "1" for your first preference and "2" for your second.

	Afternoon 1 to 4 P.M.	Evening 6 to 9 P.M.
Tuesday, November 12	_____	_____
Wednesday, November 13	_____	_____
Thursday, November 14	_____	_____

Please return by _____

Notes confirming the exact time and date of the conference should be sent home. This ensures that both teacher and parent have the same understanding of the conference time. This confirmation note from the teacher to each parent could be personal, or a form could be used (see Figure 6.8).

Private and Comfortable Meeting Places

How often have you gone into a school, walked down the halls, and seen parents and teachers trying to have a private conversation in the midst of children and other adults? To achieve open, two-way communication, parent and teacher need to talk in confidence. Select a room designed for conferences or use an empty classroom, and attach a note to the door so people won't interrupt. Give the parents adult-size chairs so they can be comfortable and on the same level as the teacher. Place a table in front of the chairs so materials, class projects, and the student's work can be exhibited. The parent, teacher, and student (if it is a three-way conference) can sit around the table and talk and exchange information. The room should be well ventilated and neither too warm nor too cold.

    Teachers also should be alert to psychological and physical barriers. People conducting interviews often set up such barriers to maintain social distance or imply a status relationship; an executive might sit behind a desk to talk with a subordinate. When teachers set themselves apart from the parents, a barrier is created.

Two-Way Communication in Conferences

Conditions necessary for effective communication during conferences include an attitude of caring shown through attentive behaviors such as smiling and other positive body language. Along with warmth is empathy, the ability to listen and respond in such a way that the parent knows you understand. Respect is key to the success of building a collaborative connection between parent and teacher. If teachers and parents respect each other and enter the conference with a warm, caring attitude, able to listen effectively and understand the other's meanings and feelings, the stage is set for a successful conference (Rotter & Robinson, 1986; Esparza, 2007).

    Some school administrators and teachers make the mistake of seeing parent–school communication as the school informing the parent about the educational process, rather than as a two-way system. During a conference, the teacher should spend only about half the time speaking. If teachers recognize the conference as a

Figure 6.8 Sample Reminder Note

This note confirms and reminds of conference times.

Dear _____:

    Thank you for your response to our request for a conference time about your child's progress. Your appointment has been set for _____ (time) on _____ (day, month, and date) in room _____.

    We have set aside _____ minutes for our chance to talk together. If the above time is not convenient, please contact the office, and we can schedule another time for you. We are looking forward to meeting with you.

                                                              Best wishes,

                                                  _____

                                                  Teacher

---

sharing time, half the burden has been lifted from their shoulders. They can use half the time to get to know the parent and child better.

During conferences, communicators need to believe that what they have to say is important to the listener. Body language can reflect feelings contrary to the spoken word, causing the verbal message to be misunderstood or missed altogether. It is important to be aware of what you are communicating. If you are rushed, pressured, or concerned about your own family, you will have to take a deep breath, relax, and concentrate on the conference. Just as important is to know cultural gender boundaries in order not to offend families.

Just as some physical gestures communicate distraction or lack of interest, some types of body language convey your interest and attention to parents' concerns. Use appropriate, attentive behavior to signal your interest, such as the following:

1. *Eye contact.* Make sure you look at the person as you communicate. Failure to do so could imply evasion, deception, or lack of commitment.

2. *Forward posture.* Leaning forward shows interest in what is being said. Be comfortable but do not slouch, which can indicate that the whole process is boring or unimportant.

3. *Body response.* A nod in agreement, a smile, and use of the body to create an appearance of interest promote empathy. If you act aware and interested, you will probably become interested. If you do not, perhaps you are in the wrong profession.

Understandable Language

Specialized language gets in the way of communication. Each year, new terms and acronyms become common language in the schools, but they freeze communication when used with people not familiar with the terms. Imagine a teacher explaining to a parent that the school has decided to use the SRA program this year in second grade, but the first grade is trying balanced literacy instruction; or one who says, "I've been using behavior modification with Johnny this year, and it has been very effective, but with Janet I find TA more helpful." Jargon can create misunderstanding and stop communication.

Sometimes terms have meaning for both communicators, but the meanings are not the same. Hymes (1974) declared that lack of communication, superficial communication, and "words and vocabulary, without friendship and trust and knowledge, get in the way of understanding" (p. 33):

> Look, for example, at "progressive education." Use those words and you have a fight on your hands. People get emotional, and wild charges fly. Yet parents will be the first to say, "Experience is the best teacher"—and there you have it! Different words, but a good definition of what progressive education stands for. (Hymes, 1974, p. 33)

Practice

To achieve the ability to listen reflectively and respond in a positive manner, practice until it becomes natural.

You can practice alone, but it is more effective if you can roleplay the conference. Having an observer present provides both practice and feedback. Teachers can choose a typical case from among their records or invent a hypothetical one. For example:

> Andy, a precocious third-grade child, spends most of the class period doodling ideas in a notebook. Although he completes his assignments, Andy takes no pride in his work and turns in messy papers. Special enrichment centers in the classroom do not attract him. Andy participates positively during recess and in physical education and music.

Each participant in the roleplay has basic information: the child's sex, the grade assigned, and the background. Assign one participant to act as the parent, another as the teacher. The third member of the team observes the interaction between the parent and teacher to check on the following:

1. Reflective listening
2. Attentive behavior (eye contact, forward posture, etc.)
3. Sensitivity to parents' feelings
4. Positive language
5. Cooperative decision making

Because no two teachers or parents are identical, there is no prescribed way to have a conference. The dialogue will be a constant flow, filled with emotions as well as objective analysis. You can prepare yourself, however, by practicing good reflective listening and positive communication. Look forward to sharing together.

Preparation for the Conference

Two types of preparation will set the stage for a successful conference. The first, an optional program, involves training teachers and parents for an effective conference. The second is essential—analyzing the child's records, current performance and attitude, and relationships with peers, and gathering examples of work along with recent standardized test results. For teachers, it is important to engage in professional development that will guide them to have successful parent–teacher conferences. Perhaps one way to do this is for the school principal or director to include this at the beginning of the school year's professional development. In addition, institutions of higher education must ensure that all students engage in professional development regarding parent–teacher conferences (Walker & Dotger, 2012).

Preconference Workshops and Guides

Workshops for parents, teachers, or a combination of both are fruitful. A discussion of what makes a conference a success or a calamity can bring forth an enormous number of tips for both parents and teachers. If parents and teachers form small groups, many ideas will emerge that can be recorded on the board for discussion later by the total group. Encourage parents to ask questions about their part in conferences. Clarifying objectives and expectations will help parents understand their responsibilities. Parents and teachers attending a workshop together can learn the art of reflective listening and communication. Role-playing during conferences can elicit discussion. Many participants will see themselves in the roles portrayed and will attempt to find alternative methods of handling conference discussions. Videos or YouTube video clips that illustrate common communication problems can also be used as starters for discussion.

At the close of the workshop, handouts or conference guides can be distributed to the participants. The guide should be designed with the school's objectives in mind. Parents can be told what to expect in the school's report and what the school expects from them. If your school does not schedule preconference workshops, put the handout in a newsletter and send it home to the parents before the conference. Questions in the conference guide should be those the school would like answered and also ones the parents might be interested in knowing. Typical questions include the following:

- How does your child seem to feel about school?
- Which activities does your child talk about at home?
- Which activities seem to stimulate your child's intellectual growth?
- How does your child spend free time?
- Is there anything that your child dreads?
- What are your child's interests and hobbies?

Some schools might also include questions about current concerns:

- What concerns do you have?
- What kinds of support or collaboration would you like from the school to help your family?

A similar memo suggests questions the parents might want to ask:

- How well does my child get along with other children? Who seem to be my child's best friends?
- How does my child react to discipline? What methods do you use to promote self-discipline and cooperation?
- Does my child select books at the proper reading level from the library?
- Does my child use study periods effectively?
- Are there any skills you are working on at school that we might reinforce at home?
- Do you expect me to help my child with homework?
- Are there any areas in which my child needs special help?
- Does my child display any special interests or talents at school that we might support at home?
- Does my child seem to be self-confident, happy, and secure? If not, what do you think the home or school can do to increase my child's feelings of self-worth?

Supplying questions before the conference is helpful in preparing parents, but it can also limit questions that develop naturally. In addition, if these questions are strictly adhered to during conferences, they can limit the scope, direction, and outcome of the conference. A checklist (Figure 6.9) can help ensure everything is covered.

Teacher Preparation

Throughout the school year, teachers should make a practice of accumulating anecdotal records, tests, workbooks, art projects, and papers that represent both academic and extracurricular areas. Folders created by students, an accordion file, or a file box or cabinet can store the papers until conference time. Students can then compile a notebook or folder of samples of their work to share with their parents during conferences.

The file is worked on periodically throughout the term, with papers placed in chronological order, thus illustrating progress in each subject. The child's work is an essential assessment tool.

Standardized tests that reveal the child's potential compared with actual performance level are useful in tailoring an education program to fit the student. With this information, parents and teachers can discuss whether the student is performing above or below potential. Parents and teachers can use the information to plan for the future.

One word of caution on the use of standardized tests: These tests are not infallible. One child might not feel well on the day of testing; another might freeze when taking tests. Standardized test results should be used to supplement informal assessment tools, such as class papers, notebooks, class observation, and informal tests, but should not be used to replace those tools. With the increasing number of tests children are now mandated to take at every grade level, it is very possible that children will "burn out" or simply refuse to complete the standardized tests. Therefore, it is important to be selective in administering tests.

If standardized test results and your informal assessment are congruent and the child scores high on aptitude tests and shows moments of brilliance in class but consistently falls short on work, you can be fairly certain that the child is not working up to his or her ability. If the child scores low but does excellent work in class, observe closely before deciding that the he or she is under too much pressure to achieve. In these cases, the test might not indicate the child's true potential. Should the child score low on the test and also show a high level of frustration when working, you may want to make plans to gear the work closer to the child's ability. The standardized test, used as a backup to the informal assessment, can help teachers and parents plan the child's educational program.

Congruent Beliefs About the Child

Have you ever had a child who constantly disrupts the class only to discover that the child behaves well during Scouts? Sometimes the disparity makes one wonder if it is the same child. It is difficult to discuss a child on common ground if the parents' and teacher's perceptions of

Figure 6.9 Conference Checklist
A checklist reviews important conference practices.

Conference Checklist

Yes	No	Did You
☐	☐	1. Review information about the child's family? Did you know the parents' last names? Were you aware of the child's educational experience?
☐	☐	2. Prepare ahead by collecting anecdotal records, tests, papers, notebooks, workbooks, and art materials from the beginning to the end of the reporting period?
☐	☐	3. Provide book exhibits, displays, or interesting reading for parents as they waited for their conferences?
☐	☐	4. Make arrangements for coffee or tea for parents as they waited for their conferences?
☐	☐	5. Prepare your room with an attractive display of children's work?
☐	☐	6. Welcome the parents with a friendly greeting?
☐	☐	7. Start on a positive note?
☐	☐	8. Adjust your conference to the parents' needs and levels of understanding?
☐	☐	9. Have clear objectives for the conference?
☐	☐	10. Say in descriptive terms what you meant? Did you avoid educational jargon and use of initials?
☐	☐	11. Listen reflectively?
☐	☐	12. Keep the communication lines open? Were you objective and honest?
☐	☐	13. Avoid comparing students or parents? Did you discuss other teachers only if it was complimentary?
☐	☐	14. Check your body language? Were you alert to the parents' body language?
☐	☐	15. Plan the child's educational program together?
☐	☐	16. Summarize your decisions? Did you make a record of your agreements and plans?
☐	☐	17. Begin and end on time? If you needed more time, did you set up another appointment?
☐	☐	18. Follow up with a note and a telephone call?

If you had the student lead the conference, in addition to the above

Yes	No	Did You
☐	☐	1. Work with the student to develop goals and objectives?
☐	☐	2. Encourage the student to achieve his/her goals and objectives?
☐	☐	3. Have the student prepare a portfolio with projects, papers, research, tests, and other achievements?
☐	☐	4. Have practice sessions in which the student developed the ability to explain objectives and progress? (Students may work with partners and/or other peers.)
☐	☐	5. Make yourself available to discuss the student's progress with the family during the conference period?

---

the child are completely different. Teachers and parents might need to compare their perceptions of the child. It is often meaningful to have students sort their own views so the perceptions of teacher, parents, and student can be compared.

Conference Membership

When children are taught by more than one teacher or have contact with numerous specialists (such as a speech teacher or physical therapist), including all professionals involved with the child is appropriate and requires cooperative planning. Beware of the effect on the parent, however, because a ratio of four professionals to one parent can be foreboding. If special care is taken to assure parents that all specialists are there to clarify and work with the teacher and parent as a team, the cooperative discussion and planning can have worthwhile results.

An alternative plan allows the parent to talk individually with each involved specialist. In some schools, the homeroom teacher reports for all the specialists, but personal contact with each person involved with the child's education is more satisfying to the parents. If time is short, the entire group could meet with the parents once in the fall and assure the parents they will be available whenever the parents have a concern.

Consider including the child in the conference. Who is better equipped to clarify why the child is doing well or needs extra help? Who has more at stake? Preschoolers make less sustained conference members, but as soon as the child becomes interested in assessment and evaluations and recognizes the goal of parent–teacher conferences, the teacher should consider including the child in the process. Initially, the child may attend for a short portion of the conference, but as interest and attention span increase, the child might be present for the entire conference. If portions of the conference need to be conducted without the child present, have a supervised play area available. If older students are included as members of the team, issues can be clarified and goals set. The student is part of the discussion and helps in setting realistic goals.

Bjorklund and Burger (1987) describe a four-phase process for collaboration with parents. *Phase 1*, scheduled early in the year, sets the stage with an overview of when conferences will take place, techniques for observation of the children, and a detailed account of the curriculum based on developmental goals. During this phase, both the teachers and parents are encouraged to consider the developmental goals of the program. *Phase 2* is based on the goals. Parents, teachers, and administrators meet and set priorities using observation, testing, anecdotal records, and work samples. Two to four goals are given priority for each child. In *Phase 3*, observations, anecdotal records, checklists, and rating scales are collected for review. *Phase 4* involves the child. The teacher sends a progress report home in which all the developmental areas are reviewed. A guide for the conference is also sent, with three questions that parents should discuss with the child before the meeting: (a) What do you like best about school? (b) Who are some of the special friends you like to play with at school? (c) Are there any things at school you would like to do more often? The teacher "begins the progress conference by sharing examples of the child's growth through anecdotes which describe some of the child's best skills or characteristics. This leads into a discussion of the three questions with the child" (Bjorklund & Burger, 1987, p. 31). The conference promotes a good self-image for the child by emphasizing the child's positive growth.

Student–Teacher–Parent Conferences

Many schools have conferences that give the task of deciding about objectives and goals to students. The advantage of this approach is that it empowers students to be responsible for their own learning. The conference planning involves the teacher, any special professionals, and the student. In a private setting, the teacher and student decide what the student is going to accomplish. Young and Behounek (2008) describe an interesting program where kindergarten students use PowerPoints to lead the parent–teacher–student conference. Every slide of the PowerPoint focuses on the child's day. The children answer questions for each slide, for example, "What do you like to do at school?" or "What's your favorite job in kindergarten?" PowerPoints provide an opportunity for young children to visually and verbally share their progress in school.

When conference time arrives, the student and teacher(s) meet in advance to decide what they will talk about at conference time and what they will put in the portfolio to share with the parents. These conferences involve more planning with the student than the traditional conference. At conference time, the student leads the discussion of what has been accomplished, what needs to be worked on, and what the future goals are. The concept behind this conference is similar to the Individualized Education Plan in that plans are made for individual students, but the pupil is more responsible for determining the objectives and goals.

Some schools organize student–teacher–parent conferences into a participatory situation with four sets of parents and children meeting at the same time. Each

Shorrocks/Getty Images

A child can participate in a parent–teacher conference.

Kali Nine LLC/Getty Images

To promote the well-being of a child, parent conferences need to be open, cooperative, and sensitive to the child's needs.

set discusses the children's achievements and goals. The teacher enters the discussion whenever a parent or child has questions or comments or when the teacher has a reason for participating in their conference. At some point during the session, each set of parents and students include the teacher in their discussion.

Different issues arise with this change in the format of the conference. With this type of conference, the child and parents are responsible for its success. Teachers must have good organizational and leadership skills so the student has established goals and direction before the conference. During the conference, the teacher will not have the opportunity to monopolize the discussion, but the student and parents must take the teacher's responsibility seriously if the conference is to be successful.

Congruent Expectations

Conferences go more smoothly when the teacher and parents have congruent expectations about the performance of the child. If the child is an excellent student and both teacher and parents are pleased with the evaluation it is easy to accept the report. If the child has a disability and both teacher and parents recognize the condition they can work together to plan an appropriate program for the child.

Too often the outward signs of good marks and pleasant personality and behavior fail to uncover how the child feels and whether the teacher can make the educational experience more satisfying and challenging. In working with a successful student, parents and teachers may fail to communicate about the child's potential and the need to have a good self-concept. Special interests of the child, friends, reading preferences, experiences, and needs are important for the teacher to know. Bring the child into the decision-making process. Together, the parents, teacher, and child can plan activities that will encourage growth and improve self-concept. Let these parents and children communicate, too.

SITUATION.   Denzel is one of those students every teacher loves to have in class. He is enthusiastic, stays on task, completes his work, and never causes a disturbance. A quiet, attractive boy with his long brown hair pulled back in a ponytail, Denzel always does the correct thing. He is polite to everyone and avoids fighting or taking sides when others are arguing.

Mrs. Jackson relaxed in her chair as she prepared for the conference with Denzel's parents. "What an easy conference," she thought. "I really don't have to talk with Denzel's parents because he fits into the routine, is well adjusted, and is progressing nicely." As she looked up, she saw Mrs. Johnson, Denzel's mother, standing outside the door. She rose to greet her and led her into the room, offering her a chair. As they sat side by side, Mrs. Jackson remarked, "It is really good to see you, Mrs. Johnson. I enjoy Denzel in class, and he is having no problems. Here are some of the papers I have collected. You can see that he completes his work and does a good job. I wish all my students were like Denzel."

After looking over the papers, Mrs. Johnson looked up and said, "It is nice not to have to worry about Denzel. I wish that Tanisha were as conscientious. I'm dreading that conference. I've really enjoyed having you be Denzel's teacher."

Mrs. Jackson and Mrs. Johnson glanced at Denzel's papers and leaned back, satisfied.

"Look at the time; we finished in 10 minutes," Mrs. Johnson said. "You have five minutes to spare. Have a good day."

"You have a good day, too," the teacher said as she escorted Denzel's mother to the door.

1. What did the conference accomplish?

2. Could there be a problem? How does Denzel feel?

3. What should Mrs. Johnson and Mrs. Jackson consider as they think about Denzel? Does Denzel feel good about himself? Is he a class leader? Does he get along well with the other children?

4. What does he enjoy doing the most? Is there anything that might make his school career even better?

SITUATION. "Welcome, Mrs. Estrada. We are so pleased to have Jaime with us this year," said Jaime's preschool teacher, Mr. López, greeting the boy's mother.

"He's just so happy to be here," Mrs. Estrada said. "He was a little anxious at first, but you have made him feel welcome."

"I'm pleased Jaime is beginning to feel comfortable. I noticed that he is interacting with the other children more—he played on the jungle gym today. His coordination is improving, and he is much more outgoing than he was three weeks ago when he first started. Let me share some of his paintings and some stories we have recorded. He illustrated this story. Look at the detail. What a great imagination!"

Mr. López and Mrs. Estrada looked at the papers together.

"What does Jaime enjoy doing at home?" Mr. López asked.

"He becomes very involved in building with his LEGO set," Mrs. Estrada said. "He loves to have us read him stories. We share stories together each afternoon and in the evening before he goes to bed. I try to limit his television viewing, though he does get to watch *Sesame Street* and *Mister Rogers* occasionally."

"Does he have any children to play with in his neighborhood?"

"There are no 4-year-old children, but Beto, who lives down the street, is in kindergarten, and he plays with Jaime about three times a week."

"I'll bet they enjoy playing together!" Mr. López said and then turned to the current class activities.

"Our theme for this month is the sun," he said. "We're studying shadows, reflections, and how the sun helps flowers to grow. These are some of the collages we have made. As you can see, a lot of the pictures were made by tearing paper but we are also working on cutting. Let me show you how we are having him hold his scissors. Do you think you can help him with this at home? I'll be sending home activity suggestions and notes that let you know what we are doing at school."

"Thank you," Mrs. Estrada said. "That way, I'll be more able to help Jaime at home if he needs it."

"Why don't you go into the observation room and watch him for a while before you leave," Mr. López said. "Don't forget that you can observe anytime, and you might want to volunteer to help in the preschool."

Jaime's mother looked surprised and answered, "I hadn't thought about that, but it might be enjoyable."

"What haven't we covered? Do you have any questions that we neglected to discuss?" Mr. López asked. After a pause, he added, "It was nice to be able to share with you about Jaime's experiences here. Be sure to call if you have any concerns or if something is happening at home that we should know about. We want to keep in touch."

"I enjoyed talking with you. I can see why Jaime enjoys school so much. *Gracias,* thank you. Goodbye," Jaime's mother said as she walked toward the observation room.

1. What was effective in this conference?
2. Did the mother get to share enough?
3. What would you suggest to make it better?

SITUATION. Ashley, a charming 7-year-old with big brown eyes, curly black hair, and a sparkling smile, seemed older than most children her age. When she came into the classroom before school started, she always went up to Miss Allen and told her about what was going on in her neighborhood. The stories were usually about fights, guns, holdups, gangs, and anger. There was reason to believe that she was relating what she had actually witnessed or heard. Ashley lived with her father; her mother had disappeared several years earlier and, although Ashley knew she was still alive, she had no contact with her. At one period in Ashley's life, she lived in a cardboard box. Life had not been easy for this child, who had experienced much change and abuse.

When school started, Ashley was unable to stay on task. She seemed to crave attention, whether it be from sharing information, describing a story in the author's chair, or acting out. Her primary method of obtaining attention was through acting out. She spoke out of turn, took pencils from other children, and shoved and pushed. Because she was large for her age, she could hurt another child with a shove.

One day, Ashley threatened an aide working in the classroom by suggesting that her older sister would beat her up. Time-outs did not help because she did not oblige, but she did seem to be threatened by a trip to the office. The school year was in its fourth week and there had been no parent–teacher conferences.

1. What would you suggest the teacher do to obtain parent collaboration?

2. Do you believe that parent–school cooperation is feasible? Why or why not?

3. What could you do as a teacher to help Ashley become a productive child?

4. Would a conference that included Ashley and her father be a good idea? Why or why not?

5. If you believed that Ashley comes from an abusive home, would you change your approach? Why or why not?

Preconference Preparation

Before the day of the conference and throughout the reporting period, you, as the teacher, prepare by getting to know the student, conducting ongoing assessment, and developing a portfolio. Before the conference, review the child's history, cultural background, family situation, successes, and concerns. Depending on which records are kept by the school, try to learn about the student's educational experience. Review the papers in the current portfolio so you can know the student's growth or delay that has occurred under your guidance.

Try to have three- to five-minute individual conferences with each child to talk about what you are going to cover in the conference. Determine if there is anything the child would like to see included, thus providing you with insight into the child's thoughts. If you recognize the children's thoughts as important, you increase their respect for self and their belief in the teacher or a caring ally.

The Day of the Conference

Relax before conference time. It is important to establish a cooperative climate. If the teacher is relaxed and poised, parents will be able to relax too, and the climate for communication will be improved. Meyers and Pawlas (1989) recommend developing a form to use for recordkeeping for planning, as well as keeping records for future conferences. The teacher is able to focus on one or two predetermined issues and keep records of the collaboration. Multiple concerns can be overwhelming; time does not allow all issues to be resolved. When determining the issues to be discussed, however, parents should have the option of helping determine the agenda. Perhaps they have a concern that is not known by the teacher. They can either share their concerns by sending back an information sheet suggesting what they would like to discuss, or during the conference the teacher can encourage them to bring up their concerns or comments.

Why do parents enter into parent–teacher conferences with apprehension? Some are worried because they want the best for their child but do not know how to achieve it. They are unsure of themselves in the discussion and might be threatened by jargon. The parent–teacher conference should be an opportunity for the exchange of ideas and information and a chance to support each other; both can enter into the conference with enthusiasm and confidence.

The Conference

Begin the conference in a relaxed, positive manner. During the conference, review your objectives, use effective communication skills, discuss concrete examples of work, and plan together.

Besides being adept at reflective listening, you need to listen intuitively to determine if parents have problems within their homes or are themselves emotionally immature. Such problems make it difficult for the child to have the home support needed for educational success. Remember that you, as the teacher, can gain a great deal of knowledge and understanding of the child from the parents and the conference is a good way to gain that knowledge.

When indicated, invite other professionals, such as the school's social worker or principal, to the conference to support and help the family and child. We want to learn more from the parents in order to understand the child's needs (Cannella, 2002).

SANDWICH APPROACH. Use the sandwich approach for the conference (Manning, 1985). Start the conference with pleasant and positive items. If you have negative comments or concerns to be discussed, bring them up during the middle of the conference. Always end with a positive summary, spend time planning with parents, and make a pleasant comment about the child.

CLEAR STATEMENT OF OBJECTIVES. Some objectives may be universal; others will be specific for the individual conference. Use the following objectives as a guide:

1. To gain a team member (the parent) in the education of the child
2. To document the child's progress for the parent
3. To explain the educational program you are using as it relates to the individual child
4. To learn about the environment in which the child lives
5. To allow the parents to express feelings, questions, and concerns
6. To get a better understanding of the expectations the parent holds for the child
7. To set up a lasting network of communication among parent, teacher, and child
8. To establish cooperative goals for the education of the child

THE PARENT AS PART OF THE TEAM. After you have made sure the room is comfortable, two-way communication will be uninterrupted, and you are ready to listen and be responsive to the parent, it is easy to recognize the parent as a part of the educational team. Parents arrive at conferences as experts on their children's history, hobbies, interests, likes and dislikes, friends, and experiences. Explain to the parents that all participants in the conference are members of a team looking at the progress of the child and working together to benefit the child. How can *we* help the child who is having a difficult time? How can *we* enrich the program for the child who is accelerated? How can *we* get the child to do the task at hand? How can *we* promote self-esteem? If the teacher and parents work as a team to answer these questions, the conference will be far more productive than if the teacher simply dictates answers to the parents. Here are some tips that will help parents feel they are part of the team:

- Review your file and know enough about the child before the parent arrives that the parent can tell you have taken a personal interest in the child's welfare.
- Know the parent's name. Do not assume that the child and parent have the same last name. Look in the record for the correct name.

- Ensure the privacy of the conference.
- Begin on a positive note. Start by praising an accomplishment of the child or a contribution the child has made to the class.
- Know the time limitations.
- Do not use terminology that might have meaning for you but not the parent.
- Do not refer to organizations, forms, tests, materials, or ideas by their initials or acronyms. Do not assume that everyone knows what the initials or acronyms mean.
- Have some questions ready about the child and show interest in the child.
- Remind parents that they may ask questions at any time and that you will be pleased to explain anything that is not clear.
- Stay on topic: the child's schooling and development.
- Encourage the parents to contribute. Try to have parents to talk at least 50% of the time.
- Show that you understand the parent by checking periodically during the conference. For example, you might ask, "Would you agree with this?" or "Do you have suggestions to add about this?"
- Make note of an idea suggested by a parent, but do not get so involved in writing that you lose the flow of the conversation.
- Keep in mind the parents' cultural background and follow culturally appropriate rules.
- Use attentive behaviors—that is, lean forward, look interested, and nod when in agreement.
- Do not ignore a parent's question.
- Be honest yet tactful and sensitive to the parent's feelings.
- Base your discussion on objective observation and concrete examples of work.
- Deal in specifics rather than generalities whenever possible.
- Evaluate needs and select methods of remediating difficulties.
- Evaluate strengths and select methods of enriching those strengths.
- Plan educational goals together.

- Talk about how you have modified your teaching to meet the needs of the child.
- Clarify and summarize the discussion.
- Make plans to continue the dialogue.

Concrete Examples of a Child's Work and Development

Both parent and teacher are interested in the child's accomplishments. By making objective observations of the child's classroom behavior along with anecdotal notes collected throughout the reporting periods, the teacher documents the child's social as well as intellectual achievements. Anecdotal records of significant behaviors are especially valuable for conferences with parents of young children. Papers and tests might not be available, so the anecdotal records become tools for evaluating the child's social, intellectual, and physical progress. In the case of children with behavioral difficulties, it is also important to be able to cite specific incidents rather than vague generalizations about incidents. Keep anecdotal records in electronic files.

The accumulated examples of the child's work with a few words from the teacher also illustrate to parents what their child is doing. It is not necessary to state when a child has not progressed, for that will be obvious. If another child has made great progress, that too will be evident from the samples collected. Consider asking parents if they have come to the same conclusion as you when comparing early and subsequent papers.

Some teachers supplement papers and anecdotal records with videos of children in the classroom. Although time-consuming, a video report is enjoyable for parents and encourages interaction between parent and teacher on the child's classroom participation.

Bringing concrete examples to the conference illustrating the child's work can prevent a confrontation and allows parent and teacher to analyze the work together. Include anecdotal records and samples of the child's work in comparison with expected behavior at that age level. In preschool, this can include fine-motor control, large-muscle activities, art, and problem solving. For school-age children, examples can include papers, artwork, projects, work in academic subjects, tests, notebooks, workbooks, and anecdotal records. It is also helpful to parents for the teacher to collect a set of unidentified "average" papers. If parents want to compare their child's work with that of the "average" child, they have a basis for this comparison.

Whatever the level of the child's performance, the parent and teacher need to form a team as they evaluate the child's educational progress and work together for the good of the child.

Use the conference form recommended by Meyers and Pawlas (1989) to keep a record. Parents and teacher—and student, if in attendance—decide on goals, highlights, or accomplishments, and plans for the future. All attendees should read and sign the conference form and retain a copy.

Postconference Plans

After the conference, write a note thanking the parents for their participation. Later, in a follow-up telephone call, let the parents know how the conference plans are being implemented and how the student is participating. Each contact increases the parent–school collaboration.

A checklist can be used for self-evaluation, as shown in Figure 6.9. If you are able to answer yes to these questions, you are ready to have productive parent–teacher conferences.

Positive Communication Calms Emotions

What do you do when an upset parent confronts you? Most professionals face such a situation at one time or another. Margolis and Brannigan (1986) list seven steps to help you control the volatile situation and allow the parent to regain composure. If you understand the dynamics of anger, you can engage in reflective listening. As a result, you can redirect the wrath and empathize with the parent. The steps include the following:

1. Remain calm and courteous, and maintain natural eye contact through the barrage. After the parents have expressed their anger, usually dominated by emotion, ask them to repeat their concerns so you can understand the situation better. The second time around, the statements are usually more comprehensible and rational.

2. Use reflective listening and give reflective summaries of their statements. You can explore the content of their messages later, but during this stage try to establish a more relaxed and trusting atmosphere.

3. Continue with reflective listening, and ask some open-ended questions that allow them to talk more as you gain greater understanding.

4. Keep exploring until you have determined what the underlying critical issues are. Do not evaluate, and do not be defensive.

5. After the issues have been fully explored, rephrase and summarize, including points of agreement. Check to see if your summary of their concerns is correct. Offer to let them add to what you have summarized. When you clearly define the concerns, they often seem more manageable.

6. Margolis and Brannigan (1986) point out that by now, listening has been used to build trust and defuse the anger. You are more likely to understand the problem from the parent's perspective. When the first five steps "are followed in an open, sincere, and empathetic manner, disagreements frequently dissolve and respect emerges" (p. 345). If such is not the case, go back and allow free exploration again.

7. Use a systematic problem-solving approach to any issues that remain unresolved. The steps in collaborative problem solving include (a) understand each other's needs and the resources available to help satisfy those needs, (b) formulate a hypothesis that might solve the problem, (c) brainstorm other solutions, (d) combine ideas and solutions to create new solutions, (e) develop criteria to judge the solutions together, (f) clarify and evaluate solutions, and (g) select the most likely solution. At the end of the confrontation, the result should satisfy both educator and parent.

SITUATION.   "I've never come to a school conference without having to wait 45 minutes to talk with you. Then, when I get in, you rush me, never let me ask questions, and just tell me how poorly Mary is doing. I know that Mary is doing poorly! I have my hands full just trying to go to work and feed my four children. Can't you do something to help Mary? Do you care?" Mary's father breathlessly expressed his anger and frustration.

"Hold on, Mr. Washington," Mr. Bonner said. "You're responsible for Mary, not me. She does poorly because she doesn't pay attention; she's more interested in her friends than in school, and she cuts class. I can work with students who come to school ready to learn. I just don't have the strength or the patience to take on your daughter until she changes her attitude."

"I waited 45 minutes to hear that?" Mr. Washington asked. "What's going on here? No wonder Mary skips school. Where's the superintendent's office? I need to talk with your supervisor." Mr. Washington stormed out of the room.

1. How could Mr. Bonner respond in a manner to reduce Mr. Washington's anger?

2. What kind of interaction should take place to promote problem solving?

3. Is there anything Mr. Bonner can do to help this situation?

4. What can Mr. Washington do to help resolve his daughter's problems?

5. What responsibility does Mary have?

Making a Contract: Parent–Teacher Communication

Most teachers have experienced working with children who do not stay on task, daydream, act out in class, or seem to be wasting their potential. Parents of these children are usually just as concerned as the teacher. In a contract arrangement, the parents are empowered to get involved in the child's school behavior. In an effort to increase the student's positive participation in school, teachers and parents have an ongoing communication system that acknowledges how the child does in school. Parents and teachers work together to establish the goals and parameters of the contract. Usually a note is sent home each day detailing how the student performed at school. This includes schoolwork as well as classroom behavior. The parents reinforce the positive behavior and help diminish the negative. By communicating each day with a focus on the goals of the contract, parents and teachers form a team to help the child become successful in school.

Kelley (1990) describes a home-based reinforcement method in her book *School–Home Notes*. It is based on behavioral theory and is similar to the contract method. This approach is beneficial for children who have difficulty staying on task or who are not performing up to their abilities. The school–home note, or daily report card, is an intervention method that requires the participation of parents as well as teachers. Together they collaborate on problem solving and determine their approach. Each day, the teacher completes a simple form and sends it home, letting the parents know how the child behaved and participated in class that day. The parent follows up with consequences. It is important that the consequences fit and that they have the desired result: "The goals in any contingency management system are to reinforce appropriate behavior (so as to increase its frequency) and to ignore or punish inappropriate or unacceptable behavior (so as to decrease its frequency)" (p. 16). If the school–home contract or notes are not working, the teachers and parents should meet again and revise their plan. Positive and productive parent-teacher conferences promote effective family engagement.

Summary

Effective communication between parents and schools allows parents to become partners in education. Communication includes speaking, listening, the reflection of feelings, and interpretation of the meaning of the message. If the receiver does not correctly interpret the message sent, then miscommunication has occurred. Miscommunication is fixed by rephrasing and checking out meanings. Talking is not the most important element in communication. The way a message is spoken and the speaker's body language account for 93% of the message. Teachers and administrators must know and understand cultural ways of communicating for all families, but especially for culturally and linguistically diverse families.

It is essential for schools to have good communication with families. One-way communication describes the method that schools use when they offer parents information through newsletters, newspapers, media, and handbooks. Two-way communication allows parents to communicate with school personnel through telephone calls, home visits, classroom visits, and school functions. It continues through the year with classroom visits and participation, back-to-school nights, parent education groups, school programs, projects, workshops, PTA carnivals, exchanges, and a suggestion box.

Parents and schools both put up roadblocks to communication. Parent roadblocks include the following roles: "my own and my child's guardian," "I don't belong," avoidance, indifferent parent, "don't make waves," and "club-waving advocate." Roadblocks put up by schools include the following roles: "authority figure," "sympathizing counselor," "pass the buck," "protect the empire," and "busy teacher."

Effective communication and trust building between parent and educator are important. The areas of communication that can be developed include positive speaking, listening, reflective listening, rephrasing, reframing, and attentive behavior. PET, STEP, and Active Parenting all include communication with an emphasis on reflective or active listening in their parent education format.

Parent–teacher conferences are the most common form of two-way exchanges. Conferences can be effective if educators and parents prepare for them in advance. Teachers need to make parents feel welcome; materials and displays should be available. Two-way conversations will build cooperation and trust. Teachers can develop expertise in conducting conferences by relating to the parents, developing trust, and learning from them about the child. A checklist is included to analyze the effectiveness of the conference.

The chapter includes suggestions for dealing with angry parents and how to deal with concerns parents may have throughout the year.

Suggested Class Activities and Discussions

1. Develop a simple newsletter, a note to parents, and a detailed newsletter.

2. Practice speaking positively. Develop situations in which a child has average ability, has a learning disability, or is gifted. Role-play the parent and the teacher. Make the interaction focus on positive speaking. Then reverse your approach and become negative in your analysis of the child. How did you feel during each interchange? You can videotape the role playing, so you can analyze the results objectively.

3. Practice listening. Divide the class into groups of three. One person is the speaker, another is the listener, and the third is the observer. Exchange roles so each person in the group gets to play each role. Have each person select a topic of interest, from something as simple as "my favorite hideaway" to something as serious as "coping with death in my family." Each person tells a story; the listener listens and then repeats or rephrases the story. The observer watches for body language, attentive behavior, interest, and correct rephrasing. A checklist is an excellent way to make sure the observer watches for all elements of listening.

4. Visit a school and obtain a copy of the school's newsletter. Analyze it. Does it communicate with parents effectively? How would you improve it?

5. Consider both your belief and value systems. What beliefs might be roadblocks in communication with parents, particularly those with a different value system?

6. Brainstorm in class for words to use in rephrasing. For example, what words could you use to describe a child who hands in sloppy work?

7. Role-play the parent putting up roadblocks to communication.

8. Role-play the roadblocks that schools put up that hinder communication.

9. Sit in on a staffing or a parent–teacher conference. Observe the parents' and the educators' interaction.

10. Compose situations that need constructive, positive answers. Make up several answers that would be appropriate for each situation.

Useful Websites

National Coalition for Parent Involvement in Education

Global Family Research Project

Glossary Terms

Communication: The active participation of the sender to convey a message or thought to the receiver who in might or might not reciprocate action.

Message: Words or verbal stimuli.

One-way communication: Information imparted in one direction.

Two-way communication: Information imparted by both individuals participating in conversation.

Chapter 7
Teacher Leadership for Family Engagement

Teacher leadership is important because it helps create a positive classroom climate that enhances partnerships with families.

Mari Riojas-Cortez

Learning Outcomes

Leadership is important to create a positive school climate to enhance partnerships with families.

7.1 Define leadership and its importance for family engagement.

7.2 Describe how styles of leadership for teachers support family engagement.

7.3 Examine teacher leadership in family education.

7.4 Explain how to conduct a needs assessment for effective school–family partnerships and how to work with groups in family trainings or meetings.

7.5 Examine how effective teacher leaders guide the process for successful meetings.

Defining Leadership and Its Effect on Family Engagement

I was recently asked to describe the meaning of leadership. Because of my training as an early childhood educator, I thought that in order to address such a question, I needed to understand children's perceptions of leadership because we all have different perceptions depending on our background and funds of knowledge. I decided to ask a group of preschoolers, and to my amazement all indicated that, "a leader is someone who tells you to stay in line!" This is a thought-provoking answer. I don't necessarily think they were referring to the teacher but to the child who is cosen (or who volunteers) to be a leader in the classroom. The children's perception of a leader is someone who seems strong and provides some guidance. Additionally, it is

important to reflect if children and parents see teachers as leaders and perhaps the answer is a positive one. A Word search for synonyms of the word **"leader"** provided the following list: chief, principal, guide, mentor, head, manager, organizer, boss, director, person-in-charge, guru, and "top dog"! Perhaps teachers do fulfill all of those roles that help them lead their classroom, although often they are not thinking in terms of all of those roles.

Leadership is a skill that helps in all facets of human interactions, particularly for the good of an organization, such as the school and classroom. When teachers are effective leaders, the students and parents follow. Unfortunately, at times leaders can be egotistic, incompetent, ignorant, reckless, cruel, and even evil (Burns, 2017). We hope that the majority of the teachers as leaders do not manifest such terrible qualities, but we must be aware so that no harm is done to children and families. In order to avoid such types of leaders, teachers must work together to develop strong and positive beliefs about children and parents. Turner, Christensen, Kackar-Cam, Fulmer & Trucano (2017) identified the importance of professional learning communities where teachers learn from one another to increase the quality of instruction. This can only happen when teachers also have a strong connection with parents. Turner et al. (2017) indicated that the important practices of a learning community with teachers include shared values and norms, collaboration, a focus on student learning, reflective dialogues, and making practice public. Professional learning communities allow teachers to develop a sense of agency in teachers as they begin to understand that their role of instructional leader is much more than the implementation of curriculum in the classroom. It is important to have teachers guiding teachers as they are much more likely to listen to one another since they see themselves as equal and understand of each other's situation. As professional development leaders, teachers can encourage others to be engaged, to have the willingness to implement change and to respond to the needs of the group (Borko, Koellner, & Jacobs, 2011).

Leadership Training

There is an increased interest in how teachers develop as leaders (Ado, 2016). The teacher leader model standards developed by ten organizations including the National Education Association or NEA consist of seven domains that teachers need in order to have leadership roles in their schools. Domain VI focuses on "Improving outreach and collaboration with families and communities" (NEA, 2018). Clearly working with parents is of importance as teachers develop as leaders.

The Regional Educational Laboratory (REL) Midwest Educator Effectiveness Research Alliance and the Center on Great Teachers and Leaders developed a self-assessment tool for teachers to assess their "knowledge, skills and competencies to serve leadership roles" (Center on Great Teachers and Leaders at American Institutes for Research, 2017, p. 1). This self-assessment tool guides teachers to self-evaluate. The domains assessed include collaboration and communication, professional learning and growth, instructional leadership, and school community and advocacy.

Schools need strong leaders that can create a positive school climate for children and families to engage in the successful development of partnerships. Partnerships are needed in schools so children can have ample opportunities to grow not only in their general development but also in their academic knowledge. When teachers are successful at creating partnerships with parents at the classroom level, they become the leaders of their classroom. Strong leaders also mentor future leaders. Principals and directors must take on the task to mentor teachers so they have the characteristics of future leaders (Krieg, Smith, & Davis, 2014). By mentoring teachers, principals or directors are helping ensure that teachers take the lead in their classrooms to create strong partnerships with parents. When teachers work effectively with parents in their classrooms, they come to know and understand why they need to work with parents.

The Five Leadership Styles for Teachers

As you read this chapter, you may be wondering about the inclusion of the five leadership styles. Just as we have different teaching styles, leadership styles help us as teachers to lead children in their learning but also create a classroom climate where parents feel welcomed and part of the classroom, as such the families begin to engage. Knowing your leadership style will not only help you with the creation of a positive school and classroom climate, but also with engaging in positive partnerships with families. A leader is much more than just someone who delegates, organizes, or manages. A leader is someone who has a vision, who cares for others, who plans ahead, is inclusive, and most of all, is not afraid of change. Teachers develop their leadership style as they begin to work with children and families. Interestingly, culture, age, and gender can also have an effect on your leadership style (Rodríguez-Rubio & Kiser, 2013). The five styles of leadership we will discuss include servant, strategic, visionary, autocratic, and transformational.

1. *Servant Leadership* involves sharing the leadership between the leader and others. The leader seeks to meet the needs of others first, thus helping to empower and help. At the local level, community activists who seek to meet the needs of the people first may be considered servant leaders. In the context of the classroom, teachers who are servant leaders seek to meet the needs of the families first. Very often, servant leaders conduct a needs assessment of the families they serve in order to better

understand their needs. An educator who is a servant leader will always look for opportunities to help and assist families not only in their immediate physical needs but also in finding ways in which families can become engaged—for example, creating a variety of opportunities for families to attend meetings or creating different venues for participation based on each family's needs. For instance, if a family cannot attend PTA meetings because they have a child with special needs, a servant leader will make sure that appropriate childcare is provided for the child so the parents can attend the meeting. Another example includes the teacher that prepares snack packs for students who face food insecurity. Teachers who provide information for immigrant families regarding ESL courses or the school system are also servant leaders. Examples of servant leaders in the global community are Mother Teresa or Dr. Martin Luther King.

2. *Strategic Leadership* consists of preparing others for future change. In this type of leadership, awareness and action are very important. Setting goals using a strong strategic plan is crucial for these leaders. In addition, strategic leaders enable their followers by preparing them to follow (Brumm & Drury, 2013). For working with families, the strategic leader employs preparation skills that will help the school or center advance. For example, if a school or center is in need of increasing family involvement, a strategic leader will seek the help of teachers and parents to create a plan to increase family involvement. In the context of the classroom, the teacher as a strategic leader is well prepared to provide meaningful learning experiences for children where their funds of knowledge are integrated. For instance, when a teacher sees the need to increase enrollment in the Parent Teacher Association or PTA, the teacher will ensure that a plan is in place that will help attract families and teachers to join the PTA. The plan might include a change in the traditional way PTA business has been conducted, creating a more contemporary plan. Another example is when the teacher creates a strategic plan to change the way parents are engaged in their classroom. I once knew a teacher that strategically visited all of her students' parents before the beginning of the school year in order to be prepared to work with the children. I recall her telling me interesting stories that helped her

understand the children she taught, pushing her to develop lessons to support that learning and engage parents at the same time. One of the goals that she had was to increase the children's interest in reading. She knew that the only way to do it was to get the families to read. She planned a visit to the library, but not just a regular visit—it was a visit that was "strategically" planned to lead parents to get a library card and select reading materials. Her strategy proved to be successful in that parents not only got their library card, but also began to read and visit the library on a weekly basis on their own.

3. *Visionary Leadership* involves the creation of a vision to challenge the status quo. A visionary leader thinks about the organization in a broad sense and guides it to a new direction with imagination, creativity, and charisma (McKeown, 2012). Visionary leaders take risks, motivate, and communicate effectively with others. In the schools, visionary leaders embrace creative change and help all stakeholders take part in the new direction. A visionary leader will "think outside of the box" for family engagement. Rather than follow the norm, teachers who are visionary will find new ways of enhancing family engagement. A visionary educator might change the way meetings are held—for instance, shorter meetings during the week are better for many families. Another example includes reaching out to the community to enhance partnerships, thus truly using the ecological systems theory developed by Bronfenbrenner. Having a vision includes planning and networking. For example, an adaptive physical education coach wanted to provide after school activities that focused on sports to children with intellectual and physical disabilities. The coach noticed that the majority of these opportunities were not available in minority and low-income communities, so he decided to create those opportunities himself. Working with a non-profit organization that focused on sports and recreation activities for children with special needs, the coach was able to persuade them to provide these activities closer to the children's communities, and to engage a higher level of parent support.

4. *Autocratic Leadership* seeks to have complete power or control of an organization. Autocratic or authoritarian leaders often can be rigid and unwilling to listen to individuals in the organization, as they believe their ideas are best. They tend to work with

individuals who do not resist change, because they believe they can best support the leader's ideas (Inandi, Tunc, & Gilic, 2013). Autocratic leadership is often seen as negative because of the level of control individuals have over the organization. Interestingly, autocratic leaders attract individuals who have identity issues such as self-uncertainty (Rast, Hogg, & Giessner, 2013). Although this style of leadership might seem negative, there are situations where it is effective, such as in schools that are in great need of direction. It is important to remember that even when using this style of leadership, the principal or director remains respectful of all stakeholders, such as families, teachers, and students. A school might need an autocratic leader if the climate is chaotic and disorganized. An autocratic leader can bring order and structure to the school or center in order to meet the immediate needs of the children. A teacher leader might need to use autocratic leadership with a class where children are facing challenges. Being autocratic does not necessarily mean being unkind or disrespectful, as many autocratic leaders in history have been. It can simply mean that the teacher as leader has to make certain decisions for the good of the students in order to help them achieve. For example, some teachers must take the initiative to start special enrichment programs for children. The teacher decides on the type of program or club that s/he thinks would be of benefit for children such as choir or robotics. As one teacher creates these opportunities, other teachers may follow his/her example—even parents can become engaged.

5. *Transformational Leadership* occurs when the leader inspires others to accomplish and achieve goals through positive energy. A transformational leader has high commitment to a vision by inspiring motivation from others. According to Williamson (2014), there are two important competencies of a transformational leader: first, contextual intelligence, which allows the leader to see necessary changes in the future before anyone else; and second, strategic intelligence, which allows the leader to change past practices to new and intellectually stimulating ones. A transformational leader is always looking for ways to move the organization ahead and change with the times. For example, a transformational principal or director creates professional development opportunities for teachers in the use of technology for teaching and learning. Similarly, a transformational principal or director uses technology (a school website, Facebook, Twitter, etc.) to enhance communication and partnerships with parents. In addition, the principal or director ensures that someone always updates the school website or Facebook page daily or regularly so families can readily access important information and announcements. A great example of a teacher who is a transformational leader is Mrs. Rosas (not her real name) a teacher at a local elementary school that offers a dual language program. This program began as a typical dual language program where the focus was mostly on the language; however, with time and leadership from Mrs. Rosas it grew into a culturally relevant dual language program where the goal is not only for children to become biliterate but also bicultural. Important to note is that Mrs. Rosas was able to lead other teachers to ensure that the goals of the program were met and expanded.

Teacher Leadership in Family Education

Leadership in family education can be viewed along a continuum (see Figure 7.1) that ranges from a lay leader, or nonprofessional with little training, to a

Figure 7.1 Continuum of Leaders in Parent Education

Parent leader with no training	Parent leader with leadership training	Parent leader with a structured curriculum	Parent leader with professional support	Professional leader with parent participation	Professional

The background and experience of the parents provide an opportunity for sharing expertise and knowledge and create an impetus for self-directed learning.

knowledgeable expert with training. As a school leader, the principal or director will always look for trained professionals (such as consultants or teachers) who will work with teachers and families in a respectful and professional manner and who will never dominate the group with didactic teaching. The lay group should not be left without direction either.

The use of lay leaders—parents leading their own groups—encourages parents to be actively engaged. Because educational growth and positive change are what is wanted in parent education groups, active involvement is highly desired. More change will occur if the parent formulates some of the educational suggestions and acts upon the information. Parents are better able to develop ways of handling parent–child relationships if they develop their expertise from their own research and interact with other members of the group. This does not mean excluding experts in the field. At times, it is necessary to have an authority give background material. After the information from experts in the field is received, however, parents need to discuss and act upon it themselves. Thus, a strong principal or director and most importantly teacher will guide the parents and families in this very important task. If the school and classroom do not have strong leaders, this collaboration will not be possible. The leadership must be at different levels at all times school-classroom.

Lay leaders benefit from having guidelines to follow in developing their leadership skills. The leader's goal is to establish an environment that facilitates and guides members in achieving the objectives. Group members can participate more effectively if they are aware of their rights and responsibilities within the group. A handout on communication skills given to members early in the school term can help eliminate problems and encourage a relaxed, productive group (Figure 7.2). Use the handout as a guide. This handout, along with a description of group roles (Table 7.1), will enable group members to grow into productive participants in group interaction.

Figure 7.2 Criteria for Group Communication

CRITERIA FOR GROUP COMMUNICATION

1. Come to the meeting ready to ask questions and share your ideas.

2. Once your ideas and thoughts are given to the group, do not feel compelled to defend them. Once shared, they become the group's property to discuss and consider. Clarify meaning if it would help the group proceed, but don't feel responsible for the idea just because you suggested it.

3. Speak freely and communicate feelings. Listen to others with consideration and understanding for their feelings.

4. Accept others in the interchange of ideas. Allow them to have opinions that differ from yours. Do not ignore or reject members of the group.

5. Engage in friendly disagreements. Listen critically and carefully to suggestions others have to offer. Differences of opinion bring forth a variety of ideas.

6. Be sincere. Reveal your true self. Communicate in an atmosphere of mutual trust.

7. Allow and promote individual freedom. Do not manipulate, suppress, or ridicule other group members. Encourage their creativity and individuality.

8. Work hard, acknowledge the contributions of others, and focus on the objectives of the group's task.

Table 7.1 Role Interaction

Both task and maintenance roles are necessary for effective group participation.

Task Roles	Group Building or Maintenance Roles	Dysfunctional Roles
Initiator–leader	Encourager	Dominator
Facilitator	Harmonizer	Aggressor
Information giver/seeker	Listener	Negativist
Clarifier	Follower	Flirtatious
Questioner	Tension breaker	Blocker
Asserter	Compromiser	Competitor
Energizer	Standard setter	Recognition seeker
Elaborator	Observer	Deserter
Orientator	Recorder	Challenger
Opinion giver	Gatekeeper	
Opinion seeker		
Summarizer		

Needs Assessment and Working with Groups

An important aspect of teacher leaders is the development or implementation of family engagement. Before you begin a parent education program—and periodically during the program—you should determine the interests and needs of the families. In order to determine the needs of families, administrators and teachers must respond to their interests by having conversations about how to make connections in children's learning contexts and by providing leadership training (Darragh, 2009). A brainstorming session is an ideal mechanism for eliciting many ideas. Write down the ideas or questions that concern and interest the families. It is important to remember to provide the sessions in the language that parents understand or have translators that know the community in order to better communicate your thoughts and their thoughts (Buysse, Castro, & West, 2005).

Once you have developed your basic list of interests and concerns, give it to a trial group and ask the members to add new ideas and concerns. Next, construct a needs-assessment tool, listing possible topics or formats for parents. Disseminate the questionnaire to adults in the school or center community. Finally, choose from the questionnaire those items that received the most requests and develop a program to meet the needs of the community.

Needs assessments are necessary when new programs are developed as well as when established parent groups reassess their needs. Less formal assessments are used frequently by ongoing groups.

Interest Finders

If a parent group is already established, members can use a number of informal methods to indicate their interests. These range from brainstorming among the members to soliciting ideas in a suggestion box. It is important to use the families' home languages when possible in order to build strong partnerships through parent programs, such as in the examples shown next for Spanish-speaking families.

BRAINSTORMING.   For a brainstorming session, choose a recorder and encourage all members to contribute ideas for programs. A list of past successful programs can be distributed. Write ideas on a whiteboard (you can use chart paper, a chalkboard, or an overhead projector if a whiteboard is not available). Caution members not to judge any suggestions as being good or bad—all suggestions are valid at this point. After all suggestions are listed, have members choose, in writing, three to six ideas that interest them most. Keep in

Jim West / Alamy Stock Photo

A needs assessment helps discover topics of interest for parents.

mind the parents' cultural backgrounds and funds of knowledge. Develop your program from the interests that receive the most votes (or are most frequently mentioned). If the group has difficulty thinking of items, you may be able to generate responses by having participants complete statements such as those illustrated in Table 7.2. Notice that the questions are written in three different languages to include diverse linguistic backgrounds.

Table 7.2 The Brainstorming Question Template

My greatest concerns are . . . (*Mis preocupaciones son . . .*
我最大的担忧是。。。)

My greatest happiness comes from . . . (*Mi mayor felicidad viene de
. . .* 我最大的快乐来自于。。。)

If I had three wishes, I would . . . (*Si tuviera tres deseos, yo pediría
. . .* 如果我能够有三个愿望的话，我希望那将是。。。)

If I could eliminate one problem from my home, it would be . . .
(*Si pudiera eliminar un problema de mi hogar, ese sería . . .*
如果我可以解决一个家中的问题，那应该是。。。)

Questions that concern me about my child's education are . . .
(*Cosas que me preocupan acerca de la educación de mi niño(a)
son . . .* 一直困扰我的有关我的孩子教育的问题是。。。)

Questions that concern me about my child's development are . . .
(*Cosas que me preocupan acerca del desarrollo de mi niño(a) son
. . .* 一直困扰我的有关我的孩子发展的问题是。。。)

As a parent, I hope to be . . .(*Como padre de familia, espero ser . . .*
作为一个家长，我希望我会是。。。)

OPEN-ENDED QUESTIONS. Parent groups can solicit requests to gain a wider knowledge of the community and find out possible ways parents can become more involved in schools and the community. The leader asks parents to respond to such topics as those listed in Table 7.3.

QUESTIONNAIRES. Develop a questionnaire, such as Test Your Know-How as a Parent, that will bring out differences in opinions in the group and show where interests and room for learning occur.

QUESTION BOX. Some parents are hesitant to make suggestions in an open meeting. They might feel more comfortable dropping questions and comments in a box

Table 7.3 Samples of Open-Ended Questions

Questions/Preguntas	Answers/Respuestas
• What do I want to know about my school? *¿Qué me gustaría saber acerca de mi escuela?*	
• What do I want to know about my community? *¿Qué me gustaría saber acerca de mi comunidad?*	
• What would I like to do for my school and/or community? *¿Qué me gustaría hacer para mi escuela o comunidad?*	

Table 7.4 The Question Box Paper Template

Please share with us your questions and then insert this sheet in the "Question Box" at the office entrance.

Favor de compartir sus preguntas y colocar el papel en la "Caja de Preguntas" en la entrada de la officina.

that is available throughout the year (see Table 7.4). Make sure the box is visible enough that parents see it, but is located in a spot where their input can be made anonymously. For example, do not place the suggestion box by the administrative assistant's desk. Instead, place it on a table near the school's entrance. In addition, schools and classrooms can use digital "suggestion boxes" as a way to reach more parents. Similarly parent organizations can also use these type of apps to entice more parents to become engaged and provide their ideas.

Developing Objectives

After the group's interests have been assessed, the program is ready to be developed. Within most programs, at least two aspects should receive attention: the content and the changes in behavior and attitudes of the participants.

Most parents know when they want help with parenting skills, although reticent parents might need special encouragement. When a new family is formed and the first baby comes home to live, parents are intensely interested in knowing how to care for the baby. An opportune time for parent education is before the birth and during the child's first 3 years of life.

Parents are also ready for exchanging information during the child's preschool years. Parent education and preschool programs bring the professional and the parents together to share concerns and experiences.

During the child's school-age years, parent education programs that focus on learning activities, building family strengths, and concerns specific to the group are beneficial. The needs of school-age children differ from those of young children; therefore, parents need help to meet those needs. Parents need to share, ask questions, and be a part of the decision-making process.

Leaders Facilitating Learning Experiences for Families

Parent educators facilitate the learning experience for parents. They design the program and the environment so the parent is an active participant in the delivery of

knowledge. Families are more apt to become involved in the learning process and more easily change their attitudes if:

- A positive climate is established.
- The family's culture and language (including funds of knowledge) are valued and respected.
- Risk is eliminated.
- Parents are recognized as having something worthwhile to contribute.
- Parents are actively involved in their own education.
- The curriculum addresses their concerns and needs and is culturally relevant.
- Parents discover the need for change on their own.
- Respect and encouragement are present.
- Real situations and analogies are used to bring theories to life.
- Positive feedback is used.
- Different approaches (role playing, short lectures, open discussion, debates, brainstorming, workshops) enable parents to learn to use a variety of techniques.
- Different approaches use a variety of sensory experiences (sight, sound, touch, taste, and smell).
- Problem solving and analysis enable the learner to continue learning beyond the personal contact.
- Parents are considered part of the learning–teaching team.
- Technology is used in a way that promotes easy and inviting engagement.

You might have noted that the way parents learn best can apply to students, professionals, or even young children. Everyone learns better in a positive environment with relevant material. Teachers as instructional leaders should create a positive learning environment or climate within the classroom that extends to the school. Teachers can assist principals or directors by enhancing opportunities for families to engage in parent education. Thus, the principals or directors and the teachers have double duty as instructional leaders not only for children but for families as well (Neumerski, 2013).

In addition, it is important to note that parents will have difficulty focusing on their children if their own immediate needs are not met. A parent at an elementary school who was also a student at a local community college was very frustrated because she wanted to engage more in her children's school. Other parents recommended that she look into the child care facilities at her community college to see if they could take her child at least part time. This parent did not know this resource was available but talking with other parents gave her that information, and she was able to enroll her son twice a week at the community college child care facility, giving her time to attend her other children's school activities and engage. Therefore, it is important to provide support, resources, and referral information to parents to help them meet their own needs. Once this has been accomplished, they will be able to focus their energy on their children.

Group Discussions

Most meetings involve group discussion, which can range from the use of open discussion as the total meeting format to a short discussion after a formal presentation. The following examples, an informal discussion plan and a problem-solving format, illustrate two uses of group discussions. The first one focuses on the informality of the process and the second requires prior development of expertise and a resolution of the issue.

The Informal Discussion Plan

A. Stems from interest or needs of group.
   Example: How can parents be more engaged in their child's school?
B. Establishes goals and objectives.
   1. Goal—parental engagement.
   2. Objectives.
      a. To determine why parents do not feel comfortable coming to school.
      b. To encourage parents to participate in school.
      c. To initiate a plan for getting parents engaged.
      d. To suggest activities in which parents can be engaged.
C. Provides for informal group meetings.
   1. Allows parents to speak freely.
   2. Emphasizes the clarification of feelings and acceptance of ideas.
   3. Encourages participation.
   4. Includes keeping a record of suggestions.
D. Selects and analyzes relevant information that emerges during the discussion.
E. Outlines a plan for action, if the group desires.

The Problem-Solving Format

A. Recognition of the problem—state the hypothesis.
   1. The problem should be selected by the group and reflect its needs and interests.
      Example: How do we keep children safe from guns in schools?
   2. The leader writes the question or problem for discussion on a chart, chalkboard, or whiteboard.
B. Understanding the problem—discuss the nature of the problem.
   Example: What are the major issues associated with guns in schools? Why?
C. Data collection—gather a wide range of ideas and determine which are relevant.
   1. Prior development of expertise—identify resources and read before meeting.
   2. Nonjudgmental acceptance—accept and record comments and ideas from participants.
D. Analysis of the problem.
   1. Focus on the subject so it can be discussed thoroughly by participants.
   2. Establish criteria for evaluation of a solution.
   3. Keep participants focused on problems.
E. Conclusion and summary.
   1. Suggest solutions.
   2. List possible conclusions.
   3. Seek an integrative conclusion that reflects the group's goals and thinking.
F. Appropriate action.
   1. Develop a timetable.
   2. Determine a method of accomplishing tasks.
   3. Delegate tasks.

Using Technology

The increased use of communication through the Internet allows parents, leaders, teachers, and students to interact virtually. The process lets participants respond to one another with the added convenience of flexible schedules and immediate discussion. This is especially true for parents who live a distance from the school or meeting place and for those whose have children at home or have a work schedule that makes it impossible for them to attend meetings. There are video conferencing tools such as Zoom, Skype, Google Handouts, Blackboard Collaborate, and Adobe Connect, among others, that enable meetings to take place virtually, giving parents more options to connect with the classroom and the school for different purposes. Teachers can meet with parents without having to stay after school and parents can also meet, engage, and plan without taking time off from work.

A concern some years ago was access to technology. The Pew Research Center (2018) indicates that today, about 95% of Americans own a cellphone of some kind. However, teachers and schools must still be cognizant that some parents, particularly those who live under the poverty level or are undocumented might not have access to technology or if the technology is limited due to financial issues some cannot make a conference call as their plan may not allow it.

E-mail

Electronic mail or E-mail can be used to communicate and provides an opportunity for an immediate response. It can be used to give information and receive parent responses and questions. E-mails can be sent to a group or individual and are fairly easy to develop through different search engines like Google or Yahoo. Receiving individual e-mails is like receiving a letter in that the sender can send very specific communication to the receiver. It is always important for teachers to know the type of information that can be sent through e-mail even when confidential. There are some schools for example that do not allow teachers to send grades through e-mail. In addition, when using the bcc feature teachers can send mass e-mails without sharing the e-mail addresses. E-mail is a good way to communicate with families through technology even those who may only have access to it through the school or the local library.

Websites

Teachers can develop websites that inform parents about events at school. Emergencies can be explained, assignments can be posted and outlined, and links that include articles about educational ideas and procedures for improving academic achievement can be included. Links to articles that concern education and child development can be placed on the website for the parents or students. If the school has had difficulties with bullying and the rejection of some students by others, information from the school can help set up programs and encourage both parents and the school to work on these concerns. When posting materials on the website, it is always good practice to check copyright laws to see

what can be posted. When in doubt, contact the author and publisher of the material selected.

For parents who cannot attend meetings because of their schedules, the Internet expands their opportunities to be involved with the school. Chat rooms or blogs are particularly helpful for parents who want to be informed but who cannot attend meetings and who have access to a computer. Schools can also become more technologically efficient by allowing parents to join in meetings online through communication such as Skype as mentioned earlier. By working with the district's technology department, schools not only are using technology to communicate with parents, but can create communities of practice or groups that share common interests for a specific goal (Jimenez-Silva & Olson, 2012) where other departments in the district help to ensure parents are involved.

Social Network

Many schools use social media to keep families informed of upcoming training sessions and meetings. Facebook, YouTube, Instagram, Snapchat, and Twitter are only a few examples that teachers can use to notify parents about the latest news or just everyday routines and grades. Leaders should use caution when posting school information on any social media, however. Figure 7.3 shows the prevalence of different social media outlets. Knowing this information will help teachers determine the best media to reach the most parents.

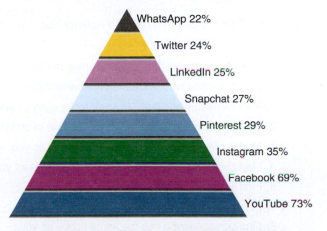

Figure 7.3 Percentage of Adults Using Social Media

WhatsApp 22%
Twitter 24%
LinkedIn 25%
Snapchat 27%
Pinterest 29%
Instagram 35%
Facebook 69%
YouTube 73%

Source: Pew Research Center. (2018). *Social media use in 2018: A majority of Americans use Facebook and YouTube, but young adults are especially heavy users of Snapchat and Instagram.* Retrieved on May 30, 2018 from http://www.pewinternet.org/2018/03/01/social-media-use-in-2018/

Establishing a Positive Climate

Icebreakers. To create an accepting and warm atmosphere, get-acquainted activities can be used to help people relax and become involved in the group. These icebreakers range from introductions of a person to mixers during breaks.

Signature Sheets. Make a form before the meeting that makes statements about people. Following each statement is a signature blank. These sheets can be made specifically for the group or can be broad enough to be used in any group. Use your imagination and make them original and interesting. It is important to select activities that are culturally relevant to parents so they can enjoy the activity. As the group arrives, give one to each participant. Encourage mixing with and meeting new people. By the time the period is complete, the members will have had an opportunity to meet and talk with a large number of people. A typical signature sheet is shown in Figure 7.4. Figure 7.5 illustrates another signature sheet design.

A word of caution regarding signature sheets: If a parent refuses to sign, don't force them as the reason may not be evident. I have met parents who did not know how to read or write in their home language, much less in English. I recall one parent signing with an X and then sitting in the back of the room. If the parents stay quiet and remain in the back of the room, this can be an indication that they do not feel comfortable with opening activities that require them to be literate. This activity can also be used as a needs-assessment activity because it can show the need to provide literacy classes for adults. Technology makes this process a lot easier. A couple of electronic tablets can be set up at the entrance of the classroom where the meeting will take place to have parents sign electronically, with assistance if needed. SignUpGenius is an example of software that can be used for meeting organization and sign up.

Bingo Card. Give each member a card that contains 12 to 25 squares, as shown in Figure 7.6. Ask members to fill each blank with a signature. Signatures may not be repeated. This encourages interaction with all members. For English language learners, make sure the bingo cards are in their language whenever possible and has photos of the items.

A variation of the bingo card includes a letter within each square. Find someone whose name begins with that letter. Check the roster ahead of time and use the members' initials in the squares. Another variation is similar to the signature sheet but asks for the signature of someone *else* who fulfills the attribute.

Who Am I? Using sticky labels, write the name of a famous person on each label and attach one to the back of each person. Members then go from person to person asking questions until they determine whose name is on their back. Questions must be phrased so that a yes or no answer is adequate. For example, the label can read something like this: "Famous anchor person who made headlines when she became the first woman to anchor the evening news in the U.S." The person who is trying to find out the answer can ask something like this: "Does this woman do documentaries?" "Does

---

Figure 7.4 Use a Get-Acquainted Activity Such as a Signature Sheet at the Beginning of a Meeting

Find people who meet the qualifications listed below and have them sign their names.

1. Find someone who is wearing the same color clothes as you. _____
2. Find someone who has the same color eyes as you. _____
3. Find someone who has the same number of children as you. _____
4. Find someone who lives in the same area as you. _____
5. Find someone who has a child the same age as yours. _____
6. Find someone who likes to go hiking. _____
7. Find someone who plays the piano. _____
8. Find someone who has the same hobby as you. _____
9. Find someone who has lived in this state as long as you have. _____
10. Find someone who was brought up in the same area you were. _____

Figure 7.5 Wheel of Friendship

During the next few minutes, find people who have the same attributes as you. Have them sign their names in the wheel of friendship between the wheel spokes.

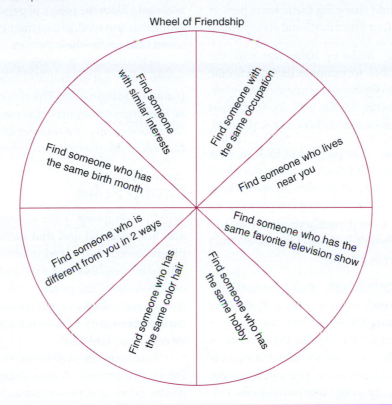

Wheel of Friendship

- Find someone with similar interests
- Find someone with the same occupation
- Find someone who has the same birth month
- Find someone who lives near you
- Find someone who is different from you in 2 ways
- Find someone who has the same favorite television show
- Find someone who has the same color hair
- Find someone who has the same hobby

Figure 7.6 Attribute Bingo

Find a person who can sign the squares. When you have completed an entire line, you can call "bingo!" Bingo games can use initials or attributes of the members of the group.

I watch television regularly.	I enjoy reading.	I have more than two children.	I like to dance.	My favorite color is orange.
I have dark hair.	I like to go shopping.	I enjoy skiing.	I enjoy hiking.	I enjoy biking.
I have red hair.	I have blonde hair.	I have brown eyes.	I have blue eyes.	I have a son.
I have two children.	I live near here.	I have lived in this area for more than one year.	I enjoy music.	I enjoy helping in school.
I exercise regularly.	I have a daughter.	I have a brother.	I have a sister.	I work outside the home.

she have blond hair?" These types of questions allow for yes/no answers. Take the context where you live in consideration and create a question that would be relevant. Variations include changing the famous person to an event, an animal, or an educational statement.

Scrambled Name Tags. Make up name tags with the names' letters out of order—for example, Ilaehs for Sheila. Have the members try to figure out each name as they talk with each person. Obviously, this has to be done at the first or second meeting, before the group becomes acquainted.

Favorite Personal Item. Ask parents to look in their purses and/or wallets and find an item that best describes them. You can send parents a letter asking them to bring an item, but there's often one person who forgets his or her item. Give parents a chance to discuss why that item is important to them. Do this in small groups and then in larger groups.

AFTER MEMBERS ARE SEATED. **Pair Introductions.** Have members talk to each other in pairs, with the idea that they will introduce each other. You can give specific instructions—for example, to ask the number of children in their family and what the member expects to gain from parent education—or you can leave the discussion completely up to the two individuals. Following the one-on-one discussion, have members introduce their partners to the group.

Allow members to introduce themselves. If a member doesn't speak English, perhaps instead of partners have groups of three, if you have others who have skills in that language, so one can translate to avoid isolating the English language learner.

It is interesting to have the pair discuss memories, such as something one partner remembers that happened during childhood a person's happiest experience, or their biggest challenge. Topics they might use include the following:

> My secret hiding place was . . .
> As a child I liked to . . . best.
> Summertime was . . .
> If I had my wish, I would be . . .
> What I liked most about school was . . .
> What I remember about walking or riding the bus
>   home from school was . . .

This activity can be used later in the year, as well as at the beginning.

I've Got a Secret. After people have become acquainted, ask each participant to write a secret on a piece of paper. (Be sure that the person does not mind having the secret revealed.) Place the pieces of paper in a bag, and as they are drawn and read, group members try to guess which secret belongs to which person.

Activities that promote good relations and allow members to get acquainted are limited only by the planner's imagination. The chairperson or leader may be in charge of this part of the program or may delegate the responsibility to a number of persons charged with the task of discovering new means of interaction.

Group Roles

Within each group, roles emerge that are functional and task oriented and that move the group forward; others are expressive and maintain the group; and still others are negative and dysfunctional and reduce the effectiveness of the group. Group members should be given descriptions of group roles to help them identify their participatory roles or roles that they would like to develop (see Table 7.1).

Roles emerge within groups and influence the interactive process. A **role**, defined as the behavioral characteristic of a person occupying a particular position in the social system, influences the actions of the person and the expectations of others toward that person. Parent groups in this text are the "social system;" members of the group expect certain norms or standards of behavior from the perceived leader of the group. These role expectations are projected in members' role behavior toward the leader. Likewise, the leader's own interpretation of the role influences the resulting role behavior or role performance.

Role continuity is easier to obtain in parent education groups with ongoing memberships. Parents are encouraged to participate for at least 2 years. New officers and leaders, already familiar with the standards of the group, may be elected in the spring and be ready to take over leadership in the fall. Although this system ensures greater continuity than the establishment of a new group each year, the returning members must be careful to be flexible, must be open to new ideas, and be sensitive to the desires of new members.

Early in the year, a session might include a discussion of roles and group dynamics. Role-playing is an excellent mechanism for clarifying role behavior. If group members are aware of the effects that roles have on the functioning of a group, they will not fall into dysfunctional roles so readily.

A leader can deter or eliminate the problem of domination or withdrawal by group members if members are aware of roles and how each member of the group can influence the group's functioning, either positively or negatively. Most people do not want to be viewed as dysfunctional members and will, therefore, refrain from acting in ways that are detrimental to group interaction. I have used this technique of discussing roles in parent groups and classes for many years and have found that the group discussion and the role-playing of group roles greatly enhance the productivity of the group.

Knowing how to handle different situations will encourage some members in the groups, but it can also inhibit others who worry about which role they are enacting. Although this is a possible negative result of discussing group roles, role definition can benefit the total group by eliminating one common problem in group dynamics—domination of the discussion by a few participants. It also benefits reticent communicators to learn that they can become productive group members despite the inability to express themselves. Asking questions, being an active listener, and being a positive member of the group are shown to be valuable contributions to a well-functioning discussion group. When balanced out, the positive aspects of discussing group roles overshadow the negative ones. One word of caution, however—do not wait until a problem has become obvious before discussing dysfunctional roles. That would embarrass and alienate the person who has been a negative contributor. It is best to handle such a problem through the leadership techniques discussed previously in the chapter.

DYNAMICS OF ROLES WITHIN GROUPS. Observation of interaction within groups shows that role behavior influences the cohesiveness and productivity of the group. Observation will be facilitated if analysis of the group is based on role interaction (Table 7.1), wherein behaviors within a group are divided into task, group building and maintenance, and dysfunctional roles.

TASK ROLES. The roles related to the task area in Table 7.1 are attributed to members of the group who initiate, question, and facilitate reaching the group's goals or objectives. The roles related to group building or maintenance are attributed to members of the group who support and maintain the cohesiveness, solidarity, and productivity of the group.

DYSFUNCTIONAL OR INDIVIDUAL ROLES. The roles in this area are attributed to members who place their own individual needs, which are not relevant to group goals, above group needs. These individual goals are not functional or productive to group achievement, but if such members are brought into the group process, they can become contributing participants.

Members of groups generally do not fit into only one role category. Members can participate in a task role and switch to a maintenance role with the next action or comment. For example, "Elena" is anxious about absenteeism and suggests that the group might improve attendance by organizing a carpool. "Lee" responds by suggesting a telephone network to contact members. Elena welcomes the idea, saying, "Good thought, Lee. We might be able to start right away." Elena, within the space of 2 minutes, has initiated an idea, acting in a task-oriented role, and has then supported Lee's contribution with a group-building or maintenance statement. There may be moments when members lapse into a dysfunctional role, but as long as the mix of interaction remains primarily positive and productive, the group will be effective.

ROLE DESCRIPTIONS. The following role descriptions are based on Beal and colleagues (1962); Benne and Sheets (1948); Borchers, (1999); King (1962); and MSU Extension (1999) and are still very relevant in today's context.

Task-Oriented Roles. Task roles are the roles that initiate and keep the group discussion meaningful and ongoing:

Initiator–leader—Initiates the discussion, guides but does not dominate, contributes ideas or suggestions that help move the group forward.

Facilitator—Helps the group stay on track and encourages member participation.

Information giver—Contributes information and facts that are from authoritative sources and are relevant to the ongoing discussion.

Information seeker—Asks for clarification or expansion of an issue from additional relevant, authoritative information.

Clarifier—Restates the discussion of an issue so that points are made clear to the group and relationships between ideas are clear.

Orientator—Takes a look at the group's position in relation to the objectives of the meetings and where the discussion is going and as a result may refocus the group discussion.

Questioner—Asks questions about issues, requests clarification, or offers constructive criticism.

Asserter—States a position in a positive manner; may take a different point of view and disagree with opinions or suggestions without attacking them.

Energizer—Stimulates and facilitates the group to action and increased output and problem solving.

Elaborator—Expands an idea or concept; brings out details, points, and alternatives that might have been overlooked.

Opinion giver—States own opinion on the situation, basing the contribution on personal experiences.

Opinion seeker—Requests suggestions from others according to their life experiences and value orientation.

Summarizer—Brings out facts, ideas, and suggestions made by the group in an attempt to clarify the group's position during the meeting and at the conclusion.

Group-Building and Maintenance Roles. Group-building and maintenance roles help the group develop and maintain the existence and quality of the group. The first six roles will emerge within the group:

Encourager—Supports, praises, and recognizes other members of the group; builds self-confidence and self-concept of others.

Harmonizer—Mediates misunderstandings and clarifies conflicting statements and disagreements; adds to the discussion in a calming and tension-reducing manner.

Listener—Is involved in the discussion through quiet attention to the group process; gives support through body language and eye contact.

Follower—Serves as a supportive member of the discussion by accepting the ideas and suggestions of others.

Tension breaker—Uses humor or clarifying statements to relieve tension within the group.

Compromiser—Views both sides of the question and offers solutions or suggestions that move the group to a position that fits conflicting viewpoints.

The following four roles are appointed or elected positions:

Standard setter—Sets standards for group performance; may apply standards as an evaluative technique for the meeting.

Observer—Charts the group process throughout the meeting and uses the data for evaluation of group interaction.

Recorder—Records decisions and ideas for group use throughout the meeting.

Gatekeeper—Regulates time spent and membership participation during various parts of the program; keeps communication open and the meeting on schedule.

Dysfunctional Roles. Dysfunctional roles interfere with achieving the goals of the group:

Dominator—Monopolizes the meeting and asserts superiority by attempting to manipulate the group.

Aggressor—Shows aggression toward the group in a variety of forms; for example, attacks ideas, criticizes others, denigrates others' contributions, and disapproves of solutions.

Challenger—Challenges other group members' ideas and suggestions.

Negativist—Demonstrates pessimism and disapproval of suggestions that emerge within the group; sees the negative side of the issue and rejects new insights.

Flirtatious—Spends time getting the attention of the opposite sex.

Blocker—Opposes decision making and attempts to block actions by introducing alternatives that have already been rejected.

Competitor—Competes with other members of the discussion group by challenging their ideas and expressing and defending his or her own suggestions.

Recognition seeker—Needs recognition and focus on himself or herself.

Deserter—Leaves the group in spirit and mind but not in body; doodles, looks around the room, appears uninterested, and stays aloof and indifferent to the group process.

PRODUCTIVE GROUPS. In productive groups, members of the group are both active and productive:

1. Members listen and pay attention to one another.

2. Members discuss the subject at hand.

3. Everyone's ideas and suggestions are welcomed.

4. Everyone has a chance to state his or her views.

5. The group uses its agenda as a guide for discussion.

6. One or two members are appointed to summarize the discussion and to see that everyone has had a chance to speak.

7. Members know and use problem-solving steps.

8. Members are clear about group decisions and are committed to them (MSU Extension, 1999).

Less-productive groups often do the following:

1. Members do not listen and everyone tends to talk at the same time.

2. The discussion jumps from one idea to another.

3. Some members' ideas don't seem to count, so those individuals feel they don't belong.

4. One or two members do all the talking.

5. The agenda is not clear, and there is no written guide for discussion.

6. No one summarizes or checks to see if everyone who wants to speak has actually spoken. Discussions go on and on until people get tired.

7. No order is followed for identifying and solving problems.

8. Decision making is muddy and people are not committed to the plan (MSU Extension, 1999).

ROLE-PLAYING GROUP ROLES. Early in the formation of a group, members can benefit from a session in which they role-play task, maintenance, and dysfunctional roles while discussing an issue of high interest. This exercise will illustrate to members how role performance can support or destroy a group. It is practical to arrange seating in two concentric circles, allowing the inner circle to discuss an issue in light of the roles assigned, while the outer circle observes and analyzes the roles being demonstrated. The session will be humorous, with members enthusiastically playing dysfunctional roles, but it should end with the understanding that each member is important to the effectiveness of the group process. It is also important

to observe the course of the session. If there is any indication that a participant is having difficulty functioning within the group, the leader needs to provide support and redirect the activity.

Observer. Analytical observation of group interaction reveals patterns that are not always obvious to the casual observer. A systematic observation can pinpoint problems and illustrate strengths to the members. One simple technique for analytical observation is the construction of a discussion wheel. A diagram of the participants is made, with names or numbers reflecting individual members. If the participants are sitting in a circle, the diagram would be similar to the one in Figure 7.7.

As members speak, the observer uses arrows to record the direction of each interaction. An arrow pointed toward the center indicates that the communicator is speaking to the group; an arrow pointed from one member to another represents a statement made to an individual rather than to the group (Beal et al., 1962). A glance at Figure 7.7 shows that Rafael did not make any suggestions; he had either withdrawn from the group or lacked its supportive encouragement. Most members contributed to the group process rather than making side comments to individual communicators. As interaction continues throughout the meeting, the observer can make cross marks on the arrows to reflect duplication of communication, thus eliminating an overabundance of lines in the observation circle (Figure 7.8).

Figure 7.7 Group Interaction Recorded on an Observation Wheel

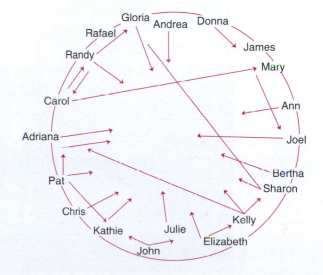

Figure 7.8 Observation Wheel
Group interaction is anonymously recorded on an observation wheel. Each time a person speaks, a mark is added to the interaction line. In this manner, one can see how often and to whom each participant communicates.

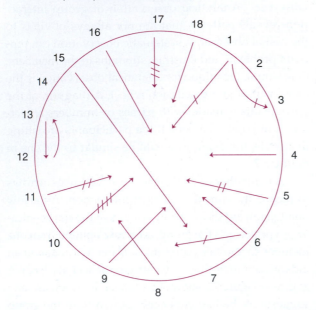

End-of-Meeting Evaluations. Evaluations are used effectively by many groups to see if the needs of the group are being met. Because every group is somewhat different, evaluations should be constructed to meet the needs of the group and should be based on the goals and objectives of the meeting. Sample evaluations are helpful, however, to guide the group in its development of evaluation methods that work for that particular group. The example in Figure 7.9 can be adapted to any group's needs.

Positive Leadership for Meaningful Meetings

Meetings can range from formal lectures to informal buzz sessions. In parent groups, informal meetings are used most often to reinforce the active involvement that proves so critical to understanding concepts and changing attitudes. The formal meeting has its place, however, if the group needs a specialist to give an organized lecture on a specific topic. Figure 7.10 illustrates types of meetings that can be used as needs, time, space, subject, and resources dictate. On the right are meetings that are the most informal and require active involvement by the participants; in the center is the panel meeting; on the left is the most formal lecture where the only audience participation is listening to the speaker. Although each type of meeting has its place in parent group meetings, the informal meeting elicits more participation by group members—a necessary ingredient for attitude clarification, learning, and change.

Arrangements for Meetings

All parent group meetings require certain procedures, regardless of the meeting format. Also, parents need to

Merrill Education

Parents actively participate in workshops that help them build on their leadership skills.

Figure 7.9 A Meeting Evaluation Form Lets You Know Exactly How the Participants Viewed the Program

Topic: _____   Date: _____

Group: _____

Put a check or x above your answer.

1. Was the meeting of interest to you?

Very much	Somewhat	Very little

2. Did you receive any pertinent ideas that will be helpful to you?

Many ideas	Some ideas	No ideas

3. Did the group participate and seem involved in the meeting?

Very involved	Somewhat involved	Not involved

4. Did the meeting give you any new insights, or did you change any of your attitudes as a result of the meeting?

New insights	Some new insights	No new insights

5. Were you able to contribute as much as you wanted?

Participation encouraged	Neutral	Left out

6. Did the leader respond to the needs of the group?

Good leadership	Neutral	No leadership

7. Was there adequate preparation by the members?

Excellent preparation	Some preparation	Poor preparation

8. Were group members encouraged to participate?

Strong	Average	No encouragement

9. Was there enough time for discussion?

Too much time	Just right	Not enough time

10. Was the atmosphere conducive to freedom of expression?

Safe environment	Neutral	Threatening environment

11. Do you have any suggestions for improvement?

12. What were the strong points of the meeting?

13. Comments:

You do not need to sign this sheet.

feel physically and emotionally comfortable at every meeting, whether formal or informal. To ensure this, the person in charge of the meeting should do the following for all meetings:

1. Check the meeting room to be sure the temperature is appropriate, the ventilation and lighting are adequate, and the room is large enough to accommodate the group.

2. As members or guests arrive, make them feel welcome. Greet them, offer nametags, and suggest they have refreshments, look at a book display, or participate in an icebreaker activity before the meeting begins. Call members or guests by name as soon as possible.

3. Have refreshments available before the meeting, during the break, or at both times. A 15-minute refreshment period before the meeting gives latecomers an opportunity to arrive before discussion commences. It also sets a relaxed tone and gives members a forum for informal interaction.

4. As participants arrive, involve them in an informal discussion through an icebreaker activity. Get-acquainted activities are important, but choose an appropriate one. For meetings at which few people know one another, it can prove beneficial to use a signature sheet or the dyad-introductions technique of asking the entire group to form into pairs, with each partner introducing the other one to the group.

Figure 7.10 Types of Meetings Range from the Informal on the Right to Very Formal on the Left

Formal	Informal
Lecture	Brainstorming
Lecture-forum	Roundtable
Symposium	Concentric circles
Audio	Buzz sessions
Audiovisual	Workshop
Book review	Dyad interaction and feedback
Debate	Role-playing
Colloquy	Dramatization
Panel	

5. In large groups where icebreakers are not appropriate, the participants can respond to group questions—where they live, what they do, how many children they have, what their interests are, and so on. Responses to the questions (by a show of hands or verbal answers) help the speaker know more about the audience to be addressed, and audience members feel they have been recognized.

6. After the group feels comfortable, the meeting can commence. Open discussion is part of all but the most formal or informal meetings, so it is important that all group leaders are able to conduct discussion sessions. Debates, panels, audiovisual aids, buzz sessions, workshops, role playing, book reviews, dramatizations, and observations can precede open discussion. The leader should gauge the time and conclude the meeting.

7. After the presentation and discussion (or question-and-answer session), thank the presenters and give appropriate recognition for their contributions.

8. Announce any specific instructions necessary for the next meeting before the group disperses.

Figure 7.11 The Roundtable Is the Basic Open Discussion Group

The descriptions of the types of meetings that follow are compiled from Eugenia Berger's experiences with parent education when she directed a parent-education and preschool program for nearly 4 years.

ROUNDTABLES (OPEN DISCUSSIONS).   Although not the most informal meeting available, the **round-table** is a true open discussion, the mainstay of group interaction (see Figure 7.11). It is used to complement most meetings, such as panels, symposia role-playing sessions, or buzz sessions. The roundtable discussion is also used for decision-making meetings and parent councils.

In a roundtable discussion, all members are encouraged to participate throughout the meeting. Care must be taken to promote good communication among all members of the group. Organizing roundtables is important in order to facilitate interactions within the groups. The following are some suggestions for leaders to use for effective round table discussions: 1) select a good topic, 2) prepare any materials needed, 3) motivate interactions, 4) keep accurate time, and 5) maintain respect for and among participants.

Problems that could emerge in a roundtable meeting include domination of the discussion by one or two members, withdrawal from the group, side discussions by two or three people, or lack of preparation by the members. Good leadership makes it possible to avoid these pitfalls. If the leader is prepared for the meeting and if members come to the meeting prepared, have relevant experiences, or have background expertise on the subject, the meeting can be a most effective means of changing attitudes and educating members. It allows all members to contribute and become involved in discussions, the clarification of issues, and decision making.

Arrangements Before the Meeting

1. Select a topic for open discussion and announce it to the group.

2. Provide members with materials and a bibliography.

   a. Duplicate and distribute background information on the topic through a distribution system or at a meeting before the roundtable.

   b. Select members to read relevant material before the meeting.

   c. Come to the meeting well prepared and ready to guide but not dominate.

Setup

1. Arrange chairs in a circle or semicircle or around tables so all participants can see each other and eye contact is possible.

2. Check the room for comfort—ventilation, lighting, and heat.

Procedure

1. The leader starts the meeting with a thought-provoking question or statement of fact. Throughout the discussion, the leader tries to keep the meeting from wandering. Before the meeting, the leader has prepared a list of questions or statements that keep the discussion moving forward.

2. During the meeting, the leader avoids dominating the discussion. Instead, the leader brings others into the discussion, helps clarify subjects, and keeps the meeting on the topic.

3. The leader summarizes at the conclusion.

4. If the members want to take action on the conclusions, the leader should call for appropriate action, help the group make plans, and assign tasks.

Appropriate Topics

1. Helping children with homework

2. Culturally appropriate guidance

3. Social media and children

4. Keeping children safe from drugs

5. Problem solving

6. Bullying in schools

7. Helping children cope with school shootings

CONCENTRIC CIRCLES.   The **concentric-circle arrangement** is a variation of the open discussion or roundtable meeting. Instead of one circle, there are two—one inside the other—with everyone facing the center. The dialogue among members is similar to that of the open discussion, but the smaller circle within the larger circle contains the first group of communicators (Figure 7.12). Divide the group so the smaller group has 6 to 12 people. The members of the smaller group discuss the issue; those in the larger group listen to the discussion. After a designated time of 5 to 10 minutes, the meeting is opened to the entire group. If you have 24 to 30 people, with people who are reticent in a large group, the concentric circle will help solve the problem. Those

Figure 7.12 Concentric Circles Encourage Those Who Might Not Participate Freely to Get Involved

within the inner circle form a small group with which to interact. This arrangement precipitates more discussion from them and succeeds in getting the whole group interested in the discussion. Those sitting in the outer circle are required to listen, but the statements, questions, and ideas offered usually promote their interest as they listen. This method is surprisingly effective in getting groups to discuss issues. By the time the discussion is opened up to the entire group, many ideas have emerged.

Setup

1. Arrange chairs with one large circle on the outside and a smaller circle within the larger circle.

2. Review the "Arrangements for Meetings" section and make appropriate preparations.

Procedure

1. The leader of the whole group might request a volunteer leader for the inner circle, or the leader can take that role.

2. The session is started with a statement or question to promote interest and dialogue.

3. The inner circle discusses the topic, using a small-group, open-discussion format. The outer circle listens. At the end of a designated period (for example, 6 minutes), the discussion may be opened to all in the room. At that time, the leader continues to control the meeting but does not dominate it.

4. For variation, reverse the roles. Those now in the outer circle move to the inner circle and so have the

opportunity for a more involved discussion, while those from the outer circle listen. A separate issue or different questions concerning the original issue can be used for each group in its discussion.

Appropriate Topics

1. How to build self-esteem in children
2. What to expect of 2-, 3-, 4-, or 5-year-olds
3. Problem solving
4. Living with change
5. Positive uses of the Internet, videogames, and television
6. Courses and workshops that could be offered at school
7. Issues and concerns of children

Buzz Sessions

Buzz sessions are an excellent means of eliciting participation from all members of the group. They must be small enough to allow interaction among all participants. The smallest session consists of two people, and the maximum size should be six to eight. This makes it possible for all members to have the chance to express their opinions easily. Even in a large group, the audience can divide into smaller groups for discussion—for instance, groups of six with a time limit of 6 minutes. The latter is called a 6–6 discussion, because six people discuss a topic for 6 minutes. Because the session time is limited, it does not allow a thorough examination of issues, but it does bring forth ideas from all involved in a very short period of time—an objective that is not accomplished in an open discussion with a large group.

Setup

1. Up to 24 people.
   a. Arrange chairs in a circle or semicircle.
   b. When the smaller group session is to begin, six people turn their chairs together to form their group. It is also possible for a group to move to another area for a quieter meeting.
2. Large auditorium.
   a. If people are seated in rows, three people turn around and discuss with three people behind them.
   b. Use some other technique to form groups of six throughout the auditorium.

Procedure

1. Buzz sessions can be formed at the beginning of the meeting, or they can be initiated later. The leader announces the formation of buzz groups either by the proximity of chairs, a common interest in specific discussion areas, or by a mechanism to distribute members, such as counting off 1 through 6 and having those with common numbers form a group.
2. Each group chooses a leader and a recorder.
3. The topic for discussion is introduced to the group, and people are encouraged to participate much as they would in any other small-group discussion.
4. The recorder keeps relevant thoughts ready to report back to the larger group. In a smaller meeting (24 people), each group might have the time to give a short report to the total group. In an auditorium 6–6 meeting, it might not be possible to have everyone report back. Allow a limited number of groups that indicate interest in doing so to report back to the total audience.

Appropriate Topics

1. Home-management tips
2. Feelings about childrearing
3. Discipline
4. Moral values
5. Vacation ideas on a budget
6. Solving problems around the home
7. Issues concerning school
8. Decisions that should be made concerning education

BRAINSTORMING SESSIONS. **Brainstorming** is a unique method of active interaction by all members of the group. It promotes interchange, encourages lateral thinking, and facilitates expansion of thought. In brainstorming sessions, all contributions are accepted. Everyone is encouraged to suggest ideas and solutions. The participants can add to, combine, or modify other ideas, or they might introduce something new. There are no value judgments on the quality of suggestions.

The free and open brainstorming session provides an environment that facilitates the production of a variety of ideas from the participants. Members who are reluctant to contribute during an open discussion because they are not sure their ideas are worthy have a guaranteed safe environment in which to contribute during brainstorming. Quantity of ideas is the object. Later, the ideas can be analyzed, judged as to quality, and reduced to selected items. The brainstorming technique, therefore, is excellent for stimulation of diversified thought and solutions to issues and problems. It also reinforces the socioemotional aspects of a group by accepting the contributions of all people freely.

Setup

1. Arrange chairs in a circle if the group has fewer than 30 members. A small group allows for more interaction.

2. Brainstorming can be used in a larger group with an auditorium arrangement of chairs. In that case, the entire group might have difficulty participating, but the mechanism is effective for bringing forth a quantity of ideas and thoughts.

Procedure

1. The brainstorming session requires a leader and a recorder.

   a. Appoint a recorder or ask for a volunteer.
   b. Appoint a leader or assume the leadership role.

2. The leader begins the brainstorming session by explaining the rules and emphasizing that all contributions are wanted and accepted. Even if ideas seem unusual, all members should contribute. Ideas should be interjected as they occur.

3. The topic or issue is explained to the group.

4. The session is opened to contributions from the group.

5. The recorder writes on a board or piece of paper all the ideas that come from the group.

6. After a predetermined amount of time—4, 6, or 10 minutes, depending on the issue and the flow of ideas—the group can begin analyzing the suggestions and pulling out the ones that seem to answer the issue or problem best.

7. A summary of the solutions and ideas gained from brainstorming is reported by the leader.

8. If this is an action meeting, plans for action should be identified at this time.

Appropriate Topics

1. Ideas to solve problems—for example, subjects for meetings, summer activities

2. How to get your child to . . . (eat or go to bed, etc.)

3. Creative activities

4. Exploring your environment

5. Nutrition

6. Ways to improve relations at the school

7. Summer offerings for families

WORKSHOPS AND CENTERS. **Workshops** are a superb means of achieving involvement by members. Most useful for demonstrating programs and curricula, they can also be used as an effective means of explaining procedures, illustrating the learning process, and developing understanding. The major ingredient in a workshop is active participation by members, whether through making puzzles and toys, working on mathematics, painting, modeling with clay, editing a newspaper, composing music, writing poetry, or planning an action. There are many appropriate topics for workshops and very often it depends on the context.

Although often confused with a workshop, a **center** is different in that it does not require participants to be actively involved in the project. Centers allow subgroups of the membership to gather simultaneously in various areas of the room, where they might see a demonstration, hear an explanation of an issue or program, or watch a media presentation. If time allows, more than one center may be visited. The variety of centers is limited only by the imagination and productivity of the planning group. The advantages of this diversified meeting are that (a) it reduces group size and thus promotes more interaction and allows individual questions, (b) participants are able to select topics of interest to them, and (c) tension and anxiety of the presenters are reduced because of the informal format.

Setup

1. Depending on available space, workshops and centers may take place in separate rooms or in one large room with designated areas.

2. Each presenter might have different requirements. The amount of space and number of tables and chairs requested should be set up according to those requirements.

Procedure

1. The chairperson explains the variety of workshops or centers available and the procedures to be used.

2. Participants choose a workshop or center. These can be assigned according to several procedures: free choice, numbers on name tags, or preregistration.

3. Participants attend one or more workshops depending on the time available. If plans include a time limit for each, the groups proceed from one to the next at a signal.

4. Members may gather together at the close of the meeting, or it may conclude with the final workshop or center.

Possible Topics

1. Learning activities
2. Art activities
3. Bookmaking
4. Games and toys
5. Math activities to do at home
6. Science activities to do at home
7. Rainy-day activities
8. Leadership training session
9. Writers' workshop
10. Learning to read
11. Guidance
12. Outdoor play
13. Traditional children's games
14. Music and songs for young children
15. The environment

OBSERVATIONS AND FIELD TRIPS. Although **observations and field trips** can be quite different in their objectives, they are similar in theory and procedure. Observations and field trips can be part of family engagement to learn more about children and education in general. The active viewing of a classroom, like a visit in the community, encourages the participant to be involved in observing activities. The opportunity to see an activity in process clarifies that process as no written or spoken word can. It is imperative, however, to discuss objectives and points to consider before the field trip or observation. It is also essential to analyze and discuss observations after the visits, to clarify the experience and bring it into focus. Many times, the end of a field trip can be the beginning of a new, expanded project for the individual or group. Remember that these are not your typical field trips where teachers and children attend a specific place. These are field

Parents work with one another, enhancing collaboration between them.

Mark Bowden/Getty Images

trips where families are engaged for a specific purpose. Some preschools for example organize family field trips and the families are provided with a learning task so that they share with others after the field trip.

Arrangements before Observations or Field Trips

1. Select the time and place for the observation or field trip.
   a. Plan classroom visits in advance. Specific objectives can be discussed prior to the observation.
   b. If the classroom has an observation area, observers can easily watch without disturbing the class. If there is no observation area, those going into the classroom should know the teacher's preferred procedure.
   c. Field trips must be planned and permission for visiting obtained.

2. Participants learn more and receive more satisfaction from field trips if background information and items to take note of are discussed before the visit.

3. If the members are going to a place different from their regular meeting area, group travel arrangements should be made.

Procedure

1. The leader plans and conducts a previsit orientation.
2. The observation or field trip is completed.
3. Discussion of the experience clarifies the issues and focuses on the learning that has taken place. Many field trips tend to be an end in themselves, but that omits the most important follow-up, where new ideas and greater understanding are generated.

Appropriate Observations and Field Trips

1. In classroom observations, look for the following:
   a. How children learn
   b. Play—child's work
   c. Interpersonal relations
   d. Aggression
   e. Fine- and gross-motor control
   f. Hand–eye coordination
   g. Stages and ages

2. Field trip options (for family engagement) include the following:
   a. Children's museums
   b. Art museums
   c. Parks
   d. Special schools
   e. Newspapers
   f. Hospitals
   g. Businesses
   h. Farms
   i. State legislature

INTERACTION AND FEEDBACK. During structured programs such as STEP and PET, interludes that allow the audience or participants to clarify, practice, and receive feedback on their interaction with others are beneficial. For example, if parents and teachers were working to improve interaction during a conference, sample statements would allow them to practice listening and other communication skills. If the topic were reflective listening, one member of each pair or small groups of three share with the others an aspect or concern. The second person would answer with a reflective listening response. The third would then critique the response. Each member of a triad would have an opportunity to play each role: speaker, listener, and observer.

Setup

1. Small group (up to 24).
   a. Arrange chairs in a circle, semicircle, or around tables.
   b. Have participants arrange their chairs so that two or three can communicate with each other.

2. Large auditorium.
   a. Start at the beginning of the row and have the aisle person turn and discuss with the person to the inside. Dyads or triads can be formed along each row.

Procedure

1. After a topic has been described or a video shown, stop the program and have the participants form dyads or triads.

2. Have the pair or small group decide who will be the speaker, the listener, and the observer.

3. Describe a situation or problem that needs to be clarified or solved. Handouts describing situations are effective in large meetings.

4. Have the participants play out their parts.

5. The observer then critiques the statement and response using positive reinforcement as well as suggestions.

Appropriate Topics

1. Communication
2. Behavior challenges
3. Determination of problem ownership
4. Reflective and active listening
5. Natural and logical consequences

ROLE-PLAYING. **Role-playing** is the dramatization of a situation where group members put themselves into designated roles. Role-playing is a very informal type of meeting, similar to presenting a drama, so it can be adapted to a variety of situations. The roles that people play can be initiated by the players, or players can follow a set format or enact a specific situation. In either situation, the people playing the roles should put themselves in those roles. They should feel that they are the characters in the roles and should respond with appropriate reactions and emotions. Spontaneous role-playing has advantages over the planned drama.

Role-playing can be used to demonstrate a problem or develop participants' sensitivities to a situation. In demonstrating a situation, the group members discuss their feelings and reactions and offer solutions. It is an excellent means for getting many people involved in a situation and is easily used to illustrate parent–child interaction.

In development of empathy, role reversal is often used. For example, a teacher plays the role of principal while a principal plays the role of teacher. Not only do participants begin to understand the obligations of the other role, but through their playing of the role they also are able to demonstrate their feelings. This clarifies feelings for both parties. Another role-reversal situation that can be used is the parent–child relationship, with one participant playing the child's role and another playing the parent's role. The parent in the child's role develops sensitivity to the child's position.

Participants in role-playing feel free to communicate their feelings and attitudes because they are not portraying themselves. This encourages greater openness and involvement. When group members begin role-playing, they tend to be hesitant to get involved emotionally with the part. After role-playing for a time, hesitancy and reluctance to be involved disappear and people enjoy the opportunity to participate. If the group progresses to a therapeutic enactment, professional counselors should be included and consulted.

Setup

1. Role-playing can be used in a variety of formats: (a) within the circle of participants—the center of the circle is the stage; (b) with chairs arranged in semicircles and the stage at the front—this is appropriate for larger groups; (c) in a large group meeting with an auditorium stage for the actors.

2. If the role-playing is planned for participation by the entire group, allow members to meet first in a circle arrangement and then break into smaller groups after an introduction.

Procedure

1. A short discussion of the topic or situation is introduced by the leader or panel.

2. The situation that will be role-played is introduced. This can be done by (a) volunteers, (b) people selected before the meeting to start the initial role-play, or (c) breaking up the total group into groups of four or five, giving each group a topic with an outline of the role situation or a challenge to develop its own role situations.

3. The role can be played in two ways:

   a. It can be done in front of the entire group with members watching and listening to the dramatization and interaction. After the role-play, the members use the open discussion method to clarify issues, study the problem, and make decisions.

   b. If the members are divided into smaller groups, it is beneficial to let each group play its roles simultaneously and have each small group

discuss the feelings and attitudes that arose while they were playing their roles. After this, the small groups can discuss alternative means, ideas, and solutions.

4. If the small groups have all met and developed specific situations, it is also meaningful to have each group perform its role-playing in front of the full group. Afterward, the larger group can discuss the role-playing together. Clarification, questions, and solutions are brought forth at this time.

5. The leader thanks those who participated in role-playing.

Appropriate Topics

1. Parent–teacher conferences
2. Behavioral problems
3. Building self-esteem
4. Reflective listening
5. Roles within groups

DRAMATIZATIONS. **Dramatizations** or **short plays**, written by group members or selected from those available from commercial companies, mental health organizations, or social agencies can be used as springboards to discussion. There are advantages to using skits composed by members. First, the skit can be kept short with parts that are easy to learn. Second, the action may be specifically related to the group's needs. Third, the preparation of the skit encourages group participants to become actively involved in the process and in the material presented.

A variation of the drama can be done through the use of puppets. Many participants like to use a puppet because it removes the threat of performing.

Setup

1. Depending on the number of people at the meeting, the room can be arranged as follows:

   a. Use a circle for a small group, with the dramatization performed as a play in the round.

   b. If the group is small, chairs can be arranged in a semicircle with the "stage" at the opening. The stage may be raised or on the same level as the group members.

   c. If the group is large, an auditorium arrangement is appropriate. The dramatization can be performed on a stage.

Procedure

1. The leader convenes the meeting and introduces the drama and the cast of characters.

2. The dramatization is presented.

3. Open discussion ensues, which clarifies the feelings, emotions, and information presented.

4. The leader thanks the performers.

Appropriate Topics

1. Domestic violence
2. Handling the stubborn child
3. Rivalry between children
4. Family rivalry
5. Family conferences
6. Communication among family members

PANELS.   A **panel** is an informal presentation by four to six presenters who discuss an issue or idea. Panel members come prepared with background material on a selected subject and, seated behind a table or in a semicircle, discuss the subject among themselves. The presentation allows informal interaction and conversation among the members.

The chairperson, although a member of the panel, has different responsibilities from the other members. The chairperson introduces members, presents the topic, and then encourages participation by the other members. Like a leader, the chairperson can clarify, keep the panel focused on the topic, and summarize the closing.

Setup

1. Place a table, or two tables slightly turned toward each other, in front of the audience. Set chairs for the panelists behind the table, allowing members to see and converse with one another easily.

2. Seat the audience or remaining members of the group in a semicircle, with the panel facing them. If the audience is large, auditorium-style seating can be used with a panel presentation.

Procedure

The chairperson does the following:

1. Clarifies the panel procedure to the audience.

2. Presents the topic for discussion and the relevance of the topic to the group's concerns.

3. Introduces the panel members.

4. Starts the discussion with a question or statement. The panelists begin a discussion, freely interacting and conversing with one another.

5. Asks for questions from the audience. Questions are discussed among panelists.

6. Summarizes the major points and the conclusions of the panel.

7. Thanks the panel members for their contributions.

Appropriate Topics

1. Child development—social, intellectual, emotional, and physical
2. New methods of classroom teaching
3. Bias-free education
4. Exceptional children
5. Influence of drugs and alcohol on children
6. Discipline
7. Emotions in children
8. Managing a home with both parents working
9. Nutrition

COLLOQUIES.   The **colloquy** is a panel discussion by an informed or expert panel where members of the audience are encouraged by the chairperson to interject questions or comments during the presentation. This allows information pertinent to the audience's interests to be discussed during the main part of the presentation instead of waiting for a question-and-answer period after the presentation.

A second form of the colloquy includes two sets of panels, an expert panel and a lay panel. The lay panel uses the procedures for a panel discussion. The expert panel gives advice when called upon by the lay panel or when it thinks pertinent information is being overlooked.

Setup

1. For a single panel, place chairs behind tables that are turned so the members of the panel can make eye contact with one another.

2. For two panels—lay and expert—seat the chairperson in the center with one panel on the left and one on the right. Both sets of panel members should be facing slightly toward the center so they can see each other and the audience.

Procedure

1. Single-panel colloquy:
   a. The leader or chairperson explains and clarifies the colloquy procedure to the audience.
   b. The topic for discussion is introduced.
   c. Panel members are introduced.
   d. The chairperson offers a stimulating comment or question to start the discussion.
   e. The chairperson encourages free interaction among panel members and takes questions and comments from the audience.
   f. An open forum follows the conclusion of the panel discussion.
   g. The leader summarizes and concludes the meeting.

2. Dual-panel colloquy:
   a. The chairperson explains and clarifies the two-panel colloquy to the audience.
   b. The chairperson introduces the subject for discussion.
   c. The expert and lay panels are presented to the audience.
   d. The leader starts the discussion with a stimulating remark or question.
   e. As expert advice is needed, the second panel is called upon to contribute.
   f. A question-and-answer period follows the presentation, with comments and questions from the audience answered and discussed by both the lay and expert panels.
   g. The chairperson summarizes, thanks the participants, and concludes the colloquy.

Appropriate Topics

1. Dealing with your child's fears
2. Handling stress
3. Drug addiction and alcoholism
4. Helping exceptional children
5. Nutrition

DEBATES. When an issue is of a pro-and-con nature, a **debate** is an effective means of presenting both sides. The debate team presents opposing views of a controversial issue.

Setup

1. Place enough chairs for the members of each debate team on either side of a podium or table.

2. Place chairs in a circle for a small audience. If the group is large, use an auditorium formation.

Procedure

1. The question to be debated is announced by the chairperson, and the issue is turned over to the speakers for each side.

2. One speaker for the affirmative begins with a 2- to 4-minute speech. The next speaker is from the opposing position. The teams alternate until each member has spoken.

3. Rebuttal following each speech is optional, or leaders of both debate teams may conclude the debate section with rebuttals.

4. The chairperson entertains questions from the audience, and the debate teams answer and discuss the issue.

Appropriate Topics

1. Sex education—home's or school's responsibility?
2. Behavior modification versus logical consequences
3. Play for learning and teaching
4. Encouragement toward achievement versus "don't push my child"
5. Back to basics versus inquiry and/or literacy-based education

Book Review Discussions

Book reviews by group members or experts provide a format that brings out stimulating new ideas or acknowledges expertise. The review can be given by one presenter or several members. An open discussion by the entire group follows.

Setup

1. Place chairs for book reviewers behind a table in front of the group.

2. Arrange chairs for the audience in a circle or semicircle.

Procedure

1. The chairperson tells a little about the book to be reviewed and introduces the book reviewer or book review panel.

2. The book reviewer discusses the author of the book.

3. The book review is given.
   a. If the book is to be reviewed by panel discussion, the group discusses issues and ideas in a conversational format.
   b. One person may give the book review.
   c. Two or three people may each review a portion of the book.
4. After the review, the entire group joins in an open discussion of the book.

Appropriate Topics for Books

1. Family values
2. Decision making
3. Building self-concept
4. Communication
5. Divorce
6. Role identification
7. Single parents

AUDIOVISUAL PRESENTATIONS.   Visual stimuli, programmed material, and film presentations can be catalysts for a good open discussion. The audiovisual format is directed toward two senses—hearing and sight—whereas an audio presentation relies solely on hearing. The addition of visual stimuli is beneficial to those who learn better through sight than sound. Accompanying charts, posters, or pictures help clarify ideas. Video presentations can present information in an interesting and succinct manner.

Techniques

1. Streamed audio and video
2. Audiovisual:
   a. DVDs
   b. PowerPoints with running commentary
   c. YouTube videos
3. Visual:
   a. Charts
   b. Posters
   c. Computers

Arrangements Before the Meeting

1. The teacher or group decides on information needed by members through interest finders.
2. Review and select DVDs or videos. (Choose only programs that are relevant, interesting, and presented well.)
3. Choose a member to give a presentation.

4. Reserve equipment—laptops, LCD projectors, chart stands, projection carts, extension cords, outlet adapters, screen, and so on. Very important to test equipment beforehand if possible.
5. Preview audiovisual and audio materials to ensure their quality and develop questions and comments relevant to the presentation. Do not use audiovisual materials as fillers; use them only as relevant additions to the curriculum.
6. Review the "Arrangements for Meetings" section and make appropriate preparations.

Setup

1. Check and prepare equipment before the meeting. Have DVDs ready to begin and have charts and posters set up. If YouTube videos will be used, make sure that the Internet connection works well.
2. Arrange chairs so everyone can see the presentation.

Procedure

1. The chairperson introduces the topic and the presenter.
2. The presenter gives background information on audiovisual material and points out important aspects of the presentation.
3. Afterward, the presenter leads an open discussion and question-and-answer period.

Appropriate Topics

1. Foundations of reading and writing
2. Emotional growth
3. Dealing with fears
4. Exceptional children—for example, those who are gifted or those with learning disabilities
5. Autism spectrum disorder
6. Attention-deficit/hyperactivity disorder
7. Drugs and alcohol
8. Drop-out problems
9. Teenage pregnancies

SYMPOSIUMS.   A **symposium** is a formal presentation by several speakers on various aspects of a topic. Each symposium presenter develops a specific talk of 5 to 15 minutes in length. The symposium is similar to a lecture, but information is given by several lecturers rather than just one. Its value—to share expert information—is the same.

Setup

1. Place chairs for the presenters behind a table in front of the audience.

2. Chairs for the audience can be in a circle or semicircle for a small group, or auditorium arrangements can be made for a large group.

Procedure

1. The chairperson or leader introduces the symposium speakers.

2. Each presenter gives a talk.

3. The chairperson or leader provides transitional statements between each speaker's presentation.

4. At the end of the presentations, questions directed to a specific speaker or to the entire symposium are entertained by the chairperson. A discussion follows.

5. The chairperson summarizes the main points of the meeting.

6. Symposium presenters are thanked for their contributions.

Appropriate Topics

1. Nonsexist education

2. Single parenthood

3. Gender-role identification

4. Cultural and linguistic diversity

5. Consumer education

6. Death and dying

7. Safety in the home (e.g., toys, storage of hazardous materials, home arrangement)

8. Special education services

9. Drugs and alcohol

10. Suicide

11. Restructuring schools

LECTURES.   A **lecture** is a talk prepared by an expert or lay presenter. No interruptions or questions are allowed during the presentation, but there may be a question-and-answer period afterward. The lecture without a forum following it results in a formal presentation with no interaction between speaker and audience. A lecture forum that includes a period for questions and answers at the end of the presentation permits some interaction and gives the audience an opportunity to ask questions, clarify points, and make comments.

The lecture is an excellent vehicle for dissemination of specific information. As a result, care must be taken to choose a speaker who not only knows the subject but also presents unbiased material.

Arrangements Before the Meeting

1. Select a topic and obtain a speaker who is recognized as an authority.

2. Communicate with the speaker on group interests and needs, time limits for speeches, and the forum environment.

3. Prepare an introduction that is based on the speaker's background and expertise.

4. Review the "Arrangements for Meetings" section and make appropriate preparations.

Setup

1. Place a podium or table at the center of the stage if the audience is large. Place chairs in a circle with a small table in front of the speaker if the audience is small.

2. Check the sound system if the area is large.

3. Obtain a glass and a pitcher of water for the speaker.

Procedure

1. The chairperson introduces the speaker and topic.

2. The speaker gives a talk for a specific period of time.

3. The chairperson conducts a forum for questions with the guest speaker, responding to comments and answering questions.

4. The chairperson thanks the speaker, and the meeting is concluded.

Appropriate Topics

1. Money management

2. Specialists in different areas of child development—for example, psychiatrists, pediatricians, dentists, nutritionists, obstetricians, special educators, speech therapists, occupational therapists, and physical therapists

3. How to manage stress

4. Dealing with illness and death

5. Preventive health measures

6. Childhood diseases and disorders

7. School finances

8. Preventing violence

Select the meeting format that fulfills your needs and is the most appropriate for the topic. Members of the group have responsibilities to themselves and to the group. After a positive group meeting, the participants should feel supportive and supported as well as fulfilled and productive. Effective teacher leaders assist in the development of effective parent meetings by using varied strategies that entice families to engage.

Summary

Parent group meetings are among the most efficient and viable forms of parent education. Positive leadership skills are essential to facilitate productive parent groups. Included in this chapter were a description of a needs assessment and a discussion of the formation of parent groups.

Leadership skills and good group interaction can be developed if groups are aware of leadership and group roles. Roles that emerge within groups affect the interaction among participants. Knowledge of task, maintenance, and dysfunctional roles improves the productivity of group interactions through the concerted elimination of dysfunctional roles. An analysis of group discussion illustrates the interaction in process.

Group meetings use a variety of meeting formats, either individually or in combination. The formats include roundtables, concentric circles, buzz sessions, brainstorming sessions, workshops, field trips, dyad or triad interaction and feedback, role-playing, dramatizations, panels, colloquies, debates, book reviews, audiovisual presentations, symposiums, and lectures. Choice of topics for the meetings should fit the interests and needs of the groups.

Evaluations are necessary in ongoing parent groups because they provide a basis for improvement of group interaction and suggestions for the continuing program.

Suggested Class Activities and Discussions

1. Conduct an opening period of a parent meeting. Include icebreakers and interest finders.
2. Attend a parent-education meeting in a community different from your own. Visit with the members. Note how the meeting is conducted, the involvement of the parents, and the feelings of the members. Talk with the director about the goals and objectives of the group. Also speak with parents about their desires for the group.
3. Conduct a needs assessment in a familiar school or child development center. From the needs assessment, develop a workshop or meeting for parents.

Include the objectives of the meeting, questions to be answered, background material on the questions, and a list of additional resources.

4. Attend a board meeting of a local district. Make note of the items that relate to family engagement.
5. Attend a parent-advisory council meeting. Present your findings to your class. How does this group promote family engagement? How is leadership displayed?
6. Attend or participate in a site-based or community management meeting. Does this group promote family engagement?

Useful Websites

Global Family Research Project
MALDEF Leadership Programs

McCormick Center for Early Childhood Leadership

Glossary Terms

Leader: Person who has a vision, who cares for others, who plans ahead, is inclusive, and most of all, is not afraid of change.
Leadership: The action of leading or guiding.

Leadership Style: The way the leader implements plans, guides, leads, motivates others to work.
Needs Assessment: Evaluation that helps determine specific needs.

Chapter 8
Family Engagement Framework in Schools

Learning at school can be more successful using children's funds of knowledge in school-based programs.

Mari Riojas-Cortez

Learning Outcomes

In this chapter on school-based education, you will read about effective family–school based programs.

8.1 Describe the components of an ideal school-based program.

8.2 List and describe nine levels of family collaboration.

8.3 Identify family engagement framework.

8.4 Examine examples of school-based programs that promote family engagement.

Components of an Ideal School-Based Program

Assume the role of a parent who visits a school committed to the involvement of other parents. As you open the school door, you notice a sign that welcomes you in English and your home language. The staff greets you with smiles when you check in at the office. If you want to have a cup of coffee or tea, look through the school's curricula, or read an article, you can visit the family center. The family center provides opportunities for parents to use computers and electronic tablets.

There, several parents are developing curriculum material for the school's resource room. One parent is making a game for the third- and fourth-grade classes. Another is downloading curriculum-related articles and saving them on the desktop computers located in the family resource room in a folder titled "articles of interest." As you sip your coffee, the sounds of young children echo down the hall from the west wing of the building. Parents and their children are arriving for parent education classes, parent–child meetings, and ESL classes. The school also offers programs for parents of infants, toddlers, and preschool children. Both parents are invited and included in the programs. For those who cannot come during the week, a Saturday session is available. On the fourth Tuesday of every month, the school has a breakfast for students' fathers and/or friends.

You came to school today to visit your child's classroom, so, after a brief visit to the family center, you walk to your child's room. On the bulletin board outside the door is a welcome notice that shows in detail what the children have been accomplishing. Here the teacher has described the events of the week, listed volunteer times for parents, and asked for contributions of plastic containers to be used in making tempera-paint prints.

Rawpixel.com/Shutterstock

Parents are active partners in education.

Studio 8/Pearson Education Ltd

A positive view of children and parents creates a healthy environment in any school or center.

Immediately aware of what is happening in the room, you make a note to start collecting "scrounge materials" for recycling in the classroom. An invitation to an evening workshop reminds you that you have saved next Tuesday evening for that very event. In the space for notes to and from parents, you write a short response to the message you received from the teacher last week.

Also attached to the bulletin board are "Tips for Visiting." These let you know that you can become involved in a classroom activity if desired. The teacher smiles and acknowledges your presence but, being involved with the class, continues teaching. The class greeter, a child chosen as a "very important person" this week, comes up and welcomes you. Later, during a center session or break, you have an opportunity to talk with the teacher and your child. Recruitment of volunteers is underway, so you are encouraged—but not forced—to contribute. Flexible hours, designated times, childcare services, and a variety of tasks make it easy to share some time in this classroom.

Knowing that the principal holds an open forum each week at this time, you stop by and join a discussion on school policy. Parents are encouraged to evaluate the "tote bag" home-learning activities that have been sent home with children. There is also a section on the school's website where parents can access literacy activities that resemble the exercises in the "tote bag" learning activities but in a digital form. Parents participate in the Parent Blog,

specifically created for sharing information regarding the home-learning activities. Most importantly, activities planned reflect the cultures represented in the school. Special programs for families of children with disabilities are also offered. In addition, plans are underway for an after-school recreation program that will include children with special needs. The principal will take the comments to the Parent Advisory Board meeting later this week. As you leave the school, you feel satisfied that this school responds to the needs of both you and your child and that the opportunities to participate are open to parents, teachers, and community members.

The preceding scenario shows a school or center that reaches out to all families and the community, creating collaboration in children's lives and thus making it a model for many schools to follow. This occurs when schools have an open mind about families because of their diversity including language. Figure 8.1 illustrates how schools reach out and collaborate with families and communities.

Schools that are serious about family engagement will invest funds to ensure that programs are successful. An important support for family engagement includes parent involvement facilitators or PIS (Ferrara, 2015), also known as family resource specialists in Early Head Start and Head Start programs. Within the ecological systems theory, these facilitators or specialists work in different capacities to support families in order for them to engage with their child and child's education to help them succeed.

Figure 8.1 Wheel of Opportunity

The spokes of the wheel radiate from the school and reveal opportunities for engaging parents, children, and the community.

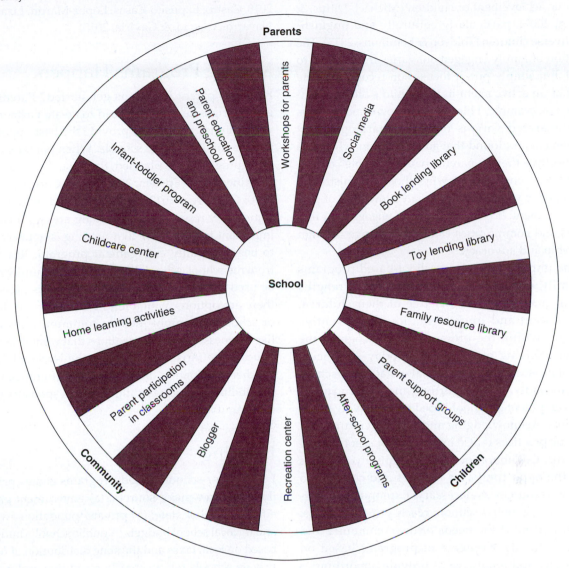

Defining School Based Family Engagement Programs

School-based programs are programs that facilitate learning for families within the school. Such programs develop from the needs assessment that effective leaders (teachers and administrators) conduct in order to meet the needs of families. School-based programs are significant for the engagement of families. **Family engagement** is demonstrated by many schools and described in a voluminous number of articles. School districts affirm the importance of family engagement across the U.S. by celebrating National Parent Involvement Day. On this day, parents are encouraged to visit the school and get involved in different duties and activities (lunch duty, fixing the classroom library, upgrading the computers in the classroom, helping the librarian, etc.). National Parent Involvement Day provides opportunities for parents to visit the school and engage in different ways for any amount of time they are able.

Family and community engagement in the schools has been linked to improved quality of school programs, better school attendance, and the increased academic achievement of children (Michael, Dittus, & Epstein, 2007), particularly culturally and linguistically diverse children (Toldson & Lemmons, 2013). The definition of family engagement varies from school to school, but simply put, it focuses on recognizing the family as an active agent in their child's life and education. For example, Hilado, Kallemeyn, and Phillips (2013) analyzed various remarks regarding family involvement and found that administrators who were more positive toward parents had a "flexible" definition of family engagement, while those administrators with negative views of parents had a low level of parent engagement. It is through family engagement that schools and communities can create change through leadership and advocacy.

The implementation of school-based programs for family engagement is based on the strengths of families and their knowledge of their children. Identification and implementation of preventive strategies within the programs that recognize the stresses affecting many families today—financial, emotional, social, and personal—make the school family-friendly and supportive, and are crucial for the development of school-based parent involvement programs. Acknowledging and valuing cultural and linguistic practices is also important for school-based programs. Collaboration with community agencies offers the opportunity for families and children to use new resources as necessary. Exploration of different models helps schools reach out to families; models that meet the needs of the community and school or the development of programs based on community and family needs provide opportunities for family engagement.

It is important to find the school-based model program that will help families understand their role in family engagement with the school. In some cultures, parent engagement in the schools is limited because of the parents' strong belief that the teacher and the school know more than they, the parents, do.

Although evidence exists that parental engagement makes a difference in the academic lives of children, considerations regarding how parents become involved, and children's reactions to parental involvement, must be taken into account (Pomerantz, Moorman, & Litwack, 2007). Indeed, the way parents engage with their children (at all levels) has shown to have an impact on their children's academic engagement particularly in the elementary years (Erdener & Knoeppel, 2018, Castro, Expósito-Casas, López-Martín, Lizasoain, Navarro-Asencio, & Gaviria, 2015).

Making Programs Happen

How can parent programs get started? Parent programs originate from the need to create partnerships with families in order to provide the best opportunities for children in the schools. When parent engagement programs are planned, they usually focus on an identified need (Epstein, 2005; Riojas-Cortez & Flores, 2010; Gutierrez, 2013). After the need is identified, community resources and funding are explored. It is important to remember that funding is not necessary to begin a family engagement program. Resources from the school, school district, and community might be used to begin a program. If funding is necessary, there are options available to the individual district or school that might include community resources like businesses and organizations that want to support education efforts. For example, the National Parent Teacher Association offers a variety of grants. Other possibilities include finding business sponsors in the community.

Funding

Funding for school-related programs comes primarily from three major sources: (a) government grants, either federal or state; (b) private foundation awards; and (c) local school budgets. A public school's budget is based on local taxes and the state distribution of funds. Private schools rely primarily on tuition and private sources for funding, although they are eligible for some federal grants. Current information on funding and grants can be obtained from your regional Department of Education or Department of Health and Human Services, as well as your state social services or education department.

The most stable funding source for public schools is the local school board. As schools begin to view the family component as worthwhile or essential, more programs will be implemented and funded through local support. Private foundations also fund special projects for parents and children. Local businesses and foundations are probably the best source of funds or information about money available in your community. For example, in Texas we have a chain of grocery stores called HEB. This grocery store funds a family literacy program that focuses on the importance of families reading to their young children. It is called HEB Read3. This program seeks to engage parents in literacy with their young children.

If a program is dependent on extra grant funding, plans must be made for financing after the grant runs out, or the program will either deteriorate or disappear. Most grants have a specified duration, usually three years. The major importance of grants is to provide the impetus for developing programs, materials, and services. Many programs that are now a permanent part of the community were started on grants. For example, a parent-engagement program in the Braintree Public Schools in Massachusetts called Parent Involvement, Inc. initiated from a U.S. Department of Education and National Science Foundation grant that focused on helping parents advocate for math, science, and technology reform for their school district and the community (Parent Involvement Program, 2010). After the grant ended, parents helped fund the program, which eventually turned into a nonprofit organization focusing on parental involvement in the schools focusing on math, science, and technology. Other programs have been developed in collaboration with higher-education institutions such as FLAME (Family Literacy: Aprendiendo, Mejorando, Educando) at the University of Illinois Champaign-Urbana (see Rodríguez-Brown, 2004), FIELD (Family Institute for Early Literacy Development; (see Riojas-Cortez, Flores, & Clark, 2003), and La Clase Mágica (Machado-Casas, 2014) from the University of Texas at San Antonio (UTSA).

When grants are not awarded, parent groups can work together with the school to seek local funding. Many organizations and community businesses are ready to provide support for programs that will meet the needs of children and their families. Teachers can work together with parents to discover the type of programs families need and want. Develop a collaborative approach to bring about a partnership. For example, volunteers can be an alternative to funding in making programs happen. Using volunteers in a positive way can help teachers and enable the school to enrich its educational offerings. Grandparents and other family members can work together with teachers to enrich the children's learning opportunities. For example, grandparents can come to the classroom to read books or make a family recipe. Other family members can assist either at school or home by creating games or finding materials for the teachers. They can also assist the school on a larger scale. You will be surprised at the amazing talents that families have. For example, when I was a teacher, the parents of my students had different skills and talents—for instance, one was a firefighter and brought a fire truck for the children during fire safety week, and his wife owned a flower shop so she sent flowers to put in the housekeeping center as a centerpiece. The key to making successful connections with families is to create a positive climate where families feel safe and comfortable enough to take advantage of a variety of opportunities.

Resources and Social Agencies

Collaboration between schools and social agencies helps develop continuity and supply the support families need. Teachers, as well as administrators, can refer families to social services, recreation districts, libraries, museums and other public agencies. If the school district does not have a list, school personnel can contact the Department of Social Services, United Way, the local chamber of commerce, or other agencies or civic groups to obtain a list of community resources. Check to see if there is a clearinghouse in the area. This information is also often available on the Internet. Libraries and museums also provide children with services, particularly increased opportunities for learning (Sirinides, Fink, & DuBois, 2017). Many work in collaboration with school districts and other educational organizations to train teachers and provide programs for children. For example, the DoSeum in San Antonio, Texas, the Children's Museum in Houston, the Boston Children's Museum, among many others provide educator workshops that focus on working with parents.

Families and children need supportive environments. Although it has been recognized that those in poverty have specific needs, families at all income levels need a sense of community and commitment. Schools, family resource centers, and families must work together. If schools and community resources communicate, cooperate, and collaborate with one another, all families and children have an opportunity to benefit from a variety of needed services and resources. For example, many working families need after-school care. Very often, families feel like they have to "settle" for the type of care their children receive. However, families can be proactive by communicating to after-school programs their child's interests, needs, and strengths (Rosenberg, Harris, & Wilkes, 2012).

Nine Levels of Family Collaboration

When developing family engagement programs, it is important to enable varying degrees of involvement and levels of family collaboration in order to include as many families as possible. Because learning occurs anytime anywhere, as indicated by Lopez and Caspe in an article from the *Family Involvement Network of Educators (or FINE) Newsletter* published by the Harvard Family Research Project[1] (2014), it is important to remember that when children are at home with their families, they are in fact learning (recall funds of knowledge). Families can be involved with schools on nine different levels, ranging from those who are active educational partners at home and school to those who participate only as recipients of education and support. (See Figure 8.2.)

1. *Parents as active partners and educational leaders at home and at school.* Parents who are actively involved at home and at school have the time and availability to participate in both aspects of their children's lives. These families want to support their children through active involvement at home as well as in the school. Their roles may end with their commitment to their children, or they may also be involved in the second level.

2. *Parents as decision makers.* The second role goes beyond active involvement to include decision making. These parents might serve on the school board, on a site-based management team, or on an advisory council. With decision making comes the power to affect the offerings and climate of the school. Power and decision making are seen in the use of policy committees, site-based collaborative decision making, advisory task forces, and school boards.

3. *Parents as advocates to help schools achieve excellent educational offerings.* Some parents are primarily involved with schools as advocates for the school and as fund-raisers. Think of the parent who spends hours setting up the booths for a school fair to earn money to buy computers or some other equipment the school needs. Think of the parent who writes letters to newspapers or administrators, supporting school programs, or who advocates forcefully for educational principles. Advocacy has spurred the development of programs for special-education students. Case advocacy, in the hands of individual parents, can give parents the opportunity to state their case and get it resolved to their satisfaction. There are many levels of advocacy and a variety of ways in which parents can advocate for their children and the concerns they have.

4. *Parents actively involved with the school as volunteers or paid employees.* Parents who work in the school

---

[1]The Harvard Research Project is now the Global Family Research Project and is not associated with Harvard University.

Figure 8.2 Parent Collaboration with Schools
Families relate to the schools in ways ranging from support of their children's education to decision making.

> **Parent Collaboration with Schools**
>
> Parent as an active partner and educational leader at home and at school
> Parent as a decision maker
> Parent as an advocate for the school
> Parent actively involved as volunteer or paid employee
> Parent as a liaison between school and home to support homework
> Parent as supporter of the educational goals of the school
> Parent as a recipient of education and support
> Parent as member of parent educational classes
> Parent as representative and activist in the community

enjoy a special position there. Through their work they can view the operations of the school, learn about the curricula, and become acquainted with teachers and administrators as friends and colleagues. They can also help as advocates for the school in the community. However, it is important for the school and parent to have specific guidelines on duties and responsibilities.

5. *Parents as liaisons between school and home to support homework and to be aware of school activities.* Parents who act as liaisons between school and home do not become involved in power or advocacy and are most interested in the school as the agency that educates their children.

6. *Parents, though not active, supporting the educational goals of the school and encouraging their children to study.* These parents, similar to those who serve as liaisons, are supportive of the schools. Perhaps they are too busy to be engaged, or perhaps they do not remember schools with fondness and prefer to keep their distance, but they do not undermine the school's objective to educate their children. Schools should reach out to these parents and make them feel welcome.

7. *Parents as recipients of support from the school.* Schools reach more families than any other agency, and so it becomes expedient to look to schools for support. Parent engagement and family education can help mothers and fathers become better informed and offer support that enables them to strengthen their families. Offerings in the school can include family literacy classes, a crisis nursery, before- and after-school programs for children, a family resource room, clothes and shoe/boot exchanges, free breakfasts and lunches for children, and parent education. Schools can also serve as referral agencies for community services if families are in need.

8. *Parents as members of parent education classes.* If parents can be encouraged to attend classes, knowledge of child development can help with child rearing. For example, knowledge of the importance of language development, based in the first 4 years of life, is essential for later school success. During parent education classes, it is sometimes a surprise to parents to learn that talking and reading with their young child are important. It is important for parents who are English language learners to know that speaking in their home language to their children builds a stronger foundation for biliteracy (Perez, 2004; Huerta & Riojas-Cortez, 2014) and helps children manage their emotions as they develop two languages.

9. *Parents as representatives and activists in the community.* Parents with knowledge of community offerings and active membership in community endeavors might have the ability to solicit information and help from organizations in the community. These community offerings might be able to help the family who is experiencing homelessness, the child whose parents are on drugs, the family who needs help in obtaining employment, the child who needs protection, or the child who needs extra help with lessons. Parents who know their community strengthen the school's ability to use community offerings, but the school must value their knowledge to increase collaboration.

Families need agencies to collaborate with each other and to help them, the families, grow or, in some cases, to survive. With the large number of parents working, all agencies involved with the family (recreation, health, social agencies, businesses, schools, and places of worship) must work together to ensure continuity. Employers should reevaluate their structure to enable more part-time, shared, and flexible hours and release time for parents to visit and engage in the schools. They should also collaborate with high schools to provide occupational internships (paid and/ or unpaid). Social agencies can provide support for parents who are unable to provide adequately for their families or who might be neglectful or abusive without that support. Schools cannot be expected to solve

Teachers are important resources to support culturally and linguistically diverse families.

Merrill Education

all of society's problems and answer all the questions involved in change, but they should work with other agencies and provide education and facilities to help strengthen families.

The emerging family resource centers and the increasing number of schools offering family literacy classes are steps in the right direction. For parents who are English language learners, it is important that the schools, together with family resource centers, offer English as a Second Language classes at times that are convenient for parents. Parents need to be given the opportunity to enhance their literacy skills so they can participate in society successfully, earn a living, and better assist in their children's development. In addition, of critical importance in early childhood is socioemotional learning. Good communication with families through conversations will allow teachers to get to know and understand the child (Arndt & McGuire-Schwarts, 2008) particularly as it relates to socioemotional learning. Understanding children's socioemotional learning and development will help educators and parents to work together to help the child develop successfully even when faced with challenges.

Family Engagement Framework

Epstein (1995, 1996, 2001, 2006) shares a framework of six types of involvement that schools can implement to increase collaboration among schools, families, and community. The framework helps teachers and schools develop effective school-based family engagement programs.

1. *Parenting*—Help parents with skills and give them an understanding of child and adolescent development that enables them to have a home environment that supports learning and school success. Examples include parenting classes; ESL or GED classes; or family workshops based on current topics such as socioemotional development, literacy development, school shootings, guidance, special needs, nutrition, and transition points, among others.

2. *Communicating*—Communicate effectively, school to home and home to school, about children's progress and the school programs. Teachers must discover the best type of communication to reach parents, either one-way or two-way. In the 21st century it is important to use technology to communicate with parents who have ready access. Email and texting are very common with texting being the preferred way of communication as being more readily available.

3. *Volunteering*—Engage parents as volunteers but be sure to provide training and flexible schedules so parents can be involved. Training and opportunities should be communicated at the beginning of the school year so parents can make arrangements to their schedule. Alternative opportunities should also be encouraged. Some of the best ideas for volunteering might come from the parents themselves.

4. *Learning at home*—Provide information and activities that parents can use in learning at home, thus connecting the family and school. Using technology, teachers can send parents ideas on how to engage with their children based on the classroom goals and objectives for each week. Activities should not overwhelm the family and should be intertwined with their daily life, perhaps using their funds of knowledge.

5. *Decision making*—Include parents in school decisions and governance and strengthen the parents' leadership skills. Decision making can also occur at the classroom level. Having brief workshops in which parents learn about the goals and objectives of the classroom and in developmentally appropriate practices can help them understand what children need and how they can engage in the decision making.

6. *Collaborating with the community*—Integrate the services and resources of the community with those of the schools to strengthen families, school programs, and children's development and learning. In the context of the classroom the teacher, in collaboration with the parents, can reach out to community stakeholders and organizations such as agencies that focus on children's well-being and health.

Epstein suggests that the six-component framework be used to further knowledge about parental engagement. This framework also shows a gap in knowledge about the topic. Epstein has suggested that there are more questions to be answered regarding parental involvement, including the teachers' views of parents and how those are different from parents' views of themselves.

Teachers who reach out to parents are more accepting of and more knowledgeable about the families than those who hesitate to be involved with parents. Studies show that teachers' involvement with families is more critical than family background in determining how students progress: "At the elementary, middle, and high school levels, surveys of parents, teachers, principals, and students reveal that if schools invest in practices that involve families, then parents respond by conducting those practices, including many parents who might not have otherwise become involved on their own" (Epstein, 1996, p. 217).

Teachers who involve parents and work well with them tend to evaluate the parents without stereotyping them, whether the parents are single or married, educated or lacking in education. When teachers involve parents, they find that the parents are helpful. When teachers do not involve parents, they often stereotype single parents and those with less education as not being helpful (Epstein, 1996).

The Center on School, Family, and Community Partnership focuses on elementary, middle, and secondary schools in their research and publications. They have guidelines to assist schools in building school–family–community partnerships.

Characteristics of Effective Collaboration

The characteristics of effective family–school collaboration include the following:

1. Principals, teachers, childcare providers, staff, and parents who believe in parent involvement.

2. Schools and childcare centers that welcome parent collaboration by encouraging parents to participate at the level that best fits their interests and time.

3. An open-door policy and climate that respond to parent concerns with effective communication.

4. Pairing children new to the school or center with a classmate to help new children with routines.

5. Conferences, with childcare available, held at times that make it possible and convenient for parents to attend.

6. A feeling of family, schools, center, and community joined together in a cooperative effort to support children's health and educational growth.

Reaching All Families

The Every Student Succeeds Act or ESSA of 2015 dictates that parents and communities play a significant role in the equation (Fenton, Ocasio-Stoutenburg, & Harry, 2017). Schools and teachers must understand that parents are collaborators in their children's education. Knowing and understanding the crucial role of parents in this process will help teachers create effective collaboration. Schools or centers can develop strategies that are culturally and developmentally appropriate for families to help children progress. Teachers must reach out to parents before the school year begins. Teachers in childcare centers should have a welcome packet as they receive new children, particularly infants and toddlers.

Moles (1996a) describes what have become classical methods and strategies to reach families that include early fall mailings, home–school handbooks, open houses, school–parent compacts, personal contacts, parent–teacher conferences, home visits, parent liaisons, homework, resource centers, family gatherings, special programs for children with special needs, and positive communication. Kraft (2017) provides more current examples regarding how families can be reached, and he focuses on the importance of communication.

First, Kraft (2017) indicates that schools should have updated parental information regarding the best way to communicate, including the preferred language. Second, teachers need to be given expectations and additional time to find ways to engage with parents, perhaps by rethinking teacher's non-instructional responsibilities and even designating a time period for "parent engagement efforts" (p. 60). Third, digital technology, including texting and mobile apps, is a critical way for teachers reach out to families. Fourth, teachers can use student information management systems to keep families informed regarding attendance, grades, and/or missing assignments. According to Kraft (2017), these systems only work when they are easily accessible for parents—and often they are not. Fifth, schools should partner with educational content organizations or create their own content in which teachers provide guidance to parents on how to talk with children about assignments or have mini lessons about what children are learning in school.

As Kraft (2017) notes, the task of educating children is too large for teachers or school to try to do it on their own; parents and families are needed to provide support. However, as Kraft (2017) recommends, schools must provide the infrastructure for parent engagement and teachers must be advocates by "providing time and support" (p. 62).

System Support for Family Engagement

The U.S. Department of Education (2018) developed a Family Engagement Team with representatives from different governmental offices to aid schools, districts, and states to engage more effectively with families. Parents, teachers, school administrators, and other team members engage in different types of communication such as policy briefings, parent forums, parent camps, webinars, Google Hangouts, tweets, Instagram posts, texts, lunch-and-learns, and listening-and-learning sessions. The team is committed to empower and give a voice to parents by

- Breaking down the "silos" within the agency, allowing for fuller exploration and integration of ideas;
- Using models and the language of legislation from early learning, special education, and Native American family engagement to share with schools, districts, and states;

Developmentally and culturally appropriate programs provide culturally and linguistically diverse children with opportunities for play, problem solving, and social learning.

Gideon Mendel/Corbis/Getty Images

- Promoting the engagement of parents, families, students, and representatives from communities to improve children's academic development;
- Making stakeholders and U.S. Department of Education (ED) staff aware of the challenges families face daily, both military and civilian;
- Sharing what each office is doing to encourage stakeholders to engage parents;
- Providing examples of effective practices that engage parents and families;
- Disseminating materials that encourage family engagement; and
- Incorporating language in grants that prioritizes engaging families in decision making and in planning school improvement programs. (U.S. Department of Education, 2018).

Reaching Reticent Parents

Parents want the best for their children. The majority of parents engage with their children but not all parents engage in the schools or with the teacher. Some parents may have a difficult time getting involved for a variety of reasons. This situation is especially common among low-income and culturally and linguistically diverse parents who may be made to feel inferior by school personnel, but it is also true for many middle- and upper class parents who receive negative feedback on their engagement in the schools.

The initiative for parent engagement must come from the school; the school must reach out to the home. The principal or director must make an effort to greet parents, particularly when they drop off their children at school. Teachers must greet all parents as they come into the classroom. In addition, a personalized message from the principal/ director or the teacher will make families feel special and valued. Furthermore, including all children in special activities also helps families feel valued. The school needs to remember that engagement of parents in children's learning in the home has a greater impact than the amount of time they spend participating in school activities (Harris & Goodall, 2008). The parents should be able to suggest their "terms of engagement" to be able to positively look at the partnership between them, the teacher and the school (Day, 2013).

Workshops at School for Parents to Use at Home: A Teacher's Sample

A workshop is one vehicle for introducing parents to home–school learning activities. Workshops allow participants to actively interact with one another and with materials that help them connect with the concepts being presented. Organization and clear directions assist teachers in creating successful workshops for parents. Real examples of successful workshops allow teachers to be creative within their own context.

The following narrative presents Ann Grimes, a first-grade teacher, who invited her students' parents to such a workshop. In order to make the parents feel welcome, Ms. Grimes greeted them, gave them nametags, and passed out a get-acquainted signature sheet for a signature game.

After the signature game, during which parents enthusiastically talked with one another, the make-and-take workshop began. Mrs. Grimes explained the program, its philosophy, and what the school expected of parents. She explained to parents that close, two-way communication helps ensure the program is meeting the needs of the child, parents, and school. If parents were interested in participating in a home–school learning project, she assured them that she would like to work with them as a member of the team.

Mrs. Grimes reminded the parents how important it is to listen to children, ask open-ended questions, and allow children the opportunity to predict and problem solve. She also reminded the parents that children, like adults, work best when they have a quiet, private work area and a regular time to work. She stressed that children should enjoy and succeed at home assignments. If a child struggles with more than 20% of the projects or problems, the activity selection should be reassessed, and new activities better geared to the child's level can be chosen. Many home activities can be recreational and enriching to family life. As she concluded her talk, Mrs. Grimes explained the plans for the evening. Parents were asked to participate in the activities located in different areas throughout the room. "If you look at your name tag, you will find a number. Go to that activity first," she instructed the parents.

The centers included games and activities, as well as directions on how to take part in them. Materials and guidelines were also available for activities that parents could make and take home. Some parents played Concentration (Figure 8.3) and made game boards, which could be easily made from cardboard, poster board, or a file folder (only an example not the actual game). Mrs. Grimes furnished decorative stickers that the parents could place on the game boards. To protect the completed board, some parents used the laminating machine, and others spread clear adhesive paper over their work. Each board was different, yet each was based on the same format—that is, children placed symbols on squares and used a spinner or die to tell them how many spaces to move. Some parents wrote letters or numbers on the spaces; others developed cards that children could take as they played their turn. If spaces were left empty, the board could be used for skill activities by developing sets of cards for phonics, numbers, or other basic skills. While some parents were busy with the game boards, others worked on language and math concepts, constructed books, or exercised their creativity at the art center.

After a busy 2-hour session, the group met again, and an animated discussion of the activities began. Two parents volunteered to make canvas tote bags for the class, and another promised to make a silk-screened print of the class emblem on each. They decided the tote bags would be reserved for home-learning activities. "Please be sure to evaluate the home-learning activities as you use them. And, please contribute your own ideas," encouraged Mrs. Grimes. "I'll keep track of each child's activities on these record sheets. If you have any questions, be sure to write or call me."

After refreshments, the parents began to leave. Some stopped by the table to sign up to volunteer in the program. Mrs. Grimes announced that she would need help implementing the home-learning program and that she could use help in the room as well. A volunteer training session was planned for the next week; the work toward a productive home–school endeavor had just begun.

The sample workshop provides an opportunity for others to see how a teacher can plan and create her/his own parent workshop. This narrative sample describes learning opportunities that can serve as a guide to develop other workshops that will meet the needs of parents within their specific contexts.

Figure 8.3 Game of Concentration

The game of concentration can be designed, constructed, and played at home or at school.

TASK SAMPLE—"CONCENTRATION"

AIM: To play a matching game with pairs of cards.

WHY: To practice visual memory, remembering the position of matching cards. To follow rules and take turns are skills used in most games.

MATERIALS: Grocery sack or small cards, five pairs of matching pictures, magazines, sales pamphlets, paste, scissors.

PROCEDURE:

1. Cut pairs of like pictures (10) from magazine and paste on circles cut from paper sacks or cards.

2. Encourage child to talk about pictures and name them. Then, together, place them in pairs.

3. Collect cards, turn them face down, and mix them.

4. Place cards in rows without looking at pictures.

5. Have child pick up one card and turn it over and say what it is. (Repeat the name if the child cannot say the name.) Then choose another card trying for a match. If no match, then both cards are turned over. Say, "That's your turn; now it's my turn."

6. The play continues until all the cards are matched. Count the matched pairs to see who is the winner.

EXTENDING THE CONCEPT:

1. Add more picture cards for pairs.

2. Play game using colors instead of pictures.

3. Use pictures of sets of objects.

Source: Project Home Base, Yakima, Washington.

Implementing Home-Learning Activities

Home-learning activities can be useful as enrichment projects, or they can be valuable as a sequential educational curriculum. If they are used to complement learning that is occurring simultaneously in the school, it is necessary to monitor the child's work at home and keep track of what is accomplished.

The process varies according to the availability of a parent coordinator or a family specialist. Depending on the program, parent coordinators or family specialists have different responsibilities such as keeping track of the home-learning activities. In some programs, parent

David Mager/Pearson Education

School activities can be reinforced in the home.

coordinators or family specialists can contact parents, make home visits and report on the progress of the child. It is the teacher's responsibility to advise the parent coordinator about the child's progress in school and recommend appropriate learning activities, if the program allows. If a parent coordinator is not available, a parent volunteer can help with recordkeeping and provide contact between the parents and the teacher. Careful considerations must be taken so that all confidential laws and policies are followed depending on the program. The following steps are appropriate for any situation:

1. Offer an orientation workshop.

2. Send learning activities home in a tote bag, deliver them personally, or give the responsibility of the delivery system to a parent coordinator.

3. Keep records of activity cards the child has taken home. Make a record card for each child with a space to indicate when each activity went home and a space for a response to the activity. This way, you will know which activity the child should be given next.

4. Get feedback from parents via notes, reports, phone calls, texts, or visits. Find out their reactions to the activities and their assessments of their child's success.

5. Continue communicating with parents. Include supplemental ideas and activity sheets on a skill that proved difficult for a particular student. Ask parents to reinforce skills up to the too-difficult level. Have them refer to previous activity cards for related projects.

6. Diversify your program to meet the needs of the parents and keep interest levels high.

7. Meet occasionally with parents or make home visits to support the monitoring system.

Communication is a basic ingredient in the success of home–school cooperation. Through talking with parents, you will know whether they consider home-learning activities to be a joy or a threat. You will want to adapt your program according to each parent's desires. Projects around the home can furnish experiences in math, language, art, music, science, and composition. The process of exploring an idea and carrying it to fruition requires problem solving.

Many teachers develop their own activities by using home learning bags or backpacks to take home. It is the responsibility of the teacher to ensure that the bags or backpacks are always ready to be sent home. It is the responsibility of the parent to send it back and provide feedback so that the child can always have a positive experience. Items that are often used for home–school activities are books, paper, and crayons. Some schools include cameras so that parents can take pictures of the activities at home, and others include digital tablets to increase digital literacy in the home.

Examples of Programs that Promote Family Engagement in Schools

A grant for $800,000 was given to the New York City system to develop strategies for parent involvement. The program by that name, the Parent Involvement Program, found that ten factors seemed important in their efforts: leadership from the schools, accessibility and open lines of communication, time to plan and implement changes, cultural awareness, active teacher roles, continuity, public recognition of those involved, broad-based support, adolescent focus, and recognition of parents as people (Jackson & Cooper, 1992). Currently, there are many examples of school-based family engagement programs. Some include those that schools and districts pay for while others are developed in-house.

Oleg Kozlov/shutterstock

Outdoor activities at home or school help children develop creativity.

Empowerment

A research project at Cornell University first worked with parents and later tied parent engagement to the schools. Working with 160 families, the team helped parents become more confident of their abilities. The researchers used a series of activities, such as role-playing, to help parents feel secure when interacting with schools. They developed a program titled Cooperative Communication Between Home and School (CCBHS) that included teachers and administrators. Parents need to view themselves as worthwhile participants to truly be able to interact with teachers and administrators, while the school personnel need to respect the parents and recognize their importance as they collaborate. In this way, they work for the greater good of families, schools, and communities (Cochran & Dean, 1991).

Perseverance, patience, and true interest in the parent are the most important factors in overcoming parents' reticence. Understanding, support, and interest usually will encourage a parent to take that first step toward collaborating with a teacher for the good of the child. However, a few parents might refuse to be involved, regardless of the teacher's efforts. Some might have serious social adjustment problems and need professional help in that area. One challenging parent or one bad experience should not destroy the commitment of the home visitor or teacher to working with others. Do what can be done and acknowledge the impossibility of reaching all parents. Do this with grace, understanding, and without recrimination. One way of involving the parents is through empowerment. **Empowerment** is a process of adult development, enhanced through participation. Family empowerment benefits parents and teachers and therefore children because it helps create a school that is responsive to the needs of all (Nelson & Guerra, 2010). Dunlap (2000) studied family empowerment in a preschool cooperative and found that "through involvement with the family component of this preschool, caregivers acquire cultural capital. Over time they translate cultural capital into human capital, or economic gain" (p. 5). This process of developing cultural capital into human capital is the process of empowerment. Dunlap found this can be accomplished without giving up the participant's sense of ethnic identity.

Necessary Communication and Support

Teachers' ability to communicate with parents provides opportunities for parents and teachers to develop a collaborative partnership of support (Schecter & Sherri, 2009). By establishing communication early in the school year, the teacher can ensure parents will be ready to receive messages throughout the year. A call from the teacher, parent coordinator, or family specialist should not always indicate that a child is in trouble. If good communication and support have been established, that call could mean the child is a strong leader or is working hard on a research project. Keep in mind that establishing communication early on does not guarantee an easy path to parent engagement. Engaging parents can remain difficult for a few reasons:

1. *Families and parents might be under a lot of stress.* In our fast-paced society, many parents are under stress. Problems might include lack of money, the illness of a loved one, unemployment, or an argument with a friend. It is possible that they cannot be actively

involved during a time of hardship, and they should not be made to feel guilty about this. Let them know you are supportive and whenever they want to be more actively involved, they may. Keep communication open through telephone calls or e-mails.

2. *Many parents feel out of their element whether coming to school or receiving home visitors.* They are unsure of themselves. They do not have confidence in their own ideas, or they believe someone else will not value them. They need their self-esteem and level of trust raised. If they have the time, let them contribute in a small way. Accept their ideas and enlist their help in an activity at which they will succeed. Build slowly; it takes time to make a change.

3. *The parents are experts in their children.* The parents' knowledge about the child is important since they are the best experts on their child. However, this can be a challenge particularly when children may be facing difficulties in school. Starting with parent–teacher conferences or home visits, the teacher can work with the parents to understand the interactions with their children and how to help with the child's education.

4. *Many teachers do not know the parents' interests, strengths, and abilities.* Keep in mind that some parents cannot help with schoolwork. They can become frustrated and angry, and the child can respond with dejection and hurt feelings. Rather than helping the child, the parent creates a battleground. It is part of your role as an educator to try to prevent this sort of situation from occurring. Suggest projects and activities that lend themselves to the capabilities of the parent, but be aware of possible misinterpretations of your recommendations. For example, in one program, a home visitor was working with an abusive parent, and suggested that the child was not using the right arm enough. At the next week's class, the home visitor found bruises up and down the child's arm. The parent, who was concerned about the teacher's comment, was "developing" the child's arm. This might seem extreme, but the response demonstrated the parent's inability to cope with everyday problems and to nurture the child in appropriate ways.

It is helpful to offer training sessions for parents where techniques and suggestions for working positively with the child are discussed. The STEP, PET, and Active Parenting programs use planned programs for parents to suggest methods for communicating with children. These resources can serve as guides in setting up sessions on working with children. YouTube videos can also be helpful in illustrating parenting skills and the role of parents as teachers. Parents also learn through modeling. Helping in the classroom can be an effective learning experience. Methods of teaching that permit observation, demonstration, and role-playing prove useful. Parents, like children, learn best through active participation.

Engaging parents when their children are young is very important because prevention is far better than trying to find a cure. If parents can be involved from the start, their resistance to programs and partnerships can be reduced or eliminated. Different approaches that meet the needs of the individual are essential.

Minnesota Early Learning Design (MELD), which started in Minneapolis in 1973 but later merged with Parents as Teachers National Center, is one such approach. This program focuses on increasing parents' self-confidence, supporting parents' connection with their children, and helping families set goals in their work and family life (MELD, 2006). MELD's mission is to provide support and information that strengthens families at critical periods during the parenting process. Initially, it focused on early childhood education, adult education, and family management (Parents as Teachers National Center, 2006), but as needs emerged, it established additional dedicated groups: New Parents for first-time parents, MELD Special for parents of children with special needs, MYM for young moms, MELD for parents who are deaf, *Nueva Familia/La Familia* for Hispanic parents, MELD for young dads, and MELD's Young Moms Plus for parents of 3- to 6-year-old children (MELD, 1988).

The Comer Process

Over 30 years ago in New Haven, Connecticut, the Yale Child Study Center and New Haven Public Schools collaborated to bring change to two public schools. Dr. J. P. Comer is a professor at Yale University who founded the Comer School Development Program. Comer focuses on the process of collaboration among parents and schools to improve the development and wellbeing of children.

Comer's School Development Program (SDP) is based on three principles—consensus, collaboration, and no fault—that are needed to develop a climate that enables schools, children, and parents to thrive. Consensus elicits discussion, brainstorming for ideas, and decision making without requiring a vote that might cause divisiveness. Collaboration encourages schools, families, and community to move forward to develop a viable, responsive environment for children (Comer, 1997, 2004). No fault means school personnel and parents can review goals and concerns without fault being assigned to anyone. The focus is on making decisions at the school and the individual student level (Fields-Smith & Neuharth-Pritchett, 2009).

Comer recognized that children's behaviors were determined by their environment, and hence they need to have positive interactions in order to develop physically, socially, and emotionally. With this in mind, he based the framework for school change on Field Theory (Lewin, 1936), Human Ecological Systems Theory (Kelly, 1966), the Population Adjustment Model (Becker, Wylan, & McCourt, 1971), and the Social Action Model (Reiff, 1966). SDP schools therefore place the child at the center, striving to meet his or her needs through the curriculum, social activities, and teaching methods, while reinforcing the positive aspects of home and building social networks.

The child-centered environment is facilitated by planning and collaboration between the professional and the community. To do this, three teams, guided by the three principles, plan and work to develop a school climate that nurtures the children. The three teams included the following:

1. *The School Planning and Management Team (SPMT).* The School Planning and Management Team plans and coordinates school endeavors, including curriculum, assessment, and instruction.
2. *The Student and Staff Support Team (SSST).* First called the Mental Health Team, the Student and Staff Support Team works to prevent concerns from becoming problems and responds to the issues and needs of individual students.
3. *The Parent Team (PT).* The Parent Team involves parents at all levels of the school and integrates the school with the community. (Comer, 2004; Emmons, Comer, & Haynes, 1996; Haynes, Ben-Avie, Squires, Howley, Negron, & Corbin, 1996)

To develop an SDP school, participants must build trust; plan well; empower parents; and continually monitor, assess, and modify as necessary (Haynes et al., 1996). For more information, refer to *Rallying the Whole Village: The Comer Process for Reforming Education* by Comer, Haynes, Joyner, and Ben-Avie (1996); or *Leave No Child Behind: Preparing Today's Youth for Tomorrow's World* by Comer (2004); or contact the School Development Program in New Haven, Connecticut.

Reggio Emilia Approach

The importance of parent involvement in education extends beyond the United States, of course. One example can be seen in the Reggio Emilia program in Italy. Malaguzzi, the founder and former director of the program, described it this way: "Our proposition is to consider a triad at the center of education—children, teachers, and families. To think of a dyad of only a teacher and a child is to create an artificial world that does not reflect reality" (Malaguzzi, 1993, p. 9). The Reggio Emilia program believes that the interaction of children with adults (both parents and teachers) and other children is essential for their development: "Interaction among children affects social, emotional, communicative, and cognitive behavior and development . . . different from those usually reached by children working in isolation" (Malaguzzi, 1993, p. 12).

Teachers in the Reggio Emilia approach have different roles that go beyond being a "pedagogista or pedagogue." Teachers are facilitators, researchers, and reflective practitioners (Hewett, 2001). Parents are a very important component of this approach (Reggio Emilia Approach, 2018). Teachers know that parents are very important in the education of their children and as such provide different levels of engagement (McNally & Slutsky, 2017). Some examples of how teachers engage parents include meetings throughout the year to discuss general events, classroom specifics, needs of children, and transitions (among others) (McNally & Slutsky, 2017).

The Project Approach

The Project Approach is method that engages children in in-depth study of real world concepts (Project Approach, 2018). The **project approach** involves the child as a constructor of knowledge and research as such it is based on the Constructivist theoretical framework. A good example of a project appeared in *Young Children* in an article by Helm, Huebner, and Long (2000) titled "Quiltmaking: A Perfect Project for Preschool and Primary." In most project approaches, there are three phases: (a) planning, researching, and organizing; (b) investigating, discovering, constructing, and working; and (c) completing the project and celebrating its success. The authors showed how both preschool and primary classrooms could use the same project theme, quilting, to successfully complete these three stages. Using quilts also provided a bridge to home and parent involvement through the use of a family participation survey. The survey included items that encourage participation between parent and child about real experiences that relate to the concept of quiltmaking. In addition, teachers built community with parents as they invited them to join in making a class quilt using paper squares, fabric, Velcro, and tie-dye. The squares were put together to create a banner. Throughout the project, children were communicating, cooperating, and constructing a knowledge base. More recent articles about projects are highlighted in the *Early Childhood Research and Practice* journal edited by Lilian Katz.

Projects also provide an opportunity for teachers to invite parents to help with the different phases, perhaps by providing their expertise. They can also be invited to assist the teacher in guiding the children in the project; to chaperone on project-related field trips; or to attend a culminating event (i.e, "Cheese Pizza" project Gallick & Lee, 2010).

School and Center Programs

The tradition of involving parents has been strong in the early childhood profession for years, as exemplified in the parent-cooperative movement and advanced by many childcare providers and educators. The following sections describe programs that have been proven effective for early childhood–age children.

EFFECTIVE PROGRAMS: RESEARCH BRIEFS. Early childhood education programs are extremely beneficial. They benefit educational progress and academic achievement, reduce delinquency and crime, and improve the potential for success in the labor market. According to research reported by Karoly, Kilburn, and Cannon (2005), the following early childhood education programs were found to be effective when combined with parent education and/or home visits: Head Start, High/Scope Perry Preschool Project, Carolina Abecedarian Project, Project CARE, Syracuse Family

Development Research, Houston Parent–Child Development Center, Early Training Project, Chicago Child Parent Center, Oklahoma Pre-K, and AVANCE.

Findings conclude that early intervention has more favorable results if the caregivers are well trained. There is also evidence to suggest that center-based programs with smaller child-to-staff ratios are more successful.

Head Start. Head Start is a federally funded program that has served over 30 million children since 1965 (Office of the Administration for Children and Families, 2018). It is a comprehensive early childhood program that provides child-development initiatives for low-income children. Although the related Early Head Start program serves infants and toddlers, Head Start is best known as a preschool program. From its inception, Head Start involved the family at the center of its outreach, with spokes of the wheel covering education; health care including medical, dental, and mental health; nutrition; social services; staff development; and parent involvement. Head Start makes a significant difference in the lives of children and their parents through these services. The U.S. Congress appropriates funds for Head Start. During 2015 Head Start was appropriated $9,168,095,000 (Office of the Administration for Children and Families, 2018). The Office of Head Start revised their Program Performance Standards in 2016. The Head Start Program Performance Standards (2016) integrate families throughout but Subpart E specifically targets Family and Community Engagement Program Services. According to the standards, "A program must integrate parent and family engagement strategies into all systems and program services to support family well-being and promote children's learning and development. Programs are encouraged to develop innovative two-generation approaches that address prevalent needs of families across their program that may leverage community partnerships or other funding sources" (p. 51). Of particular importance is the shared responsibility between the program and families regarding the child's learning and development and the importance given to parent-child relationships. The standards include strategies for parent engagement programs as shown in the following statements:

1. Offering activities that support parent-child relationships and child development including language, dual language, literacy, and bi-literacy as appropriate.

2. Providing parents with information about the importance of their child's regular attendance, and partner with them as necessary to promote attendance; and,

3. For dual language learners, information and resources for parents about the benefits of bilingualism and bi-literacy (p. 51).

In addition, the standards also include the importance of having a parenting curriculum developed with input from parents in order to meet the specific needs of families. This is a great way to promote parent engagement while at the same time validating parents' experiences and cultural background.

Early Head Start.   Early Head Start, a program that serves low-income families who have infants and toddlers, was created with the reauthorization of the Head Start Act in 1994. From 68 programs in 1995, it grew to 635 programs serving 45,000 children in 2001. In 2002 and 2003, Early Head Start (EHS) received 10% of the Head Start funding appropriation. In January 2001, a national evaluation of the first two years of 3,000 children showed that EHS children performed significantly better on cognitive, social–emotional, and language development. In addition, the parents scored higher than the control group on knowledge of infant–toddler development, parenting, and quality of home environment. It was also found that parents of children were more likely to go into job training or attend school, and that family conflict declined (Fenichel & Mann, 2001). Parents' contributions to children's linguistic and social development through a positive early learning environment demonstrated positive correlations with emotion regulation and vocabulary development, whereas depressive symptoms and parenting stress were associated with behavior problems (Chazan-Cohen, Raikes, Brooks-Gunn, Ayoub, Pan, Kisker, Roggman, & Fuligni, 2009). According to the National Head Start Association there were a total of 154,352 Early Head Start Slots in 2016-2017 (National Head Start, 2018).

Families can be served in center-based or home-based environments or a combination of the two. Programs need to meet or exceed federal Head Start performance standards (Buell, Hallam, & Beck, 2001). For children from birth to 36 months who are enrolled in center programs, the EHS standard is a maximum of eight children and a child ratio of one to four. This standard helps ensure the high-quality care and nurturing

environment that infants and toddlers need. Early Head Start provides intensive and comprehensive family support services for families (Early Head Start Programs, 2018).

HighScope Perry Preschool Program.   In November 2004, the HighScope Educational Research Foundation reported a long-term study of adults at age 40 who, as low-income 3- and 4-year-old children, had participated in a 2-year early education and care program provided by HighScope. From 1962 through 1967, HighScope operated the HighScope Perry Preschool Program. A limit of eight children were permitted per teacher. A sample of 123 low-income African American boys and girls were randomly assigned to five preschools or to a group who received no preschool program. Classes were held 5 days a week for two and a half hours. Teachers were college graduates certified in early childhood, special education, or elementary education.

Research Results.   HighScope Educational Research Foundation staff studied these children every year from the age of 3 until they were 11, and then at ages 14, 15, 19, 27, and 40. They found that more students who had preschool graduated from high school than did those in the no-program group (65% versus 45%), with the number of women graduates being significantly higher than men (84% versus 32%). Sample comparisons of the HighScope Program versus no program at age 40 showed that 70% of those who had been enrolled in a program versus 50% of those who had not been enrolled in a program were employed; 37% of program participants versus 28% of non-participants owned their own home; 76% of program participants versus 50% of non-participants had savings accounts; 2% of participants versus 12% of non-participants committed violent felonies; and 3% of participants versus 20% of non-participants were cited for having illegal drugs.

Curriculum Research.   The Foundation conducted a HighScope Preschool Curriculum Comparison study after the HighScope Perry Preschool study and found that the HighScope model was successful compared with other preschool programs as well. The researchers studied the direct instructional model, in which teachers taught the children academic skills and rewarded them for correct answers. They also examined the traditional nursery school model in which teachers responded to the children's self-initiated activities in a supportive and loosely structured environment. In the

HighScope model, teachers designed their classrooms with both large- and small-group activities, emphasizing self-initiated learning. The children, with help from the teacher, planned their own activities and reviewed these activities after they carried out their plans (Schweinhart, 2009). Research conducted on 23-year-olds who had participated in nursery school and HighScope showed that nursery school and HighScope had similar outcomes (Schweinhart & Weikart, 1997). Although the direct instructional model shows early improvement in academics, the improvement is temporary, and the research also demonstrates loss of opportunity in long-term social behavior improvement (Schweinhart et al., 2005).

Parent Involvement. High Scope (2018) philosophy is to help teachers cultivate connections that will help parents to participate in meaningful opportunities in their child's education through six indicators:

1. Welcoming atmosphere—atmosphere should reflect respect through physical space. Parents should always be greeted cordially.

2. Sharing information about children—arrival and departure routine is important teachers must be available for parents to welcome and send them on a positive note sharing observation about children.

3. Welcoming families to participate—it is important for children to see adults interested in their learning and education teachers should provide expectations, talk to parents about the importance of adult-child interactions, and provide time for parents to debrief at the end of the day or be available through phone calls or emails.

4. Strategize for home visits—home visits help to make connections with families as teachers learn about them and their child. Teachers should make a list that guides them to remember what happens in a home visit and they can share it with parents so that they are prepared. Invite parents to engage by discussing child's strengths and interests.

5. Prepare parent workshops—demonstrate through workshops how children learn in a High Scope classroom.

6. Resources—Books available through the High-Scope store for purchase for parent workshops.

The Carolina Abecedarian Project. The North Carolina Abecedarian Project was a program in which children from low-income families had high-quality full-time educational intervention, from infancy through age 5, for children born between 1972 and 1977. Individualized education enhanced development, with the activities consisting of "games" included in the children's regular day. The activities emphasized language development with social, intellectual, and emotional development also included (Campbell et al., 2008).

The Woodcock-Johnson Achievement Test was given to children in the Abecedarian Project in the fall and spring of their third year of school. The children were monitored and had follow-up studies during the summer following their seventh-grade year (age 12), tenth-grade year (age 15), and at 21 years of age. It was found that high-quality intervention and education during early childhood can carry over academically as the child progressed through school. The children had higher cognitive test scores beginning as toddlers, and the scores continued to be above average through the last study at age 21. Improved language development seems to have enhanced the resulting cognitive test scores. Other major findings included the following: intervention children on average were older when they had their first child, academic achievement in both reading and math was higher from early grades to young adulthood, and the children were more likely to attend a four-year college (University of North Carolina, FPG Child Development Institute, n.d.).

Carolina Approach to Responsive Education (Project CARE). A study related to the Abecedarian Project was the Carolina Approach to Responsive Education (Project CARE). The program recruited children who were born between 1978 and 1980 and they were randomly assigned to one of three groups: educational childcare plus home visits from 6 weeks until school entry, home visits from 6 weeks until school entry, and the control group. The first two groups received home–school resource services during the first three years of school. Extensive testing was done during the period the children were in school, with testing including quality of family environment, maternal measures (mother's characteristics and other information), and cognitive and academic achievement. The Woodcock-Johnson Achievement Test was administered in the fall and spring during the first three years of school, and in the summer after their seventh year of school. Based on Woodcock-Johnson test scores, Rand Corporation identified Project CARE as a successful program

(Karoly, Kilburn, & Cannon, 2005). This evidence, along with evidence from the Abecedarian Project, strengthened the case to provide quality early childhood intervention, particularly for families in need (Campbell et al., 2008).

Syracuse Family Development Research Program. The Syracuse Family Development Research Program (FDRP) was a comprehensive early childhood program that included home visits, parent training, and a children's center with a program of education, health, nutrition, and other human services, from prenatal to the beginning of elementary school. The targeted program participants were low-income families of young African American single parents. Honig, Lally, and Mathieson assessed the program in 1982, finding that the FDRP kindergarten children had emotional functioning superior to those in the control group and were more flexible, purposeful, energetic, social, relaxed, and affectionate to others than the children in the control group. In addition, the FDRP groups had more children who attained an IQ score above 89. The first-grade group continued to exhibit positive behavior toward other children, but they showed more negative and positive behavior toward adults than the control group (Promising Practices Network, n.d.). In 1988, the research found that by eighth grade, none of the FDRP girls had failing grade averages, whereas 16% of the control group did. Seventy-two percent of the FDRP girls maintained a C average or better, compared to only 47% of the control group. There were no significant differences in achievement between FDRP boys and the control group. Research on delinquency reported by Lally, Mangione, and Honig in 1988 found that three of the control group had committed violent crimes, compared to none of the FDRP group. An analysis reported in 2001 by Aos, Barnoski, and Lieb found that the FDRP children committed fewer crimes than the control group, but of those who committed crimes, there was no difference in the number of offenses that were committed (Promising Practices Network, 2011).

Houston Parent–Child Development Center Infant Health Development Program. The Houston Parent–Child Development Center focused on very young Latino children. The first year included 25 home visits. Each 90-minute visit focused on infant development. Small groups met together on weekends for family workshops in which they discussed communication, decisions, and issues chosen by the participants. English as a second language classes were also offered to the mothers of the children. Information on child and public health was furnished by a visiting nurse. Transportation and information on ways to obtain resources were provided.

During the second year, there were center-based classes for mothers and their 2-year-olds for four hours, four mornings a week. Transportation and lunch were provided, group discussion continued and information on home management and childcare was ongoing. Fathers attended monthly meetings, which strengthened their paternal roles (Johnson, 1990).

The Early Training Project. The Early Training Project was an early (1962–1965) research project in which 65 African American children 4 to 5 years old were chosen to participate in a study to improve educational achievement. The children were chosen from families based on education, occupation, housing, and income. The children were randomly assigned to a group that attended a 10-week summer program for two summers, a group that attended for three summers, or a control group (no program attendance). Those in the intervention programs also received weekly home visits throughout the school year. Assessments of the program participants were conducted during the intervention period, and in 1965, 1966, 1968, 1975, and 1978. In 1965, at the end of first grade, the children scored high on three of the four subtests of the Metropolitan Achievement Test (Karoly, Kilburn, & Cannon; 2005). Significant differences were found, but they faded as the children matured. Participants were less likely to be placed in special education, be retained in grade, or drop out of high school (Karoly et al., 2005). The reduction in special education placements at age 12 showed that only 5% of Early Training Project students were in special education compared to 29% of the control group, and that 8% graduated compared to 52% of the control group (Currie, 2000).

Chicago Child–Parent Centers. Chicago Child–Parent Centers are integrated with primary schools in Chicago. When it began in 1967, the program was a half-day preschool program for 3- to 4-year-old children. Using federal Title I funds, the center provided health services, social services, and a preschool, and encouraged parent participation and involvement. The preschool program was designed to prepare children for school with a focus on language skills and preparation for reading.

In 1978, with the addition of state funding, the kindergarten was increased to full day and the program was extended through third grade. The children also received free breakfasts, lunches, and health screenings. Class sizes were kept relatively small, with the adult-to-child ratio in preschool being one to eight in a class of 17, and in kindergarten, 1 to 12 in a class of 25. The class size was further reduced, and the primary program added coordinated instruction and parent involvement to its offerings. Findings based on children at 9 years of age showed that CPC children had significantly higher math and reading achievement scores, less retention, and more significant parent involvement. There was no difference in special education placement, but the number of years spent in special education was significantly lower (Karoly et al., 2005).

It is important to note here that parent involvement was strong. Activities included parenting classes, clerical assistance by parents, and parent involvement in school activities such as developing resources and coordinating school projects (Chicago Longitudinal Study, 2004).

Oklahoma Pre-K. Oklahoma has been a leader in providing public school prekindergarten offerings. As early as 1980, Oklahoma was considering standards for a program for 4-year-old children. In 1990, Head Start–eligible students could attend prekindergarten without cost and, if space was available, others could pay tuition and attend. The standards for a prekindergarten program include early childhood–certified teachers who have a bachelor's degree and who pass an early childhood education–subject-area competency test. The pre-K teachers are paid on the same salary scale as the K–12 teachers. Pre-K has small class sizes of 20 students and an adult-to-child ratio of 1 to 10. The program also encourages family involvement and requires developmentally appropriate curricula and the continued professional development of certified personnel (Garrett, 2004; Gormley, Gayer, Phillips, & Dawson, 2004).

In September 2003, the Woodcock-Johnson Achievement Test was given to 1567 pre-K children and 3148 kindergarteners in Tulsa, Oklahoma. The pre-K students were ready to begin their program for the year, and nearly half of the kindergarten students had participated in the pre-K program the year before. Key findings included a 52% gain in letter word identification, a 27% gain in spelling test scores, and a 21% gain in applied problems. These were percentages above the average gain that occurs over one year. Gains for minority students were even more impressive. Hispanic students showed a 79% gain in letter and word identification. There was also a 39% gain in spelling, and a 54% gain in applied programs (Gormley et al., 2004).

AVANCE. This program is one of the oldest and most distinguished parenting and early childhood programs in the United States. The word *avance* in Spanish means "to advance," and that is what the program strives for through parent education. The program assists parents in creating cognitively stimulating environments that enable children to develop their five senses to explore their world. Developed in 1973, AVANCE uses a wide variety of methods of reaching families and their children, including three hours of class time weekly, consisting of play and toy curricula, a parent-education curriculum, and community-resource awareness (AVANCE, 2018). The AVANCE model also teaches participants that the home must provide a language-rich environment because through language, learning occurs.

AVANCE shows parents how they can transmit the values associated with their culture to encourage appropriate behavior within their family and society at large. In addition, AVANCE trains parents to develop homes that are safe havens for children, free from violence and abuse. Many AVANCE parents have been victims of abuse and neglect; therefore, it is imperative that parents attend the scheduled classes for optimal success. Johnson, Walker, and Rodriguez (1996) found that mothers who participated in the program with their infants became highly skilled teachers even after a one-year follow-up. In fact, after participating in the training, AVANCE parents often become center teachers themselves.

Other Examples of Successful Programs—School on Saturday. The Ferguson-Florissant School District in St. Louis, Missouri, worked with parents to offer a Saturday school. The program consisted of 3-hour preschool sessions for 4-year-olds on Saturdays throughout the school year. Although the program is no longer available in the school district, the concept behind it is appropriate for districts that could have a Saturday program, especially if they are unable to furnish full-time preschools. The program had three major objectives:

- To provide an education program that will help 4-year-old children succeed in school.
- To involve parents in the education of their children.
- To provide support for families.

These objectives were accomplished by providing the following:

- Diagnostic screening at the beginning of the school year to establish appropriate goals.
- Half-day preschool each Saturday in a public kindergarten.
- Opportunities for participation by parents in the preschool. (Parents had to participate every 4 to 6 weeks as parent helpers in the preschool.)
- Home visits, one hour each week, with a group of two or three children and their parents.
- Home activity guides that provided ideas for projects and other activities for the 4-year-old child—and younger siblings, if any—to do at home. These activities fostered skills needed for success in school.
- Consultants in child development, who were available to consider specific concerns as well as provide parent meetings.

Although the program was discontinued in Ferguson-Florissant, while it was in operation Saturday school seemed to work: Children gained cognitive skills, language, and eye–hand coordination. Parents gained in their ability to communicate with their children, to use appropriate reinforcement techniques, and to sense a child's learning readiness. The program reached out to fathers as well as mothers. The curriculum, dealing with motor-coordination development, goes hand in hand with positive interaction between child and father. The National Fatherhood Initiative (NFI) provides free resources for fathers, including eBooks that suggest a variety of tips for working and connecting with their children. The eBooks also describe child protection

cases, among other subjects. The NFI also includes free electronic tools that help fathers track their children's development, as well as radio podcasts that fathers might find helpful.

What can other programs gain from the Saturday school and organizations such as NFI? These aspects seem especially important:

- Active participation by both parents in teaching their own children.
- Diagnostic and prescriptive activities for children with disabilities.
- Observation and participation by parents in a school setting.
- Guidance and activities that support parents' efforts.
- Teacher visits to the home, establishing a team rapport between teachers and parents.
- Opportunities for the child to experience routine school activities and an enriched curriculum each week.
- Home-learning activity booklets to be used by parents of children from birth through age 3.

The varied approaches of the Saturday school met many more needs than a program with only one dimension—for example, preschool without the parent component.

Brookline Early Education Project.   An excellent example of how the public school system can collaborate with a health organization was the Brookline Early Education Project (BEEP). In 1972, Brookline Public Schools, Children's Hospital Medical Center, and researchers from Boston-area universities joined to develop a coordinated plan for physical checkups and educational programs for young children up to kindergarten age (Figure 8.4). Together, the hospital and school supplied a reassuring support system.

Based on the theory that parents are the child's most influential teachers, BEEP had three interrelated components:

1. *Parent education and support.* Three levels of support were provided, ranging from frequent home visits and meetings to parent-initiated support. Home visits, parent groups, and center visits were available.

Figure 8.4 Diagnosis and Education Support Wheel
The hospital and school work together to provide for the child's health, education, and development.

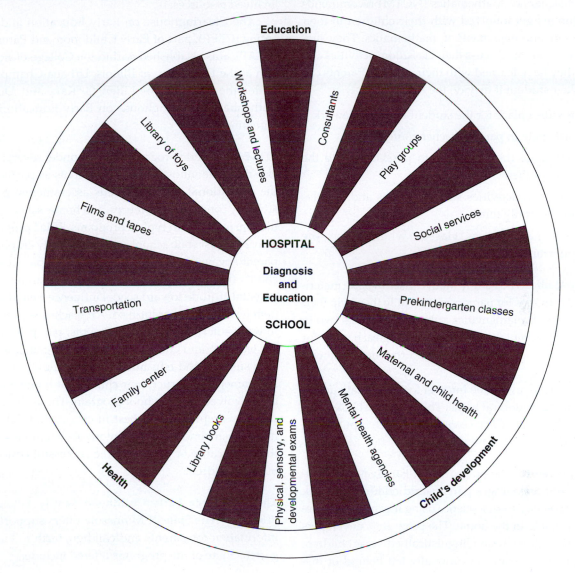

2. *Diagnostic monitoring.* Children were periodically screened by staff at Children's Hospital Medical Center from age 2 weeks until entry into kindergarten.

3. *Education and enrichment.* The 2-year-old children attended weekly play group sessions in the BEEP project center.

In addition to these services, the BEEP program offered a parent center; consultants to answer questions; library books and pamphlets, films and videotapes on child development; a series of special events such as workshops, films, and lectures; and transportation for the parents of the children enrolled in BEEP (Pierson, Walker, & Tivnan, 1984). Home visits were reported as being the most valuable in terms of support for the parents. Over 95 percent of the mothers would recommend the BEEP program to their own children (Palfrey, Bronson, Hauser-Cram, & Warfield, 2002).

A study begun in 1996 and published in 2002 found that the young adults who had participated in BEEP had higher incomes and reported higher health ratings and lower levels of depression. They attained more years of education and were more likely to be employed or in school.

MATH AND SCIENCE ASSOCIATIONS THAT SUPPORT FAMILY INVOLVEMENT. The National Council of Teachers of Mathematics (NCTM) recommends that parents get involved with their children in their success in, and enjoyment of, mathematics. They suggest that students discuss their classroom activities and what they have learned with their parents. Parents can help their student if they do the following:

- Provide a place for the student to do homework.
- Participate in parent–teacher conferences.
- Encourage their children to persist, not do the work for them.
- Engage in activities such as games and puzzles during family time.
- Visit mathematics classes when given the opportunity.

Family Math. The Family Math classes include materials and activities for parents to use while they help their children with mathematics at home. Meetings two to three hours long take place one evening each week for four to six weeks. Children attend the meetings with their parents.

Families can use the Internet to obtain math activities that can be done at home. There is also a book available, *Helping Your Child Learn Math*, which is published by the U.S. Department of Education.

Family Science. An outgrowth of Family Math, Family Science encourages parents and children to work together on day-to-day science using inexpensive materials available in the home. The program's developers hope that culturally and linguistically diverse children, and girls in general—traditionally left behind or discouraged from scientific pursuits—will be encouraged to develop their abilities in math and science if they learn about them in a nonthreatening environment.

The Education Resources Information Center (ERIC). The Education Resources Information Center (ERIC), located at the University of Illinois under the direction of Lilian G. Katz, was an educational resource for areas of education including elementary and early childhood education. The service commenced in 1967 and continued until December 2003, when a new ERIC was established. At that time, all the divisions of ERIC continued as a digital library of education resources under the Institute of Education Sciences of the U.S. Department of Education. The digital library was opened for public use in 2004 with a focus on providing current and archived resources.

The Clearinghouse on Early Education and Parenting (CEEP), part of Early Childhood and Parenting (ECAP), was established within the College of Education at the University of Illinois, Urbana-Champaign, under the direction of Lilian G. Katz and Dianne Rothenberg (Clearinghouse on Early Education and Parenting, 2011).

TITLE I. Federal programs funded under several titles also illustrate innovative use of parents as partners in the educational process. Needs assessments, parent advisory councils, conferences, and home–school activities are included in typical programs. Title I programs, active in most state school systems, heavily emphasize parent engagement, recognizing that the parent is the child's first teacher and that home environment and parental attitude toward school influence a child's academic success. A parent-resource teacher is provided to work solely with parents. Parents, paraprofessionals, teachers, and administrators work together to provide support and education for the children. Parents are trained to instruct their children at home and are also involved in the school program. These successful programs represent the best in curriculum development. Their concern for parent involvement illustrates the significance of parents in the successful education of their children.

The Minnesota Early Childhood Family Education Program. The State of Minnesota offers support and information for parents and children, birth to kindergarten. Some of the programs offered include:

1. *Early childhood screening* is for children before they enter kindergarten. Because it is important that any potential problems be identified early, it is recommended that screening be done by the time the child is 3.

2. *Early Childhood Family Education* is a program that parents of children, birth until enrollment in kindergarten, can attend for information, activities, and support. A typical day has the parent and child doing an activity, followed by the parent and child doing their own activities, the child active in preschool, and the parent attending a parent-education session.

3. *The High-Five* kindergarten is a program for 4-year-olds who will start kindergarten the following year.

4. *Early childhood special education* is for children from birth to kindergarten who have been identified as having a disability.

5. *Parents in Community Action (PICA)* has operated a Head Start program for over 30 years.

6. *Home-based programs* include Way to Grow, a program that builds school readiness for children ages 3 to 5. It focuses on future school success by focusing on cognitive, emotional, and social development and is delivered through home visits. In addition, Minneapolis offers Home Instruction Program for Preschool Youngsters (HIPPY). See Chapter 9 for a description of HIPPY (Minneapolis Public Schools, 2006).

Minneapolis.   Minneapolis is a good example of the greater involvement of parents with schools. The Early Childhood Family Education program welcomes the enrollment of all families living in Minneapolis who have children from birth to enrollment in kindergarten. Programs for the children include Early Reading First, a full-year program for children who are 3; Minneapolis Kids Fours Explore is a full-day program for 4-year-olds; and High-Five is a prekindergarten school year for children who are 4 years old. Programs are varied; early childhood special education serves children from birth to kindergarten. Screening is provided to assess if children need a special-education program. The New Families Center is a year-long all-day program for families whose second language is English. There is also the Teenage Pregnant and Parenting Program, which provides services to support teenagers who are pregnant or are already parents. In Minneapolis, pledges or covenants are signed by all involved—students, parents or representatives, teachers and other staff members, the superintendent, school board members, and community members. All participants have specific ways in which they can help (Minneapolis Public Schools, 2006).

Institute for Responsive Education.   The Institute for Responsive Education or IRE (2006) continues with its emphasis on connecting school, family, and community. In April 2005, the program moved to Cambridge College, School of Education, in Cambridge, Massachusetts. The mission of the IRE focuses on providing support for partnerships between schools, families, and communities.

The various activities of the Institute for Responsive Education include the Parent Leadership Exchange, which provides networking for parent leaders in three New England states; the Boston Parent Organizing Network (BPON); and Family Involvement in After School Study, a study of family centers nationwide. The changes in the Institute illustrate the ebb and flow of family involvement with schools. New programs are developed, flourish, meet the needs of the schools, change the environment, become a part of the total program, or diminish when they are no longer needed, something replaces them, or the funding source is lost (Institute of Responsive Education, 2006).

National Association of State Boards of Education

The National Association of State Boards of Education (NASBE, 1991, 2006) recommends continual communication between parents and schools, with parent involvement in decision making on program policy, curriculum, and evaluation. The NASBE also encourages more time for teachers to plan and carry out home visits, for home activities and materials to be provided for parents to use with their children, and for schools to provide leadership in developing family support services in collaboration with existing community agencies. They would also like to see businesses encouraged to give parents time off to attend parent–teacher conferences and volunteer in the classroom. The NASBE suggests parents get involved by coming to the classroom to observe and volunteer and to tutor their children at home; strong parent involvement is also important to accommodate the family in before- and after-school programs. Administrators often try to have parents involved in the planning of before- and after-school programs through parent advisory committees, workshops, and orientation sessions, though the task force of the NASBE suggests further in-service training for administrators and teachers on parental involvement. With this mission of cooperation between home and school, the task force supports provision of sufficient staff, training, and time to work together (National Association of State Boards of Education, 2006).

In 2001, NASBE, with financial support from the Kellogg Foundation, started Early Childhood Education Network, a project to increase the ability of six states (Kansas, Illinois, Massachusetts, Louisiana, Ohio, and Wyoming) to implement early childhood education programs and services. The goal was to help states "create integrated, high-quality early childhood education policies, programs, and services to children" (National Association of State Boards of Education, 2006, p. 1). The results were outstanding, with the states able to define school readiness and unify their standards. It included an outreach to early childhood education programs in higher education and aligned the college course content to the program. In 2006, NASBE received a grant allowing the organization to add five new states to the Early Childhood Education Network (National Association of State Boards of Education, 2006).

Parent Education for Teenagers

The U.S. Department of Health and Human Services (2018) notes that in 2016 there were 20.3 births for every 1,000 teen females between the ages of 15 and 19, but it also mentions the decline of teen pregnancies in the last eight years. The importance of prevention by educating teens and their parents is crucial. However, families and schools must be ready in case teen pregnancies do happen by providing support systems that will assure the healthy development of the child as well as the teen or school-aged parents.

Teen or school-aged parents have unique needs that include socioemotional and financial, among others. The most important message that families and schools need to give to teen parents is that support is going to be provided for them, particularly in the form of parenting programs. Such programs enable teen parents to understand their child and achieve stability. In particular, programs must incorporate the following for teen mothers and fathers to be not only successful with their children but also engaged, according to the Family and Youth Services Bureau tip sheet (n.d.):

- Self-sufficiency
- Housing stability
- Financial stability
- Successful and engaged parenting attachment
- Healthy relationships

The Office of Adolescent Health (OAH) Teen Pregnancy Prevention (TPP) Program funds new and innovative programs that that target adolescents 10–19 years old. The programs include many topics focusing on sexual health such as pregnancy and birth, STDs, sexual partners, sexual initiation and abstinence, contraceptives, and parent engagement. Examples of such programs that include parent engagement include the following:

- Aban Aya Youth Project
- Children's Aid Society (CAS) Carrera Program
- Draw the Line/Respect the Line
- FOCUS
- Nu-Culture Healthy Futures
- Safer Choices

Teen parents must know that they are not alone. Resources and support can be found through different programs that will help them learn how to balance life between being a teen and a parent. Examples of programs that support teens in such efforts include: For Young Parents, A Home Within, The National Parent Helpline: Strengthening Families All Across America, Parental Support for Pregnant Teens, Partnering with Teens, Teen Parenting Service Network, and Teen Pregnancy and Parenting Support Groups (Child Welfare Information Gateway, 2018).

Family Support Programs

Three programs—Family Support America (formerly Family Resource Centers), Family and Child Education (FACE), and The National Center for Family Literacy—illustrate the types of services that support centers provide. These three programs were developed because of families' obvious need for support to survive and provide the nurturing environment their children need. Family Support America is a national coalition of groups that work for resources and provisions to strengthen families. Family and Child Education is a support and literacy program for children who are Native Americans. The National Center for Family Literacy focuses on literacy development for the total family. School personnel are becoming increasingly aware that families are the underlying support for the child and that the school must work with both to be successful in the education of the child.

Premises and principles of family support include the following:

a. Primary responsibility for the development and well-being of children lies within the family, and all segments of society must support families as they rear their children.

b. Ensuring the well-being of all families is the cornerstone of a healthy society and requires universal access to support programs and services.

c. Children and families exist as a part of an ecological and reciprocal system.

d. Child-rearing patterns are influenced by parents' understanding of child development and of their children's unique characteristics, personal sense of competence, and cultural and community traditions and mores.

e. Enabling families to build on their own strengths and capacities promotes the healthy development of children.

f. The developmental processes that make up parenthood and family life create needs that are unique at each stage in the lifespan.

g. Families are empowered when they have access to information and other resources and take action to improve the well-being of children, families, and communities. (Family Support America's Shared Leadership Series, 2000).

The centers focus on families' strengths and respond to parents (whether young or mature) according to their needs, linking them with social services that will help ensure they have the basic necessities. They help the families cope with stress; they offer prenatal classes, child development, and parent education to help them with their children; they work to prevent crises; they sponsor drop-in services; and they arrange opportunities for parents to develop support networks.

Family and Child Education (FACE)

In 1990, the Bureau of Indian Affairs, Office of Indian Education, wanted an integrated program for early childhood parental involvement for American Indian families and children. The goals of FACE include the following: to support parents and primary caregivers in their role as their child's first and most influential teacher; to increase family literacy; to strengthen family–school–community connections; to promote the early identification of, and services to, children with special needs; to increase parent participation in their child's learning; to support and celebrate the unique cultural and linguistic diversity of each American Indian community served by the program; and to promote lifelong learning.

The Family and Child Education (FACE) training program provides training sessions and on-site assistance. The program includes the integration of language and culture in two settings: home and school. Family services are provided to parents of children from prenatal through 5 years old. The focus is to support parents as teachers with a special emphasis in language development. In 2009, FACE services were provided to 2327 adults and 2349 children, ages birth to 5 years from 1866 families. Seventy percent of adults and children participate in home-based services, 24% participate in center-based services, and 4% participate in both home- and center-based services (United States Department of Health and Human Services, 2009).

Family Literacy

The federal definition of **family literacy services** is as follows:

Services that are of sufficient intensity in terms of hours and of sufficient duration, to make sustainable changes in a family and that integrate all of the following activities:

a. Interactive literacy activities between parents and their children.

b. Training for parents regarding how to be the primary teacher for their children and full partners in the education of their children.

c. Parent literacy training that leads to economic self-sufficiency.

d. An age-appropriate education to prepare children for success in school and life experiences. (U.S. Department of Health and Human Services, Administration for Children and Families 2000)

The inability to read and write hinders men and women in fulfilling their roles in society and their roles as parents. Parents should become literate not only to ensure self-sufficient employment, but also to engage in interactive literacy activities with their children and to be the primary teachers for their children and become full partners in their children's education. Parents who cannot read books or notes that their children bring home are unable to collaborate effectively with the school for the betterment of their children. Comprehensive family literacy programs and family-centered literacy programs provide the support that parents need to fulfill their parental roles (Dail & Payne, 2010).

The federal government supports family literacy through a few programs, including Title I and Head Start. The Head Start program initiated its focus on family literacy programs in 1992 with three goals: (a) helping parents realize their own needs and working to overcome their own literacy concerns; (b) helping them increase their access to literacy services, programs, and materials; and (c) supporting them in their role as their child's teacher (Potts, 1992). The federal government also offers Even Start, which links parents of children under 8 with combined adult-literacy and preschool programs, with the goal of reducing illiteracy and poverty (National Even Start Association, 2014). Home visits are also used to bring activities and new books to the parents and visit with them on their home territory.

There are, of course, many programs offered in addition to those available through the federal government. The Education and Human Services Consortium is a coalition interested in connecting families with the services they need, and many nonprofit organizations, workplace literacy programs, and colleges and universities also promote adult literacy. Two major nonprofit associations have made great strides in supporting families: Family Support (Family Resource Center) in Chicago spearheaded the move toward more centers, whether federally, state, or privately funded, and the National Center for Family Literacy received a grant from the Kenan Trust in support of its efforts to promote family literacy through programs and training. The National Center for Family Learning offers a directory of National Literacy programs such as GED and English as a Second Language. Studies show that literacy programs assist individuals to realize the value of education and the need to realize their own potential (Prins & Schaff, 2009).

All family literacy programs—whether federal, state, or nonprofit—focus on building family programs based on the strengths of families rather than on their deficits. It is recommended that literacy programs should be of sufficient duration to provide sufficient support to the family to enable success. Literacy programs use methods of teaching adults that have been tested over time and work very well with parents and families.

Summary

Parent engagement is increased when the climate of the school allows for parents to feel welcomed and valued. School-based programs that involve parents are varied. The Comer process is based on three principles—consensus, collaboration, and no fault—which are needed to develop a climate that allows children, parents, and schools to thrive. Effective programs that have a strong parental involvement component include Head Start, HighScope Perry Preschool Program, Carolina Abecedarian Project, Project CARE, Syracuse Family Development Research, Houston Parent–Child Development Center, Early Training Project, Chicago Child–Parent Centers, and Oklahoma Pre-K. School-based programs are diversified, but each type of involvement is essential if the needs of families are to be met. Many parent involvement programs begin with grants and develop and change as the needs of the families they serve change. Family literacy programs, particularly for English language learners and other minorities, are crucial in helping children be successful in school and life.

Suggested Class Activities and Discussions

1. Visit schools in different areas and find out how they engage families. Analyze the different approaches.

2. Design a family blog for your classroom. Ask a parent volunteer to be the "blogger" by discovering themes of interest to other parents.

3. Do a Google search on current parent engagement programs.

4. Develop digital backpacks that families can use with their children at home.

5. Search the community for resources that can be used in the school. Include specialists, materials, and places to visit.

Useful Websites

Family Support America
National Center for Family Literacy

The Annie E. Casey Foundation
AVANCE, Inc.

Glossary Terms

Family engagement: Collaborative process to create home-school partnerships.

School-based program: A program that provides goals and objectives for family engagement through different themes based in a school.

Chapter 9
Home Programs

The child's first learning environment is the home and when needed educators collaboratively work with families to provide support for children's healthy development.

Mari Riojas-Cortez

Learning Outcomes

In this chapter, you will learn about home-based education, homeschooling, and homework.

9.1 Identify characteristics of home-based programs.

9.2 Examine a home-based program example.

9.3 List components of home-visiting activities.

9.4 Identify characteristics of homeschooling.

Imagine yourself as the parent of an infant or toddler living in the country at least a mile from the nearest neighbor. Or, pretend you are a parent in a core-city apartment house with no friends or family living close by. If you had an infant or toddler with a disability or special need, what would you do? Some parents in urban and suburban areas have no more contact with support networks than those isolated by distance in the country, as are many Native Americans. Immigrant families can face the same sort of challenges, living in a different country from their friends and relatives. Urban and rural residents, as well as immigrant families, need educational support and knowledge to provide an enriched, positive environment for their children, for parents to be effective as their children's first teachers. Most programs that serve these families are known as home-based visiting programs. According to the organization Zero to Three (2018a), home-visiting programs include parenting and health education, child abuse prevention, early intervention, and general education. Most home-based visiting programs are voluntary in nature (Finello, Terteryan, & Riewerts, 2016). Home-based visiting programs and home-based programs are different from homeschooling, which is a choice that many parents make (Guterman & Neuman, 2018), usually when children begin formal schooling.

Home-based programs began in the 1800s in the U.S. and were largely focused on populations that needed the most support, which is very similar to what we have today (Finello, Terteryan, & Riewerts, 2016). When immigrants from southern and eastern Europe began to come in great numbers to the United States in the later 1800s, visiting nurses and settlement houses were part of the response to "encourage" the new arrivals to use "proper" hygiene and health. The growth of government intervention and services came a bit later, beginning in the 20th century, and parent education provided outside the home became prominent in the 1920s. The trend toward home visiting was renewed after World War II, and since the 1970s, the programs have moved from working with individuals to working with and empowering families (Wasik & Bryant, 2001). Most programs have a theoretical underpinning, which might include Bronfenbrenner's Ecological System Theory and others (Finello, Terteryan, & Riewerts, 2018).

In 2010, Congress established the Maternal, Infant, and Early Childhood Visiting Program (MIECHV), through the Health Resources and Services Administration (HRSA) and the Administration for Children and Families (ACF). The following are examples of programs that operate with the financial assistance from the federal government: Child FIRST, Early Head

Start–Home Visiting, Early Intervention Program for Adolescent Mothers, Family Check-Up, Healthy Steps, Home Instruction for Parents and Preschool Youngsters (HIPPY), Nurse Family Partnership (NFP), Parents as Teachers (PAT), and Play and Learning Strategies (PALS) (Health Resources and Services Administration Maternal and Child Health, 2018).

Currently, programs such as Early Head Start have a home-visit component for healthy infant development and parenting skills (Roggman, Boyce, & Cook, 2009). Other programs focus on working with parents on couple relationships, father involvement, and parenting interactions to decrease instances of child maltreatment and strengthen family relationships (Sar, Antle, Bledsoe, Barbee, & Van Zyl, 2010).

Home-visiting programs can assist families with different areas of development.

Characteristics of Home Programs

Numerous programs have proved effective in a variety of projects throughout the United States. They range from programs specifically designed to educate children and bring positive parenting practices into the home to those that provide support for the entire family's physical health, mental health, housing, income, child development, and education. Descriptions of selected programs illustrate the scope and variety of parent involvement in the educational process, and families can take from them the ideas and procedures that fit their situation. These are known as home-visiting programs and often the focus is on infants and toddlers. Such programs serve underrepresented and marginalized populations, such as those living in poverty and people of color (usually Blacks, Latinos, and Native Americans).

Home-based programs were developed on the premise that parents are a child's first and most influential teachers; therefore, parents must be supported in order to fulfil this role. Many of these programs were developed to reduce the impact of child abuse by assisting parents to relate constructively to their children and to guide parents to support the physical, emotional, and cognitive development of their children, which is especially important during a child's first three years, when brain development is most rapid. Programs that help parents during these early years offer great benefits in the cognitive and language development of their children. Currently, some of these programs focus on early intervention for children with special needs or

disabilities with therapists providing speech, occupational, or physical therapy during home visits.

Home-visiting programs provide different services for families in their home. A sample list of home-visiting programs that meet the Department of Health and Human Services criteria for effectiveness (National Home Visiting Resource Center, 2017) are listed in Table 9.1. In 2015, more than a quarter of a million families participated in some type of home-visiting program (National Home Visiting Resource Center, 2017).

In addition, grant funds are awarded to the Tribal Maternal, Infant, and Early Childhood Home Visiting

Table 9.1 Evidence-Based Models, According to National Home Visiting Center (2017)

Attachment and Biobehavioral Catch-Up (ABC) Intervention	Healthy Families America (HFA)
Child FIRST	HealthySteps
Early Head Start—Home Visiting (EHS)	Home Instruction for Parents of Preschool Youngsters (HIPPY)
Early Intervention Program for Adolescent Mothers	Maternal Early Childhood Sustained Home-Visiting Program (MECSH)
Early Start (New Zealand)	Minding the Baby
Family Check-Up for Children	Nurse–Family Partnership (NFP)
Family Connects	Oklahoma's Community-Based Family Resource and Support (CBFRS) Program (no longer in operation)
Family Spirit	Parents as Teachers (PAT)
Health Access Nurturing Development Services (HANDS) Program	Play and Learning Strategies (PALS)
Healthy Beginnings	SafeCare Augmented

Stockbyte/Getty Images

Figure 9.1 Tribal Maternal, Infant, and Early Childhood Home Visiting Program for American Indian and Alaskan Native Communities

Different states where the program is available. Between 2012-2016, 54,801 home visits were provided serving 3,477 parents and children.

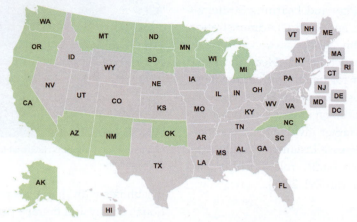

Source: Early Childhood Development. (2018). Tribal home visiting grantees. Office of the Administration for Children and Families. Retrieved on November 20, 2018 from https://www.acf.hhs.gov/ecd/home-visiting/tribal-home-visiting/map

Program for American Indian and Alaskan native communities. Figure 9.1 shows the states where the program is available. Between 2012 and 2016, 54,801 home visits were provided, serving 3,477 parents and children. The success of this program is shown by the 80% family retention rate in 2016. The majority of participants were under the age of 21 (Tribal Home Visiting, 2018). Of importance is how the programs connect cultural experiences with early learning, as does the Partnership for Anishnaabe Binoojiiyensag Tribal Home Visiting Program (Early Childhood Development, 2018). The lessons developed in this program were based on relevant cultural traditions that form part of daily family life.

Parents as Teachers Program

The Parents as Teachers Program is an international organization that promotes the optimal early learning and healthy development of children. The Parents as Teachers (PAT) program was developed in four districts in Missouri in the early 1980s and extended to the entire state in 1985. For 37 years, the PAT program has worked in 50 states and 6 countries to provide high-quality early learning opportunities for families and young children (Parents as Teachers, 2018). PAT operates in all 50 U.S. states and in 100 Tribal organizations. It serves more than 195,000 children in different schools and communities in the U.S., as well as five other countries and one U.S. territory (Parents as Teachers, 2018).

The PAT program secured a $14.23 million i3 grant from the U.S. Department of Education to support the BabyFACE project, which provides home visits and family services to high-need Native American families and children (Parents as Teachers, 2014). The PAT program meets the criteria of the Maternal, Infant, and Early Childhood Home Visiting Program and those of the Tribal Home Visiting Grantees (Parents as Teachers, 2014). Recently, the PAT program (2018) and the University of Southern California Suzanne Dworak-Peck School of Social Work and Telehealth Clinic received a $1 million in prize funding to use interactive videoconferencing for developmental screenings for children.

The PAT program services include four components:

1. Personal visits
2. Group connections
3. Resource network
4. Child screening (Parents as Teachers, 2018)

The objectives for the program include:

1. increase parent knowledge of early childhood development and improve parent practices,
2. provide early detection of developmental delays and health issues,
3. prevent child abuse and neglect, and
4. increase children's school readiness and success (Parents as Teachers, 2018).

The Parents as Teachers Program is for all families who need it. In particular, the model provides universal access home visiting for those families who are most vulnerable and have high needs, such as those suffering from homelessness, domestic violence, substance abuse, mental illness, and other challenges. Figure 9.2 shows the Parents as Teachers logical model.

Research conducted in 1985 on first-time parents who participated in PAT validated the parents' positive responses to the program. It showed that children participating in the Parents as Teachers project scored significantly higher on all measures of verbal ability, intelligence, language ability, achievement, and auditory comprehension than did children in a comparison group. The program proved so successful it was adopted by the Missouri Department of Elementary and Secondary Education for use by 543 school districts throughout the state. Revisions and updates to the PAT curriculum were accomplished in 1996, in addition to the development of the Born to Learn curriculum. The new curriculum was field-tested and became part of the standard PAT Program for prenatal to 3-year-olds for Missouri in 1999. In a later study, Pfannenstiel and Ziegler (2007) found that parents in the PAT program read more to their children, a large percentage of children entered school ready to learn, and the majority of low-income third-graders who had attended PAT performed at the benchmark on the Missouri state-mandated test.

A 2009 study by Wookfolk and Unger focused on the relationships between low-income African American mothers and their home visitors. The findings indicated that the mothers' perspectives regarding the program were linked to their relationship with the home visitor. Another study by Chaiyachati et al (2018) showed that home visiting can prevent child neglect. The strong stance on family welfare is demonstrated in the program's Statement on Separating Children from Families. The statement focuses on the lasting damage that the zero tolerance policy from the Department of Homeland Security has on families seeking asylum or shelter from poverty and other dire conditions (Parents as Teachers, 2018).

HIPPY—Home Instruction Program for Preschool Youngsters

The HIPPY (Home Instruction for Parents of Preschool Youngsters) program was developed in 1969 at the Hebrew University of Jerusalem in Israel, and is now used in at least eight countries. The first U.S. programs were established in 1984. There are 129 HIPPY programs in 21 states and the District of Columbia (Home Instruction for Parents of Preschool Youngsters, 2018).

The basic assumptions of the program are that all children can learn and that all parents want the best for their children. The mission of HIPPY is to "help parents empower themselves as their children's first teacher by giving them the tools, skills, and confidence they need to work with their children in the home" (Home Instruction for Parents of Preschool Youngsters, 2014).

The skill areas included in the curriculum are tactile, visual, auditory, and conceptual discrimination, in addition to language development, verbal expression, eye–hand coordination, premath concepts, logical thinking, self-concept, and creativity. The HIPPY curriculum targets 3-, 4-, and 5-year-olds and includes storybooks, activity packets, and manipulative shapes (HIPPY, 2014). The curriculum focuses on parents working with children using play and hands-on learning (Doyle, 2005). Figures 9.3A and 9.3B illustrate the type of study materials offered to parents in the program (Baker, Piotrkowshi & Brooks-Gunn, 1998; BarHava-Monteith, Harre, & Field, 1999). Enrichment activities that focus on health, nutrition, and problem solving for 5-year-olds have been added to the curriculum (HIPPY, 2014).

Home visitors role-play strategies for engaging children in learning activities. There are also group meetings with parents to encourage socialization. A HIPPY site with no more than 180 children can be served by one coordinator and 12–18 part-time home visitors. A professional coordinates the program, but home visitors are paraprofessionals selected from parents who were in the program. They visit bimonthly, or at least 15 times a year to instruct the parents in the use of HIPPY educational materials (Baker, Piotrkowski, & Brooks-Gunn, 1999).

The HIPPY program is open to parents from rural and urban areas, giving these families an opportunity to help their children succeed in school. The University of South Florida hosts The National Research & Evaluation Center for HIPPY USA, which focuses on the design and implementation of national research strategies (HIPPY, 2014).

Healthy Families America

The Healthy Families America (2018) program was established by the Prevent Child Abuse America (formerly known as the National Committee to Prevent Child Abuse) organization. The mission of the HFA program is "to work with families who might have histories of trauma, intimate partner violence, mental health and/or substance abuse issues" (Healthy Families

Figure 9.2 Parents as Teachers Logical Model

 Parents as Teachers® **Evidence-Based Home Visiting Logic Model**

Guiding Theoretical Framework

Human Ecology and Family Systems | Tenets of Child Development | Developmental Parenting | Attribution Theory | Empowerment and Self-Efficacy

Inputs

- Implementing agency leadership and support
- Qualified supervisors and parent educators trained in Foundational and Model Implementation
- Participants (families with children ranging from prenatal to kindergarten)
- Technology (database, phones, etc.)
- Sustainable funding
- Policies, procedures and protocols
- Community support and partnerships
- The Foundational curricula, Model Implementation and Supervisor's Handbook
- Comprehensive Affiliate Plan with design elements that meet Parents as Teachers Essential Requirements and Quality Standards
- Program management, evaluation and Continuous Quality Improvement (CQI)
- Implementation, advocacy, data collection and management resources with support from state and national offices

Activities

- **Reflective Supervision and Professional Development**
- **Personal Visits**
- **Group Connections**
- **Child Screening**
- **Resource Network**
- **Family-Centered Assessment and Goal Setting**
- **Stakeholder Engagement**
- **Evaluation and Continuous Quality Improvement**

Approach: Partner, Facilitate, Reflect

Outputs

- Staff receive regular reflective supervision and participate in professional development.
- Families have regular personal visits that include the areas of emphasis and follow the Foundational curricula.
- Group connections are provided for families.
- Children receive regular developmental screening and a health review, including hearing and vision.
- Families are connected to needed community resources.
- Parent educators complete family-centered assessment and support families to set goals.
- Advisory committee meetings are held regularly and advocacy work is conducted.
- Measurement of outcomes and participant satisfaction and participation in the Quality Endorsement and Improvement process.

Outcomes

Short-term

- Increased healthy pregnancies and improved birth outcomes.
- Increased early identification and referral to services for possible developmental delays and vision, hearing and health issues in children.
- Increased parent knowledge of age-appropriate child development, including language, cognitive, social-emotional and motor domains.
- Improved parenting capacity, parenting practices and parent-child relationships through the demonstration of positive parenting skills and quality parent-child interactions.
- Improved family health and functioning as demonstrated by a quality home environment, social connections and empowerment.

Intermediate

- Improved child health and development.
- Reduced rates of child abuse and neglect.
- Increased school readiness.
- Increased parent involvement in children's care and education.

Long-term

- Strong communities, thriving families and healthy, safe children who are ready to learn.

Vision | Mission | Core Values | Approach

ParentsAsTeachers.org

Figure 9.3A HIPPY Domains

YEAR 2: WEEK 3

Contents

Domains

You will need ...

Activity 1: Literacy

The book, *Sounds I Hear,* by Ophra Gelbart, paper plate or cover from a pan, Activity Sheet 1, crayons or markers, scissors, envelope with pictures you saved from Week 2

Activity 2: Math

54 small objects (dried beans, cereal, pasta, buttons, coins, or pebbles); an egg carton with the last two spaces cut off or 10 small containers; Activity Sheet 2; scissors

Activity 3: Science

A heavy sheet of 8.5x11 sheet of paper (an old HIPPY Activity Sheet works); crayons, markers or watercolors; 24" string or yarn, 10-12" strips of tissue paper or crepe paper, ribbon, or yarn or string; glue; scissors or pencil

Activity 4: Motor

A large open space; Activity Sheets 3 and 4; a wrapped up treat to hide for your child; crayons; scissors

Activity 5: Language

The book, *Sounds I Hear,* by Ophra Gelbart, Activity Sheet 5; envelope with pictures you saved from Week 2

Activity 6: Alphabet

Pencil; Activity Sheets 6 and 7

Tip

As you read the HIPPY books to your child and work on the activities that go with them your child will gain **Book Knowledge**. Your child will not only learn to comprehend the stories, but is also learning how books are constructed and used: including title, author, and recognizing concepts such as front and back cover, top and bottom of page, beginning, middle and end of story and knowing that print goes from left to right and top to bottom.

Tip

Many of the HIPPY activities will focus on **Language Development**. This is the process of your child building vocabulary for understanding words either spoken and/or heard.

• **Building Vocabulary (Vocabulary Development)** is learning new words and using them to express one's self.
• **Expressive Language** is explaining one's ideas clearly in complete sentences (speaking).
• **Receptive Language** is understanding the meaning of words that one hears spoken (listening).

America, 2014). The aims of the program include the following:

- Reduce child maltreatment
- Improve parent-child interactions and children's social-emotional well-being
- Increase school readiness
- Promote child physical health and development
- Promote positive parenting
- Promote family self-sufficiency
- Increase access to primary care medical services and community services
- Decrease child injuries and emergency department use (Healthy Families America, 2018)

Figure 9.3B HIPPY Sample Activities

YEAR 2: WEEK 3

Activity 3: Science, Weather

Science

What your child will learn from this activity

Today your child will be using *fine motor skills* to color and glue paper to make a windsock. Then your child will *observe* what happens to the windsock by *experimenting* with it being blown and *predicting* what will happen if there is no wind. These are all important skills in the process of *scientific exploration*.

You will need

- A heavy sheet of 8.5x11 sheet of paper (an old HIPPY Activity Sheet works)
- Crayons, markers, or watercolors
- 24" of string or yarn
- 10 – 12" strips of tissue paper, newspaper, crepe paper, ribbon, yarn or string
- Glue
- Scissors or pencil to poke holes in the windsock

What to do

1. (Place all of the materials on the table in front of your child.)

   We have been checking our weather everyday with our weather chart. Today we are going to make a windsock. It is something that will help us to decide if it is a windy day. Here is a picture of a windsock. We will make one like this.

   First we will take the sheet of paper and decorate it for our windsock. You can use crayons (or markers or water colors) to decorate the paper. Draw whatever you would like to draw and color it with your favorite colors.

   (When your child has finished decorating the paper, point to one of the short sides of the paper where your child will put the glue.)

   Put glue all along this short side of the paper.

These goals support improved parenting skills, the enhancement of child health and development, the reduction of family stress, and improved family functioning, as well as the prevention of child abuse and neglect. Recently, the program has added "e-parenting," which is a computer-based intervention to augment home visiting. Results show that mothers are utilizing the program in a therapeutic manner (Zero to Three, 2010).

Families are selected primarily through the use of a standardized assessment tool by participating hospitals or physicians, public health nurses, midwives, support groups in areas where access to hospital records is unavailable, or by self or family referral. The HFA staff helps expectant parents and the parents of newborns learn how to properly take care of oneself during pregnancy, soothe a crying baby, ensure the child receives the appropriate nutrition, promote healthy development and bonding, and assist in creating a safe home environment (Healthy Families America, 2014).

Considering the stress new parents face daily, especially without family or community supports, a key strategy to prevent child abuse and neglect is to provide the support that is missing (Daro, McCurdy, Falconnier, & Stojanovic, 2003; Rogers & O'Connor, 2003). Home visitors are trained to provide supportive, culturally appropriate services beginning prenatally or at the birth of a child and continuing until the child is 5. The program begins with level 1, weekly visits; progresses to level 2, which consists of two visits a month; and completes at levels 3 and 4 with monthly or quarterly visits.

Research findings published on the Prevent Child Abuse America website provide results of program outcomes in various state settings. For example, in Pinellas County, Florida, the rate of child maltreatment for participants in the HFA program was 1.6%, compared to 4.9% for the county as a whole. In Maryland, there were only two reports of neglect among the 254 families served in 4 years (a rate of 0.8%). Results from a study in Alaska show modest benefits to children's cognitive development and behavior as well as an increase in the quality of the home environment (Gomby, 2007). In other studies, HFA proved effective in preventing teen repeat births and rapid repeat births (Ownbey, Ownbey, & Cullen, 2011).

In general, the Healthy Families program has demonstrated the following:

- Mothers achieve higher levels of confidence.
- Home environment is better organized.
- Parents engage in neglectful behavior less often.
- Parents show greater acceptance of their children's behavior.
- Significantly lower levels of distress arise for parents and children.
- Significantly fewer reports of abuse and neglect occur within the first year of life.

Early Head Start

Early Head Start (EHS) is a federally funded program that serves low-income pregnant women and families with infants and toddlers. It is designed to serve children until their third birthdays, with transition plans made for preschool services, either in Head Start or other community services for which the families are eligible. Children participating in EHS live in poverty and have at least one of the disability indicators (Peterson, Mayer, Summers, & Luze, 2010). Early Head Start seems to also help in the prevention of child maltreatment (Green, Ayoub, Bartlett, Von Ende, Furrer, Chazan-Cohen, Vallotton, & Klevens, 2014).

The EHS program has four service areas in which outcomes are measured: child development, which includes health, language, cognitive and social-emotional development; family development, which includes parenting skill development and economic self-sufficiency; staff development; and family–community partnerships, which include establishing collaborations between the EHS program and other community organizations. Services are provided through visits by home visitors that represent the parent populations served by the program (Raikes, Green, Atwater, Kisker, Constantine, & Chazan-Cohen, 2006). Program services include the following:

- Weekly home visits that last 90 minutes. Home visitors work with parents to guide them in using daily routines to promote child development. Parents are encouraged to plan each week's activities; one example might be cooking to enhance nutrition habits, language and literacy skills, number awareness, and social skills such as turn taking and sharing.
- Screening of children to determine if they are meeting developmental milestones in language, cognitive, and social-emotional areas, physical growth, and nutrition.
- Assessment of the home environment to determine if it is supportive of children's safety, health, and cognitive, language, and socioemotional development.
- Assessment of the children's and family's medical needs.
- Development of family partnership agreements through which parents plan strategies to develop self-sufficiency through participation in education and training activities, job search strategies, and advocacy skills to attain services needed by their children.
- Assistance to parents in preparing their children for transitioning from the EHS program to preschool programs when their children reach 3 years of age.

Reports from the Early Head Start Research and Evaluation Project (EHSREP) show that when families participate in home-based and center-based approaches or mixed programs, there is a significant positive impact on parents and children through age 3 (Robinson, Klute, Faldowski, Pan, Staerkel, Summers, & Wall, 2009). Twice a month, families have the opportunity to participate in group activities that encourage children and parents to socialize with others and to observe staff modeling appropriate child–adult interactions. Parents also have the opportunity to identify other participants within the program with whom they can develop supportive relationships.

Programming of parent–child socialization activities is decided by a parent committee, which is a subcommittee of the parent policy council, a decision-making group overseeing the EHS program. The EHS program maintains a parent policy council, which is an elected group made up of present and past parents and some community representation. The policy council reviews the EHS budget, hiring and firing of staff, selection of curricula and screening tools to be used by home visitors, annual community needs-assessment activities, and performs a federally mandated self-evaluation. Participation on the parent policy council provides interested parents with many opportunities to develop skills in public speaking, committee work, business skills, communication skills, and enhanced understanding of the functioning of the program (Lane, Kesker, Ross, et al., 2005; McCallister, Wilson, Green, & Baldwin, 2005).

Nurse Family Partnership Program

The Nurse Family Partnership Program (formerly the Nurse Home Visitation Program) is a home-visiting nurse program that serves low-income, first-time mothers by improving their health and social functioning. Public-health nurses begin providing service when mothers are 20 to 28 weeks into their pregnancy. The nurse provides support to the mother through the child's first two years of life. The program was begun as a research project in Elmira, New York, and was expanded to six demonstration cities. In 1999, the National Center for Children, Families, and Communities was established to disseminate the program, which now operates in 42 states and serves more than 280,000 families (Nurse Family Partnership Program, 2018). The goals of the program are to do the following:

- Improve prenatal, maternal, and early childhood health
- Improve family functioning in health, home, and neighborhood environments
- Build family and friend support networks
- Build parental roles
- Build skills to improve coping with major life events

Home visits target the following risk areas:

- Health behaviors that affect preterm delivery, low birth weight, and infant neurodevelopmental impairment, such as tobacco and other substance abuse
- School dropout prevention
- Welfare dependence
- Unintended subsequent pregnancies

Nurse home visitors follow a structured intervention plan that involves assessing attitudes, skills, knowledge, and support available to the mother in the home environment. Mothers are encouraged to work toward personal goals, attain behavior changes, and cope with challenges. Activities are assigned between home visits. Visits are scheduled to coincide with the progression of the pregnancy and the child's development. Nurse home visitors use the Clinical Information System to track family characteristics, needs, services received, and progress attained by the mother (Nurse Family Partnership, 2014).

A follow-up evaluation has demonstrated several positive outcomes. They include the following:

- A decrease in arrests and convictions of 15-year-old target children
- A decrease in sexual partners among 15-year-old target children
- Improved birth outcomes
- Reduced child abuse and neglect
- Savings of $4 for every dollar invested due to reduced welfare, fewer arrests, and lower health-care costs (Karoly, Kilburn, & Cannon, 2005)

Studies have shown that the program has helped children born to mothers with low psychological resources not only reduce mental-health problems and the use of substances, but also improve their academic achievement (Kitzman et al., 2010). Other studies also show the importance of training the nurses to adapt the visit to the family's needs (Ingoldsby, Baca, McClatchey, Luckey, Ramsey, Loch, Lewis, et al., 2013), making the program culturally relevant for families.

The Parent–Child Home Program

The Parent–Child Home Program (PCHP) is a home-based family literacy program that relies on positive verbal interaction between the child 2 to 4 years old and the primary caregiver. This program serves the following types of families (Parent–Child Home Program, 2018):

- Families facing poverty, low literacy, limited education, language barriers, geographic isolation, and/or homelessness
- Families with annual incomes of under $25,000
- Families with multiple children
- Single parent households
- Non-English speaking

The goal of the program is to build school readiness in the home. Parent-child interaction is critical in helping with the development of language skills. The PCHP program early learning specialists visit twice a week with parents and children to show them how to use appropriate books and toys while using verbal language. The focus is to model for parents how a natural dialogue that enhances and enriches the child's language is possible through books and toys (Parent-Child Home Program, 2018).

The program is based in the child's home; trained home visitors ("early learning specialists") come twice weekly for half-hour sessions from the time the child is 2 until they are 4. The twice-a-week visits to the home are set up at the parent's convenience (Levenstein et al., 1998; Nievar, Van Egeren, & Pollard, 2010). During the biweekly visits, the home visitor demonstrates toys and books in a play session with parent and child. Parenting behavior emphasizing verbal interaction is modeled instead of being taught directly. Language interactions are encouraged in the family's native language (Mann, Sandoval, Garcia, & Calderon, 2009). The parent and child participate as they learn through play. Books and toys are given to the families so the learning can continue. There are no specific tasks other than enjoying the play and resultant verbal interaction. Guide sheets cover such concepts as colors, shapes, and sizes and such cognitive skills as matching, pretending, and differentiating.

Children learn through play.

The Parent–Child Home Program is grounded on a constructivist philosophy in which the importance of parent or adult interaction with children is a significant component in healthy development (Parent–Child Home Program, 2018).

The method, curricula, and delivery of the program include the following:

- 46 half-hour sessions twice a week spread over 7 months each year for 2 years
- A guide sheet, a one-page list of concepts, and developmentally appropriate labels for actions or words applied to the toy or book brought by the home visitor to the toddler
- A 20-item VIP-created instrument called "Child's Behavior Traits," a measure as well as a guide to the child's socioemotional goals
- A "Parent and Child Together" curriculum of 20 traits that measure and guide positive parent behavior, modeled by the home visitor and achieved by the parent
- Curriculum materials including 12 illustrated books and 11 toys—with a different set for each year of the 2-year program, for a total of 46 books and toys given to the family
- Modeling involvement in the child's play by the home visitor and inviting the parent to be involved

Jupiterimages/Stockbyte/Getty Images

- Home visitor modeling (without directly teaching) of a positive response to the child by reading to the child, encouraging the family's literacy in addition to the child's

- Sessions arranged at the parents' convenience

- Program coordinators who are college graduates and work with home visitors to develop the necessary nondidactic skills and respect for family privacy and lifestyles, and to prepare written reports (Levenstein et al., 1998).

More recent studies indicate the success of the visitation program in increasing language interactions, play, story book readings, and other skills and positive behaviors (Nievar, Van Egeren, & Pollard, 2010; Organizational Research Services, 2010).

The Portage Project

The Portage Project was developed in 1969 as a home-based, family-centered demonstration program providing service to children with disabilities and their families. The model worked with children from birth to age 6 and with their families through weekly home visits by a home teacher. The project originally covered 3600 square miles in south-central Wisconsin (The Portage Project, 2014). Successful evaluation of the model and validation by the National Diffusion Network led to other areas setting up the program.

Over the years, The Portage Project has adhered to the principles upon which it was based:

1. Intervention for children with disabilities should begin as early as possible. The earlier work begins, the greater the probability of having a significant effect on the child and the greater the chance this effect will be maintained over time.

2. Parent/primary caregiver involvement is critical to successful early intervention.

3. Intervention objectives and strategies must be individualized for each child and support the functioning of the family.

4. Data collection is important to reinforce positive change and to make ongoing intervention decisions.

The Portage Project works in collaboration with community agencies to provide comprehensive services to children and families. Referral from individuals and local agencies leads to a play-based assessment conducted by a multidisciplinary team. This assessment is conducted in the family's home and is designed to provide information on parent–child interaction patterns, parent perceptions, and the developmental functioning level of the child.

If the team, including parents, determines that a child is eligible, the process to develop an Individual Family Service Plan is initiated. This process includes extensive observation and communication with the family. The plan might include weekly home visits by a member of The Portage Project transdisciplinary staff, therapy or counseling from community providers, consultation with childcare providers or other caregivers, participation in parent support groups or play groups, or other activities requested by the family.

An interventionist is the care coordinator for the family who maintains regular communication with other service providers. This interventionist can be an educator, a speech and language therapist, or a motor specialist, but his or her role in working with families is transdisciplinary.

The Portage Project staff has developed materials to support early childhood programs. These materials include the *Portage Guide to Early Education*, developed in the late 1970s and used in the United States and internationally, and *Growing: Birth to Three* (The Portage Project, 2014).

The *Portage Guide* includes a checklist of 580 developmentally sequenced behaviors for children up to 6 years old. The behaviors are divided into six areas: infant stimulation, self-help, language, cognition, motor skills, and socialization. The guide includes ideas for teaching each of the behaviors to assist parents and teachers. The new version of the *Portage Guide* is currently available, both in print and on The Portage Project's website.

Growing: Birth to Three offers materials to support family-centered interactive intervention. The materials are designed to be used as a package, as each piece contributes to the intervention process. The materials are designed to encourage flexibility in working with families as well as act as a stimulus to expand beyond the specific suggested intervention strategies.

Ecological Planner. Part I of the Ecological Planner suggests guidelines for observation and communication, provides a way to document transactions over time, and offers a selection of formats for individualized intervention planning. Part II of the Ecological Planner is called the Developmental Observation

Guide. It provides an in-depth developmentally sequenced series of behaviors that children frequently display from birth through 36 months.

Nurturing Journals. These journals are designed for use by parents or primary caregivers. Each book contains open-ended questions or statements to help parents reflect on the process of parenting.

Interactive Grow Pack. This section represents the heart of interactive intervention. It offers strategies for interactive communication with parents as well as ways to enhance and encourage mutually satisfying interactions between caregiver and child.

Interactions and Daily Routines Books. This collection offers activity suggestions for each skill or behavior listed in the Developmental Observation Guide. Activity suggestions are embedded in daily routines, rituals, play, and interactions.

Master Forms Packet. This packet of reproducible forms is designed to assist in family-guided intervention. The forms can be used to document communications and observations, develop a family-generated service plan, and develop intervention suggestions responsive to each individual family being served (CESA 5, Portage Project, 1998). Figures 9.4A and 9.4B are examples of activities used by home visitors in The Portage Project. Figure 9.4C shows an example of the observation form called the Child Development Tool for Observation and Planning.

A variety of home-based programs are operating in the United States and in other countries. The programs included here are just a sample of them. The shared premise is working with families and children in their own homes, but there is great variety in the requirements for staff and the manner in which services are provided.

Making a Difference in Families' Lives: A Home Based Program

Since 1903, Family Services Association of San Antonio has been providing services for children, families, and seniors in need. It is funded through the United Way, the United States Department of Human Services, private foundations, grants, client fees, and outpatient mental health insurance. This organization provides services including childcare resources and referrals, counseling services, early childhood well-being, financial empowerment center, teen tech center, Head Start, marriage and relationship enrichment, rural services, special services, and outpatient treatment services, as well as other services for families, children, and seniors. Some of the programs are home based. The fees are on a sliding scale and no one is denied help for lack of funds (Family Services Association, 2018).

Of the many programs that are provided by Family Services Association, the home-based program for families referred to parenting classes by child protective services is among the most successful. The following two parents, "Jeremiah" and "Jennifer," share their respective stories of how the home-based program and the parent educator from Family Services Association helped them become better parents to their children. The interviews are provided as the parents spoke to show their reality and perhaps for us to better understand them in their own words.

Jeremiah's Story

Jeremiah is a veteran diagnosed with PTSD who is a single parent of three children: a son who is 7 years old, a daughter who is 12 months old, and a former stepdaughter, who is 5 years old. His children live with their mothers but he works with both of them to have the children whenever possible. There is no formal custody arrangement and no custody papers between them.

My ex-girlfriend she has her 5-year-old daughter and basically that was the reason for me taking this class. Me and her [the stepdaughter] didn't see eye-to-eye we always were at each other's throats. The class basically it got me to where enough with the ego step down off my little podium and talk to her and try to understand where she's coming from. It got me to ok actually talk to her it got me to stop spanking her [the stepdaughter] for not apparent reason. I thought it was a good reason but it wasn't she only knows me as her father. So it finally got to that point where me and her started building a relationship thanks to this class and it got the point to where we sat down talked everything out we took turns talking why she was upset why she was screaming and yelling and then she realized she didn't even know why she was screaming and then me and her talked it out and now its you need to calm down go to time-out sit down and think about it and you can come talk to me instead of just me "yanking" the kid out and start whipping her for no apparent reason.

Figure 9.4A Sample Activities from *The Portage Guide: Birth Through Six*

Communication/Language/Literacy

Developmental Strand: Early Reading

 7 UNDERSTANDS LEFT TO RIGHT AND TOP TO BOTTOM ORIENTATION AND FAMILIAR CONCEPTS OF PRINT

Why Is This Important?

These skills are a necessary pre-requisite for learning to read and write.

Interactive Activities:

Modeling: Over time I have learned how to handle books by watching you handle books. You have modeled how to hold the book; pointed out that we start reading the words on the left side of the page and that the story starts at the front of the book.

Daily Routine Activities:

Storytime: Any time I am looking at a story book, a Big Book, a chart story or flannel board story be sure to point out that we are starting the story at the left side and at the top of the page. Leave out flannel board story pieces and books for me to use during choice time.

Continued on back

5 to 6 years

PORTAGE GUIDE: BIRTH TO SIX © 2003 Portage Project

Communication/Language/Literacy

Developmental Strand: Early Reading

 8 RECITES STORY FROM BOOK WITH REASONABLE ACCURACY OR TELLS A 3-5 PART SEQUENCED STORY

Why Is this Important?

The child's story-reading behavior is moving from a not formed story e.g., relating a sequence of events, to a formed story e.g., the story has causal connections that gives it cohesiveness.

Interactive Activities:

Expanding: Reading me age appropriate books from the earliest years gives me a wealth of book reading and handling experience. This knowledge is the basis for my own storytelling abilities.

Daily Routine Activities:

Storytime/Anytime: I love telling stories from familiar books. Let me tell stories to the other children in the class or to my siblings at home. I like to sit on a chair and hold up the book like you do. I'm pretty good at remembering the beginning, middle and end of the story although I'm using the picture and word cues to help me.

Continued on back

5 to 6 years

PORTAGE GUIDE: BIRTH TO SIX © 2003 Portage Project

Source: From *Portage Guide to Early Education*, by CESA5, Portage Project, 1998, Portage, WI: Author. Copyright 1998 by the Portage Project. Reprinted with permission.

I was slightly abused as a child back in the day, physically abused, and now I almost put that towards her and my son and I backed away and started saying okay no that's not the way it should be so it actually takes different perspectives in life to understanding your kids including if they're not your kids to actually build a relationship with them and it actually helped us it helped me out very much.

The class was an hour long for twelve weeks we extended a little bit longer than that because I wanted the classes at

Figure 9.4B Sample Activities from *The Portage Guide: Birth Through Six*

Social Emotional Development

Developmental Strand: Interactions with Others

 14 TALKS ABOUT HAVING FRIENDS

Why Is This Important?

Friendships provide opportunities to learn how to interact *with* similar age peers; they facilitate the transition from mother to others and enhance the child's self esteem.

Interactive Activities:

Expand: There are many things that you can do that will facilitate the development of play and friendship in my life. You can model being a friend by demonstrating how to approach another child and ask her to play. Or, you can give me the words or an idea of how to approach other children to play, e.g., say to them *I can carry the groceries for you* or *I can be the dog.* You also model friendship for me by your friendly interactions with other adults that you work with.

Reinforcing: Sometimes I've noticed that if you play with me, e.g., sitting with me at the play dough table, other children will also get interested and join us. Then as our play develops you can move away from the situation.

Daily Routine Activities:

Playtime: Play games that encourage cooperative behaviors rather than competitive behaviors. In *Musical Shares* a child and the chair are not eliminated, but the child who is *it* sits on another child's lap and the music starts over. *Touch green* on another child is a color game that encourages gentle touching as

Continued on back

4 to 5 years

PORTAGE GUIDE: BIRTH TO SIX © 2003 Portage Project

Social Emotional Development

Developmental Strand: Interactions with Others

15 TALKS OCCASIONALLY ABOUT OWN OR OTHER'S FEELINGS

Why Is This Important?

The child now has the words that can describe how she or someone else might be feeling. Being able to communicate these feelings contributes positively to the social interactions she has with other children.

Interactive Activities:

Reinforcing: By providing me with feedback you can help me maintain verbal exchanges and sustain social interaction with other children. Give me words for expressing affection. For example, *Your hug is telling Maria, I like you for playing with me*; expressing appreciation, *The way you are laughing and doing what Roberto did, tells him you like his game*; or unhappiness, *Look at Martin's tears. They tell you he is unhappy because you hit him.*

4 to 5 years

PORTAGE GUIDE: BIRTH TO SIX © 2003 Portage Project

Source: From *Portage Guide to Early Education*, by CESA5, Portage Project, 1998, Portage, WI: Author. Copyright 1998 by the Portage Project. Reprinted with permission.

first I wasn't taking anything seriously I was like "once I'm done with the class I can just go about my life" and then I had some financial issues and everything started hitting me all at once and I realized that the class is there to help me it is there to help me understand me better to understand my kids and it is there to help my child as well to understand where I'm coming from that yes I am the father I am the head of the household but at the same time I am here to help you I am not here to get after you for every single thing and it helped me from being an aggressive parent to more of a

Figure 9.4C Sample from the Child Development Tool for Observation and Planning (TOP). *Portage Project Guide: Birth Through Six*

Child Development Tool for Observation and Planning (TOP)

CODE:
Always or consistently (✓)
Occasionally (O)
Cannot do/not observed (N)
Mark date and code

Social Emotional Development

4 to 5 years

Strands		Things to Consider	OBSERVATION Dates	Code
Relationships	10 Sometimes resolves problems with peers, without physical aggression, with adult support	She will rely more on yelling than on hitting to make a point. Help the child make other choices; persuasion, negotiation, substitution.	1 2 3 4	
Emotional Response	11 Manages emotional responses with adult support	Adults can give childern language for their strong feelings and then offer coping strategies.	1 2 3 4	
	12 Willingly tries new experiences	Trust and security developed through meaningful relationships with others allows the child to have the courage to try new things.	1 2 3 4	
	13 Works alone at a task fro 15-20 minutes	The child can attend to self-selected activities for a longer period of time.	1 2 3 4	
Interactions with Others	14 Talks about having friends	Children at this age are beginning to find people outside the family more interesting; your interest will encourage new relationship.	1 2 3 4	
	15 Talks occasionally own or other's feelings	Beginning to have the words to talk about more complex emotional thinking. You help build understanding of complex emotional issues when you talk about the feelings you see the child expressing.	1 2 3 4	

Comment:

NEW PORTAGE GUIDE: BIRTH TO SIX   21   © 2003 Portage Project

subtle it basically matured me to the point I understand that I can sit down and talk to them regardless if they're screaming I say ok when you're done yelling we'll talk and we had a bunch of sessions where she [stepdaughter] would start screaming and I go like why are you screaming and she just keeps screaming.

My son and me because of this whole transition before me and my ex broke up before the whole transition he was trying to get accustomed to being the brother to two sisters an adopted one and a baby girl and I was there trying to be the medium so the class actually pushed me to the side basically and helped me understand basically this is where he's coming from this is where she's coming from well the baby on the other hand she doesn't know where she's at right now but it helped me with both of them now well since the break up it doesn't really hurt us any more but before it helped them cope with each other a lot more because I was starting to see that I was basically praising my son more than I would my stepdaughter and it helped me balanced that out.

Basically my son would sit right next to me and I wouldn't care but the moment she sat next to me I was "no like you can't scoot over a little bit [I would tell her]." I realized that was pushing her away more than I was actually accepting her. The only thing I can possibly say is that I was doing that was because she wasn't really mine and I wanted her to be mine but I was going about it the whole wrong way. I would let my son get away with something and her I would not let her get away with anything to grabbing stuff without permission, grabbing a snack without permission I would let him but I wouldn't let her.

The spanking, I have a very long leash, the spanking didn't come until she started yelling at me. We would talk and talk and talk then I would start screaming and she would start screaming and then we would just yell at the top of our lungs and she was pissed off at me I was like no and turn around and give her one whacking I realized that was the wrong thing to do what I should have done was I should have just stopped and listen to what she had to say before I tried to intervene. So we had our own little disputes here and there but now it's a lot more understanding my ex now starting to realize is that I am trying to talk to her now including that since we separated yes I am still trying to be there for her maybe not as a father figure but as someone who actually cares for her. So on top of that too me and her have different ways of treating our children but at the same time when we do praise them we praise them the same . . .

It was actually CPS [Child Protective Service] was actually called on me by a friend of the family that we no longer talk to and the only reason why I was able to find this out was because she does make-up art and she put make up on her [the daughter] to make it look like she had a bruise beautiful art work to the point where it looked like she was bruised and I got CPS called on me the school saw her and they said that she was getting beat up by her father I said I have not even touched her not on the face but if you want you can check her butt though. But you know what I said, I only spanked her once on her "cheeks" I never spanked her more than twice never more than once because to me I got your attention now I'm talking to you there's no reason to be screaming the course that we took was. They investigated and everything like that they didn't find any violence in the household at least not that amount of violence that was being accused towards me and what ended up happening was there's nothing we can do at this point but we do recommend at least a parenting class and I was like. I was like I really don't want to I really don't but if it's something that would help me I would. They recommended a bunch of stuff and you don't have to take it but I was like you know what if they can come to the house I take it and they came to the house first two or three weeks that I took it I didn't take anything seriously at all.

Basically "Sarai" was my teacher and she came and she would bring coloring books for the kids or little shirts or gave us passes for things for us to do like the zoo that's the way she basically she introduced herself to us we took a survey that told her where we were and we did homework that was basically was what you learned from that day was talking to your kid or playing with your kid just talking with your kid. I saw a change in my stepdaughter she went from basically being terrified of me to where she wanted to be near me every single minute of the day. She started acting differently she started to respond differently instead of me yelling at her to finally get her attention. Every week since it was a different homework assignment . . . some where kind of odd because sometimes it would never come around like one of them was how to sustain an argument needless to say I didn't have to do to that one because by the time we hit that teaching assignment me and her never had those arguments anymore so what was funny about it was like why don't you put this one at the very beginning so that we can actually go through it she [parent educator] said "well you won't know how to take care of it." Because the homework before it teaches you how to take care of it and it as ok well it's already messed up because I can't take care of the argument there's no argument and she was like don't worry there will be and needless to say as soon as everything is all set and good there happened to be a little dispute at school but we were able to work it out . . . I'm there when she needs me there . . . right now I'm just working on myself so right now I have two beautiful kids you know they're the ones that make me happy in life right now. I would say to other fathers that I know that it's going to be hard for the first couple of weeks I say stick with it at the very end you're going to learn so much that new doors to understanding your kids are going to open up and the relationship that you and your kids will have will flourish it will be a lot better than what it is right now regardless if you think you have the best relationship with your kids this program actually helped make it a lot better. It's just a basic understanding something that should come sense wise it opened those doors with me and my kids and it's actually helped me tremendously because of it. It helped me broaden up my work ethic somewhat not too much but enough to where I want to be out there I want to be there with my kids I want to be done fast enough not to go home to my wife or my significant other but to be there for my kids . . . This program helped me realized that."

When Jeremiah completed the course he framed his certificate and put it up in his parents' home. He felt that the class helped him to create a special bond with his children that he didn't have before. The many systems in Jeremiah life helped him understand his role as a father and encouraged him to be better for them.

Jennifer's Story

Jennifer is a mother of two children, a 12-year-old daughter and an 11-year-old son. Jennifer is bipolar and has been in and out of hospitals dealing with her disorder. The program at Family Services Association created pathways among the different systems of support so that she could be well enough to take care of her children. The school, community agencies, the case worker, and a friend became important systems that helped her find peace in her life. Jennifer's friend "Stephen" would come to her house to help her, not only with the children, but also with the household, and with herself spiritually. She is grateful to the school because she would not have found this program without it. Jennifer's voice is clearly heard in the following raw interview that I conducted at her home.

MC: Tell me: how did you hear about this program?

JK: I had somebody call on me, a worker came over here and checked everything out, and at the end of the visit I guess they gave me a little test and they found that there were some areas that I could use a little help in parenting, and they offered me the parenting classes and asked me if I wanted to take them, and I said yes.

MC: And what were those areas they recommended you take parenting classes?

JK: They said that since I grew up a military brat, my whole family is military, [and] that the way that I discipline my children is sort of like corporal punishment. Because I would make my kids get in the push-up position when they were bad instead of putting them on time-out, or I would make them run or . . . do jumping jacks or make them exercise when they got in trouble.

MC: What were some of the things that the kids would do that would get them into that type of trouble?

JK: Hmm . . . fighting with each other, not doing maybe what I asked them to do after the tenth time I asked them to do it. Lying. Talking back. Stuff like that, doing bad in school.

MC: How did you get in trouble? Who reported you?

JK: I was living with my kids and their father and he was cheating on me with another girl, and this had been going on for about five years, and I guess me and her got into it one time and she got mad and she called CPS on me.

MC: When you were growing up, did you experience the same type of discipline? Did your parents do the same thing to you?

JK: No my parents hit me.

MC: So you didn't want to do that to your kids.

JK: No I didn't want to do that.

MC: After they reported you, who gave you the information for Family Services Association?

JK: The caseworker who came to inspect the house and everything . . . gave me the number and said that they were going to call me for my classes.

MC: And was this recommended or required?

JK: It was recommended.

MC: It was recommended. So what got you to actually do the program?

JK: Because I wanted to be a better mom. If I was doing something wrong I didn't want to do that anymore.

MC: What was the next step?

JK: The next step was just to set up an appointment with my caseworker and have her come over and explain, you know, pretty much the outline of why she was here and what she was going to be helping me with.

MC: And what are some of the things that she said she was going to help you with?

JK: She told me that [I] was going to be able to communicate with my kids easier and so maybe not get so frustrated and to find a better way of disciplining them.

MC: What are some of the strategies that she showed you?

JK: She showed me first of all that how you speak to your kids has a lot to do with how they speak to you back. And when dealing with my kids, instead of disciplining them at first while I'm angry, I need to take a step back, you know, remove myself for a minute, just so that I can calm down and deal with the situation. So that was a big thing for me.

MC: Were there lessons that she taught you?

JK: Yes ma'am. Every week she would come she would give us a lesson that we would work on.

MC: And this was for how many weeks?

JK: Twelve weeks?

MC: Once a week?

JK: Once a week. I think it was supposed to be for an hour but most of the time she would stay longer.

MC: Why do you think she stayed longer?

JK: She became my friend.

MC: How did that happen?

JK: We became friends because when all of this was going on with the kids . . . this was going with the father of my kids too . . . Throughout the years there had been a lot of cheating . . . I would get rid of him and I would take him back, and she pretty much, like, talked to me a lot and she would she made me feel like I did not need to take him back, that I could do this with my kids . . . that it was probably better for my kids because for him to be here and for my kids to see us fighting all the time was making things worse. So she pretty much just gave me like a shoulder to hold on to while I got through it. You know what I mean? And I did get through it.

MC: So give me some examples of the things that she would tell you when she was here. Would she give you any homework?

JK: Yes ma'am, she would give us [homework] to do for me and for my son . . . Every week, the next week we would go over . . . the homework that we did through the week or whatever, and she would talk to my son about how he felt and how things had went over the week, and did we put any of what we learned into practice.

MC: And what would your kids say?

JK: My kids said yes, they said that they could see a big difference, that I wasn't as angry and I took more time to understand how they were feeling and I wasn't just like acting up about how I felt at the moment.

MC: Were they surprised to see that change?

JK: Yes, I think so, because I had been like that for a long time.

MC: Did they come and approach you when they would see that change?

JK: They didn't come and approach me or tell me anything specific but the way that they act towards me now, I can see them a lot more loving and coming to me and talking to me about stuff a lot more than they were before, because before it was just like they were fighting or it was just an attitude. It was just a whole lot of turmoil.

MC: Did you see any changes in them, in their behavior at school, in the way they were behaving at school?

JK: Not really. At school my kids are really good. My kids are really really good at school but another thing that helped us is that my boy was being bullied at school and I didn't really know. . . . One day my caseworker came and she was talking to him and she got it out of him that he was being bullied.

MC: How did she get it out of him?

JK: She just kept asking him a lot of questions about why did he look the way he looked, and why was he making the faces that he was making. He looked like he wasn't happy and something was bothering him, and she just kind of picked a little bit, you know what I mean? And she finally got it out of him . . . It was something that I didn't even know it was going on, and eventually by the end of the day she showed me . . . he had a big bruise on his arm from the girls. It was girls that were beating him up at school and I was mad. I wanted to go to the school and go like [makes a fist] . . .

MC: Like any mom.

JK: It's worse because I have bipolar. Once I get things they switch like that, and I wanted to go to the school . . . she [the caseworker] didn't let me. She gave me like a plan. [She said,] this is what you need to go in there, and this is what you need to say, and if they don't do what you need them to do then you need to tell them this, and if they still don't then you [say], I'm going to call CPS on y'all because my kids are being hurt over here at school. You know, she helped me a lot with that too, because now I could go in there and call the principal or call teachers, call whoever I needed to call into a meeting and sit down and have a conversation and say, this is what's happening, without it turning into something ugly. You know what I mean?

MC: Yes, right. So then you were taking these classes. Were there any classes that made you say, "I don't know about this"? That you were getting ready to say "I don't think I want to do this anymore, it's too hard"?

JK: No. I looked forward to her coming every week, and actually, I looked forward to her coming so much that even after I finished the program I started taking the classes at the school on my own.

MC: At your children's school? What kind of classes did they provide?

JK: Through Family Services, and I just kept going. Yes, ma'am, I know that I had already finished the program but I thought maybe with another teacher too there's something else that I can pick up that I didn't pick up before.

MC: And was there something else that you learned?

JK: I'm still learning! I'm still learning.

MC: What is the one thing that you learned that you say really helped you? Something that they taught you that made you feel so good about it that it makes you so much more comfortable and a better parent?

JK: I think the fact that they made me want to be a better parent makes me proud. When I walk into my classes every week I feel proud because I don't have to be there—I choose to be there. Some people have to be there. . . . I want to be there because I want to do better and it's gotten me to be more involved at my kids' school . . . I went to represent my son's school in the 2014 parent summit for SAISD (San Antonio Independent School District) and I'm going to all the parent meetings and I'm involved in the parent room now. It helped me a lot.

MC: That's wonderful. So how do your children see you? If they see you at school, how do they feel?

JK: I think they like to see me there. 'Cause every time I'm at the school their friends go "Hi Ms. Kerr, hi Ms. Kerr! Hi Jackelyn's mom! It makes me feel good, you know, because they like me. I go to eat lunch with my boy too at school, and as soon as I sit down the whole class comes around and we sit there talking. You know, I like to be there, I like to be around kids.

MC: If you had to recommend this program to a parent, what would you tell them?

JK: I would tell them don't put your guards up, lower your guards, don't look at it like they're trying to hurt you. Look at it like they're trying to help you, 'cause I was one of those people . . . before I was like [if there was] somebody trying to tell me [I'm] not a good mom I got defensive. I am a good mom even though I wasn't the best that I could be. I would be defensive and I just closed off, you know what I mean? What I would say is, keep an open mind, like don't be defensive. I think they're here to help.

MC: And so what are your plans now, what are your future plans? You've taken two classes?

JK: Yes, I go every Wednesday and my plan is just keep getting involved in the school I want to get a job in the school now, and I want to be part of the parent room. I want to be one of the parents that run the parent room who helps the other parents.

MC: And how would you do that? By going through Family Services or the school district?

JK: I think both because the Family Services, they are there in our parent room. It's like a big coordinated effort. It's just a bunch of different people from different agencies and so I think it's probably both.

MC: Where would you go and say I want to work here?

JK: I would go straight to the principal. Yes ma'am, I'm pretty good with all the staff at the school. They know me. I'd go to the principal.

MC: Is there something else that you would like to say? What would you recommend for a home-based program?

JK: I think that the parent is the main thing and when you work with the parents it trickles down to the kids because a happy parent makes happy kids. It's hard to make your kids happy when you are just miserable and that's how I was for a long time. I was miserable and now I'm not. I feel so much better. I haven't felt this good in 15 years. It's the best I ever felt for a long time, and also you know, I've even learned things in this program that helped me aside from my kids, because I did grow up with bipolar. I was in and out of hospitals my whole life, counselors, and I never knew how to deal with some of the issues that I had, like with the anger. They would just put me on medication, and that's not what I needed. I didn't need medication. I needed someone to talk to me and say this is how you deal with it, not just cover it with the medication. So it's helped me more than just with my kids.

MC: So for you, are you able to handle your relationships a little bit differently?

JK: I haven't had too many relationships [laughs]. I think the fact that I'm taking my time and making sure not to get involved with people who are not good for me, that's something new, so that's a positive for me . . . I don't want to bring anybody around me or [the] kids who's going to bring trouble or drama or bring me down back to where I was before. I want positive people around me.

In "Jeremiah's" and "Jennifer's" experiences, the Family Services Association home-based program turned a negative situation into a positive situation, where the parents not only learned to interact with their children in different situations but also gave the parents an opportunity to better themselves as individuals. These two cases show the importance of different systems working together to help families achieve a better quality of life. These are great examples of how the Ecological Systems Theory works to assist children's development. The cases also show the importance of home-school collaborations through strong partnerships.

Components of Home Activities for Home-Visiting Programs

The development of home activities depends on the objectives and philosophy of the program. Materials and experiences are based on the home environment, the children's interests, and the parents' enthusiasm. This provides an excellent opportunity to involve parents in creating learning activities for their children. It can also enable the parents to change their approach to childrearing through encouragement and acceptance of their contributions. Figure 9.5 is an example of an activity that was done with parents regarding home remedies. It is an easy activity to do in the home, thus making it culturally responsive (Huerta & Riojas-Cortez, 2011).

Throughout the year, home visitors involve parents in teaching their children at home. As the home visitor suggests activities for the child, additional ideas might occur to both the visitor and the parent. In addition, children themselves can elaborate on old ideas or create new activities. The home visitor should bring these ideas back to the office, where they can be classified and cataloged. Parents receive a boost if home visitors recognize their contributions. They will also continue to develop activities for children if they are reinforced. Write down their suggestions and file them for future use or include them in the program for the coming week.

Parent Engagement during Home Visits

Children learn best when they are actively engaged particularly from their parents. Piaget (1976) asserts that learning stems from the active involvement of the person doing the inventing; once invented, the theory or steps are not forgotten. Piaget recommends "the use of active methods which give broad scope to the spontaneous research of the child or adolescent and require that every new truth to be learned be rediscovered or at least reconstructed by the student and not simply imparted to him" (pp. 15–16). Kamii (1985a, 1985b) recommends a Piagetian approach in constructivism, meaning the belief that children construct their own knowledge if given the opportunity.

Experiential activities that afford children an opportunity to learn by discovery are facilitated best in a relaxed, natural, and rich learning environment. The setting can be either in the home or in the community. It is important to guide and support parents so they can fulfill their role as their child's first teacher—and constant support system—to ensure that children are able to reach their full potential. The steps to developing a home-learning activity, as suggested by Gordon's program in Florida (Gordon & Breivogel, 1976), reflect the use of the natural environment. Most important is the attitude that learning is possible everywhere for the child.

The home is a learning center. Children learn to talk without formal instruction. They learn as they interact with others and participate in interesting events. Through play at home, children become active learners (Parlakian & Lerner, 2010). Learning tasks at home can and should be intriguing rather than simply difficult. A parent who reads stories to children is actually teaching reading—the development of an interest in and love of reading is the first step toward acquisition of proficient reading skills.

Activities and Resources at Home

Brainstorm for a moment about all the learning opportunities in the home. Record the ideas that can be used during home visits or to share with parents. The following ideas can lead to many more:

Figure 9.5 Family Lesson Plan

Sample lesson from a culturally relevant family literacy program. Translation for the title of the lesson is provided to show how this lesson can be done in two languages.

Example of a Family Lesson that can be used by the Home Visitor
Family Institute for Early Literacy Development (FIELD)—
Science with a Home Flavor/*Las Ciencias con Sabor Casero*

Home Remedies/Los Remedios Caseros

Objectives:
Children will be able to:
1. Develop and use vocabulary
2. Compare language and oral traditions such as family stories that reflect customs, regions, and culture by discussing ideas with their parent
3. Respond to a narrative by writing and illustrating their own personal story of home remedies

Materials
Plants and herb samples
Markers
Paper to create books

Children's Books
(Use books that are appropriate for family's culture and language)
Prietita and the Ghost Woman/Prietita y la Llorona
Family Pictures/Cuadros de Familia

Activity for Families
(Home visitor will guide discussion)
1. Interactive discussion to activate prior knowledge regarding home remedies: what do families remember about home remedies?
2. Ask to make a list of home remedies used in the past and present.
3. Families compare and contrast plants and herbs that can be used for medicinal purposes.
4. Home visitor asks family to create a book about their home remedies (parents and children working together to write and illustrate using materials provided).

- *Art and crafts.* Have tempera paint, watercolors, crayons, chalk, white paper, colored paper, scissors, glue or paste, Play-Doh, and modeling clay available for spontaneous art projects. Draw, paint, or make rubbings and collages. Try painting outdoors with water.

- *Read together.* Children begin learning to read at home. To help children with language and reading development, parents need to talk with and read to their infants. Include a range of literature from nursery rhymes and poems to stories that adults enjoy in their native language. Infants hear the voice, develop sensitivity to the sounds, and set out on their way to literacy. The proximity to the reader helps develop trust and attachment. Read aloud with preschoolers and school-age children. Discover and emphasize the many situations in which children can be engaged in reading and writing.

- *Publishing.* Make a publishing center and include paper, pencils, pens, or a computer, and cardboard for the covers of books.

For very young children, transcribe their stories for them and let them illustrate the story or book. If children are older, help them brainstorm ideas for a book or make a history book of their family. Let them write in journals or diaries. Encourage them to write to a relative, pen pal, or friend. Create poetry, cinquains, haiku, free verse, rhymes, and limericks. Help them edit their work in a cooperative spirit.

Write a cooperative newsletter for the neighborhood or relatives. Make a form with areas for writing by each person or descriptions of each project. Let someone, like a family member or friend fill in the information.

- *Games.* Take time to play games. The list is long: Concentration, hopscotch, jacks, jump rope, basketball, table tennis, toss a ball, lotto, Monopoly, word or letter bingo, anagrams, and matching. Games that are culturally appropriate are also recommended, such as Lotería for Latino children. Some games are still popular; other games parents might need to introduce children to, such as jacks, which helps with visual perception.

- *Backyard science.* Examine the ground for insects and vegetation. Examine bugs with a microscope. Classify leaves by shape, size, and color. Categorize plants or animals.

- *Front yard business.* Have a garage sale and let your child be the cashier.

- *Listening center.* Collect read-along books so the child can listen to the books and read along using e-books in e-readers like Nook, Kindle, Kobo, and others.

- *Music center.* Using iTunes, download music to computers, phones, and other digital devices so the child can listen to various types of music. Use the center for singing, moving, and dancing. If you have songs with written words, the activity can also be a reading experience.

- *Communicate.* Talk with each other. Let children describe all the things that are happening. Help them predict and observe by showing interest in their predictions. Make the home a safe place to express feelings.

- *Homemaking activities.* Chores are not chores if you have fun doing them. Cooking is fun and can be used as an intellectual endeavor as well as a functional activity. Practice mathematics by dividing a recipe in half. Research where and how the ingredients were grown using different websites on the Internet.

Activities Away from Home

Trips around and away from home can also be adventures.

- *Take a walk.* Collect water from a stream or puddle. Examine the water through a microscope when you return home. Describe or draw the creatures found in a drop of water.

- *Visit the library.* Go to the library. Help children get library cards if they don't have them. Choose and check out books. If the library has a storytime or program for older children, attending can make the library a wonderful place to visit.

- *Visit a store.* It can be the grocery store, post office, department store, or hardware store. Before going, make a shopping list together. Keep it simple. Let the child help with the selection and cost of the products.

- *Explore museums.* Art, natural history, historical, or other specialty museums might have pictures or artifacts that lend themselves to artwork at home. To increase observational powers, let the child look for something specific, such as a color or materials. Talk about how the art materials were used or which shapes were selected.

- *Visit historical buildings.* Take along paper, pen, and crayons. Draw the shape of the building. Make a crayon rubbing of the placard that tells about the building's dedication.

- *Visit the airport and bus station.* Watch the people. Imagine where they are going. Count the people who walk by. Find out how the station or airport is managed. Note how many buses, trains,

Funds of knowledge include learning opportunities in the home.

Chad Baker/Jason Reed/Ryan McVay/getty Image

Parents can devise a practical educational experience from everyday projects such as planting a garden.

or airplanes you can see. How are they different from each other? Compare the costs of the different methods of travel.

- *Go to a garage sale.* Determine how many articles you can buy for $5 or $10.
- *Visit a flea market.* Find out how many different items are sold that are from other countries and other cultures. How many toys can you purchase with $1 or $2?

Using intriguing and exciting activities benefits the family in two ways: learning takes place, and the parent–child relationship is enhanced. This will help parents understand the importance of a rich home environment, but they still need to be reinforced for their positive teaching behaviors. Although good times together can be reinforcement enough, schools can help support productive parent–child interaction by encouraging parents, offering workshops, and supplying home-learning activities.

Home-Learning Strategies for the Home Visitor

Each home-based program has developed its own approach to home-learning activities. The Portage Project developed a systematic program for its home visitors that can be used by others. HIPPY provides a specific curriculum design with storybooks and activity packets. The Nurse–Family Partnership Program includes a curriculum that emphasizes maternal health, mental health issues, and infant/toddler development. Other programs focus on giving the families support, building family self-sufficiency, and encouraging improved parenting skills.

As parents and home visitors work together to develop the children's curriculum, the following tips will help:

- Choose an emerging skill that the child has shown an interest in or one in which an interest can be developed.
- Choose some skills that the parent considers important.
- Choose a skill the child needs to learn.
- Choose a developmentally appropriate task that is easily accommodated at home (U.S. Department of Health and Human Services, Office of Human Development Services, 1985).

In the implementation of a home-based program, both home visitors and parents can develop activities related to individual families or they can be supported by learning activities developed by commercial companies and school districts. Appropriate learning activities can be purchased or found in the library.

Home visitors should remember that the relationship they establish with parents is the most critical means of helping parents support their children's development. They should acknowledge each parent's experience, be respectful at all times, and be a constant learner. While they might establish closer ties with some parents than others, objectivity and an awareness of professional boundaries are of equal importance for all families they serve (U.S. Department of Health and Human Services, Office of Human Development Services, 1987). It is also important to provide professional development for the home visitor in order to perform his or her job more effectively (Harden, Denmark, & Saul, 2010).

Establishing a Home-Based Program

Before a program is established, the reasons for and needs of such a program must be examined. The primary goals of home-based programs include the following:

- To enable parents to become more effective teachers of their children.
- To support the parents in the roles of caregivers and homemakers.
- To strengthen the parents' sense of autonomy and self-esteem.

- To reach the child and family early in the child's formative years.

- To respond to the family's needs and thus improve the home environment.

Educators expect home-based programs to increase a child's sense of well-being, improve educational success, and help the child realize optimum development. Individual goals for programs vary according to the needs of the area. For instance, an overriding concern in one area might be health; in another, language development; in still another, nutrition. Although all three are important in varying degrees in every home-based program, the intensity of involvement can vary.

The concern for serving families and children in their homes as an intervention strategy is ongoing. A series of reports and policy briefs titled "Building Community Systems for Young Children" included a policy brief, Home Visiting: A Service Strategy to Deliver First 5 Results (Thompson, Kropenske, Heinicke, Gomby, & Halfon, 2003). The policy brief discussed strategies to strengthen program quality. Three principles identified as essential were that (a) interventions should be grounded in research that identify adverse outcomes to be addressed and factors necessary to change the outcome, (b) interventions should be based on theories of behavior change, and (c) interventions should be viewed as relevant and needed by the community. In addition, the U.S. Advisory Board recommends as imperative that programs monitor the implementation of the program services by the staff and monitor the

impact of the interventions on holistic client outcomes. Program monitoring should be embedded in program implementation efforts in order to support continued funding and to determine what contributes to effective delivery of services to children and families. A recent study showed the effects of home-based programs were more effective for parents than for children, and their effects were sustained two years after the completion of the program (Chazan-Cohen, Raikes, & Vogel, 2013). Furthermore, home-based programs seem to be effective for improving a child's health and decreasing instances of maltreatment and abuse across ethnic groups (see Avellar & Supplee, 2013; Gresl, Fox, & Fleischmann, 2014).

Determining the Need for a Program

Community groups, schools, and centers should consider the needs of children and their families and the availability of community resources as they determine the need for a home-based program. They should also examine the variety of programs available before embarking on a home-based program. The following questions can be used as guidelines for choosing a program:

1. Are there children and families who could be helped by early intervention in the home?

2. What can the community agency or school do in a home-visitation program that cannot be accomplished through other programs?

3. Could early intervention help children go to school?

4. Are there children with disabilities who could be diagnosed and given service before they enter school?

5. Will the preventive program help eliminate later educational problems, offsetting the cost to the public?

6. Will the prevention of later educational problems reduce emotional problems, also offsetting the cost to the public?

7. Are there parents who could be helped by an adult-literacy program?

8. Do parents need support to develop self-sufficiency so they can provide for their children's long-term needs?

Robin Sachs/Photo Edit

Home-based programs focus on the socioemotional and academic well-being of children.

9. Are immigrant families in need of resources that will help them improve their quality of life, such as ELL programs for adults or medical services and education for young children?

If "yes" is the answer to most of these questions, the next step is to consider the feasibility of a home-based program. The following questions must be addressed:

1. Has there been a thorough assessment of needs to establish community interest in home-based services?

2. Are there enough families in the community who are definitely interested and eligible to participate in a program that emphasizes home visits and the role of the parents?

3. Do staff members already have the skills and interests needed to work effectively with parents in their own homes? If not, does the program have, or can it obtain, the considerable training necessary to prepare staff members for their new roles? Is the staff willing to receive such training? Is the staff culturally and linguistically compatible with families to be served?

4. Can transportation needs be met? Public transportation is often an inefficient mode of travel and is not available in many areas. Home visitors need a car to get around quickly, transport materials, and take parents and children for special services needed from local resource agencies.

5. Will the program include family members who are away from home during the day? The answer to this usually involves meetings and home visits in the evenings and on weekends. In some ways, home-based programs require a staff selflessness and dedication that goes beyond the demands of the workload and schedules of center-based services (U.S. Department of Health and Human Services, 1985).

Before a questionnaire or needs assessment is devised, data should be gathered from school files, social-service agencies, city surveys, or census reports. Social services will be particularly helpful in determining services and the number of children in families. School figures, questionnaires, and surveys will supplement those data so that services can be offered to all those who want or need them. Make every effort to establish a good working relationship with the various agencies. You will need to coordinate your efforts later, and initial communication and rapport are essential to subsequent implementation of the program.

Involving Others in the Program

The four components of an effective home-based program are: (a) education, (b) social services, (c) health services (physical and mental health, dental care, nutrition, and safety), and (d) parent involvement. It is only through comprehensive services to children and their families that pervasive family-based problems can be solved. Although the project will be fully responsible for education and parent involvement, social and health services will need the support of other agencies.

The Recruitment of Families

Many families can be identified through cooperative agreements with existing programs, such as Head Start, schools, and social-service agencies. Churches can also help identify families who are in need. Articles in newspapers about the new home-based program will alert other parents, and flyers can be delivered by students. The most effective method, however, is a door-to-door canvass. Home visitors can go from house to house to chat with parents and explain the program and its benefits. This personal approach seems to encourage parents to participate when a notice through the mail might not. Families new to the area or unknown to social agencies probably will be reached only by a door-to-door campaign.

Published articles can increase parents' interest. Curriculum and child development can be communicated through newsletters as well as personal visits. It is also a good idea to combine the two and give the parent a handout at the end of a home visit.

Parents to be served in a home-based program should be actively involved in the initial planning. Many schools and preschool programs have parent advisory councils or citizen advisory councils that can give input on the needs of the community and suggest relevant questions. If a council is not functioning in your area, it might be worth it to start one. You can work through the existing PTO or PTA, or you can establish an entirely new council with the parents you will serve.

The formation or election of the board should be advertised. Parents then have an opportunity to nominate themselves or others, and an election is scheduled to determine who will represent the community on the council. You could advertise the formation of an advisory council by sending notes home with children; explaining the council at meetings of Boy Scouts, Camp Fire Girls, PTA, YMCA, and YWCA; and distributing flyers throughout the community. All nominations should be accepted. Using a democratic process will ensure that everyone has an opportunity to participate in the selection process.

Distinct advantages to using a democratic selection process rather than appointment to an advisory council include: (a) interest in the program is generated and maintained, (b) the parents feel a sense of self-determination and autonomy, (c) the council becomes a source of relevant information and feedback from those affected, and (d) cooperation between schools and parents increases.

The Selection of Home Visitors

Before selecting home visitors, the choice must be made whether to use professionals, professional parent teachers, paraprofessionals, or volunteers. Although the director, coordinator, and special services specialists will probably be professionals, such as therapists for children with special needs, many programs use paraprofessionals or volunteers as the home-visit specialists. The home visitor is crucial as she or he helps develop a strong partnership with parents to empower them in their relationship with their children (Butcher & Gersch, 2014). The home visitor should ideally be someone who cares, respects, values, and is willing to empower families. Criteria for selection will be determined by the needs of your program.

Five criteria often considered are as follows:

1. Experience, age, and maturity—good judgment and flexibility
2. Race, ethnicity, culture, and language—a key consideration should be to the home visitor who has respect for the values and beliefs of other cultures
3. Professional education
4. Gender
5. Helping skills (Wasik, 1993)

COMMUNICATION SKILLS. The skills needed for an effective home-visitor program (Figure 9.6) also include collaboration and effective communication in which the home visitor is able to do the following:

1. Listen empathetically.
2. Affirm the family.
3. Recognize and affirm the family's funds of knowledge.
4. Maintain appropriate boundaries.
5. Individualize for each family's needs.
6. Demonstrate and model effective parenting skills.
7. Interpret the purpose of activities and child–parent interactions.
8. Problem solve with the parents. (Klass, Pettinelli, & Wilson, 1993)

RECRUITING.   When recruiting paraprofessional home visitors, the positions should be advertised throughout the community. Announcements must be clear and include the following:

1. An explanation of the program. Explain what your home-based program entails, indicating its goals and objectives.
2. The job description of the position. List the duties and responsibilities, workday schedule, salary range, and benefits.
3. The qualifications required. Indicate whether a high school diploma, college degree, or specific competencies is required. Also include reliable transportation.
4. An equal opportunity employment announcement. Make a statement of nondiscrimination.
5. Instructions for applying. Give instructions on how to apply, whom to contact, and the deadline for application.
6. Bilingual ability. Include a statement in which the qualifications include being bilingual depending on the language spoken in the community (i.e., Spanish/English, Vietnamese/English). This can also include the ability to use sign language.

The announcement should be posted in public places, such as libraries, schools, stores, and social agencies like Head Start, as well as other Internet websites including but not limited to monster.com or Craig's list. Wide dissemination of information about available positions encourages individuals in the community to become involved and alerts others to the upcoming home-based program.

Figure 9.6 A Self-Evaluation Form for Home Visitors

Are YOUR Home Visits Parent-Focused?		
• Do you involve the parents in the assessment of the child?	Yes	No
• Do you provide the parent with a copy of the checklist for their own use?	Yes	No
• When you arrive for the weekly home visit, do you direct your attention and greeting toward the parent?	Yes	No
• Do you discuss the previous week's visit and follow up on the weekly activities with the parent?	Yes	No
• Does the parent co-plan the activities for the home visit?	Yes	No
• Do you make sure that the child is sitting beside the parent?	Yes	No
• Does the parent demonstrate EACH new activity?	Yes	No
• Do you review each activity with the parent before presenting it?	Yes	No
• Do you hand all materials to the parent?	Yes	No
• Do you identify and reinforce the parent's teaching strengths?	Yes	No
• When the parent has difficulty, do you intervene with the parent rather than the child?	Yes	No
• Do you let the parent be the primary reinforcing agent?	Yes	No
• Do you help the parent problem solve when problems do arise instead of jumping to the rescue?	Yes	No
• Do you work on activities the parent feels are important?	Yes	No
• Do you ask the parent to provide as many materials as possible?	Yes	No
• Do you give the parent the lead, when appropriate?	Yes	No
• Do you incorporate the parent's ideas into each activity?	Yes	No
• Do you let the parent present new and exciting experiences?	Yes	No
• Do you individualize parent education activities for each parent?	Yes	No
• Do you accept the parent's values?	Yes	No
• Do you involve the parent in evaluation of the home visit?	Yes	No

Source: From *The Head Start Home Visitor Handbook*, by U.S. Department of Health and Human Services, Office of Human Development Services, Administration for Children, Youth, and Families, Head Start Bureau, 1987, Washington, D.C.: U.S. Government Printing Office.

In-Service Training After the Program Has Started

Learning by both the family and the home visitor comes to fruition during the development of the program. During this period, the home visitor responds to the needs, desires, and styles of the parents and children. Close contact with the program's coordinator or trainers supports the home visitor and allows administrators to keep track of what is happening in the field. Reports on each visit, with copies for the home visitor and for the program's administrators or trainers, will enable people from both levels of the program to keep in touch with developments and needs. In doing so, in-service training can be directed to enrich weak areas and clarify procedures. At the end of each visit, home visitors can reflect on the questions presented in Figure 9.6. A home visitor's answers to these questions can also provide the basis for in-service training.

SMALL GROUPS. Throughout the year, questions and needs for training will arise. Training sessions are more effective when small groups of home visitors—rather than all members of the program—meet together as needs emerge. The individualized meeting is beneficial because the session has been set up especially for the participants, and small numbers allow for a more personalized response by the trainer or coordinator.

George Dodson/Pearson Education

Professionals must maintain open communication with parents.

COMMUNITY RESOURCES. Although lists of community resources are given to home visitors early in the program, more definite descriptions and procedures are useful when specific problems arise. During the year, specialists from a variety of community agencies can be invited to share their experiences and knowledge of procedures with the staff. Have them come to training meetings, meet the staff, and answer questions concerning use of their programs.

Program Evaluation

Ongoing evaluations of contacts, visits, and services rendered are essential. Home-visit reports give data that can be used to measure progress. If the home visitor systematically completes each report, the administrator will be able to evaluate progress throughout the training period.

PARENT QUESTIONNAIRES. Statements by parents and responses to questionnaires concerning the effect of the program on the child and family are valuable in analyzing the effects of the program. Collect these throughout the program as well as at the completion of the year.

Evaluation is a tool to be used during the development of the program, as well as a means to assess accomplishments. Include a variety of evaluations to improve the program and demonstrate its effectiveness.

Screening for Better Understanding

As home visitors and parents work with children, they informally assess the child's characteristics and skills.

Informal assessments with checklists can be used while the child is playing. It is always best to view the child in a natural setting unrestricted by contrived tasks. A portfolio containing collections of art activities and projects, teacher comments, and the child's comments can aid in assessing the child's development. These kinds of assessment are essential—they provide the parent and teacher with guidelines for developmentally appropriate activities for each child.

Parent educators also need to be able to recognize if families under their guidance need special help. Screening for potential problems in both the developmental status of children and the children's environment—especially if they are growing up in a low socioeconomic area—will help the parent educator identify problems early and thus more effectively serve children and their families (Fandal, 1986).

Several instruments are available to screen the developmental progress of children. Two of the most widely used are the Denver Prescreening Developmental Questionnaire and the Denver Developmental Screening Test. There are also standardized methods of assessing the home environment of children, such as the Home Screening Questionnaire and the Home Observation for Measurement of the Environment.

Home Observation for Measurement of the Environment

The Home Observation for Measurement of the Environment (HOME) Inventory is used by schools, child-care centers, and other social-service agencies to help them determine the quality of the home environment as it relates to the child's development. Current studies using the HOME Inventory show the association between maternal education and reading and math achievement (Zadeh, Farnia, & Ungerleider, 2010). Home visitors can use the HOME Inventory to analyze the family's home environment.

The HOME Inventory was developed "to get a picture of what the child's world is like from his or her perspective—from where he or she lies or sits or stands or moves about and sees, hears, smells, feels, and tastes that world" (Caldwell & Bradley, 1984, p. 8). In addition to the standardized HOME Inventories for birth to 3-year-olds and 3- to 6-year-olds, an inventory for elementary school children also is available.

When using the program, the interviewer should:

- Know the HOME Inventory well before using it.
- Contact the parents and arrange a visit.
- Visit when the child is awake and available.
- Start the interview with friendly, relaxed interaction.

A suggested technique for starting the interview is described by the following statement:

> You will remember that we are interested in knowing the kinds of things your baby (child) does when he is at home. A good way to get a picture of what his days are like is to have you think of one particular day— like yesterday—and tell me everything that happened to him as well as you can remember it. Start with the things that happened when he first woke up. It is usually easy to remember the main events once you get started. (Caldwell & Bradley, 1984, p. 3)

The administration and scoring of each item in the inventory are clearly described in the Administration Manuals, so the interviewer can make correct judgments on the scoring of HOME.

Home Screening Questionnaire (HSQ)

Coons, Gay, Fandal, Ker, and Frankenburg (1981) and Frankenburg and Coons (1986) recognized the value of an earlier version of the HOME Inventory but were concerned about the length of time needed for a skilled interviewer to make a home visit. Coons et al. developed the Home Screening Questionnaire (HSQ), which could be answered by parents. With the cooperation of the authors of the HOME Inventory, items were selected and turned into two questionnaires that correspond to the two HOME scales (for children from birth to 3 years and those from 3 to 6 years of age). Each takes about 15 minutes for a parent to complete. The questionnaires have been validated as effective screening tools to identify environments that would benefit from a more intensive assessment.

Homeschooling

Homeschooling is defined as "a form of private education that is parent-led and home-based (Ray, 2013). Homeschooling is not new. Many of our nation's early

leaders were taught at home. The common school movement began about 1830 and 1840, but it was usual for children to attend for only 3 months out of the year for 3 or 4 years.

The last half of the 19th century saw a greater transformation of schooling. Eighty-six percent of children ages 5 to 14 were attending public schools by 1890 (Carper, 1992). During the 20th century, parents sent their children to public and private schools, and schools became more and more centrally administered. It was not until the 1980s that the increase in homeschooling began to be noticed.

Estimates of the number of children who were being schooled at home in the 1970s ranged from 1,000 to 15,000; in 1983, estimates ranged from 60,000 to 125,000; by 1988, the homeschool "student body" was thought to be 150,000 to 300,000 (Lines, 1991). The number increased rapidly in the 1990s—estimates of homeschooled children ranged up to 2 million. But in 1999, the 95% confidence interval for the number of homeschoolers was 709,000 to 992,000. Subsequent data gathered have determined that homeschoolers account for 1.7 percent of the students in the United States (Kaplan-Leiserson, 2002; National Center for Education Statistics, 2001). It is projected that the number of children homeschooled will increase by 15% each year (Kaplan-Leiserson, 2002). A report from The National Home Education Research Institute (Ray, 2011) indicates that 2.04 million students were homeschooled in 2010. According to the National Center for Education Statistics (2014), in 2010–2011 approximately 3% of the school-age population were home-schooled (Table 9.2 shows the number and percentage of children homeschooled from 2011–2012).

Characteristics of Homeschooling and Homeschooled Children

The U.S. Department of Education indicates that home-schooled children are between the ages of 5 and 17 in grades ranging from those similar to kindergarten but not higher than 12th grade (*Fast Facts*, National Center for Statistics, 2014). The majority of the students who are homeschooled are White. Parents make decisions to homeschool based on the quality of local schools, the constraints of income, and available leisure time, as well as religious preferences (Isenberg, 2007; Lubienski, Puckett, & Brewer, 2013). In most cases of homeschooling, the mother is the teacher, and she usually teaches

Table 9.2 Number and Percentage Distribution of All Children Ages 5–17 Who Were Homeschooled and Homeschooling Rate, by Selected Characteristics: 2011–2012

Characteristic	Number (thousands)	Percentage distribution	Homeschooling rate[1]
Total Locale of student's household[2]	1,770	†	3.4
City	489	28	3.2
Suburban	601	34	3.1
Town	132	7	2.7
Rural	548	31	4.5
Student's sex			
Male	876	49	3.3
Female	895	51	3.6
Student's race/ethnicity			
White, non-Hispanic	1,201	68	4.5
Black, non-Hispanic	139	8	1.9
Hispanic	267	15	2.3
Asian or Pacific Islander, non-Hispanic	73	4	2.6
Other, non-Hispanic[3]	90	5	3.2
Student's grade equivalent			
Kindergarten–2nd grade	415	23	3.1
3rd–5th grade	416	23	3.4
6th–8th grade	425	24	3.5
9th–12th grade	514	29	3.7
Parents' highest education level			
Less than high school	203	11	3.4
High school graduate or equivalent	355	20	3.4
Vocational/technical or some college	525	30	3.4
Bachelor's degree	436	25	3.7
Graduate or professional school	252	14	3.3
Poverty status[4]			
Poor	348	20	3.5
Nonpoor	1,422	80	3.4

†Not applicable.

[1]The homeschooling rate is the percentage of the total subgroup that is homeschooled. For example, in 2012, some 3% of all school-age males were homeschooled.

[2]Locale of student's household classifies the residential ZIP code into a set of four major locale categories: city, suburban, town, rural.

[3]"Other, non-Hispanic" includes children who were multiracial and not of Hispanic ethnicity, or who were American Indian or Alaska Native, or who were not Hispanic, White, Black, Asian, or Pacific Islander. The different groups mentioned here are not shown separately because the sample sizes do not support stable estimates. Those reported as Asian and Pacific Islander who are not Hispanic are included in the "Asian or Pacific Islander, non-Hispanic" group.

[4]Students are considered poor if living in households with incomes below the poverty threshold, which is a dollar amount determined by the federal government to meet the household's needs, given its size and composition. Income is collected in categories in the survey, rather than as an exact amount, and therefore the poverty measures used in this report are approximations of poverty. Detailed information on the poverty status calculation used in this report is available in Appendix B.

Note: Detail may not sum to totals because of rounding. Homeschooled students are school-age children (ages 5–17) in a grade equivalent to at least kindergarten and not higher than 12th grade who receive instruction at home instead of at a public or private school either all or most of the time. This excludes students who were enrolled in public or private school more than 25 hours per week and students who were homeschooled only because of temporary illness.

Source: U.S. Department of Education, National Center for Education Statistics, Parent and Family Involvement in Education Survey of the National Household Education Surveys Program (NHES), 2012.

her own children, spending 20 to 30 hours each week in school activities. Homeschool teachers are reported to have a more controlling style of teaching than other teachers. They have fewer years of formal education and are more conservative in their political views (Cai, Reeve, & Robinson, 2002). There is no one curriculum that parents use, although they can buy curriculum programs from a variety of organizations.

Testing for academic achievement and effective development has indicated that most homeschooled children do well in academics. Homeschoolers score higher on state-mandated tests, indicating that although some score below average, "a large number test above that mark" (Lines, 1996). Some studies show that home-schooled students have higher SAT and ACT scores, and higher grade point averages (Cogan, 2010). In 2002, the average SAT score for public school children was 1020, but was 1092 for homeschooled children. In 2004, the average ACT score for public school children was 20.9, but was 22.6 for homeschooled children (Beato, 2005). There also seems to be little risk to their social-ization, psychological development, and self-esteem (Lines, 1996; Ray & Wartes, 1991; Ray, 2013).

In the past decade, proponents have been successful in advocating for homeschool, and state legislatures have been responding to parental demands. When there have been court cases, the proponents of homeschooling are able to rely on court decisions and the Bill of Rights (Guterson, 1992). All states allow homeschooling. Typically, a state's statutes—through a court ruling, an attorney general's opinion, or a regulation that interprets a school attendance law to include homeschooling—consider homeschooling a legitimate option for meeting compulsory education requirements. Because each state regulates homeschooling differently, parents should examine local laws and consult other homeschoolers before proceeding. In every state, parents must, at a minimum, notify a state or local education agency of their intent to educate their children at home and identify the children involved (Lines, 1996). Current research indicates that there are more positive learner outcomes from homeschooling than negative outcomes (Ray, 2013).

Reasons for Homeschooling

The National Center for Education Statistics (2007) indicates that the largest single reason for homeschooling is parents' concern about the environment of the school their child would attend (85%). Religious reasons follow (72%), with dissatisfaction with the academic instruction being offered making up the third-highest reason for selecting homeschooling (68%). Parents might homeschool because they believe they can do a better job in teaching their children; they may have the need to instill stronger family values that children may not get in school; some might want to avoid what they believe may be negative influences and teachings; and others might not like the idea of public schools (Lubien-ski, Puckett, & Brewer, 2013). Table 9.3 indicates some of the reasons for home schooling according to the National Center for Statistics. Parents who homeschool do not appear to use packaged curricula, as the major-ity are not certified teachers (Ray, 2013), but many use the Internet as a source for information.

School–Parent Cooperation

The Cupertino Union School District in California has given parents options for collaboration between public schools and homeschoolers for over 25 years. Parents enroll their child in the district school system, but they educate the child at home. The school receives the rev-enue from the state, and parents are given curricula, services, materials, software, and money for books. Each family has a resource teacher who holds a confer-ence with them monthly, or more often if desired. They also have access to a library of materials and books for homeschooling. They can use the school's supplies and equipment, and children can be enrolled in extended day classes (Berger, 1997; Lamson, 1992).

Another example is the San Diego City School Dis-trict, which offers support to homeschooled children. The school offers a structured curriculum for families to use. Educators are assigned as homeschool teachers, who meet with the families on a trimester basis. Families can con-tact the teacher assigned to them as often as they desire. Parents can take advantage of services, field trips, special education, and counseling, educating their own children with the support of the school district (Dalaimo, 1996).

In collaboration, schools can furnish resources and services for homeschool families. These can include offering the use of resource centers; enrollment in spe-cial classes such as music, art, and science; participation of homeschooled parents in school district programs; advisory and facilitating services; in-service work-shops; and participation of homeschooled students in extracurricular activities, summer programs, and large-group or team activities (Knowles, 1989).

Table 9.3 Number and Percentage of School-Age Children Who Were Homeschooled, by Reasons Parents Gave as Important and Most Important for Homeschooling: 2011–2012

Reason	Important[1]		Most important	
	Number	Percent	Number	Percent
A desire to provide religious instruction	692,299	64	76,338	16
A desire to provide moral instruction	831,842	77	51,210	5
A concern about environment of other schools[2]	986,643	91	268,628	25
A dissatisfaction with academic instruction at other schools	799,336	74	204,312	19
A desire to provide a nontraditional approach to child's education	474,545	44	56,045	5 !
Child has other special needs	186,157	17	18,107	‡
Child has a physical or mental health problem	166,878	15	50,652	5
Other reasons[3]	404,313	37	226,423	21

‡Reporting standards not met.

!Interpret data with caution; coefficient of variation is 30 percent or more.

[1]Respondents could choose more than one reason.

[2]Based on the response to the question, "You are concerned about the school environment, such as safety, drugs, or negative peer pressure?"

[3]Parents homeschool their children for many reasons that are often unique to their family situation. "Other reasons" parents gave for homeschooling include family time, finances, travel, and distance.

Note: Homeschooled students are school-age children (ages 5–17) in a grade equivalent to at least kindergarten and not higher than grade 12. Excludes students who were enrolled in public or private school more than 25 hours per week and students who were homeschooled only because of temporary illness.

Source: U.S. Department of Education, National Center for Education Statistics, Parent and Family Involvement in Education Survey of the National Household Education Surveys Program (NHES), 2012.

By allowing the student to be schooled at home, but providing support and an opportunity to participate with other children in activities, the school helps parents achieve their goals of educating their children themselves while giving children opportunities to interact socially with other students.

A newer choice of home schooling for the 21st century is virtual schooling. Parents now have the option of children being homeschooled through virtual academies. Some choices are faith-based, while others are secular, but most charge a fee or tuition. A Google search will give you a variety of choices. Most virtual schools hire certified teachers that work individually with children at their own pace. The curriculum and materials are included in the tuition fee and families choose when children "attend school."

Supporting Children's Homework

The need for homework for children in the early grades has been questioned by parents, educators, and children. The Child Study Movement of 1890 and the early 1900s believed that children should be children and not start school until they were 7. In the mid-1920s to 1940s, homework was limited or abolished in New York City, Chicago, and San Diego. The reform of homework, rather than its elimination, was the call after World War II. When the Soviet Union launched Sputnik in 1957, the educational system felt challenged and set out to educate the young so that the nation could compete. The result was increased homework nationwide (Winerip, 1999). In 1986, the report "What Works," stated that homework "worked." Since then, homework has been seen as necessary and beneficial: "Assignments become common as early as first grade, and some schools require it every day. Parents' grumbling is heard across the land" (Winerip, 1999, p. 32). In today's society, the argument of whether homework is needed or not has turned into an argument for the quality of homework given by teachers and the impact in children's learning. School policies that promote high homework expectations because of homework's impact on learning seem to be more important than whether teachers should give homework or not (Watkins & Stevens, 2013).

Studies show that although all parents are interested in the well-being of their children, parents of diverse backgrounds support children with their homework in different ways (Thelamour & Jacobs, 2014). For example, in a study conducted by Joshi (2005, p. 30), it was found that "At first and second grade, the Chinese-American families averaged 31 minutes in homework versus 11 minutes for Euro-Americans." Another example includes the emotional support and encouragement that Latino parents give their children during homework, which seems to help students in their motivation to finish (Martinez, 2011). Another study found that Indian parents supported their children in their homework depending on their educational, cultural, and socioeconomic background, and this varied from intense to complex (Vidya, 2014).

Assisting children with homework is one way to build a bridge between home and school. Homework varies according to the age of the child. For young children, the home environment, the interaction, and intense work with toys make up the child's learning experience—the home is the child's school and what the child does is homework. As children get older and the location of school goes outside the home, suddenly what they do at home is not considered school unless they bring home an assignment. But the home is still part of the child's learning experiences, and parents can support children by learning about the child's school experience and what he or she is learning to do. Real-life experiences, including funds of knowledge, serve as a purposeful context where family literacy and numeracy can take place (Kennedy, 2010).

An alternative to homework has been the development of after-school programs in which children can do schoolwork under supervision and with the help that they might need. This is especially helpful for families in which both parents work. Many after-school programs, however, have been careful to avoid being seen as an extension of the school day. The recurrent concern is how best to support and extend children's learning opportunities.

Home–School Collaboration for Successful Homework

The satisfactory use of homework requires communication and planning on the part of the school and the parent. While homework has long been used as a tool by schools to reinforce classroom instruction, many teachers do not see the opportunity or responsibility to communicate with parents about homework. Much greater cooperation and collaboration will occur if a teacher communicates with parents about the importance of homework. Teachers must reach out to parents, as part of establishing a partnership with them, to find out how the parents respond to the opportunity to support their child's educational growth through homework. Teachers

must also determine if parents have the language and educational background to understand information that comes from schools. If necessary, written material sent to parents might need to be translated into the child's home language. If parents are not literate in their first language, school staff needs to attempt to make phone contact to speak with the parents in their first language. In many schools, this can present quite a challenge as many languages may be represented in any particular elementary school. In addition, parents might have disabilities that require alternative methods of communication. If the school has a stated policy about homework, the school staff needs to make this information available to parents in a manner that parents can understand. If the school leaves homework up to individual teachers, each teacher is responsible for communicating with parents, through translators if necessary, about specific requirements for homework in their classes.

Parents have a shared responsibility to communicate with their child's teacher. They need to ask questions: Will there be homework each night? How long should the average amount of homework take? Will the assignments be explained before the student is sent home with them? Will the student understand the assignment? What are the rules and regulations regarding homework? Can homework be made into "homefun," where both student and parent enjoy the challenge?

If parents resent homework or are not able to assist their children, it can become a negative experience. Instead of strengthening the family, it can become divisive and fail to strengthen the child's academic achievement. At a minimum, parents should be guided by the teacher to talk to their children, in their home language if appropriate, about their school day and what they are learning. This will convey a strong message to children that school is important and that their parents care about their experience.

Homework must be handled with care. The teacher should do the following:

- Send homework that reinforces or enriches what was learned in class. In either case, the assignment should be something the child is able to accomplish. Assignments that are short and frequent rather than long and infrequent appear to have a more significant effect on the child's learning (Cooper, 1999).

- Create meaningful assignments. Homework should not be haphazard busy work. It should instead be well planned and well designed. Clearly explain the homework assignment. If it is new or extension material, review several of the issues or problems so the student knows what is expected.

- Explain the rules and regulations of homework. Do you take off points for late homework? Is the homework grade figured into the grade for the grading period?

- Provide a homework form that the student fills out in class that states the assignment, pages, or worksheets that go along with the homework. This could include a signature line for the parent to sign so the teacher knows the parent knows about the assignment.

- Grade all homework personally. Display homework on the bulletin board to show the student it is recognized and that it is important. Only assign homework on which students will be given feedback.

- Communicate with parents to explain the process and respond to any difficulties that the family might be having with the homework.

- Teach study skills (Canter & Hausner, 1987; Cooke & Cooke, 1988; Hodapp & Hodapp, 1992; Paulu, 1995; Radencich & Schumm, 1996).

Homework can provide immediate retention of recent learning and can reinforce learning during leisure time. In addition, homework can support great self-direction, self-discipline, and time organization. Some children feel that homework should provide them with opportunities to practice areas of weakness and push them to practice what has not been learned (Cushman, 2010).

Homework can have negative outcomes also. It can promote satiation of interest in learning, encourage parental interference in learning, lead to cheating, and can increase the differences between low-income and more affluent students. Teachers and parents must work together to ensure that homework produces positive outcomes and avoids pitfalls.

How Can Parents Help?

Children of all ages can be helped with their homework. It is important that parents make sure they observe their children and try to determine if the homework is developmentally appropriate. A rule of thumb is that homework should take about 10 minutes per grade level (Cooper, 2001). The following tips can be provided to parents by their child's teacher. However, teachers should recognize that parents who live in crowded quarters might not be able to provide a positive environment for homestudy. A staffed study hall for after

school might be essential. For homework, parents can help by providing the following:

- Set up a specific place to study that is:
  - Well lighted.
  - Quiet, but not too isolated.
  - Comfortable, with an appropriate chair and table.
  - Equipped with materials—paper, pencils, pens, erasers, pencil sharpener, clock, and/or computer.

- Set aside a regular time for homework, or make a schedule for the week so parents or children can fill in activities, study periods, dinner time, recreation, and bedtime for each school day.

- Be supportive and give appropriate help. Parents should not do their children's homework, but parents can engage in problem solving with them, guide them, and help them over the rough spots.
  - Consider the child's learning style. Does the child learn best through seeing, hearing, or manipulating the material?
  - Talk about the assignments. Does the child understand the homework? What does the child need in order to complete the work?
  - Help the child structure the time and assignment, and help the child get started. Recognize that the responsibility for completing the homework belongs to the student.

- Show interest in and encourage the child's efforts.

- Be a parent who is both loving and firm.

- Refer the child to a homework hot line or website to get an explanation of the assignment if needed.

- Contact the teacher if further help is needed (Canter & Hausner, 1987; Cooke & Cooke, 1988; Hodapp & Hodapp, 1992; Paulu, 1995; Radencich & Schumm, 1996).

The setting for homework should be determined by the learner's preferences and the conditions under which the student learns best (Hong & Milgram, 2000). For example, some learners find background music helpful. Parents may adjust the study area to the child's preference of temperature, lighting, and sound, as "It has been clearly established that higher academic achievement and improved attitude result from tailoring the learning experiences to the cognitive and personal social characteristics of the learner" (Hong & Milgram, p. 17). Training parents how to work with their children on homework assignments seems to help children complete their homework, have fewer homework problems, and improve academic performance, at least in elementary school (Patall, Cooper, & Robinson, 2008). In addition, the Internet provides a wealth of resources that parents can use to provide homework help for their children.

Other examples of resources include local libraries where children can either talk on the phone or chat online with a tutor who helps them with their homework, or schools that provide their own online homework help.

Summary

Home-based education, initiated in the 1960s, saw continued and increased use in the 1980s, 1990s, and the 21st century. Programs developed include Parents as Teachers, Home Instruction Program for Preschool Youngsters, Healthy Families America, and Early Head Start, which joined earlier programs such as The Portage Project, Parent–Child Home Program, and the Nurse–Family Partnership Program.

If the school is interested in developing a home-based program, it should (a) show a need for the program, (b) involve others in planning, (c) develop a parent advisory council, and (d) decide on a program format.

Home-learning activities to be used by the home visitor and the family can be obtained through development of individualized activities, commercial offerings, or activities developed by demonstration programs. Use materials that are readily available to the parents because the parent is the primary teacher in the home-based program. The focus in a home-based program is on the parent interacting with and teaching the child after the home visitor is gone. Screening instruments can be selected to guide teachers in their work with parents and children and to serve as a basis for referrals for more thorough evaluation.

Concern about excellence in education has brought added emphasis on homework and the question of what amount shows the greatest benefit. Parents and teachers must work together as partners to support and extend children's learning to ensure their success in school.

Suggested Class Activities and Discussions

1. Brainstorm home situations that would be positive experiences for children.
2. Itemize household equipment that can be used as home learning tools. How would you use each?
3. Write role-playing opportunities based on families in several home situations.
4. Discuss the guidelines related to home visits.
5. Discuss value systems that might vary from your own. How can you work with parents and refrain from infringing on their beliefs?
6. Compare the strengths and weaknesses of home-based programs.
7. Discuss how to establish a working relationship with parents to support out-of-school learning.

Useful Websites

Early Head Start
Family Services Association

Home School Legal Defense Association

Glossary Terms

Home based program: A program that provides home visits focusing on different parent-child interactions that may focus on social skills, language, early literacy and play, among others.
Home visits: Teachers or specialists visiting families in their home for the purpose of building relationships.

Homeschooling: Formal education that happens in the home usually by a parent but tutors or online programs may also occur.
Early intervention: Home based program for children with disabilities or special abilities.

Chapter 10
Supporting Families of Children with Special Needs

with Allegra Montemayor

Respect, empathy, interest, motivation, care, and value create strong partnerships with families of children with special needs.

Mari Riojas-Cortez

 ## Learning Outcomes

This chapter provides ideas about how to engage families of children with special needs and reviews legislation and policies that help support children with special abilities in educational settings.

10.1 Review historical views of special abilities.

10.2 Examine special education legislation in the United States and its impact on families.

10.3 Identify and describe different special needs including disabilities and giftedness.

10.4 Briefly explore Autism Spectrum Disorders, learning disabilities, and intellectual disability.

10.5 Investigate resources that help families of children with special abilities.

10.6 Identify strategies to enhance family–school partnerships for children with special abilities.

Every summer I drive my son to a daily summer camp for children with special needs. He has autism.[1] The facility is a beautiful place, with cottages, trees, gardens, educational buildings, a chapel, and a swimming pool. Each morning I see children and adults with different abilities participate in many different activities. Each is cared for depending on his or her needs. I see parents dropping off their children, happy that such a wonderful place exists for their kids, particularly during the summer when inclusive activities are difficult to find, a lack felt by families who want the best for their children. Families of children with special needs in many ways occupy a different world that only other special-needs families and caretakers truly understand.

Across the United States we have seen an increase in the care and respect for individuals with special needs. Our government has passed laws and policies to improve the lives and opportunities of people with special needs. Many people have changed their perception about individuals with special needs. However, families still need help in finding resources that will help them care for their child's health. There is a lack of childcare centers that accept young children with special needs. Often, parents have to quit working to care for their child. Better health-care programs are needed that cover the variety of therapies that many children need. Churches of different

---

[1]For more information about one family's story regarding autism see Riojas-Cortez, M. (2011). Culture, play, and family: Supporting children on the autism spectrum. *Young Children*, 66(5), 94–99.

faiths need to find ways for special-needs families to feel welcome and participate in their services and events. Furthermore, teacher preparation programs must embrace the philosophy of inclusion where the child with special needs is included within the context of courses.

In summary, families need the community to help them engage their children in society. The ecological systems theory helps us understand that different systems are needed to support families so their children can also have a chance for a better future because of their ability. The terms special needs, special abilities and disabilities will be used throughout the chapter but are all terms that are often used in the schools by teachers.

Historical Perspectives of Special Needs

Throughout history, there have been many tales of cruel and inhumane treatment of people with special abilities. However, this information from the past helps us understand the need to provide services for individuals with special abilities. Recalling the story of *The Hunchback of Notre Dame* quickly brings to mind these cruelties. The Spartans were known to force parents to abandon imperfect babies by leaving them out in the cold (Greenleaf, 1978). There were people in very early history, however, who had a more positive view of those who were different. Hippocrates, who lived around 400 B.C., believed that emotional problems were caused not by supernatural powers but by natural forces. Plato (375 B.C.) defended those with mental disabilities as not being able to account for their deeds. The temples built by Alexander the Great provided asylum for mentally ill persons. In 90 B.C., Asclepiades made the first attempt at classifying mental illness, advocating humane treatment of those with the illness.

The period of A.D. 1450 to 1700 was an especially difficult time for those who special needs. Belief in demonology and superstition resulted in the persecution of those who were intellectually or developmentally disabled, or had other special needs. John Locke, concerned about harsh discipline, cultivated the "blank tablet" concept of the newborn's mind to overcome the popular belief that a child was born full of evil ideas.

In the late 1700s, Jean Marc Gaspard Itard (1775–1838) sought new methods to teach those with special needs. He was a physician and an authority on diseases of the ear and the education of the deaf. He found a boy in the forest of Auvergne, France, naked and apparently without upbringing, whom he attempted to raise and educate. He produced behavioral changes in the boy, Victor, but was unable to teach him to talk or to live independently. Itard believed he was a failure, but others followed his methods, which began a movement in treatment and education that had a profound effect on the development of special education (Cook, Klein, & Tessier, 2004; Hallahan & Kauffman, 1997).

In the early 1900s, individuals with disabilities were excluded from the community and public school systems. Residential facilities were built with the intention of providing educational services to individuals with intellectual disabilities and physical disabilities. Samuel Howe established the first state school for individuals with intellectual disabilities in the United States in 1848. However, by the turn of the 20th century these institutions functioned to protect the community and control individuals with disabilities (Vitello & Soskin, 1985, pp. 25–27).

By the mid-1900s, concerns over quality of care, inadequate funding, and overcrowding was substantiated by a report from the President's Panel on Mental Retardation[2] (1963). In an attempt to facilitate the changes documented by the President's Panel, a series of exposés were made public including Geraldo Rivera's *Willowbrook* (1972) and Burton Blatt and Fred Kaplan's *Christmas in Purgatory* (1974). Both exposés documented the severe conditions of overcrowding, which ultimately led to the "deinstitutionalization" movement. This movement was based on Wolf Wolfensberger's (1972) philosophy of normalization.

Children with special needs thrive in a playful environment.

---

[2]Derogatory term that is no longer used.

Early Educational Opportunities for Individuals with Special Needs

During the 1800s, residential schools for individuals with special needs began to emerge. The first American residential school for those who were deaf was established in 1817 in Hartford, Connecticut, by Thomas Hopkins Gallaudet (1787–1851). Most early schools avoided severely disabled students or those with multiple disabilities and worked only with those who were deaf, blind, or intellectually challenged. Those with more serious disabilities were typically ineligible for admission to any school and were often placed in what was known as asylums. Private schools were usually expensive, and state-operated schools were limited in their facilities (Murdick et al., 2014; Hallahan & Kauffman, 1990).

The Perkins School for the Blind, founded in Watertown, Massachusetts, was the first school for the blind. Samuel G. Howe (1801–1876) demonstrated that those who were blind could be taught when Laura Bridgman, who was blind and deaf, was educated in the manual alphabet and taught to write. (Hallahan & Kauffman, 1997). Seeking education for his daughter Helen Keller (1880–1968), who was deaf and blind, Arthur H. Keller consulted the director of the Perkins Institution. It was from this institution that Anne Mansfield Sullivan came to teach Helen when Helen was almost 7 years of age (Keller, 1991). Helen Keller's fame and her successful life with disabilities did much to persuade parents and professionals that, indeed, persons with disabilities could be educated.

It was not until the beginning of the 20th century that community-based programs for children with special needs began to appear. Gallaudet College, still the only college for those who were deaf, started a teacher-training program in the 1890s. In 1904, summer training sessions for teachers of children who had special needs began at the Vineland Training School in New Jersey. The community-based programs, however, often became "sunshine" rooms, in which such activities as arts and crafts were pursued, with little attempt to educate the children. In some cases, expectations were unrealistic and disappointment in the programs ensued. Few parents or professionals were optimistic about educating those who had special needs (Hallahan & Kauffman, 1990). Grassroots organizations also began to emerge and focus on providing support for individuals with special needs and their families.

Organizations Supporting Individuals with Special Needs

Organizations to help individuals with special needs have often developed because their families believe in the individual's potential to live a fulfilling and productive life. These families use their funds of knowledge for the benefit of those who need it the most. Families who commit to a specific cause often do so because a family member has a particular **disability**.

The Easterseals organization has been helping individuals with disabilities and their families for nearly 100 years. Edgar Allen was a businessman who lost his son in a streetcar accident in 1907 and decided to sell his business and build a hospital in his hometown in Ohio. As he became involved in this endeavor, he realized that children with disabilities were often hidden from public view. He engaged in a campaign that created what is now one of the exceptional organizations that offers hope and answers to millions of children, adults, and their families affected by a disability. Currently, inclusive services are offered through a network of 73 local Easterseals communities nationwide including Puerto Rico as well as international partners including Australia, Mexico, and Canada (Easterseals, 2018).

Another example of an organization that serves individuals who have special needs and their families is The Joseph Kennedy Jr. Foundation, created by the Kennedys, a powerful and influential family who had a daughter with a disability. The Foundation "aims to improve the way society deals with its citizens who have intellectual disabilities . . . and to help identify and disseminate ways to prevent the causes of intellectual disabilities" (The Joseph Kennedy, Jr. Foundation, 2018). The Foundation particularly emphasizes the need to assist families by informing them of resources and including children and adults with special abilities in the community. The specific goals of the Foundation comprise the following:

1. Enhance the quality of life of persons with intellectual disabilities and their families.

2. Provide seed funding to capitalize on federal and/or state or local spending on behalf of persons with intellectual disabilities and their families by funding initiatives that reach beyond existing programs, and do not duplicate public efforts.

3. Increase professional and public awareness of the needs of persons with intellectual disabilities and their families.

4. Work to reduce the incidence of intellectual disabilities (The Joseph Kennedy, Jr. Foundation, 2018).

The Special Olympics, established in 1968 by Eunice Kennedy Shriver, is an athletic program for people with intellectual disabilities. It is the world's largest sports program, with 172 countries, 4.9 million athletes and families, and over one million volunteers and coaches participating (Special Olympics, 2018). Thus, parents, educators, and influential families reinforce the growing concern of all parents of children with disabilities: that their children should have opportunities to develop to their highest potential.

The Arc of the United States (The Arc), previously the National Association for Retarded[3] Children (NARC), was chartered in 1953 and became active in influencing state legislatures and Congress. This organization was created by a small group of parents and other concerned individuals to act as voices for change (The Arc, 2018). In 1957, along with other organizations, it supported such important legislative action as the federal establishment of national special education programs and governmental support of research and leadership training in the field. In 1963, support was extended to other individuals with special needs, except individuals who were considered gifted, who did not receive support until 1979. The Bureau of Education for the Handicapped was established in 1966. It is important to note that ARC changed its name to "The Arc for People with Intellectual and Developmental Disabilities" in order to remove the terminology "retarded" that is derogatory and demeaning (The Arc, 2018).

Bob and Suzanne Wright founded Autism Speaks in 2005 when their grandchild was diagnosed with autism. Autism Speaks is the largest nonprofit science and advocacy organization that funds research which focuses on the causes, prevention, treatment, and cure of autism, increasing awareness of autism spectrum disorders, and advocating for support for individuals with autism and their families (Autism Speaks, 2018). One of their greatest efforts to increase awareness is the international initiative called Light It Up Blue, which is held during Autism Awareness Day on April 2. For this initiative major landmarks across the world are illuminated in blue, which is the official color for autism awareness.

Best Buddies is an important organization that focuses on ending the isolation of people with intellectual and developmental disabilities such as down syndrome, autism, Fragile X, Williams syndrome, cerebral palsy, traumatic brain injury, and other undiagnosed disabilities. Their vision is to integrate people with intellectual disabilities into schools, workplaces, and communities through the use of buddies from middle school, high school, college students, community members, corporations, and other employers. This organization was founded in 1989 by Anthony K. Shriver and it currently has 2,498 chapters across 50 states, 48 countries, and 6 continents (Best Buddies, 2018).

The last example of a unique organization created by parents of a child with special needs is the Gordon Hartman Foundation in San Antonio, Texas, which created the only amusement park in the world for children and adults with disabilities and their families; it is called Morgan's Wonderland and the only waterpark for individuals of all abilities, Morgan's Inspirational Island (Gordon Hartman Foundation, 2018). The mission of Morgan's Wonderland is to "provide a park that will nurture the minds and bodies of individuals

Best Buddies.

Mari Riojas-Cortez

---

[3]Derogatory term that is not longer used.

with special needs and their families (Hollingsworth, 2009, p. 24). Individuals with special needs have free admission to both parks. Both parks were created to provide full access to all children regardless of disability including the fully accessible splash pad at Morgan's Inspirational Island, which was named one of TIME's World's Greatest Places to visit in 2018. Gordon Hartman and his wife Maggie were inspired to create a space for children with different abilities and their families to enjoy the benefits of play. The Hartmans have a daughter named Morgan with physical and cognitive disabilities.

Organizations such as the ones described previously have provided children with special needs opportunities to learn to live with their special ability, and also assist parents to furnish a variety of experiences for their children.

The government has also ensured that individuals with special abilities are protected. The following section focuses on the development of special-education laws.

Legislation for People with Disabilities

Legislation for people with disabilities has been developing since the 1960s. With each new law or amendment to existing legislation, the programs for children and adults with disabilities have become more encompassing. During the 1960s, parents organized advocacy groups that became vocal and attracted enough attention to result in legislation to provide educational support to children with disabilities. In 1971, the Pennsylvania Association for Retarded Children (PARC) won a landmark case against the Commonwealth of Pennsylvania. It was a decision based on the 14th Amendment and it assured all children, including those with disabilities, the right to a free and appropriate education. Decisions such as this one led to the passage of other important laws.

Elementary and Secondary Education Act of 1965 (P.L. 89-10)

The first federal legislation, the Elementary and Secondary Education Act (ESEA), was intended to improve the education for elementary and secondary aged students that were "educationally disadvantaged," including students with disabilities. Its initial budget of $1.3 billion was designed to assist disadvantaged students and included funds to cover instructional materials, state agencies, and centers for educational innovation and research (Martin, 1968). Succeeding amendments to ESEA including P.L. 89-313 (1965) and P.L. 89-750 (1966) extended funding and established federal grants that were used to establish resources, including the Bureau of Education for the Handicapped (BEH), for the education of students with disabilities. The funding went towards regional resource centers, centers for deaf-blindness, media programs, assistance for new educational programs, training of personnel for students with disabilities, and research and training efforts.

The Rehabilitation Act of 1973, Section 504

Section 504 of the Rehabilitation Act of 1973, which relates to nondiscrimination under Federal Grant, P.L. 93-112, required that "no otherwise qualified handicapped individual in the United States shall, solely by reason of his handicap, be excluded from the participation in, be denied the benefits of, or be subjected to discrimination under any program or activity receiving Federal financial assistance" (29 U.S.C. § 794). At the time, Section 504 specifically applied to discrimination in employment. The Rehabilitation Act Amendments of 1974 extended coverage to all civil rights, including education, health, welfare, and other social-services programs.

Under Section 504, all recipients of Department of Education funds that operate public elementary and secondary programs must provide a free appropriate public education (FAPE) to each qualified individual with a disability who is in the recipient's jurisdiction, regardless of the nature or severity of the person's disability (Office of Civil Rights, 2010). This ensures the availability of programs and physical access for individuals with disabilities.

Since the legislation was passed, there has been confusion about implementation and compliance of the regulations. As a result of the confusion, the Office of Civil Rights has issued policies and rulings that clarify many issues.

A person is considered disabled under the definition of Section 504 if the individual:

1. Has a physical or mental impairment that substantially limits one or more of such person's major life activities.
2. Has a record of such impairments.
3. Is regarded as having such an impairment.

Major life activities include functions such as caring for oneself, performing manual tasks, walking, seeing, hearing, speaking, breathing, learning, and working. When a condition does not substantially limit a major life activity, the individual does not qualify for services under Section 504.

Much confusion also exists regarding the relationship between Section 504 and special education laws and regulations. It must be emphasized that administration of Section 504 is under the management of regular education. Students who have disabilities but who do not qualify for special education might still be eligible for accommodations under Section 504.

Section 504, which covers a broader range of disabilities than the special education law (which will be covered later), also requires public schools to provide students with a "free appropriate public education" and, in addition, ensures that students with disabilities are afforded an equal opportunity to participate in school programs. A student who is found to be disabled under Section 504 should be served by the resources provided through regular education. The exception to this is a student who has been determined to be disabled under the Individuals with Disabilities Education Act (IDEA). Such a student could receive special education services under IDEA and accommodations required under Section 504 of the Rehabilitation Act of 1973.

For students with disabilities or who qualify for Section 504 services, this means that schools are required to make special arrangements so that the students have access to the full range of programs and activities offered, as determined at a multidisciplinary team meeting to determine students' service needs. At the meeting, the use of "evidence-based assistive technology," as mandated by IDEA 2004, is to be identified, since all students receiving special education services qualify for it (Quinn et al., 2009). Assistive technology, a means to provide the support needed to increase, maintain, or improve a student's functioning, can include a range of devices, from "low tech," such as a pencil grip, to "high tech," such as a voice synthesizer or Braille reader that helps students with disabilities be successful in the classroom (Dyal, Carpenter, & Wright, 2009; Copenhaver, 2004; Families Together, 1993).

Other students might need technology to provide physical access to the school facilities. One example is that a student who needs a wheelchair lift to get on a school bus must be provided with this technology. Other examples of modifications that might be required under Section 504 include installing ramps in buildings and modifying restrooms to provide access for individuals with physical disabilities.

Determination of a student's eligibility for Section 504 services must be based on the use of tests and other evaluations that evaluate specific areas of need, not solely a single intelligence quotient test. These tests and evaluations should not be culturally or linguistically biased. Subsequent assessments to determine progress made toward individualized goals should also provide appropriate accommodations so they reflect the student's achievement without the impact of the student's disability (Chicago Office of the Office for Civil Rights, 2005).

Enforcement of Section 504 of the Rehabilitation Act of 1973 in programs and activities that receive funds from the U.S. Department of Education is provided by the Office for Civil Rights (OCR). There are 12 enforcement offices and a headquarters in Washington, D.C. Section 504, like other civil rights laws, is monitored by OCR. It is a goal of OCR to foster partnerships between school districts and parents to address the special education needs of students attending programs that receive federal funds. Enforcement procedures include administrative remedies, a private right of action in federal court, monetary damages, injunctive relief, attorney's fees, and defunding by the U.S. Department of Education (Chicago Office of the Office for Civil Rights, 2005).

The Americans with Disabilities Act

The Rehabilitation Act of 1973 was made more comprehensive by the Americans with Disabilities Act of 1990. In it, childcare centers were designated as public accommodations, which must be available to all who desire to use them. They must serve all children, including those who are disabled, unless (a) the child is a direct threat to self or others, (b) the facility cannot provide childcare without it being an undue burden, or (c) the childcare center would have to change the services it provides. New updates for this act were passed by Congress and signed by the President in 2008 in relation to student eligibility standards (Zirkel, 2009).

The act specifically defines discrimination, including various types of intentional and unintentional exclusions, such as the following: segregation; inferior or less effective services, benefits, or activities; architectural, transportation, and communication barriers; failure to make reasonable accommodations; and discriminatory qualifications and performance standards. Actions that do not constitute discrimination include unequal treatment unrelated to a disability or that results from legitimate application of qualifications and performance standards necessary and substantially related to the ability to perform or participate in the essential components of a job or activity.

The act stipulates that the Architectural and Transportation Barriers Compliance Board will issue minimum accessibility guidelines. Other regulations will be issued by the attorney general, the U.S. Equal Opportunity Commission, the secretary of Housing and Urban Development, the secretary of Transportation, the Federal Communications Commission, and the secretary of Commerce. The act does not repeal Sections 503 and 504 of the Vocational Rehabilitation Act of 1973, and all regulations issued under those sections remain in full force.

In order to make this act even stronger, the U.S. Department of Justice has revised ADA regulations revising Title I and Title III (U.S. Department of Justice, 2011a). The 2010 ADA Standards for Accessible Design "set minimum requirements for newly designed and constructed or altered State and local government facilities, public accommodations, and commercial facilities to be readily accessible to and usable by individuals with disabilities" (U.S. Department of Justice, 2011b). In addition, the ADA also requires access to medical care and services and the facilities where the care is provided (U.S. Department of Justice, 2011c). It is not enough for buildings to comply with ADA standards; the entire facility must meet the needs of people with all disabilities.

The Education for All Handicapped Children Act of 1975 (P.L. 94-142)

The most far-reaching and revolutionary legislation related to education was P.L. 94-142, the Education for All Handicapped Children Act of 1975.

This federal law ensures that all people between the ages of 3 and 21 residing in the United States must be provided with free and appropriate public education (FAPE). The term *appropriate* means suited to the disability, age, maturity, past achievements of the child, and parental expectations. The education must be in a program designed to meet the child's needs in the least restrictive environment (Section 504 Regulations). This means that the child will be placed in the classroom that will benefit the child the most (Wagner & Katsiyannis, 2010). If the student would benefit more from a regular classroom, the child is to be placed there.

The terms *mainstreaming* and *inclusion* have become synonymous with placing children with disabilities in the regular classroom. However, meeting the child's needs in the *least restrictive environment* can also refer to moving the child with disabilities with justification out of a regular classroom and into a resource room or self-contained special-education room (Hyatt & Filler, 2011; Rozalski, Stewart, & Miller, 2010), and some to an alternative school, as in the case of children who exhibit severe emotional disturbances (Hoge, Liaupsin, Umbreit, & Ferro, 2014). The law requires diagnosis and individualization of the educational program. Legal mandates for more participation of students with disabilities in general education classrooms have prompted teachers to participate in collaborative planning and teaching, particularly for children with special needs who are culturally and linguistically diverse (Nevin, Thousand, & Villa, 2009).

The ultimate goal for all individuals with disabilities is that they have access to the general education curriculum. Additional terms that reflect the delivery of services in the least restrictive environment include "pull out" and "push in" services. "Pull out" services are those in which children with similar needs are "pulled out" of their base classroom to meet with a teacher for small-group teaching. "Push in" services are those in which the teacher assigned to children with disabilities works in their base classroom. The teachers work with students with and without disabilities so that children with disabilities are not separated from their peers. Reverse inclusion is a type of program in which typically developing children are brought to the special education classroom for short periods of time to interact with children with disabilities (Schoger, 2006). This type of model ensures that children with disabilities have an opportunity to interact with others, but it also gives the typically developing children an opportunity to see how special needs children learn.

Amendments of 1983 (P.L. 98-199)

The Education of the Handicapped Act Amendments of 1983, P.L. 98-199, extended fiscal authorization for federal aid to state and local school systems through 1987; improved reporting and information dissemination requirements; increased assistance to children who are deaf and blind including diagnosis and evaluation, programs, consultations, and training services for the families; provided grants for transitional programs; and expanded services for children from birth through 5 years of age (*Congressional Record*, 1983).

Amendments of 1986: Infants and Toddlers with Disabilities (P.L. 99-457)

The Education of the Handicapped Act Amendments of 1986, P.L. 99-457, established statewide, comprehensive, coordinated, multidisciplinary, interagency programs of early-intervention services for infants and toddlers with disabilities ages 3 through 5, as well as their families (*Congressional Record*, 1983). This law addressed easily recognized needs of the very young with disabilities.

However, there are many conditions that are not immediately recognized, so services early in life can be delayed for those with genetic conditions associated with mental challenges, congenital syndromes associated with delays in development, sensory impairments, metabolic disorders, prenatal infections (AIDS, syphilis, cytomegalic inclusion disease), and low birth weight. There are also concerns for infants whose parents are developmentally delayed, have severe emotional disturbances, or are 15 years old or younger.

Parents or caretakers might have difficulty finding the programs and services they need to help them care for these young children. These services are provided through the Department of Education in each state, so the first contact should be through the local school. Another group that might be able to offer information about services for rural families is the American Council on Rural Special Education (ACRES) P.L. 99-457, which provides for public supervision at no cost (except where federal and state laws allow), and helps meet the needs of special needs infants and toddlers, with family training, counseling, special instruction, physical therapy, stimulation therapy, case management, diagnosis-qualified personnel, and conformance with the Individualized Family Service Plan.

Individuals with Disabilities Education Act Amendments (1997 P.L. 105-17 and 2004 P.L. 108-446)

This federal law—formerly the Education for All Handicapped Children Act, P.L. 94-142—mandated that all children receive an education regardless of the severity of their disability. An amended IDEA was reauthorized in June 1997 and went into effect on July 1, 1998, and was reauthorized again in 2004 and went into effect July 1, 2005. IDEA '97 and 2004 are organized into four parts: (a) general provisions; (b) school-aged and preschool (3- to 5-year-olds); (c) infants and toddlers (birth through 2-year-olds); and (d) support. Part C relates to the education of infants and toddlers, birth to age 3 (Early Childhood Technical Assistant Center, 2018). Although alike in many ways, the differences include "zero reject" in Part B. "Zero reject" means there can be no exclusion of children ages 3 through 21, and public school systems are responsible for including all these children in an educational program, regardless of the extent or the kind of disability.

Part C for infants gives discretion to the states to develop a program that best serves the needs of infants and toddlers. Each state determines which agency can work most effectively with parents and their infants and toddlers. States use different agencies such as the Departments of Education or Health and Human Services. For infants and toddlers with identified disabilities, there must not be a break in service as they transition from Part C to Part B services.

Terms used in the act include the following:

- The term *handicapped child* was changed to *child with disabilities* because it was recognized that the children are handicapped by the limitations placed on them rather than by their abilities. The child has a disability, which might not be a handicap, depending on the situation.

- All children with disabilities will have an education that is individualized to meet their needs. This is written in an Individualized Education Program (**IEP**) for children ages 3 to 21, and in an Individualized Family Service Plan (IFSP) for infants and toddlers, birth to age 2 (Utah Parent Center, 1997). Teachers, special education teachers, administrators, parents, and others who are concerned with the child's education are involved in the development of the IEP. If appropriate, the child is also included. The law provides for a hearing that can be initiated by

Educators must communicate effectively with parents of children with special needs.

Figure 10.1 Usual Components for an ARD Meeting

Sample ARD Meeting Agenda
Each school district has the capability of developing a standard form for the ARD meeting agenda. These are the most common topics covered at an ARD meeting that are important for the Individualized Education Program, or IEP.

1. Welcome and Introductions
2. Purpose of the meeting
3. Presentation by specialists (present levels of academic achievement and functional performance, goals, objectives, and evaluations)
   a. Occupational therapist
   b. Speech therapist
   c. Physical therapist
   d. Adaptive physical education teacher
   e. General education teacher
   f. Special education teacher
   g. Licensed specialist school psychologist
4. Recommendations of goals and objectives for next year
5. Placement of services and consideration of least restrictive environment
   a. Determine how you will measure progress toward the goals and develop a schedule for reporting a student's progress to his or her parents.
   b. Base services on peer-reviewed research.
   c. Implement program modifications in the general education classroom.
   d. Provide related services when applicable.
6. Parents' rights
7. Deliberations
8. Signatures (agree/not agree with committee decisions)

the parents if they do not agree with the diagnosis of the child, the placement, and/or the IEP. This is due process, and it is the responsibility of the school to inform the parents of their rights.

The school district is responsible for serving or seeing that children aged 3 to 5 are served in preschools. The primary focus of the IEP is the education of the student, although the family may receive some services. Figure 10.1 shows an agenda with some general topics that must be covered in the Admissions, Review, Dismissal, or **ARD** meeting where the IEP is discussed.

In the birth-to-2 program, an Individualized Family Service Plan (IFSP) is written to serve both student and family. One of the requirements for the IFSP is to provide documentation of family priorities, resources, and concerns. It is also used to provide services to the families based on their individual preferences to meet the child's exceptional needs (Turnbull et al., 2014).

IDEIA

The Individuals with Disabilities Education Improvement Act, or IDEIA, created new regulations in 2006 that are still in effect. Yell, Katsiyannis, Ryan, McDuffie, and Mattocks (2008) provide 20 ways to ensure compliance. Here are a few of their suggestions.

1. Meet the procedural requirements of IDEA.
2. Convene legally correct IEP meetings.
3. Develop educationally meaningful IEP.
4. Conduct relevant assessments.
5. Link assessment results to goals and services.
6. Develop measurable annual goals.

Development of the Individualized Education Program (IEP)

An Individualized Education Program (IEP) is a written plan that illustrates the goals that schools and parents want for their children with disabilities.

Three pages of an IEP for a kindergarten child diagnosed with autism are illustrated in Figures 10.2A, 10.2B, and 10.2C. Notice that the IEP form focuses on instructional services and the skills that teachers should focus on with this child.

Figure 10.2A A Page of the Individualized Education Program (IEP) for Math

Student Name: _Rodrigo Cortez_ DOB: _12-10-18_ Date of Meeting: _12-15-18_   Page_____ of_____

☒ *INSTRUCTIONAL SERVICES   ☐ DRAFT_____
                                                                                       Date
                          *INDIVIDUAL EDUCATIONAL PLAN (IEP)[1] [2]

☐ *RELATED SERVICES   ☐ ACCEPTED BY ARD COMMITTEE
    SPECIFY: _____

*Duration of services from: ____ _12-15-18_ ____   to: ____ _12-15-18_ ____
                              MONTH / DAY / YEAR   MONTH / DAY / YEAR

The student will demonstrate measurable progress toward mastery of _Math_ skills at   Language of delivery: _English_
the _____ developmental/age level or _K_ grade level as measured by specified   ESL Required   ☐ YES ☒ NO
evaluation procedures addressing these specific needs: _____

*BENCHMARKS OR SHORT-TERM OBJECTIVES THE STUDENT WILL BE ABLE TO:	*INDICATED LEVEL OF MASTERY CRITERIA	*EVALUATION PROCEDURE	*SCHEDULE FOR EVALUATION	EVALUATION CODES DATE C/M	DATE C/M	DATE C/M	DATE C/M	DATE REGRESSION YES / NO ?
• sort objects by object, color, or shape	75%	1,2	6 wks					☐ Y / N ☐
• follow and complete an AB and ABC pattern	75%	1,2	6 wks					☐ Y / N ☐
• recognize and name numbers 10-20	75%	1,2	6 wks					☐ Y / N ☐
• ~~name 4 shapes~~	~~80%~~	~~1,2~~	~~6 wks~~					☐ Y / N ☐
• show one to one correspondence for numbers 1-10	75%	1,2	6 wks					☐ Y / N ☐
• recognize penny, nickel, quarter, dime	75%	1,2	6 wks					☐ Y / N ☐
								☐ Y / N ☐
								☐ Y / N ☐

EVALUATION PROCEDURE CODES:

1. Teacher-made tests
2. Observations
3. Weekly Test
4. Unit Tests
5. Student Conferences
6. Work Samples
7. Portfolios
8. Baseline Data
9. Weekly Consult
10. Other: _____

EVALUATION CODES

C - Continued
M - Mastered

*Denotes required items

10/25/2007
ARD-5

[1] Goals and objectives for English as a second language and/or primary language development shall be included for limited English proficient students as appropriate.
[2] Criteria and schedule must allow for determining student's eligibility for participation in extracurricular activities.

Figure 10.2B A Page of the Individualized Education Program (IEP) for Social Studies

Student Name: _Rodrigo Cortez_ DOB: _12-10-18_ Date of Meeting: _12-15-18_ Page____ of ____

☑ *INSTRUCTIONAL SERVICES

☐ DRAFT ____
Date

*INDIVIDUAL EDUCATIONAL PLAN (IEP)[1] [2]

☐ *RELATED SERVICES

☐ ACCEPTED BY ARD COMMITTEE

SPECIFY: _____

*Duration of services from: _____12-15-18_____
MONTH / DAY / YEAR

to: _____12-15-19_____
MONTH / DAY / YEAR

Social Studies

The student will demonstrate measurable progress toward mastery of _____ skills at the _____ developmental/age level or _K_ grade level as measured by specified evaluation procedures addressing these specific needs: _____

Language of delivery: _____

ESL Required   ☐ YES ☐ NO

*BENCHMARKS OR SHORT-TERM OBJECTIVES THE STUDENT WILL BE ABLE TO:	*INDICATED LEVEL OF MASTERY CRITERIA	*EVALUATION PROCEDURE	*SCHEDULE FOR EVALUATION	EVALUATION CODES				DATE
				DATE C / M	DATE C / M	DATE C / M	DATE C / M	REGRESSION YES / NO ?
Follow a two-step direction	75%	2	6 wks					☐Y / N☐
respond to "STOP"	80%	2	6 wks					☐Y / N☐
come to an activity when called	75%	2	6 wks					☐Y / N☐
put things away upon request	75%	2	6 wks					☐Y / N☐
begin to identify warning signs in the environment	80%	1, 2	6 wks					☐Y / N☐
								☐Y / N☐
								☐Y / N☐
								☐Y / N☐

EVALUATION PROCEDURE CODES:

1. Teacher-made tests
2. Observations
3. Weekly Test
4. Unit Tests
5. Student Conferences
6. Work Samples
7. Portfolios
8. Baseline Data
9. Weekly Consult
10. Other: _____

EVALUATION CODES

C - Continued
M - Mastered

*Denotes required items

10/25/2007
ARD-5

[1] Goals and objectives for English as a second language and/or primary language development shall be included for limited English proficient students as appropriate.
[2] Criteria and schedule must allow for determining student's eligibility for participation in extracurricular activities.

Figure 10.2C A Page of the Individualized Education Program (IEP) for Self-Help

Student Name: _Rodrigo Cortez_ DOB: _12-10-18_ Date of Meeting: _12-15-18_ Page _____ of _____

☒ *INSTRUCTIONAL SERVICES

☐ DRAFT _____
Date

*INDIVIDUAL EDUCATIONAL PLAN (IEP)[1] [2]

☐ *RELATED SERVICES
SPECIFY: _____

☐ ACCEPTED BY ARD COMMITTEE

*Duration of services from: _12-15-18_ to: _12-15-19_
MONTH / DAY / YEAR   _Self-Help_   MONTH / DAY / YEAR

The student will demonstrate measurable progress toward mastery of _____ skills at the _____ developmental/age level or _____ grade level as measured by specified evaluation procedures addressing these specific needs: _____

Language of delivery: _____

ESL Required   ☐ YES ☐ NO

*BENCHMARKS OR SHORT-TERM OBJECTIVES THE STUDENT WILL BE ABLE TO:	*INDICATED LEVEL OF MASTERY CRITERIA	*EVALUATION PROCEDURE	*SCHEDULE FOR EVALUATION	EVALUATION CODES				DATE
				DATE C/M	DATE C/M	DATE C/M	DATE C/M	REGRESSION YES / NO ?
• follow a toileting schedule using a visual schedule	90%	2	6 wks					☐Y / N☐
								☐Y / N☐
• zip and button pants	80%	2	6 wks					☐Y / N☐
• use a "spork" to eat	75%	2	6 wks					☐Y / N☐
• independently open wrapped items and milk carton								☐Y / N☐
								☐Y / N☐
								☐Y / N☐
								☐Y / N☐

EVALUATION PROCEDURE CODES:

1.	Teacher-made tests	6.	Work Samples
2.	Observations	7.	Portfolios
3.	Weekly Test	8.	Baseline Data
4.	Unit Tests	9.	Weekly Consult
5.	Student Conferences	10.	Other: _____

EVALUATION CODES

C - Continued
M - Mastered

*Denotes required items

10/25/2007
ARD-5

---

[1] Goals and objectives for English as a second language and/or primary language development shall be included for limited English proficient students as appropriate.
[2] Criteria and schedule must allow for determining student's eligibility for participation in extracurricular activities.

All children (ages 3 through 21) with disabilities receiving any type of special education services must have an Individualized Education Program, or IEP, prepared specifically for them (Christle & Yell, 2010). The IEP is developed and reviewed in the annual ARD meeting. The IEP must be the product of the joint efforts of members of a child multidisciplinary study team. The team forms part of the ARD committee as follows:

Required Members of the ARD Committee

1. Child's parent(s) or guardian.
2. General education teacher (at least one).
3. Special education teacher
4. Therapists. Depending on the services needed by the child and provided by the school district these can include speech, occupational, or physical therapists. Other specialists include Adapted PE teachers or music therapists.
5. Administrator such as the principal, vice principal, or assistant principal.

Many requirements must be met when dealing with the child with disabilities. The IEP should be reviewed periodically, and not less than annually, to determine if progress toward the goals is advancing as expected and to reevaluate and assess the program. For students who are transitioning, it is a good idea to "triangulate" the IEP goals to ensure that academic goals, content standards, and postsecondary goals are strong and coincide with each other (Peterson, Burden, Sedaghat, Gothberg, Kohler, & Coyle, 2013). The 2004 IDEA reauthorization changed attendance requirements so all members of the IEP do not need to attend a reevaluation meeting if the area they represent is not being

IEPs must avoid jargon and be clearly explained to all parents.

discussed. Administrators and teachers must be aware of all procedures that the schools are responsible for administering. These procedures include the following: definitions, opportunity to examine records, independent educational evaluation, prior notice, parental consent, procedures when parent refuses consent, content of notice, formal complaint resolution, impartial due-process hearing, reasonable attorney's fees, impartial hearing officer, appointment of hearing officer, access rights, records, children's rights, and more (Burns, 2006; Family and Advocates Partnership for Education Project, 2006; Gartin & Murdick, 2005).

Rights and Responsibilities for Parents—2004

IDEA 1997 and 2004 addressed the participation of parents in the development of their child's program. It stated that the Local Education Agency (LEA) or the State Education Agency (SEA) will ensure that parents are members of any group that makes decisions on the educational placement of their child. Parents can examine all records and participate in meetings regarding the evaluations, placement, and the free and appropriate public education that the child will receive. Specifications include the following:

- Parents must receive an explanation and copy of the procedural safeguards.
- Public agencies must notify parents when the agencies propose or refuse to initiate or change the identification, evaluation, or educational placement of the child or the provision of FAPE to the child.
- Parents have the right to inspect and review all records relating to their child that a public agency collects, maintains, or uses regarding the identification, evaluation, or educational placement of the child or the provision of FAPE to the child.
- Parental consent is required before a child can be evaluated for the first time.
- Parents have the right to obtain an independent educational evaluation (IEE) of their child.
- Parental consent is required for a child's initial special education placement.
- Parents have the right to challenge or appeal any decision related to the identification, evaluation, or educational placement of their child, or the provision of FAPE to their child.

- Parents are responsible for notifying the public agency if they plan to remove their child from the public agency for placement in a private school at public expense.

- Parents are responsible for notifying the public agency if they intend to request a due-process hearing (Center for Parent Information and Resources (CPIR), 2017; Family and Advocates Partnership for Education Project, 2006; PEAK Parent Center, 1997).

NOTIFICATION. There are procedural safeguards that require written notification to parents prior to any proposed action. The notification must be in the parents' native language or preferred mode of communication—for example, Braille or sign language. There is protection of the child's rights when parents cannot be located. The United States Department of Education has a free example of a procedural safeguards notice that you can find online.

MEDIATION. According to the Committee on Education and Workforce, U.S. House of Representatives (2005), mediation is "defined as an attempt to bring about a peaceful settlement or compromise between parties to a dispute through the objective intervention of a neutral party" (p. 13). If disagreements arise, a mediation system employing a qualified, impartial mediator must be available. Parents might be required to attend a mediation meeting.

DEVELOPMENTAL DELAY. The developmental delay category, previously used for placement of children 3 to 5 years old, was recognized as appropriate for those ages 3 to 9 and was therefore extended to cover that age group. There are five areas of development that can be affected, which include cognitive, physical (vision and hearing), communication, social or emotional, and adaptive.

CHARTER SCHOOLS. Charter schools, new since the original IDEA, were included in the provisions. They must follow the same guidelines as other publicly funded schools. They offer public elementary and secondary services just like traditional schools. Charter schools offer parents "school of choice" and provide small class size, high academic standards, and advanced teaching and learning approaches.

Definitions of Disabilities and Giftedness

The following descriptions of children with disabilities as defined in IDEA (34 Code of Federal Regulations, Section 300.7) clarify those who need special programs. If a student in a classroom fits into any of the following categories, special services should be provided.

1. *Autism.* A developmental disability significantly affecting verbal and nonverbal communication and social interaction, generally evident before age three, that adversely affects a child's educational performance. Other characteristics often associated with autism are engagement in repetitive activities and stereotyped movements, resistance to environmental change or change in daily routines and unusual responses to sensory experiences.

2. *Deafness–blindness.* Concomitant hearing and visual impairments, the combination of which causes such severe communication and other developmental and education problems that a child cannot be accommodated in special education programs solely for children who are deaf or for children who are blind.

3. *Deafness.* A hearing impairment so severe that a child is impaired in processing linguistic information through hearing, with or without amplification, that adversely affects a child's educational performance.

4. *Emotional disturbance.*

   a. A condition exhibiting one or more of the following characteristics over a long period of time and to a marked degree and that adversely affects educational performance: (a) an inability to learn that cannot be explained by intellectual, sensory, or health factors; (b) an inability to build or maintain satisfactory interpersonal relationships with peers and teachers; (c) inappropriate types of behavior or feelings under normal circumstances; (d) a general pervasive mood of unhappiness or depression; or (e) a tendency to develop physical symptoms or fears associated with personal or school problems.

   b. The term includes children who have schizophrenia. The term does not include children who are socially maladjusted, unless it is determined that they have an emotional disturbance.

5. *Hearing impairment.* An impairment in hearing, whether permanent or fluctuating, that adversely affects a child's educational performance but is not included under the definition of *deafness.*

6. *Intellectual disabilities.* Significantly subaverage general intellectual functioning existing concurrently with deficits in adaptive behavior and manifested during the developmental period, which adversely affects a child's educational performance; formerly known as "mental retardation." In 2010, a 9-year-old girl named Rosa Marcellino with Down Syndrome and her family advocated for a change in the terms used for individuals with mental challenges. As a result, Rosa's Law, P.L. 111-256 authorized the change from "mental retardation" to "intellectual disability" (Hallahan, Kauffman, & Pullen, 2015). The term "mental retardation" is derogatory and should no longer be used.

7. *Multiple disabilities.* Concomitant impairments (such as intellectual disabilities–blindness or intellectual disabilities–orthopedic impairment), the combination of which causes such severe educational problems that the child cannot be accommodated in a special education program solely for one of the impairments. The term does not include children with deaf–blindness.

8. *Orthopedic impairment.* A severe orthopedic impairment that adversely affects a child's educational performance. The term includes impairments caused by a congenital anomaly (e.g., clubfoot or absence of a limb), impairments caused by disease (e.g., poliomyelitis or bone tuberculosis), and impairments from other causes (e.g., cerebral palsy, amputations, or fractures or burns that cause contractures).

9. *Other health impairment.* Having limited strength, vitality, or alertness, due to chronic or acute health problems—such as a heart condition, tuberculosis, rheumatic fever, nephritis, asthma, sickle-cell anemia, hemophilia, epilepsy, lead poisoning, leukemia, or diabetes—that adversely affects a child's educational performance. According to the Office of Special Education and Rehabilitative Services' clarification statement of September 16, 1991, eligible children with Attention Deficit Hyperactivity Disorder, often referred to as ADHD, may also be classified under "other health impairment."

10. *Specific learning disabilities.* A disorder in one or more of the basic psychological processes involved in understanding or in using language, spoken or written, that might manifest itself in an imperfect ability to listen, think, speak, read, write, spell, or do mathematical calculations. The term includes such conditions as perceptual disabilities, brain injury, minimal brain dysfunction, dyslexia, and developmental aphasia. The term does not include children who have learning problems that are primarily the result of visual, hearing, or motor disabilities, of intellectual disabilities, of emotional disturbance, or of environmental, cultural, or economic disadvantage.

11. *Speech or language impairment.* A communication disorder, such as stuttering, impaired articulation, a language impairment, or a voice impairment, that adversely affects a child's educational performance.

12. *Traumatic brain injury.* An acquired injury to the brain caused by an external physical force, resulting in total or partial functional disability or psychosocial impairment, or both, that adversely affects a child's educational performance. The term applies to open or closed head injuries resulting in impairments in one or more areas, such as cognition; language; memory; attention; reasoning; abstract thinking; judgment; problem-solving; sensory, perceptual, and motor abilities; psychosocial behavior; physical functions; information processing; and speech. This term does not apply to brain injuries that are congenital or degenerative, nor does it include brain injuries induced by birth trauma.

13. *Visual impairment, including blindness.* A visual impairment that, even with correction, adversely affects a child's educational performance. The term includes both children with partial sight and those with blindness.

Visually impaired children and youth shall be identified as those whose limited vision interferes with their education and/or developmental progress. Four divisions for the visually impaired shall be made:

Partially sighted indicates some type of visual problem has resulted in a need for special education.

Low vision generally refers to a severe visual impairment, not necessarily limited to distance vision. Low vision applies to all individuals with sight who are unable to read the newspaper at a normal viewing distance, even with the aid of eyeglasses or contact lenses. They use a combination of vision and other senses to learn, although they may require adaptations in lighting or the size of print and sometimes Braille.

Legally blind indicates that a person has less than 20/2000 vision in the better eye or a very limited field of vision (20 degrees at its widest point).

Totally blind students learn via Braille or other nonvisual media.

Visual impairment is the consequence of a functional loss of vision, rather than the eye disorder itself. Eye disorders that can lead to visual impairments can include retinal degeneration, albinism, cataracts, glaucoma, and muscular problems that result in visual disturbances, corneal disorders, diabetic retinopathy, congenital disorders, and infection.

Attention Deficit Hyperactivity Disorder

According to the Centers for Disease Control and Prevention (2014a), Attention Deficit Hyperactivity Disorder or ADHD is one of the most common neurodevelopmental disorders. Changes in the number of children with ADHD have occurred through the years, as well as the treatments. Figure 10.3 provides a timeline that describes the changes over the years, starting in the 1900s and continuing until now (CDCP, 2017).

Symptoms that are a sign of ADHD are persistent inattention, hyperactivity, and impulsivity. There are three different subtypes of ADHD, including predominantly inattentive, predominantly hyperactive-impulsive, and combined. Table 10.1 lists some possible ADHD symptoms. Causes for ADHD are unknown, but according to the CDCP, research indicates it is linked to genetics or other possible risk factors such as brain injury, toxins exposure, alcohol and tobacco use during pregnancy, low birth weight, and premature delivery (2017). The National Institute of Mental Health (2018) states a comprehensive evaluation is required to test for ADHD. Most professionals agree on four mechanisms to assess whether a student has ADHD. This includes, first, a medical examination to eliminate any medical conditions including thyroid problems, brain tumors, or seizures, as the cause of the hyperactivity and/or inattention (Barkley & Edwards, 2006). Second, a

clinical interview is conducted with the parent regarding the child's psychological and physical characteristics, family dynamics, and interactions with his or her peers. Third, teacher and parent rating scales are conducted to verify how often the child gets easily distracted, does not pay attention to details, fidgets, and so on. The child may be asked to fill out a rating scale. Lastly, whenever possible, it is important to observe the child in the classroom to have a better understanding of how the child performs different tasks that require their complete attention.

Teachers in particular must find ways to help children with ADHD have successful experiences in school. Murphy (2014) lists some possible ways, including making eye contact, providing brief instructions, asking the child to repeat instructions aloud, and using cues to redirect attention.

A Brief Look at Autism Spectrum Disorders, Learning Disabilities, and Intellectual Disability

Autism Spectrum Disorders

Known as a complex neurobiological disorder, autism impacts communication, behavior, and social relationships. According to the organization Autism Speaks, autism is the fastest-growing serious developmental disability in the United States (Autism Speaks, 2018). The Centers for Disease Control and Prevention (CDC) provided new data (April, 2018) on the number of children affected. Their study showed that 1 in 59 children (1 in 37 boys and 1 in 151 girls) have autism spectrum disorders. The cause of autism is unknown. Although some organizations and celebrities have wrongly blamed vaccines for the development of autism, the American Academy of Pediatrics studies (2013) affirm that there is no link between vaccines and autism. An updated study from 2014 indicated again that there is no connection between vaccines, particularly MMR, and autism (Maglione et al., 2014). A study regarding causes for autism indicates that there is a genetic basis for this disorder (Pinto et al., 2010), but the cause is still undetermined. Some researchers

Figure 10.3 Timeline of ADHD Diagnostic Criteria, Prevalence, and Treatment

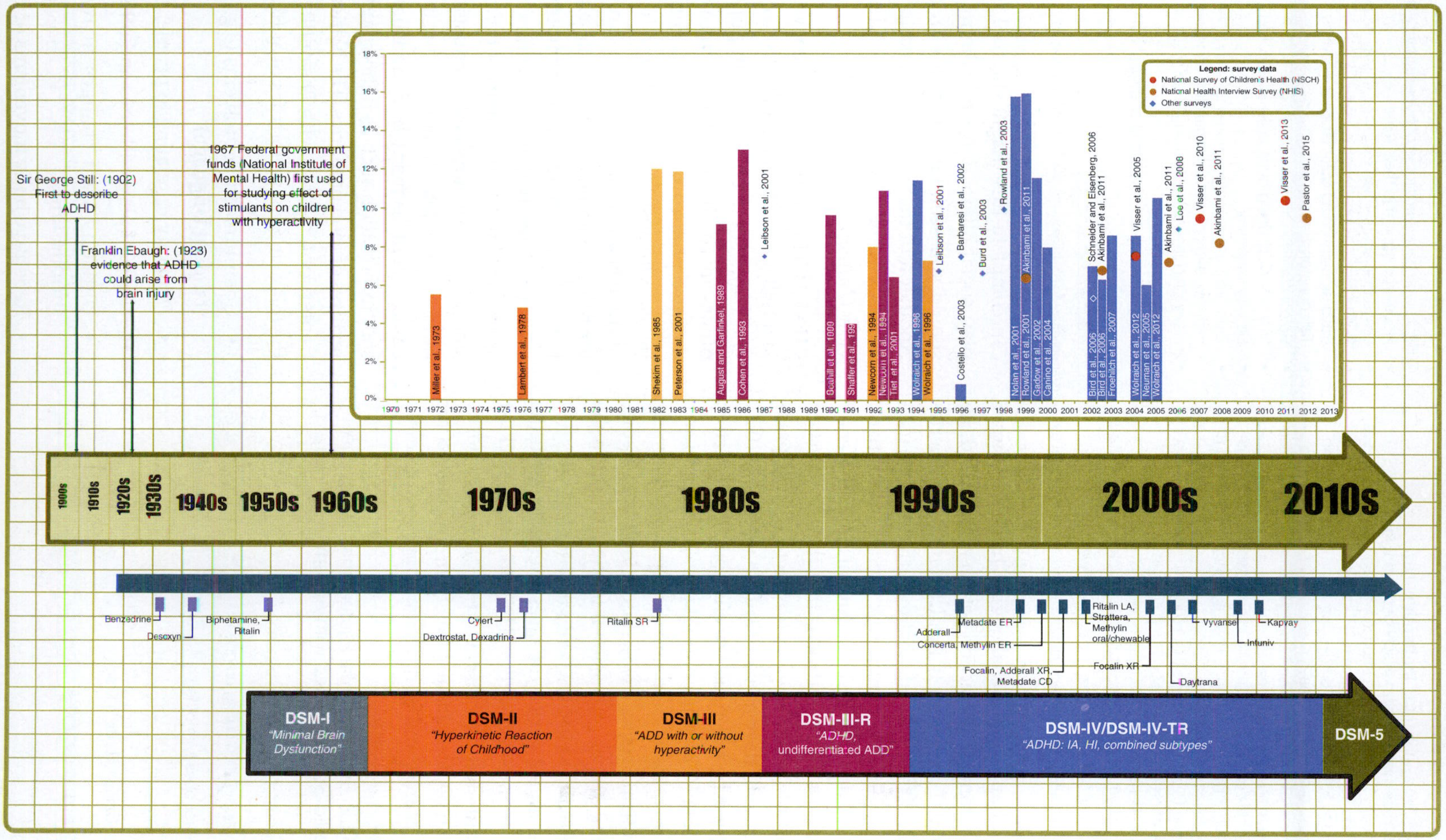

Table 10.1 ADHD Symptoms

Children who have symptoms of **inattention** may:	Children who have symptoms of **hyperactivity-impulsivity** may:
• Make careless mistakes across school or work tasks • Have difficulty with sustaining attention on play or task activities • Not seem to listen when spoken to • Be unable to follow through on directions and unable to finish schoolwork, duties, or chores • Have difficulty focusing attention on organizing and completing a task or learning something new • Have trouble completing or turning in homework assignments, often losing things (e.g., pencils, toys, assignments) needed to complete tasks or activities • Be unwilling to complete tasks that require an extensive amount of mental effort and time • Daydream, become easily confused, and move slowly • Have difficulty processing information as quickly and accurately as others	• Fidget and squirm in their seats • Leave their seats when expected to stay seated • Run or climb when inappropriate • Have difficulty doing quiet tasks or activities • Talk nonstop • Be constantly in motion • Have difficulty doing quiet tasks or activities • Be very impatient • Blurt out inappropriate comments, show their emotions without restraint, and act without regard for consequences • Have difficulty waiting for things they want or waiting their turns in games • Often interrupt conversations or others' activities

Source: National Institute of Mental Health, http://www.nimh.nih.gov/health/publications/attention-deficit-hyperactivity-disorder/index.shtml#pub2

indicate that autism is a challenging human disorder that occurs from an interaction between genes and the environment (LaSalle, 2013). Lyall, Schmidt, and Hertz-Picciotto (2014) also indicate that maternal lifestyle may be linked to environmental risk factors for autism. Furthermore, the National Institute of Environmental Health Sciences (2014) indicates that there are certain exposures to toxins in the environment during pregnancy that could have a link to autism (see Table 10.2). Caution must be taken, as the environmental factors listed in Table 10.2 alone are unlikely to cause autism.

Currently, there are no medical tests to diagnose autism (Autism Speaks, 2018). A developmental pediatrician is the proper professional to diagnose it. In the school districts, licensed school psychologists are also certified to give a variety of assessments to see if the child has an autism disorder. The Modified Checklist for Autism in Toddlers (M-CHAT-R™) is a diagnostic tool that can be downloaded free from the Internet for clinical, research, and educational purposes. Parents

can complete this diagnostic tool, which focuses on play, social interaction, and communication, but they should still seek an expert for an official diagnosis. Another tool that was developed to improve the test's accuracy is the M-CHAT-R/F™, the Follow Up Interview (Autism Speaks, 2018).

CHARACTERISTICS.   Children with autism will vary in intelligence, abilities, and behaviors.

While some children with autism do not speak, others might have limited language that includes repeated phrases. Children with autism often have difficulty with abstract concepts and have a limited range of interests. Lately TV shows such as the Good Doctor bring awareness to the social challenges faced by individuals with autism. It is important to note, however, the diversity that exists within the children on the spectrum. Some will be able to attend college (and possibly become doctors and scientists). Others will hold other types of jobs, if they are able and can tolerate the environment, as many have unusual responses to sensory information such as lights, loud noises, and some textures of food or fabrics. The National Dissemination Center for Children with Disabilities (2011) describes the following characteristics of autism:

Table 10.2 Environmental Factors that Researchers Believe Could Be Associated with Autism

Age of parents at the time of conception
Exposure to air pollution during pregnancy
Diabetes and/or obesity (mother)
Premature birth and low-birth weight
Oxygen deprivation to baby's brain
Parents' exposure to pesticides

Source: Autism Spectrum Disorder (National Institute of Environmental Health Sciences, 2014).

• Communication problems (e.g., using and understanding language)

• Difficulty in relating to people, objects, and events

• Unusual play with toys and other objects

• Difficulty with changes in routine or familiar surroundings

• Repetitive body movements or behavior patterns

Autism can be characterized by a broad range of behaviors, which has led diagnosticians to describe autism as a broad-spectrum disorder. This has resulted in the need for teachers and parents to recognize the differences in the needs of children, from mild to severe, depending on how their disability manifests itself (Hallahan, Kauffman, & Pullen, 2015).

RECOMMENDATIONS. Children with autism respond best in a predictable and consistent program. Public schools offer different types of programs including self-contained autistic units, life skills units, or inclusion. There are private schools that focus on applied behavior therapy based on the principles of Applied Behavior Analysis (ABA). Applied behavior analysis focuses on teaching functional skills with progress monitoring and applies emphasis on positive reinforcement (e.g. reward appropriate behavior) (Hallahan, Kauffman, & Pullen, 2015). A Google search will help you find schools in your area. Many professionals that work in such schools are Board Certified Behavior Analysts (BCBA®), which is a certification for individuals who want to be independent practitioners, and to practice principles of learning to address behavioral needs with individuals with autism and other developmental disabilities (Behavior Analyst Certification Board, 2018).

STRATEGIES.   There are several common strategies that teachers of children with autism use. Social Stories™ by Carol Gray is one such strategy. A Social Story helps to explain what to expect and the behaviors expected. There are many templates for Social Stories that can be purchased on the Internet. Autism Speaks uses PowerPoint to create Social Stories. Another strategy is the Picture Exchange Communication System (PECS®) that is used by many speech therapists and also by teachers. The PECS is an augmentative/alternative communication strategy that uses pictures.

This system has pictures that can be used in sentences for communication. The Premack principle, also known as "First and Then strategy," helps children complete specific tasks. For the "First and Then" strategy children are motivated to do a task first (that they may or may not enjoy) and then they get to do something they truly enjoy or like. The cards are easy to make, as you can see in Figure 10.4.

Learning Disabilities

The most common types of disabilities that often are not diagnosed are learning disabilities.

CHARACTERISTICS

1. Children with learning disabilities are primarily typically developing children. They are not chiefly visually impaired, hearing impaired, environmentally disadvantaged, mentally challenged, or emotionally disturbed. In spite of the fact that these children have adequate intelligence, adequate sensory processes, and adequate emotional stability, they do not learn without special assistance.

2. Children with learning disabilities show wide discrepancies in inter-individual and intra-individual differences in a profile of their development. Learning disabilities affect children in different ways. Some might have difficulties in math while others have difficulties in reading. In intra-individual differences it is often shown by marked discrepancies in one or more of the specific areas of academic learning or a serious lack of language development or language facility. These disabilities can affect the child's behavior in such areas as thinking, conceptualization, memory, language, perception, reading, writing, spelling, or arithmetic.

3. The concept of deviation of a child with learning disabilities implies that the child deviates so markedly from the norm of the child's group as to require specialized instruction. Such specialized instruction required for these children can be of value to other children. However, the population to be served with special education funds does not include children with learning problems that are the result of poor instruction or economic or cultural deprivation (Kearns, 1980).

4. Other characteristics include academic achievement problems in reading, written language, perceptual,

Figure 10.4 First and Then Strategy

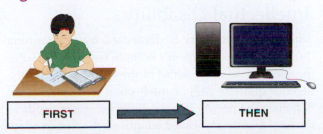

FIRST   →   THEN

perceptual-motor, memory, socio-emotional challenges, and lack of motivation (Hallahan, Kauffman, & Pullen, 2015).

SIGNS OF LEARNING DISABILITIES.   Learning disabilities are generally recognized when the child enters school and specific learning tasks are expected. There is no one sign that says that the child has a learning disability, but you can watch for the difference between what a child accomplishes in school and what that child should be able to do given the child's intellect and ability.

Silver and Hagin (2002) describe and discuss learning disorders, research, and the various curriculum designs used to help students develop. Planning for students requires an understanding of the factors that affect them, including cognitive, emotional, social, neuropsychological, and educational factors.

Identification of the problems that hinder a child's learning need to be analyzed by a specialist, but if a child has several of the following problems, the parent or teacher can assume the child has a learning disability. Clues include the following:

- May have trouble learning the alphabet, rhyming words, or connecting letters to their sounds.
- May make many mistakes when reading aloud, and repeat and pause often.
- May not understand what he or she reads.
- May have significant trouble with spelling.
- May have very messy handwriting or hold a pencil awkwardly.
- May struggle to express ideas in writing.
- May learn language late and have a limited vocabulary.
- May have trouble remembering the sounds that letters make or hearing slight differences between words.
- May have trouble understanding jokes, comic strips, and sarcasm.
- May have trouble following directions.
- May mispronounce words or use a wrong word that sounds similar.
- May have trouble organizing what he or she wants to say, or may not be able to think of the word he or she needs for writing or conversation.
- May not follow the social rules of conversation, such as taking turns, and may stand too close to the listener.
- May confuse math symbols and misread numbers.
- May not be able to retell a story in order (what happened first, second, or third).
- May not know where to begin a task or how to go on from there.

TIPS FOR TEACHERS AND PARENTS

1. Learn as much about learning disabilities as you can.
2. Observe the child playing and "working." Make note of progress the child has made and tell the child what you have seen. This helps confirm for the child that you know when he or she works hard or does well. Give positive feedback.
3. Recognize the child's strengths and interests. Find out how the child learns best. Give the child opportunities to use his or her talents and strengths.

TIPS FOR PARENTS

1. Give your child with learning disabilities the opportunity to excel or just enjoy activities outside the classroom, such as dancing, music, sports, or computers. Give your child opportunities to participate in areas of interest and/or talent. Encourage friendships with children whom they meet in these activities.
2. Help your child learn through areas of strengths. Talk with your child's teacher and observe for yourself how the child learns best. Establish a special place where the child can do homework and prioritize its importance.
3. Meet other parents who have children with learning disabilities. Share concerns and successes with others, as well as advice and emotional support.
4. Help develop an educational plan for your child with the school. Establish a positive working relationship and communicate regularly with your teacher, discuss questions, and exchange information about successes and progress (NICHCY, 2011).

Intellectual Disability

Intellectual Disability is diagnosed by determining (a) the ability of a person's brain to learn, think, solve problems, and make sense of the world (called intelligence quotient [IQ] or intellectual functioning); (b) whether the person has the skills he or she needs to live independently (called adaptive behavior, or adaptive functioning) (CPIR, 2017).

The average score of an IQ test is 100, and those classified as mentally challenged score 70 to 75 or below. To look at the skills needed to live independently, the child is compared to others of the same age. The adaptive skills are (a) daily living skills, such as dressing, using the bathroom, and feeding oneself; (b) communication skills—understanding what is said and being able to respond; and (c) social skills with adults, friends, and family (CPIR, 2017).

More than 425,000 children ages 3 through 21 with an intellectual disability have a need for special education. Seven percent of those who need special education have some form of intellectual disability (U.S. Department of Education, 2016).

TIPS FOR PARENTS

- Learn about intellectual disabilities in order to give your child the help he or she needs.
- Encourage your child to be independent, learning daily care skills such as dressing, grooming, eating, and using the bathroom.
- Give your child chores, but make each chore one in which she or he can be successful. Use them as teaching tools. For example, in setting the table, have the child count out the number of napkins. Give the child one task at a time, and help when assistance is needed.
- Praise, praise, praise when the child has worked hard and accomplished the task. Give feedback and build your child's abilities.
- Have your child join outside activities, such as scouts, sports, and recreational activities.
- Review the IEP and see how you can support your child's learning at home. Work with the school and your child's teacher. Apply what he or she is learning at school with activities at home and in the community.
- Volunteer in the classroom or in another classroom. See how the teachers work with the children. Contribute to the success of the class by cooperating with the teacher (CPIR, 2017).

Implications of Disabilities on Learning

For years, the popular philosophy has been that we can best motivate young people in pleasing and attractive settings. The lesson will stimulate interest, be fun, and be relevant to the learner. Because students enjoyed doing it, they would be willing to learn. This is an excellent theory, and there is no quarrel with its premise. However, we have produced some youths who have not met their potential because, in real life, work is not always pleasing, and for children with disabilities, it is even more of a challenge to achieve.

Work involves diligence, tenacity, endurance, sacrifice, discipline, and repetition. It requires deep concentration and dedication. Work is *not* always fun—it is often boring. Most of us spend our lives doing work. We are willing to make this sacrifice not only for the extrinsic values of status, income, and fringe benefits but also for the intrinsic values of self-worth, dignity, and contribution to society. It is important to help children identify the intrinsic value of what they are learning. It is important for teachers and parents to communicate explicitly with children how what they are learning relates to what is important to them. This will help establish a pattern of lifelong learning—a very valuable lesson indeed.

Children with disabilities often work harder and longer to accomplish what other children do easily and quickly. It is not always easy for them to accept this. It is hard for parents to refrain from expecting the school and the teacher to lighten the load, to expect less because the child has a disability. But this deprives children of the feeling of accomplishment, of striving for and reaching their full potential. The Individualized Education Program (IEP) provides for the appropriate level of accommodation. Use this tool effectively to ensure that all exceptional children are given the opportunity to reach their goals.

Just as the parent feels warmth and joy at the progress of a child with a disability, so will the professional whose help and guidance leads to better family relations, improved schoolwork, and an ability to participate in life more fully for the child with a disability. It is a worthy and mighty undertaking.

Students Who Are Gifted and Talented

Students who are gifted and talented have the potential for superior performance and excel in unique ways compared to other students of the same age. This can include intellectual achievement, special aptitudes, or creative thinking and performing abilities.

The Gifted and Talented Children's Education Act, P.L. 95-561, gave states and local education agencies financial incentives to identify and educate students who are gifted and talented, provide in-service training, and conduct research (Heward & Orlansky, 1988). None of the federal legislation has mandated educational opportunities for children who are gifted. Approximately 30 states mandate educational opportunities for youngsters who are gifted, and other states have legislation permitting establishment of such classes (Karnes & Marquardt, 1997).

The Jacob K. Javits Gifted and Talented Students Education Act of 1988 was followed by the Jacob K. Javits Gifted and Talented Education Act of 1992. In 1998, the Javits Act was the only federal funding earmarked for gifted education. Funding not earmarked for gifted education can still be used to benefit students who are gifted. In funding for children with disabilities, meeting the child's needs is required, but children with gifts and talents do not have legislation that requires support. The purpose of the federal acts is to encourage rich education for gifted and talented students and to have special programs broadened and expanded into the regular classroom (Boren, 1994).

According to the Council of State Directors of Programs for the Gifted, 50 states administer gifted and talented programs under special education or exceptional children divisions. Some may administer programs under curriculum and instruction, general education, or gifted-and-talented divisions. Twenty-one states provide funding for gifted children; however, most other states do not require school divisions to provide services to children with high abilities (Council of State Directors of Programs for the Gifted, 2018).

According to analysis by the Davidson Institute for Talent Development, more states are offering gifted education. These include the following:

- Four states mandated fully funded gifted programs: Florida, Georgia, Iowa, and Oklahoma.
- Twenty-four states mandated partially funded gifted programs: Alabama, Arkansas, Colorado, Hawaii, Idaho, Indiana, Kansas, Kentucky, Louisiana, Maine, Minnesota, Mississippi, Nebraska, Nevada, New Mexico, North Carolina, Ohio, South Carolina, Tennessee, Texas, Virginia, Washington, West Virginia, and Wisconsin.

- Nine states mandated gifted programs but had no gifted funding available: Alaska, Arizona, Delaware, Maryland, Montana, New Jersey, Oregon, Pennsylvania, and Rhode Island.
- Five states do not mandate gifted programs and are partially funded: California, Missouri, North Dakota, Utah, and Wyoming.
- Eight states and the District of Columbia do not mandate gifted programs and no gifted funding is available: Connecticut, District of Columbia, Illinois, Massachusetts, Michigan, New Hampshire, New York, South Dakota, and Vermont.

Each state makes its own decision on gifted education, but with the help of foundations and the Jacob K. Javits Gifted and Talented Students Education Act, there is an increase in gifted education. It continues to need support.

The increase of children that speak languages other than English in the education system has created a challenge for educators of gifted and talented children. Children who are second-language learners often are not included in gifted programs because educators might not know how to assess them. Appropriate testing tools, multiple sources of assessment information, and strong parental involvement are strategies that educators must use in order to fully meet the needs of gifted second-language learners (Council for Exceptional Children, 2001, 2003).

Resources for Families of Children with Disabilities

Parents of children with disabilities want to help their children be successful and get an education but sometimes feel overwhelmed by the challenges a child with special needs has. These are some statements I have heard parents of children with special needs say:

I don't know how to help my child.
I just want to make sure she gets an education.
His teacher says that he can do so much more if he could just focus.
I don't know who to talk to about his disability.
Is there someone who can help me?
I don't know what else to do.

Parents often rely on educators to assist them in how to best help their child by providing them with important information regarding their children's rights and those strategies they can use at home. The majority of parents of children with special needs are not familiar with special education programs and very often they have a variety of misconceptions. Teachers and administrators can create a different picture of special education from what it has been historically: that it can help children reach their full potential and increase their quality of life (Van Haren & Fiedler, 2008). Special education teachers can help parents navigate the overwhelming process of special education services. In order to do this, teachers need to believe in parents, exhibit patience and flexibility, and look at children and families from an asset-based perspective—one in which the family's funds of knowledge are valued. Additionally, teachers must learn to communicate with parents so that parents can effectively communicate with them. In other words, teachers can be a very important resource for families particularly if they know how to communicate effectively.

The following essay by a special education teacher in San Antonio, Texas shows her commitment to communicating and working with parents; she is a good resource for them. Her name is Lucía Martínez and she has been teaching children with special needs for 19 years.

Throughout my 19 years in teaching, I have learned that parents are the most important component of the team, when working with children. It is an even greater importance for children who have special needs. I have seen a large range of involvement from parents. Some parents appear to not be involved at all or do not have the time to be as involved as they would like. Some parents appear to be completely committed to participating in their child's education. Building a relationship with parents is crucial. They need to get to know you as a teacher and as a person. They need to know that teachers care about them and that they are not being judged. Good communication is the key to working with parents. I have learned to use all modes of communication, from making phone calls, writing notes, sending text messages, and making home visits. The most important thing I have learned when dealing with parents is to ask questions and not make assumptions. I have daily communication with parents. I have learned that parents are empowered when I take the time to teach them by modeling, writing about, or describing strategies that are working in the classroom. It is very effective when parents visit or volunteer in the classroom. They get hands-on training.

I would like parents to know they are the most important teachers in their child's life. They make a huge difference in the success of their child when they work with them at home and extend learning through play, everyday routines, consistency in routines, and use of vocabulary.

I would like parents to know that behavior can be shaped and changed through establishing rules and consequences at home.

Teachers also learn from the parents. I send home a reinforcer checklist with every student. Parents have a wealth of information for teachers. They need to share this information, as it helps their child at school. It is important for parents to tell teachers about situations that a child is going through, for example, when a parent starts working, a death in the family, illness, or even a change in sleeping or eating patterns. Effective teachers use parent strengths and build on them, just as with our students. I meet parents where they are, and help them to learn and grow because it is in the best interest of the child.

I have seen children progress and reach goals successfully when parents are involved and work in partnership with the teacher. It has made a big difference for many of my students. These students have been able to participate and function in inclusion and mainstream settings.

Lucía H. Martínez
San Antonio, Texas 2014

Special education teachers have the responsibility to teach and care for children regardless of the severity of the disability. Just as parents might seem frustrated, teachers also experience frustration as they navigate a system that can be full of paperwork in addition to meeting individual children's needs. See Jamie Teixeira's thoughts in the following essay. She has been a special education teacher for over 6 years in South Central Texas. She teaches special education because she likes working with the children and she can also empathize with the parents, which is something that helps her be a good resource for parents.

As a special education teacher and a parent of a child with autism, I have the benefit of understanding both sides. Similar to most parents, I am always worried about my daughter being treated properly and fairly. I also want to ensure that she is given all of the same opportunities that non-disabled students have. I in turn, provide my students with the same care and respect. Being responsible for someone else's child, more importantly a special needs student, is an enormous and extraordinary task. Unlike general education teachers, who stay in the comfort of their classrooms, special education teachers often "float" class to class, servicing various students with diverse disabilities in several different subject areas. One year, as an inclusion teacher, I was placed in 6th grade Math and Science, 7th grade English and Texas History, as well as a 6th grade math resource teacher. This was in addition to case-managing 15 students, which required me to be responsible for IEPs, modifications, attendance, grades, and referrals. Even so, special education teachers are often viewed as less significant to general education teachers and as a result, are regarded by the students and parents as a teacher's aide, rather than a certified teacher. To label us as less than equal demeans our profession and the students we service. I have been very fortunate to have some wonderful interactions with parents, but often my experiences have left me feeling frustrated, hurt, and discouraged. The most important suggestion I would give a parent with a special needs child is to never stop communicating with your child's teacher. I call frequently, visit my students often, handle a child's outburst then give them a shoulder to cry on because I truly care. Daily, special education teachers face different difficult obstacles with limited resources and support. Yet we still handle any situation that arises with genuine smiles, hope in our hearts, and caring love for every special needs student.

The Child Find Project

Concern about reaching parents and their children with disabilities resulted in the federal funding of the Child Find Project. In this program:

> All children with disabilities residing in the State, including children with disabilities attending private schools, regardless of the severity of their disabilities, and who are in need of special education and related services are identified, located, and evaluated and a practical method is developed and implemented to determine which children with disabilities are currently receiving needed special education and related services. (NICHCY, 1998; Smith, 2005)

Child Find is designed to locate children with disabilities using any feasible methods available, such as door-to-door surveys, media campaigns, dissemination of information from the schools, and home visits by staff and/or volunteers (Cook et al., 2004; Lerner, Mardell-Czudnowski, & Goldenberg, 1987).

Table 10.3 summarizes the special education process starting from Child Find or other referrals to the placement and evaluation team meeting.

In recent years, other names such as *Count Your Kid In* and *Make a Difference* have been used to designate this type of program. In many cases, this program is funded by both federal and state governments. Preschool screenings have been very successful in finding children in need and informing parents that help is available.

EVALUATION. When parents believe that their child needs special assistance, or if a child is identified through Child Find, the subsequent evaluations must

Table 10.3 A Summary of the Special Education Process

Child Find/Referral	Referral of child for diagnosis may be formal or informal; may come from parent or from others.
Assessment/Diagnosis	Multidisciplinary, non-biased comprehensive battery of tests. (Complete re-evaluation for classification required every 3 years.)
Classification (includes parent)	Team reviews assessment/diagnostic data and classifies for special education based on test results. Parent signature required.
IEP Meeting (includes parent)	Individualized Education Program developed by team. Must be updated yearly, but team or parent may request as needed. Parent signature required.
Placement (includes parent)	Team decides placement based on the IEP. Parent signature required.
Evaluation Team Meeting	Team evaluates child's total special education program and progress at least yearly. (Teacher evaluates daily as child works on short-term objectives.)

be evaluated in a fair and unbiased manner. Parents must be informed and must give their consent to have the original evaluation.

For initial evaluations:

- Notice must be provided to evaluate a child, and informed consent of parents must be obtained.
- No single procedure shall be the sole criterion for determining eligibility.
- The child must be assessed in all areas of suspected disabilities.
- Determination of eligibility shall be made by a team of qualified professionals and the child's parents. Children are not eligible if the only deciding factor is a limited English proficiency or a lack of math or reading instruction (National Association of State Directors of Special Education, 1997; Turnbull, Turnbull, & Wehmeyer, (2007)).

Figure 10.5 illustrates the special education cycle. A good resource to share with parents is the *The Everything Parent's Guide to Special Education: A Complete Step-by-Step Guide to Advocating for Your Child with Special Needs* by Amanda Morin (2014). This book provides parents with guidelines that are easy to follow regarding special education and how to advocate for their children.

The phrase *infant or toddler with a disability* means any child under 3 who needs early intervention services because the child is at risk of substantial developmental delays if intervention is not provided to the child. The areas of delay can be in cognitive development, physical development, communicative development, social or emotional development, adaptive development, or a diagnosed physical or mental condition that would probably cause developmental delay (National Association of State Directors of Special Education, 1997).

Conditions that are associated with significant delays in development include the following:

- Chromosomal conditions (such as Down syndrome, Fragile X)
- Congenital syndromes or conditions (such as spina bifida)
- Sensory impairments (such as hearing or visual impairments)
- Metabolic disorders (such as PKU or lactic acidosis)
- Prenatal and/or perinatal infections or conditions (such as AIDS, CMV, or exposure to toxic substances)
- Significant medical problems (such as cerebral palsy)
- Low birthweight (less than 1,200 grams, or 2 lb. 10 oz.)
- Postnatal conditions (such as attachment disorder) (Hallahan, Kauffman, & Pullen, 2015; Colorado Department of Education, Early Childhood Initiatives, The Arapahoe Early Childhood Network, PEAK Parent Center, The Colorado Consortium of Intensive Care Nurseries, 1997)

REACHING INFANTS AND TODDLERS WITH DISABILITIES. The importance of development while a child is an infant or a toddler is increasingly recognized. Recently developed brain-scan techniques have made it possible to see how synapses and connections develop during the first years of life. If this is a critical time for children without disabilities, one can immediately recognize how important it is for a child with a disability. This is a period in which great change and intervention become crucial (Bruder, 2010).

Figure 10.5 The Special Education Cycle

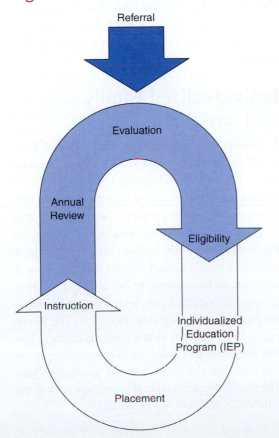

Child Find is one method of reaching parents of infants or toddlers with disabilities. Health agencies, doctors, visiting nurses, and hospitals are important sources in finding infants who need services.

Part C of IDEA 97 and 2004

Part C of the Individuals with Disabilities Education Act Amendments of 1997 and 2004 focuses on infants and toddlers with disabilities, ages birth to age three or "zero to three." An at-risk infant or toddler is an individual younger than 3 who would be at risk of experiencing substantial developmental delay if early intervention services were not provided to the individual.

Each state sets up its own program, but the program is expected to have the following:

- A comprehensive child-find system, including a system to make referrals to service providers.

- An Individualized Family Service Plan, including family-centered services and service coordination.

- A comprehensive, multidisciplinary evaluation of the infant or toddler with a disability.

- A family-directed identification of the needs of each family with an at-risk infant or toddler to assist the child's development.

- A public-awareness program that focuses on early identification of infants and toddlers with disabilities. This emphasizes that hospitals and physicians need to be provided with information about the services so parents will know about their availability.

- A comprehensive system of personnel development. Qualified personnel include special educators, speech–language pathologists and audiologists, occupational therapists, physical therapists, psychologists, social workers, nurses, nutritionists, family therapists, orientation and mobility specialists, and pediatricians and other types of physicians. Part C also includes the training of paraprofessionals and primary referral sources—recruitment and retention of early education service providers; early intervention providers, fully and appropriately qualified to provide early intervention; personnel to work in rural and inner-city areas; and personnel to coordinate transition services for infants and toddlers to preschool or other

Children with Down syndrome can live independent and productive lives with the support of their families.

appropriate services. Nothing prohibits the use of paraprofessionals and assistants who are appropriately trained and supervised, and states were given three years to develop the qualified staff.

Part C also requires states to provide early intervention services in the child's natural environment including the home and community-based settings with and without children with disabilities (Turnbull et al., 2014). These services are provided at no cost to families, except where federal or state law provides for a system of payment by families, including a schedule of sliding fees.

The Individualized Family Service Plan (IFSP)

The Individualized Family Service Plan (IFSP) differs from the IEP in format because it is designed to focus on programs for infants and young children. IDEA 97 and 2004 place preschoolers under the school system and do not differentiate between preschooler programs and elementary and secondary programs, which leaves the IEP as the format to decide on the child's program. If it appears that a family would benefit from services, it seems appropriate to continue to use the IFSP for that family as was indicated in previous IDEA legislation. Each state can make its own determination. The intent is the same—to serve individuals with disabilities. The IFSP gives attention to family concerns and needs, as well as services for the child. Federal guidelines also require the family be involved in the development of the IFSP (Hallahan, Kauffman, & Pullen, 2015).

The IFSP is designed to be flexible, family-focused, and unintrusive for families. It includes the following elements:

- A statement of the infant's or toddler's present levels of attainment in physical or motor, sensory, cognitive, communication, psychosocial, and adaptive behavior. The law requires that this statement be based on objective criteria acceptable to both parent and provider.

- A statement of the family's resources, priorities, and concerns related to enhancing the development of the child with special needs and/or related to broader family issues.

- A statement of the major outcomes expected for the child and family. This includes how, when, and methods the team will use to evaluate whether progress is being made and whether changes or updates in outcomes or services are needed.

- A statement of specific supports and services necessary to meet the unique strengths and needs of the infant/toddler and family, including options and a variety of all community supports and services available.

- A statement describing the environments in which services will be provided, and the location of services.

- Dates when services will start and how long services will be used.

- The name of the service coordinator. This person is responsible for seeing that the IFSP is carried out and for coordinating the process among all involved parties.

- The steps to be taken to support the child's transition to home, community, or preschool services, if appropriate.

- Parents or legal guardian must provide written consent to the IFSP (Hallahan, Kauffman, & Pullen, 2015).

The IFSP is evaluated once a year, and the family is given a review of the plan at six-month intervals, or more often if appropriate, based on the infant's and family's need.

A number of states have established statewide mandated forms for IFSPs. Examples of these forms, and guidance for completing them, can be found at the Early Childhood Technical Assistance Center. There are many commonalities between the states, but there are also a few specific individual differences.

Procedural Rights for Infants and Toddlers

Each state has flexibility in how it sets up Part C for Infants and Toddlers, IDEA 97, and 2004. Most programs should have the following components.

First, a program should have *multidisciplinary evaluations*. A team consisting of the family and two or more qualified professionals looks at how the child is doing in physical or motor, sensory, cognitive, communication, social-emotional, and adaptive development. This evaluation is the procedure used to determine initial and continuing eligibility for services. Evaluations are provided at no cost to the parent.

Second, an *Individualized Family Service Plan* (IFSP) is needed, consisting of a team of people, including family members, who jointly plan supports and services and identify resources that will meet the family's concerns and priorities about the child's development. This plan is documented. A *transition plan* for the child's dismissal is also included in the IFSP at least 90 days before the child's third birthday.

Other components include a *service coordinator* who works with the family to identify resources, supports, and services and coordinates agencies and people involved. Parents are given *prior written notice* about any changes that service providers want to make, and parents are given the chance to approve or reject those changes.

Information, both written and spoken, will be given in the child's native language or, if that is impossible, will be translated orally or by another mode of communication so parents understand the information. Native language refers to the language routinely used by the parents of the child. Qualified personnel will determine whether it is developmentally appropriate to use the language normally used by the child when conducting evaluations. Parents have the right to accept or deny service and must have *informed consent*. *Confidentiality* is ensured by keeping private any information about the child and the family. Parents will have *access to records* with the ability to change incorrect information.

Support and services are provided in a *natural environment,* the environment typically used for children who are the same age but do not have disabilities. Parents will also have *access to services,* helped by the service coordinator.

Parents can use an *appeals process* to resolve any disagreements they have with providers. The appeals process can involve mediation and due process. Finally, *mediation* will be used to find a solution satisfactory to all involved in the dispute. Due process is employed in resolving complaints (Colorado Department of Education et al., 1997).

Children with Disabilities in Head Start and Childcare

In 1974, with the passage of the Community Services Act (P.L. 96-644), Congress stipulated that 10 percent of Head Start's enrollment must be children with disabilities. Head Start developed procedures and policies to answer the needs of these children by offering individualized and appropriate education. When Early Head Start was initiated, the same requirement for 10 percent enrollment of children with disabilities was mandated for that program.

The Local Education Agency (LEA) is responsible for ensuring that services are provided to children with disabilities from birth to 21 years of age, but it is not responsible for providing all services. IDEA's policy is to ensure that all children with disabilities, beginning as soon as diagnosed for infants and toddlers and continuing through age 21, have the right to a free appropriate education in either public or private institutions. This includes Early Head Start, Head Start, and private childcare facilities. Early Head Start and Head Start facilities were directed to use IDEA's definition of children with disabilities.

The coordinator of services for children with disabilities must have a plan containing the following: (a) procedures for timely screening; (b) procedures for making referrals to the LEA for evaluation; (c) procedures to determine whether there is a need for special education and related services for a child as early as the child's third birthday; (d) provisions to ensure accessibility of the facilities and appropriate special furniture, equipment, and materials as needed; and (e) the transition of children from Early Head Start to Head Start or into other appropriate preschool program placements.

The Early Head Start and Head Start's service delivery plans must include options to meet the needs and take into consideration the strengths of each child based upon the IFSP or IEP so that a continuum of services available from various agencies is considered.

Eligibility requirements are similar to those cited in the discussion of IDEA 2004, with the addition of developmental delays. These include health impairment, hearing impairment, orthopedic impairment, visual impairment (including blindness), learning disabilities, autism, and traumatic brain injury. The developmental delays are in physical development, cognitive development, communicative development, socioemotional development, or adaptive development, as discussed in IDEA 97 and 2004's Part C for Infants and Toddlers.

Early Head Start and Head Start and Parents

The Early Head Start and Head Start staff must do the following ten things:

1. Support parents of children with disabilities.

2. Provide information to parents on how to foster their child's development.

3. Provide opportunities for parents to observe large-group, small-group, and individual activities described in their child's IFSP or IEP.

4. Provide follow-up assistance and activities to reinforce program activities at home.

5. Refer parents to groups of parents of children with similar disabilities who can provide peer support.

6. Inform parents of their rights under IDEA.

7. Inform parents of resources that might be available from the Supplemental Security Income (SSI) Program; the Early Periodic Screening, Diagnosis, and Treatment (EPSDT) Program; and other sources, as well as assist them with initial efforts to access such resources.

8. Identify needs (caused by the disability) of siblings and other family members.

9. Provide information that might help prevent disabilities among younger siblings.

10. Build parents' confidence, skill, and knowledge in accessing resources and advocating to meet the needs of their children (Federal Register, 1993).

SpecialQuest

In 1997, SpecialQuest, a partnership between the Hilton Foundation and Early and Migrant Head Start programs, was begun. It is the first public/private partnership with the Administration for Children, Youth, and Families. This partnership was established to improve services to infants and toddlers with disabilities by an intensive team-based program with on-site support to implement new learning strategies. From 1997 to 2004, in an effort to include Early Head Start administrators, teachers, early intervention specialists, parents, and community members, 250 teams of service providers met at four-year intervals to receive training, develop plans, and monitor improvements to the service-delivery systems in their respective communities.

In February 2004, the Conrad Hilton Foundation was given an award by the Administration for Children, Youth, and Families (ACF) for its contribution to infants and toddlers (ACF Press Office, 2004).

From 2004 to 2007, 263 SpecialQuest teams and 128 Learning Coaches exposed their work to 100,214 individuals that did not attend trainings. The growth of SpecialQuest was evident across the nation and findings demonstrated that more infants and toddlers with disabilities were enrolled, targeted practices towards inclusion were increased, and families and staff reported an increase of knowledge and skills including becoming informed decision makers (Special Quest, 2008).

Funding for this project ended in 2010. SpecialQuest operates under the Napa County Office of Education in collaboration with the Frank Porter Graham Child Development Center at Chapel Hill.

Rights and Services Available to Families

Many parents of children with exceptionalities are unaware of the rights they have and the services available to them. The Buckley Amendment (Family Educational Rights and Privacy Act or FERPA) is a right for all parents, but it is especially important for parents who have children with disabilities.

Filing a complaint of discrimination for children with disabilities can help advocate for those who need it the most. If parents and friends of the disabled do not stand up for these rights, they will be lost. Whenever discrimination occurs, it hurts not just the people involved but our nation as well. Complaints should be directed first to the person in charge. If a satisfactory conclusion is not reached, take the complaint to the next highest level of responsibility. Follow the chain of command. If this is not satisfactory, contact the regional Office of Civil Rights (OCR) for your area. The complaint can be filed by mail or through their OCR Complaint portal online. The following items are important to include in a complaint:

- Your name
- Full address
- Telephone numbers (include area code)
- E-mail address (if available)
- Name, full address, and telephone number of the person, agency, or organization you believe discriminated against you
- A brief description of what happened, including how, why, and when you believe your (or someone else's) civil rights were violated
- Any other relevant information
- Your signature and date of complaint
- The name of the person on whose behalf you are filing if you are filing a complaint for someone else

  You may also include:

- Any special accommodations for us to communicate with you about this complaint
- Contact information for someone who can help us reach you if we cannot reach you directly
- If you have filed your complaint somewhere else and where you've filed (Office of Civil Rights, 2018)

Each state has Parent Training and Information Centers that provide training and information to parents of children with disabilities. A directory is listed on *Exceptional Parent Magazine*'s web site.

Inclusive Family–School Partnerships

Helping Young Children Develop

Developmental delays need special consideration, but very young special-needs children in particular benefit from a nurturing and responsive home or childcare center. Children ages 3 to 5 should attend a good, developmentally appropriate class that has supplemental intervention that meets the needs of each child. They need an appropriate nurturing environment where language, movement, creativity, and discovery support their physical, socioemotional, and cognitive development. Individual concerns for such things as autism, Fragile X, and Down syndrome need to be addressed in relation to appropriate intervention. Because there is not enough space in this text to include all the information and recommendations, care providers should contact the Special Education Early Childhood program and the parent center for children with disabilities in their home state. The Center for Parent Information and Resources, formerly referred to as The National Dissemination Center for Children with Disabilities (NICHCY), furnishes information on each area of the child's disability and can also furnish the names of other references.

COMMUNICATE WITH THE CHILD. Communication is how children learn their language, and they must be given opportunities to practice that skill across multiple settings. Talk naturally so the child can understand and develop language. When your child talks, listen. How do you feel when you talk to someone who will not listen to what you are saying? Most adults don't waste time talking to people who do not listen to them. Children don't either. If you want your children to develop skills to appropriately express themselves, let them initiate conversations and respond by giving them your attention.

GIVE PRAISE AND ENCOURAGEMENT. Praise can have a powerful effect on a child. Praise reinforces learning and behaviors, and encouragement helps children continue working. Let children know when you are pleased with what they are doing. We all work for rewards, and praise is one of the most important rewards you can give. Be patient with children. It takes many trials and many errors to learn skills. Encouragement emphasizes effort and helps build self-esteem and confidence. Adults forget over the years how it was to be a child. If the situation gets out of hand and you become impatient or angry, reset by leaving the situation, do something else, and come back to it when you are in control of yourself.

NEVER COMPARE. Don't compare your children with others. Allow for individuality. Every child is exceptional and has unique characteristics that make up his or her personality and no one else's. No two children are every the same and will have different talents, interests, and strengths. Stress, anxiety, and low self-esteem are just some of the negative effects from comparing your child to other children. As an alternative, praise the child's strengths on the tasks he or she performs well, always support your child, and encourage him or her to do their best.

OFFER ENRICHMENT ACTIVITIES. Help increase your children's knowledge by taking them to places such as zoos, libraries, or airports. Use television as a learning tool by selecting appropriate programs, viewing them together, and discussing them afterward. Another learning experience that is often overlooked is the family mealtime. Sharing experiences, talking about interesting subjects, and improving conversational skills can happen around the dining table. Using digital tablets with educational apps helps children with the development of a variety of academic, language, and social skills.

ENCOURAGE PLAY. Play is as important for children with disabilities as it is for children without. It is especially important for children who are deaf or blind. These disabilities do not interfere with the natural phenomenon of learning about the world and growing and developing while doing so. Activities that are appropriate for normal babies are appropriate for the infant with disabilities, too. Clapping hands, cooing, singing, playing peekaboo, and cuddling are not only helpful but necessary. Provide the baby or small child with tactile objects to grasp. Firm cushions can be used for crawling babies. Rock children back and forth or play with them on a swing so they will have the same experiences needed to develop as other children. Babies and small children must have the opportunity to think, experiment, investigate, and learn about their environment. Of course, infants should never be left unsupervised.

READ AND TALK TOGETHER. Read to your children, have them read to you, and listen to them read. Let them tell you about what they have been reading. Magazines, newspapers, comics, and books can all be used to increase a child's knowledge and reading ability.

For school-age children add the following:

Develop Good Work Habits. Set the stage for good homework habits. A well-lighted place to study that is quiet, with room for books, pencils, and papers, helps. Schedule regular home study.

Get Sufficient Rest. Set a bedtime and stick to it. Children need a lot of rest to be able to do good mental work. Rest is necessary for proper growth.

Attend School Regularly. See that your child attends school regularly and on time. Regularly visit with teachers to learn how your child is getting along in school and listen to what they have to tell you about your child. It would be helpful if you keep a hard copy of the school's calendar to keep track of school days and holiday breaks.

Families Assisting Children at Home

For teachers and parents alike, the goal is to have all children reach their full potential. Students with disabilities might need extra help at home to keep up their schoolwork. Special tutoring by someone outside the family might be very effective. If the parents are planning to work with their child, the following suggestions should help guide them.

KNOW YOUR CHILD. You are your child's first teacher and often know better about his or her abilities than anyone else. Communicate your hopes, long term goals, and plans to your child's teacher.

ACTIVELY PARTICIPATE IN YOUR CHILD'S SCHOOL INCLUDING CAMPUS ACTIVITIES AND FIELD TRIPS. Treat all students and other members of the school community with respect (Educational Resources Information Center, 1996). Develop relationships and networks with the other families in your child's classroom.

CONDUCT AN INITIAL VISIT WITH THE TEACHER. Explain that you want to help increase your child's abilities at home by being notified on the latest curricular topics. Suggest how you can assist with your child's schoolwork. Ask the teacher to explain the material the class will be covering and how assignments should be done. Try to get a schedule for assignments if your child doesn't already have one.

SET A DEFINITE WORK TIME FOR THE CHILD. Set a time to work with your child at home. Go over the day's experiences including the topics he or she learned, and listen to how your child felt about her or his experiences in the classroom. Reinforce the expectations while at school including how assignments can be completed and turned in on time.

MONITOR PROGRESS. Keep a record of your child's progress including the assignments that are handed in and the scores received, so you have a record of how your child is doing in school. If the grades are low or you do not understand them, visit with the teacher to find out exactly the teacher's expectations of the children.

PROMOTE SUCCESS. Your child will be more likely to succeed in a home–school collaboration if you do the following:

- Use a pleasant, firm approach that says, "Yes, this must be done, and we will do it as quickly and pleasantly as we can."

- Set up a token economy reward system. Few of us will work hard at a job we do not receive satisfaction from or get paid for. Your praise and approval are your children's pay for a job well done. If they get scolded all the time, they are unlikely to want to work for another scolding.

- Make sure your child has time for work, play, and rest. There must be some work, play, and rest in everyone's life. If we do too much of one, the other two will suffer. Parents are the best ones to determine how to keep this balance.

Parents can be the most important force in seeking the correct educational placement for their children. It is important they be aware of the various ways their children can be served. Different labels for placement can exist in different regions. The *interrelated classroom* is a popular term for a classroom in which children are placed according to their level of academic achievement rather than according to their diagnosed disabilities.

Inclusive Family Engagement

In addition to an advocacy role, parents should also take an active role in the education of their children. Parent involvement in the classroom is an asset that is often overlooked or mismanaged. The parent is involved in planning the IEP and has the right of input and due process. Although parents are aware of these rights, many probably do not feel self-assured enough to fully capitalize on them. They rely on the teacher, the administrator, or the psychologist to keep them informed of what they, as parents, should be doing. Many parents believe the teacher, or some other person in an authority role, knows what is best and that it is up to that person to decide whether the parent can be of assistance. The counterpart is the teacher who fears parent involvement, perhaps because of misconceptions or a bad experience. Thus, there can be a lack of communication or overt action that prevents application of an influential force—the parents—for the education of the student with disabilities. Many families of children with disabilities cannot participate in the typical activities for different reasons. The school, however, needs to find ways to include families within the scheduled school events. The following include suggestions for successful inclusive partnerships:

- *Parent Teacher Association (PTA) meetings.* Include families by providing care for children with special needs. Invite local organizations or university teacher preparation programs to volunteer to help families during PTA meetings. Create a SEPTA (Special Education Parent Teacher Association) or a chapter within the existing PTA (Parent Teacher Association, 2014).

- *Reverse volunteer group.* Recruit other families to volunteer for special education classrooms for school events such as fundraisers, carnivals, talent shows, and so on. Invite families from the inclusion classrooms to help out the special education classroom.

- *Special highlights.* Include news about special needs children on the school's website or Facebook page, in its newsletter, or through Twitter—for example, when children attend the Special Olympics or they go on a field trip. Highlight the special academic projects that the children with special needs participate in so that their progress is valued.

- *Inclusive committee membership.* Ensure that families of children with special needs are included in committees so that the children's voices are always acknowledged and represented in school matters.

- *Workshops and seminars.* Special guest speakers for workshops and seminars should always include children with special needs in their presentation. This should be part of the mission of the school.

How Families Can Support Children's Schoolwork at Home

Parents may find that a digital voice recorder is one of the most valuable instruments available to help the student learn at home or at school. With a digital recorder, parents can put exactly what they want in a lesson and determine its format. A set of headphones further enhances the learning situation.

The digital recorder is excellent for recording spelling words and for having children practice taking spelling tests as they would in a classroom. If the children can read the words, have them record the words on the recorder and use them as in a spelling lesson. When the students listen to the words, they automatically monitor the sound of the word, the inflection, and the phrasing. Corrections are made unconsciously as the mind corrects errors that the ear hears.

Another important use is letting children record a reading lesson on the recorder and then asking them to correct their own errors. A chart of the time, number of words read, and errors made can be kept to show progress.

The digital recorder that records video can also be valuable for recording a model of a lesson or giving instructions for a task or activity. Instructions on how to set a table, tie shoelaces, or make a bed can be recorded to give a child valuable experience in learning to follow directions.

SUGGESTIONS FOR DIGITAL LESSONS

- Make the length of your lesson five minutes shorter than the period you want the lesson to last. This gives flexibility for handling interruptions.

- Arrange the tasks sequentially. Check the order by doing the lesson once yourself.

- Speak more slowly than your normal rate of speech. Children with learning disabilities do not process words and thoughts as quickly as most people do. The same applies to children with developmental delays, autism, and intellectual disabilities. Check to see if children know what the recorder is saying by asking them to repeat what they hear. Be careful not to ask if they understand the information. They might think they do, but testing might reveal they don't.

- When the child successfully completes a task or activity, provide him or her with praise and/or a tangible reward, if appropriate.

- Include a set of questions at the end of the recorded lesson for immediate review of the material. (This is also helpful for the teacher with students who have missed reading lessons or lectures.)

- Monitor the child's progress.

A Few Things to Remember

When working with children with special abilities, teachers and parents should follow these suggestions:

- Model best way for children to respond to questions.
- Use formal assessments as learning instruments. More learning takes place when tests are answered and corrected soon after being given.
- Learning occurs more effectively when more channels of learning are involved. Involving the visual and hearing channels is more effective than involving just vision or just hearing.
- Putting what has been learned into action through verbal or physical reaction increases the learning experience.
- Learning is reinforced by repetition, reviewing often at first and then again at varying intervals.
- Begin with concrete items and move gradually to teaching abstract concepts. Many children with disabilities do not learn by observation so adults will have to model expectations and show picture icons. Make sure to model expectations for children that need to learn by observing before they can internalize expectations.
- Ask the child to help make a "to-do" list so the child begins to practice organizing what needs to be done and the most efficient order in which to do them. The child can dictate them or record them if writing is a problem. Checking off completed tasks is very rewarding.
- Color-code folders at home and school to help children organize their materials: homework, worksheets, notes, and so forth. Make sure to put the folders in the same place so children can consistently get and put their materials away.
- Establish a consistent schedule so children can pace themselves and can anticipate how much time it takes to complete tasks. Time management is an issue whether a child has disabilities or not. Help the child become aware of time spent doing tasks by using a clock or egg timer.
- Children with disabilities, like all children, need downtime. It is important to plan unstructured time that allows the child to make constructive leisure choices. Life is about balancing needs, and an overworked child will be resentful and unproductive. Children should be encouraged to work hard and play hard.

The Importance of Communication Between Families and Professionals

Teachers may be confronted with dispirited parents experiencing considerable doubt, confusion, and anxiety about their child with a disability and their reactions to the child. A troubled parent may enlist the help of a teacher to discuss problems that are related to a child's performance at school or about other, more personal concerns regarding the child. A parent's inability to cope effectively with a child is often a motivating factor in seeking help (Seligman, 2000, p. 9).

Parents react differently and sometimes unpredictably to the birth or the diagnosis of a child with a disability. Reactions are a result of feelings. Parents can experience frustration, hurt, fear, guilt, disappointment, ambivalence, or despair. For the professional to work effectively with parents of children with disabilities, there must be an ability to recognize these feelings and a willingness to honor them (Chinn, 1984; Chinn et al., 1978). It takes skill, tact, and ingenuity for a professional to communicate with people who have children with different needs. It is also very important to choose the best words to assist in conveying an understanding of parents' feelings. Mistakes to avoid include "talking down" to the parents, assuming an understanding exists where in fact none does, and using jargon or technical language. People First Language (Clarke, Embury, Knight, & Christensen, 2017).) offers suggestions for phrases and terms that can facilitate lines of communication and it's a positive way to highlight the person first rather than the disability.

Parents of a child with a severe disability or an intellectual disability can be faced with a lifetime of caring for the child. There is a need to offer parents relief from the constant care that is often required. Foster parents, substitute grandparents, and knowledgeable volunteers are becoming more available to give these parents helpful breaks (Chinn, 1984; Chinn et al., 1978). Respite care is another way to provide relief for parents.

Parents are receptive to open and direct communication. Messages should be clear and in language the parents can understand. The teacher or professional will deal with a wide variation in language efficiency, so they should acquaint themselves with the parents' backgrounds. Listen to the words parents use to guide how to best communicate information about their child. The professional should also be receptive to clues from the parents to determine if the message is being received and accommodated as intended. Ask a leading question to let the parents express their understanding of the topic being discussed. You might be surprised to find the interpretations are different from what you intended.

The professional should include the support and consultation of the medical and theological professions if the parents exhibit a need for these services. Be aware of the agencies and organizations that assist parents and professional workers in the community, as well as national organizations.

Ways to Reach Parents

DAILY COMMUNICATION LOG. Use a form like the one in Figure 10.6 to let the parents know how their child performed in school on a daily basis. The teacher can provide feedback for the parent by writing comments of great things and challenges that faced the child. This is a good way to also keep a record of the progress of the child for later use because it has a space not only for instructional information but also for behavioral information.

NEWSLETTERS. Implement a monthly newsletter to document upcoming school events and field trips. Newsletters are also a great way to offer tips for parents. There are things that all parents can do to help their children in school that are important to parents of children both with disabilities and without.

LETTERS AND E-MAIL. Letters are another effective means of communicating an idea or message to parents. Letters should state the concern, then present methods or suggestions for dealing with or changing the situation, include any guidelines or datelines that are pertinent, and finally, end with a conclusion and an offer for assistance if needed. If parents have access to a computer and have an e-mail account, they can readily communicate with their child's teacher without exceptional effort. Teachers in return can keep the parent informed by simply sending an e-mail with pertinent information.

FACEBOOK AND TWITTER. The use of Facebook and Twitter should be done carefully by special education teachers because there is a great amount of confidential information that should not be shared with the general public. Teachers might want to create a classroom website that offers parents an opportunity to look at the information teachers need to share, such

as suggested activities, homework, and reading lists, among others, and also perhaps a blog where parents can communicate with one another and share ideas. Technology can enable parents of children with special needs to share resources to help one another help their children.

There are as many ways to write the message you wish to convey as there are teachers. Each will need to adapt the contents to the concerns of the situation.

Family Perceptions of Special Abilities

It is important for professionals to understand how families perceive having a child with special abilities, the impact it has on the family, and the unique ways each family deals with it. This is important as teachers and schools begin to create partnerships. Research has suggested that parents go through psychological stages after learning their child is diagnosed with a disability. The stages include denial, blame, fear, guilt, grief, withdrawal, rejection, and acceptance as the last stage. Parents might experience some or all of these stages at one point in time. Grief, loss, and guilt are the most reported reactions by parents (Goldman, 2013). The usual progression to acceptance can vary, but most parents experience guilt and grief before they reach acceptance and compassion.

PARENTS' INITIAL RESPONSE

Denial. Parents who deny the existence of a child's disability feel threatened. Their security is uncertain, and they are defending their egos or self-concepts. This is a difficult reaction for the professional to deal with. Time, patience, and support will help these parents see that much can be gained through helping children with disabilities realize their potential. Parents in denial might also make excuses for their child's delays or deficits because of their lack of acceptance of his or her disability.

Projection of Blame. A common reaction is to blame the situation on something or someone else—the psychologist, the teacher, the doctor. Often parents' statements begin with "If only . . ." Feelings of doubt about what caused the child's disability further lead parents to speculate that they are to blame. Again, patience, willingness to listen to the parent, and tact will help the professional deal with a potentially hostile situation.

Figure 10.6 An Example of a Teacher's Daily Log

Daily Log

Student: *Rodrigo*   Teacher: *Mrs. Acosta*

Date: *1-7-19*   Teaching Assistant: *Mr. Jones*

Instructional

Workstations	On task	hand/hand	constantly redirected
Sensory	☑	☐	☐
Vocational	☑	☐	☐
P.E.	☐	☐	☑
Library	☐	☐	☑
Music	☐	☐	☑
Math	☑	☐	☐
Reading	☑	☐	☐
Language Arts	☐	☑	☐
Science	☐	☑	☐
Social Studies	☐	☑	☐

Comments: *Good job in math!*

Breakfast

Ate Well	☐
Ate Little	☑
Did Not Eat	☐

Comments:

Rodrigo drank half of his Pediasure

Lunch

Ate Well	☑
Ate Little	☐
Did Not Eat	☐

Comments:

Rodrigo loves his peanut butter sandwich.

Behaviors

Excellent	☐	Needs Improvement	☐
Good	☐	Time Out/*Cool out*	☑ *Brief*

Comments: *Thought spitting water was funny, so he went to cool out. Did better in the afternoon.*

Medical

Seizures	☐	Asthma	☐
Meds	☐		
Other:	☐	*N/A*	

Comments:

My Day Was

Happy	☑ *for the most part*	Not Feeling Well	☐
Good	☐	Not Good	☐

Comments: *In the morning we were not communicating, we worked together and Rodrigo accomplished his tasks.*

Toileting

Urine	☐ *0*	# of Accidents:
B.M.	☐ *0*	# of Accidents:

Comments:

Great job!

Supplies Needed

Diapers	☐	Wipes	☐	Change of Clothes	☐	Other	☐
Toothbrush	☐	Toothpaste	☐	Other	☐	Other	☐

My Body

Comments: *No marks*

Rodrigo earned a dollar today because he stayed on task and worked hard.

Don't forget picture day tomorrow!

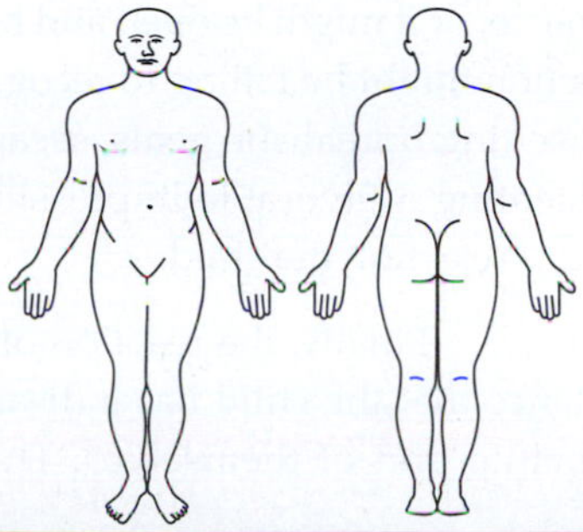

Fear. The parents might not be acquainted with the cause or characteristics of the disability. They might have unfounded suspicions or erroneous information, which causes anxiety or fear. It is important to get to know the parents. For example, when providing information be sure to give the information in amounts the parents can handle. A positive communication process helps the professional judge when it is time to offer additional information.

Guilt. Guilt is one of the most common emotions reported by parents with a child with a disability. This is probably because many disabilities' causes are not known. Parents' feelings of guilt—thinking they should have done something differently or believing the disability is retribution for a misdeed—are difficult to deal with. The professional can help by encouraging guilt-ridden parents to channel their energies into more productive activities after genuine communication has been established.

Grief. Grief is a natural reaction to a situation that brings extreme pain and disappointment. Feelings of guilt and fear go hand in hand because parents feel that their children will not be as successful and will have a harder life given their challenges. Parents who have not been able to accept their child as having a disability may become grief-stricken. In such a case, it is necessary to allow the parents to go through a healing process before they can learn about their child and how the child can develop.

Withdrawal. Being able to withdraw and collect oneself is a healthy, necessary response. It is when one begins to shun others, avoid situations, and maintain isolation that it becomes potentially damaging. Parents can often feel vulnerable to criticism from the public because children with disabilities often have to deal with unfortunate reactions from others.

Rejection. There are many reasons for rejection and many ways of exhibiting it. It might be subtle, feigning acceptance, or it might be open and hostile. Some forms of rejection might be failing to recognize positive attributes, setting unrealistic goals, escaping by desertion, or presenting a favorable impression to others while inwardly rejecting the child.

Acceptance. Finally, the reaction of parents might be acceptance that the child has a disability—acceptance of the child and of themselves. This is the goal and realization of maturity. The parents and the child can then grow and develop into stronger, wiser, and more compassionate human beings (Chinn, 1984; Chinn et al., 1978). Acceptance is important not only for parents but for many family members who are close to the child with special needs. Read the following essay written by an 86-year-old Mexican grandmother "Eliaeber" as she reflects on her grandson who has autism. It has taken a while to accept that her grandson has a disability but she loves him nonetheless.

> *Soy la abuelita de un niño tan querido por mi y que tiene autismo. Y me preguntan, ¿Qué siente que su nieto tiene autismo? Al principio triste, con llanto, desesperado. Pero . . . atravez de su vida y la mía he comprendido y he aprendido a ques es mejor estar al pendiente de él y no mostrar desaliento, es un niño hermoso y cariñoso y le pido al Altísmo que lo proteja para sentirnos major. Yo me siento amada por él.*

[I am the grandmother of a child so dear to me and who has autism. And someone asks me, how does it feel that your grandson has autism? At the beginning sad, weeping, desperate. But . . . right through his life and mine I have understood and learned that it is best to be vigilant of him and not show discouragement, he is a beautiful and loving child and I ask the Almighty to protect him so that we can feel better. I feel loved by him.]

Although other family members as well as parents may have some of these feelings, one of the most important components in handling their feelings is the knowledge that there are things they can do to help their child. When parents are able to focus on the positive and design a program that will enable their child to develop to full potential, they then have a challenge and an answer to the crisis they might have felt initially. Too often, professionals and friends respond with sympathy rather than suggestions for ways to face the future and meet the challenges.

Reaching Out with Programs

When parents are confronted with the task of rearing a child with a disability, they need both emotional support and specific information. The first step is the establishment of attachment between parent and infant. The second step is the development of parenting qualities in one or both parents. This ability is acquired when the parent is able to read cues and understand the baby's behavior. The cues and behavior patterns of a child with a special ability might not be the same as those of a typically developing infant. If misinterpreted by the parents, a certain behavior can confuse and frustrate the parents, causing them eventually to withdraw from meaningful relationships. The end result can be that the attachment process between parent and child is disturbed.

Most school districts offer parent program services for parents and families of children with disabilities. They are in charge of hosting weekly and monthly workshops and training. Topics include the IEP process in Special Education, disability awareness training, and mental health information. Oftentimes parent programs work with the teachers to assign social workers to families in need of additional support in the home setting.

Other programs for fathers of children with special needs include the Fathers Network, whose website, fathersnetwork.org, shares information on fathers and their children. Included are current news articles from sources such as *The Seattle Times, Seattle Post-Intelligencer, The New York Times,* and the Associated Press that provide information pertinent to fathers of children with disabilities. Topics include planning for the future of children with disabilities, experiences of siblings of children with disabilities, and personal experiences of fathers coping with their children's disabilities. An events calendar lists upcoming conferences and seminars offered in Washington State, the Northwest, the rest of the United States, and Canada.

Students Speak Out

The National Council on Disability (2002) asked youths to respond to questions about their school experiences in IDEA. The questions were:

- When you think about your years in school, what comes to mind about special education and related services?
- If your school was reluctant to provide special-education services because of financial concerns, which services were disputed? Did you receive the services that your IEP team said you needed?
- If the discipline procedures under IDEA need to be clearer, how would you change the way the discipline policy is explained to students and their parents?

- How could schools do a better job before students leave high school to help you and other young people with disabilities prepare in areas such as employment, transportation, housing, managing finances, health care, independent living, connecting to resources in the community, and/or postsecondary (college or vocational) education? (pp. 8–9)

One student's experience was as follows:

I am a 12-year-old who has been diagnosed with Chronic Fatigue Syndrome (CFS) and Postural Orthostatic Tachycardia Syndrome (POTS). I am currently finishing the 6th grade and have been ill with these illnesses for most of my life. By the 3rd grade I was unable to attend school at all and my parents worked with the school to have me classified as Other Health Impaired so that I could receive services under the IDEA. The problem that they had initially was that my test scores showed that I was at the high end of my ability, even though my education was being severely affected by the illness . . . . I have been very fortunate in my school system because once my eligibility was accepted the CSE has been very supportive. They have been very open to our suggestions and those of the tutor to services that may benefit me, and have stuck by my IEP in following through with services. My parents have had to maintain an active role and remind the school of things we needed, such as extra textbooks, or use of a word processor, but the school has accommodated when reminded. Individual teachers have been our great allies and our worst enemies. If they try to understand my illness and limitations they bend over backwards to help me out. But some teachers have been totally unwilling to teach me via a tutor. They will not grade my work and resist modifying my workload. We have been fortunate to be able to find ways to work around these situations . . . . Most of my teachers have been willing to offer help in modifying and consolidating the workload to a manageable level for me to complete. (National Council on Disability, 2002, pp. 11–12, 17)

While not all students interviewed had positive experiences, positive communication that acknowledges an understanding of a student's experience can make a significant impact on a student's performance.

Craft and Howley (2018) conducted a study to explore how African American students with learning disabilities in secondary special-education programs perceived their experiences in schools. The researchers also explored the challenges, benefits, and disadvantages associated with students' disability labels and their placement in special education. Findings demonstrated that the African American students felt that their negative experiences outweighed the benefits from being placed in special education. The students reported feelings of stigmatization by peers, limited academic progress because of the change in pace of curriculum, and barriers that kept them from transitioning back into general education.

This study proved that institutional racism and placement in special education stigmatizes students with disabilities. It also further emphasizes the importance for educators to recognize all students as effective learners and understand that all students, including students who are African American, are capable of communicating the kinds of supports they need to be successful. Educators must also not lower their expectations for their students because of their weaknesses but enhance their strengths in the classroom (DeFur & Korinek, 2010).

Parents' Reflections

Hilaria Bauer is the mother of a young adult with a disability. She shares her feelings and thoughts about this so others might benefit from her experiences.

Because Asperger's Syndrome was not really coined until the early 80's, we never knew what was wrong with my daughter. We knew she was a bit "different" since she was a toddler, and we took her to many doctors, who diagnosed her from having Cerebral Palsy to Motor Delay, but nobody knew what was really wrong. When she entered school, she had no problems learning to read, but we knew that there was "something." Her fine motor skills never caught up as she developed. She had problems climbing stairs, throwing a ball, and learning how to write. She never learned how to ride a bike. As she grew, she had a very hard time trying to "fit in." She was tested for Special Education services twice and never qualified. She was "high functioning" for her IQ. The school system was not ready to address any of her needs.

Because my daughter did not fit any of the school's labels, we went through a 504 process, to safeguard her rights as a student. Through 504, she was able to obtain some modifications to her school experience, especially when taking a test or completing a project. However, there were no specialized services to help her cope with her condition. Administrators and teachers did not, just like doctors, know what to do with her. She was reading, somewhat writing, and learning all the factual information school imparts, but she was left out of the learning experience whenever abstract concepts were addressed. As she matured, this became painfully real. She was not able to understand

literary devices, she was not able to comprehend algebra or other high mathematical concepts, she could not get mature humor. Little by little, her body aged, but her social mind and some of her cognitive skills stayed at the level of someone about 9 or 10 years old.

We learned what her condition was when she entered junior college. At the age of 18, we found out that she had something called Asperger's Syndrome. I became friends with someone who had a Psychiatric Social Work background. In one of my conversations with my friend, I described some of my daughter's symptoms. My friend suggested to have her checked for Asperger's Syndrome. When we took my daughter to a diagnostician, we were finally given a "label." Most people frowned when they saw how happy I was with the "label." For me, it was not knowing what was wrong that prevented us from providing more appropriate help. We read many books about Asperger's, including Songs of the Gorilla Nation *by Dr. Dawn Prince-Hughes. Although my daughter didn't have autism, Asperger's was considered in the same kind of social challenges as Autism. She is now trying to finish her Associate Arts degree from our community college at the age of 26.*

The only uncertainty we have for her as an adult are her job prospects. We are committed as parents to provide for her as long as we live; however, we don't know what will happen when we are not around. As of now, she has not been able to hold a steady job. She has tried a couple of things without success, so any conversation around work makes her very anxious. She loves school, she has a couple of acquaintances, and she fulfills all of her responsibilities, at school, home, and church. She is a very caring, responsible, and smart individual. But, as of now, the workplace doesn't appear to be a safe environment for someone who is an adult with a child-like perception.[4]

I never heard from the author but we had used this on the previous edition and we had permission.

1 OUT OF 59: A FATHER'S PERSPECTIVE   Armando is a father of three. His middle child was diagnosed with autism. Here he shares his experience as a father of a child with autism.

My Rodrigo is a 7-year-old diagnosed with autism and sensory processing dysfunction. At 11 months Rodrigo stopped eating solid foods, cried constantly, and played with his toys differently than other children, such as lining up toys and fixation with items other than toys such as leafs. My wife and I were given a packet of resources and were told to go and find help but we did not know where to begin. Although Rodrigo has gone through speech, occupational,

---

[4]Reprinted by permission of Hilaria Bauer, October 25, 2010.

and applied behavior analysis therapy, it is what I do with him that I can see making a difference for him. To have a child with a disability is to know him as my boy. When I say my boy it means a love from my heart. My Rodrigo is the son I have always wanted, and his disability is to overcome what the world has put in front of him, and my job is to not allow for anyone's prejudice, skewed ideas, ignorance, limits, and their own life, to keep my boy from reaching his own potential. He is my inspiration to become the best father, role model, friend, teacher, coach, and a shelter when he is tired and wants to be next to his dad. I am proud of him and want him to always know that wherever we go he will always be with us. No matter what the future brings Rodrigo will always be my boy and I want to be in his world and make the world a better place for him and others.

Armando

Texas

November 1, 2010

Rodrigo's father explained that his son is in second grade in an autistic unit because he is able to learn his academic content more effectively in a setting with fewer children and with a teacher who has a special-education certificate. He is able to go to inclusion twice a day every day—once during physical education for motor development and socialization and once in the general second-grade classroom for science and social studies. His father explains that the special-education teachers, as well as the inclusion teachers, want to do more for him because he is a "smart boy." Rodrigo has an older sister and a younger brother. Both love their brother and wish they could do more with him as explained on a letter written by his older sister "Marisol":

Dear Mom:

Times can be hard and fun when you have a brother with autism. It's hard to imagine him missing out on things like him going to the movies with my friends and getting into fights like what a typical brother and sister do. I was once thinking while I was at my youth camp at church that if Rodrigo didn't have autism he would be having a blast going to the pool, worshipping, and socializing with other kids there. When I was thinking about this in my dorm I almost broke my tears just thinking about it. Some hysterical moments that I've had with my brother are just having this look on his face whenever he is going to do a "travesura" [mischief] and he just makes you smile.

Autism is a disability that affects social and language skills but also family relations. Siblings have to also learn to navigate the world of autism. There are also organizations that provide services such as support groups for siblings of children with a disability. One example of this is Sibshops (Meyer & Vadasy, 2008). Check your local listings for specific agencies.

Update about Armando's Son

Rodrigo is now in high school. He is 15 years old. He attends a public high school and is in a life-skills unit. The ARD team concluded that Rodrigo had made sufficient progress and that he would benefit from being in a life-skills unit rather than an autistic unit. He is in inclusion for physical education and art. He takes all of his subjects but they are modified. His challenging behaviors have decreased because his neurologist prescribed him medication to control his violent rages. Rodrigo's IEP was created to help him become self-sufficient and hopefully find a job upon graduation. The district representatives indicated that their job is to ensure that high school prepares Rodrigo for the world and if he is successful at graduating at 18 with a job, then they have accomplish their goal. As parents we share and appreciate this goal.

Parents are the best advocates for children with autism.

Armando Cortez

Caring for Families of Children with Disabilities

BURNOUT. *Burnout* is a term applied to the loss of concern and emotional feeling for people you work with or live with (Schaufe et al., 2017; Maslach, 1982). Both teachers and parents experience burnout. It is felt most when what you are trying to do seems unproductive or when you think you have few alternatives that would change or improve the course of events. This frustration can lead to a feeling of being trapped. It can happen to any teacher and any parent. The obligations of teaching and parenting are similar. Both are in an authoritarian role and are responsible for setting up the child's program. Balancing the student's needs with time constraints, the mechanical constraints of running a classroom or a home, and the constraints of the personal needs of the authoritarian figure is a role for a magician. Indeed, when parents and teachers are successful, the result does seem to be magical. Both teacher and parent know, however, that their success was produced by hard work, good planning, cooperation, and perseverance.

Those who set high standards and aim for perfection are more likely to experience burnout, as are those who feel a need to be in control. Feelings of anger, guilt, depression, self-doubt, and irritability are symptoms of burnout. When these occur, take a hard look at what is really going on and what needs to be going on. Are you neglecting yourself? Are the things you want to do essential? Do some things need to be changedBe willing to give yourself and others credit where credit is due. Build in rewards so that you and others feel good about what you are doing. Always have some goals that are short term and accessible. Nothing feels better than success. This is one of the best methods to combat burnout. Remember, burnout is reversible.

DEPRESSION AND SUICIDE.   People who parent or work with exceptional children need to know that these children are in a high-risk group for depression and suicide. Children with learning disabilities are particularly at risk because of the frustration they often encounter in trying to learn. Children with giftedness are also at risk because they often find it difficult to feel comfortable in the school and home environment.

Parents and teachers must recognize the child's symptoms of depression and impending suicide and be willing to take appropriate action. Generally, the

Working with children of special needs requires teachers to maintain a positive attitude.

Jules Selmes/Pearson Education Ltd

child will be depressed or irritable, lacking enjoyment in normally pleasurable activities. Changes in weight, appetite, or eating habits can be signals. Sleeplessness, hyperactivity, loss of energy, and/or fatigue are also signals that something is wrong. Loss of self-esteem and feelings of inadequacy or a decreased ability to concentrate should alert teachers and parents to a very real need for help. Thoughts of death or suicide should not be taken lightly. Recognize these as very serious symptoms and get professional help. Mental-health centers and public schools have programs for crisis intervention and can give guidance and help in a time of need.

Although many families find support from other family members, caring for children with disabilities is a full-time job and help is always needed. Respite care provides temporary relief for families of children with special needs. Although the need for respite care is enormous, it is often a need that is not met (Whiting, 2014).

Culturally and Linguistically Diverse Families of Children with Disabilities

Culturally and linguistically diverse children, particularly those of African American, Latino, and Native American descent, are often overrepresented in special-education classrooms and are underrepresented in gifted-and-talented programs (Cartledge, Gardener, & Ford, 2009). For many culturally and linguistically diverse families, the school system is very overwhelming. Many have had negative experiences or are simply not familiar with the way the system works (Harry, 2008). When a child with special needs is involved, the situation very often becomes more distressing because not only are parents learning to help their child but they are learning to accept the child's disability.

Sometimes teachers complain that culturally and linguistically diverse parents are not involved in their child's education, but very often parents feel disrespected and belittled in the meetings they attend (Lo, 2008). This results in outcomes that do not consider the cultural values of the family (Sheehy, Ornelles, & Noonan, 2009); thus, children suffer cultural and language loss. Cultural reciprocity allows for educators and parents to share information about cultural values and beliefs to promote effective communication and collaboration (Sheehy et al., 2009). When teachers know a child's native language it helps increase communication and break down cultural barriers (Columna, Senne, & Lytle, 2009).

Culturally relevant pedagogy helps teachers include culturally and linguistically diverse parents in the educational decisions that affect their child. A teacher must gain a family's trust in order to successfully work with their child (Pewewardy & Fitzpatrick, 2009). The following list includes issues faced by culturally and linguistically diverse families in schools (Cartledge et al., 2009, pp. 136–139) and suggestions for teachers:

Perceptions. Very often, families face negative perceptions from teachers and administrators. SUGGESTION—Discover the family's funds of knowledge by getting to know the family and the child. Avoid making judgments about the family and focus on the child's needs.

Trust. Parents sometimes do not trust educators, and educators can feel that parents are not involved enough because they don't care. SUGGESTION—Create an environment of trust by inviting parents to visit their child's classroom often. Allow them to stay and observe the different techniques that you use as a teacher so they can use them at home. Make them feel welcome.

Adaptation to the child's special needs. Culturally and linguistically diverse families appear to have less of a "grief cycle": They seem to be more resilient in accepting their child's disability. SUGGESTION—Form a parent support group in which parents can talk with one another. Let parents guide the meeting and learn to listen.

Goals for their child. Every family has different goals for their children. SUGGESTION—Respect parents' wishes and work with them to help the child be successful in your classroom without infringing on the parents' cultural beliefs.

Parenting issues. Usually referred to as *parenting styles*, many culturally and linguistically diverse families' approaches differ from teachers who may be of a different culture and linguistic background. SUGGESTION—Be understanding of the different parenting styles. Learn from the parent the type of values they have and see how those affect the child.

Economic issues. Many culturally and linguistically diverse families have to work hard to provide for their children as such they must find support systems such as grandparents and other extended family members take care of the child while they are at work. SUGGESTION—Provide parents with a list of resources that they can use. This list can be derived from the United Way directory or from the school district.

Cultural discontinuities. Culturally and linguistically diverse parents need to communicate with teachers and other professionals that work with their child, particularly in their native language. Parents want professionals to value and respect their culture, including their language, and to not have deficit views. SUGGESTION—Develop respect for families' funds of knowledge and cultural traditions by discovering reasons why families practice what they do. Dismiss deficit thinking. Find qualified translators (rather than the children) for parent conferences, particularly for Admission, Review, and Dismissal (ARD) meetings.

Summary

Parents, teachers, and other professionals are effective forces in influencing the life of the exceptional child. It is important that all be able and willing to work together for the benefit of the child with disabilities. Special education terms, once crude, have been replaced with more inclusive educational terms.

During the 20th century, the special education movement grew, and in 1971, the Pennsylvania

Association for Retarded Children (PARC) won a court case against the Commonwealth of Pennsylvania, affirming the right of all children to a free and appropriate education. This included children with disabilities. The Vocational Rehabilitation Act of 1973, the Education of All Handicapped Children Act of 1975 (P.L. 94-142), the Education of the Handicapped Act Amendments of 1983 (P.L. 98-199), Americans with Disabilities Act, Individuals with Disabilities Education Act, and IDEA 97 are some of the far-reaching laws passed since the landmark PARC case of 1971.

From the Education of All Handicapped Children Act of 1975 to IDEA 97 (P.L. 105-17) and IDEA 04 reauthorization, the Individualized Education Program (IEP) and the Individualized Family Service Program (IFSP) have been instrumental in addressing the needs of children with disabilities. These plans are developed by the parents, the child, teachers (special and regular), administrators, psychologists, and any others involved with the child's education. The plans ensure a continuum of services appropriate to age, maturity, handicapping condition, achievements, and parental expectations. The child or student with a disability includes those with autism, deafness, deafness–blindness, hearing impairments, intellectual disabilities, multiple disabilities, orthopedic impairments, other health impairments (including ADHD), emotional disturbances, learning disabilities, speech or language impairments, traumatic brain injury, and visual impairments. For children 3 to 9 years old, developmental delays are also used for placement. IDEA 97 and 04 also provide for due process—the right to a hearing—if parents disagree with the educational placement.

Parents have been effective forces in securing this legislation. Parents should and do have an important role in the life and education of their exceptional children. The parent's role begins as one of nurturing in the home but can become an effective force in the school as the parent supports the teacher at home as a tutor or at school as a volunteer. Value parents' funds of knowledge to help in the development of their child with special needs.

Suggested Class Activities and Discussions

1. Write a brief review of the development of special education.

2. Describe in your own words what *least restrictive* means.

3. List and describe briefly the 13 categories of exceptional students.

4. A *staffing* refers to the meeting that takes place when an exceptional student's IEP is developed or changed. Who is included on the IEP team? What are their responsibilities?

5. *Mainstreaming* and *inclusion* are terms used quite frequently. Read carefully about them and write in your own words what you think they mean.

6. List ways the general classroom can adapt to and support a child with a disability.

7. Study the legislation that has developed for children with disabilities. How has it progressed? List changes.

8. Choose one of the problems a parent of an exceptional child might encounter and describe how you as a professional would try to help that parent. Examples could include a parent who is an English language learner or one who has a disability.

Useful Websites

Council for Exceptional Children
Autism Speaks
Easterseals
Center for Parent Information and Resources
Centers for Disease Control and Prevention
Individuals with Disabilities Education Act

National Center for Learning Disabilities
National Association for Parents with Children in Special Education
The National Dissemination Center for Children with Disabilities
Council of State Directors of Programs for the Gifted

Glossary Terms

ARD: Admission, Review, Dismissal.

Disability or special ability: An impairment that can be physical, emotional, linguistic, sensory, or intellectual.

IEP: Individualized Education Program.

Chapter 11
Family Violence and Child Abuse

Keeping children safe from violence is ensuring an emotionally stable future.

Mari Riojas-Cortez

Learning Outcomes

In this chapter, you will recognize how family violence leads to child abuse and neglect.

11.1 Discuss domestic violence and how it leads to abuse.

11.2 Define child abuse and identify warning signs.

11.3 Describe and explain child abuse categories.

11.4 Describe the procedures for child abuse reporting.

11.5 Identify ways to communicate with parents about child abuse and neglect.

John Lennon's song "Imagine" talks about living life in peace. Living in peace is something we all want, not just those unfortunate enough to be living in war zones. Many children face a war of abuse, and the offenders are usually those whom they trust and love. Over the years, we have heard about mothers drowning their children while battling depression, other parents who are under the influence of drugs injuring and even killing their infant children, and still more offenders, including educators and members of the clergy and recently coaches, who take advantage of their role and treat children in the most horrendous manner. Imagine a world where we, as educators and parents, advocated for those children who are suffering from abuse, neglect, and domestic violence.

Domestic Violence

Many daily headlines we see on the news and Internet may look something like this:

"Triple murder-suicide . . . father and husband murders wife and child and then kills himself."

"Boyfriend strangles girlfriend."

"Wife runs husband down with car."

"Athlete rapes young girl."

"Children found alone in their apartment dirty and hungry while parents out drinking."

"Doctor accused of abusing female athletes."

These headlines show us the urgency in understanding and educating people about domestic violence. In my hometown of San Antonio, Texas, daily we hear stories about domestic violence and/or child abuse and neglect. We have seen cases where the violence occurs not only between mother and father, but between other family members, such as children hurting their parents. Domestic violence is considered a major health problem that affects tens of millions of families in the United States (Smith, Slep, & O'Leary,

Table 11.1 Early Warning Signs of Abusers

Tells you to stop seeing your friends and family	Always blames others and you
Tells you to stop participating in things that interest you	Extremely jealous
Gets upset and aggressive easily	Criticizes former partner/spouse
Requires to know where you are at all times	History of domestic abuse
Does not respect your space	Raised in a violent home

Source: Adapted from *Red Flags of Abuse*. National Network to End Domestic Violence (2014). http://nnedv.org/resources/stats/gethelp/redflagsofabuse.html

2009) and around the world (McGarry, Westbury, Kench, & Furse, 2014). Very often, victims of domestic violence are victims of abuse or their children are victims of abuse. The Centers for Disease Control and Prevention (2014b) lists five types of domestic violence: sexual, physical, stalking, psychological/emotional aggression, and control of reproductive or sexual health. Power and control seem to drive the need for the perpetrator to abuse the victim. Table 11.1 shows some red flags developed by the National Network to End Domestic Violence (2018) that are important in helping individuals identify possible abusers.

When domestic violence is present within the family unit, the entire family suffers. Children from violent homes often continue the cycle of violence as adults if help is not provided. Afolabi (2015) conducted a systematic review of the literature which indicates that children that come from backgrounds of domestic violence develop biological and psychological health problems.

Teachers and other educators often see signs of domestic abuse in the children they teach. Throughout my years of teaching, I encountered children who lived in violent homes. I could often determine the child who experienced domestic violence by their drawings, conversations, and behaviors (some sad and withdrawn, and others overly aggressive). Recently I was visiting one of my students who was placed in a Head Start Center as part of her field work assignment. As I looked around, I noticed that there was a child who had a bruise on his cheek. I asked him what he had on his cheek. The teacher assistant quickly indicated that they had talked with the mother. Since the bruise was in an unusual place, I had to ask; it was my responsibility. As educators we must always question to keep children safe even if it is uncomfortable to do so.

Effects of Domestic Violence on Children

According to the National Network to End Domestic Violence (2018), 30 to 60% of individuals who are violent toward their partner also abuse their children. Medically fragile infants appear to be at high risk for abuse, particularly if their family has a history of social problems, including domestic violence, mental illness, or substance abuse (Fullar, 2008). Studies have shown how children are at high risk of maltreatment when parents psychologically abuse each other (Chang, Theodore, Martin, & Runyan, 2008). The children are also disempowered and intimidated (Thornton, 2014). It is imperative, therefore, to provide resources and crisis intervention to families who are experiencing domestic violence so that children and their parents do not become yet another statistic.

Many organizations are ready to help families end the cycle of domestic violence. A Google search can help you find local resources. Table 11.2 lists four organizations and their mission, as examples that can help

Table 11.2 Organizations Against Domestic Violence

Organization	Mission
National Coalition Against Domestic Violence	"The Mission of the National Coalition Against Domestic Violence (NCADV) is to organize for collective power by advancing transformative work, thinking and leadership of communities and individuals working to end the violence in our lives." (NCADV, 2014)
National Center on Domestic Violence, Trauma & Mental Health	"The mission of the National Center on Domestic Violence, Trauma & Mental Health is to develop and promote accessible, culturally relevant, and trauma-informed responses to domestic violence and other lifetime trauma so that survivors and their children can access the resources that are essential to their safety and well-being. Our work is survivor defined and rooted in principles of social justice." (NCDVTMH, 2014)
STAND! For Families Free of Violence	"STAND! For Families Free of Violence is a catalyst for breaking the multi-generational cycle of violence, promoting safe and strong relationships, and rebuilding lives." (SFFFV, 2014)
National Network to End Domestic Violence	"The National Network to End Domestic Violence (NNEDV), a social change organization, is dedicated to creating a social, political, and economic environment in which violence against women no longer exists." (NNEDV, 2018)

you find resources for families in need. Some of these organizations, such as the National Network to End Domestic Violence or NNEDV, have coalitions in each state to help end domestic violence.

Defining Child Abuse

What is **child abuse**? According to the Child Abuse Prevention and Treatment Act of 1974, or P.L. 93-247 (1977), it is "The physical or mental injury, sexual abuse, negligent treatment or maltreatment of a child under the age of 18 by a person who is responsible for the child's welfare under circumstances which indicate that the child's health or welfare is harmed or threatened thereby" (p. 1826). The Centers for Disease Control and Prevention (2014b) indicate that "**child maltreatment** includes all types of abuse and neglect of a child under the age of 18 by a parent, caregiver, or another person in a custodial role (e.g., clergy, coach, teacher)."

Background

For centuries, child abuse and neglect have been prevalent in many societies. In fact, child abuse used to be considered quite normal (deMause, 1988). The child was considered the property of the father to be worked, sold, loved, or killed as the father willed. In the 1500s, a case of child abuse was reported when authorities began to be suspicious of two parents who claimed that their son was a "monster," taking him from town to town and making considerable amounts of money by putting him on display. The child was disfigured but the parents had created injuries that made the disfigurement worse for financial gain. The parents were found guilty and put to death for the atrocity they had committed (Kompanje, 2007).

In the 1800s, it was common for children to work 12 hours a day under the threat of beatings. Children were cheap and useful laborers. They "continued to be the property of their parents who could choose to beat them, neglect them, or send them out to work" (Crosson-Tower, 2002, p. 4). Actions that would be called child abuse today were overlooked or considered to be the parent's right to discipline. The child had no rights (Jalongo, 2006).

It was not until 1874, in New York City, that the first case of abuse was reported. It involved a 9-year-old girl, Mary Ellen, who was beaten daily by her parents and was severely undernourished when found by church workers. Because there were no agencies to deal with child abuse, the workers turned to the American Society for the Prevention of Cruelty to Animals.

One year later the New York Society for the Prevention of Cruelty to Children was organized (Fontana & Besharov, 1979; Lazoritz, 1990). The Children's Division of what is now the American Humane Association began addressing the issue in 1877 (American Humane Association, 2014). Soon there were other indications of growing concern for children. National groups such as the Child Study Association of America and the National Congress of Parents and Teachers were formed. Mounting concern over working conditions and care of children culminated in 1909 with the first White House Conference on Children, which resulted in the 1912 legislation establishing the Children's Bureau.

What happened between 1913 and recent decades to focus attention on the child at risk? Dr. John Caffey, a radiologist, began collecting data that indicated child abuse in the early 1920s. It was not until after World War II that he published the first of several studies relating to fractures in young children (American Humane Association, 1978; Elmer, 1982). Caffey's first medical paper, written in 1946, reported the histories of six traumatized infants and questioned the cause of their injuries. In it, he reported that fractures of the long bones and subdural hematomas occurring concurrently were not caused by disease.

Dr. Frederick Silverman, who had been a student of Caffey's, followed in 1953 with an article that indicated that skeletal trauma in infants could be the result of abuse (American Humane Association, 1978; Elmer, 1982). Reports began appearing more frequently (Altman & Smith, 1960; Bakwin, 1956; Fisher, 1958; Silver & Kempe, 1959; Woolley & Evans, 1955), but it was an article by Kempe, Silverman, Steele, Droegemueller, and Silver (1962), "The Battered-Child Syndrome," that brought national attention to the abused child, a problem that had occurred for years but somehow never got the needed attention (Levine & Levine, 2012). The authors charged physicians with the duty and responsibility to do a full evaluation of the child, including the use of X-ray imaging in determining abuse. Another researcher, Dr. Vincent Fontana, argued that the deprivation of food and clothing should also be included and thus the term should change to "child abuse and neglect" (Nelson, 2012).

National Response

The term *battered* and the picture it evoked aroused the nation. By 1967, all 50 states had legislation to facilitate the reporting of child abuse. There was, however, no provision for the coordination of procedures, nor was there a standard definition of abuse and neglect. Other conditions that precluded standardized reporting included the inconsistent ages of children covered by law, hesitation of professional and private citizens to report cases, different systems of official recordkeeping, and varied criteria on which to judge abuse.

National Center on Child Abuse and Neglect

The National Center on Child Abuse and Neglect (NCCAN) was created in 1974 by P.L. 93-247. The NCCAN disseminates information through the Clearinghouse on Child Abuse and Neglect.

After the establishment of NCCAN, regional centers on child abuse were funded. Their purpose was to conduct research to determine the cause of child abuse and neglect, its identification and prevention, and the incidence of child abuse in the nation. Reporting of child abuse and neglect has been conducted by a variety of organizations. From 1973 until 1986, the American Association for Protecting Children (the

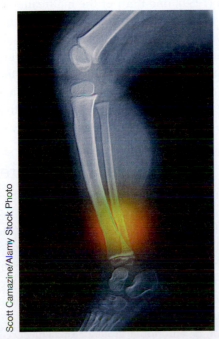

When X-rays became available, doctors began noticing recurring breaks that revealed abuse.

Scott Camazine/Alamy Stock Photo

American Humane Association) supplied data on abuse and neglect. The National Committee for the Prevention of Child Abuse did a survey of the 50 states in 1991. At that time, NCCAN established the National Child Abuse and Neglect Data System (NCANDS) to be responsible for providing comprehensive data on abuse and neglect.

Currently, the Administration for Children and Families under the U.S. Department of Health and Human Services created the Child Welfare Information Gateway which "provides resources on training to identify child abuse and neglect, locating funding sources for child protection and child abuse treatment, and connecting with Federal agencies, national and State organizations, and [the] State hotline" (2014). In addition, the Child Welfare Information Gateway lists statistics regarding the different types of abuse and neglect, the number of fatalities, characteristics of perpetrators, risk and protective factors, and impact on families.

Why Is There Abuse?

As we continue to hear horrendous cases of child abuse and neglect, we can't help but wonder why parents and other adults continue to do acts of violence to children. Research indicates that perpetrators have been victims of abuse themselves; some have endured sexual, emotional, and physical abuse and neglect; while others experience no love or love was conflated with sex (Thomas, Phillips, Carlson, Shieh, Kirkwood, Cabage, & Worley, 2014).

Perpetrators range from parents to family members and friends. In the case of parents, perhaps abuse occurs because they did not have a childhood that allowed them to become independent, productive, functioning adults. Generally, they had to disregard their own needs and desires for the wishes of an authority figure. Perhaps they were unable to develop inner controls and looked to outside figures for direction. Such parents also exhibit dependence on others in their search for love and affection. Ultimately, parents who become abusive can have different reasons or motives, such as the following explanations found in literature.

1. *Inappropriate expectations.* Abusive parents often perceive the child's abilities to be greater than they are, and they expect children to take on responsibilities that are not appropriate for their ages. These parents can have expectations such as

toilet training the child at 6 to 12 months, talking by age 2, and taking on housekeeping chores at an early age. Young or inexperienced parents, who do not know child development, might interpret an infant or toddler's appropriate behavior as stubbornness and rebellion. Combine this with a belief that physical punishment will help the child behave, and you have the conditions for abuse. Children in these families develop a poor self-concept and feel incapable, unacceptable, and worthless (Bavolek, 1989; Hamilton, 1989).

2. *Lack of empathy.* Abusive parents often did not experience loving care when they were growing up, so they do not have a model to follow. They cannot change their own personality traits until they receive the support and love they need. These parents usually have dependency needs and are unable to empathize with their children. The child's basic needs are ignored. Such parents might justify cruel and abusive behaviors under the guise of teaching and guiding their children. Mothers who were brought up by uncaring, inattentive mothers will tend to mother their own children in the same way. Their children grow up with a low sense of self-esteem and inadequate identity (Bavolek, 1989; Hamilton, 1989; Steele, 1986, 1987).

3. *Belief in physical punishment.* Abusive parents often believe that physical punishment is necessary to rear their children without spoiling them. This once common belief in the United States seems to be evolving because of heightened awareness of child abuse, but abusive parents can still go to extremes and believe that babies and children should not be allowed to get away with anything. They punish to correct perceived misbehavior or inadequacy on the part of their child. The child does not live up to expectations and is considered "bad." The parents think they have the moral duty to correct their child's behavior any way they choose.

4. *Parent–child role reversal.* In these abusive families, children are looked upon by the parents as providing the love and support that the parent needs. The parent is like a needy child, so the child must play the role of the adult. If the child is able to take on some of the parental roles, abuse may be avoided, but only at the expense of the child's normal development. This is destructive to children—they do not go through normal developmental stages, do not develop their own identities, and see themselves as existing to meet the needs of their parents (Bavolek, 1989; Hamilton, 1989).

5. *Social isolation.* Social isolation is recognized by most child abuse researchers as a factor that perpetuates neglect and abuse. Either the absence of social support or inability to accept any support has the same effect. The abusive family isolates itself, attempts to solve its problems alone, and avoids contact with others. Isolation is a defense against being hurt and rejected. Although abusive parents might act self-sufficient and sure of themselves, they are dependent, frightened, and immature. Cross-cultural research indicates that child maltreatment occurs less often in cultures with multiple caregivers, including extended families (Hamilton, 1989). This seems to be a natural process as other caregivers provide the support that parents often need when raising children.

6. *Difficulty experiencing pleasure.* In other abusing families, the parents do not enjoy life. Their social relationships are minimal and unrewarding. They do not feel competent, have difficulty planning for the future, and do not trust their own performances. Children in these families exhibit similar behavior.

7. *Intergenerational ties.* According to Vondra and Toth (1989), one-third of the maltreated are abusive to their children (p. 13). If abuse and neglect are viewed in a broad sense, however, an alarming number of parents did not receive adequate parenting or develop a positive attachment to their parents and other loved ones and thus have a difficult time providing the kind of environment that nourishes and cares for a child adequately (Steele, 1986).

Child Abuse in a Global Context

Around the world, many children endure all kinds of abuse, including maltreatment, neglect, exploitation, physical labor, commercial sex exploitation, child wedlock, child soldiering, and child trafficking (UNICEF, 2010). Those who are the most vulnerable are very young children and children with disabilities. According to the World Health Organization (2018), about one billion children ages 2–17 have been subjected to physical, sexual, or emotional violence or neglect. UNICEF reports that there is a higher incidence of mortality

(80%) for those children who have a disability, particularly in poor countries. UNICEF works diligently to eradicate violence and abuse from the lives of children around the world (UNICEF, 2013). It is the responsibility of parents and other caregivers to protect children from abuse, neglect, maltreatment, and oppression. Failure to do so results in a society without compassion, morals, or ethical standards.

It is important for all nations around the world to help fight child abuse because its existence ails society and its citizens. The Convention on the Rights of the Child (CRC), created by UNICEF and adopted by the United Nations General Assembly, appears to be the only international human rights treaty that has almost universal ratification, except in Somalia and the United States, which appear to be working toward formally approving it (Svevo-Cianci & Lee, 2010). The Declaration of the Rights of the Child Principle #9 indicates that, "The child shall be protected against all forms of neglect, cruelty and exploitation. He shall not be the subject of traffic, in any form" (UNICEF, 2014). Difficulty arises when cultural practices are abusive and lead to neglect of children. This can be considered the "dark side of culture," and unfortunately, it is present in all cultures in all countries. The voice of children in this case should be heard rather than keeping traditions that hurt them. The journal *Child Abuse and Neglect* provides an international and multidisciplinary perspective on child abuse and neglect.

Information regarding child abuse and neglect in an international context is increasing. Many countries are beginning to truly advocate for children, mostly because of the work that UNICEF and the United Nations are doing for children's rights. For example, in Saudi Arabia, it was not until 1990 that the first case of child abuse was reported in a medical journal (Eissa & Almuneef, 2010). The most common type of child abuse in Saudi Arabia is physical abuse, followed by neglect, with the majority of the children abused being males about 5 years of age. In Australia, it is estimated that the most common form of abuse is emotional followed by neglect (Goebbels, Nicholson, Walsh, & DeVries, 2008). For many Gypsy children in Albania, trafficking appears to be a major incidence of child abuse since it is connected to contextual issues of poverty, internal and external migrations, discrimination, and problems with the legal system (Gjermeni, VanHook, Gjipali, Xhillari, Lungu, & Hazizi, 2008).

Similarly, children who live in the streets in India endure all kinds of abuse, with young males reportedly being abused more than young females (Mathur, Rathore, & Mathur, 2009). Other children who look for a better place to live outside of their country end up being abused by the caregivers whom they begin to trust, as shown in an example of sexual maltreatment of unaccompanied asylum-seeking minors from the Horn of Africa to the United Kingdom (Lay & Papadopoulos, 2009).

Neglect and corporal punishment are two issues related to abuse that seem to be prevalent in many countries. For instance, in a study conducted in Botswana, Mexico, and Vietnam, it was found that parents leave their children home alone many times not by choice but out of necessity (Ruiz-Casares & Heymann, 2009). Many countries, including Mauritania, Kenya, Barbados, Thailand, and Tanzania (among others), are seeking to change attitudes and implement positive discipline rather than corporal punishment (UNICEF, 2010).

The examples provided here represent a small fraction of the global epidemic of child abuse. There are many organizations that are working closely with many governments to stop child abuse.

Who Are the Victims?

Child abuse strikes children at all ages, but those who are the youngest seem to be the most at risk. Childhelp indicates that more than 3.6 million referrals are made to child protective agencies that involve more than 6.6 million children (Childhelp, 2018). It is estimated that child abuse is reported every 10 seconds. Neglect is the most frequent type of abuse, followed by physical abuse. In 2007, the National Child Abuse and Neglect Data System (NCANDS) reported an estimated 1,760 child deaths due to abuse (Child Welfare Information Gateway, 2010). Children with disabilities are at a higher risk of being abused not only in the United Stated but also around the world (UNICEF, 2014).

It is also important to recognize that although some children overcome barriers related to child abuse and neglect, the majority of them suffer many consequences through adulthood (Zielinski, 2009). Support systems such as the extended family must be agents of change and help when their relatives are involved in the cycle of child abuse.

Who Are the Abusers?

Home appears to be the most dangerous place for abused children to be (Cetin & Ozozen Danaci, 2016). In most reports from NCANDS, over 80% of abusers are the victim's parents. Harsh discipline seems to be prevalent in abusive parents (Belsky, Conger, & Capaldi, 2009), particularly those with substance abuse problems (Bailey, Hill, Oesterle, & Hawkins, 2009). Perpetrators of maltreatment are defined by most states as parents and other caregivers including relatives, foster parents, babysitters and clergy (i.e. minister, priest, pastor, etc.). Recently we have heard of doctors who have been accused of sexually molesting athletes for years.

Child Abuse Categories

Different organizations may have different terms for child abuse categories. The most common terms include neglect, physical abuse, sexual abuse, psychological maltreatment, and medical neglect. Figure 11.1 shows the percentage of each type of abuse.

Neglect

Child neglect occurs when there is failure to care for the child's basic needs. Physical neglect is the area most frequently identified, but there can also be educational and emotional neglect. Neglect can also include medical neglect, abandonment, or not allowing a runaway to return home. The parents are not always indifferent.

Instead, they might not recognize the importance of medical care or a developmental environment, or they might be incapable of furnishing them. Young children under the age of 3 who have been severely neglected may have serious language delays because of the lack of interaction in the environment (Sylvestre & Mérette, 2010).

Physical neglect refers to the parents' failure to provide the necessities—adequate shelter, care and supervision, food, clothing, and protection. Physical neglect is the most common type of child abuse, accounting for more than half of maltreatment. The child shows signs of malnutrition, usually is irritable, and may need medical attention. The child often goes hungry and lacks supervision after school. The parents are either unable or unwilling to give proper care. In this type of neglect, parents refuse to provide the basic necessities (American Humane Association, 2014).

Educational neglect occurs when parents permit chronic truancy, fail to make sure their child attends school, or fail to tend to any special educational needs of the child. Both physical neglect and educational neglect result in the child's inability to develop fully.

Emotional neglect includes refusal to provide psychological help if the child needs it, exposure of the child to abuse of someone else (e.g., spousal abuse in the child's presence), and permission for use of drugs and alcohol by the child (American Humane Association, 2014).

Neglect is a serious concern in the United States. In order for our society to prosper, we need adults to take care of children wholeheartedly.

Figure 11.1 Types of Child Abuse and Neglect

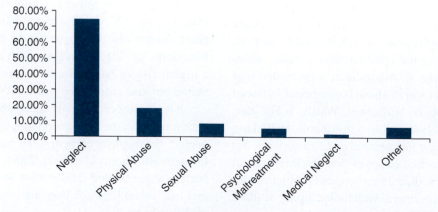

Source: Numbers and Trends. (2016). Child maltreatment 2016: Summary of Key Findings. Child Welfare Information Gateway. Children's Bureau. Retrieved on August 9, 2018 from https://www.childwelfare.gov/pubPDFs/canstats.pdf

Physical Abuse

The physically abused child shows signs of injury—welts, cuts, bruises, burns, or fractures. An update from the American Academy of Pediatrics (2014) indicates that the cause of fractures is physical abuse in 12–20% of the cases. Educators should be aware of repeated injuries, untreated injuries, multiple injuries, and new injuries added to old. Multiple maltreatment often occurs in a child who suffers abuse or neglect. Although emotional maltreatment can be isolated, instances of physical abuse or neglect usually are accompanied by emotional abuse. Potential predictors of physical child abuse include depression, alcoholism, life stress, and perceptions of the child's behavior problems (Haskett, Neupert, & Okado, 2014).

RECOGNIZING PHYSICAL ABUSE. Although many bruises and abrasions are accidental, others give cause for the teacher to believe that they were intentionally inflicted. Bruises are the most common symptoms of physical abuse. Other signs include welts, lumps, or ridges on the body, usually caused by a blow; burns, shown by redness, blistering, or peeling of the skin; fractured bones; scars; lacerations or torn cuts; and abrasions.

Many schools and early childhood programs provide guidance regarding how to recognize abuse. For example, Head Start personnel are mandated reporters and as such are given guidelines for identifying abuse of the preschool child (U.S. Department of Health and Human Services, 2015). These guidelines are useful for detection of abuse in children of any age.

The first is location of the injury. As illustrated in Figure 11.2, bruises on the knees, elbows, shins, and—for the preschool child—the forehead are considered normal in most circumstances.

The second criterion is evidence of repetition of injury. A significantly large number of bruises or cuts and injuries in various stages of healing should be suspect. There are instances, however, when repetition could be accidental: The child could be accident prone,

---

Figure 11.2 Comparison of Typical and Suspicious Bruising Areas

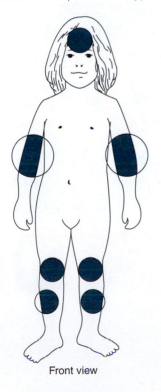

Front view

Normal bruising areas

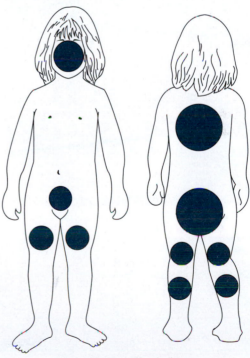

Front and back views

Suspicious bruising areas

Note: The bruises children receive in play are depicted on the left. The bruises on the right would not normally happen in everyday play.

Source: From *Child Abuse and Neglect: A Self-Instructional Text for Head Start Personnel*, by the U.S. Department of Health, Education and Welfare, Head Start Bureau and Children's Bureau, 1977, Washington, DC: U.S. Government Printing Office.

so the correlation between the injury and an explanation of its cause—the fourth criterion, described later—needs to be kept in mind.

The third criterion is the injury. If it is obvious that an object, such as a belt, stick, or cigarette inflicted the bruise, cut, or burn then the caregiver or teacher should suspect abuse. It is also important to work with a child protection team to confirm the severity of the injury, which many times goes untreated (Lane, Dubowitz, & Langenberg, 2009).

The fourth criterion is the correlation between the injury and the explanation given by the child or the parent. The accident as described should be likely to produce the resultant injury. For example, could round burns shaped like the end of a cigarette be caused by the child playing too near the stove?

In ascertaining the extent of suspected physical abuse, the teacher should not remove any of the child's clothing. That should be done only by such personnel as a nurse or doctor who would undress a child as part of their professional responsibilities.

After checking school policy and reviewing the four criteria—the suspicious placement of the injury, the severity and repetition of injuries, evidence of infliction by an object, and inconsistent explanation (or consistent if the child reports the abuse)—the educator must report a suspected injury to the appropriate authorities.

SHAKEN BABY SYNDROME.   Parent educators and teachers should discuss shaken baby syndrome with parents and those who care for infants, because violent shaking is extremely dangerous for infants and young children. Children under 2 have undeveloped neck muscles, and sudden motion can result in the brain pulling away and tearing blood vessels and brain cells. The force with which an angry person might shake a child is 5 to 10 times greater than if the child had simply fallen (American Humane Association, 2014). Even pushing a young child on a swing is cause for concern. Critical questions to ask: Is the baby able to hold its head upright? Is the head bobbing back and forth? If it is, the jarring of the brain might cause

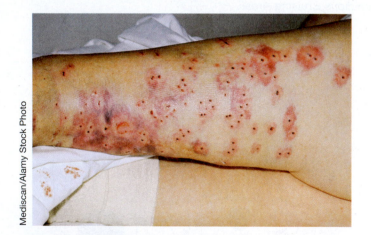

Mediscan/Alamy Stock Photo

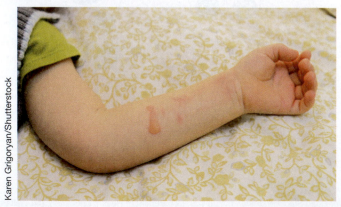

Karen Grigoryan/Shutterstock

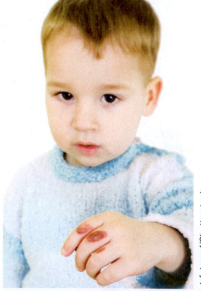

st-fotograf/Shutterstock

Cigarette burns on the hands or body, puncture wounds, scald marks, and bruises are recognizable signs of physical abuse.

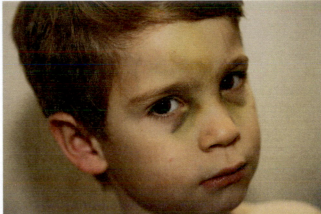

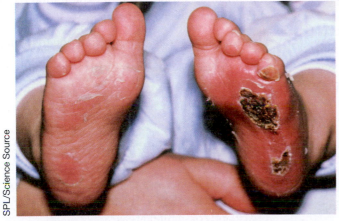

Scalded and battered, these children were victims of child abuse.

injury. Tossing a baby in the air results in jarring and should be avoided. In fact, shaken baby syndrome is the leading cause of death in the U.S.. It is estimated that about 25% of babies die each year due to shaken baby syndrome (National Center on Shaken Baby Syndrome, 2018a).

Shaken baby syndrome appeared in medical literature in 1972 and has since been recognized as a cause of injury or death for young children. In the United States every year, 1,200 to 1,400 children are shaken, and 25 to 30 percent die as a result (National Center on Shaken Baby Syndrome, 2006). Shaking can cause subdural hemorrhage, brain swelling, and damage that can also result in developmental delays, intellectual

disability, blindness, paralysis, or hearing loss (American Humane Association, 2014).

Shaking usually occurs when a frustrated caregiver loses control with a crying child. Parents and caregivers need to know that it is all right for a baby to cry if the caregiver checks and knows that all the child's needs are met. It is also very important to acknowledge that some children cry more than others, particularly newborns between 1 month and 4 months of age (Barr, Rivara, Barr, Cummings, Taylor, Lengua, & Benitz, 2009). When this is the case, respite needs to be given to caregivers so they can maintain control of their own emotions. Three states (Texas, New York, and Utah) have legislation regarding the prevention of shaken baby syndrome.

Training regarding the dangers of shaking infants and young children is mandatory for caregivers to maintain their license (National Center on Shaken Baby Syndrome, 2018).

The Period of PURPLE Crying is a prevention program that includes an 11-page booklet and a 10-minute DVD to be given to new parents. The focus is to help parents understand the reasons for an infant's cry. It is culturally sensitive to a variety of groups (National Center on Shaken Baby Syndrome, 2018b).

Emotional Abuse

Compared to physical neglect and abuse, it is more difficult to identify emotional neglect and abuse, defined as a "pattern of behavior that can seriously interfere with a child's positive emotional development" (American Humane Association, 2014). Children who have been emotionally abused during childhood have problems with attachment and will have difficulty with maladaptive issues toward the self and others in adulthood (Wright, Crawford, & Del Castillo, 2009).

Parents of emotionally abused children are usually overly harsh and critical. They withhold love and acceptance and do not give the child physical or verbal encouragement and praise. Although they expect performance, they do not support the child's endeavors. While physical abuse damages a child's body, emotional abuse damages a child's psyche: "Children who are constantly shamed, terrorized, humiliated, or rejected suffer at least as much if not more than if they had been physically assaulted" (American Humane Association, 2014). Patterns can include the following:

- Terrorizing
- Continued rejection of the child
- Refusal to provide needed nurturance
- Refusal to provide help for a child's psychological problems
- Lack of needed mental or physical stimulation
- Forced involvement with drugs, criminal activities, and other corruptive forces

Children who are not nurtured and who live in an emotionally insecure environment can show signs of low self-esteem, slow educational growth, and insecurity (Dowling, 2010). The difficulty of identifying psychological unavailability and emotional neglect makes it doubly difficult for the schools to respond to the concern. It also is impossible for teachers to overcome a student's childhood that is devoid of emotional security. Children's self-confidence and self-esteem can be either enhanced or diminished. They can either feel good about themselves or view themselves as incapable, unlikable people.

Sexual Abuse

Sexual abuse is defined under the Child Abuse Prevention and Treatment Act (CAPTA, 2003) as follows:

A. the employment, use, persuasion, inducement, enticement, or coercion of any child to engage in, or assist any other person to engage in, any sexually explicit conduct or simulation of such conduct for the purpose of producing a visual depiction of such conduct; or

B. the rape, and in cases of caretaker or inter-familial relationships, statutory rape, molestation, prostitution, or other form of sexual exploitation of children, or incest with children.

Categories of sexual abuse include the following:

1. *Incest.* Physical sexual activity between members of the extended family.

2. *Pedophilia.* Sexual preference by an adult for prepubertal children.

3. *Exhibitionism.* Exposure of genitals to someone of the opposite gender.

4. *Molestation.* Fondling, touching, masturbation in front of, or kissing of the child, especially on the breast and/or genital areas.

5. *Sexual intercourse (statutory rape).* Includes penile–vaginal intercourse, fellatio (oral–genital contact), and sodomy (anal–genital contact).

6. *Rape.* Sexual intercourse or attempted sexual intercourse without consent.

7. *Sexual sadism.* Infliction of bodily harm for sexual gratification.

8. *Child pornography.* Photographs, videos, or films showing sexual acts featuring children.

9. *Child prostitution.* Children in sex acts for profit. (Kempe & Kempe, 1984)

10. *Child trafficking.* Occurs when children are sold and imprisoned and requires timely identification (UNICEF, 2018).

Sexual conduct becomes abuse when activities are instigated through trickery or force with the instigator—one who has caretaking relations with the child or has age and maturational advantage over the child. Abuse also includes a perpetrator who has a power advantage over a child (Putman, 2009) physically and mentally. Most sexual abuse is committed by someone who is close to the child, placing the child at high risk for repeat attacks.

Abuse can be categorized as contact and noncontact sexual abuse. Contact includes touching sexual parts of a child's body or having the child touch parts of the sexual partner's body, which may include penetration (into the vagina, mouth, or anus) and nonpenetration. Nonpenetration contact involves fondling, kissing, or touching sexual parts of the body by either the child or the partner. Noncontact sexual abuse occurs when the victims are forced to watch sexual acts or private parts of body or also read or look at sexually explicit materials such as videos, photographs, magazines, etc.

An estimated 300,000 children are involved in child pornography. Although historically most societies have had taboos against such behavior, sexual abuse and incest have always existed. But sexual abuse generally has been concealed, mythicized, or ignored. Not until the late 1970s and early 1980s did its existence become realistically recognized. Even then, most people gathering information on the problem believed that, as in reported incidents of other kinds of child abuse, only the tip of the iceberg had been revealed. According to Martin & Alaggia (2014), cyberspace has added a new dimension to the distribution of child pornography, as it is unfortunately readily available for perpetrators.

Incest and other sexual abuse occur in all socioeconomic groups, and therefore teachers in all schools or childcare settings should be aware of the indicators. Sexually abused children often exhibit some of the following physical and behavioral characteristics (Krugman, 1986; Riggs, 1982):

Physical signs

- Bruises or bleeding in external genitalia or anal area
- Uncomfortable while sitting
- Difficulty walking
- Pregnancy
- Torn, bloody, or stained underclothing
- Sexually transmitted disease

Behavioral signs

- Appetite disorders
- Phobias
- Guilt
- Temper tantrums
- Neurotic and conduct disorders
- Truancy
- Suicide attempts
- Confides with teacher or nurse that he or she has been sexually mistreated
- Reports by other children that their friend is being sexually mistreated
- Displays precocious sexual behavior and/or knowledge
- Unwilling to change for gym
- Withdrawn
- Depressed, sad, and teary eyed
- Confused about own identity
- Frequent absences justified by caregiver or parent
- Acts out in a seductive manner
- Reluctant to go home
- Young child regresses to earlier behavior by engaging in thumb-sucking and/or bed wetting, has difficulty eating and/or sleeping, and is fearful of the dark
- Older child turns to drugs, tries to run away, and has difficulty doing schoolwork

Concern about sexual abuse has steadily risen because of its deleterious effects on the child and, later, the adult. Psychological and emotional reactions are common. Children feel trapped, confused, betrayed, and disgraced. They might have fears, phobias, somatic complaints, mood changes, anxieties, hysterical seizures, multiple personalities, or nightmares (Rafanello, 2010).

According to RAINN (Rape, Abuse, Incent, National Network), sexual abuse occurs every 8 minutes. Unfortunately sexual abuse is often not reported. Statistics by RAINN (2018) show that each year between 2009 and 2013 there were 63,000 victims of child sexual abuse. Figure 11.3 provides parents with ideas from the Child Welfare Information Gateway (2014a) for talking with children about sexual abuse.

Figure 11.3 Suggestions to Parents for Preventing Child Sexual Abuse

What You Can Do

- Take time at the end of each day to connect with your children with a hug, a smile, a song, or a few minutes of listening and talking.
- Find ways to engage your children while completing everyday tasks (meals, shopping, driving in the car). Talk about what you are doing, ask them questions, or play simple games (such as "I spy").

- Explore parenting questions with your family doctor, your child's teacher, family, or friends.
- Subscribe to a magazine, website, or online newsletter about child development.
- Take a parenting class at a local community center (these often have sliding fee scales).
- Sit and observe what your child can and cannot do.
- Share what you learn with anyone who cares for your child.

- Take quiet time to reenergize: Take a bath, write, sing, laugh, play, drink a cup of tea.
- Do some physical exercise: Walk, stretch, do yoga, lift weights, dance.
- Share your feelings with someone you trust.
- Surround yourself with people who support you and make you feel good about yourself.

- Participate in neighborhood activities such as potluck dinners, street fairs, picnics, or block parties.
- Join a playgroup or online support group of parents with children at similar ages.
- Find a church, temple, or mosque that welcomes and supports parents.

- Make a list of people or places to call for support.
- Ask the director of your child's school to host a Community Resource Night, so you (and other parents) can see what help your community offers.
- Dial "2-1-1" to find out about organizations that support families in your area.

- Provide regular routines, especially for young children. Make sure everyone who cares for your child is aware of your routines around mealtimes, naps, and bedtime.
- Talk with your children about how important feelings are.
- Teach and encourage children to solve problems in age-appropriate ways.

Source: Child Welfare Information Gateway (2014a). Retrieved from https://www.childwelfare.gov/preventing/

Boys and girls have similar responses to sexual abuse, both long term and short term, including fears, sleep problems, and distractedness (Finkelhor, 1990). Whereas boys may act out more aggressively, girls may act more depressed. The differences show boys are less symptomatic when evaluated by teachers and parents, but equally symptomatic when evaluated by themselves.

Children who are sexually abused present lower interpersonal trust. They have a sense of loneliness, feel different from others in their peer group, and display social difficulties (Blanchard-Dallaire & Hébert, 2014). To understand a child's predicament, one must understand the helplessness the child feels in responding to the adult who is more physically powerful and supposedly more knowledgeable. The adult first approaches the child with the need for secrecy: "Everything will be all right if you do not tell. No one else will understand our secret." "Your mother will hate you." "If you tell,

it will break up the family." "If you tell, I'll kill your pet." "If you tell, I'll spank you." Whatever the secret, the child is in a no-win position: If he tells the secret, he might get hurt, and even if he does tell, the reaction is often disbelief.

The teacher or childcare giver who suspects sexual abuse must report those suspicions—social service and child protection agencies are established in every state. In Texas, for example, the law protects children by providing a process that includes the involvement of different agencies in order to keep them safe (Texas Attorney General, 2018).

The teacher's role is a supportive one. Continue to have normal expectations for the child, keep a stable environment for the child, and do not make the child feel ostracized or different. Treat the child with understanding, be sensitive to the child's needs, and help build the child's self-esteem. Several programs have been developed to help the child develop defenses against personal abuse.

Reviewers and teachers have asked for more help in responding to a child who tells about an abusive situation. An article by Austin (2000) gives suggestions to help teachers respond to a sexually abused child. The topics include the following:

- Remain calm and reassuring. Speak quietly; do not panic.
- Take the child to a private place like the nurse's office.
- Position yourself at the child's eye level.
- Speak on the child's level. Use language the child understands.
- Listen intently.
- Take the child seriously.
- Obtain only the information necessary to make a report.
- Do not put words in the child's mouth.
- Do not use words that the child has not already used. (Don't use words describing sex that are not in the child's vocabulary.)
- Allow the child to have feelings.
- Reassure the child that the abuse is not his or her fault.

- Start your conversation with general open-ended questions and allow the child to tell the story without interrupting.
- Do not condemn the abuser.
- Let the child know that he or she is not alone and that you are willing to help.
- Do not touch the child without permission.
- Tell the truth—do not make promises you will not be able to keep.
- Tell the child about the process, that others will be told about the abuse.
- Thank the child for confiding in you.
- Help the child devise a safety plan if abuse occurs again. Have the child tell someone immediately—a reliable person at home or a teacher or school professional.
- Assure the child that she or he will remain with someone safe until authorities come. Do not allow the child to return to the home of the abuser.

Approximately 1,770 children died from child abuse and neglect in 2016 (Child Welfare Information Gateway, 2018). Figure 11.4 shows the fatality victims by age with the youngest children being the most vulnerable. Figure 11.5 shows that neglect is the most common type of abuse that leads to fatalities.

Figure 11.4 Child Abuse and Neglect Fatality Victims by Age, 2016

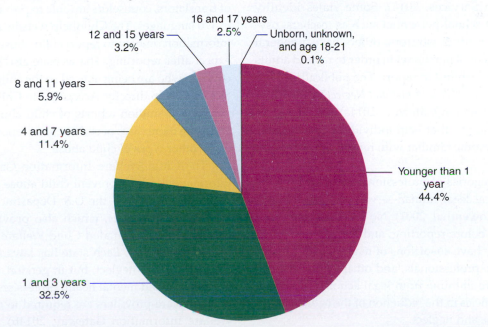

- 16 and 17 years 2.5%
- 12 and 15 years 3.2%
- Unborn, unknown, and age 18-21 0.1%
- 8 and 11 years 5.9%
- 4 and 7 years 11.4%
- Younger than 1 year 44.4%
- 1 and 3 years 32.5%

Figure 11.5 Child Abuse and Neglect Fatalities by Maltreatment Type, 2016

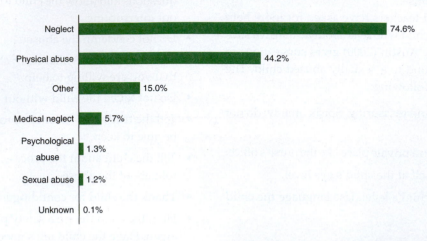

Source: Child Welfare Information Gateway. (2018). Child abuse and neglect fatalities 2016: Statistics and interventions. Retrieved on November 2, 2018 from https://www.childwelfare.gov/pubPDFs/fatality.pdf.

Responsibility to Report

School personnel and childcare staff members have more than a moral responsibility to report suspected abuse. Reporting abuse helps with the early detection and even prevention of abuse (Goebbels, Nicholson, Walsh, & DeVries, 2008). Laws in each state require childcare workers to report suspected cases of abuse (Horton & Cruise, 2001; U.S. Department of Health and Human Services, 2014). Some states identify categories of school personnel such as teachers, psychologists, or administrators; others have a general category of school personnel in order to remind adults of their responsibility to report. The publication *Mandatory Reporters of Child Abuse and Neglect* by the Child Welfare Information Gateway (2014a) provides state statute summaries that help individuals, particularly educators, become familiar with reporting laws within their state.

Four categories of professional-mandated reporting are medical, legal, human-service professionals, and educators (Lowenthal, 2001). No states require proof of the abuse before reporting, and the reporters must report if they have suspicions of maltreatment. Teachers, childcare professionals, and others who report in good faith are immune from legal action. Schools are essential agencies in the reduction of the national crisis of child abuse and neglect.

Reporting Child Abuse and Neglect

The nonprofit organization Childhelp provides the National Child Abuse Hotline, which is dedicated to the prevention of child abuse (Childhelp, 2018). This hotline serves the United States, its territories, and Canada. It is staffed 24 hours a day, seven days a week, by crisis professional counselors. With the use of translators, counselors are able to provide assistance in 170 languages. The Childhelp website also provides information on how to report child abuse and what to expect after reporting. The website also has a link for children who are being abused so the children can contact Childhelp directly. According to Childhelp, every year over 3 million reports of child abuse are made. There are more cases of child neglect reported than any of the other types of child abuse.

The Child Welfare Information Gateway gives information to help prevent child abuse. This organization is a service of the U.S. Department of Health and Human Services, which also provides links to the Statewide Automated Child Welfare Information System (SACWIS). Each state has laws for reporting child abuse and neglect, but in general, social workers, medical and mental health professionals, teachers, and childcare providers are required to report (Child Welfare Information Gateway, 2014b). The hotline

Figure 11.6 Professionals Responsible for Child Maltreatment Reporting

Professionals submitted the majority of screened-in referrals (reports) that received an investigation or alternative response

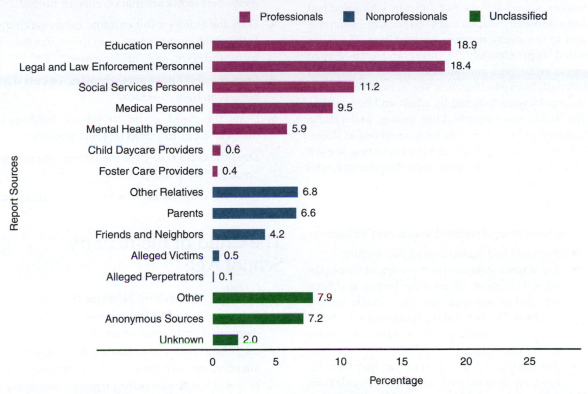

Source: U.S. Department of Health & Human Services, Administration for Children and Families, Administration on Children, Youth and Families. Children's Bureau. (2018). Child Maltreatment. Retrieved on October 23, 2018 from https://www.acf.hhs.gov/cb/research-data-technology/statistics-research/child-maltreatment

numbers are included in the Child Welfare Information Gateway website; live chat is also available during business hours. The information is also provided in Spanish. When a child is in immediate danger, everyone is required to call 911.

Who Reports Maltreatment Cases?

Cases of child maltreatment must be reported by both nonprofessionals and professionals. Educators have become much more aware of their responsibility, and most reports come from this group (16.5% in 2004), as shown on Figure 11.6. Professionals—including educators as well as law enforcement, social services, and medical personnel—made 55.7% of the reports. Friends and family members reported 19.6% of the cases (U.S. Department of Health and Human Services, 2004). Situations related to teachers and schools are described in *Child Abuse and Neglect: A Shared Community Concern* (U.S. Department of Health and Human Services, 1992). Two examples follow.

REPORT

When Cindy was 8 years of age, her teacher called Child Protection Services (CPS). Cindy was the only child in her family who wore old, tattered clothing to school and was not given the same privileges and opportunities as her brothers and sisters. The other children were allowed to join in after-school activities; however, Cindy was not allowed to participate in any outside activities. Cindy became very withdrawn at school. She stopped speaking in class and would not engage in play activities with her classmates. Her academic performance declined rapidly. Finally, Cindy became incontinent and had "accidents" in class.

REASONS

The reasons the teacher reported this case to CPS were:

- Serious differential treatment of one child in the family.
- Marked decline in academic performance and class participation.
- Incontinence.

REPORT

Susan, age 7, was in her first-grade class when her teacher noticed that she had difficulty sitting and had some unusually shaped marks on her arm. Susan was sent to the school nurse to be examined. The nurse noted approximately 12 linear and loop-shaped marks on her back and buttocks. These marks ranged in length from 6 to 10 inches. The nurse believed that the marks were inflicted by a belt and belt buckle. The marks were purple, blue, brown, and yellow, indicating that the bruises were sustained at different times. Susan said she did not know how she got the bruises. The nurse spoke with the principal, who called CPS.

REASONS

The school principal reported this case to CPS because:

- The child had sustained a physical injury.
- The bruises were inflicted at different times, perhaps days apart. (Even if the bruises had been inflicted at one time, this case should still be reported. The fact that the bruises were in different stages of healing raises greater concern for the child's safety.)
- The nurse's clinical opinion was that the injuries were inflicted by a belt and belt buckle (U.S. Department of Health and Human Services, 1992).

Indicators that a child has the potential need for protections is described in Figure 11.7.

Parent and Child Behaviors as Indications of Abuse and Neglect Abuse

Specialists working with child abuse have developed some guidelines to help educators determine the existence of child abuse (Fontana, 1973a; Helfer & Kempe, 1987). The following information has been modified from publications by Head Start, the U.S. Department of Health and Human Services, and the American Humane Association.

The Child of Preschool Age

1. Does the child seem to fear his or her parents?
2. Does the child miss preschool or the childcare center often?

3. Does the child bear evidence of physical abuse? Are there signs of battering, such as bruises or welts, belt or buckle marks, cuts, or burns?
4. Does the child exhibit extreme behavior changes? Is the child very aggressive at times and then fearful, withdrawn, and/or depressed?
5. Does the child have sores, bruises, or cuts that are not adequately cared for?
6. Does the child come to school inadequately dressed? Does the child look uncared for?
7. Does the child take over the parent role and try to "mother" the parent?
8. Does the child seem to be hungry for affection?

The Child of Elementary School Age

1. Does the child exhibit behavior that deviates from the norm? Is the child (a) aggressive, destructive, and disruptive or (b) passive and withdrawn? The first might be a child who is shouting for help, demanding attention, and striking out, whereas the second might be out of touch with reality, remote, submissive, and subdued, but crying for help in another way.
2. Does the child miss classes, or is the child often tardy? Does the child come to school too early and stay around after hours? In the first instance, the child's behavior suggests problems at home. In the second, the child might be pushed out in the morning and have nowhere to go after school.
3. Does the child bear evidence of physical abuse? Are there obvious signs of battering: bruises, belt or buckle marks, welts, lacerations, or burns?
4. Does the child lack social skills? Is the child unable to approach other children and play with them?
5. Does the child have learning problems that cannot be diagnosed? Does the child underperform? If intelligence tests show average academic ability and the child is not able to do the work, there might be problems at home.
6. Does the child show great sensitivity to others' feelings? Does the child get upset when another person is criticized? Abused children often have to "mother" their abusive parents, and some are overly sensitive to the feelings of others.

Figure 11.7 Indicators of a Child's Potential Need for Protection

	Physical Indicators	*Behavioral Indicators*
Physical Abuse	• Unexplained bruises (in various stages of healing), welts, human bite marks, bald spots • Unexplained burns, especially cigarette burns or immersion burns (glovelike) • Unexplained fractures, lacerations, or abrasions	• Self-destructive • Withdrawn and aggressive—behavioral extremes • Uncomfortable with physical contact • Arrives at school early or stays late as if afraid to be at home • Chronic runaway (adolescents) • Complains of soreness or moves uncomfortably • Wears clothing inappropriate to weather, to cover body
Physical Neglect	• Abandonment • Unattended medical needs • Consistent lack of supervision • Consistent hunger, inappropriate dress, poor hygiene • Lice, distended stomach, emaciated	• Regularly displays fatigue or listlessness, falls asleep in class • Steals food, begs from classmates • Reports that no caretaker is at home • Frequently absent or tardy • Self-destructive • School dropout (adolescents)
Sexual Abuse	• Torn, stained, or bloody underclothing • Pain or itching in genital area • Difficulty walking or sitting • Bruises or bleeding in external genitalia • Venereal disease • Frequent urinary or yeast infections	• Withdrawal, chronic depression • Excessive seductiveness • Role reversal, overly concerned for siblings • Poor self-esteem, self-devaluation, lack of confidence • Peer problems, lack of involvement • Massive weight change • Suicide attempts (especially adolescents) • Hysteria, lack of emotional control • Sudden school difficulties • Inappropriate sex play or premature understanding of sex • Threatened by physical contact, closeness
Emotional Maltreatment	• Speech disorders • Delayed physical development • Substance abuse • Ulcers, asthma, severe allergies	• Habit disorders (sucking, rocking) • Antisocial, destructive • Neurotic traits (sleep disorders, inhibition of play) • Passive and aggressive—behavioral extremes • Delinquent behavior (especially adolescents) • Developmentally delayed

Source: From *Guidelines for Schools to Help Protect Abused and Neglected Children*, by the American Association for Protecting Children (n.d.), Denver, CO: American Humane Association. Reprinted with permission. Adapted in part from *Early Childhood Programs and the Prevention and Treatment of Child Abuse and Neglect* (The User Manual Series), by D. D. Broadhurst, M. Edmunds, and R. A. MacDicken, 1979, Washington, DC: U.S. Department of Health, Education, and Welfare.

7. Does the child come to school inadequately dressed? Is the child unwashed and uncared for? These can be signs of neglect.

8. Does the child seem tired or fall asleep in class?

9. Does the child appear undernourished? Does the child attempt to save food? Is there real poverty in the home, or do the parents not care?

10. Does the child seem to be afraid of his or her parents?

The Secondary-Level Student

Most of the traits just mentioned are relevant to detection of abuse in the middle school and high school student, but there are additional signs to watch for in the upper levels. High school students may experience abuse from fellow students, boyfriends/girlfriends, and unfortunately teachers. In addition to evidence of physical abuse, neglect, truancy, and tardiness, the older student might experience the following:

1. Does the student have to assume too much responsibility at home?

2. Does the parent expect unrealistic and overly controlled behavior?

3. Does the student have difficulty conforming to school regulations and policies?

4. Does the student have problems communicating with his or her parents?

5. Does the student have a history of running away from home or refusing to go home?

6. Does the student act out sexually?

7. Does the student lack freedom and friends?

The Child with Special Needs

The most vulnerable children are those with special needs, particularly those who suffer intellectual disabilities. In a study conducted in Canada by Dion, Paquette, Tremblay, Collin-Vézina, and Chabot (2018) the researchers found that children with intellectual disabilities, or ID, experienced more severe maltreatment and were referred more frequently to child protection services. In the U.S. and the rest of the world, children with intellectual disabilities are more susceptible to abuse and neglect. The Division for Early Childhood of the Council of Exceptional Children or DEC developed a position statement that focuses on how to "prevent and reduce instances of maltreatment as well as how to support young children with disabilities and their families who have experienced maltreatment" (DEC, 2016).

The School System and Child Abuse

Although some children recover from maltreatment without serious consequences, the evidence is clear that maltreatment often has deleterious effects on children's mental health and development, both short- and long-term (Child Welfare Information Gateway, 2014b). The quality of life that a child is entitled to is one without suffering inflicted by others. Although most victims of serious and fatal child abuse are very young, to regard older children and adolescents as invulnerable to the severe consequences of abuse and neglect is a mistake.

Because of required school attendance and an increase in the use of childcare centers, caregivers and teachers have an expanded opportunity for contact with families and children. These professionals work closely with children and families over extended periods. In so doing, they are also the people most able to detect and prevent abuse and neglect. The responsibilities are great, but an affirmative response by schools is vital to the well-being of thousands of children throughout the United States.

School has not always been recognized as an important agency in the detection of child abuse, but with more than 70% of the children who are abused or neglected having contact with schools or childcare centers, the school's role in detecting and preventing child abuse is vital. Through Parents as Teachers, Early Head Start and Head Start, and private and public preschool programs, it has become easier to detect abuse of 2- to 6-year-olds.

Better Information and Education on Reporting

The U.S. Advisory Board on Child Abuse and Neglect (1993) made 27 recommendations for responding to this crisis. Recommendation D-4a refers to Child Protection and the Schools as follows:

STRENGTHENING THE ROLE OF ELEMENTARY AND SECONDARY SCHOOLS IN THE PROTECTION OF CHILDREN. The federal government should take all necessary measures to ensure that the nation's elementary and secondary schools, both public and private, participate more effectively in the prevention, identification, and treatment of child abuse and neglect. Such measures should include knowledge building, program development, program evaluation, data collection, training, and technical assistance. The objective of such measures should be the development and implementation by State Educational Agencies (SEAs) in association with Local Educational Agencies (LEAs) and a consortia of LEAs of the following:

- Inter-agency multidisciplinary training for teachers, counselors, and administrative personnel on child abuse and neglect;

- Specialized training for school health and mental health personnel on the treatment of child abuse and neglect;

- School-based, inter-agency, multidisciplinary supportive services for families in which child abuse or neglect is known to have occurred or where children are at high risk of maltreatment, including self-help groups for students and parents of students;

- Family life education, including parenting skills and home visits, for students and/or parents; and

- Other school-based inter-agency, multidisciplinary programs intended to strengthen families and support children who may have been subjected to maltreatment, including school-based family resource centers and after-school programs for elementary and secondary school pupils which promote collaboration between schools and public and private community agencies in child protection (p. 164).

Both public and private schools are considered essential to the child-protection system and have responsibilities to effectively provide for the children who attend schools.

The school professionals must take into account legal considerations (mandated reporting), ethical considerations (confidentiality), and moral considerations (commitment to the child's well-being) (Horton & Cruise, 2001). When a professional reports suspicions of maltreatment, "families may move away from the school or at least cancel their children's participation in any counseling relationships" (p. 55). The parents might feel that their belief and trust in the school have been destroyed. Reporting, however, can prevent severe physical injury, psychological harm, or inadequate nourishment and health care. However, "reports may protect children from severe physical injury or even death. Psychological suffering may be lessened and dysfunctional patterns interrupted. Families may get needed services" (p. 56).

The school must serve as a defense against child abuse in three basic ways: (a) as a referral agency to child protection agencies—reporting suspected abuse is required by law; (b) as an educational institution offering parent education, family-life education, and home visitations to adults and students; and (c) as a support system for families and as a collaborator with other agencies in providing a total protection system.

Internet Safety

In recent years, children using the Internet have become vulnerable to pedophiles and pornographers. Children can inadvertently become exposed to pornography by simply typing the word *legs,* for LEGOS. Several steps must be taken to protect children by teachers, parents, and children themselves. It has been recommended that preventive software such as filtering, monitoring, or blocking be installed as an Internet safety plan for children, particularly those younger than 15 years of age (Ybarra, Finkelhorn, Mitchell, & Wolak, 2009). First, parents and teachers must monitor children's use of computers. At school, teachers can set up safe websites that control what children will be able to access. Parents can contact their Internet service providers to block certain materials from coming into a child's computer. The filtering programs can also restrict personal information from being sent online. In addition, children can be guided to discriminate between appropriate sites and those that make them feel uncomfortable. All three steps are necessary to safeguard children (Kids Health, 2006).

Dombrowski and Gischlar (2014) provide a set of strategies for families to follow to keep children safe while on the Internet. Some of the strategies include discussing dangers (use age-appropriate conversations), teach children not to give personal information, do not allow children to download games unless you know the source and you download for them, and create a contract (see Figure 11.8).

Figure 11.8 Family Contract for Social Media Safety

I, _____ (write your name) understand that the rules for using social media apply not only at home but any location where I can gain access. I have read and understand the importance of keeping myself safe from potentially dangerous situations. I will contact an adult, preferably my parents, teachers, or a family member should I encounter suspicious activities. This contract will be posted on my door so that I can remember to follow my promise.

Child's signature _____

Parent's signature _____

Bullying and Violence in Schools

Bullying is "a relationship-based form of aggression, which involves the use of various behaviors to humiliate, dominate, and oppress others" (Burkhart, Knox, & Brockmyer, 2013). Bullying appears in early childhood and at the same rate for males and females (Burkhart et al., 2013). According to Stopbullying.gov (2018), there are three types of bullying: verbal, social, and physical. Emotional bullying is also a type of bullying as it includes teasing, threatening, taunting, calling names, or starting negative rumors about someone. Children's reactions to bullying depend on the context and the bullying episode (Fox, Jones, Stiff, & Sayers, 2014).

The Centers for Disease Control, or CDC (2018), indicates that bullying is usually associated with children who have defiant or disruptive behaviors, harsh parenting by caregivers, and attitudes accepting of violence. Furthermore, the CDC explains that the victims are usually children who have low self-esteem, poor peer relationships, and who are perceived by others as shy or quiet.

Teaching children tolerance and acceptance is teaching them to avoid bullying. It is disheartening to see a child feeling unsafe at school. My daughter had two "friends" that constantly taunted her until she learned that such "friends" were not really friends and she was able to get away from them. The unfortunate fact is that these two girls will continue to bully others if they are not helped. The CDC (2014b) has four steps for bullying prevention:

Step 1: Define and monitor the problem

Step 2: Identify risk and protective factors

Step 3: Develop and test prevention strategies

Step 4: Ensure widespread adoption

Being bullied can lead to drastic occurrences such as school shootings. In the first half of 2018 we heard of 23 school shootings (Strickland, 2018). Children and families are afraid to attend school because of the threat of gun violence. We often hear that emotional reasons such as bullying may cause students to break down and cause harm to others. Mental health is a very real threat and with the high incidence of child abuse that threat becomes even more real.

Awareness of Abuse, Child to Child

Another area of concern that has been evident in schools and playgrounds for many years, but which is most often overlooked as a process of growing up, is degradation of one child by another, whether it is defined as bullying or teasing. Research by the Family and Work Institute, conducted from October to December 2001 on children grades 5 through 12, found that 67% of the children in the study experienced being teased or negatively gossiped about during a one-month span. The study cannot say which came first, being hurt or hurting, but 68% of those who were gossiped about or teased in the month turned around and did the same to others. Sixty-one percent of the students in the study had been rejected or ignored, and 32% had been bullied (Galinsky & Salmond, 2002). More children are bullied, hit, kicked, and shoved between fifth and eighth grade than high school, where there is more gossip and students are more often teased.

Programs designed to reduce devastating experiences for children in school need to be implemented. Action steps to end violence include the following:

1. Help establish norms where differences are not put down but are celebrated.

2. Work toward the creation of a civil society where there is more caring and respect.

3. Improve the relationships that children have in all aspects of their lives—at home and at school.

4. Include young people's views of how to end violence in violence prevention efforts.

5. Establish, invest in, and evaluate violence prevention efforts as well as positive youth development efforts (Galinsky & Salmond, 2002).

6. Do *not* victimize the child who has already been bullied and victimized.

TEACHERS AND BULLYING. Teachers are extremely important to a child's feeling adequate, competent, and cared for. One way teachers can lose this and add to a child's insecurity is by using children as scapegoats in a class. They control the rest of the class by focusing on one or two children who are targeted for discipline and negative reinforcement. I have observed classrooms in which teachers cause emotional abuse in their efforts to control the classroom. Teachers can have an attitude toward a child that fosters prejudice and discrimination against that child by the child's classmates. They do not recognize that they are, in effect, emotionally abusing the child. Their actions are not occasional disciplinary decisions; they are caused by a repeated pattern as described by James Garbarino, past Executive

Director of the Erikson Institute, as "the chronic pattern that erodes and corrodes a child . . . that persistent, chronic pattern of behavior toward a child" (American Humane Association, 1992c, p. 2).

Garbarino was speaking about parents and children, but this chronic pattern is also damaging when it is used in the schools. An occasional loss of control by parents (or teachers) does not indicate emotional abuse. Human beings can lose control and say hurtful things from time to time, but a person who consistently destroys a child's self-esteem is extremely hurtful to the child and is emotionally abusing the child.

The International Bullying Prevention Association also provides conferences, resources, and training to guide adults in effective strategies to develop environments to protect victims of bullying. The organization also recognizes the need to guide and redirect children that bully others, so they have the chance to develop constructive interpersonal relations (International Bullying Prevention Association, 2006).

Corporal Punishment in Schools

Does there seem to be an element of inconsistency in our work to eliminate abuse in the schools with the policy of corporal punishment still in place in many schools? Every industrialized country in the world prohibits school corporal punishment except the United States and one state in Australia (Center for Effective Discipline, 2006). According to Gershoff and Font (2016) school corporal punishment is still legal in 19 states in the U.S. and over 160,000 children are disciplined by this method every year. The report highlights that males are more likely to experience corporal punishment and that racial disparities exist as Black children have a higher rate of experiencing corporal punishment in general.

By 2007, 29 states and the District of Columbia had banned corporal punishment: Alaska, California, Connecticut, Delaware, Hawaii, Illinois, Iowa, Maine, Maryland, Massachusetts, Michigan, Minnesota, Montana, Nebraska, Nevada, New Hampshire, New Jersey, New York, North Dakota, Oregon, Pennsylvania, Rhode Island, South Dakota, Utah, Vermont, Virginia, Washington, West Virginia, and Wisconsin. Many cities in states that have not abolished corporal punishment have abolished the practice in their schools (Center for Effective Discipline, 2007; U.S. Department of Education, 2005). In general, schools have been alarmingly slow to join the national movement to reduce abuse—a movement that began in the 1960s and has continued into the 21st century. Thus, schools perpetuate the use of force to discipline children.

Why Do Abuse and Neglect Continue to Happen?

The National Center on Child Abuse and Neglect identified the following factors to determine which contribute to ongoing abuse and neglect of children:

- *Family income.* Children who come from families with incomes below the poverty level are seven times more likely to be abused than those at a higher income level.

- *Gender.* A child's gender has no effect on whether the child is neglected. However, girls are more likely to be abused than boys. The rate of sexual abuse is three times higher for girls than for boys.

- *Family size.* Children in families with four or more children are more likely to be neglected or abused.

- *Race or ethnicity.* There was no significant difference among children of different ethnic groups.

- *Type of community.* Abuse and neglect occur in rural, suburban, and urban communities (U.S. Department of Health and Human Services, 1992).

- *Exposure to violence.* Personal experience and exposure to media reports, television programs, Internet, and movies expose the child and the school to excessive violence.

Characteristics and Risk Factors of Abusive Parents

Three approaches for understanding abusive parents have been investigated: the psychological model, the sociological model, and the parent–child interaction model.

In the psychological model, lack of empathy distinguishes the abusive parent. In the sociological model, cultural attitudes toward violence, social stress, family size, and social isolation are factors that relate to child abuse. Prevention and treatment based on the sociological model focus on the effect the community and society have on the family. Environmental stress is a sociological risk factor in the abuse of children. Stress from poverty or in the workplace can cause anxiety in parents, and they might lash out at their child.

In the parent–child interaction model, the parents lack skill in interacting with their children, disciplining them, and teaching them appropriate behavior (Wiehe, 1989). Parents might have had inadequate exposure to positive parenting and lack information on child development. If raised by maladaptive parents or if raised with cultural beliefs that are compatible with mistreatment, the parent might not be capable of adapting to the child's needs.

The U.S. Department of Health and Human Services (1992) offered these reasons why parents might be more likely to abuse their children:

> Parents may be more likely to maltreat their children if they abuse drugs or alcohol (alcoholic mothers are three times more likely and alcoholic fathers are eight times more likely to abuse or neglect their children than are nonalcoholic parents); are emotionally immature or needy; are isolated, with no family or friends to depend on; were emotionally deprived, abused or neglected as children; feel worthless and have never been loved or cared about; or are in poor health. Many abusive and neglectful parents do not intend to harm their children and often feel remorse about their maltreating behavior. However, their own problems may prevent them from stopping their harmful behavior and may result in resistance to outside intervention. It is important to remember that diligent and effective intervention efforts may overcome the parents' resistance and help them change their abusive and neglectful behavior.

Children are more likely to be at risk of maltreatment if they are unwanted, resemble someone the parents dislike, or have physical or behavioral traits which make them different or especially difficult to care for. Family interactions and environmental conditions are two situations that may cause families to abuse and neglect children.

- *Family interactions.* Each member of a family affects every other member of that family in some way. Some parents and children are fine on their own, but just cannot get along when they are together, especially for long periods of time. Some characteristics commonly observed in abusive or neglectful families include social isolation and parents turning to their children to meet their emotional needs.

- *Environmental conditions.* Changes in financial condition, employment status, or family structure can shake a family's stability. Some parents might not be able to cope with the stress resulting from the

changes and can experience difficulty in caring for their children (U.S. Department of Health and Human Services, 1992, p. 5).

The National Center on Child Abuse and Neglect suggests these guiding principles:

- Child maltreatment is a family problem. Consequently, our treatment efforts must focus on the family as a whole as well as the individual family members. Treatment must be provided to abused and neglected children as well as their parents. Unless children receive the support and treatment for the trauma they have suffered, they could suffer permanent physical, mental, or emotional handicaps, and as adults they might continue the cycle of abuse with their own family or other children. In addition, abused and neglected children are more likely than other children to have substance abuse problems.

- Although we cannot predict with certainty who will abuse or neglect their children, we do know the signs indicating *high risk*. People at high risk include parents who abuse drugs and alcohol, young parents who are ill-prepared for the parenting role, families experiencing great stress who have poor coping skills and have no one to turn to for support, and parents who have difficulty with or who have not developed an emotional bond with their infant. We need to be alert to these and other high risk indicators and offer assistance, support, counseling, and/or parent education to families at risk before their children are harmed.

- Families at risk may be most receptive to help soon after the birth of their first child.

- Child sexual abuse prevention programs aimed at school-aged children appear to be useful in helping children avoid sexually abusive situations and to say no to inappropriate touch by adults. However, prevention programs must be carefully examined and selected. These programs must be responsive to the learning capacities and developmental stages of the children involved. Inappropriately designed programs can frighten young children or fail to teach them what they can do to protect themselves.

- Volunteers can be very effective with some abusive and neglectful parents—especially with those parents who are experiencing stress, who have been emotionally deprived, and who lack knowledge of child development and effective parenting skills. Volunteers must be carefully screened, trained, and supervised.

Clearly, if we are going to stop child abuse and neglect and help the child victims and their families, we all must work together. Efforts must occur at the federal, state, and local levels (U.S. Department of Health and Human Services, 1992, pp. 10–11).

The following behavioral characteristics can help the professional determine the likelihood of abuse or neglect:

1. Do the parents fail to show up for appointments? Do they stay away from school? When they come to school, are they uncooperative and unresponsive?

2. Do the parents have unrealistically high expectations for themselves and their child? Do the parents describe the child as "different" or "bad"?

3. Do the parents have expectations for the child that are inconsistent or inappropriate for the child's age?

4. Do the parents become aggressive or abusive when school personnel want to talk about the child's problems?

5. Do the parents isolate themselves? Do they know other parents in the school? Are they known by other parents?

6. Do they lack knowledge of child development and the child's physical and psychological needs?

7. Do the parents report that they were abused or neglected as children?

8. Do the parents refuse to participate in school events?

9. Do the parents ignore the child and avoid touching?

10. Do the parents show little interest in the child's activities or concern for the child's well-being?

Development of Policies

School districts and childcare centers need to develop the policies and training programs vital to successful child abuse intervention. If there is no policy, the teacher should see the school nurse, psychologist, director, counselor, social worker, or principal, depending on the staffing of the school. Even in a school district with a policy statement, each school or childcare center should have one person who is responsible for

receiving reports of child abuse. Making one person responsible results in greater awareness of the problem of abuse and facilitates reporting. It is also helpful to establish a committee to view evidence and support the conclusions of the original observer. A written report contains the details of the situation.

All states require reporting of suspected child abuse. Evidence of violent physical abuse must be reported immediately. If school officials refuse to act, you should call social services, law enforcement, or a family crisis center. The person making the report should have the right to remain anonymous. When reporting in good faith, the person reporting is protected by immunity described in state legislation. Colorado law, for example, specifically states: "Any person participating in good faith in the making of a report or in a judicial proceeding held pursuant to this title shall be immune from any liability, civil or criminal, that otherwise might result by reason of such reporting" (Denver Public Schools, 1992).

Needs Assessment

Schools and childcare centers first must determine the prevention and protection delivery systems that are already available in the community. They should consider social-service departments, child-protection teams, child-welfare agencies, law enforcement, juvenile court systems, Head Start, childcare centers, hospitals, clinics, public-health nurses, mental-health programs, public and private service groups, fundraising agencies such as United Way, and service organizations that might be unique to their community.

Following assessment of the community, the schools and childcare centers have to determine their roles in an integrated approach to abuse and neglect. Communication lines must be kept open at all times. A representative of the schools should serve on the child-protection team. One role that is mandated is identification of abuse and neglect. Other roles will be individualized according to the needs of the community, the resources in the schools and childcare centers, and the commitment of the personnel.

Policy

Child abuse is found in all socioeconomic groups in the United States, so all school districts must be prepared to work with interdisciplinary agencies in the detection and prevention of this national social problem.

Policies should be written in compliance with the requirements of each state's reporting statute, details of which can be learned by consulting the state's attorney general. Because reporting is required in all states, the policy should include a clear statement of reporting requirements. The policy should also inform school personnel of their immunity and legal obligations. Dissemination of the policy should include the community as well as all school employees. Not only is it important that the community realize the obligation of the school or childcare center to report suspected abuse or neglect, it also is vital that the community become aware of the extent of the problem.

Communication with Families

Just as there are varieties and levels of abuse and neglect, there should be variations in the school's interaction with parents. Talking to a parent regarding observed behaviors that could be linked to abuse is very challenging. When I was a prekindergarten teacher, I had to tell a parent that her daughter had touched another child inappropriately while playing in the housekeeping center. Although the school counselor became involved as well as child protective services, no evidence was found of child abuse (although my observation that the child touched other children inappropriately should have been enough evidence). Unfortunately, when this child entered first grade, the abuse had become more prevalent as shown by the physical signs the child exhibited—she was always tired and sleepy. When the first-grade teacher took her to the nurse, the nurse was able to see the signs of abuse by the way she walked and her urges to urinate. It was found that the uncle had been molesting her for a few years! Thankfully, he was sentenced and convicted, but the child never fully recuperated.

Childcare workers and school personnel who want to help an abused child must exercise good judgment. Their first response might be to want to call the parent to determine how the injury occurred, but in the case of violent abuse, the child might be in danger of being permanently injured or killed. With serious abuse, do not call the parents or try to handle the situation by yourself. Contact the appropriate authorities immediately. Calling the family to discuss the problem not only fails to help the family, but also can precipitate more abuse. In addition, the family can become alarmed and move away. Then, the child might be abused for many more months before a new school or center detects the problem.

When the problem appears to be neglect rather than abuse, as when a child comes to school hungry or inappropriately dressed, a supportive visit or call to the family is in order. The school can provide emotional support and food and clothing. Working *with* parents shows them they are not alone with their overwhelming problems. If providing services is beyond the capability of the school, or if the family needs professional help, social services should be called.

How to Talk with Children and Parents

Knowing how to communicate with parents for different situations is important. Care must be taken in talking with or interviewing children or parents. The conversation should take place in a private, relaxed, and comfortable atmosphere. Children should not feel threatened, nor should they be pressed for information or details they do not want to reveal. Parents should be aware of the school's legal obligation to report suspected neglect and abuse. If they believe the school is supportive of the family, the interaction between parents and school will be more positive. It is best to contact child protective services when child abuse is suspected Tower (1992) provides some guidelines:

When Talking with the Child

Do:

Make sure the interviewer is someone the child trusts.

Make sure the educator is the most competent person in the school to talk with children.

Conduct the interview in private.

Sit beside the child, not across a table or desk.

Tell the child that the interview is confidential, but that child abuse and neglect must be reported.

Conduct the interview in language the child understands.

Ask the child to clarify words or terms you do not understand.

Tell the child if any future action will be required.

Don't:

Allow the child to feel "in trouble" or "at fault."

Disparage or criticize the child's choice of words or language.

Suggest answers to the child.

Probe or press for answers the child is unwilling to give.

Display horror, shock, or disapproval of the parents, the child, or the situation.

Pressure or force the child to remove clothing.

Conduct the interview with a group of interviewers.

Leave the child alone with a stranger (e.g., a CPS worker).

When Talking with the Parents

Do:

Select the person most appropriate to the situation.

Conduct the interview in private.

Tell the parents why the interview is taking place.

Be direct, honest, and professional.

Tell the parents the interview is confidential.

Reassure the parents of the support of the school.

Tell the parents if a report has been made or will be made.

Advise the parents of the school's legal responsibilities to report.

Don't:

Try to prove abuse or neglect; that is not an educator's role.

Display horror, anger, or disapproval of parents, the child, or the situation.

Pry into family matters unrelated to the specific situation.

Place blame or make judgments about the parents or child.

There are organizations that have developed parenting programs in order to prevent child abuse. Prevention for many experts is the key to stopping child abuse. Many programs focus on the parent before they begin to focus on the children. Some programs focus on meeting the physical and emotional needs of the parent to increase the child's chances of a strong childhood.

The Childhelp Approach (2018) to ending abuse encompasses prevention programs. These prevention programs work with children, families, and communities to raise the awareness of abuse and neglect. They seek to prevent abuse and educate parents. Some examples include Childhelp Speak Up Be Safe for Educators, Childhelp Speak Up Be Safe for Athletes, and Childhelp Community Centers (such as the one in Arizona). The Childhelp Intervention programs seek to protect children and implement the seven steps to

conflict resolution. For children who have been abused, Childhelp provides treatment programs.

Support Offered by Schools

The position statement by the American School Counselor Association supports programs to help eliminate child abuse. The association hopes to provide children with coping skills; help teachers understand abuse; provide continued counseling to the child and the family; and offer workshops for parents that focus on handling anger, parenting skills, and methods of discipline other than corporal punishment (American School Counselor Association, 1988). Some of the school-based programs include life-skills training, socialization skills, problem solving, and coping skills (Tower, 1992).

If the public were aware of how essential it is for teenagers who have not received these skills at home to be able to learn and model life skills, there would not be the demand to eliminate these types of courses. Although academic basics (reading, writing, and arithmetic) are essential, the focus away from life skills could be detrimental to the next generation. Offering workshops or courses on conflict resolution, consequences of actions, and seeking alternatives should be recognized as essential. It should be possible for schools to provide all the needed academic skills as well as the necessary skills for parenthood, self-protection, and life skills.

Many schools are developing family resource centers. Offerings for parents who are no longer students include parent education and family literacy.

Checklist for Schools and Centers

Having a checklist available for teachers and administrators helps the school or center maintain accountability for preventing child abuse and neglect. Public schools should work with their school district's office to ensure they are following the appropriate policy.

The following questions can be used to create a checklist:

- Does the school have a policy on reporting child abuse and neglect?

- Did the school do a needs assessment that shows the resources in your area and the status of child abuse and neglect in the school district?

- Does the school or center coordinate activities and resources with other social agencies?

- Does the school or center hold periodic meetings for improved communication and coordination among agencies?
- Does someone in the school district serve on the child protection team?
- Does the school or center have a training program?
- Do parents feel welcome in the school?
- Does the school or center have a parent education program for parents of preschoolers?
- Does the school or center have a parent education program for parents of infants and toddlers?
- Is the PTA or any other parent group involved with the school or center in a meaningful way for parents?
- Is there a parent resource room in the school?
- Do parents feel welcome to visit the school?
- Is there regular contact with parents, the teacher, and the school or center? Do the teachers have frequent communication with parents when there is something good to report?

Professionals who work with the abusive parent must first understand themselves and their values so they can come to peace with their feelings toward abuse and neglect of children. To help the family, professionals should not have a punitive attitude toward the parents. It can help to remember that many abusive or neglectful parents are rearing their children the same way they were reared. It is a lifelong pattern that must be broken (Bavolek, 1989; Reppucci, Britner, & Woolard, 1997; Steele, 1987; Vondra & Toth, 1989).

Although the parents might resist intrusion or suggestion, they desperately need help in feeling good about themselves. They need support, comfort, and someone they can trust and lean on. They need someone who will come when they have needs. Instead of criticism, they need help and assurance that they are worthwhile. Because they are unable to cope with their child, someone must help them understand the child. Parents need to feel valuable and adequate.

Parents Anonymous

Parents Anonymous (2006) is a self-help program that gives parents the chance to share their feelings with others who have had similar experiences. Parents can use Parents Anonymous (PA) and its crisis-intervention hotlines without fear of public disclosure.

The members help one another avoid abuse by providing the opportunity to talk out problems. Each group has a group facilitator who is trained in Parents Anonymous standards and practices. They also have a parent group leader, selected by the group. Weekly meetings are held and both the group leader and group facilitator are available between the weekly meetings. PA believes that abuse happens because parents have unresolved issues about their own childhood, stressful current problems and unmet needs, and a precipitating crisis that brings about the abuse.

Community Help

Help from social services or nonprofit organizations can include treatment that is offered by parent-aides, homemakers, and health visitors (Hamilton, 1989). The helper can serve as an advocate for the family to get the extra assistance it needs. This might include family therapy (Pardeck, 1989), assertiveness training, Healthy Start, Parents as Teachers, Community Resource Centers, Family Resource Centers, and Building Family Strengths programs. These programs try to bolster the positive elements in the family and eliminate the destructive elements.

Many abusive parents want help. When they reveal their desires, they indicate that they want another parent to help them develop childrearing skills through modeling and friendship. Professionals can give them psychiatric help and other support, but because these parents may have missed a childhood with nurturing parents, their greatest need is the opportunity to have an active experience with a nurturing model. The importance of bonding and of a close relationship between parent and infant has been recognized as necessary for the child's emotional and physical growth. Severe deprivation can result in failure to thrive and marasmus (Skeels & Dye, 1939; Spitz, 1945). Failure to develop close and trusting bonds as infants and children results later in parents who need special help in learning to relate to their own child. These parents are still looking for someone to mother them. The supportive help of another parent can function as a nurturing model for both parent and child.

Summary

The wave of child abuse cases reveals a phenomenon that is not new but that must be stopped. Child abuse has been with society since very early times, but it was not recognized as a problem until the second half of the 20th century, and no concerted effort was made to stem the crisis until the 1960s.

Legislation requires schools to report cases of abuse and neglect. Schools work with children more than any other agency, so they need to be in the forefront in preventing child abuse.

Child abuse and neglect include physical, sexual, and emotional abuse. It is important to note the characteristics of families who tend to be abusive, ways to identify the abused or neglected child, and psychological characteristics of abusive parents and abused children in order to keep children safe. Prevention programs provide ideas about how to work with families that have experienced abuse and/or neglect.

Ways schools can work to help potentially abusive parents include recognition of and response to the problem by the school, parent-education groups, school curricula, resource rooms, crisis nurseries, and/or parent-to-parent support groups.

Suggested Class Activities and Discussions

1. Attend a meeting of the Child Protection Council or similar group. What is the composition of the council—for example, doctors, educators, social workers, or judges? How does the wide spectrum of specialists show the need for cooperation among agencies working with families?

2. Go to the UNICEF website and explore different videos that deal with child abuse around the world. Think about how volunteers, particularly those who are teachers or are going to be teachers, can help this organization with this epidemic.

3. Based on the information you have read in this chapter, create a public service announcement in which you talk about a type of abuse and provide local, state, and national resources that can be helpful for families.

4. Visit with the director of a women's shelter and ask how they serve families who are victims of domestic violence. Remember to use pseudonyms to protect everyone's identity.

5. Working in four groups, students create four scenarios that deal with child abuse. The students dramatize each scenario and ask the audience to help find solutions and resources.

6. Read an article from one of the volumes of the journal *Child Abuse and Neglect*. Write a one-page paper that discusses these efforts.

Useful Websites

Child Welfare Information Gateway
Child Welfare League of America (CWLA)

i-SAFE
Prevent Child Abuse America

Glossary Terms

Child abuse: Action that physically or emotionally causes injury or death to a child.
Child neglect: Failure to provide care for a child.

Child maltreatment: Includes all types of abuse and neglect.

Chapter 12
Families and Child Advocacy

Children need strong advocates for a promising future.

Mari Riojas-Cortez

Learning Outcomes

In this chapter, you will find ideas about child advocacy and how to collaborate with families using different levels of advocacy.

12.1 Define advocacy as it relates to children and families.

12.2 Identify advocacy issues for young children and their families.

12.3 Provide guidelines for advocacy.

12.4 Describe the power of advocacy for family engagement.

Advocacy is a sign of caring for something, standing up for our views on a particular cause, supporting that which matters to us. I like to think of advocacy as an act of devotion that will help others live a better life because we care. Advocacy involves action, taking a stand particularly to make the lives of others better. Children's advocacy focuses on enhancing their development.

The theories of funds of knowledge and ecological systems help families and teachers find ways to work together to advocate for children's rights. We must value children's cultural capital given by their families to enhance their development. Systems in the community can provide services that help families optimize children's development. Understanding our role in child advocacy as educators and parents will help us advocate for our children, but we must work together and give children a voice.

Advocacy for Children and Families

When thinking of children's advocacy, we must first remember human rights. According to Hessle (2014), there are three categories of rights that must be respected: civil and political rights; social, economic, and cultural rights (such as education, health care, housing, and language rights); and those pertaining to the natural world (for instance, living in a healthy environment). The rights that guard children here in the United States are derived from the U.S. Constitution, the Bill of Rights, our social customs, federal and state legislation, the rulings of state and federal courts, and the United Nations. Advocacy is the strong belief in, and active involvement for, a cause.

Child advocacy grows from an emotional involvement in the lives of children, caring, a recognition of need, and a willingness to do something about that need. Sometimes advocacy is not successful, but the process and the voices behind it resonate more strongly because we know advocates exist who care (Royea & Appl, 2009). Children's advocates must grasp the needs of the child and the resources available within the different systems (such as the ones in the Ecological Systems Theory). Different types of advocates include the following:

1. *Leaders*—people with vision who help keep advocacy efforts on track.

2. *Advisers*—people who share their expertise with advocates and policymakers.

3. *Researchers*—people who collect data and synthesize research reports to support advocacy efforts.

4. *Contributors*—people who make phone calls, stuff letters, and make visits or write letters to legislators (National Association for Education of Young Children, 2004).

Qualifications for Personal Advocates

One quality that helps a person to be a good child advocate is the intrinsic ability to be truly motivated to help children. The help must be systematic, knowledgeable, and thorough. The advocate must be committed to finding out all the needs of the child or children being helped. Although it is time consuming and difficult, advocacy, when supported by the best available data, is most beneficial to the community, parents, and schools. For advocates, becoming change agents in the lives of children is the ultimate goal (McDonald, 2010).

Parents are their child's first advocates.

Geo Martinez/Shutterstock

Making a Personal Contribution

There are three different types of advocacy: personal, public policy, and private sector (Robinson & Stark, 2004). The most common kind of advocacy is one that many teachers and parents do every day—personal advocacy. Parents and teachers often recognize that children cannot advocate for themselves and thus find ways to advocate for children to live full and meaningful lives. Individual advocates who work for children in their own childcare programs or classrooms can have a huge effect on children's lives. If everyone who works or lives with a child assumed the important role of an advocate for that child, the lives of all children would be improved.

Teachers' Personal Advocacy

One of the best reasons to be a teacher is to make a difference in children's lives. But how can teachers do that? It is actually quite simple. You must care enough to offer the best for children, which is part of advocacy. Teachers must respect children, and treat children and their families with kindness. In addition, teachers should talk to children in such a way as to build their self-confidence. Children who feel respected will grow to respect others and make a difference in others' lives. Similarly, children need a chance to grow and make mistakes, particularly in early childhood as children develop socioemotional skills.

As early childhood teachers, we must be cognizant of children's development as well as their background. This helps to advocate for developmentally and culturally appropriate practices. Teachers should advocate for school settings that give children room to grow and develop. An environment where children are allowed and encouraged to play indoors and outdoors benefits children in all areas of development (Elkind, 2007). Children should not be deprived of play since this will harm their development (Belknap & Hazler, 2014). Every child has the right to play. In particular, children with special needs such as ADHD benefit from exploring and playing outdoors in nature (Gomes, 2013). Lastly, schools should offer a developmentally and culturally appropriate curriculum that is devoid of worksheets and full of project learning, exploration, play, and authentic children's literature.

Family Personal Advocacy

Family advocacy for children begins by providing them with basic needs, such as food and shelter. Caring for children includes ensuring that emotional needs are also met. This type of advocacy for families must follow the family's cultural norms; therefore, advocacy needs will vary between families. When my middle sister was in elementary school she would often get in trouble for talking in the classroom. One day, as my mother and I were walking back home from running errands we went by my sister's school and noticed that she was standing outside of the classroom. My mother worried and so we walked back to the school. In the early 1970s in Mexico, we never had to stop by the school's office so we went directly to the classroom. My mother asked the teacher why my sister was standing outside. The teacher told her that it was because she was talking when she was told not to. My mother told the teacher that a first grader should never be shamed but should be guided to understand her mistake. My mother decided to go to the principal to discuss the issue as the teacher did not agree with her. The common practice of having children stand outside of the classroom because of challenging behavior stopped at that school. The teacher apologized to my mother. My mother in turn told her that she was going to remind my sister to listen to the teacher and follow rules. My mother advocated for my sister and for other children. For us as a family, shaming children in front of others was not tolerated as children needed to be respected and valued.

The concept of funds of knowledge becomes very important in family personal advocacy. For instance, the way families discipline children differs greatly and very often is culturally based (Riojas-Cortez & Flores, 2009b) as the example above showed. However, as we have seen in previous chapters, harsh discipline can lead to child abuse, when families hurt children physically and emotionally. Families can advocate for their children by using different ways of guiding children and understanding child development. This includes children who have special needs.

What can the school do to help? A school that has a positive school climate allows families to advocate for their children. The school should help parents know their rights and responsibilities, as in the case of immigrant families who are English language learners and who might not know how to navigate the school system. For example, a study about Burmese refugee children and their families found that while parents encouraged children's learning, the school did not know how to meet the unique needs of this population (Isik-Ercan, 2012). Knowing their rights will help families advocate for their children in school-related issues.

Table 12.1 shows how families and teachers can advocate on a personal level.

Public Policy Advocacy

Individuals work together and separately to advocate on the public level. Most successful advocacy requires a broad-based approach, whether it is achieved through the responses of many individuals, the advocacy work

Table 12.1 Ways Families and Teachers Can Help Advocate for Children

Families	Teachers
Use funds of knowledge to provide a stimulating environment where children grow and play.	Acknowledge the family's funds of knowledge and how those help children with their development.
Spend time with children, listening to what concerns or interests them.	Provide a stimulating environment where children are free to speak and adults listen.
All children have the right to an education. Speak to teachers and administrators when that is not happening.	Maintain educational and social equity for culturally and linguistically diverse children.
Develop a love for the environment by taking children to parks and other natural areas where they can play.	Seek out interesting excursions and activities that will benefit the child.
Look for resources for children who have special needs. Ask the teacher and/or social worker for help.	Determine the most appropriate education for a child with special needs.
Report physical, sexual, and emotional abuse.	Report physical, sexual, and emotional abuse.
Attend meetings and speak out on issues.	Attend meetings and take a stand on issues.
Become active in your community.	Become active in professional organizations.
Write and contact your legislator.	Write and contact your legislator.

of professional organizations, or the lobbying efforts of political action committees.

Different organizations advocate for children's lives and well-being. Currently the Children's Defense Fund (2014), founded and headed by Marion Edelman, advocates vehemently for children's rights. In particular, the Children's Defense Fund seeks to develop policies to end poverty, child abuse, and neglect. In addition, the Children's Defense Fund advocates for policies to improve health care and education for children, as well as provide children with a moral and spiritual foundation.

UNICEF is another organization that works for children's rights around the world. They strive to improve the lives of children because they see them as the "cornerstone of human progress." Their stated mission is "to work with others to overcome the obstacles that poverty, violence, disease and discrimination place in a child's path" (UNICEF, 2014). Their advocacy largely focuses on girls' rights to an education. Girls who are educated become better thinkers, citizens, and mothers. Furthermore, immunization against childhood disease is another UNICEF advocacy project, prompted by their strong belief that children should not suffer due to preventable diseases.

Lately, we have seen an increase in the number of immigrant children coming from El Salvador, Honduras, and Guatemala. Humanitarian aid and advocacy (including legal counsel) need to be provided for those children (in this instance, called "unaccompanied minors") who come to the United States for a variety of reasons (King, 2013). Many children came to the United States when they were infants and toddlers and really do not know their country of origin. Many see themselves as "Americans" even though they do not have the required legal documents. The National Law Immigration Center (NLIC), founded in 1979, focuses on defending and advancing the rights of low-income immigrant families. The center has worked in different states to enact inclusive policies for immigrants (NLIC, 2013). Other organizations include: RAICES, the CARA Project, Kids in Need of Defense, and Justice for our Neighbors, among others. An important policy is the Deferred Action for Childhood Arrivals (DACA) program. DACA was created in 2012 as an effort from President's Obama Administration to help individuals who immigrated to the U.S. as children without documents. The policy provides a consideration for deferred action for a period of two years. There are guidelines that need to be met when requesting DACA status. The future of DACA is unknown but a federal court order mandates that the U.S. Citizenship and Immigration Services or USCIS accept requests to renew a grant of deferred action. Unfortunately, new requests are not being accepted if individuals have never submitted requests under DACA (U.S. Citizenship and immigration Services, 2018).

Early childhood organizations, such as the National Association for the Education of Young Children or NAEYC, have specific advocacy based on public policy, such as NAEYC Children's Champions, which addresses social, humanitarian, and educational advocacy at the national level but also has tremendous impact at all levels (NAEYC, 2014). The Association for Childhood Education International (ACEI) sees advocacy as a vital element of their mission, which includes "a sustainable future for children and youth worldwide" (ACEI, 2018). Zero to Three is an organization that focuses on early connections with children "birth to age three" and their families. They indicate that their agenda is: promoting good health, strong families, and positive early learning experiences for all infants and toddlers, with special emphasis on those who are the most vulnerable and in need (Zero to Three, 2018).

In San Antonio, Texas, the Child Advocates San Antonio or CASA is a non-profit organization that works with court-appointed volunteers who advocate for neglected and abused children (Child Advocates San Antonio, 2018). Volunteers go through a rigorous training process as preparation and knowledge of their duties is important to be able to advocate for children. At the national level, other associations work to provide equal educational opportunities for all children regardless of ability, ethnicity, or gender, such as the Center on Families, Communities, Schools, and Children's Learning; the Family Resource Coalition; the Institute for Responsive Education; the National Center for Family Literacy; The National Children's Advocacy Center; The Child Welfare League of America; The National Association for the Advancement of Colored People; the National Council of La Raza; and the National Parent and Teacher Association. All of these organizations have a strong impact on families as advocates.

Private Sector Advocacy

Many businesses and individuals like to advocate for their special causes through philanthropy, which is defined as a gift or act that is provided for humanitarian purposes. Organizations such as the YMCA receive money from foundations that helps them run their organization. Many businesses provide financial assistance to organizations that provide a humanitarian service to families in need, such as the American Red Cross. Businesses such as Bank of Americ a have charitable foundations that provide grants and other financial opportunities to enhance the causes they believe in, such as workforce development, education, housing, and preventing hunger (Bank of America, 2014). Other businesses believe in the value of learning and families, such as Toyota, which has provided more than a billion dollars to philanthropic programs in the United States (Toyota Family Learning, 2014). There are many other donors that advocate for a cause that is meaningful to them.

The different types of advocacy encompass the systems mentioned by Bronfenbrenner in his ecological systems theory. Within the child's microsystem, teachers can advocate for appropriate practices by being active participants in children's learning and understanding their development, including their culture. Similarly, families personally advocate for their children in different situations and for different purposes using their funds of knowledge. Public policy as well as private sector advocacy form part of the exosystem which, depending on the organization or business, can have a positive impact. For example, the Children's Health Insurance Program, or CHIP, provides low-cost health coverage to children of families that earn too much money to qualify for Medicare (HealthCare. gov, 2018). In my hometown, the local grocery store HEB created an early literacy program called the HEB Read3 that focuses on working with families and their young children to develop early reading skills. Families attend workshops for 6 weeks at different early childhood center sites. These examples are also part of the macrosystem, which focuses on attitudes and ideologies of the culture because it shows individuals how to think about the importance of advocating for children.

Advocacy Issues for Children and Families

There are many issues that affect children and families today. As advocates, we look at the immediate issues (at the microlevel) as well as the global issues (at the macrolevel). Table 12.2 gives us some questions to reflect upon at the macrolevel.

Table 12.2 Critical Questions for Reflection in Children's Lives

1. How can children's rights be valued and protected?
2. How can children's cultural and language backgrounds be valued?
3. How can we provide healthy environments where children grow and thrive?
4. How do we keep children safe from abuse and neglect?
5. How can we ensure that all children have health care?
6. How do we provide quality early childhood programs for all children?
7. How do we protect immigrant children and families, particularly those who are undocumented?
8. How can we keep children safe from guns?
9. How do we ensure that children have proper nutrition?
10. How do we embrace children with special needs and their families?

Often, when we see social issues such as these, we feel powerless, as these issues appear overwhelming and not easy to solve. However, it is imperative that as educators we understand the guidelines that will show us the how to become advocates for families and children.

Concern about children's welfare occurred beginning at the end of the 18th century, and several philanthropic, charitable, and government organizations have looked into different aspects of children's welfare, including infant mortality, orphans, child labor, and child abuse, among others (Jablonka, 2013). Later, the civil rights movement and the rights of people with disabilities focused on fair and equal treatment and provided the foundation for important laws that protect our children today.

Parents and educators can develop a list of possible topics to advocate for their children. Usually those topics have some type of immediate impact on young children and their families. For example, parents of children with autism can advocate for inclusion, particularly in spaces that are sensory friendly. Some public libraries have implemented sensory rooms so that children with autism can also enjoy this community organization. Another important topic that many working parents highly need is universal prekindergarten. Universal prekindergarten is a topic of great debate, but one that can help alleviate childcare challenges for working families (Casto & Sipple, 2009). Children's health also includes the right to live in clean environments. Families can advocate for green space by planting trees and working with government officials to stop unplanned development. A similar issue is the need to create safe and accessible play environments for all children. Many children in the inner city do not enjoy the benefits of playgrounds because their families are afraid to take them to the park, worried about unforeseen dangers. Another important issue is to advocate for the rights of immigrants (Olson, 2009). Very often, we forget that many of us, or perhaps our ancestors, also came to the U.S. to pursue a dream, and that others today harbor a similar dream. Immigrants have the right to appropriate education, health care, and jobs. Together, we can make the U.S. an even better place to live so that we can turn our advocacy lens to the rest of the world.

A Sleeping Giant: The Child Advocate

The issues of the new century vividly illustrate why children need advocates. Poverty, homelessness, and child abuse continue to be problems. In addition, there's a growing demand for quality childcare and green spaces for children to play. All of these issues require advocates, as well as a great deal of attention and action. But children also need advocates at a personal level. Educators need the tools to advocate for parents, particularly those who are English language learners (Campos, Delgado, & Soto Huerta, 2011) and those who have special needs.

Children face many challenges, and they need teachers and parents to work together to help them meet their individual needs and create opportunities for healthy development. Both teachers and parents must stand up for children and advocate at all levels. If they don't, who will? Lately in the U.S., we have seen numerous individuals and organizations advocating to put an end to the many school shootings in which children and teachers have lost their lives. Although there are no excuses for these unthinkable events, researchers like Sommer, Leuschner, and Scheithauer (2014) found that in the majority of cases, the perpetrator experienced some type of social conflict in school. Social conflicts included experiencing bullying, peer rejection, and conflicts with teachers. Advocacy in these cases can include students organizing walkouts, parents meeting with government officials, anti bullying campaign, and politicians advocating to either create stronger gun laws or arm our teachers! (this is a very controversial view). Indeed, gun violence is an epidemic and public health crisis (Katsiyannis, Whitford, & Parks Ennis, 2018) that requires advocates for children.

Preparing for Advocacy

Procedure

Teachers advocate for their students to see that the children's needs are met. At times, this is just part of the role of a teacher. At other times, objectives and preparation must be established to advocate effectively.

To achieve their objectives, advocates must systematically study the issue and proceed with a sound foundation. They first list the needs of the child and justify these needs by making certain they have been professionally determined. They read the literature and speak to experts in the field so their views are supported by reputable observations. Good advocates make sure their positions are based not on their own beliefs alone but on the true needs of the individual child, of all children, and society at large.

The following guidelines describe the steps to take when working on an individual advocacy case:

1. *Know your facts.* Be sure they are correct. Find out who, what, where, when, and why.

2. *Know the rights.* This includes the rights of the child, the parent, or other parties in the case. Contact an advocacy organization or lawyer if you have any questions.

3. *Know the policy.* Make sure you know the policies and procedures that relate to the problem. Get them in writing; don't accept just an oral version.

Monkey Business Images/Shutterstock

The rights that guard these children are derived from the U.S. Constitution, the Bill of Rights, social customs, legislation, and rulings of state and federal courts.

4. *Keep accurate notes.* Document as much evidence as possible. Date everything. Remember that when notes are kept as a personal memory aid they are not educational records, but that notes taken as educational records must be shared.

5. *Discuss various options.* Do not tell the young person or parent what to do. Rather, let the people you are helping choose the option and course of action that is wisest and that they are willing to live with.

6. *Never go alone to a meeting with officials.* Unless it is an unusual circumstance, take the young person, the parent, or another concerned person with you.

7. *Keep to the point when meeting with officials.* Be firm but not antagonistic and keep focused on the problem and the need to resolve it. Steer clear of personality conflicts.

8. *Follow channels.* Don't go over someone's head without first talking to that person about the problem. It is wise to let the person know you are dissatisfied with the result of your meeting and that you intend to go to the next person in authority.

9. *Send a letter.* If appropriate, send a letter to indicate your understanding of what took place at a meeting with officials or administrators (Fernandez, 1980).

Steps to Take for Public Advocacy

These are the basic steps involved in advocacy at the public level:

1. *Write to federal officials.* Individual letters written by constituents are more effective than letters with many signatures. You can also use e-mail and telephone contact. Federal officials have websites that provide citizens with an opportunity to communicate via e-mail (which is preferred). Officials to contact include:
   President of the United States
   Representatives: The Honorable *(name)*, U.S. House of Representatives.
   Senators: The Honorable *(name)*, U.S. Senate.
   For representatives' and senators' telephone numbers and e-mail addresses, visit the U.S. Capitol's website.

2. *Talk with and write to state legislators.* On the state level, write or call your state representative or state senator. Work with your representative before the assembly or legislature meets if you or your group has a bill you want introduced.

If you plan to write to your state representative or senator, here are a few tips to follow:

- State your purpose in the first paragraph, including the number of the legislation, such as HR _____ or S _____.
- Be courteous but to the point.
- Address only one issue in the letter.
- Follow up your letter with a phone call (Children's Defense Fund, 2014).

If you will be communicating with the media, remember to do the following:

- Know what you want to say.
- Say it well by using a brief but powerful anecdote.
- Say it clearly. Avoid jargon.
- Say it again, clearly and simply (National Association for the Education of Young Children, 2004).

3. *Get involved before elections.* Campaign for legislators who agree with your position on childcare, families, and children.

4. *Stay involved after elections.* After an election, invite elected officials to meet with your organization.

5. *Join professional organizations in your region.* For example, you can join and collaborate with the National Association for the Education of Young Children and its local chapter, Zero to Three, the Council for Exceptional Children, the National Association for Children with Learning Disabilities, and the National Council on Family Relations.

6. *Get firsthand experience.* Visit childcare centers, homeless shelters, schools, and other facilities.

Children's Ombudsman Offices / Office of the Child Advocate

Many organizations including universities, businesses, and government have established an **ombudsman** office, which acts as an agent to assist in finding resolutions and which represents the public, particularly when rights are violated. For example, at a university, the office of the ombudsman may assist students as well as faculty in different situations, such as when a student needs to talk about a problem with a faculty member but wants to maintain anonymity.

Best practices for an ombudsman office developed by the United States Ombudsman Association indicate that the office should be independent, impartial, confidential,

Table 12.3 Types of Children's Ombudsman Office by State

Independent and autonomous—child welfare	Colorado Connecticut Georgia Indiana Maine Massachusetts Michigan Missouri Rhode Island Tennessee Washington
Operates within, and autonomous of, state agency providing child welfare services	California Texas Utah
Supervision of all governmental agencies within the state including child welfare services	Alaska Arizona Hawaii Iowa Nebraska
Non-Independent Children's Ombudsman that take complaints and resolve disputes	Arkansas Kentucky Illinois Oklahoma New Hampshire New Jersey New York Oregon
Some Ombudsman programs may or may not operate within an agency	Delaware Maryland Minnesota Nevada
Programs that may operate by the county or specific programs	Montana Ohio South Carolina Virginia

Source: National Conference of State Legislators. Children's Ombudsman Offices/Office of the Child Advocate Retrieved August 6, 2014 from http://www.ncsl.org/research/human-services/childrens-ombudsman-offices.aspx

and should include a credible review process (Nowak, 2014). The Children's Ombudsman Office was established at the state level to handle complaints by citizens, to provide an accountability system, protect children's rights, and monitor programs (Nowak). Table 12.3 provides a list of different ombudsman systems within each state.

World Ombudsmanship

The United Nations Convention on the Rights of the Child has made a strong impact on the development of programs concerned about children's rights and their need to be protected. The European Network of Ombudspersons for Children (ENOC) was established in 1997 to ensure the implementation of the Convention on the Rights of the Child, as well as advocating for children's

rights from 27 European countries (Thomas, Gran, & Hanson, 2011). Similarly, the Asian Ombudsman Association was established in 1996 to promote Ombudsmanship principles protecting human rights (Vital Speeches International, 2010). It currently has 27 members from 17 countries (Asian Ombudsman Association, 2014).

Children's rights movements have occurred at a slow pace (Maclure, 2014). Currently, there is no Ombudsman Office established throughout Latin America. Some countries such as Mexico have social organizations that advocate for children's rights and at the same time act as an ombudsman, such as the Red por los Derechos de la Infancia en Mexico, or REDIM (Network for the Rights of Children). This is part of the initiative that was developed in 1990 with the Convention on the Rights of Children (Renobales Barbier, Corés Jarrín, Meseguer Lemus, & Barquera Medina, 2013). Other organizations such as UNICEF and the Child's Right International Network (CRIN) mostly advocate for children's rights in the majority of Latin American countries. The absence of social advocacy organizations creates gaps where children's rights are violated, as we see in the issue of children immigrating alone to the U.S., or in the case of Bolivia passing a law where children as young as 10 years old can work legally, which is a step back from years of advocacy against child labor (NPR, 2014).

Strong Family Engagement for Advocacy

The need for advocacy at all levels is crucial. How can professionals ensure that families will feel empowered and become involved? The following suggestions are adapted from *Community Mobilization: Strategies to Support Young Children and their Families,* a book from the Families and Work Institute (Dombro, O'Donnell, Galinsky, Melcher, & Farber, 1996):

- If you provide ongoing support to parents from the beginning—showing respect, using a buddy system, encouraging them to ask questions, and introducing them into the school program—you will promote feelings of competence and empowerment. The parents will be more comfortable and confident and will see how they can contribute.

- Help parents see that they are an important part of the organization. Parents come to the table with

Creativa Images/Shutterstock

Parents use their funds of knowledge to advocate for their children.

If you include parents as partners in the education process, you are advocating for them and their children. When teachers create partnerships with families, they are in fact being advocates for children. Effective school leaders, teachers and administrators, must create a positive climate in order to increase advocacy efforts.

Schools and school districts that lack leadership do not have a positive school climate and thus do not engage in advocacy such as in the example of a school district that cut librarians in the secondary schools. One librarian's persistence, the support of parent advocates, and a new leadership allowed the school district to keep the librarians in the secondary schools (Kaaland, 2013). Schools that have a positive school climate will not only provide a great environment for families but will also allow families to engage in advocacy for different purposes. For example, at the school where I used to work, the PTA was very involved in ensuring that all teachers had enough help developing materials for their classrooms, so they enlisted a group of families who could not come to school for different reasons. These families were asked to take the materials home and work on them, and then return them to the teachers in a timely manner. The school climate was very positive because the principal and the teachers valued families and their children. Thus, advocacy became the norm in the school as strong partnerships developed between families and teachers.

different skills and experiences. "When parents define roles with which they are comfortable, they are more likely to be effective and remain involved in the process" (Dombro et al., 1996).

- Parents have unique skills, but you can offer them training and workshops to develop their skills and leadership potential.

- Recognize that parents have limited time. If possible, reimburse them for expenses such as transportation or try to assist with their transportation needs so they can participate. Provide childcare to permit parents with younger children to attend meetings. Reach out to single parents with their special needs and help them get representation in the political process.

Summary

Families are the best advocates for children. Support systems like schools and teachers help families advocate at different levels. Legal rights and responsibilities of parents, students, and professional educators are crucial to the success of advocacy. Current criticisms of schools make cooperation between home and schools even more essential than previously.

Families and teachers keep children safe by being aware of the types of advocacy. Public policy advocacy is a broad-based approach used by professional organizations and or political action committees. This type of advocacy in the context of children, finds ways to increase their well being including educational opportunities. Private sector advocacy includes businesses

Wavebreakmedia/Shutterstock

The Buckley Amendment (Family Educational Rights and Privacy Act) gives this child's parents the right to see her school records.

and individuals that advocate for their special cause through philanthropy.

Three levels of advocacy involvement between home and school include the following: (a) development and periodic review of a code of rights and responsibilities for each class, school, or local school district; (b) election of and active involvement with a parent or citizen advisory council; and (c) implementation of the educational program in a classroom community. Development of a code involves the identification of interests, researching and gathering background material, the formulation of a draft code, feedback, approval, implementation, and review.

Parents and teachers must advocate for children's rights. This can be accomplished by organizing, planning, and advocating for a more caring and healthy environment. Parents and schools working together can provide a wholesome, intellectually stimulating, and challenging environment for families and children.

Suggested Class Activities and Discussions

1. Discuss what free speech is and how its boundaries are defined.
2. Discuss the rights parents and students have to see school records.
3. Discuss the concept that rights are also accompanied by responsibilities.
4. How have schools responded to the need to eliminate racial discrimination? Investigate the changes that have occurred in schools in your area because of affirmative action.
5. Contact a school in your area and find out what alternative education programs exist.
6. Follow the legislative action in your state, choose a bill that you strongly support, and advocate for its passage.
7. Brainstorm and come up with a list of needs that should be addressed by an advocate or advocacy groups.
8. Research the status of the United Nations Convention on the Rights of the Child in the United States.
9. Design an ombudsman program for children. What would be needed?

Useful Websites

Child Advocate
Child Welfare League of America (CWLA)

Children's Defense Fund

Glossary Terms

Activism: The action to make social change.
Advocacy: To speak up or take action for a cause.

Ombudsman or ombudsperson: Person appointed to investigate complaints within an organization.

References

ACF Press Office. (2004). Administration for Children, Youth, and Families. Conrad Hilton Foundation Award. (2004, February 5). Press release.

Active Parenting Publishers. (2018). *Active parenting publishers.* Retrieved on May 2, 2018 from http://www.activeparenting.com/

Adair, J. K. (2016). Creating positive contexts of reception: The value of immigrant teachers in U.S. early childhood education programs. *Education Policy Analysis Archives, 24*(1), 1–33.

Adair, J. K., Tobin, J., & Arzubiaga, A. E. (2012). The dilemma of cultural responsiveness and professionalization: Listeing closer to immigrant teachers who teach children of recent immigrants. *Teachers College Record, 114*(12), 1.

Ado, K. (2016). From pre-service to teacher leader: The early development of teacher leaders. *Issues in Teacher Education, 25*(1), 3–21.

Afolabi, O. E. (2015). Domestic violence, risky family environment and children: A bio-psychology perspective, *International Journal of Special Education, 30*(2), 44–56.

Ainsworth, M. D. (1973). The development of infant–mother attachments. In B. M. Caldwell & H. N. Ricciuti (Eds.), *Review of child development research.* Chicago: University of Chicago Press.

Akers, P. (2005). Conferencing the SMART way. *Principal, 84*(3), 47.

Aldoney, D., & Cabrera, N. J. (2016). Raising American citizens: Socialization goals of low-income immigrant Latino mothers and fathers of young children. *Journal of Child and Family Studies, 25*(12), 3607–3618.

Altman, D. H., & Smith, R. L. (1960). Unrecognized trauma in infants and children. *Journal of Bone and Joint Surgery, 42A*(1), 407–413.

Amato, P. R. (1994). Life-span adjustment of children to their parents' divorce. *The Future of Children: Children and Divorce 4*(1), 143–164.

American Academy of Pediatrics. (2013). *Vaccine safety: Examine the evidence.* Retrieved on November 29, 2018 from http://www.aap.org/en-us/Documents/immunization_vaccine_studies.pdf

American Academy of Pediatrics. (2014). AAP Updates recommendations on evaluating fractures in children. Retrieved July 8, 2014, from http://www.aap.org/en-us/about-the-aap/aap-press-room/Pages/AAPUpdates-Recommendations-on-Evaluating-Fractures-in-Children.aspx#sthash.B2yS7XbJ.dpuf

American Association for Protecting Children. (n.d.). *Guidelines for schools to help protect abused and neglected children.* Denver, CO: American Humane Association.

American Humane Association. (1978). *National analysis of official child neglect and abuse reporting.* Denver, CO: Author.

American Humane Association. (1992c, October). *Fact sheet: Child abuse and neglect data.* Englewood, CO: Author.

American Humane Association. (1998). *Children's division.* Englewood, CO: Author.

American Humane Association. (2014). *About us.* Retrieved from American Hume Society, July 8, 2014, from http://www.americanhumane.org/about-us/

American Psychological Association. (2018). The changing role of the modern day fathers. Retrieved on November 28, 2018 from http://www.apa.org/pi/families/resources/changing-father.aspx

American School Counselor Association. (1988). The school counselor and child abuse/neglect prevention. *Elementary School Guidance & Counseling, 22*(4), 261–263.

Ancell, K. S., Bruns, D. A., & Chitiyo, J. (2018). The importance of father involvement in early childhood programs. *Young Exceptional Children, 21*(1), 22–33.

Araujo, B. E. (2009). Best practices in working with linguistically diverse families. *Intervention in School and Clinic, 45*(2), 116–123.

Arndt, J. S., & McGuire-Schwarts, M. E. (2008). Early childhood school success: Recognizing families as integral partners. *Childhood Education, 84*(5).

Asher, L. J., & Lenhoff, D. R. (2001). Family and medical leave: Making time for family is everyone's business. *The Future of Children: Caring for Infants and Toddlers, 11*(1), 115–121.

Ashiono, B. L, & Mwoma, T. B. (2015). Does marital status influence the parenting styles employed by parents? *Journal of Education and Practice, 6*(10), 69–75.

Asian Ombudsman Association. (2014). About AOA. Retrieved on August 7, 2014, from http://asianombudsman.com/index.php?option=com_content&view=article&id=57&Itemid=95

Association for Childhood Education International (ACEI). (2018). Our mission. Retrieved on September 4, 2018 from https://www.acei.org/.

Austin, J. S. (2000). When a child discloses sexual abuse: Immediate and appropriate teacher responses. *Childhood Education, 77*(1), 2–5.

Autism Speaks. (2018). Home. In *Autism Speaks.* Retrieved July 6, 2014, from http://www.autismspeaks.org/

AVANCE. (2018). About us. Retrieved on September 27, 2018 from https://www.avance.org/about-avance/history/.

AVANCE. (2018). *Fatherhood: Fathers in Action.* Retrieved on October 13, 2018 from https://www.avancehouston.org/index.php/fatherhood/.

Avellar, S. A., & Supplee, L. H. (2013). Effectiveness of home visiting in improving child health and reducing child maltreatment. *Pediatrics, 2*, 90–99.

Backhouse, J. & Graham, A. (2012). Grandparents raising grandchildren: Negotiating the complexities of role–identity conflict. *Child & Family Social Work, 17*, 305–315.

Barhava-Montieth, G., Harre, N., & Field, J. (1999, July). Hippy New Zealand: An evaluation overview. *Social Policy Journal of New Zealand, 106*–122.

Bailey, J. A., Hill, K. G., Oesterle, S., & Hawkins, J. D. (2009). Parenting practices and problem behavior across three generations: Monitoring, harsh discipline, and drug use in the intergenerational transmission of externalizing behavior. *Developmental Psychology, 45*(5), 1214–1226. doi: 10.1037/a0016129

Baker, A. J., Piotrkowski, C. S. & Brooks-Gunn, J. (1998). The effects of the Home Instruction Program for Preschool Youngsters (HIPPY). *Early Childhood Research Quarterly, 13,* 571–588.

Baker, A. J., Piotrkowski, C. S., & Brooks-Gunn, J. (1999). The Home Instruction Program for Preschool Youngsters. *The Future Child, 9*(1), 116–123.

Bakwin, H. (1956). Multiple skeletal lesions in young children due to trauma. *Journal of Pediatrics, 49*(1), 7–15.

Bank of America. (2014). Bank of America charitable foundation funding opportunities. Retrieved August 5, 2014, from http://about.bankofamerica.com/en-us/globalimpact/charitable-foundationfunding.html#fbid=ItxIseYO1TC

Barahona Collection. (2018). *University library*. California State University, San Marcos. Retrieved on June 13, 2018 from https://biblio.csusm.edu/barahona-collection

Barhava-Monteith, G., Harre, N., & Field, J. (1999). An evaluation of the HIPPY program in New Zealand. *Early Child Development and Care, 159*, 145–157.

Barkley, R. A., & Edwards, G. (2006). Diagnostic interview, behavior rating scales, and medical examination. In R.A. (Ed.). *Attention-deficit hyperactivity disorder: A handbook for diagnosis and treatment* (3rd ed., pp. 337–368). New York: Guilford Press.

Barr, R. G., Rivara, F. P., Barr, M., Cummings, P., Taylor, J., Lengua, L. J., & Benitz, M. (2009). Effectiveness of educational materials designed to change knowledge and behaviors regarding crying and shaken-baby syndrome in mothers of newborns: A randomized, controlled trial. *Child: Care, Health and Development, 35*(4), 587–588.

Barr, R. G., Rivara, F. P., Barr, M., Cummings, P., Taylor, J., Lengua, L. J., & Meredith-Benitz, E. (2009). Effectiveness of educational materials designed to change knowledge and behaviors regarding crying and shaken-baby syndrome in mothers of newborns: A randomized, controlled trial. *Pediatrics, 123*(3), 972–980. doi: 10.1542/peds.2008–0908.

Barratt-Pugh, C., Anderson, K., & North, S. (2013). The changing perspectives of librarians in the "Better Beginnings" family literacy program. *Australian Library Journal, 62*(3), 183–195.

Bassuk, E., L. (1991). Homeless families. *Scientific American, 264*(6), 66–74.

Bassuk, E., & Rubin, L. (1987). Homeless children: A neglected population. *American Journal of Orthopsychiatry, 57*(22), 279–285.

Bavolek, S. J. (1989). Assessing and treating high-risk parenting attitudes. *Early Child Development and Care, 42*, 99–111.

Beal, G., Bohlen, J. M., & Raudabaugh, J. N. (1962). *Leadership and dynamic group action*. Ames: Iowa State University.

Beato, G. (2005). Homeschooling alone. *Reason, 36*(11), 32–39.

Becker, A., Wylan, L., & McCourt, W. (1971). Primary prevention: whose responsibility? *American Journal of Psychiatry, 128*, 412–417.

Behavior Analyst Certification Board. (2018). *Board Certified Behavior Analyst: About the credential*. Retrieved on August 31, 2018 from https://www.bacb.com/bcba/.

Bekerman, Z. (2009). The complexities of teaching historical conflictual narratives in integrated Palestinian-Jewish schools in Israel. *International Review of Education, 55*(2/3), 235–250.

Bell, R. Q., & Harper, L. V. (1980). *Child effects on adults*. Lincoln: University of Nebraska Press.

Belknap, E. & Hazler, R. (2014). Empty playgrounds and anxious children. *Journal of Creativity in Mental Health, 9*(2), 210–231.

Belsky, J., Conger, R., & Capaldi, D. M. (2009). Intergenerational transmission of parenting: Introduction to the special section. *Developmental Psychology, 45*(5). doi: 10.1037/a0016245

Benne, K. D., & Sheets, P. (1948). Functional roles of group members. *Journal of Social Issues, 4*(2), 41–49.

Berger, E. H. (1997). Home schooling. *Early Childhood Education Journal, 24*(3), 205–208.

Bernier, A., Calkins, S.D., & Bell, M. A. (2016). Longitudinal associations between the quality of mother-infant interactions and brain development across infancy. *Child Development, 87*(4), 1159–1174.

Berrueta-Clement, J. R., Schweinhart, L. J., Barnett, W. S., Epstein, A. S., & Weikart, D. P. (1984). *Changed lives: The effects of the Perry Preschool Program on youths through age 19*. Monograph of the High/Scope Educational Research Foundation, No. 8. Ypsilanti, MI: High/Scope Press.

Best Buddies. (2018). *Best Buddies: Friendship, Jobs & Leadership Development*. Retrieved on August 31, 2018 from https://www.bestbuddies.org/.

Bester, G., & Brand, L. (2013). The effect of technology on learner attention and achievement in the classroom. *South African Journal of Education, 33*(2), 1–15.

Bigner, J. J. (1985). *Parent–child relations*. New York: Macmillan.

Bjorklund, G., & Burger, C. (1987). Making conferences work for parents, teachers, and children. *Young Children, 42*(2), 26–31.

Blanchard-Dallaire, C., & Hébert, M. (2014). Social relationships in sexually abused children: Selfreports and teachers' evaluation. *Journal of Child Sexual Abuse, 23*(3), 326–344.

Blatt, B. & Kaplan F. (1974). *Christmas in purgatory. A photographic essay on mental retardation*. Syracuse, NY: Human Policy Press.

Block, N. C. (2012). Perceived impact of two-way dual immersion programs on Latino students' relationships in their families and communities. *International Journal of Bilingual Education and Bilingualism, 15*(2), 235–257.

Bloom, B. S. (1964). *Stability and change in human characteristics*. New York: Wiley.

Borchers, T. (1999). *Small group communication: Roles in groups*. Retrieved August 28, 2002 from http://www.abacon.com/commstudies/groups/roles.html

Boren, S. (1994). *Education of the gifted and talented reauthorization fact sheet*. Washington, DC: U.S. Department of Education. (ERIC Document Reproduction Service Nos. ED371526 and EC303113).

Boutte, G. S., & Strickland, J. (2008). Making African American culture and history central to early childhood teaching and learning. *The Journal of Negro Education, 77*(2), 131–132.

Bower, T. G. R. (1982). *Development in infancy* (2nd ed.). San Francisco: W. H. Freeman.

Bowlby, J. (1966). *Attachment*. New York: Basic Books.

Bowlby, J. (1982). *Maternal care and mental health*. New York: Schocken Books.

Bowlby, J. (1988). *A secure base*. New York: Basic Books.

Boyer, W. (2013). Getting back to the woods: Familial perspectives on culture and preschoolers' acquisition of self-regulation and emotion regulation. *Early Childhood Education Journal, 41*, 153–159.

Brazelton Institute. (2005). *The Newborn Behavioral Observation system: What is it?* Retrieved from http://www.touchpoint.brazelton-institute.com/clnbas.html

Brazelton Institute. (2017). Research. Retrieved August 25, 2018 from http://www.childrenshospital.org/research-and-innovation/research/centers/brazelton-institute/nbas

Brazelton, T. B., & Greenspan, S. I. (2000). *The irreducible needs of children: What every child must have to grow, learn, and flourish*. Cambridge, MA: Perseus.

Brazelton, T. B., & Yogman, M. W. (1986). *Affective development in infancy*. Norwood, NJ: Ablex.

Brim, O. (1965). *Education for child rearing*. New York: Free Press.

Bronfenbrenner, U. (1979). *The ecology of human development*. Cambridge, MA: Harvard University Press.

Bronfenbrenner, U. (1986). Ecology of the family. Research perspectives. *Developmental Psychology, 22*, 723–742.

Bronte-Tinkew, J., Burkhauser, M., & Metz, A. J. R. (2012). Elements of promising practices in fatherhood programs: Evidence based research findings on interventions for fathers. *A Journal of Theory, Research & Practice about Men as Fathers, 10*(1), 6–30.

Brooks, K., & Karathanos, K. (2009). Building on cultural and linguistic capital of English learner (EL) students. *Multicultural Education, 16*(4), 47–51.

Bruder, M. E. (2010). Early childhood intervention: A promise to children and families for their future. *Exceptional Children, 76*(3), 262–264.

Brumm, C. A., & Drury, S. (2013). Leadership that empowers: How strategic planning relates to followership. *Engineering Management Journal, 25*(4), 17–32.

Buell, M. J., Hallam, R. A., & Beck, H. L. (2001, May). Early Head Start and child care partnerships: Working together to serve infants, toddlers, and their families. *Young Children, 56*(3), 7–12.

Burkhart, K., Knox, M., & Brockmyer, J. (2013). Pilot evaluation of the ACT Raising Safe Kids program on children's bullying behaviors. *Journal of Child and Family Studies, 22*(7), 942–951.

Burns, E. (2006). *IEP-2005. Writing and implementing individualized education programs (IEPs)*. Springfield, IL: Charles Thomas Ltd.

Burns, W. A. (2017). A descriptive review of harmful leadership styles: Definitions, commonalities, measurements, negative impacts, and ways to improve these harmful leadership styles. *Creighton Journal of Interdisciplinary Leadership, 3*(1), 33–52.

Bursal, M. (2013). Longitudinal investigation of elementary students' science academic achievement in 4–8th grades: Grade level and gender differences. *Educational Sciences: Theory & Practice, 13*(2), 1151–1156.

Butcher, R. L., & Gersch, I. S. (2014). Parental experience of the "Time Together" home visiting intervention: Attachment theory perspective. *Educational Psychology in Practice, 30*(1), 1–18.

Buysse, V., Castro, D. C., & West, T. (2005). Addressing the needs of Latino children: A national survey of state administrators of early childhood programs. *Early Childhood Research Quarterly, 20*(2), 146–163.

Byers, L. (2010). Native American grandmothers: Cultural tradition and contemporary necessity. *Journal of Ethnic & Cultural Diversity in Social Work, 19*(4), 305–316.

Caffey, J. (1946). Multiple fractures in long bones of infants suffering from chronic subdural hematoma. *American Journal of Roentgenology, 56*, 163–173.

Cai, Y., Reeve, J., & Robinson, D. T. (2002). Homeschooling and teaching style: Comparing motivational styles of homeschool and public school teachers. *Journal of Educational Psychology, 94*(2), 372–380.

Calderon, M., Slavin, R., & Sanchez, M. (2011). Effective instruction for English learners. *Immigrant Children, 21*(1), 103–128.

Caldwell, B. M., & Bradley, R. H. (1984). *Administration manual: Home observation for measurement of the environment*. Little Rock: University of Arkansas.

California Department of Education. (2018). Migrant education Family Biliteracy Program. Retrieved on October 16, 2018 from https://www.cde.ca.gov/sp/me/mt/mefbpbackground.asp.

Campbell, F. A., Wasik, B. H., Pungello, E., Burchinal, M., Barbarin, O., Kainz, K., Sparling, J. J., & Ramey, C. T. (2008). Young adult outcomes from the Abecedarian and care early childhood educational interventions. *Early Childhood Research Quarterly, 23*, 452–466.

Campos, D., Delgado, R. & Soto Huerta, M. E. (2011, July). *Reaching out to Latino parents of English learners*. Alexandria, VA: ASCD.

Cancian, M., & Danziger, S. (2009). Changing poverty and changing antipoverty policies. *Focus, 26*(2), 1–5.

Cancian, M., & Reed, D. (2009). Family structure, childbearing, and parental employment: Implications for the level and trend in poverty. *Focus, 26*(2), 21–26.

Cannella, G. S. (2002). *Deconstructing early childhood education: Social justice & revolution*. New York: Peter Lang.

Canter, L., & Hausner, L. (1987). *Homework without tears*. New York: Harper & Row.

Carlisle, R. P. (2011). *The Native Americans*. New York: Infobase Publishing.

Carper, J. C. (1992). Home schooling: History and historian: The past and present. *The High School Journal, 75*(4), 252–257.

Cartledge, G. Y., Gardener, R., III., & Ford, D. Y. (2009). *Diverse learners with exceptionalities: Culturally responsive teaching in the inclusive classroom*. Ohio: Merrill.

Casper, V., Cooper, R. M., & Finn, C. D. (2003). Culture and caregiving: Goals, expectations & conflict. *Zero to Three, 25*(3), 4–54.

Casto, H. G., & Sipple, J. W. (2009). Who and what influences school leaders' decisions: An institutional analysis of the implementation of universal prekindergarten. *Educational Policy, 25*, 134–165.

Castro, M., Expósito-Casas, E., López-Martín, E., Lizasoain, L., Navarro-Asencio, E., & Gaviria, J. L. (2015). Parental involvement on student academic achievement: A meta-analysis. *Educational Research Review, 14*, 33–46.

Cataldo, C. Z. (1987). *Parent education for early childhood*. New York: Teachers College Press.

Center for Effective Discipline. (2006, July). *Facts about corporal punishment worldwide*. Retrieved from http://www.stophitting.com/disatschool/facts.php

Center for Effective Discipline. (2007). U.S.: *Corporal punishment and paddling statistics by state and race*. Retrieved from http://www.stophitting.com/disatschool/statesBanning.php

Center for Family Strengths. (1986). *Building family strengths: A manual for facilitators*. Lincoln, NE: University of Nebraska.

Center on Great Teachers and Leaders at American Institute for Research. (2017). *Teacher leadership: Teacher self-assessment tool*. American Institute for Research.

Center for Parent Information & Resources (CPIR). (2017). *Supporting the parent centers who serve families of children with disabilities*. Retrieved on August 31, 2018 from https://www.parentcenterhub.org/.

Centers for Disease Control and Prevention (2014b). Child maltreatment prevention. Retrieved from Injury Prevention and Control Center for Disease Control and Prevention on July 9, 2014, from http://www.cdc.gov/ViolencePrevention/childmaltreatment/

Centers for Disease Control and Prevention (2018). Prevent bullying. Retrieved on August 28, 2018 from https://www.cdc.gov/features/prevent-bullying/index.html.

Centers for Disease Control and Prevention (2018, April 26). Autism Spectrum Disorder (ASD). Retrieved on April 26, 2018 from https://www.cdc.gov/ncbddd/autism/data.html

Center on Great Teachers and Leaders at American Institutes for Research (2017). Teacher self-assessment tool. Teacher Leadership. *American Institute for Research*. Retrieved on October 17, 2018 from https://www.gtlcenter.org/sites/default/files/TeacherLeadership_TeacherSelf-Assessment.pdf.

Centre for Europe's Children. (2001 December 13). *Annual report on the activities of the French ombudsman for children/Defenseur des enfants*. Retrieved from http://www.ombudsnet.org/Ombudsmen/France/Activities_00_01.htm

CESA 5, Portage Project. (1998). *Growing: Interactions/daily routines*. Portage, WI: Author.

Cetin, Z., & Ozozen Danaci, M. (2016). A multivariate examination of the child-abuse potential of parents with children aged 0–6. *Eurasian Journal of Educational Research, 66*, 71–86.

Chaiyachati, B. H., Gaither, J. R., Hughes, M., Foley-Schain, K., & Leventhal, J. M. (2018). Preventing child maltreatment: Examination of an established statewide home-visiting program. *Child Abuse & Neglect, 79*, 476–484.

Chandler, D., & Munday, R. (2016) *Oxford: A dictionary of media and communication* (2nd ed). Oxford University Press.

Chang, J. J., Theodore, A. D., Martin, S. L., & Runyan, D. K. (2008). Psychological abuse between parents: Associations with child maltreatment from a population-based sample. *Child Abuse & Neglect, 32*, 819–829.

Charlesworth, R. (2014). *Understanding child development* (9th ed.). Boston, MA: Cengage Learning Publishers.

Chazan-Cohen, R., Raikes, H., Brooks-Gunn, J., Ayoub, C., Pan, B. A., Kisker, E. E., Roggman, L., & Fuligni, A. S. (2009). Low-income children's school readiness: Parent contributions over the first five years. *Early Education and Development, 20*(6), 958–977.

Chazan-Cohen, R., Raikes, H. H., & Vogel, C. (2013). Program subgroups: Patterns of impacts for home-based, center-based, and mixed-approach programs. Monographs of the Society for Research in Child Development, 78, 93–109. doi: 10.1111/j.1540-5834.2012.00705.x

Chen, F. & Abenyega, J. (2012). Chinese parents' perspectives on home–kindergarten partnership: A narrative research. *Australasian Journal of Early Childhood, 37*(2), 95–105.

Chicago Longitudinal Study. (2004). *Parent program*. Retrieved from http://www.waisman.wisc.edu: 8000/cls/parent.htm

Chicago Office of the Office for Civil Rights. (2005). *Protecting students with disabilities*. Chicago: Author.

Child Abuse Prevention and Treatment Act of 1974. (1977). *United States Code, 1976, The Public Health and Welfare, Section 5101* (Vol. 10). Washington, DC: U.S. Government Printing Office.

Child Advocates San Antonio. (2018). About us. Retrieved on May 17, 2018 from https://www.casa-satx.org/about/who-we-are

Child Trends Data Bank. (2014). Immigrant children: Indicators of child and youth well-being. Child Trends. Retrieved on November 28, 2019 from https://www.childtrends.org/wp-content/uploads/2013/07/110_Immigrant_Children.pdf

Child Welfare Information Gateway. (2010). *About us*. Retrieved from http://www.childwelfare.gov/

Child Welfare Information Gateway. (2014a). Mandatory reporters of child abuse and neglect. U.S. Department of Health and Human Services, Children's Bureau. Retrieved July 10, 2014, from https://www.childwelfare.gov/responding/mandated.cfm

Child Welfare Information Gateway. (2014b). Tipsheets. Retrieved from Child Welfare Information Gateway July 9, 2014, from https://www.childwelfare.gov/pubs/guide2014/tipsheets_en.pdf#page=4

Child Welfare Information Gateway. (2018). Supporting pregnant and parenting teens. Retrieved on June 16, 2018 from https://www.childwelfare.gov/topics/preventing/promoting/parenting/pregnant-teens/

Childhelp. (2018). Child abuse statistics and facts. Retrieved on May 26 from https://www.childhelp.org/child-abuse-statistics/.

Children's Bureau Centennial. (2018). Children's Bureau timeline. *U.S. Department of Health and Human Services. Administration for Children and Families*. Retrieved on November 28, 2018 from http://cb100.acf.hhs.gov/childrens-bureau-timeline.

Children's Defense Fund. (1989). *A vision for America's future*. Washington, DC: Author.

Children's Defense Fund. (2010). The State of America's Children. http://www.childrensdefensefund.org

Children's Defense Fund. (2014). About us. Retrieved on August 5, 2014, from http://www.cdc.gov/ViolencePrevention/childmaltreatment/

Chinn, P. C. (Ed.). (1984). *Education of culturally and linguistically exceptional children*. Reston, VA: Council for Exceptional Children.

Chinn, P. C., Winn, J., & Walters, R. H. (1978). *Two-way talking with parents of special children: A process of positive communication*. St. Louis, MO: C. V. Mosby.

Christle, C. A., & Yell, M. L. (2010). Individualized education programs: Legal requirements and research findings. *Exceptionality, 18*(3), 109–123.

Clark, B. (2013). Supporting the mental health of children and youth of separating parents. *Pediatrics & Child Health, 18*(7), 373–377.

Clark, E. R., & Flores, B. B. (2001). Who am I? The social construction of ethnic identity and self-perceptions of bilingual preservice teachers. *The Urban Review, 33*(2), 69–86.

Clarke, L. S., Embury, D. C., Knight, C., & Christensen, J. (2017). People-furst lantuage, equity and inclusion: How do we say it and why does it matter? *Learning Disabilities: A Multidisciplinary Journal, 22*(1), 74–79.

Clearinghouse on Early Education and Parenting. (2011). Retrieved on September 27, 2018 from http://www.eclearningil.org/resources/clearinghouse-early-education-and-parenting.

Cochran, M., & Dean, C. (1991). Home–school relations and the empowerment process. *Elementary School Journal 91*(3), 261–269.

Cogan, M. (2010). Exploring academic outcomes of home-schooled students. *Journal of College Admission, 208*, 18–25.

Collie, R., Shapka, J. D., & Perry, N. E. (2012). Predicting teacher commitment: The impact of school climate and social-emotional learning. *Psychology in the Schools, 48*(11), 1034, 1048.

Collier, M., Keefe, E. B., & Hirrel, L. A. (2015). Listening to parents' narratives: The value of authentic experiences with children with disabilities and their families. *School Community Journal, 25*(2), 221–243.

Comer, J. P., Haynes, N. M., Joyner, E., & M. Ben-Avie, M. (Eds.). (1996). *Rallying the whole village*. New York: Teachers College Press.

Colmer, K., Rutherford, L., & Murphy, P. (2011). Attachment theory and primary caregiving. *Australasian Journal of Early Childhood, 36*(4), 16–20.

Colorado Department of Education, Early Childhood Initiatives, The Arapahoe Early Childhood Network, PEAK Parent Center & The Colorado Consortium of Intensive Care Nurseries. (1997). *From one parent to another.* Denver, CO: Author.

Columna, L., Senne, T. A., & Lytle, R. (2009). Communicating with Hispanic parents of children with and without disabilities. *Journal of Physical Education, Recreation & Dance, 80*(4), 1–58.

Comenius, J. A. (1967). *The great didactic of John Amos Comenius* (M. W. Keatinge, Ed. & Trans.). New York: Russell & Russell. (Original work published 1657.)

Comer, J. P. (1997). *Waiting for a miracle.* New York: Dutton.

Comer, J. P. (2004). *Leave no child behind: Preparing today's youth for tomorrow's world.* New Haven: Yale University Press.

Emmons, C., Comer, J., & Haynes, N. (1996). Translating Theory into Practice: Comer's Theory of School Reform. In J. P. Comer, N. M. Haynes, E. Joyner, & M. Ben-Avie (Eds.), *Rallying the Whole Village.* New York: Teachers College Press.

Committee on Education and the Workforce, U.S. House of Representatives. (2005, February). *Individuals with Disabilities Education Act (IDEA): Guide to "frequently asked questions."* Washington, DC: Author. (Available online at: http://www.doe.in.gov/sites/default/files/individualized-learning/ideafaq.pdf)

Conderman, G., Walker, D. A., Neto, J. R., & Kackar-Cam, H. (2013). Student and teacher perceptions of middle school climate. *Clearing House, 86*(5), 184–189.

Congressional record. (1983). 98th Congr., Vol. 129, pt. 24: 33310–33329, 98–199.

Consortium for Longitudinal Studies. (1983). *As the twig is bent.* Hillsdale, NJ: Erlbaum.

Cook, R. E., Klein, M. D., & Tessier, A. (2004). *Adapting early childhood curricula for children in inclusive settings* (6th ed.). Upper Saddle River, NJ: Merrill/Prentice Hall.

Cooke, G., & Cooke, S. (1988). Homework that makes a difference in children's learning. Personal communication.

Coons, C. E., Gay, E. C., Fandal, A. W., Ker, C., & Frankenburg, W. K. (1981). *Home screening questionnaire.* Denver, CO: JFK Child Development Center.

Cooper, G. (2017). Circle of security in child care: Putting attachment theory into practice in preschool classrooms. *Zero to Three, 37*(3), 27–34

Cooper, H. (2001). Homework for all. *Educational Leadership, 58*(7), 34–38.

Cooper, J. M. (1999). *Classroom teaching skills* (6th ed.). Boston: Houghton Mifflin.

Copenhaver, J. (2004). *Assistive technology for students with disabilities: Information for parents and educators.* Logan, UT: U.S. Department of Education.

Council for Exceptional Children. (2001). *Nurturing young children.* Retrieved from http://www.cec.sped.org

Council for Exceptional Children. (2003). *GT-English as a second language.* Retrieved from http://www.cec.sped.org

Council of State Director of Programs for the Gifted. (2018). Home. Retrieved on August 31, 2018 from https://csdpg.weebly.com/.

Craft, E., & Howley, A. (2018). African American Students' Experiences in Special Education Programs. *Teachers College Record, 120*(10).

Crawford, E., & Witherspoon, A. N. (2017). "We don't talk about undocumented status . . . We talk about helping children": How school leaders shape school climate for undocumented immigrants. *International Journal of Educational Leadership and Management, 5*(2), 116–147.

Crosson-Tower, C. (2002). *Child abuse and neglect* (5th ed.). Boston: Allyn & Bacon.

Cummins, J. (1979). Cognitive/academic language proficiency, linguistic interdependence, the optimum age and some other matters. *Working Papers on Bilingualism, 19,* 121–129.

Currie, J. (2000). *Early childhood intervention programs: What do we know?* Retrieved from http://www.jcir.org/wpfiles.currie.EARLYCHILDHOOD.Psd

Cushman, K. (2010). Show us what homework is for. *Educational Leadership, 68*(1), 74–78.

Daft, R. L., & Lengel, R. H. (1986). *Organizational information requirements, media richness and structural design. Management Science. 32* (5): 554–571. *doi:10.1287/mnsc.32.5.554.*

Dail, A. R., & Payne, R. L. (2010). Recasting the role of family involvement in early literacy development: A response to the NELP report. *Educational Researcher, 30*(4), 330–333.

Dalaimo, D. M. (1996). Community home education: A case study of public school-based home schooling program.

Daro, D., McCurdy, K., Falconnier, L., & Stojanovic, D. (2003). Sustaining new parents in home visitation services: Key participation and program factors. *Child Abuse and Neglect, 27*(10), 1101–1126.

Darragh, J. (2009). Informal assessment as a tool for supporting parent partnerships. *Exchange, 31*(3), 22–25.

Day, S. (2013). "Terms of engagement" not "hard to reach parents." *Educational Psychology in Practice, 29*(1), 36–53.

DeFur, S. H., & Korinek, L. (2010). Listening to student voices. *The Clearing House: A Journal of Educational Strategies, Issues and Ideas, 83,* 15–19.

Delpit, L. (1996). *Other people's children: Cultural conflict in the classroom.* New York: New Press.

deMause, L. (Ed.). (1988). *The history of childhood: The untold story of child abuse.* New York: Harper & Row.

DeNavas-Walt, C., Proctor, B. D., & Smith, J. C. (2010). Income, poverty, and health insurance coverage in the United States: 2009. *Current Population Reports,* U.S. Census Bureau.

Denver Public Schools, Emily Griffith Opportunity School. (n.d.). *Parent education and preschool department leadership handbook.* Denver, CO: Author.

Derman-Sparks, L., & Olsen Edwards, J. (2012). Anti-bias Education for young children and ourselves. Washinton, DC: NAEYC.

Diamond, A. (2009). The interplay of biology and the environment broadly defined. *Developmental Psychology, 45*(1), 1–8.

Dickerson, M. (1992). Later leaders in education: James L. Hymes, Jr., Advocate for young children. *Childhood Education, 68*(3), 164–171.

Dike, V. E. (2017). Poverty and brain development in children: Implications for learning. *Asian Journal of Education and Training, 3*(1), 64–68.

Dinkmeyer, D., McKay, G. D., & Dinkmeyer, D., Jr. (1997). *Parent's handbook. Systematic training for effective parenting.* Circle Pines, MN: American Guidance Service.

Dinkmeyer, D., McKay, G. D., Dinkmeyer, J. S., & Dinkmeyer, D., Jr. (1992). *Teaching and leading children.* Circle Pines, MN: American Guidance Service.

Dion, J., Paquette, G., Tremblay, K. N., Collin-Vézina, D., & Chabot, M. (2018). Child maltreatment among children with intellectual disability in the Canadian incidence study. *American Journal on Intellectual and Developmental Disabilities, 123*(2), 176–188

Division for Early Childhood, Council for Exceptional Children (DEC). (2016). *Child maltreatment: A position statement of the Division for Early Childhood* (DEC). Washington, D.C.

Doggett, D., Marken, D. M., & Caldwell, D. (2014). Impact of education on grandparents' actions in raising grandchildren, *Journal of Extension, 52*(3).

Dombro, A. L., O'Donnell, N. S., Galinsky, E., Melcher, S. G., & Farber, A. (1996). *Community mobilization: Strategies to support young children and their families.* New York: Families and Work Institute.

Dombrowski, S. C., & Gischlar, K. L. (2014). Keeping children safe on the Internet: Guidelines for parents. *Comuniqué, 34*(2).

Dowling, M. (2010). *Young children's personal, social & emotional development* (3rd ed.). Los Angeles: SAGE.

Doyle, M. E. (2005). HIPPY: Home instruction for parents of pre-school youngsters program. *New England Reading Association Journal, 41*(2), 28–29.

Dutro, E., Kazemi, E., Balf, R., & Lin, Y. S. (2008). "What are you and where are you from?": Race, identity, and the vicissitudes of cultural relevance. *Urban Education, 43*, 269–300.

Dyal, A., Carpenter, L. B., & Wright, J. V. (2009). Assistive technology: What every school leader should know. *Education, 129*(3), 556–560.

Early Childhood Development. (2018). *Connecting cultural experiences with early learning.* An Office of the Administration for Children & Families. Retrieved on June 30, 2018 from https://www.acf.hhs.gov/ecd/success-story/connecting-cultural-experiences-with-early-learning

Early Childhood Technical Assistance Center (ECTA). (2018). *Part C of IDEA.* Retrieved on November 29, 2018 from http://ectacenter.org/partc/partc.asp.

Early Head Start Programs. (2018). *About Early Head Start Program.* Retrieved on November 30, 2018 from https://eclkc.ohs.acf.hhs.gov/programs/article/early-head-start-programs.

Easterseals. (2018). *The story of Easterseals.* Retrieved on August 3, 2018 from http://www.easterseals.com/who-we-are/history/.

Eddowes, E. A. (1992). Children and homelessness: Early childhood and elementary education. In E. H. Stronge (Ed.), *Educating homeless children and adolescents: Evaluating policy and practice.* Newbury Park, CA: Sage.

Educational Resources Information Center, U.S. Department of Education. (1996, Fall). Inclusion. *ERIC Review, 4*(3).

Eissa, A. M., & Almuneef, M. (2010). Child abuse and neglect in Saudi Arabia: Journey of recognition to implementation of national prevention strategies. *Child Abuse & Neglect, 34*(1), 28–33.

Ek, L. D., Machado-Casas, M., Sánchez, P., & Smith, H. (2011). Aprendiendo de sus comunidades/Learning from their communities: Bilingual teacher candidates use research to explore language views and the literacy environments of urban Latino neighborhoods. In V. Kinlock (Ed.), *Critical perspectives on education in urban settings.* New York: Teachers College Press.

Elkind, D. (2007). *The power of play: Learning what comes naturally.* Philadelphia, PA: De Capo Press.

Elmer, E. (1982). Abused young children seen in hospitals. In S. Antler (Ed.), *Child abuse and child protection: Policy and practice.* Silver Springs, MD: National Association of Social Workers.

Elmore, M. (2008). Effective parent conferences. *Principal Leadership (Middle School Ed.), 8*(6), 7–8.

Epstein, J. L. (1994). Theory to practice: School and family partnerships lead to school improvement and student success. In C. L. Fagnano & B. Z. Werber (Eds.), *School, family, and community interaction: A view from the firing lines.* CO: Westview Press.

Epstein, J. L. (1995). School/family/community partnerships: Caring for the children we share. *Phi Delta Kappan, 76*(9), 701–712.

Epstein, J. L. (1996). Perspective and previews on research and policy for school, family and community partnerships. In A. Booth & J. F. Dunn (Eds.), *Family-school links: How do they affect educational outcomes?* Mahwah, NJ: Erlbaum.

Epstein, J. L. (2001). *Schools, family, and community partnerships: Preparing educators and improving schools.* Boulder, CO: Westview Press.

Epstein, J. L. (2005). Attainable goals? The spirit and letter of the No Child Left Behind Act on parental involvement. *Sociology of Education, 78*, 179–182.

Epstein, J. L. (2006). Families, schools, and community partnerships. *Young Children, 61*(1), 40.

Epstein, J. L. (2008). Improving family and community involvement in secondary schools. *The Education Digest, 73*(6), 9–12.

Epstein, J. L. & Sheldon, S. B. (2002). Present and accounted for: Improving student attendance through family and community involvement. *Journal of Educational Research, 95*, 308–318.

Erdener, M. A., & Knoeppel, R. C. (2018). Parents' perceptions of their involvement in school. *International Journal of Research in Education and Science, 4*(1), 1–13.

Ergler, C. R., Kearns, R. A., & Witten, K. (2013). Seasonal and locational variations in children's play: Implications for well-being. *Social Science and Medicine, 91*, 178–185.

Erikson, E. (1986). *Childhood and society.* New York: W. W. Norton.

Esparza, R. (2007). Personalizing my school: Perfect parent attendance. *School Administrator, 64*(8), 1–2.

European Network of Ombudspersons for Children. (2013). European Network of Ombudspersons for Children (ENOC). Retrieved on August 6, 2014, from http://crinarchive.org/enoc/

Eyyam, R., & Yaratan, H. S. (2014). Impact of use of technology in mathematics lessons on student achievement and attitudes. *Social Behavior & Personality, 42*, 31–42.

Families together. (1993, Summer). Newsletter. Topeka, KS: Author.

Family and Advocates Partnership for Education Project. (2006). *The IEP process.* Minneapolis, MN: Pacer Center.

Family Services Association, 2018. About us. Retrieved on October 18, 2018 from https://family-service.org/about-us/.

Family Support America's Shared Leadership Series. (2000). *From many voices: Consensus what American needs for strong families and communities.* Chicago: Family Support America.

Fandal, A. (1986, February). Personal correspondence. Denver: University of Colorado Medical Center.

Farrell, A. F., & Collier, M. A. (2010). School personnel's perceptions of family—school communication: A qualitative study. *Improving Schools, 13*(1), 4–20.

Federal Interagency Forum on Child and Family Statistics. (2013). *America's children: Key national indicators of well-being.* Washington, DC: U.S. Government Printing Office.

Federal Register. (1993, January 21). *Part VI Department of Health and Human Services: Administration for Children and Families, 58*(12), 1304–1305, 1308.

Feinstein, S., Driving-Hawk, C., & Baartman, J. (2009). Resiliency and Native American teenagers. *Reclaiming Children and Youth, 18*(2), 12–17.

Feldman, J. (2012). Best practice for adolescent prenatal care: Application of an attachment theory perspective to enhance prenatal care and diminish birth risks. *Child & Adolescent Social Work Journal, 29*(2), 151–166.

Fenichel, E., & Mann, T. L. (2001). Early Head Start for low-income families with infants and toddlers. *The Future of Children: Caring for Infants and Toddlers, 11*(1), 135–141.

Fenton, P., Ocasio-Stoutenburg, L., & Harry, B. (2017). The power of parent engagement: Sociocultural considerations in the quest for equity. *Theory into Practice, 56*(3), 214–225.

Fernandez, H. C. (1980). *The child advocacy handbook.* New York: The Pilgrim Press.

Ferlazzo, L. (2011). Involvement or engagement? *Educational Leadership, 68*(8), 10–14.

Ferrara, M. M. (2015). Parent involvement facilitators: Unlocking social capital wealth. *School Community Journal, 25*(1), 29–51.

Fields-Smith, C., & Neuharth-Pritchett, S. (2009). Families as decision-makers: When researchers and advocates work together. *Childhood Education, 85*(4), 237–242.

Fierman, A., Dreyer, B., Quinn, L., Shulman, S., Courtlandt, C., & Guzzo, R. (1991). Growth delay in homeless children. *Pediatrics, 88*, 918–925.

File, T. (2013). Computer and Internet use in the United States. *Current Population Survey Reports, P20–568.* U.S. Census Bureau, Washington, D.C.

Finello, K. M., Terteryan, A., & Riewerts, R. J. (2016). Home visiting programs. What the primary care clinical should know. *Current Problems in Pediatric and Adolescent Health Care, 46*(4), 101–125.

Finkelhor, D. (1990). Early and long-term effects of child sexual abuse: An update. *Professional Psychology: Research and Practice, 21*(5), 325–330.

Fisher, M. (1933). Parent education. In *Encyclopedia of the social sciences* (Vol. 2). New York: Macmillan.

Fisher, S. H. (1958). Skeletal manifestations of parent-induced trauma in infants and children. *Southern Medical Journal,* 956–960.

Fisher, M. M. J. (2006). Culture and cultural analysis. *Theory, Culture & Society, 23*(2–3), 360–364.

Fletcher, R., St. George, J., & Freeman, E. (2013). Rough and tumble play quality: Theoretical foundations for a new measure of father–child interaction. *Early Child Development & Care, 183*(6), 746–759.

Flores, B. B., Clark, E. R., Guerra, N., Casebeer, C. M., Sánchez, S. V., & Mayall, H. (2010). Measuring the psychosocial characteristics of teacher candidates through the Academic Self-Identity: Self-Observation Yearly (ASI SOY) Inventory. *Hispanic Journal of Behavioral Sciences, 32*(1), 136–163. Retrieved from http://dx.doi.org/10.1177/0739986309353029.

Flynn, G. & Nolan, B. (2008). What do school principals think about current school–family relationships? *NASSP Bulletin, 92*(3), 173–190.

Fontana, V. (1973). The diagnosis of the maltreatment syndrome in children. *Pediatrics, 51*, 780–782.

Fontana, V. J., & Besharov, D. J. (1979). *The maltreated child: The maltreatment syndrome in children.* Springfield, IL: Charles C. Thomas.

Ford, A. C., & Sassi, K. (2014). Authority in cross-racial teaching and learning (re)considering the transferability of warm demander approaches. *Urban Education, 49*(1), 39–74.

Fox, C. L., Jones, S. E., Stiff, C. E., & Sayers, J. (2014). Does the ender of the bully/victim dyad and the type of bullying influence children's responses to a bullying incident? *Aggressive Behavior, 40*(4), 359–368.

Francis, G. L., Haines, S. J., & Nagro, S. A. (2017). Developing relationships with immigrant families: Learning by asking the right questions. *Teaching Exceptional Children, 50*(2), 95–105.

Frankenburg, W. K., & Coons, C. E. (1986). HOME screening questionnaire: Its validity in assessing home environment. *Journal of Pediatrics, 108*, 624–626.

Freeman, D. E., & Freeman, Y. S. (2001). *Between worlds: Access to second language acquisition.* Portsmouth, NH: Heinemann.

Fullar, S. A. (2008). Babies at double jeopardy. *Zero to Three, 28*(6), 25–32.

Gadsden, V., Fagan, J., Ray, A., & Davis, J. E. (2001). The fathering indicators framework: A tool for quantitative and qualitative analysis. *National Center on Fathers and Families. Graduate School of Education University of Pennsylvania.* Retrieved on November 28, 2018 from https://files.eric.ed.gov/fulltext/ED454942.pdf

Galinsky, E. (1987). *The six stages of parenthood.* Reading, MA: Addison-Wesley.

Gay, G. (2010). Acting on beliefs in teacher education for cultural diversity. *Journal of Teacher Education, 61*(1–2), 143–152.

Galinsky, E., & Salmond, K. (2002, July). *Youth & violence.* Denver: Colorado Trust and Families and Work Institute.

Gallick, B., & Lee, L. (2010). "Cheesy pizza": The pizza project. *Early Childhood Research & Practice, 11*(2).

Gamble, T. K., & Gamble, M. (1982). *Contacts: Communicating interpersonally.* New York: Random House.

Garrett, S. (2004). *Oklahoma #1 in pre-kindergarten program participation.* Retrieved from http://www.sde.state.ok.us/pro/prek/default.htm

Gartin, B., & Murdick, N. (2005, November/December). IDEA 2004: the IEP. *Remedial and Special Education, 26*(6), 327–332.

Geertz, C. (1973). *The interpretation of cultures.* New York: Basic Books.

Gershoff, E. T. & Font, S. A. (2016). Corporal punishment in U.S. public schools: Prevalence, disparities in use, and status in state and federal policy. *Social Policy Report, 30*(1), 1–25.

Gillanders, C., McKinney, M., & Ritchie, S. (2012). What kind of school would you like for your children? Exploring minority mothers' beliefs to promote home–school partnerships. *Early Childhood Education Journal, 40*(5), 285–294.

Ginott, H. G. (1965). *Between parent and child.* New York: Macmillan.

Gjermeni, E., VanHook, M. P., Gjipali, S., Xhillari, L., Lungu, F., & Hazizi, A. (2008). Trafficking of children in Albania: Patterns of recruitment and reintegration. *Child Abuse & Neglect, 32*(10), 941–980.

Goebbels, A. F., G., Nicholson, J. M., Walsh, K., & DeVries, H. (2008). Teachers' reporting of suspected child abuse and neglect: Behaviour and determinants. *Health Education Research, 23*(6), 941–951.

Goldberg, W. A., Tan, E. T., Davis, C. R., & Easterbrooks, M. A. (2013). What predicts father involvement by young fathers at psychological risk? *Fathering, 11*(3), 280–291.

Goldenberg, C. (2014). Unlocking the research on English language learners: What we know—and don't yet know—about effective instruction. *Education Digest, 79*(6), 36–46.

Goldman-Rakic, P. (1996). What can neuroscience contribute to education? In *Education Commission of the States: Bridging the gap between neuroscience and education.* Denver, CO: Author.

Goldman, M. (2013). Bridging joy and sorrow: A basic guide for developing partnership with parents of children with disabilities. *International Journal of Child health and Human Development, 6*(4), 439.

Gomby, D. S. (2007). The promise and limitations of home visiting: Implementing effective programs. *Child Abuse & Neglect, 31*(8), 793–799.

Gomes, M. (2013). It's not just child's play: Nature's powerful effect on children's well-being. *Tikkun, 28*(4), 7–12.

Gonzales Bertrand, D. (1999). *Family/Familia.* Piñata Books Arte Público Press.

Gonzalez, V., Yawkey, T. D., & Minaya-Rowe, L. (2006). *English-as-a-second-language (ESL) teaching and learning: Pre-K-12 classroom applications for students' academic achievement and development.* Upper Saddle River, NJ: Pearson.

Goodykoontz, B., Davis, M. D., & Gabbard, H. F. (1947). Recent history and present status in education for young children. In *National Society for the Study of Education, 46th yearbook, part II.* Chicago: National Society for the Study of Education.

Gordon, I. J., & Breivogel, W. F. (Eds.). (1976). *Building effective home–school relationships.* Boston: Allyn & Bacon.

Gordon, T. (1975). *P.E.T.: Parent effectiveness training.* New York: Wyden.

Gordon, T. (2000). *P.E.T.: Parent effectiveness training: The proven program for raising responsible children.* New York: Three Rivers Press.

Gordon Hartman Foundation. (2018). *The Foundation.* Retrieved on August 31, 2018 from http://gordonhartman.com/.

Gormley, W. T., Jr., Gayer, T., Phillips, D., & Dawson, B. (2004). *The effects of universal pre-k on cognitive development.* Retrieved from http://www.crocus.georgetowm.edu/reports/oklahoma9z.pdf

Gort, M., & Pontier, R. W. (2013). Exploring bilingual pedagogies in dual language preschool classrooms. *Language and Education, 27*(3), 223–245.

Grall, T. S. (2009). *Custodial mothers and fathers and their child support: 2007.* U.S. Census Bureau.

Gray, S. W., Ramsey, B. K., & Klaus, R. A. (1982). *From 3 to 20: The early training project.* Baltimore: University Park Press.

Gray L, Thomas N, Lewis L. 2010a. *Educational technology in U.S. public schools: Fall 2008.* NCES 2010-034. Washington, DC: National Center for Education Statistics. https://nces.ed.gov/pubs2010/2010034.pdf.

Green, B. L., Ayoub, C., Dym Bartlett, J., Von Ende, A., Furrer, C., Chazan-Cohen, R., Vallotton, C. & Klevens, J. (2014). The effect of Early Head Start on child welfare system involvement: A first look at longitudinal child maltreatment outcomes. *Children and Youth Services Review, 42,* 127–135.

Greenleaf, B. (1978). *Children through the ages: History of childhood.* New York: McGraw-Hill.

Greenspan, S. (2002, January). *Emotional origins of intelligence. Special presentation.* Retrieved from http://www.lcweb.loc.gov/loc/brain/emotion/Greenspan.html

Gregg, K., Rugg, M., & Stoneman, Z. (2012). Building on the hopes and dreams of Latino families with young children: Findings from family. *Early Childhood Education Journal, 40*(2), 87–96.

Gresl, B. L., Fox, R. A., & Fleischman, A. (2014). Home-based parent–child therapy in low-income African American, Caucasian, and Latino families: A comparative examination of treatment outcomes. *Child & Family Behavior Therapy, 36*(1), 33–50.

Griffith, P. L., Kimmel, S. J. & Biscoe, B. (2010). Teacher professional development for at-risk preschoolers: Closing the achievement gap by closing the instruction gap. *Action in Teacher Education, 31*(4), 41–53.

Gruenberg, B. C. (Ed.). (1927). *Outlines of child study.* New York: Macmillan.

Gruenert, S., & Whitaker, T. (2017). *School culture recharged: Strategies to energize your staff and culture.* Alexandria, VA: ASCD.

Guitart, M. E., & Moll, L. (2014). Funds of identity: A new concept based on the funds of knowledge approach. *Culture & Psychology, 20*(1), 31–48.

Guo, Y. (2009). Communicating with parents across cultures: An investigation of an ESL parents' night. *Journal of Educational Thought, 43*(2), 171–190.

Gutek, G. L. (1968). *Pestalozzi and education.* New York: Random House.

Guterman, O., & Neuman, A. (2018). Personality, socio-ecnomic status and education: Factors that contribute to the degree of structure in homeschooling. *Social Psychology of Education, 21*(1), 75–90.

Guterson, D. (1992). *Family matters: Why homeschooling makes sense.* New York: Harcourt Brace Jovanovich.

Gutierrez, S. (2013). Parents as agents of change. *Family Involvement Network of Educators (FINE), 5*(3). Retrieved June 14, 2014, from http://www.hfrp.org/family-involvement/publications-resources/parents-asagents-of-change

Hallahan, D., & Kauffman, J. M. (1990). *Exceptional children: Introduction to special education* (5th edition). Boston, MA: Pearson.

Hallahan, D., & Kauffman, J. M. (1997). *Exceptional learners: Introduction to special education* (7th ed.) Boston: Allyn & Bacon.

Hallahan, D. P., Kauffman, J. M., & Pullen, P. C. (2015). *Exceptional learners: An introduction to special education* (13th ed.). Boston: Pearson.

Halme, N., Astedt-Kurk, P., & Tarkka, M. T. (2009). Fathers' involvement with their preschool-age children: How fathers spend time with their children in different family structures. *Child Youth Care Forum, 8,* 103–119. DOI 10.1007/s10566-009-9069-7

Hamilton, L. R. (1989). Child maltreatment: Prevention and treatment. *Early Child Development and Care, 42,* 31–56.

Hampden-Thompson, G., Galindo, C. (2017). School-family relationships, school satisfaction and academic achievement of young people. *Educational Review, 69*(2), 248–265.

Hanson, J. L., Hair, N., Shen, D. G., Shi, F., Gilmore, J. H., Wolfe, B. L., & Pollak, S. D. (2013). Family poverty affects the rate of human infant brain growth. *PLoS ONE, 8*(12), 1–10.

Hanson, R. A. (1975). Consistency and stability of home environmental measures related to IQ. *Child Development, 46*(2), 470–480.

Harden, B. J., Denmark, N., & Saul, D. (2010). Understanding the needs of staff in Head Start programs: The characteristics, perceptions, and experiences of home visitors. *Children & Youth Services Review, 32*(3), 371–390.

Harris, A., & Goodall, J. (2008). Do parents know they matter? Engaging all parents in learning. *Educational Research, 50*(3), 277–289.

Harry, B. (2008). Collaboration with culturally and linguistically diverse families: Ideal versus reality. *Exceptional Children, 74*(3), 372–388.

Harvard Research Project. (2014). Making it real—Connected learning in the digital age. *Family Involvement Network of Educators (FINE), 6*(2). Retrieved June 29, 2014, from http://www.hfrp.org/family-involvement/fine-familyinvolvement-network-of-educators/fine-newsletter-archive/aprilfine-newsletter-making-it-realconnected-learning-in-thedigital-age

Haskett, M. E., Neupert, S. D., & Okado, Y. (2014). Factors associated with 3-year stability and change in parenting behavior of abusive parents. *Journal of Child and Family Studies, 23,* 263–274.

Health Resources and Services Administration Maternal and Child Health. (2018). *Home visiting.* Retrieved on October 20, 2018 from https://mchb.hrsa.gov/maternal-child-health-initiatives/home-visiting-overview

Healthcare.gov. (2018). Children's health insurance program (CHIP). https://www.healthcare.gov/medicaid-chip/childrens-health-insurance-program/

Healthy Families America. (2014). About us. In *Healthy Families America.* Retrieved on June 26, 2014, from http://www.healthyfamiliesamerica.com/home/index/shtml.

Healthy Families America. (2018). The Healthy Families America Strategy. Retrieved on June 30, 2018 from http://www.healthyfamiliesamerica.org/the-hfa-strategy-1/

Helfer, R. E., & Kempe, R. S. (Eds.). (1987). *The battered child* (4th ed.). Chicago: University of Chicago Press.

Helm, J., Huebner, A., & Long, B. (2000). Quiltmaking: Perfect project for preschool and primary. *Young Children, 5*(3), 44–49.

Herman, K. C., & Reinke, W. M. (2017). Improving teacher perceptions of parent involvement patterns: Findings from a group randomized trial. *School Psychology Quarterly, 32*(1), 89–104.

Hernandez-Sheets, R. (2005). *Diversity pedagogy: Examining the role of culture in the teaching-learning process.* Upper Saddle River, NJ: Pearson.

Hessle, S. (2014). Introduction. In S. Hessle (Ed.), *Human rights and social equality: challenges for social work.* Farnham: Ashgate Publishing Ltd.

Heward, W. L., & Orlansky, M. D. (1988). *Exceptional children: An introductory survey of special education* (3rd ed.). Upper Saddle River, NJ: Merrill/Prentice Hall.

Hewett, V. M. (2001, Winter). Examining the Reggio Emilia approach to early childhood education. *Early Childhood Education Journal, 28*(4), 95–99.

High Scope. (2018). Family engagement: For Teachers. Retrieved on November 30, 2018 from https://highscope.org/families/teachers

Hilado, A. V., Kallemeyn, L., & Phillips, L. (2013). Examining understanding of parent involvement in early childhood programs. *Early Childhood Research and Practice, 15*(2). Retrieved June 30, 2014, from http://ecrp.uiuc.edu/v15n2/hilado.html

Hill, R. (1960). The American family today. In E. Ginsberg (Ed.), *The nation's children.* New York: Columbia University Press.

Hodapp, A. F., & Hodapp, J. B. (1992). Homework: Making it work. *Intervention in School and Clinic, 27*(4), 233–235.

Hodges, J. (1996). The natural history of early non-attachment. In B. Bernstein & J. Brannen (Eds.), *Children Research and Policy.* Bristol, PA: Taylor and Francis.

Hoerr, T. R. (2014). Tips for better parent–teacher conferences. *Educational Leadership,71*(7), 86–87.

Hoge, M. R., Liaupsin, C. J., Umbreit, J., & Ferro, J. B. (2014). Examining placement considerations for across three alternative schools. *Journal of Disability Policy Studies, 24*(4), 218–226.

Hoffman, L., Podikunju-Hussain, S., & Ridout, S. (2015). Don't stop stuffing the backpacks! Parents of English language learners share school-home communication preferences. Retrieved on September 5, 2018 from https://files.eric.ed.gov/fulltext/ED566954.pdf.

Hollingsworth, J. C. (2009). Morgan's Wonderland: An oasis of fun and accessibility for children with special needs and their families. *The Exceptional Parent Magazine.* Retrieved from http://www.eparent.com

Homes for the Homeless. (2011). America Family Inns. http://www.hfhnyc.org/programs/americanfamilyinns.asp

Home Instruction for Parents of Preschool Youngsters (HIPPY). (2014). The HIPPY model. In *The Home Instruction for Parents and Preschool Youngsters.* Retrieved July 2, 2014, from http://www.hippyusa.org/

Home Instruction for Parents of Preschool Youngsters (HIPPY). (2018). *Find a program.* Retrieved on June 30, 2018 from https://www.hippyusa.org/find-a-program/

Hong, E., & Milgram, R. M. (2000). *Homework: Motivation and learning preference.* Westport, CT: Bergin & Garvey.

Honig, A. S., Lally, J. R., & Mathieson, D. H. (1982). Personal-social adjustment of school children after five years in a family enrichment program. *Child Care Quarterly, 11*(2), 138–146.

Horn, W. F. (1997, July, August). You've come a long way, daddy. *Policy Review,* No. 84, 24–30.

Horton, C. B., & Cruise, T. K. (2001). *Child abuse and neglect.* New York: Guilford Press.

Howard, E. F. (1991). *Aunt Flossie's Hats (and Crab Cakes Later).* Clarion Books.

Howard, T. C. (2003). Culturally relevant pedagogy: Ingredients for critical teacher reflection. *Theory into Practice, 42*(3), 195–202.

Huerta, M. E., & Riojas-Cortez, M. (2011). *Santo Remedio*: Latino parents and students foster literacy through a culturally relevant folk medicine event. *Multicultural Education, 18*(2).

Huerta, M. E., & Riojas-Cortez, M. (2014). Playful dialogues of a bilingual child in every day conversation. *International Multilingual Research Journal, 8,* 231–249.

Hughes, L. (2009). *My people: My people with photographs.* Atheneum Books.

Huhtanen, S., & Huhtanen, M. (2008). Bridging the gap: Advocating for your child with autism. *The Exceptional Parent, 38*(12), 7–73.

Hulit, L. M., Howard, M. R., & Fahey, K. R. (2011). *Born to talk: An introduction to speech and language development* (5th ed.). Upper Saddle River, NJ: Pearson.

Hunt, J. M. (1961). *Intelligence and experience.* New York: Wiley.

Hunter, W. (January 16, 2018). The story behind the poem on the Statute of Liberty. *The Atlantic.* Retrieved on March 13 from https://www.theatlantic.com/entertainment/archive/2018/01/the-story-behind-the-poem-on-the-statue-of-liberty/550553/

Hyatt, K. J., & Filler, J. (2011). LRE re-examined: Misinterpretations and unintended consequences. *International Journal of Inclusive Education,15*(9), 1031–1045.

Hymes, J. L., Jr. (1974). *Effective home–school relations.* Sierra Madre: Southern California Association for the Education of Young Children.

Hymes, J. L., Jr. (1987). *Early childhood education: The year in review: A look at 1986.* Carmel, CA: Hacienda Press.

Inandi, Y., Tunc, B., & Gilic, F. (2013). School administrators' leadership styles and resistance to change. *International Journal of Academic Research Part B, 5*(5), 196–203.

Ingoldsby, E. M., Baca, P., McClatchey, M. W., Luckey, D. W., Ramsey, M. O., Loch, J. M., Lews, J., Blackaby, T. S., Petrini, M. B., Smith, B. J., McHale, M., Perhacs, M., & Olds, D. L. (2013). Quasi-experimental pilot study of intervention to increase participant retention and completed home visits in the Nurse-Family Partnership. *Prevention Science, 14*(6), 525–534.

Institute for Children, Poverty & Homelessness. (2018). *Quick facts.* http://www.icphutsa.org

Institute for Responsive Education. (2006). *IRE: Connecting school, family and community.* Retrieved from http://www.responsive education.org

Interagency Council on Homelessness. (2010). *Opening doors: Federal strategic plan to prevent and end homelessness: 2010.*

International Bullying Prevention Association. (2006). *Our mission.* Retrieved from http://stopbullyingworld.com/

Isenberg, E. J. (2007). What have we learned about homeschooling? *Peabody Journal of Education, 82*(2–3), 387–409.

Ishimaru, A. (2014). Rewriting the rules of engagement: Elaborating a model of district-community collaboration. *Harvard Educational Review, 84*(2), 188–216.

Isik-Ercan, Z. (2012). In pursuit of a new perspective in the education of children of the refugees: Advocacy for the "family." *Educational Sciences: Theory & Practice, Special Issue, 3025–2038.*

Jablonka, I. (2013). Dependent children, social welfare, and the rights of children. In P. S. Fass (Ed.), *The Routledge history of childhood in the Western World.* New York: Routledge.

Jackson, B. L., & Cooper, B. S. (1992). Involving parents in improving urban schools. *NAASP Bulletin, 76*(543), 30–38.

Jalongo, M. R. (2006). The story of Mary Ellen Wilson: Tracing the origins of child protection in America. *Early Childhood Education Journal, 34*(1), 1–4.

Johnson, D. L. (1990). Developing family environments with families. In F. Kaslow (Ed.). *Voices in family psychology.* Beverly Hills, CA: Sage.

Jimenez-Silva, M., & Olson, K. (2012). A community of practice in teacher education: Insights and perceptions. *International Journal of Teaching and Learning in Higher Education, 24*(3), 335–348.

Johnson, D. L., Walker, T. B., & Rodríguez, G. G. (1996). Teaching low-income mothers to teach their children. *Early Childhood Research Quarterly, 11*(1), 101–114.

Joshi, A. (2005). Understanding Asian Indian families—facilitating meaningful home-school relations. *Young Children, 60*(3), 75–78.

Kaaland, C. (2013). The power of parent advocacy. *School Library Monthly, 30*(2), 26–28.

Kamii, C. (1985a). Leading primary education toward excellence: Beyond worksheets and drills. *Young Children, 40*(6), 3–9.

Kamii, C. (1985b). *Young children reinvent arithmetic.* New York: Teachers College Press.

Kaplan-Leiserson, E. (2002). Education evolution: How many other institutions look exactly as they did 40 years ago? *T&D, 56*(4), 16–18.

Karnes, F. A., & Marquardt, R. (1997, February). *Know your legal rights in gifted education.* Reston, VA: The ERIC Clearinghouse on Disabilities and Gifted Education, The Council for Exceptional Children.

Karoly, L. A., Kilburn, R., & Cannon, J. (2005). *Early childhood interventions: Proven results, future promise.* Santa Monica, CA: Rand Books & Publication.

Katsiyannis, A., Whitford, D. K., & Parks Ennis, R. (2018). Historical examination of United States intentional mass school shootings in the 20th and 21st centuries: Implications for students, schools, and society. Journal of Child and Family Studies, http://dx.doi.org/10.1007/s10826-018-1096-2

Katz, K. (1999). *The color of us.* Henry Holt and Company LLC Publisher.

Katz, L. G. (n.d.). Clearinghouse on early education and parenting. *The Project Approach Catalog: The Importance of Projects.* Retrieved from http://ceep.crc.ululc.edueecearchive/books/projappl/initial.html#incorporating

Kayser, T. (2013). Six ingredients for collaborative partnerships. *Leader to Leader, 61,* 48–55.

Kearns, P. (Ed.). (1980). *Your child's right for a free public education: Parent's handbook.* Topeka: Kansas Association for Children with Learning Disabilities.

Keller, H. (1991). *The story of my life: With her letters (1887–1901) and supplementary account of her education including passages from the reports and letters of her teacher, Anne Mansfield Sullivan.* CA: Temecula American Biography Series, Reprint Services Co.

Kelley, M. L. (1990). *School–home notes: Promoting children's classroom success.* New York: Guilford Press.

Kelly, J. G. (1966). Ecological constraints on mental health services. *American Psychologist, 21,* 535–539.

Kelly, J. (2012). Two daddy tigers and a baby tiger: Promoting understandings about same gender parented families using picture books. *EarlyYears: Journal of International Research & Development, 32*(3), 288–300.

Kelly, L. (2018). Interest convergence and hegemony in dual language: Bilingual education, but for whom and why? *Language Policy, 17*(1), 1–21.

Kempe, C. H., & Kempe, R. (1984). *The common secret: Sexual abuse of children and adults.* San Francisco: W. H. Freeman.

Kempe, C. H., Silverman, F. N., Steele, B. F., Droegemueller, W., & Silver, H. (1962). The battered-child syndrome. *Journal of the American Medical Association, 181,* 17–24.

Kennedy, A. (2010). Family support for early literacy and numeracy: Examining events in the home and community. *Exchange, 32*(1), 18–22.

Khailova, L. (2012). Every child "off to a good start": Hispanic/Latino family literacy workshops in an academic library setting. *Illinois Reading Council Journal, 40*(2), 23–30.

Khan, H. (2012). Golden Domes and Silver Lanterns: A Muslim Book of Colors. Chronicle Books.

Kids Health. (2006). *Internet safety.* Retrieved from http://kidshealth.org/kid/

King, C. E. (1962). *The sociology of small groups.* New York: Pageant Press.

King, S. M. (2013). Alone and unrepresented: A call to Congress to provide counsel for unaccompanied minors. *Harvard Journal of Legislation, 50,* 331–384.

Kitzman, H. J., Olds, D. L., Cole, R. E., Hanks, C. A., Anson, E. A., Arcoleo, K. J., Luckey, D. W., Knudtson, M. D., Henderson, C. R. Jr., & Holmberg, J. R. (2010). Enduring effects of prenatal and infancy home visiting by nurses on children. Follow-up of a randomized trial among children at age 12 years. *Archives of Pediatrics & Adolescent Medicine, 164*(5), 412–418.

Klass, C., Pettinelli, D., & Wilson, M. (1993). Home visiting: Building linkages. Personal correspondence.

Klein, T., Bittel, C., & Molnar, J. (1993). No place to call home: Supporting the needs of homeless children in the early childhood classroom. *Young Children, 48*(6), 22–31.

Knopf, H. T., & Swick, K. J. (2007). Using our understanding of families to strengthen family involvement. *Early Childhood Education Journal, 35*(5), 419–427.

Knowles, J. G. (1989, January). Cooperating with home school parents: A new agenda for public schools? *Urban Education, 23*(4), 392–411.

Koch, P. K., & McDonough, M. (1999, March). Improving parent–teacher conferences through collaborative conversations. *Young Children, 54*(2), 11–15.

Kompanje, E. J. O. (2007). A case of malingering by proxy described in 1593. *Child Abuse & Neglect, 31*(9), 1013–1017.

Koellner, Jacobs & Borko, H. (2011). Mathematics professional development: Critical features for developing leadership skills and building teachers' capacity. *Mathematics Teacher Education and Development, 13*, 115–136.

Kraft, M. A. (2017). Engaging parents through better communication systems. *Educational Leadership*, 58–62.

Krashen, S. D. (1981). *Principles and practice in second language acquisition.* English Language Teaching Series. London: Prentice Hall International (UK) Ltd.

Kreider, R. M., & Ellis, R. (2011). Living Arrangements of Children: 2009, Current Population Reports, P70–126, U.S. Census Bureau, Washington, DC, 2011.

Krieg, S., Smith, K. A., & Davis, K. (2014). Exploring the dance of early childhood educational leadership. *Australasian Journal of Early Childhood, 39*(1), 73–80.

Kroth, R. L., & Edge, D. (2007). Parent–teacher conferences. *Focus on Exceptional Children, 40*(2), 1–8.

Krugman, R. D. (1986). Recognition of sexual abuse in children. *Pediatrics in Review 8*(1), 25–30.

Ladson-Billings, G. (1995). Toward a theory of culturally relevant pedagogy. *American Educational Research Journal, 32*(3), 465–491.

LaFave, D., & Thomas, D. (2014). "Extended families and child well-being." Working Paper 20702. National Bureau of Economic Research.

Lally, J. R. (2001). Infant care in the United States and how the Italian experience can help. In L. Gandini & C. P. Edwards (Eds.), *Bambini: The Italian approach to infant/toddler care.* New York: Teachers College Press.

Lamb, M. E. (Ed.). (1997). *The role of the father in child development.* New York: Wiley.

Lamson, P. A. (1992). Home schooling: A choice the Cupertino district supports. *The School Administrator, 49*(1), 26–27.

Landale, N.S., Thomas, K. J. A., & Van Hook, J. (2011). The living arrangements of children of immigrants. The *of Children, 21*(1), 43–70.

Lane, J., Kesker, E. E., Ross, C., et al. (2005). The effectiveness of Early Head Start for 3-year old children and their parents. *Developmental Psychology, 41*(6), 885–902.

Lane, W. G., Dubowitz, H., & Langenberg, P. (2009). Screening for occult abdominal trauma in children with suspected physical abuse. *Pediatrics, 124*(6), 1595–1602.

LaSalle, J. (2013). Epigenomic strategies at the interface of genetic and environmental risk factors for autism. *Journal of Human Genetics, 58*(7), 396–401.

Laukkanen, J., Ojansuu, U., Tolvanen, A., Alatupa, S., & Aunola, K. (2013). Child's difficult temperament and mother's parenting styles. *Journal of Child and Family Studies, 23*, 312–323.

Lau v. Nichols, 414 U.S. 563. (1974).

Lay, M., & Papadopoulos, I. (2009). Sexual maltreatment of unaccompanied asylum-seeking minors from the Horn of Africa: A mixed method study focusing on vulnerability and prevention. *Child Abuse & Neglect, 33*.

Lazar, I., Darlington, R., Murray, H., Royce, J., & Snipper, A. (1982). Lasting effects of early education: A report from the Consortium for Longitudinal Studies. *Monographs of the Society for Research in Child Development, 47*(2–3).

Lazoritz, S. (1990). Whatever happened to Mary Ellen? *Child Abuse and Neglect, 14*(2), 143–149.

Lemmer, E. M. (2012). Who's doing the talking? Teacher and parent experiences of parent–teacher conferences. *South African Journal of Education, 32*(1), 83–96.

Leon, K., & Cole, K. (2004, March). *Helping children understand divorce.* University of Missouri Extension. Retrieved from http://muextension.missouri.edu/xplor/hesguide/humanrel/gh600.htm

Lerner, J., Mardell-Czudnowski, C., & Goldenberg, D. (1987). *Special education for the early childhood years.* Upper Saddle River, NJ: Prentice Hall.

Levenstein, P. (1988). *Messages from home: The mother-child program.* Columbus: Ohio State University Press.

Levenstein, P., Levenstein, S., Shiminski, J. A., & Stolzberg, J. E. (1998). Long-term impact of a verbal interaction program for at-risk toddlers: An exploratory study of high school outcomes in a replication of the mother-child home program. *Journal of Applied Developmental Psychology, 19*(2), 267–285.

Levine, J. A., Murphy, D. T., & Wilson, S. (1993). *Getting men involved: Strategies for early childhood programs.* New York: Scholastic.

Levine, M., & Levine, A. G. (2012). The misuse of abuse: Restricting evidence of battered child children. *American Journal of Orthopsychiatry, 82*(2), 167–173.

Lin, M., Lake, V. E., & Rice, D. (2008). Teaching anti-bias curriculum in teacher education programs: What and how. *Teacher Education Quarterly, 35*(2), 187–200.

Lines, P. (1996). *Homeschooling.* Washington, DC: Office of Educational Research and Improvement, U.S. Department of Education. (ERIC Document Reproduction Service No. ED965033)

Litcher, D. T., & Crowley, M. (2002, June). Poverty in America: Beyond welfare reform. In *Population Bulletin 57.* Washington DC: Population Reference Bureau.

Livingston, G., & Parker, K. (2010). Since the start of the Great Recession, more children raised by grandparents. *Pew Research Center Social & Demographic Trends.* Retrieved on November 28, 2018 from http://www.pewsocialtrends.org/2010/09/09/since-the-start-of-the-great-recession-more-children-raised-by-grandparents/

Lopez, M. E., & Caspe, M. (2014). Family engagement in anywhere, anytime learning. *Family Involvement Network of Educators (FINE),6*(3). Retrieved June 29, 2014, from http://www.hfrp.org/publications-resources/browse-our-publications/family-engagement-inanywhere-anytime-learning

López, G., & Radford, J. (2017). Facts on U.S. immigrants, 2015: Statistical portrait of the foreign-born population in the United Sates. *Pew Research Center Hispanic Trends.* Retrieved on March 13, 2018 from http://www.pewhispanic.org/2017/05/03/facts-on-u-s-immigrants/

Loucks, H. (1992). Increasing parent/family involvement: Ten ideas that work. *NASSP Bulletin, 76*(543), 19–23.

Lowenthal, B. (2001). Abuse and neglect: The educator's guide to the identification and prevention of child maltreatment. Baltimore, MD: Paul H. Brooks.

Lubienski, C., Puckett, T., & Brewer, T. J. (2013). Does home-schooling "work"? A critique of the empirical claims and agenda of advocacy organizations. *Peabody Journal of Education, 88*(3), 378–392.

Lyall, K., Schmidt, R. J., & Hertz-Picciotto, I. (2014). Maternal lifestyle and environmental risk factors for autism spectrum disorders. *International Journal of Epidemiology, 43*(2), 443–464.

Machado-Casas, M. (2014). *El mundo en la palma de la mano* [The world in the palm of the hand]: Bridging families' multigenerational technology gaps through *La ClaseMágica*. In B. B. Flores, O. A. Vásquez & E. R. Clark (Eds.), *Generating Transworld Pedagogy: Reimagining La ClaseMágica*. Lexington Publishers, Rowman Littlefield Publishing Group.

Maclure, R. (2014). Introduction. *International Journal of Children's Rights, 22*(2), 235– 239.

Maglione, M. A., Das, L., Raaen, L., Smith, A., Chari, R., Newberry, S. .& Gidengil, C. (2014). Safety of vaccines used for routine immunization of US children: A systematic review. *Pediatrics, 134*(2), 1–15.

Magruder, E. S., Hayslip, W. W., Espinosa, L. M., & Matera, C. (2013). Many languages, one teacher: Supporting language and literacy development for preschool dual language learners. *Young Children, 68*(1), 8–15.

Malaguzzi, L. (1993, November). For an education based on relationships. *Young Children, 49*(1), 9–12.

Mann, V., Sandoval, M., Garcia, L., & Calderon, D. (2009). Using Spanish in the home to promote school readiness in English. In A. Harrison (ed.), *Speech disorders: Causes, treatment and social effects* (pp. 97–118). USA: Nova Science Publishers, Inc.

Manning, B. H. (1985). Conducting a worthwhile parent-teacher conference. *Education, 105*(4), 342–348.

Manning, D. T., & Wootten, M. D. (1987). What stepparents perceive schools should know about blended families. *The Clearing House, 60*(5), 230–235.

Margolis, H., & Brannigan, G. G. (1986). Relating to angry parents. *Academic Therapy, 21*(3), 343–346.

Martin, A., Ryan, R. M., & Brooks-Gunn, J. (2010). When fathers' supportiveness matters most: maternal and paternal parenting and children's school readiness. *Journal of Family Psychology, 24*(2), 144–155.

Marian, V., Shook, A., & Schroeder, R. S. (2013). Bilingual two-way immersion programs benefit academic achievement. *Bilingual Research Journal, 36*, 167–186.

Marsh, S., Waniganayake, M., & De Nobile, J. (2014). Improving learning in schools: The overarching influence of "presence" on the capacity of authoritative leaders. *International Journal of Leadership in Education, 17*(1), 23–39.

Martin, E. (1968). Breakthrough for the handicapped: Legislative history. *Exceptional Children, 34*, 493–503.

Martin, J., & Alaggia, R. (2013). Sexual abuse images in cyberspace: Expanding the ecology of the child. *Journal of Child Sexual Abuse, 22*(4), 398–415.

Martinez, S. (2011). An examination of Latino students' homework routines. *Journal of Latinos in Education, 10*(4), 354–368.

Maslach, C. (1982). *Burnout: The cost of caring.* Upper Saddle River, NJ: Prentice Hall.

Mathur, M., Rathore, P., & Mathur, M. (2009). Incidence, type and intensity of abuse in street children in India. *Child Abuse & Neglect, 33*(12), 907–913.

Mayer, A. P., Donaldson, M. L., LeChasseur, K., Welton, A. D., & Cobb, C. D. (2013). Negotiating site-based management and expanded teacher decision making: A case study of six urban schools. *Educational Administration Quarterly, 49*(5), 695–731.

McCallister, C., Wilson, P., Green, B., & Baldwin, J. (2005). "Come take a walk": Listening to Early Head Start parents on school readiness as a matter of child, family and community health. *American Journal of Public Health, 95*(4), 617–626.

McCormick, L., & Holden, R. (1992). Homeless children: A special challenge. *Young Children, 47*(6), 61–67.

McCoy, D., Roy, A., & Sirkman, G. (2013). Neighborhood crime and school climate as predictors of elementary school academic quality: A cross-lagged panel analysis. *American Journal of Community Psychology, 52*(1/2), 128–140.

McDonald, L. (2010). Advocacy in reading: To be or not to be an advocate? *Reading Improvement, 47*(2), 71–73.

McGarry, J., Westbury, M., Kench, S., & Furse, B. (2014). Responding to domestic violence in acute hospital settings. *Nursing Standard, 28*(34), 47–50.

McNally, S. A., & Slustky, R. (2017). Key elements of the Reggio Emilia approach and how they are interconnected to create the highly regarded system of early childhood education. *Early Child Development and Care, 187*(12), 1925–1937.

Mead, M., & Wolfenstein, M. (1963). *Childhood in contemporary cultures.* Chicago: University of Chicago Press.

MELD. (1988). *MELD's Young Moms (MYM): Information and support for teen mothers.* Minneapolis, MN: Author.

MELD. (2006). *What is MELD?* Retrieved from http://www.meld.org

Mesman, J., van Ijzendoorn, M., Behrens, K., Carbonel, O. A., Cárcamo, R., Cohen-Paraira, I., de la Harpe, C., Ekmekçi, Emmen, R., Heidar, J., Kondo-Ikemura, K., Mels, C., Mooya, H., Murtisari, S., Nóblega, M., Ortiz, J. A., Sagi-Schwartz, A., Sichimba, F., Soares, I., Steele, H., Steele, M., Pape, M., van Ginkel, J., van der Veer, R., Wang, L., Selcuk, B., Yavuz, M., & Zreik, G. (2016). Is the ideal mother a sensitive mother? Beliefs about early childhood parenting in mothers across the globe. *International Journal of Behavioral Development, 40*(5), 385–397.

Meyer, D. J., & Vadasy, P. F. (2008). *Sibshops: Workshops for siblings of children with special needs.* Baltimore, MD: Paul H. Brookes Pub.

Meyerhoff, M. K., & White, B. L. (1986). New parents as teachers. *Educational Leadership, 44*(3), 42–46.

Meyers, K., & Pawlas, G. (1989). Simple steps assure parent-teacher conference success. *Instructor, 99*(2), 66–67.

Michael, S., Dittus, P., & Epstein, J. L. (2007). Family and community involvement in schools: Results from the school health in policies and programs of study 2006. *Journal of School Health, 77*(8).

Miller, J. W., Kuykendall, J. A., & Thomas, S.A. (2013). Are we in this together? An analysis of the impact of individual and institutional characteristics on teachers' perceptions. *School Community Journal, 23*(2), 137–159.

Milner, H. R. IV. (2013). Culturally relevant pedagogy in a diverse urban classroom. *Urban Review: Issues and Ideas in Public Education, 43*(1), 66–89.

Minneapolis Public Schools. (2006). *School readiness.* Retrieved from http://schoolchoice.mpls.k12.mn.us/School_Readiness.html

Moles, O. C. (1987). Who wants parent involvement? Interest, skills, and opportunities among parents and educators. *Education and Urban Society, 19*(2), 137–145.

Moles, O. C. (Ed.). (1996a). *Reaching all families: Creating family-friendly schools.* Washington, DC: U.S. Department of Education, Office of Educational Research and Improvement.

Moles, O. C. (1996b). New national directions in research and policy. In A. Booth & J. F. Dunn (Eds.), *School–family links: How do they affect educational outcomes?* Mahwah, NJ: Erlbaum.

Moll, L. C., Amanti, C., Neff, D., & Gonzalez, N. (1992). Funds of knowledge for teaching: Using a qualitative approach to connect homes and classrooms. Theory into Practice, 31(2), 132–141.

Morgan, J. K., Shaw, D. S., & Forbes, E. E. (2014). Maternal depression and warmth during childhood predict age 20 neural response to reward. *Journal of the American Academy of Child & Adolescent Psychiatry, 53*(1), 108–117.

Morin, A. (2014). *The Everything Parent's Guide to Special Education: A Complete Step-by-Step Guide to Advocating for Your Child with Special Needs.* Adams, MA: Adams Media.

MSU Extension. (1999). *Group effectiveness: Understanding group member roles.* Retrieved from http://www.msue.msu.edu/msue/imp/modii/ii719202.html

Muhammad, A. (2017). *Transforming school culture: How to overcome staff division.* Bloomington, IN: Solution Tree Press.

Murdick, N. L., Gartin, B. L., & Fowler, G. A. (2014). Special education law (3rd edition). Boston, MA: Pearson.

Murphy, S. (2014). Finding the right fit: Inclusive strategies for students with characteristics of ADHD. *Young Children, 69*(3), 66–71.

Napier, C. (2014). How use of screen media affects the emotional development of infants. *Primary Health Care, 24*(2), 18–25.

National Association for the Education of Young Children (NAEYC). (2011). *NAEYC Code of ethical conduct and statement of commitment*: A position statement of the National Association for the Education of Young Children. Retrieved on March 17, 2018 from https://www.naeyc.org/sites/default/files/globally-shared/downloads/PDFs/resources/position-statements/Ethics%20Position%20Statement2011_09202013update.pdf

National Association for the Education of Young Children (NAEYC). (2014). Technology and interactive media as tools in early childhood programs serving children from birth through age 8. Retrieved from http://www.naeyc.org/files/naeyc/PS_technology_WEB.pdf.

National Association for the Education of Young Children (NAEYC) & National Association of Early Childhood Specialists in State Departments of Education. (1991). Guidelines for appropriate curriculum content and assessment in programs serving children ages 3 through 8. *Young Children, 46*(3), 21–38.

National Association of State Boards of Education (NASBE). (1988). *Right from the start.* Alexandria, VA: Author.

National Association of State Boards of Education. (1991). *Caring communities: Supporting young children and families.* Alexandria, VA: Author.

National Association of State Boards of Education. (2006). *NASBE awarded grant to replicate successful early*

National Association of State Directors of Special Education. (1997). *1997 amendments to the Individuals with Disabilities Education Act.* Washington, DC: Author.

National Center for Education Statistics (2010). Educational technology in U.S. public schools: Fall 2008. *U.S. Department of Education.*

National Center for Fathering. (2018). *Trends in fathering.* Retrieved on November 28, 2018 from http://fathers.com/statistics-and-research/trends-in-fathering.

National Center on Shaken Baby Syndrome. (2018a). Learn more. Retrieved on August 28, 2018 from https://dontshake.org/learn-more.

National Center on Shaken Baby Syndrome. (2018b). PURPLE Crying. Retrieved on August 28, 2018 from https://dontshake.org/purple-crying.

National Center for Children in Poverty. (2018). Child poverty. Retrieved on October 21, 2018 from http://www.nccp.org/topics/childpoverty.html.

National Center for Education Statistics. (2001, March). *National assessment of educational progress history—Time spent on homework.* Retrieved from http://nces.ed.gov/nationsreportcard/ushistory/findhomework.asp

National Center for Education Statistics. (2007). *1.1 million home-schooled students in the United States in 2003.* Retrieved from http://nces.ed.gov/nhes/homeschool.

National Center for Education Statistics. (2014). Homeschooling. In *Fast Facts.* Retrieved from http://nces.ed.gov/FastFacts/display.asp?id=91

National Center for Families Learning. (2018). About us. *National Center for Families Learning.* Retrieved on March 24, from http://www.familieslearning.org/about-us/about-us.html

National Center on Shaken Baby Syndrome. (2006). *Prevention and legislation.* Retrieved from http://www.dontshake.com

National Center on Shaken Baby Syndrome. (2018). About. Retrieved on October 21, 2018 from https://dontshake.org/.

National Coalition Against Domestic Violence (2014). About us. Retrieved on July 11, 2014, from http://www.ncadv.org/aboutus.php

National Council on Disability. (2002, July). *Individuals with Disabilities Education Act reauthorization: Where do we really stand?* Retrieved from http://www.ncd.gov/newsroom/publications/synthesis_07-05-02.html

National Dissemination Center for Children with Disabilities. (2011). *All about the IEP.* Retrieved from www.nichy.org/educatechildren/ieppages

National Education Association. (2018). *Teacher leader model standards.* Retrieved on May 28, 2018 from http://www.nea.org/home/43946.htm

National Even Start Association. (2014). *Programs: Even Start.* Retrieved on November 30, 2018 from https://www2.ed.gov/programs/evenstartformula/index.html.

National Head Start Association. (2018). Access to Head Start in the United States of America. *National Head Start Fact Sheet.* Retrieved on September 27, 2018 from https://www.nhsa.org/facts.

National Home Visiting Resource Center. (2017). *2017 Home Visiting Yearbook.* Arlington, VA: James Bell Associates and the Urban Institute.

National Information Center for Children and Youth with Disabilities. (1998). IDEA amendments of 1997. *NICHCY News Digest 26* (Rev. ed.). Washington, DC: Author.

National Information Center for Children and Youth with Disabilities. (2000, February). *Reading and learning disabilities.* Retrieved from http://www.nichy.org/pubs/factshe/fs17text.htm

National Information Center for Children and Youth with Disabilities, 2011

National Institute of Environmental Health Sciences. (2014). Autism. In *National Institute for Environmental Health Science.* Retrieved on July 5, 2014, http://www.niehs.nih.gov/health/topics/conditions/autism/

National Institute of Mental Health. (2014). Attention deficit hyperactivity disorder. In *National Institute for Mental Health.* Retrieved July 7, 2014, from http://www.nimh.nih.gov/health/publications/attention-deficithyperactivity-disorder/index.shtml#pub2

National Institute of Mental Health. (2018). *Attention Deficit Hyperactivity Disorder.* Retrieved on August 31, 2018 from https://www.nimh.nih.gov/health/topics/attention-deficit-hyperactivity-disorder-adhd/index.shtml

National Law Center on Homelessness & Poverty. (2002a). *Homelessness and poverty in America.* Retrieved from http://www.nlchp.org/FA_HAPIA/

National Law Center on Homelessness & Poverty. (2002b). *McKinney-Vento 2001 reauthorization—at a glance.* Retrieved from http://www.nlchp.org/FA_Education/mckinneyGlance.cfm

National Law Center on Homelessness & Poverty. (2018). Homelessness in America: Overview of data and causes. Retrieved on November 28, 2018 from https://www.nlchp.org/documents/Homeless_Stats_Fact_Sheet

National Law Immigration Center. (2013). Annual report. Retrieved on August 5, 2014, from http://nilc.org/.

National Network of Schools in Partnership. (2018). What is NSSP? *National Network of Schools in Partnership.* Retrieved on March 24, 2018 from http://schoolsinpartnership.org/about-us

National Network to End Domestic Violence. (2018). Red flags of abuse. Retrieved on August 28, 2018 from https://nnedv.org/content/red-flags-of-abuse/

National Network to End Domestic Violence. (2018). About us. Retrieved on May 25 from https://nnedv.org/

National Parent Teacher Association. (2018a). National PTA launches center for family engagement. *National PTA.* Retrieved on March 24, from https://www.pta.org/home/About-National-Parent-Teacher-Association/PTA-Newsroom/news-list/news-detail-page/2018/03/23/national-pta-launches-center-for-family-engagement

National Parent Teacher Association. (2018b). History. *National PTA.* Retrieved on June 13, from https://www.pta.org/home/About-National-Parent-Teacher-Association/Mission-Values/National-PTA-History

National Public Radio. (2014). Bolivia makes child labor legal in an attempt to make it safer. *Morning Edition.* Retrieved on September 5 from https://www.npr.org/2014/07/30/336361778/bolivia-makes-child-labor-legal-in-an-attempt-to-make-it-safer.

National Society for the Study of Education. (1929). *Twenty-eighth year book. Preschool and parent education (parts 1 and 2).* Bloomington, IL: Public School Publishing.

Nelson, J., Leerkes, E. M., Perry, N., O'Brien, M., Calkins, S. D., & Marcovitch, S. (2013). Associations between mothers' emotion socialization practices and child competence vary in African American and European American families. *Social Development, 22,* 485–498.

Nelson, K. (2012). Coming full circle: A social context for Henry Kempe's work, *Law & Contemporary Problems, 75*(1), 187–210.

Nelson, S. W., & Guerra, P. L. (2010). Empowered parents partner with schools to meet student needs. *Journal of Staff Development, 31*(1), 67–68.

Neumerski, C. M. (2013). Rethinking instructional leadership, a review: What do we know about principal, teacher, and coach instructional leadership, and where should we go from here? *Educational Administration Quarterly, 49*(2), 310–347.

Nevin, A. I., Thousand, J. S., & Villa, R. A. (2009). Collaborative teaching for teacher educators—what does the research say? *Teaching and Teacher Education, 25,* 569–574.

Newman, F. (1996). Introduction. In *Education Commission of the States, Bridging the gap between neuroscience and education.* Denver, CO: Author.

Nieto. S. (2008). Culture and education. *Yearbook of the National Society for the Study of Education, 107*(1), 127–142.

Nievar, A. M., Van Egeren, L. A., & Pollard, S. (2010). A meta-analysis of home visiting programs: Moderators of improvement in maternal behaviors. *Infant Mental Health Journal, 31*(5), 499–520.

Nimnicht, G. P., & Brown, E. (1972). The toy library: Parents and children learning with toys. *Young Children, 28*(2), 110–116.

No Child Left Behind Act of 2001. (2001).

Nowak, K. B. (2014). What is an ombudsman? Retrieved August 6, 2014, from http://www.ncsl.org/research/human-services/childrensombudsman-offices.aspx

Nuñez, R. D. (1996). *The new poverty: Homeless families in America.* New York: Plenum Press.

Nurse Family Partnership. (2014). About. In *Nurse Family Partnership.* Retrieved June 27, 2014, from www.nursefamilypartnership.org/

Nurse Family Partnership. (2018). *About us.* Retrieved on June 30, 2018 from https://www.nursefamilypartnership.org/about/

O'Callaghan, J. B. (1993). *School-based collaboration with families.* San Francisco: Jossey-Bass.

O'Connell, M., & Bloom, D. E. (1987). Juggling jobs and babies: America's child care challenge. *Population Bulletin,* No. 12. Washington, DC: Population Reference Bureau.

Office of Civil Rights. (2010). *Free and appropriate education for students with disabilities: Requirements under Section 504 of The Rehabilitation Act of 1973.* U.S. Department of Education, http://www2.ed.gov/about/offices/list/ocr/docs/edlite-FAPE504.html

Office of Civil Rights, 2018. How to file a civil rights complaint. Retrieved on August 30 from https://www.hhs.gov/civil-rights/filing-a-complaint/complaint-process/index.html.

Office of the Administration for Children and Families. (2018). *Office of the Head Start.* Retrieved on September 20 from https://www.acf.hhs.gov/ohs/about.

Olson, L. (2009). The role of advocacy in shaping immigrant education: A California case-study. *Teachers College Record, 111*(3), 817–850.

Organizational Research Services. (2010). *Evaluation of the parent–child home program/play & learn group demonstration project 2005–2010: Final report.* Seattle: Business Partnership for Early Learning.

Osborn, D. K. (1991). *Early childhood education in historical perspective* (3rd ed.). Athens, GA: Education Associates. P.L., 94–142, Part B of the Education of All Handicapped Children Act, Title 20 of the *United States Code,* Sections 1400–1420. Regulations, Title 34 of the *Code of Federal Regulations,* Sections 300.1–300.754 and Appendix C, IEP Notice of Interpretation.

Ovando, C. J., Combs, M. C., & Collier, V. P. (2006). Bilingual and ESL classrooms: Teaching in multicultural contexts (4th ed.). Dubuque, IA: McGraw-Hill

Ownbey, M., Ownbey, J., & Cullen, J. (2011). The effects of a Healthy Families home visitation program on rapid and teen repeat births. *Child & Adolescent Social Work Journal, 28*(6), 439–458.

Ozcinar, Z., & Ekizoglu, N. (2013). Evaluation of a blog based parent involvement approach by parents. *Computers and Education, 66,* 1–10.

Palfrey, J., Bronson, M. B., Hauser-Cram, P., & Warfield, M. E. (2002). *Beepers come of age. The Brookline early education project follow-up study.* Retrieved from http://www.bc.edu/bc_org/avp/soe/beep/bpmajorfindings.htm

Palts, K., & Harro-Loit, H. (2015). Parent-teacher communication patterns concerning activity and positive-negative attitutes. *Trames: a Journal of the Humanities and Social Sciences, 19*(2), 139–154.

Papernow, P. (1998). *Becoming a stepfamily. Patterns of development of remarried families.* Mahwah, NJ: Analytic Press.

Papernow, P. L. (1993). *Becoming a stepfamily.* San Francisco: Jossey-Bass.

Parent-Child Home Program. (2018). *Who we serve.* Retrieved on October 9, 2018 from https://www.parent-child.org/our-program/who-we-serve/.

Parent Teacher Association. (2014). Special Education Parent Teacher Association. In *Parent Teacher Association.* Retrieved on July 8, 2014, from http://www.pta.org/content.cfm?ItemNumber=2100

Parenting in America. (2015). *The American family today.* Pew Research Center Retrieved on February 3, 2018 from http://www.pewsocialtrends.org/2015/12/17/1-the-american-family-today/.

Parents Anonymous. (2006). *Strengthening families around the world.* Retrieved from http://www.parentsanonymous.org

Parents as Teachers. (2014). *Parents as Teachers 30th anniversary.* In *Parents as Teachers.* Retrieved June 25, 2014, from http://www.parentsasteachers.org/about/30thanniversary

Parents as Teachers. (2018). Statement on separating children from families. Retrieved on June 30, 2018 from https://parentsasteachers.org/news/2018/6/18/statement-on-separating-children-from-families

Parents as Teachers. (2018).*Who we are.* Retrieved on June 30, 2018 from https://parentsasteachers.org/who-we-are

Parents as Teachers National Center. (2002). *What's new.* Retrieved from http://www.patnc.org/forpatprograms-whatsnew.asp

Parents as Teachers National Center. (2006). *Fact sheet.* Retrieved from http://www.parentsasteachers.org/site/pp.asp?c=eklRLcMZJxE&B=1802131

Parker, K., & Livingston, G. (2017). 6 facts about American fathers. FactTank News in the Numbers. Pew Research Center. Retrieved on February 3, 2018 from http://www.pewresearch.org/fact-tank/2017/06/15/fathers-day-facts/

Parlakian, R., & Lerner, C. (2010). Beyond twinkle, twinkle: Using music with infants and toddlers. *Young Children, 65*(2), 14–19.

Patall, E. A., Cooper, H., & Robinson, J. C. (2008). Parent involvement in homework: A research synthesis. *Review of Educational Research, 78*(4), 1039–1101.

Paulu, N. (1995). *Helping your child with homework for parents of elementary and junior high school-aged children.* Washington, DC: Office of Educational Research and Improvement, U.S. Department of Education.

PEAK Parent Center. (1997). *IDEA 97 and the tie to the general curriculum: Module 9–1.* Colorado Springs, CO: Parent Education and Assistance for Kids (PEAK).

Pedro, J. Y., Miller, R., & Bray. P. (2012). Teacher knowledge and dispositions towards parents and families: Rethinking influences and education of early childhood pre-service teachers. *Forum on Public Policy, 2012*(1), 1–15.

Pegram, T. (2011). *One hundred percent American: The rebirth and decline of the Ku Klux Klan in the 1920s.* New York: Ivan R. Dee Publisher.

Pennsylvania Department of Public Instruction. (1935). *Parent education. Bulletin 86.* Harrisburg: Author.

Perez, B. (2004). *Becoming biliterate: A study of two-way bilingual immersion education.* New York: Routledge.

Petersen, S. (2012). School readiness for infants and toddlers? Yes, really. *Young Children, 67*(4), 10–13.

Peterson, C. A., Mayer, L. M., Summers, J. A., & Luze, G. J. (2010). Identifying and preventing disabilities among vulnerable children. *Early Childhood Education Journal, 37,* 509–517.

Peterson, L. Y., Burden, J. P., Sedaghat, J. M., Gothberg, J. E., Kohler, P. D., & Coyle, J. L. (2013). Triangulated IEP transition goals. *Teaching Exceptional Children, 45*(6), 46–47.

Pew Research Center. (2018). Mobile fact sheet. *Internet & Technology.* Retrieved on May 30, 2018 from http://www.pewinternet.org/fact-sheet/mobile/

Pfännestiel, J., & Ziegler, E. (2007). The Parents as Teachers program: Its impact on school readiness and later school achievement: A research summary. In *The Parents as Teachers Program: Its Impact on School Readiness and Later School Achievement All Children Will Learn, Grow and Develop to Realize Their Full Potential.* Report. Parents as Teachers National Center.

Piaget, J. (1976). *To understand is to invent.* New York: Penguin Books.

Pierson, D. E., Walker, D. K., & Tivnan, T. (1984). A school-based program from infancy to kindergarten for children and their parents. *The Personnel and Guidance Journal, 62*(8), 448–455.

Pinto, D., Pagnamenta, A. T., Klei, L., Anney, R., et al. (2010). Functional impact of global rare copy number variation in autism spectrum disorders. *Nature, 466,* 368–372. PMID 20531469.

Plato. (1953). *The dialogues of Plato* (4th ed., B. Jowett, Trans.). London: Oxford University Press. (Original work published 1871.)

Pomerantz, E. M., Moorman, E. A., & Litwack, S. D. (2007). The how, whom, and why of parents' involvement in children's schooling: More is not necessarily better. *Review of Educational Research, 77,* 373–410.

Popkin, M. H. (2002). *Active parenting now.* Marietta, GA: Active Parenting. Retrieved from http://www.activeparenting.com/xapn.htm.

Potts, M. (1992, March). Strengths model. *National Center for Family Literacy, 4*(1), 5.

Posey, L. (2017). Race in place: Black parents, family-school relations, and multispatial microaggressions in a predominantly White suburb. *Teachers College Record, 119*(12).

Prins, E., & Schaff, K. A. (2009). Individual and structural attributions for poverty and persistence in family literacy programs: The resurgence of the culture of poverty. *Teachers College Record, 111*(9), 2280–2310.

Promising Practices Network. (2011). *Syracuse family development research program.* Retrieved from http://www.promisingpractices.net/program.asp?programid=133# overview

Putman, S. E. (2009). The monsters in my head: Posttraumatic stress disorder and the child survivor of sexual abuse. *Journal of Counseling and Development, 87*(1), 80–89.

Qiu, W., Schvaneveldt, P. L., & Sahin, V. (2013). Children's perceptions and definitions of family in China, Ecuador, Turkey, and the United States. *Journal of Comparative Family Studies, 64*(5), 1–23.

Quinn, B. S., Behrmann, M., Mastropieri, M. A., & Chung, Y. (2009). Who is using assistive technology in schools? *Journal of Special Education Technology, 24*(1), 1–13.

Radencich, M. C., & Schumm, J. S. (1996). *How to help your child with homework* (2nd ed.). Minneapolis, MN: Free Spirit.

Rafanello, D. (2010). Child sexual abuse prevention and reporting: It's everyone's responsibility *Exchange, 32*(1), 50–53.

Raikes, H., Green, B. L., Atwater, J., Kisker, E., Constantine, J., & Chazan-Cohen, R. (2006). Involvement in Early Head Start home visiting services: Demographic predictors and relations to child and parent outcomes. *Early Childhood Research Quarterly, 21,* 2–24.

RAINN (Rape, Abuse, Incent, National Network). (2018). Children and teens statistics. Retrieved on August 28, 2018 from https://www.rainn.org/statistics/children-and-teens.

Rast, D. E., Hogg, M. A., & Giessner, S. R. (2013). Self-uncertainty and support for autocratic leadership. *Self & Identity, 12*(6), 635–649.

Ratcliffe, C., & Kalish, E. (2017). Escaping poverty: Predictors of persistently poor children's economic success. *US Partnership on Mobility from Poverty.* Retrieved on October 18, 2018 from https://www.urban.org/sites/default/files/publication/90321/escaping-poverty.pdf.

Ray, B. D. (2011). 2.04 million homeschool students in the United States in 2010. National Home Education Research Institute. Retrieved from http://www.nheri.org

Ray, B. D. (2013). Homeschooling associated with beneficial learner and societal outcomes but educators do not promote it. *Peabody Journal of Education, 88*(3), 324–341.

Ray, B. D., & Wartes, J. (1991). The academic achievement and affective development of home-schooled children. In H. Van Galen & M. A. Pitman (Eds.), *Home schooling: Political, historical, and pedagogical perspective* (pp. 43–62). Norwood, NJ: Ablex.

Redford, J., Battle, D., and Bielick, S. (2017). *Homeschooling in the United States: 2012* (NCES 2016-096.REV). National Center for Education Statistics, Institute of Education Sciences, U.S. Department of Education. Washington, DC.

Reggio Emilia Approach. (2018). *Reggio Emilia Approach.* Retrieved on September 20, 2018 from http://www.reggio-children.it/identita/reggio-emilia-approach/?lang=en.

Reiff, J. (1966). Mental health manpower and institutional change. *American Psychologist, 21,* 540–548.

Renobales Barbier, A., Cortés Jarrín, A., Meseguer Lemus, X., & Barquera Medina, L. (2013). La infancia cuenta en Mexico 2013: Hacia la construcción de un sistema de información sobre los derechos de infancia y adolesencia en México. *Red por los Derechos de la Infancia en Mexico.* Retrieved on August 8, 2014, from http://derechosinfancia.org.mx/index.php?contenido=listado_documentos&clas=1&id_opcion=75

Reppucci, N. D., Britner, P. A., & Woolard, J. L. (1997). *Preventing child abuse and neglect through parent education.* Baltimore: Brookes.

Richardson, J., & Parnell, P. (2005). And Tango makes three. Little Simon.

Riggs, R. C. (1982). Incest: The school's Gutierrez, role. *The Journal of School Health, 52,* 365–370.

Riojas-Cortez, M. (2017). *La familia como sistema de apoyo para el desarrollo y bienestar de los niños Latinos bilingües.* In M. Guerrero, K. Escamilla, M. C. Guerrero, L. González-Sotero, & D. Rogers, *Fundamentos de la Educación Bilingüe.* Dual Language Education of New Mexico.

Riojas-Cortez, M. (2008). Trying to fit in a different world. Acculturation of Latino families with young children in the United States. *International Journal of Early Childhood Education, 40*(1).

Riojas-Cortez, M. (2011). Culture, play and family: Three elements assisting in the development of a child on the autism spectrum. *Young Children, 66*(5), 94–99.

Riojas-Cortez, M. & Cataldo, R. (2016). Using children's literature to understand values, traditions, and beliefs within Latin family systems. In Clark, E. R., Smith, H. L., & Flores, B. B. *Multicultural Literature for Latino Bilingual Children: Their words, their worlds.* Lanham, MD: Rowman & Littlefield.

Riojas-Cortez, M., & Flores, B. B. (2009a). Sin olvidar a los padres: Families as collaborators within the school and university partnership. *Journal of Latinos in Education, 8*(3), 231–239.

Riojas-Cortez, M., & Flores, B. B. (2010). Música, versos y juegos: Familias Latinas desarrollando el lenguaje oral con sus niños. *Novedades Educativas: Publicación de Nivel General y Educación, 22*(230), 46–49. (Journal published in Buenos Aires, Argentina).

Riojas-Cortez, M., Flores, B. B, & Clark, E. R. (2003). Los niños aprenden en casa: Valuing and connecting home cultural knowledge with the school's early childhood education program. *Young Children, 58*(6), 78–83.

Riojas-Cortez, M., Huerta, M. E., Flores, B. B., Clark, E. R., & Pérez, B. (2007). Using cultural tools to develop scientific literacy of young Mexican American preschoolers. *Early Child Development and Care, 178*(5), 527–536.

Risko, V., & Walker-Dalhouse, D. (2010). Making the most of assessment to inform instruction. *Reading Teacher, 63*(5). 420–422.

Rivera, G. (1972). *Willowbrook: The last great disgrace.* WABC-TV documentary film.

Robinson, A., & Stark, D. R. (2004). *Advocates in action: Making a difference for young children.* Washington, DC: NAEYC.

Robinson, J. L., Klute, M. M., Faldowski, R., Pan, B., Staerkel, F., Summers, J. A., & Wall, S. (2009). Mixed approach programs in the Early Head Start research and evaluation project: An in-depth view. *Early Education & Development, 20*(6), 893–919.

Rodriguez-Brown, F. V. (2004). Project FLAME: A parent support family literacy model. In B. Wasik (Ed.), *Handbook of Family Literacy.* Mahwah, NJ: Erlbaum.

Rodríguez-Rubio, A., & Kiser, A. I. T. (2013). An Examination of Servant Leadership in the United States and Mexico: Do Age and Gender Make a Difference? *The Global Studies Journal, 5*(2), 127–150.

Rogers, P., & O'Connor, R. E. (2003). How to build a better mother: A successful program prevents child abuse by teaching the art of being a mother. *People Weekly, 59*(15), 137.

Roggman, L. A., Boyce, L. K., & Cook, G. A. (2009). Keeping kids on track: Impacts of a parenting- focused Early Head Start program on attachment security and cognitive development. *Early Education & Development, 20*(6), 920–941.

Rosado, L., Amaro-Jiménez, C., & Kieffer, I. (2015). Stories to our Children: A program aimed at developing authentic and culturally relevant literature for Latina/o children. *School Community Journal, 25*(1), 73–93–.

Rosenberg, H., Harris, E., & Wilkes, S. (2012). Joining forces: Families and out-of-school programs as partners in supporting children's learning and development. *Family Involvement Network of Educators (FINE), 4*(2). Retrieved June 29, 2014, from http://www.hfrp.org/family-involvement/publicationsresources/joining-forces-familiesand-out-of-school-programs-aspartners-in-supporting-children-slearning-and-development

Rotter, J. C., & Robinson, E. H. (1986). *Parent-teacher conferencing: What research says to the teacher.* Washington, DC: National Education Association of the United States.

Rousseau, J. J. (1979). *Emile: Education* (A. Bloom, Trans.). New York: Basic Books. (Original work published 1762.)

Royea, A. J., & Appl, D. J. (2009). Every voice matters: The importance of advocacy. *Early Childhood Education Journal, 37,* 89–91.

Rozalski, M. E., Stewart, A., & Miller, J. (2010). How to determine the least restrictive environment for students with disabilities. *Exceptionality, 18*(3), 151–163.

Ruiz-Casares, M., & Heymann, J. (2009). Children home alone unsupervised: Modeling parental decisions and associated factors in Botswana, Mexico, and Vietnam. *Child Abuse & Neglect, 33*(5), 312–323.

Rutter, M. (1981). *Maternal deprivation reassessed.* Harmondsworth, England: Penguin Books.

Rychly, L., & Graves, E. (2012). Teachers' characteristics for culturally responsive pedagogy. *Multicultural perspectives, 14*(1), 44–49.

Sanders, M. G. (2014). Principal leadership for school, family, and community partnershps: The role of a systems approach to reform implementation. *American Journal of Education, 120*(2), 233–255.

Sar, B. K., Antle, B. F., Bledsoe, L. K., Barbee, A. P., & Van Zyl, M. A. (2010). The importance of expanding home visitation services to include strengthening family relationships for the benefit of children. *Children & Youth Services Review, 32*(2), 198–205.

Sawchuck, S. (2011). Through home visits, teacher recruiting parents as partners. *Education Week, 31*(1), 299–303.

Saylor, R. S. (2007). Take the time to communicate with parents: Build a relationship of respect and cooperation with students' families. *American Teacher, 92*(2), 7.

Schaufe, W. B., Maslach, C., & Marek, T. (2017). *Professional Burnout: Recent Developments in Theory and Research.* Taylor & Francis.

Schecter, S. R., & Sherri, D. L. (2009). Value added? Teachers' investments in and orientations toward parent involvement in education. *Urban Education, 44*(1), 59–87.

Schlossman, S. L. (1976). Before Home Start: Notes toward a history of parent education in America, 1897–1929. *Harvard Educational Review, 46*(3), 436–467.

Schoger, K. D. (2006). Reverse inclusion: Providing peer social interaction opportunities to students placed in self-contained special education classrooms. *Teaching Exceptional Children Plus, 2*(6), Article 3. Retrieved from http://escholarship.bc.edu/education/tecplus/vol12/iss6/art3/

Schorr, L. B., & Schorr, D. (1988). *Within our reach: Breaking the cycle of disadvantage.* New York: Doubleday.

Schueler, B. E., Capotosto, L., Bahena, S., McIntyre, J., & Gehlba, H. (2014). Measuring parent perceptions of school climate. *Psychological Assessment, 26*(1), 314–320.

Schweinhart, L. J. (2009). Designing a curriculum for EC teachers and caregivers. *Exchange, 31*(2), 34–37.

Seligman, M. (2000). *Conducting effective conferences with parents of children with disabilities.* New York: Guilford Press.

Shapley, K., Sheehan, D., Maloney, C., & Caranikas-Walker, F. 2011. Effects of technology immersion on middle school students' learning opportunities and achievement. *The Journal of Educational Research, 104*(5), 299–315.

Shatkin, G., & Gershber, A. I. (2007). Empowering parents and building communities: the role of school-based councils in educational governance and accountability. *Urban Education, 42*(6), 582–615.

Sheehy, P., Ornelles, C., & Noonan, M. J. (2009). Biculturalization: Developing culturally responsive approaches to family participation. *Intervention in School and Clinic, 45*(2), 132–139.

Sheridan, S., & Gjems, L. (2017). Preschool as an arena for developing teacher knowledge concerning children's language learning. *Early Childhood Education Journal, 45*(3), 347–357.

Shipman, V. C., Boroson, M., Bidgeman, B., Gart, J., & Mikovsky, M. (1976). *Disadvantaged children and their first school experiences.* Princeton, NJ: Educational Testing Service.

Shonkoff, J. P., & Phillips, D. H. (2000). *From neurons to neighborhoods: The science of early childhood development.* Washington, DC: National Academy Press.

Shore, R. (1997). *Rethinking the brain.* New York: Families and Work Institute.

Silver, A. A., & Hagin, R. A. (2002). *Disorders of learning in childhood,* New York: Wiley.

Silver, H. K., & Kempe, C. H. (1959). Problems of parental criminal neglect and severe physical abuse of children. *American Journal of Diseases of Children, 95,* 528.

Simmons, T., & Dye, J. L. (2003, October). *Grandparents living with grandchildren: 2000.* Washington, DC: U.S. Department of Commerce, Economics and Statistics Administration, U.S. Census Bureau.

Sirinides, P., Fink, R., & DuBois, T. (2017). A study of early learning services in museums and libraries. *Early Childhood Education Journal, 45*(4), 563–573.

Skeels, H. (1966). *Adult status of children with contrasting early life experiences: A follow-up study.* In Monographs of the Society for Research in Child Development (Vol. 31). Chicago: University of Chicago Press.

Skeels, H. M., & Dye, H. B. (1939). A study of the effects of differential stimulation on mentally retarded children. *Proceedings and Addresses of the American Association on Mental Deficiency, 44,* 114–136.

Sleeter, C. (2012). Confronting the marginalization of culturally responsive pedagogy. *Urban Education 47*(3), 562–584.

Smith, H. L., & Riojas-Cortez, M. (2010). Cartitas de cariño: Little notes to say you care. *Language Arts, 88*(2), 125–133.

Smith, S. (2012). Cultural replay in early childhood education: Methods of teaching school behavior to low income children. *Urban Review, 44,* 571–588.

Smith Slep, A. M., & O'Leary, S. G. (2009). Distinguishing risk profiles among parent-only, partner-only, and dually perpetrating physical aggressors. *Journal of Family Psychology, 23*(5), 705–16.

Smith, T. (2005, November/December). IDEA 2004: Another round in the reauthorization process. *Remedial and Special Education, 26*(6), 314–320.

Smith, V. (1986). Listening. In O. Hargie (Ed.), *A handbook of communication skills* (pp. 246–265). Washington Square: New York University Press.

Söderstörm, M., Boldemann, C., Sahiln, U., Martensson, F., Raustorp, A., & Blennow, M. (2012). The quality of the outdoor environment influences children's health – a cross-sectional study of preschools. *Acta Paediatrica, 102*(1), 83–91.

Soley, G., & Hannon, E. E. (2010). Infants prefer the musical meter of their own culture: A cross-cultural comparison. *Developmental Psychology, 46*(1), 286–292.

Sollberger, D. (2013). On identity: From a philosophical point of view. *Child and Adolescent Psychiatry & Mental Health, 7*(1), 1–10.

Sommer, F., Leuschner, V., & Scheithauer, H. (2014). Bullying, romantic rejection, and conflicts with teachers: The crucial role of social dynamics in the development of school shootings—A systematic review. *International Journal of Developmental Science, 8*(1–2), 3–24.

Soska, K. C., Adolph, K. E., & Johnson, S. P. (2010). Systems in development: Motor skill acquisition facilitates three-dimensional object completion. *Developmental Psychology, 46*(1), 129–138.

Special Olympics. (2018). *Our work*. Retrieved on August 31, 2018 from https://www.specialolympics.org/.

Special Quest. (2008). *SpecialQuest birth-five: Head Start/Hilton Foundation Training Program vision*. Retrieved on November 29, 2018 from http://ectacenter.org/~pdfs/meetings/national 2009/sq_brochure_7308.pdf

Spitz, R. A. (1945). Hospitalism: An inquiry into the genesis of psychiatric conditions in early childhood. In A. Freud et al. (Eds.), *The psychoanalytic study of the child* (Vol. 2). New York: International Universities Press.

Spitz, R. A. (1965). *The first year of life*. New York: International Universities Press.

Spock, B. (1957). *Baby and child care*. New York: Pocket Book.

Spodek, B. (Ed.). (1982). *Handbook of research on early childhood education*. New York: Free Press/Macmillan.

STAND! for Families Free of Violence (2014). Mission. Retrieved on July 11, 2014, from http://www.standagainstdv.org/aboutus/mission.html

Steele, B. F. (1986). Notes on the lasting effects of early child abuse throughout the life cycle. *Child Abuse and Neglect, 10*, 283–291.

Steele, B. F. (1987). C. Henry Kempe memorial lecture. *Child Abuse and Neglect, 11*, 313–318.

Stendler, C. B. (1950). Sixty years of child training practices. *Journal of Pediatrics, 36*(1), 122–134.

STEP Publishers. (2018). *Step into Parenting*. Retrieved on May 2, 2018 from https://www.steppublishers.com/

Stephens, K. (2007). Parent meetings: Creative ways to make them meaningful. *Exchange, 175*.

Strickland, A. (2018). Bullying is a serious public health problem expert say. *CNN* Retrieved on August 28, 2018 from https://www.cnn.com/2016/05/10/health/bullying-public-health-zero-tolerance/index.html

Stronge, J. H. (Ed.). (1992). *Educating homeless children and adolescents: Evaluating policy and practice*. Newbury Park, CA: Sage.

Stronge, J. H., & Helm, V. M. (1991). *Residency and guardianship requirements as barriers to the education of homeless children and youth*. Paper presented at the Annual Meeting of the American Research Association. Retrieved on November 28, 2018 from http://files.eric.ed.gov/fulltext/ED319845.

Stopbullying.gov. (2018). Types of bullying. Retrieved on August 28, 2018 from https://www.stopbullying.gov/what-is-bullying/index.html#types.

Suárez-Orozco, C., Gaytán, F. X., Bang, H. J., Pakes, J., O'Connor, R., & Rhodes, J. (2010). Academic trajectories of newcomer immigrant youth. *Developmental Psychology, 46*(3), 602–618.

Subero, D., Vujasinovic, E., & Guitart, M. E. (2017). Mobilising funds of identity in ana nd out of school. *Cambridge Journal of Education 47*(2), 247–263.

Svevo-Cianci, K., & Lee, Y. (2010). Twenty years of the Convention of Rights of the Child: Achievements in and challenges for child protection implementation, measurement and evaluation around the world. *Child Abuse & Neglect, 34*(1), 1–4.

Schweinhart, L. J., & Weikart, D. P. (1997). The high/scope preschool curriculum comparison study through age 23. *Early Childhood Research Quarterly, 12*, 117–143.

Schweinhart, L. J., Montie, J. Xiang, Z., Barnett, S. W., Belfield, C. R., & Nores, M. (2005). *Lifetime effects: The High/Scope Perry Preschool study through age 40*. High Scope Press.

Swick, K. J., Da Ros, D. A., & Kovach, B. A. (2001). Empowering parents and families through a caring inquiry approach. *Early Childhood Education Journal, 29*(1), 65–71.

Swick, K., & Williams, R. (2006). An analysis of Bronfenbrenner's bio-ecological perspective for early childhood educators: Implications for working with families experiencing stress. *Early Childhood Education Journal, 33*(5), 371–378.

Sylvestre, A., & Mérette, C. (2010). Language delay in severely neglected children: A cumulative or specific effect of risk factors? *Child Abuse and Neglect, 34*(6), 414–428.

Taylor, K. W. (1981). *Parent and children learn together: Parent cooperative nursery schools*. New York: Teachers College Press.

Texas Attorney General. (2018). What we can do about child abuse. Retrieved on August 28, 2018 from https://www.texasattorneygeneral.gov/cvs/what-we-can-do-about-child-abuse-2#responsible.

The Arc. (2018). History of the ARC. Retrieved on November 29, 2018 from https://www.thearc.org/who-we-are/history.

The Child Abuse Prevention and Treatment Act. (2003). The child abuse prevention and treatment act. *U.S. Department of Health and Human Services. Office of Child Abuse and Neglect.* Retrieved on August 28, 2018 from https://www.acf.hhs.gov/sites/default/files/cb/capta2003.pdf

The Fatherhood Project. (2018). *About us*. Retrieved on February 8, 2018 from http://www.thefatherhoodproject.org/about/

The Joseph Kennedy, Jr. Foundation. (2018). *Joseph P. Kennedy, Jr.* The John F. Kennedy Presidential Library and Museum. Retrieved on August 31, 2018 from https://www.jfklibrary.org/JFK/The-Kennedy-Family/Joseph-P-Kennedy-Jr.aspx.

The Project Approach. (2018). *About the Project Approach*. Retrieved on November 30, 2018 from http://projectapproach.org/about/.

The Portage Project. (2014). About. In *The Portage Project*. Retrieved June 30, 2014, from https://sites.google.com/a/cesa5.org/portageproject/history.

The President's Panel on Mental Retardation. (1963). Report of the taskforce on law. *Library of Congress Catalogue* Card No. 63-60030

The United States Conference of Mayors. (2016). *The U.S. conference of mayors' report on Hunger and homelessness: A status report on homelessness and hunger in American's cities*. Retrieved on November 28, 2018 from https://endhomelessness.atavist.com/mayorsreport2016

Thelamour, B., & Jacobs, D. L. (2014). Homework practices of English and non-English-speaking parents. *Urban Education, 49*, 528.

Thomas, A. J., & Blackmon, S. M. (2015). The influence of Trayvon Martin shooting on racial socialization practices of African American parents. *Journal of Black Psychology, 41*(1), 75–89.

Thomas, N. A., Gran, B. B., & Hanson, K. C. (2011). An independent voice for children's rights in Europe? The role of independent children's rights institutions in the EU. *International Journal of Children's Rights, 19*(3), 429–449.

Thomas, S. P., Phillips, K., Carlson, K., Shieh, E., Kirkwood, E., Cabage, L., & Worley, J. (2013). Child experiences of perpetrators of child sexual abuse. *Perspectives in Psychiatric Care, 49*, 187–201.

Thomas-Duckwitz, C. M., Hess, R. S., & Atcherly, E. (2013). "Las Siete Historias": Perceptions of parent involvement among Mexican immigrant women. *Multicultural Learning and Teaching, 8*(1), 133–154.

Thompson, L., Kropenske, V., Heinicke, C., Gomby, D., & Halfon, N. (2003, July). *Home visiting: A service strategy to delivery first 5 results*. Policy Brief Number 15, Building Community Systems for Young Children, Los Angeles: UCLA Center for Healthier Children, Families and Communities, California Policy Research Center.

Thompson, B. C., Mazer, J. P., & Grady, E. F. (2015). The changing nature of parent-teacher communication: Mode selection in the smartphone era. *Communication Education, 64*(2), 187–207.

Thornton, V. (2014). Understanding the emotional impact of domestic violence on young children. *Educational & Child Psychology, 31*(1), 90–100.

TIME. (2018). World's greatest places 2018. Retrieved on August 29, 2018 from http://time.com/collection/worlds-greatest-places-2018/.

Tizard, B., & Hodges, J. (1978). The effect of early institutional rearing on the development of eight year old children. *The Journal of Child Psychology and Psychiatry, 19*(2), 99–118.

Tobin, B. (2017). Understanding the direct involvement of parents in policy development and school activities in a primary school. *International Journal for Transformative Research, 4*(1), 25–33.

Toldson, I. A., & Lemmons, B. P. (2013). Social demographics, the school environment, and parenting practices associated with parents' participation in schools and academic success among Black, Hispanic, and White students. *Journal of Human Behavior in the Social Environment, 23*(2), 237–255.

Tower, C. C. (1992). *The role of educators in the protection and treatment of child abuse and neglect.* Washington, DC: U.S. Department of Health and Human Services, National Center on Child Abuse and Neglect.

Toyota Family Learning. (2014). Welcome to Toyota family learning. Retrieved on August 5, 2014, from http://toyota-familylearning.org/

Trawick-Smith, J. W. (2010). *Early childhood development: A multicultural perspective* (5th ed.). Upper Saddle River, NJ: Pearson.

Tribal Home Visiting. (2018). *Tribal Home Visiting in Action.* Retrieved on June 30, 2018 from https://www.acf.hhs.gov/ecd/home-visiting/tribal-home-visiting

Turbiville, V., Umbarger, G. T., III, & Guthrie, A. C. (2000, July). Fathers' involvement in programs for young children. *Young Children, 55*(4).

Turnbull, A. P. Turnbull, R., & Wehmeyer, M. L. (2007). *Exceptional lives: Special education in today's schools.* Upper Saddle River, NJ: Pearson Merrill Prentice Hall.

Turnbull, A. P., Turnbull, H. R., Erwin, E. J., Soodak, L. C., & Shogren, K. A. (2014). *Families, professionals, and exceptionality: Positive outcomes through partnerships and trust* (7th ed.). Upper Saddle River, NJ: Pearson.

Turner, J. C., Christensen, A., Kackar-Cam, H. Z., Fulmer S. M., & Trucano, M. (2017). The development of professional learning communities and their teacher leaders: An activity systems analysis. *The Journal of the Learning Sciences, 27*(1), 49–88.

UNICEF. (2010). The state of the world's children special edition: Celebrating 20 years of the convention on the rights of the child. Retrieved from http://www.unicef.org/publications

UNICEF. (2013). *The state of the world's children 2013: Children with disabilities.* Retrieved on August 28, 2018 from https://www.unicef.org/sowc2013/files/SWCR2013_ENG_Lo_res_24_Apr_2013.pdf.

UNICEF. (2014). Who we are. Retrieved on August 5, 2014, from http://www.unicef.org/about/who/index_introduction.html.

UNICEF. (2018). Child trafficking. Retrived on May 26 from https://www.unicef.org/protection/57929_58005.html

United Nations. (1989). *United Nations convention on the rights of the child.* New York: Author.

University of North Carolina, FPG Child Development Institute. (2004). *The Carolina Abecedarian Project.* Retrieved from http://www.childcareresearch.org/location/ccrca4716

Utah Parent Center. (1997). *Parents as partners in the IEP process: Information booklet.* Salt Lake City, UT: Author.

U.S. Advisory Board on Child Abuse and Neglect. (1993, April). In Department of Health and Human Services, Administration for Children and Families, *The continuing child protection emergency: A challenge to the nation.* Washington, DC: U.S. Government Printing Office.

U.S. Census Bureau. (2010). *Publications.* Retrieved from http://www.census.gov/

U.S. Census Bureau. (2018) 2016 Current population survey annual social and economic supplement. Retrieved on November 9, 2018 from https://www.census.gov/library/visualizations/2016/comm/cb16-192_living_arrangements.html

United States Census. (2018). Grandparents still work to support grandchildren. Retrieved on November 9, 2018 from https://www.census.gov/content/dam/Census/library/visualizations/2017/comm/grandparents-day.pdf

U.S. Department of Education, National Center for Education Statistics. (2016). Digest of Education Statistics, 2015 (NCES 2016–014). Washington, DC: Author. Retrieved from https://nces.ed.gov/fastfacts/display.asp?id=64

U.S. Department of Education. (2016). 38th annual report to Congress on the implementation of the Individuals with Disabilities Education Act, 2016. Washington, DC: Author. Retrieved from https://www2.ed.gov/about/reports/annual/osep/2016/parts-b-c/38th-arc-for-idea.pdf

U.S. Department of Education. (2018). The family and community engagement team. Retrieved on June 13, 2018 from https://www.ed.gov/family-and-community-engagement/team

United States Department of Health and Human Services. (2009) FACES: 2009 Cohort [United States]. Administration for Children and Families. Office of Planning, Research and Evaluation. Head Start Family and Child Experiences Survey Ann Arbor, MI: Inter-university Consortium for Political and Social Research [distributor], 2018-07-26. https://doi.org/10.3886/ICPSR34558.v3

U.S. Department of Health and Human Services. (2018). Working with pregnant and parenting teens tip sheet. *Family and Young Services Bureau.* Retrieved on June 16 from https://www.acf.hhs.gov/sites/default/files/assets/pregnant-parenting-teens-tips.pdf.

U.S. Department of Health and Human Services. (2018). Early Head Start Programs. Head Start /ECLKC. Retrieved on September 27, 2018 from https://eclkc.ohs.acf.hhs.gov/programs/article/early-head-start-programs.

U.S. Department of Health and Human Services, Administration for Children and Families. (2000). *Information memorandum: Family literacy services in Head Start and Early Head Start programs.* Retrieved from http://www.headstartinfo.org/publications/im00/m00_25.htm

U.S. Department of Health and Human Services. (1992). Child abuse and neglect: A shared community concern. *Administration for Children, Youth and Families. National Center on Child Abuse and Neglect.* Washington, DC: U.S. Government Printing Office.

U.S. Department of Health and Human Services, Office of Human Development Services. (1985). Administration for Children, Youth and Families, Head Start Bureau. *A guide for operating a home-based child development program.* Washington, DC: U.S. Government Printing Office.

U.S. Department of Health and Human Services, Office of Human Development Services. (1987). Administration for Children, Youth and Families, Head Start Bureau. *The Head Start home visitor handbook.* Washington, DC: U.S. Government Printing Office.

U.S. Department of Health, Education and Welfare. (1974). *Home Start/Child and family resource programs. Reports of a joint conference—Home Start, child, and family resource programs.* Washington, DC: U.S. Government Printing Office.

U.S. Department of Justice. (2011a). *Americans with Disabilities Act of 1990, as amended.* Retrieved from http://www.ada.gov

U.S. Department of Justice. (2011b). *2010 ADA standards for accessible design.* Retrieved from http://www.ada.gov

U.S. Department of Justice. (2011c). *Access to medical care for individuals with mobility disabilities.* Retrieved from http://www.ada.gov

U.S. Department of Labor. (2013). Family and Medical Leave Act: Protections expanded for military families and airline flight crews. Retrieved from http://www.dol.gov/WHD/fmla/2013rule/militaryDate.htm

Valdés, G. (1996). *Con respeto: Bridging the distances between culturally diverse families and schools.* New York: Teachers College Press.

Valencia, R. (2002). *Chicano school failure and success: Past, present, and future.* New York: Routledge/Falmer.

Vandewalker, N. C. (1971). *The kindergarten in American education.* New York, NY: Arno Press.

Van Haren, B., & Fiedler, C. R. (2008). Support and empower families of children with disabilities. *Intervention in School and Clinic, 43*(4), 231–235.

Venegas, K., Cadena, M., Galan, C., Park, E., Astudillo, S., Acuña Avilez, A., Ward, J. D., Lanford, M., & Tierney, W. G. (2017). *Understanding DACA and the implications for higher education.* Pullias Center for Higher Education, University of Southern California.

Veseley, C. K., Levine Brown, E., & Mehta, S. (2017). Developing cultural humility through experiential learning: How home visits transform early childhood preservice educators' attitudes for engaging families. *Journal of Early Childhood Teacher Education, 38*(3), 242–258.

Vidya, T. (2014). Homework, homework everywhere: Indian parents' involvement with their children's homework. *Childhood Education, 90*(2), 83–90.

Villegas, A. M., & Lucas, T. (2007). The culturally responsive teacher. *Educational Leadership, 64*(6), 28–33.

Vincent, C. E. (1951). Trends in infant care ideas. *Child Development, 22*(3), 199–209.

Visher, E. B. (2001). *A systemic examination of stepfamily relationships.* First Annual Ohio State University Extension Family Life Electronic Inservice. Columbus, OH. Ohio State University.

Vital Speeches International. (2010). Role of ombudsman of Uzbekistan in human rights protection. *Vital Speeches International, 2*(2), 74–77.

Vitello, S. J. & Soskin, R. M. (1985). *Mental retardation: its social and legal context.* Upper Saddle River: NJ: Prentice-Hall.

Vondra, J. I., & Toth, S. L. (1989). Child maltreatment research and intervention. *Early Child Development and Care, 42,* 11–24.

Wagner, J. Y, & Katsiyannis, A. (2010). Special education update: Implications for school administrators. *NASSP Bulletin, 94*(1), 40–52.

Walker J., & Dotger, B. (2012). Because wisdom can't be told: Using comparison of simulated parent–teacher conferences to assess teacher candidates' readiness for family–school partnership. *Journal of Teacher Education, 63*(1).

Warner, I. (1991). Parents in touch: District leadership for parent involvement. *Phi Delta Kappan, 73*(5), 372–375.

Wasik, B. H. (1993). Staffing issues for home visiting programs. *The Future of Children: Home Visiting, 3*(3), 140–157.

Wasik, B. H., & Bryant, D. M. (2001). *Home visiting: Procedures for helping families* (2nd ed.). Thousand Oaks, CA: Sage.

Watkins, P. J., & Stevens, D. W. (2013). The Goldilocks dilemma: Homework policy creating a culture where simply good is just not good enough. *Clearing House, 86*(2), 80–85.

Weigel, D. J. (2008). The concept of family: An analysis of lay people's views of family *Journal of Family 29*(11), 1426–1447.

Wherry, J. H. (2009). Enter the new generation of parents. *Principal, 52.*

White, B. L., Kaban, B. T., Attanucci, J., & Shapiro, B. B. (1973). *Experience and environment: Major influences on the development of the young child* (Vol. 1). Upper Saddle River, NJ: Prentice Hall.

Whiting, M. (2014). Support requirements of parents caring for a child with disability and complex health needs. *Nursing Children & Young People, 26*(4), 24–27.

Wiehe, V. R. (1996). *Working with child abuse and neglect: A primer.* Thousand Oaks, CA: Sage.

Williamson, D. (2014). Transformational leadership. *Leadership Excellence, 31*(2), 19.

Williamson, R., & Blackburn, B. R. (2010). Supporting student learning. *Principal Leadership, 10*(8), 65–67.

Winerip, M. (1999). Homework Bound. New York Times.

Woo, Jeong-Gil. (2016). Revisiting "Orbis Sensualium Pictus": An iconographical reading in light of the Pampaedia of J. A. Comenius. *Studies in Philosophy and Education, 35*(2), 215–233

Woolley, P. V., Jr., & Evans, W. A. (1955, June). Significance of skeletal lesions in infants resembling those of traumatic origin. *Journal of American Medical Association,* 539–543.

Wolfenstein, M. (1953). Trends in infant care. *American Journal of Orthopsychiatry, 23*(1), 120–130.

Wolfensberger, W. P. (1972). *The principle of normalization in human services.* Toronto: National Institute on Mental Retardation.

Wong-Fillmore, L. (1991). When learning a second language means losing the first. *Early Childhood Research Quarterly, 6,* 323–346.

Wong-Filmore, L. (2000). Loss of family languages: Should educators be concerned? *Theory into Practice, 39*(4), 203–210.

World Health Organization. (2018). Violence against children. Key facts. Retrieved on May 25 from http://www.who.int/news-room/fact-sheets/detail/violence-against-children

Wright, M. O., Crawford, E., & Del Castillo, D. (2009). Childhood emotional maltreatment and later psychological distress among college students. The mediating role of maladaptive schemas. *Child Abuse and Neglect, 33*(1), 59–68.

Ybarra, M. L., Finkelhorn, D., Mitchell, K. J., & Wolak, J. (2009). Associations between blocking, monitoring, filtering software on the home computer and youth-reported unwanted exposure to sexual material online. *Child Abuse & Neglect, 33*(12), 857–860.

Yell, M. L., Katsiyannis, A., Ryan, J. B., McDuffie, K. A., & Mattocks, L. (2008). Ensure compliance with the Individuals with Disabilities Education Improvement Act of 2004. *Intervention in School and Clinic, 44*(1), 45–51.

Young, D., & Behounek, L. (2008). Kindergarten students use PowerPoint to lead conferences. *Principal, 87*(5), 58–59.

Youngquist, J., & Martínez-Griego, B. (2009). Learning in English learning in Spanish: A Head Start program changes its approach. *Young Children.* Retrieved from http://www.naeyc.org/yc.

Zadeh, Z. Y., Farnia, F., & Ungerleider, C. (2010). How home enrichment mediates the relationship between maternal education and children's achievement in reading and math. *Early Education & Development, 21*(4), 568–594.

Zeanah, C. H., Berlin, L. J., & Boris, N. W. (2011). Clinical applications of attachment theory and research for infants and young children. *Journal of Child Psychology and Psychiatry, 52*(8), 819–833.

Zero to Three. (2001). *Brain wonders.* Retrieved from http://zerotothree.org/brainwonders/faq.html

Zero to Three. (2010). *Parenting infants and toddlers today: Key findings from a Zero to Three 2099 National Parents Survey.* Retrieved from http://www.zerotothree.org

Zero to Three. (2018a). Home visiting. Retrieved on June 20 from https://www.zerotothree.org/espanol/home-visiting.

Zero to Three. (2018b). Policy and advocacy. Retrieved on May 17, 2018 from https://www.zerotothree.org/policy-and-advocacy.

Zielinski, D. S. (2009). Children maltreatment and adult socioeconomic well-being. *Child Abuse & Neglect, 33*(10), 666–678.

Zirkel, P. A. (2009). What does the law say? New Section 504 student eligibility standards. *Teaching Exceptional Children, 41*(4), 68–71.

Index